Nonparametric and
Distribution-Free Methods
for the Social Sciences

Roger E. Kirk, Consulting Editor

Exploring Statistics: An Introduction for Psychology and Education
Sarah M. Dinham
The University of Arizona

Methods in the Study of Human Behavior
Vernon Ellingstad and Norman W. Heimstra
The University of South Dakota

An Introduction to Statistical Methods in the Behavioral Sciences
Freeman F. Elzey
San Francisco State University

Experimental Design: Procedures for the Behavioral Sciences
Roger E. Kirk
Baylor University

Statistical Issues: A Reader for the Behavioral Sciences
Roger E. Kirk
Baylor University

The Practical Statistician: Simplified Handbook of Statistics
Marigold Linton
The University of Utah
Philip S. Gallo, Jr.
San Diego State University

Nonparametric and Distribution-Free Methods for the Social Sciences
Leonard A. Marascuilo
University of California, Berkeley
Maryellen McSweeney
Michigan State University

Basic Statistics: Tales of Distributions
Chris Spatz
Hendrix College
James O. Johnston
University of Arkansas at Monticello

Multivariate Analysis with Applications in Education and Psychology
Neil. H. Timm
University of Pittsburgh

Nonparametric and Distribution-Free Methods for the Social Sciences

Leonard A. Marascuilo
University of California, Berkeley

Maryellen McSweeney
Michigan State University

Brooks/Cole Publishing Company
Monterey, California
A Division of Wadsworth Publishing Company, Inc.

ISBN: 0–8185–0202–9
L. C. Catalog Card No.: 76–19452
Printed in the United States of America

10 9 8 7 6 5 4 3 2 1

Preface

This book on nonparametric and distribution-free statistical methods can be used as a learning source for advanced undergraduate and graduate students as well as a bountiful reference source for the researcher. Our goal is to present a statistically sound cookbook with easy-to-follow recipes. We recognize that, just as an understanding of basic cooking principles encourages successful modification of the recipes and improvisation, so, too, an understanding of the rationale for various statistical analyses and the assumptions upon which they depend is essential to data analysts who want to adapt nonparametric procedures to their specific analytic needs. Our attempts to provide flexibility have resulted in some occasionally wordy explanations and the inclusion of some algebraic demonstrations, but we have also included more than 250 completely worked examples and more than 200 chapter-end problems focusing on simple theory and/or data analysis. We believe that students, instructors, and researchers can use the book selectively to satisfy personal needs and interests.

As a working principle, we have included in the text only those methods and techniques that have broad utility for social-science research. We identify "useful" techniques as those that (1) have potential applicability to common data-analysis problems in fields such as education, sociology, and psychology, (2) are capable of being implemented without reliance on extensive computer software, and (3) exist in exact form or in a form for which evidence is available concerning the validity of applying large-sample approximations to small-sample data. The first criterion has led us to focus primarily on the analysis of location or homogeneity, goodness of fit, and association for qualitative and quantitative data and to omit, for example, questions of dispersion. The second criterion has led to the exclusion of several practical nonparametric techniques that require either extensive matrix operations or iteration to converge to solution. Application of the third criterion has resulted in the omission of many multivariate nonparametric techniques, the small-sample properties of which have not been adequately investigated.

We have excluded some currently used methods of questionable validity (such as the Wald–Wolfowitz runs test used for location problems) and have included some new methods that are generally unknown to contemporary researchers. To facilitate our selection process, we have studied recent journals in education, sociology, and psychology to determine what techniques are commonly in use. We have also made an investigation of the methods generated by statisticians and presented in the technical statistical literature. From these two searches, we made our choices. Familiar methods like the two forms of the Wilcoxon test, the Mann–Whitney test, the McNemar test of change, the Kruskal–Wallis test, the Friedman test, the Karl Pearson Chi-square test, the Kolmogorov–Smirnov test, and others have been included. In addition, the unfamiliar and newer Goodman procedures for the analysis of multidimensional contingency tables, the Hodges–Lehmann alignment procedures for one- and two-way nonparametric analysis-of-variance designs based on ranks or normal scores, the Bowker test, and others have also been included.

Early in our writing, we adopted a second working principle. We chose to emphasize estimation rather than the more familiar hypothesis-testing models, provided that estimation procedures existed for the methods included in the book. Both of us find hypothesis testing an incomplete model for data analysis. To know that a tested hypothesis is false or that a result is statistically significant at $\alpha \leq 0.01$ is rarely sufficient for an understanding of what has gone on in an experimental or observational study. The reasons for rejection of a tested hypothesis are truly what a researcher wants to know. Location and estimation of the size of meaningful effects are needed. It is probably for these reasons that the post hoc, or data-snooping, procedures of Tukey and Scheffé for classical analysis-of-variance models have become so widely adopted for the analysis of normally distributed variables. Perhaps unknown to some researchers is the fact that corresponding procedures exist for contingency tables of two or more dimensions and for tests based on the substitution of ranks or normal scores for the original data. These methods and their extensions are emphasized in this book. In fact, these and related procedures constitute the focus of the book, together with planned and *post hoc* comparisons based on nonparametric, distribution-free, or assumption-freer contrasts. We believe that the techniques described and illustrated here are the most useful procedures for behavioral science research.

Finally, the book contains another set of unique procedures that are of major concern in contemporary behavioral studies. Researchers have been in the habit of applying the Karl Pearson Chi-square test to any contingency table of interest, even when it is known that the independent variable or the dependent variable satisfies an ordered relationship. When ordered dependent or independent variables are encountered, the Karl Pearson test is not optimum, because it ignores completely the ordered relationships in the data. There are a number of new solutions to this problem and we have included some of them in this book.

A book with such a variety of techniques owes its existence to the suggestions and contributions of many people. In addition to our special gratitude to Douglas Penfield of Rutgers University, who contributed to several early drafts of the manuscript, we want to thank Andrew Porter of Michigan State University and the National Institute of Education, Michael Subkoviak of the University of Wisconsin at Madison, Steven Lawton of the University of Ontario, David Wright of the National Assessment of Educational Progress, and James Maas of Ferris State College, all of whom tested the teachability of our instructional materials and contributed substantially to their improvement. We would also like to thank the many researchers who attended our workshops and helped us test the materials for clarity and understandability.

In addition, Arthur L. Dudycha of West Virginia College of Graduate Studies, J. Barnard Gilmore of the University of Toronto, Alfred Hexter of the University of California at Berkeley, Joel Levin of the University of Wisconsin at Madison, William L. Sawrey of California State University at Hayward, Neil Timm of the University of Pittsburgh, and Hans Ury of Kaiser Medical Center deserve our thanks for their many helpful suggestions in the manuscript stage. Roger Kirk of Baylor University was a conscientious and encouraging editor who aided us substantially in making the transition from workshop syllabus to textbook. He, as well as Bill Hicks of Brooks/Cole, are deserving of our thanks for their assistance and forebearance. We are especially indebted to Tom Little for his patience and great care in typing the manuscript again and again, and yet again, in its various versions. We are most appreciative of his usually good-humored acceptance of such an apparently endless and inadequately recompensed task.

Finally, we are grateful to the Literary Executor of the late Sir Ronald A. Fisher, F.R.S., to Dr. Frank Yates, F.R.S., and to Longman Group, Ltd., London, for permission to reprint Tables III and XXIII from their book *Statistical Tables for Biological, Agricultural and Medical Research* (6th edition, 1974).

Leonard A. Marascuilo
Maryellen McSweeney

CONTENTS

x

Part I

Statistical Principles Underlying Nonparametric Methods

Part I serves as a review of basic statistical concepts that are usually included in a first-year course in elementary statistics.

Chapter 1 introduces the notions of nonparametric, distribution-free, and assumption-freer tests. The problems encountered in the use of these terms are discussed.

Chapter 2 begins with rules on counting and includes the familiar notions of permutations and combinations. The nature of qualitative and quantitative variables is investigated and a brief presentation of probability theory is made. The algebra of linear compounds, their expected value, and variance is presented. A discussion of planned and post hoc comparisons precedes the presentation of the role of the normal, the t, the X^2, and the F distributions.

Chapter 3 contains an extensive presentation of the one-sample binomial and matched-pair sign test. Confidence intervals and power are discussed. Special cases of these tests in the form of the one-sample median test and the Cox-Stuart test for trend are illustrated.

Chapter 4 provides a discussion of estimate and test efficiency and principles for choosing between competing tests that can be used in the analysis of a specific set of data.

Nonparametric and Distribution-Free Procedures

A first glance at the title of this book might suggest that the book is divided into two parts, with the first part devoted to a presentation of nonparametric tests and the second part devoted to a presentation of distribution-free tests. Such a division of subject matter is impossible because "nonparametric" and "distribution-free" tests are imperfect synonyms rather than polar opposites. The two terms are treated synonymously throughout the book, even though distinctions can be drawn between the two types of methods. According to Bradley (1968), "A nonparametric test is one which makes no hypothesis about the value of a parameter in a statistical density function, whereas a distribution-free test is one which makes no assumptions about the precise form of the sampled population."

Consider the classical two-independent-sample Student's *t* test used to test the hypothesis that two normal distributions with equal variances have identical centers, against the alternative hypothesis that the centers are different in numerical value. If X_1 and X_2 represent the same variable of interest in populations 1 and 2, respectively, then the population distributions of scores on this variable can be characterized by the statements:

1. X_1 is normally distributed with mean μ_1 and variance σ^2.
2. X_2 is normally distributed with mean μ_2 and variance σ^2.

The Student's *t* test of equality of the population means is clearly parametric because the hypothesis under test states that the parameters that define the centers of the two

3

distributions are identical, while the alternative states that the parameters are numerically different. In standard statistical form, it is stated that:

$$H_0: \mu_1 = \mu_2 \text{ is tested against the alternative } H_1: \mu_1 \neq \mu_2.$$

As a specific example in which the t test would be used, suppose Population One with population mean or expected value $E(X_1) = \mu_1$ corresponds to scores made on a spelling test by students who would ordinarily be taught by a standard teaching method, and that Population Two with population mean or expected value $E(X_2) = \mu_2$ corresponds to scores made on the same spelling test by students taught with a new method. The hypothesis under test is parametric since it states that the means or expected values of the two normal populations of test scores are identical.

As another but related example, suppose that, in the same study in which the two methods for the teaching of spelling were being compared, it was decided to count only the number of students who obtained scores exceeding a specified cutoff point. If this were done, then it would be impossible to test directly the hypothesis that $\mu_1 = \mu_2$, since the exact numerical measurements would not be obtained for each subject in the study. If the proportion of students who score above a specified cutoff point for each procedure were determined, one could test the substitute hypothesis of:

$$H_0: p_1 = p_2 \text{ against the alternative } H_1: p_1 \neq p_2,$$

where p_1 and p_2 designate the proportions of students in populations 1 and 2, respectively, that exceed the cutoff point. Although this hypothesis focuses on a legitimate population characteristic of interest, that characteristic is not one of the parameters of the original populations, which are known to be normally distributed with location parameters μ_1 and μ_2 and common variance σ^2. For this reason, the test of $p_1 = p_2$ can, in this case, be viewed as a *nonparametric* test of identical location parameters.

The distinction between parametric and nonparametric tests is blurred by the reappearance of the test of $p_1 = p_2$ as a *parametric* test of equality of proportions in two independent binomial populations. For example, consider a psychological experiment that compares the maze-learning ability of $n_1 = 20$ "maze-bright" and $n_2 = 20$ "maze-dull" rats. If, at a single choice point, a rat may make either a correct or incorrect choice and if each of the $n_1 + n_2$ rats is run independently, the number of correct choices made by rats from the two populations can be described by independent binomial distributions with parameters (n_1, p_1) and (n_2, p_2), respectively, where p_1 and p_2 denote the respective probabilities of correct choice for the two populations. In this context, a test of $H_0: p_1 = p_2$ is *parametric*.

The same problem of describing a test as parametric or nonparametric, relative to the populations of interest, occurs when rank tests are used. The Wilcoxon–Mann–Whitney test of Chapter 11 is a test of equality of centers or identity of two independent populations, against the alternative that they differ in location. This test is generated by rank-ordering the observations and then substituting the first N integers for the ordered observations. The hypothesis of equal means or equal expected values is replaced by an apparent parametric hypothesis of equal expected-rank values with:

$$H_0: E(\overline{R}_1) = E(\overline{R}_2) \text{ against the alternative } H_1: E(\overline{R}_1) \neq E(\overline{R}_2).$$

This test is *parametric* in the distribution of *ranks*, but is *nonparametric* in the distribution of *scores*.

In summary, a statistical test is termed *nonparametric* if it does *not* test a hypothesis characterizing one of the parameters of the parent variable of interest. In this sense, the tests of $H_0 : p_1 = p_2$ and $H_0 : E(\overline{R}_1) = E(\overline{R}_2)$ are nonparametric tests with respect to the variables X_1 and X_2, which are each independent normal, with expected values μ_1 and μ_2 and variance σ^2.

Unfortunately, the confusion between parametric and nonparametric is increased by the introduction of the term *distribution-free*. A statistical test is distribution-free if the sampling distribution of the statistic on which the test is based is completely independent of the parent distribution of the variable. For example, the test of $H_0 : p_1 = p_2$ provided by the Irwin–Fisher exact test of Chapter 5 is distribution-free, because the sampling distribution of the criterion variable for testing $H_0 : p_1 = p_2$ is entirely independent of the values of p_1 and p_2. The Wilcoxon–Mann–Whitney rank test of $H_0 : E(\overline{R}_1) = E(\overline{R}_2)$ is valid for any distribution of scores and is, therefore, distribution-free.

As the illustrations have noted, the tests of $H_0 : p_1 = p_2$ and $H_0 : E(\overline{R}_1) = E(\overline{R}_2)$, as well as many other tests in this book, can be considered parametric, nonparametric, *or* distribution-free. The specific hypothesis tested and the use of the test statistic determine the classification of the test. Because the nonparametric–distribution-free distinctions are situation–specific and frequently blurred, the terms *nonparametric* and *distribution-free* are used interchangeably in this book and by many statisticians.

The issue of parametric/nonparametric/distribution-free tests is clouded even more by the realization that many classical *parametric* tests that assume normality are approximately distribution-free for very large samples. Their stated significance levels are approximately correct and their power approaches unity even when the data are drawn from non-normal populations. Moreover, the power of some nonparametric tests depends on the characteristics of the distributions sampled, so that these tests are not totally distribution-free.

It has been suggested by Ury (1967) that perhaps *nonparametric* and *distribution-free* procedures are better titled *assumption-freer*. This more accurate term is used occasionally in this book with its two *synonyms* nonparametric and distribution-free. However, these tests will never be called *quick and dirty*. Some of them require excessive amounts of arithmetic calculations, and some of them are actually cleaner and more appropriate than the classical tests encountered in much behavioral research.

In many respects, the precise classification of a particular test as parametric, nonparametric, or distribution-free is unimportant. Far more important to the researcher is the selection of a test for which the power of rejection is maximized when the hypothesis tested is false. If the data adhere to the assumptions required for a classical, normally based t or F test, a researcher would be foolish if he did not use them, since they are optimum, when justified. If the variables require an analysis based on the binomial or related distributions, then they should be used because they, too, are optimum for their own special cases. It is when the assumptions for the classical tests cannot be satisfied that one should seek out substitute tests. In most cases, the final choice as to which test to use will depend upon how much a researcher knows about alternative statistical methods, and the relative power of these methods, that could be used as substitute procedures. The question as to whether the tests are nonparametric or distribution-free will be of little importance. If the test selected does the job, and does it more efficiently than competing procedures, then the most relevant choice of test has been made.

While this discussion has centered upon nonparametric and distribution-free methods as possible replacements for classical or parametric tests, it should not be assumed that this is their sole justification for existence. Many of the tests presented in the following chapters are not substitutes for any other test, but are actually the optimum tests for the hypotheses they test. This is true for the Irwin–Fisher test and its large two-sample binomial, chi-square, or normal approximations. It is also true for the Wilcoxon–Mann–Whitney two-sample test if the data are observed as ranks and not as test scores or some other measured variable. Other examples could be cited, but such a listing would be of little value at this point in the book. Instead, one should note, while studying the examples, tests, and estimation procedures presented on the following pages, that this basic property of the tests described is, indeed, true. In almost all cases, the described tests are optimum for the hypotheses they are used to test. Since the hypotheses are frequently broad in nature, other hypotheses can be reformulated to fit different models, and under this condition these tests can be used as substitute tests. Even so, one should never think that nonparametric or distribution-free tests are exclusively substitutes for parametric tests.

Probabilistic and Statistical Concepts Necessary for Nonparametric and Distribution-Free Procedures

2–1. Structure of Nonclassical Statistical Methods

While most researchers are able to perform a two-sample t test on a desk calculator, or a three-way analysis of variance with replication and interaction with an electronic computer, it is perhaps true that many do not comprehend the theoretical basis of the computations that lead to a final test statistic. This is because most elementary texts are actually statistical cookbooks filled with a finite number of recipes that can be imitated, step by step. In this sense, many researchers perform classical tests in a programmed manner, sometimes utilizing a wrong procedure, or else abandoning the investigation of the original research questions for less specific alternatives that they know how to analyze.

Though nonparametric and distribution-free methods are less familiar to research workers, they are, in general, easier to understand and use correctly than are the classical methods, which are actually based on a knowledge of calculus for their derivation and comprehension. Almost all nonparametric methods are based on principles of elementary arithmetic, and anyone who has had a course in high-school algebra should find the derivation and application of most nonparametric tests simple and, it is to be hoped, interesting. For the most part, all that one need know to understand the basis of most nonparametric tests is how to count, but at a sophisticated level that includes knowledge of permutations and combinations.

EXAMPLE 2–1.1. As an example, consider a psychologist who has 10 rat cages lining the wall of his laboratory and who, one Monday morning, finds that the four rats in adjacent cages 6, 7, 8, and 9 died over the weekend, while the rats in cages 1, 2, 3, 4, 5, and 10 were still alive and active. His immediate thought might be that an epidemic is spreading through the cages. If he is familiar with the algebra of permutations and combinations, he knows that the number of different ways one could find four dead rats and six living rats among 10 rats is given by:

$$T = \begin{bmatrix} 10 \\ 4 \end{bmatrix} = 210 \quad \text{or} \quad T = \begin{bmatrix} 10 \\ 6 \end{bmatrix} = 210$$

Of these 210 combinations, only seven consist of four dead rats in adjacent cages. These seven combinations are given by:

$$\{1, 2, 3, 4\}, \quad \{2, 3, 4, 5\}, \quad \{3, 4, 5, 6\}, \quad \{4, 5, 6, 7\},$$
$$\{5, 6, 7, 8\}, \quad \{6, 7, 8, 9\}, \quad \text{and} \quad \{7, 8, 9, 10\}.$$

Given that four dead rats have been observed, the probability that all four are in adjacent cages is given by:

$$p = \frac{7}{210} = 0.033$$

To most researchers this represents a very low probability of occurrence of an event on the basis of chance alone. As a result, most would be willing to conclude that there is a strong possibility that an epidemic has spread through the rats and, in this case, the psychologist would be well advised to take precautions to save the rest of the animals.

It should be noted that $p = 0.033$ represents a conditional probability based on the psychologist's prior knowledge that four rats are dead. The dependence of this model on the after-the-fact definition of an epidemic can be completely avoided by noting that each rat can be dead or alive at the time of observation. Under this model, the number of different possible outcomes is given by:

$$T = 2^{10} = 1024$$

If an epidemic is operationally defined as the death of two or more rats in adjacent cages, we see that there is only one way to observe 10 dead rats in adjacent cages, two ways to observe nine dead rats in adjacent cages, three ways to observe eight dead rats in adjacent cages, etc. Thus the number of ways of observing two or more dead rats in adjacent cages is given by:

$$1 + 2 + 3 + 4 + 5 + 6 + 7 + 8 + 9 = 45$$

so that the *a priori* probability of finding two or more dead rats in adjacent cages is given by:

$$p = \frac{45}{1024} = 0.044$$

Since the finding of two or more dead rats in adjacent cages has such a low probability of occurrence by chance alone, it may be concluded that an epidemic has taken place. This decision can be justified, because the appearance of four dead rats in adjacent cages represents an outcome that is compatible with the *a priori* definition of an epidemic.

Many of the nonparametric tests presented in this book distinguish between conditional and unconditional probability models. Once the model is agreed upon, all one does is count the favorable or unfavorable outcomes and then compute the probabilities of these outcomes. Decisions are then made on the basis of the magnitude of the probabilities of the observed events treated as chance events. If the probabilities are small, the events are treated as representing factors other than chance, and the hypothesis of chance occurrence is rejected. If the probabilities are high, the explanation based on chance factors is retained. As with classical test theory, chances for the making of a Type I or Type II error exist.

EXAMPLE 2–1.2. For the previous example, the hypothesis under test states:

H_0: Death of rats in 10 adjacent cages is a random or chance process.

while the alternative states:

H_1: Death of rats in 10 adjacent cages is not a random or chance process.

A Type I error occurs if it is concluded that the appearance of dead rats in adjacent cages is not a chance event when, in fact, it is. This occurs whenever H_0 is rejected when it should really be retained. A Type II error occurs if it is concluded that the appearance of dead rats in adjacent cages is a chance error when in reality it is not but is actually the result of an epidemic. For the conditional and the unconditional models, the probabilities of a Type I error are given by $p = 0.033$ or $p = 0.044$, respectively. Unfortunately, the probability of a Type II error cannot be evaluated, since the *exact* statistical nature of the alternative cannot be specified with any degree of precision. As will be seen, this inability to define the alternative is a common property of most nonparametric or distribution-free tests, and so the determination of β, the probability of a Type II error, is treated less effectively. For this reason, minimal discussion is given to this important topic in this book; however, where it can be discussed and illustrated, attempts are made to make the results understandable and usable to practitioners.

2–2. Rules on Counting

Many of the nonparametric and distribution-free methods described in later pages of this book are based upon the counting rules presented in this section. In fact most, if not all of them, are based on the repeated application of a simple idea that can be expressed as the *fundamental rule of counting*. According to this principle, the total number of ways that two consecutive actions E_1 and E_2 can be performed, one action followed by the other, is simply the product of the number of ways E_1 and E_2 can be performed separately. Stated as a rule, this principle of counting reduces to:

Rule One. If action E_1 can be performed in n_1 ways, and if action E_2 can be performed in n_2 ways, then their joint action, E_1 followed by E_2, can occur in $T_1 = n_1 n_2$ ways.

EXAMPLE 2–2.1. As an example of the use of Rule One, consider the psychologist of the previous section who, at the time his study began, had to assign the rats to their respective cages. Since the first rat could be assigned to any of the

$n_1 = 10$ cages, this means that the second rat could be assigned to any of the $n_2 = 9$ remaining cages. Thus, the total number of ways the psychologist could assign the two rats to two of the ten cages is given by $T_1 = n_1 n_2 = 10(9) = 90$.

The extension of Rule One to the performance of K consecutive actions is given by:

Rule Two. If action E_1 can be performed in n_1 different ways, action E_2 in n_2 different ways, ..., and action E_K in n_K different ways, then the K actions can be performed in $T_2 = n_1 n_2 \cdots n_K$ ways.

EXAMPLE 2–2.2. Suppose that the psychologist has constructed a maze consisting of a runway that branches into three identical runways, each of which branches into two more identical runways, which finally branch into four other runways. This entire maze is as illustrated in Figure 2–1. The number of different

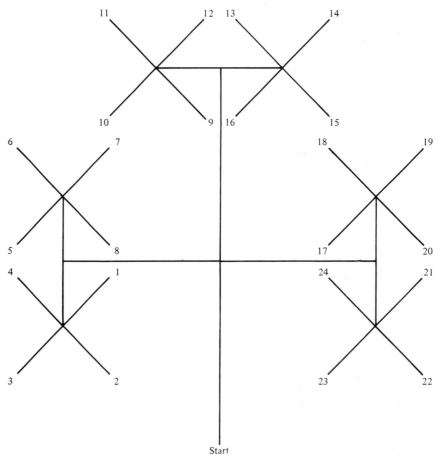

FIGURE 2–1. Maze with 24 different direct paths with choice points of size 3, 2, and 4.

direct paths and goal boxes available to a rat at the beginning of a test period is given by $T_2 = n_1 n_2 n_3$, where $n_1 = 3$, $n_2 = 2$, and $n_3 = 4$, so that the number of different direct paths is given by $T_2 = 3(2)(4) = 24$. Of course, in this counting it is assumed that no rat returns to any choice point and then selects a different runway as a continuation of his final path.

The direct application of Rule Two to the ordering of n different objects produces a rule on permutations that is used in the derivation of many of the nonparametric and distribution-free tests presented in later pages. Rule Two essentially defines the total number of arrangements of n distinct elements as $n(n-1)(n-2)(n-3)\cdots(3)(2)(1)$. Since products of this form are of frequent occurrence, a special notation has been developed, which defines the product of n consecutive decreasing integers as $n!$, which is read as n *factorial*. Thus, one has:

Rule Three. The number of permutations or orderings of n distinct objects is given by:

$$T_3 = n! = n(n-1)(n-2)(n-3)\cdots(3)(2)(1)$$

The reason for this repeated multiplication of decreasing integers follows from Rule Two. When there are n objects, any one of the n objects may be selected for the first position; once it is removed, $(n-1)$ objects are available for the second position. Thus, the number of arrangements of the first two selected objects is given by $n(n-1)$. Once the second object is removed, there are $(n-2)$ objects left for the third position. Thus, any one of the remaining $(n-2)$ objects may be aligned with the first two objects. This produces $n(n-1)(n-2)$ ways for accomplishing the first three ordered selections. Under repeated applications of this reasoning, the total number of permutations is given by $n!$.

EXAMPLE 2–2.3. Since the psychologist had 10 cages arranged sequentially, the total number of ways of assignment of the 10 rats to 10 cages is given by $T_3 = n! = 10! = 10(9)(8)(7)(6)(5)(4)(3)(2)(1) = 3,628,800$.

In some cases, the ordering of all n objects is not wanted. Instead, one may wish to select only t of the n objects and then to order the t objects actually selected. The number of ways of accomplishing this selection and arrangement is:

$$n(n-1)(n-2)\cdots(n-t+1).$$

By noting that this set of products is identical to:

$$\frac{n(n-1)(n-2)\cdots(n-t+1)(n-t)\cdots(3)(2)(1)}{(n-t)\cdots(3)(2)(1)} = \frac{n!}{(n-t)!}$$

one obtains the following:

Rule Four. The number of permutations of t objects selected from n objects is given by:

$$T_4 = \frac{n!}{(n-t)!}$$

EXAMPLE 2–2.4. Suppose that the psychologist can test only four animals a day on the maze illustrated in Figure 2–1. The total number of ordered ways that he has for choosing four of the 10 rats for a day's testing is given by:

$$T_4 = \frac{n!}{(n-t)!} = \frac{10!}{(10-4)!} = \frac{10!}{6!} = 10(9)(8)(7) = 5{,}040$$

In other cases, once the objects are selected, ordering may be of no interest. For these situations, one would like to know how many different groups of t objects can be selected from n objects. Since $n!/(n-t)!$ represents the number of ways of selecting t objects and then permuting them, it follows that the number of unique groups is given by dividing by $t!$. Thus:

$$T_s = \frac{n!/(n-t)!}{t!} = \frac{n!}{t!(n-t)!}$$

Since fractions of this type are frequently encountered in statistics, a special symbol has been proposed for them. The symbol is $\begin{bmatrix} n \\ t \end{bmatrix}$ and is read as "the number of combinations of t objects selected from n objects." With this symbol, the following rule is obtained:

Rule Five. The number of unique groups of t objects or combinations of unordered selections from n objects is given by:

$$T_s = \begin{bmatrix} n \\ t \end{bmatrix} = \frac{n!}{t!(n-t)!}$$

EXAMPLE 2–2.5. Suppose the psychologist wished to select five rats for use in an experiment where they would be deprived of food for two days. The number of different groups of five rats that he could select from the group of 10 rats is given by:

$$T_s = \frac{n!}{t!(n-t)!} = \frac{10!}{5!5!} = \frac{10(9)(8)(7)(6)(5)(4)(3)(2)(1)}{(5)(4)(3)(2)(1)(5)(4)(3)(2)(1)} = 252$$

The formula of Rule Five is also used in counting the permutations of n objects, t of which are of one kind and $(n-t)$ of which are of a second kind. If all n objects were different, then they could be arranged in $n!$ ways. However, if t of them are alike, their $t!$ indistinguishable arrangements reduce to a single arrangement. If the $(n-t)$ objects in the second group are identical to each other but different from the first t objects, their $(n-t)!$ indistinguishable arrangements reduce to a single arrangement. Thus, the number of unique arrangements is given by:

$$\begin{bmatrix} n \\ t \end{bmatrix} = \frac{n!}{(n-t)!t!}$$

When applied to counting permutations of two sets of different but identical objects, $\begin{bmatrix} n \\ t \end{bmatrix}$ is referred to as the *binomial coefficient* and is associated with Rule Six.

Rule Six. The number of permutations of n objects in which t of one kind are identical and the remaining $(n - t)$ of another kind are identical is given by:

$$T_6 = \begin{bmatrix} n \\ t \end{bmatrix} = \frac{n!}{t!(n-t)!}$$

EXAMPLE 2–2.6. In the example of the previous section, the psychologist was interested in knowing the number of ways 10 rats could be divided into two groups of four dead rats and six living rats. Since the four dead rats are identical with respect to death, as are the six living rats:

$$T_6 = \begin{bmatrix} n \\ t \end{bmatrix} = \begin{bmatrix} 10 \\ 6 \end{bmatrix} = \frac{10!}{4!(10-4)!} = \frac{10!}{4!6!}$$
$$= \frac{10(9)(8)(7)(6)(5)(4)(3)(2)(1)}{4(3)(2)(1)(6)(5)(4)(3)(2)(1)}$$
$$= 210$$

Often one requires, for some nonparametric or distribution-free tests, an extension of Rule Six to the case in which the objects belong to K different groups, but in which the objects in each group are identical. The number of such permutations is given by:

Rule Seven. The number of permutations of n objects in which n_1 are alike, n_2 are alike, ..., and n_K are alike, where $n = n_1 + n_2 + \ldots + n_K$, is given by:

$$T_7 = \begin{bmatrix} n \\ n_1 n_2 \cdots n_K \end{bmatrix} = \frac{n!}{n_1! n_2! \cdots n_K!}$$

The symbol $\begin{bmatrix} n \\ n_1 n_2 \cdots n_K \end{bmatrix}$ is called the *multinomial coefficient.*

EXAMPLE 2–2.7. If three of the rats are solid grey, if two are solid black, and if five are white, then the number of ways the rats can be assigned to the 10 cages with respect to fur color, only, is given by:

$$T_7 = \begin{bmatrix} 10 \\ 3,2,5 \end{bmatrix} = \frac{10!}{3!2!5!}$$
$$= \frac{10(9)(8)(7)(6)(5)(4)(3)(2)(1)}{3(2)(1)(2)(1)(5)(4)(3)(2)(1)}$$
$$= 2,520$$

As might be expected, Rule Five can be extended to the case in which n objects are assigned to K groups of size $n_1, n_2, \ldots, n_K$, where $n = n_1 + n_2 + \ldots + n_K$. This is given by Rule Eight.

Rule Eight. The number of unique groupings of n objects into K groups of size $n_1, n_2, \ldots, n_K$ is given by:

$$T_8 = \begin{bmatrix} n \\ n_1 n_2 \cdots n_K \end{bmatrix} = \frac{n!}{n_1! n_2! \cdots n_K!}$$

EXAMPLE 2–2.8. The number of different groupings of the 10 rats into $K = 3$ groups of size $n_1 = 4, n_2 = 4$, and $n_3 = 2$ is given by:

$$T_8 = \begin{bmatrix} 10 \\ 4,4,2 \end{bmatrix} = \frac{10(9)(8)(7)(6)(5)(4)(3)(2)(1)}{4(3)(2)(1)(4)(3)(2)(1)(2)(1)} = 3,150$$

Thus, there are 3,150 different groups of rats that permit the psychologist to test four rats on one day, four on a second day, and two on a third day.

These eight rules will find repeated applications in the development of most of the nonparametric tests appearing in this book. The tests of Chapter 3, for example, are built entirely from the application of Rules Two and Six as applied to permuting n objects in which t are identical and in which the remaining $(n - t)$ are identical, but different, from the first t. The tests of Chapter 5 will be seen to depend upon Rules One and Five as applied to combinations of t objects selected from n objects. Other examples of the application of these rules are given in subsequent chapters.

2–3. Types of Statistical Variables

An on-going controversy in measurement theory has focused on the issue of whether the use of statistical techniques is limited by the scale of measurement of the outcomes of interest. Writers who were heavily influenced by S. S. Stevens' early discussion of the issue of scale of measurement and permissible arithmetic operations identified the use of certain statistical tests with the associated scales of measurement (e.g., Siegel, 1956). Some statisticians countered by emphasizing that the validity of the statistical techniques depended on the distributional properties of the variables of interest, and not their scale of measurement. The statement of I. R. Savage (1957) is illustrative of this point of view:

> The erroneous statement is frequently made that arithmetic operations should not be performed if the results are not meaningful in terms of the phenomenon the data measure. . . . I know of no reason to limit statistical procedures to those involving arithmetic operations consistent with the scale properties of the observed quantities . . .
>
> It is probably true, however, that sophisticated assumptions about the distribution of the observations are commonly unsupportable in situations where very few arithmetic operations with the data lead to numbers that are meaningful in terms of the phenomena under study. (p. 333)

Readers who are interested in following this controversy will find the writings of Stevens (1946, 1968), Lord (1953), Savage (1957), Anderson (1961), Baker, Hardyck, and Petrinovich (1966), and Gardner (1975) informative. This book sides with Savage and emphasizes the dependence of the statistical techniques on the distributional properties of the variables, not the scale of measurement. Consequently, the statisticians' classification of variables will be examined, rather than the classification by scale of measurement as nominal, ordinal, interval, or ratio. Statistical variables are of two types: they are either *qualitative* or *quantitative*.

Qualitative variables can be subclassified as *ordered* or *unordered*, while quantitative variables can be subclassified as *discrete* or *continuous*.

Qualitative variables are variables whose states or levels are defined by a set of mutually exclusive and exhaustive subclasses . The classes are usually defined in verbal terms. Examples of qualitative variables are:

1. Race: {Asian, Black, Caucasian, Other}
2. Sex: {Male, Female}
3. Marital status: {Single, Married, Widowed, Divorced}
4. Social class: {High, Medium, Low}
5. Attitude toward school integration: {Strongly opposed, Moderately opposed, Neutral, Moderately supportive, Strongly supportive}
6. Area of residence: {Central core city, Suburban area, Rural town, Rural farm}

The first three examples represent qualitative variables for which the classes are not ordered, whereas the last three examples represent variables ordered from high to low social class, from strongly opposing to strongly supportive of school integration, and from maximum to minimum urbanization. Statistical methods for qualitative variables which are not ordered are presented in Chapters 3, 5, 6, 7, 8, 9, and 10. Procedures for ordered qualitative variables are presented in Chapters 6, 8, 12, and 16.

Quantitative variables are variables whose states or numerical values are determined by counting or measuring. Examples of quantitative variables are:

1. Number of daily visits to a health clinic during the month of January: {0, 1, 2, 3, . . . , 31}
2. Score on a 25-item reading test: {0, 1, 2, . . . , 25}
3. IQ score: {68, 69, 70, 71, . . . , 199, 200}
4. Weight of male children at birth: {3 lbs., 0 oz. to 25 lbs., 15 oz.}
5. Amount of time to run the 100-yd dash: {0 seconds to 20 seconds}
6. Age at death: {0 yrs to 120 yrs}

The first three variables are examples of *discrete* variables. All values of the variable can be listed and put into a one-to-one correspondence with some or all of the positive integers. For these examples, the one-to-one correspondence is achieved with only part of the integers. When this occurs, the variable is said to cover a finite set of values. There are statistical variables for which the correspondence must be made with the entire infinite set of integers. Such variables are not commonly encountered in behavioral research and are, in this sense, of academic interest only.

The set of values that the last three variables can actually assume is, in practice, infinite, but the number of values is uncountable. There is no way to put the entire set of possible values into a one-to-one correspondence with the set of integers.

One way to appreciate the impossible nature of counting the number of possible values for a continuous variable is to consider the set of decimals between 0 and 1. Between 0 and 1 there is at least one other value. For example, .31726 is between 0 and 1. Similarly, between 0 and .31726 there are other values, including .31725. In a like manner, between .31725 and .31726 there are other values such as .317257. Since this process can be continued forever between any two decimals, it is seen that it is impossible to put all possible values of the decimals between 0 and 1 into a one-to-one correspondence with the set of integers. If the correspondence cannot be established for the decimals between 0 and 1, surely it cannot be established for the decimals between any two limits. For this reason, such variables are called *continuous* variables.

In a certain sense, continuous variables are mainly of academic interest because, even though constructs such as weight, time, age, and height are perceived as continuous, the measurement operation limits the possible numerical values to a discrete or countable set of values. For example, if weight scales are calibrated in ounces, then male weights at birth are reported as {3 lbs. 0 oz., 3 lbs. 1 oz., 3 lbs. 2 oz., . . . , 25 lbs. 15 oz.}. This set of numerical values really represents a discrete set of values that can be placed into a one-to-one correspondence with a subset of integers. This is also true of reported times to run the 100-yard dash. Most stopwatches used at track meets are calibrated to the one-hundredth of a second. Thus, times are reported at 0.01, 0.02, . . . , 59.99 seconds. This set of numbers can be put into a one-to-one correspondence with a subset of the full set of integers; so what is in theory a continuous variable is actually measured on a scale that produces a discrete outcome. This is true for the measurement of all continuous variables.

At times, it becomes important to distinguish between the theoretical nature of a variable and its measurement nature. For example, most psychologists believe that the variable *intelligence* is continuously distributed throughout a population, even though *intelligence quotients* are reported on a discrete scale. In order to avoid unnecessary confusion, the *concept of intelligence* is referred to as a *hypothetical construct*, whereas the IQ score is referred to as the *operational definition* of a hypothetical construct. In a similar manner, attitude toward school integration is a hypothetical construct probably extending from positive attitudes toward integrating all schools to negative attitudes for keeping all schools segregated. Between the two extremes are a myriad of attitudes, which could not be put into a one-to-one correspondence with the set of integers. Thus, while attitude toward integration of schools represents a hypothetical construct that extends along a continuous scale, all operational definitions of the attitude produce either an ordered qualitative variable or a discrete quantitative variable that is used for analysis. For example, an ordered qualitative variable is produced if subjects are asked to respond to the question:

What is your attitude toward the integration of schools?
1. I strongly oppose it.
2. I moderately oppose it.
3. I don't care.
4. I moderately support it.
5. I strongly support it.

On the other hand, a discrete quantitative variable is produced by asking subjects to respond to the item:

Indicate how much you support or oppose school integration by circling the number that best describes your point of view. Let 0 mean complete opposition and let 10 mean complete support.

0 1 2 3 4 5 6 7 8 9 10

As will be seen, statistical procedures are dependent upon the way a researcher chooses to define the hypothetical constructs of his study. This should be given careful attention because statistical power and efficiency are greatly influenced by the nature of the underlying variable. If a construct can be defined in only one way, then no choice exists. However, if a number of procedures can be generated to give operational meaning to the construct, and if they are of equal explanatory value to the researcher, then the one that leads to the most powerful statistical method should be selected. Usually, this means that ordered qualitative variables are preferable to unordered qualitative variables, and, going one step further, that quantitative variables, typically discrete quantitative variables, are preferable to ordered qualitative variables. If a researcher has a choice, he should give serious thought to these recommendations and follow them, if at all possible.

2–4. Continuity, Treatment of Ties and Corrections for Continuity in Nonparametric and Distribution-Free Ties

Almost all of the tests of Chapters 10, 11, 12, 13, 14, 15, and 16 assume that the underlying variables are continuously distributed in the populations of interest. As indicated in Section 2–3, even though a variable is continuous in theory, all measurement of it must be made on a discrete scale or set of values. The conflict between the theoretical assumption of continuity of the data and the empirical reality of data measured on a discrete scale must be considered by the user of these tests. Because of this incongruity, adjustments are often required on the original data or on the data that have been transformed to a different level of abstraction or quantification. A number of ways have been proposed to handle this problem, but none of them is thoroughly adequate. Rather than present the pros and cons for the proposed methods, only the procedures that are actually recommended and used in the later pages of the book are described. Other procedures are examined in some of the exercises that follow each chapter.

If a variable is continuous, the probability of selecting two or more values that are exactly equal in numerical value is zero. In other words, it is not possible to generate tied scores or observations for variables that are continuous. Such is not the case for discrete variables. For discrete variables, ties can occur in great abundance. Statistical tests that appear in Chapters 10 through 16 frequently require a rank ordering of the variables and then an assignment of the integers $\{1, 2, 3, \ldots, n\}$ to the ranked values.

EXAMPLE 2–4.1. Suppose X: $\{0, 0, 0, 2, 3, 3, 6, 9, 12, 12\}$ represents the number of wrong turns taken, before reaching the final goal, by each of the 10 rats tested on the maze of Figure 2–1.

If the psychologist would like to assign the rank values

$$R: \{1, 2, 3, 4, 5, 6, 7, 8, 9, 10\}$$

to the errors, he is faced with the problem of ties, since three rats made zero errors, two rats made three errors, and two rats made 12 errors. One way he could break the ties is to assign midranks to the tied values. For the three rats that made zero errors, the midrank value is given by $\frac{1}{3}(1 + 2 + 3) = 2$; for the two rats that made three errors, the midrank values are $\frac{1}{2}(5 + 6) = 5.5$, while for the two rats that made 12 errors, the midrank values are $\frac{1}{2}(9 + 10) = 9.5$. With these values, the assigned ranks are given by

$$R: \{2, 2, 2, 4, 5.5, 5.5, 7, 8, 9.5, 9.5\}$$

The major disadvantage of this midrank procedure for the breaking of tied observations is that it tends to reduce the number of possible values that a test statistic can assume. For the exact ranking, the total number of permutations of the ranks is given by Rule Three as

$$10! = 10(9)(8)(7)(6)(5)(4)(3)(2)(1) = 3{,}628{,}800$$

whereas, for the midrank assignment, the total number of permutations is given by Rule Seven as:

$$\begin{bmatrix} 10 \\ 3,1,2,1,1,2 \end{bmatrix} = \frac{10!}{3!\,1!\,2!\,1!\,1!\,2!} = 151{,}200$$

With the reduction in the number of possible assignments of rank values, there occurs a reduction in the number of different values that the corresponding statistical variable can assume. This in turn has a tendency to reduce the number of unique values that constitute the critical region of the resulting test. With a reduction of the critical values there also occurs a reduction in the power of the test. Thus, this method of correction for ties can produce a test with less power than desired. Fortunately, for most of the tests presented, additional corrections are available that compensate for the reduced number of possible values of the test statistic and that thus restore the power to near the original level occurring in the absence of ties.

Tied values also create problems for the tests discussed in Chapters 3, 5, 6, 7, 8, and 9, but for different reasons. The tests in these chapters are designed mainly for qualitative variables, but they can be used for quantitative variables that have been categorized. The problem with ties occurs when an observation is numerically equal to a value that defines the boundary of one of the categories constituting the set of mutually exclusive and exhaustive classes that define the variable.

EXAMPLE 2–4.2. To illustrate, consider the number of errors made by the 10 rats in running the maze of Figure 2–1, but according to whether or not they were in the control or experimental conditions of the study. Suppose the results are as shown in Table 2–1. The median number of errors made by the 10 rats is given by $\hat{M} = 3$, a value that equals the numbers of errors made by one rat in each sample. If the psychologist wished to classify the rats in the experimental and control groups according to whether the number of errors made in running the maze was less than or greater than the median number of errors, he would be unable to classify the two rats that made the median number of three errors. The question he must answer is

TABLE 2–1. *Number of errors made by ten rats running the maze of Figure 2–1.*

Control group	Experimental group
2	0
3	0
9	0
12	3
12	6

how he should handle the two rats whose scores are tied at the boundary points of his classification scheme.

An obvious option is to discard them from the study and reduce the total sample size from 10 to 8. This may not be acceptable on practical grounds since the collection of data is expensive. It is also questionable on statistical grounds if the researcher wishes to test the hypothesis that the median numbers of errors for the two conditions are equal, for the discarded pieces of information are compatible with the hypothesis of no difference in medians.

Another way to handle the problem is to take each piece of information that occurs at the category boundary and assign it *at random* to the category *above* the boundary or to the category *below* the boundary by flipping a coin, or by selecting an odd or even number in a table of random numbers. This is the method prescribed by most mathematical statisticians, since it maintains the basic probability structure of the resulting test statistic. Naturally, it also means that if the experiment were to be repeated and if the same set of outcomes were to be observed, it is possible that a different decision might be made, since the assignment of the two tied observations to the categories above or below the boundary might differ. For this reason, the statistically optimum procedure has not found much acceptance among researchers.

Another option, and the one that is most frequently used in this book, is to assign the tied values to the categories so as to make the rejection of the hypothesis of *no difference* in medians *most difficult*. This makes the resulting statistical test conservative, thereby reducing the power of the test. However, it does place an upper limit on the size of a Type I error, the error of false rejection of a null hypothesis. With this method of breaking ties, the resulting two-by-two table for the observed data is as shown in Table 2–2.

TABLE 2–2. *Two-by-two frequency table for the data of Table 2–1, with values tied at median assigned above and below the median, to produce a conservative test of no difference in median.*

Number of errors	Control group	Experimental group	Total
Above median	3	2	5
Below median	2	3	5
Total	5	5	10

Continuity also creates a problem in the large-sample form of many nonparametric and distribution-free tests since they are generally based on the continuous normal or chi-square distribution, while the sampling distribution of the test statistic assumes a discrete set of values. To overcome this problem, one makes what is called the *correction for continuity* by adding or subtracting $\frac{1}{2}$ of the distance between adjacent possible values for the discrete criterion variable. In general, an addition of $\frac{1}{2}$ of a unit is made to the observed value if the outcome variable is below the expected value, while a subtraction of $\frac{1}{2}$ unit is made if the observed value is above the expected value. This correction makes the test slightly conservative and its utility has been questioned by some (Grizzle, 1967). No example is presented here since many examples will be encountered in later pages.

2–5. Probability Model for Equally Likely Events

Most of the probability computations for nonparametric or distribution-free tests are based upon the assumption that all permutations of the outcomes are equally likely. Under this model, probability computations reduce to simple applications of the eight rules of counting and a substitution of the resulting counts into the following definition of probability.

Let S denote the set of all possible outcomes of an experiment. Let the individual outcomes that constitute S be called the *elements* of S. Let the number of elements of S, $n(S) = N$. Consider an event, E, which can occur in $n(E)$ different ways in the total set of N possible outcomes. If the outcomes are all equally likely, then *the probability of E* is given as the simple ratio of $n(E)$ to N and is written as:

$$P(E) = \frac{n(E)}{N}$$

EXAMPLE 2–5.1. In the example described in Section 2–1, the number of different ways of finding four rats dead in adjacent cages is given by $n(E) = 7$, while the total number of different ways of finding four dead rats is given by Rule Six as $N = \begin{bmatrix} 10 \\ 4 \end{bmatrix} = 210$, so that the probability of four deaths in four adjacent cages is given by $P(E) = 7/210 = .0333$.

Although the definition of probability for equally likely events is frequently applied in the development of nonparametric statistics, an algebra for probability computations can be developed without its use. Some of the principal rules of that algebra are stated as Probability Rules One through Six, and are explained in terms of the probabilities of equally likely events.

If E denotes the event of interest, then $\overline{E}$ will be used to denote the non-occurrence of E or the occurrence of the *complementary event*. Since S can be partitioned into two mutually exclusive and exhaustive sets, E and $\overline{E}$, it follows that $n(E) + n(\overline{E}) = N$. Thus, upon division by N:

$$\frac{n(E)}{N} + \frac{n(\overline{E})}{N} = 1$$

so that:

$$\frac{n(\overline{E})}{N} = 1 - \frac{n(E)}{N}$$

This gives rise to Probability Rule One.

Probability Rule One. If the probability of E is given by $P(E)$, then the probability of its complement is given by:

$$P(\overline{E}) = 1 - P(E)$$

EXAMPLE 2–5.2. If the probability of running the maze of Figure 2–1 correctly on the first try is given by $P(E) = .3$, then the probability of making one or more errors on the first try is given by $P(\overline{E}) = 1 - .3 = .7$.

If some of the elements of S can be partitioned into two sets E_1 and E_2 such that each element can be assigned to only one of the two sets, the sets are said to be *mutually exclusive*, or *disjoint*. The elements that are members of E_1 or E_2 are said to constitute the *union* of E_1 with E_2. Since $n(E_1 \text{ or } E_2) = n(E_1) + n(E_2)$, it follows that:

$$\frac{n(E_1 \text{ or } E_2)}{N} = \frac{n(E_1)}{N} + \frac{n(E_2)}{N}$$

This is essentially a statement of Probability Rule Two.

Probability Rule Two. If the events E_1 and E_2 are mutually exclusive, the probability of their union is given by:

$$P(E_1 \text{ or } E_2) = P(E_1) + P(E_2)$$

EXAMPLE 2–5.3. If the probability of making one error in the running of the maze of Figure 2–1 is given by $P(E_1) = .3$, and if the probability of making two errors is given by $P(E_2) = .2$, then the probability of making one *or* two errors is given by:

$$P(E_1 \text{ or } E_2) = .3 + .2 = .5.$$

If the events E_1 and E_2 have elements in common, they are said to *intersect*. If the number of elements in the intersection is denoted by $n(E_1 \text{ and } E_2)$, then the number of elements in their union is given by $n(E_1 \text{ or } E_2) = n(E_1) + n(E_2) - n(E_1 \text{ and } E_2)$, so that:

$$\frac{n(E_1 \text{ or } E_2)}{N} = \frac{n(E_1)}{N} + \frac{n(E_2)}{N} - \frac{n(E_1 \text{ and } E_2)}{N}$$

This is the corresponding probability rule for nondisjoint events.

Probability Rule Three. If the events E_1 and E_2 are not mutually exclusive, then:

$$P(E_1 \text{ or } E_2) = P(E_1) + P(E_2) - P(E_1 \text{ and } E_2)$$

EXAMPLE 2–5.4. If, in Table 2–2:

$$P(E_1) = P(\text{Rat is in the control group}) = \frac{5}{10}$$

$$P(E_2) = P(\text{Rat is above median}) = \frac{5}{10}$$

and

$$P(E_1 \text{ and } E_2) = P(\text{Rat is in the control group and above the median}) = \frac{3}{10}$$

then:

$$P(E_1 \text{ or } E_2) = P(\text{Rat is in the control group or above the median})$$
$$= \frac{5}{10} + \frac{5}{10} - \frac{3}{10} = \frac{7}{10}$$

In many texts, the intersection of two sets E_1 and E_2 is denoted by $E_1 \cap E_2$, the union of two sets is denoted by $E_1 \cup E_2$, and if two sets are mutually exclusive, one writes $E_1 \cap E_2 = \phi$. These notations are used sparingly in this book. Instead, intersection is usually indicated by *and* and union by *or*. In most cases, probabilities will be defined on disjoint sets, so that Probability Rule Three will not be encountered too frequently.

If, following each run of a rat in the maze of Figure 2–1, the psychologist allowed the runways to air, so that the path taken by previously run rats could not influence the paths taken by rats run at a subsequent time, it is said that runs between the rats are *statistically independent*. In a like manner, in repeated tosses of a coin, the appearance of heads or tails is not determined by previous tosses because the coin does not have a memory, and it is said that outcomes on consecutive tosses are statistically independent. Independence of events is assumed for most of the statistical tests presented in this book. Since it is so important, it is stated as a definition in Probability Rules Four and Five.

Probability Rule Four. If two events E_1 and E_2 are statistically independent, then the probability of their intersection is given by:

$$P(E_1 \text{ and } E_2) = P(E_1)P(E_2)$$

Probability Rule Five. If K events are involved, statistical independence means that:

$$P(E_1 \text{ and } E_2 \text{ and } E_3 \ldots \text{ and } E_K) = P(E_1)P(E_2)P(E_3) \cdots P(E_K)$$

and that all 2-element, 3-element, 4-element, $\ldots$, $(K - 1)$-element intersections also satisfy a corresponding product probability statement.

EXAMPLE 2–5.5. If the choice points made by rats running the maze of Figure 2–1 are statistically independent, then the probability that a rat will make a correct run of the maze strictly on the basis of chance is given by:

$$P(E_1 \text{ and } E_2 \text{ and } E_3) = P(E_1)P(E_2)P(E_3)$$

$$= \frac{1}{3} \times \frac{1}{2} \times \frac{1}{4} = \frac{1}{24}$$

In addition,

$$P(E_1 \text{ and } E_2) = \frac{1}{3} \times \frac{1}{2} = \frac{1}{6}$$

$$P(E_1 \text{ and } E_3) = \frac{1}{3} \times \frac{1}{4} = \frac{1}{12}$$

and

$$P(E_2 \text{ and } E_3) = \frac{1}{2} \times \frac{1}{4} = \frac{1}{8}$$

If events are *not* statistically independent, they are said to be statistically *dependent*. For example, suppose the psychologist, in running the rats through the maze, always placed food pellets in platform 8, and suppose he did not give the entire maze a chance to air, so a tested rat might be able to smell and detect the path taken by his predecessor. If this were to happen, the runs between the two rats would *not* be independent; instead they would be *correlated*. When this occurs, the probability of the joint occurrence of the two events is influenced to some degree by the occurrence of the first event. It is also said that the occurrence of E_2 is *conditional upon* the occurrence of E_1. To see what the probability of the intersection is under such conditions, note that:

$$P(E_1 \text{ and } E_2) = \frac{n(E_1 \text{ and } E_2)}{N} \frac{n(E_1)}{n(E_1)}$$

$$= \frac{n(E_1)}{N} \frac{n(E_1 \text{ and } E_2)}{n(E_1)}$$

By definition, $n(E_1)/N = P(E_1)$. But notice that $[n(E_1 \text{ and } E_2)]/n(E_1)$ is the ratio of the number of times E_1 and E_2 occur together to the number of times E_1 occurs altogether.

This ratio satisfies the definition of a probability, not in the entire set of outcomes S, but within the set of outcomes defined by E_1. It is called the *conditional probability* of E_2 under the condition that E_1 has occurred. This is denoted by:

$$P(E_2|E_1) = \frac{n(E_1 \text{ and } E_2)}{n(E_1)}$$

Thus, one has Probability Rule Six.

Probability Rule Six. If E_1 and E_2 are not statistically independent, the probability of their intersection is given by:

$$P(E_1 \text{ and } E_2) = P(E_1)P(E_2|E_1)$$

In a similar fashion, the probability of the intersection can also be computed from:

$$P(E_1 \text{ and } E_2) = P(E_2)P(E_1|E_2)$$

EXAMPLE 2–5.6. For the data of Table 2–2:

$$P(\text{Rat is in the control group}) = \frac{5}{10}$$

$$P(\text{Rat is above the median, given that the rat is in the control group}) = \frac{3}{5}$$

Thus:

$$P(\text{Rat is in the control group and is simultaneously above the median})$$

$$= \frac{5}{10} \times \frac{3}{5} = \frac{3}{10}$$

While the six probability rules of this section have been derived under the model of equally likely outcomes, such a restriction is not necessary. Generally, the equally likely model is all that is required for most nonparametric and distribution-free tests. Where differential probabilities of events are encountered, no hesitation will be noted in applying the six probability rules of this section. They can be used safely and without fear of error since, under a more general model, the same equations or formulas are encountered.

2–6. Discrete Random Variables

Earlier, two types of variables, qualitative and quantitative, were contrasted in terms of their states or levels. The levels of a qualitative variable were either ordered or unordered categories, while the quantitative variable was characterized by its numerically-valued outcomes. Variables may also be described as *random variables* or *variates*. The term *random variable* is used to represent a variable that may assume any of a specified set of values with a specifiable probability. If each possible outcome of an experiment can be associated with one and only one numerical value, and if a probability distribution can be defined for those numerically-valued outcomes, then the set of ordered pairs consisting of the experimental outcomes and their associated numerical values is a *random variable*.

EXAMPLE 2–6.1. For example, if a rat maze provides a choice point with a left or right turn, and if it is assumed that the choices of a left or right turn are equally likely, then a random variable $X = \{(\text{left turn, 1}), (\text{right turn, 0})\}$ can be defined. The assumption of equally likely choices results in the assignment of probabilities of $\frac{1}{2}$ to each turn or to the associated numerically-valued outcomes. The random variable X is the function $X = \{(\text{left turn, 1}), (\text{right turn, 0})\}$; however, random variable is often used to describe the *observed value* or the numerically-valued outcome of the experiment. Thus, the abbreviated terminology "the value of the random variable is 1" is used to imply the statement that "the experiment has yielded an outcome for which the associated numerical value is 1."

Most of the random variables that are encountered in the nonparametric or distribution-free methods presented in this book are discrete. In almost all cases, probabilities of occurrence can be determined, and then summary measures that specify the *location* or *center of gravity* of the distribution and its degree of *spread* can be calculated. These measures are called the *expected value* and *variance*, respectively. Once these are known, the large-sample form of most nonparametric or distribution-free tests can be specified.

Consider a discrete random variable that can assume the set of values X: $\{x_1, x_2, \ldots, x_K\}$ with the following probabilities of occurrence, P: $\{p_1, p_2, \ldots, p_K\}$. By definition, the *expected value of X* and the *variance of X* are given by:

$$E(X) = \sum_{k=1}^{K} x_k p_k = \mu$$

$$\text{Var}(X) = \sum_{k=1}^{K} (x_k - \mu)^2 p_k$$

A computing formula for $\text{Var}(X)$ is given simply as:

$$\text{Var}(X) = \sum_{k=1}^{K} x_k^2 p_k - \mu^2$$

The square root of the variance is called the *standard deviation* and is denoted as:

$$\sigma = \sqrt{\text{Var}(X)}$$

EXAMPLE 2–6.2. As an example, consider a perfectly balanced six-sided die with faces marked as X: $\{1, 2, 3, 4, 5, 6\}$, and probabilities given by P: $\{\frac{1}{6}, \frac{1}{6}, \frac{1}{6}, \frac{1}{6}, \frac{1}{6}, \frac{1}{6}\}$. When the die is rolled one time, the expected number on the upper face is given by:

$$E(X) = \sum_{k=1}^{6} x_k p_k$$

$$= 1 \cdot \frac{1}{6} + 2 \cdot \frac{1}{6} + 3 \cdot \frac{1}{6} + 4 \cdot \frac{1}{6} + 5 \cdot \frac{1}{6} + 6 \cdot \frac{1}{6} = 3.5$$

By the computational formula, the variance is given by:

$$\text{Var}(X) = \sum_{k=1}^{6} x_k^2 p_k - \mu^2$$

$$= \left[(1)^2 \left[\frac{1}{6}\right] + (2)^2 \left[\frac{1}{6}\right] + \ldots + (6)^2 \left[\frac{1}{6}\right] \right] - (3.5)^2$$

$$= \frac{35}{12} = 2.92.$$

Since the arithmetic involved in the computational formula is simpler than that encountered in the definitional formula, its use is preferred.

Closely allied to the notion of the variance of a single random variable is the parallel idea of the *covariance* between two random variables. By definition:

$$\text{Cov}(X_1, X_2) = \sum_{k=1}^{K} \sum_{k'=1}^{K'} (x_{1k} - \mu_1)(x_{2k'} - \mu_2)P_{kk'}$$

where

$$P_{kk'} = P(X_1 = x_{1k} \quad \text{and} \quad X_2 = x_{2k'})$$

A computing formula for $\text{Cov}(X_1, X_2)$ is given simply as:

$$\text{Cov}(X_1, X_2) = \sum_{k=1}^{K} \sum_{k'=1}^{K'} x_{1k} x_{2k'} P_{kk'} - \mu_1 \mu_2$$

EXAMPLE 2–6.3. Suppose two dice are thrown simultaneously. Since all tosses are independent, it follows from Probability Rule Four that:

$$P_{kk'} = P(X_1 = x_{1k} \quad \text{and} \quad X_2 = x_{2k'})$$
$$= P(X_1 = x_{1k})P(X_2 = x_{2k'})$$
$$= \left[\frac{1}{6}\right]\left[\frac{1}{6}\right] = \frac{1}{36}$$

Thus, for all values of k and k', by the computing formula for covariance:

$$\text{Cov}(X_1, X_2) = \sum_{k=1}^{K} \sum_{k'=1}^{K'} x_{1k} x_{2k'} \left[\frac{1}{36}\right] - (3.5)(3.5)$$
$$= \left[(1)(1) + (1)(2) + \ldots + (6)(6)\right]\left[\frac{1}{36}\right] - (3.5)(3.5)$$
$$= 0$$

In this example, the covariance of X_1 with X_2 is identical to zero because the tosses of the individual die are statistically independent of one another. If the events were not independent, then the covariance would be expected to differ from zero. However, it should not be concluded that a zero covariance between two random variables necessarily implies that the variables are independent. Examples in which the covariance is zero and yet the variables are not independent are not difficult to find, but in any case one can always state that if two variables are independent, their covariance is zero.

Most researchers do not employ covariance measures when speaking of the dependence that exists between two random variables. Instead, they prefer to employ the *correlation coefficient*, which is defined as a standardized covariance:

$$\rho = \frac{\text{Cov}(X_1, X_2)}{\sigma_{x_1}\sigma_{x_2}}$$

The covariance can range from large negative to large positive values, and is expressed in the squared metric of interest (e.g., squared feet, squared score units, ...). On the other hand, the correlation coefficient is limited to a range of -1 to $+1$ and is a metric-free or dimensionless measure. Both of these properties result from the division of the covariance by the product of the two standard deviations.

2-7. Linear Compounds and the Algebra of Expected Values

Many of the random variables encountered in classical and nonparametric statistics have a *linear form* and are often referred to as *linear compounds*. As a result, one of the commonly occurring problems of both classical and nonparametric statistics is to determine the sampling distribution of such variables. Often, the determination of the distribution is greatly simplified by the direct application of the following theorem, which is stated without proof.

If $X_1, X_2, \ldots, X_p$ are random variables with

$$E(X_i) = \mu_i, \qquad \text{Var}(X_i) = \sigma_i^2, \qquad \text{and} \qquad \text{Cov}(X_i, X_{i'}) = \rho_{ii'}\sigma_i\sigma_{i'}$$
$$i \neq i'$$

and if $a_1, a_2, \ldots, a_p$ are arbitrary constants, then the linear compound:

$$L_p = a_1 X_1 + a_2 X_2 + \ldots + a_p X_p$$

has as its expected value:

$$E(L_p) = a_1\mu_1 + a_2\mu_2 + \ldots + a_p\mu_p = \sum_{i=1}^{p} a_i\mu_i$$

and variance:

$$\text{Var}(L_p) = a_1^2 \ \text{Var}(X_1) + a_2^2 \ \text{Var}(X_2) + \ldots + a_p^2 \ \text{Var}(X_p)$$
$$+ a_1 a_2 \ \text{Cov}(X_1 X_2) + a_1 a_3 \ \text{Cov}(X_1 X_3)$$
$$+ \ldots + a_p a_{p-1} \ \text{Cov}(X_p X_{p-1})$$

$$= \sum_{i=1}^{p} a_i^2\sigma_i^2 + \sum_{i=1}^{p}\sum_{i'=1}^{p} a_i a_{i'} \rho_{ii'}\sigma_i\sigma_{i'}, \qquad i \neq i'$$

If the X_i are statistically independent, then each $\rho_{ii'} = 0$, so that the $\text{Var}(L_p)$ is given simply as:

$$\text{Var}(L_p) = \sum_{i=1}^{p} a_i^2 \ \text{Var}(X_i) = \sum_{i=1}^{p} a_i^2\sigma_i^2$$

If a linear compound has the added property that the sum of the coefficients is zero, the compound is said to be a *contrast* of the variables. Contrasts play a significant role in both classical and nonparametric data analysis, especially when the variables are estimates of the population parameters. Thus, consider the set of K parameters $(\theta_1, \theta_2, \ldots, \theta_K)$ measured on K independent populations. A contrast in these parameters will be denoted by:

$$\psi = a_1\theta_1 + a_2\theta_2 + \ldots + a_K\theta_K$$

where

$$a_1 + a_2 + \ldots + a_K = 0$$

2-8. Planned and Post Hoc Comparisons

Classical hypothesis-testing techniques for K-sample problems focus on testing an omnibus null hypothesis:

$$H_0: \theta_1 = \theta_2 = \ldots = \theta_K$$

against an unspecified alternative:

$$H_1: H_0 \text{ is false}$$

Rejection of the null hypothesis does not result in an identification of the location and magnitude of the departures from group identity. Moreover, the omnibus hypothesis does not allow a direct test of specific relationships involving fewer than K groups. Post hoc comparison techniques are addressed to the problem of locating and estimating the magnitude of group differences after rejection of the omnibus null hypothesis. The techniques of Tukey and Scheffé are probably the most familiar classical post hoc procedures. Planned comparisons enable the researcher to substitute several specific hypotheses and their associated tests for the test of the omnibus null hypothesis.

Both planned and post hoc comparisons are available for many K-sample nonparametric tests. The greater part of this book is devoted to the development and illustration of these methods. In addition, point and interval estimation is emphasized, instead of traditional hypothesis testing, because the former yields a more complete analysis of data than does the latter.

Nonparametric post hoc investigations are performed in a manner very similar to that used for post hoc comparisons in the analysis of variance. Contrasts in the parameters are defined as specified in Section 2–7, and they are surrounded with a confidence interval similar to that used in the application of the Scheffé method in the analysis of variance. Whereas the Scheffé method uses the F distribution, the nonparametric tests employ the chi-square distribution. For most of the tests, the corresponding Scheffé-type coefficients are given by

$$S^* = \sqrt{X^2_{K-1:1-\alpha}},$$

where $X^2_{K-1:1-\alpha}$ represents the $(1 - \alpha)$ percentile of the chi-square distribution with $\nu = K - 1$ degrees of freedom.

In some special cases, analogs to Tukey's method for pairwise comparisons are available, but for the most part they are rare. If, instead of testing a large number of comparisons on a post hoc basis, the researcher wants to test a small number of specified contrasts (typically no more than $\left[\frac{K}{2}\right]$ for a K-group design), the method of planned comparisons will be preferred. The researcher can control the probability of making one or more Type I errors in the entire set of planned comparisons by controlling the alpha level per comparison.

Let $P(E_q)$ denote the probability of making a Type I error on the qth planned comparison, and assume that a total of Q planned comparisons will be made. The probability of making at least one Type I error in the set of Q planned comparisons is given by what is called the first-order *Bonferroni inequality*:

$$P(E_1 \text{ or } E_2 \text{ or } \ldots \text{ or } E_Q) \leq P(E_1) + P(E_2) + \ldots + P(E_Q)$$

If the probability of at least one Type I error is denoted by α_T, then:

$$\alpha_T \leq \sum_{q=1}^{Q} P(E_q)$$

The probability of a Type I error is usually equalized across the Q comparisons, so that:

$$P(E_1) = P(E_2) = \ldots = P(E_Q) = \alpha_0$$

Under this condition,

$$\alpha_T = P(\text{At least one Type I error in } Q \text{ contrasts})$$
$$\leq \alpha_0 + \alpha_0 + \ldots + \alpha_0$$

or, in simpler terms,

$$\alpha_T \leq Q\alpha_0.$$

To control α_T at any desired level, each contrast should be tested at $\alpha_T/Q = \alpha_0$. When the Dunn–Bonferroni procedure (Dunn, 1961) is used with the normal distribution, the critical values are given by $Z = \pm Z_{(1-\alpha/2Q)}$, where Q equals the number of planned comparisons and where $(1 - \alpha/2Q)$ refers to the $(1 - \alpha/2Q)$-percentile value of the $N(0, 1)$ distribution. A table of critical values from the standard normal distribution for varying values of K, Q, and α is reported in the last column of Table A–1 of the Appendix. Many examples of the use of the Dunn–Bonferroni inequality appear in later chapters of this book.

2–9. The Role of the Normal Distribution

Classical statistical methods are based, for the most part, upon normal probability distribution theory. Random variables that are normally distributed are known to be symmetrical about their centers, continuous in nature, and are characterized by two parameters, μ and σ^2. The first, μ, is generally associated with the mean value of the distribution and is often called the *expected value* of the underlying variable, $E(X)$, or the location parameter of the distribution. The second, σ^2, is a parameter characterizing the *dispersion* about μ and is called the *variance* of the distribution, $\text{Var}(X) = \sigma^2$, or the scale parameter of the distribution. The standard deviation of the distribution, σ, is simply the square root of the variance.

The basic shape of a typical normal distribution is as shown in Figure 2–2. The points along the X-axis at which the curve changes direction from concave up to concave down, or from concave down to concave up, are called the *inflection points* of the curve, and are defined at the 16th- and 84th-percentile values of the variable. These percentile values occur at $P_{16} = \mu - \sigma$ and $P_{84} = \mu + \sigma$.

In the remainder of this book, a variable that is normally distributed with expected value μ and variance σ^2 is denoted as $N(\mu, \sigma^2)$. Thus, the shorthand notation $N(25, 100)$ means that the variable under study has a normal distribution with expected value equal to 25, variance equal to 100, and standard deviation equal to 10.

Many nonparametric procedures require the use of normal probability distribution calculations. To assist in making these computations, a table of the standard normal distribution, with expected value of zero and variance of one, is presented as Appendix Table A–2. All normal distributions can be related to this particular normal distribution by a simple transformation:

$$Z = \frac{X - \mu}{\sigma}$$

Probabilistic and
Statistical
Concepts
Necessary for
Nonparametric
and Distribution-
Free Procedures

29

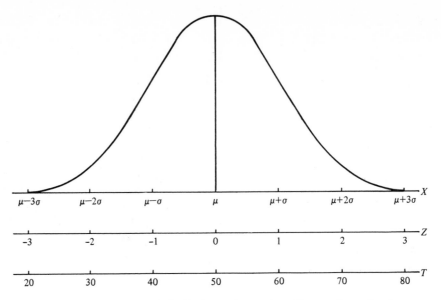

FIGURE 2–2. The normal distribution and examples of its transformed scales.

EXAMPLE 2–9.1. If X is $N(80, 4^2)$, then the probability that X is less than 85 is given by:

$$P(X < 85) = P\left[Z < \frac{85 - 80}{4}\right] = P(Z < 1.25) = .8944$$

and the probability that X is between 73 and 83 is given by:

$$P(73 < X < 83) = P(X < 83) - P(X < 73)$$
$$= P\left[Z < \frac{83 - 80}{4}\right] - P\left[Z < \frac{73 - 80}{4}\right]$$
$$= P(Z < .75) - P(Z < -1.75)$$
$$= .7734 - .0401$$
$$= .7333$$

Test scores are often transformed to a scale with $\mu = 50$ and $\sigma = 10$, to minimize the occurrence of negative values. These scores, known as McCall's T scores, are defined by:

$$T = 50 + 10\left[\frac{X - \mu}{\sigma}\right]$$
$$= 50 + 10Z$$

EXAMPLE 2–9.2. If $\mu = 80$ and $\sigma = 4$, then $X = 88$ is equivalent to a T score with:

$$T = 50 + 10\left[\frac{88 - 80}{4}\right] = 50 + 20 = 70$$

Since $T = 50 + 10Z$, it follows that $Z = (T - 50)/10$. If the T scores possess a normal distribution, then this transforming equation can be used to enter the standard normal table, A–2, to determine the percentile rank of an individual T score. For example, if the T scores are on a discrete scale that can be approximated by a normal variable, then the percentile rank for $T = 70$, corrected for continuity, is given by:

$$P(T < 70) = P\left[T < \frac{69.5 - 50}{10}\right] = P(Z < 1.95) = .9744$$

Thus, a counselor speaking to a layman might say that 98 percent of the persons tested had T scores below 70, or that a T score of 70 corresponds to the 98th percentile, P_{98}, of the distribution.

The sampling distribution of many of the random variables encountered in classical and nonparametric statistics approaches a normal distribution when the sample size is large, even if the population distribution of the underlying variable is not normal. This approach to a normal form can occur under a number of different models. The model that is most frequently used in this book assumes that there exists a linear compound of the form:

$$L_p = \sum_{i=1}^{p} a_i X_i$$

where the X_i are independently and identically distributed with $E(X_i) = \mu$, $\text{Var}(X_i) = \sigma^2$, and $\text{Cov}(X_i, X_{i'}) = 0$.

According to the algebra of expected values:

$$E(L_p) = a_1 \mu + a_2 \mu + \ldots + a_p \mu = \sum_{i=1}^{p} a_i \mu = \mu \sum_{i=1}^{p} a_i$$

$$\text{Var}(L_p) = \sum_{i=1}^{p} a_i^2 \sigma^2 = \sigma^2 \sum_{i=1}^{p} a_i^2$$

In addition, if the individual X_i are normally distributed, then L_p is also normally distributed with parameters given by $E(L_p)$ and $\text{Var}(L_p)$ as defined above. On the other hand, if the X_i are not normally distributed, then the distribution of L_p is also not normally distributed. However, if p is large, then the distribution of L_p can be approximated by a normal distribution with parameters $E(L_p)$ and $\text{Var}(L_p)$, as defined above. This statement follows from the Central Limit Theorem, stated without proof in the special case in which it will be most frequently encountered in this book.

The Central Limit Theorem. Consider the sequence of random variables $L_1, L_2, L_3, \ldots, L_p, \ldots$ such that:

$$L_p = a_1 X_1 + a_2 X_2 + \ldots + a_p X_p$$

and such that each X_i is independently and identically distributed with

$$E(X_i) = \mu, \qquad \text{Var}(X_i) = \sigma^2, \qquad \text{and} \qquad \text{Cov}(X_i, X_{i'}) = 0$$

then the sequence of random variables $L_1, L_2, \ldots,$ approaches a normal form with parameters given by:

$$E(L) = \mu \sum_{i=1}^{p} a_i \quad \text{and} \quad \text{Var}(L) = \sigma^2 \sum_{i=1}^{p} a_i^2$$

It should be noted that the Central Limit Theorem is a *limit* theorem, relating to a sequence of variables L_1, L_2, L_3, ..., and not to a weighted sum, for which p is finite. In all applications, p is *finite* and unless each X_i is normal, L_p cannot be normal. Thus, normality is a hypothetical construct that frequently serves as a good approximation for L_p. When it is reported that a particular variable has a normal distribution with a large sample size, remember: This phrase implies that the approximation resulting from normal-curve theory is sufficiently close to the true probability that would be found if it were to be actually computed. This interpretation is quite important with many of the nonparametric tests described in this book, since most of them are based on random variables that possess a discrete probability distribution. Because normal probabilities are computed under the assumption that the underlying variable is continuous, the corrections for continuity described in Section 2–6 can be used to improve the approximation to the correct discrete probability distribution.

2–10. The Role of the Chi-square Distribution

While the normal distribution plays the dominant role in the large-sample form of the one- and two-sample nonparametric and distribution-free tests, the chi-square distribution plays the dominant role when the number of samples is three or larger. This is to be expected because of the close ties between the chi-square distribution and the normal distribution. As a definition of the chi-square distribution, consider a set of K independent random variables $(Z_1, Z_2, ..., Z_K)$ that are each $N(0, 1)$. The random variable

$$X_v^2 = Z_1^2 + Z_2^2 + ... + Z_K^2$$

is distributed as a chi-square with parameter given by $v = K$. The parameter v that characterizes X^2 is called its *degrees of freedom.*

As a special case of this definition, consider K populations with parameters $[\theta_1, \theta_2, ..., \theta_K]$, which are estimated by $[\hat{\theta}_1, \hat{\theta}_2, ..., \hat{\theta}_K]$. Assume that each $\hat{\theta}_k$ is approximately $N(\theta_0, \sigma_{\hat{\theta}k}^2)$. For each of the estimates, define:

$$Z_1 = \frac{\hat{\theta}_1 - \theta_0}{\sigma_{\hat{\theta}_1}}, \quad Z_2 = \frac{\hat{\theta}_2 - \theta_0}{\sigma_{\hat{\theta}_2}}, \quad ..., \quad Z_K = \frac{\hat{\theta}_K - \theta_0}{\sigma_{\hat{\theta}K}}$$

where θ_0 is a known parameter value, and let:

$$X_v^2 = Z_1^2 + Z_2^2 + ... + Z_K^2 = \sum_{k=1}^{K} \frac{(\hat{\theta}_k - \theta_0)^2}{\sigma_{\hat{\theta}k}^2}$$

By the definition of chi-square, this random variable is distributed as X^2 with $v = K$. In many of the applications, X^2 as so formulated cannot be computed since

θ_0 is, in general, unknown. If θ_0 is estimated by

$$\hat{\theta}_0 = \frac{\dfrac{\hat{\theta}_1}{\sigma^2_{\hat{\theta}_1}} + \dfrac{\hat{\theta}_2}{\sigma^2_{\hat{\theta}_2}} + \ldots + \dfrac{\hat{\theta}_K}{\sigma^2_{\hat{\theta}_K}}}{\dfrac{1}{\sigma^2_{\hat{\theta}_1}} + \dfrac{1}{\sigma^2_{\hat{\theta}_2}} + \ldots + \dfrac{1}{\sigma^2_{\hat{\theta}_K}}} = \frac{w_1\hat{\theta}_1 + w_2\hat{\theta}_2 + \ldots + w_K\hat{\theta}_K}{w_1 + w_2 + \ldots + w_K}$$

where

$$w_1 = \frac{1}{\sigma^2_{\hat{\theta}_1}}, \qquad w_2 = \frac{1}{\sigma^2_{\hat{\theta}_2}}, \ldots, \qquad w_K = \frac{1}{\sigma^2_{\hat{\theta}_K}}$$

and if X^2 is redefined as

$$U = \sum_{k=1}^{K} \frac{(\hat{\theta}_k - \hat{\theta}_0)^2}{\sigma^2_{\hat{\theta}_k}} = \hat{Z}_1^2 + \hat{Z}_2^2 + \ldots + \hat{Z}_K^2$$

it can be shown that U is approximately distributed like X_ν^2 with $\nu = K - 1$. Estimating θ_0 from the data is said to use one degree of freedom. Actually, it restricts the value of U, reducing its ability to fluctuate freely. If, in addition, the individual $\sigma^2_{\hat{\theta}}$ are unknown, one estimates them from the data and substitutes the estimated values into U. While the distribution of U is not exactly chi-square, its approximation to chi-square is quite adequate for most research questions.

In other cases encountered in later chapters, the estimators of the individual θ_k are correlated because of restrictions placed on the observations and estimates. For the special case in which the $\rho_{\hat{\theta}_k, \hat{\theta}_{k'}}$ are all equal to a common value, ρ, the approach to X^2 is achieved by the statistic:

$$U = \frac{1}{1 - \rho} \sum_{k=1}^{K} \frac{(\hat{\theta}_k - \hat{\theta}_0)^2}{\sigma^2_{\hat{\theta}_k}} = \frac{1}{1 - \rho} \left[\hat{Z}_1^2 + \hat{Z}_2^2 + \ldots + \hat{Z}_K^2 \right]$$

which tends to a chi-square form with $\nu = K - 1$.

Since the derivation requires advanced statistical techniques, the results have been cited without proof. Many illustrations of the use of the statistic U will be given throughout this book which, while not a standard "cookbook" of recipes, does contain many examples that can be used in other contexts by imitation. On the other hand, principles are emphasized so that variations of the statistics can be developed by the more sophisticated reader.

2–11. Student's t Distribution and the F Distribution

Closely related to the normal and the chi-square distributions are the t and F distributions. These distributions are encountered in inference procedures related to univariate statistical hypothesis testing and interval estimation. Tables of significance probabilities for the chi-square distribution, the t distribution, and the F distribution are presented in the Appendix as Tables A–3, A–4, and A–5. The four distributions are interrelated in the following set of statements:

Pearson's chi-square. If Z_1, Z_2, ..., Z_K are independently distributed random variables, each $N(0, 1^2)$, then the random variable:

$$X^2 = Z_1^2 + Z_2^2 + \ldots + Z_K^2$$

is distributed like Pearson's chi-square with parameter given by $v = K$.

Student's t. If Z is $N(0, 1^2)$ and if X_v^2 is chi-square with $v = K$, then

$$t = \frac{Z}{\sqrt{\dfrac{X_v^2}{v}}}$$

is distributed like Student's t, with parameter given by $v = K$.

Snedecor's F. If X_v^2 is chi-square with $v_1 = p$ and if $X_{v_2}^2$ is also chi-square with $v_2 = q$, and if they are statistically independent, then

$$F = \frac{X_{v_1}^2/v_1}{X_{v_2}^2/v_2}$$

is distributed like Snedecor's F with parameters $v_1 = p$ and $v_2 = q$.

2–12. The Sampling Distribution of an $\overline{X}$ in Finite and Infinite Populations

The most important applications of the Central Limit theorem involve the sampling distribution of

$$\overline{X} = \frac{1}{n}(X_1 + X_2 + \ldots + X_n)$$

where $(X_1, X_2, \ldots, X_n)$ is a random sample from a population in which $E(X_i) = \mu$ and $\text{Var}(X_i) = \sigma^2$. If the population is infinite in size, then, by the Central Limit theorem, the sampling distribution of $\overline{X}$ is approximately normal, with:

$$E(\overline{X}) = \mu \qquad \text{and} \qquad \text{Var}(\overline{X}) = \frac{\sigma^2}{n}$$

It follows, from the formulas of Section 2–7, that $\overline{X}$ can be represented by the linear compound:

$$L = \overline{X} = \frac{1}{n}X_1 + \frac{1}{n}X_2 + \ldots + \frac{1}{n}X_n$$

and

$$E(L) = E(\overline{X}) = \mu \sum_{i=1}^{n} \frac{1}{n} = \mu n \left(\frac{1}{n}\right) = \mu$$

Since the X_i are independent in a random sample from an infinite population, it follows that:

$$\text{Var}(L) = \text{Var}(\overline{X}) = \sigma^2 \sum_{i=1}^{n} \left(\frac{1}{n}\right)^2 = \sigma^2 n \left(\frac{1}{n^2}\right) = \frac{\sigma^2}{n}$$

If the population is finite in size, then observations in a random sample are not independent, so the $\text{Var}(\bar{X})$ is not equal to σ^2/n. Instead, it is defined by:

$$\text{Var}(\bar{X}) = \frac{\sigma^2}{n}\left(\frac{N-n}{N-1}\right)$$

where n is the size of the sample and N is the size of the population. This population model is employed in the derivation of many nonparametric or distribution-free tests; however, $\bar{X}$ is not often used in direct computations. Instead, $T = n\bar{X}$ is the preferred criterion. Under this model for finite populations:

$$E(T) = nE(\bar{X}) = n\mu$$

and

$$\text{Var}(T) = n^2 \, \text{Var}(\bar{X}) = n^2\frac{\sigma^2}{n}\left[\frac{N-n}{N-1}\right] = n\sigma^2\left[\frac{N-n}{N-1}\right]$$

EXAMPLE 2–12.1. As an example, consider selecting a random sample of size $n = 2$ from the uniform distribution $(1, 2, 3, 4, 5, 6)$, for which $N = 6$. As shown in Section 2–6, $\mu = 3.5$ and $\sigma^2 = 35/12$. For this finite population model, and $T = X_1 + X_2$:

$$E(T) = n\mu = 2(3.5) = 7$$

and

$$\text{Var}(T) = n\sigma^2\left[\frac{N-n}{N-1}\right] = 2\left[\frac{35}{12}\right]\left[\frac{6-2}{6-1}\right] = 2\left[\frac{35}{12}\right]\left[\frac{4}{5}\right] = \frac{14}{3}$$

Exercises

An asterisk before a problem number means that the problem will appear later under a different context, or that the problem is based on examples appearing in the text.

1. Define the following statistical terms. Illustrate each with an example.

a) Random variable	g) Permutations
b) Qualitative variable	h) Combinations
c) Ordered qualitative variable	i) Statistical independence
d) Discrete variable	j) Contrast
e) Continuous variable	k) Expected value
f) Fundamental rule of counting	l) Variance
	m) Standard deviation

*2. Mr. Adams, who teaches elementary statistics and probability at a West Coast university, returned to his home town in the midwest for a visit. Before he left home, there were 15 healthy elm trees lined along the city block where his parents lived. During the last few years, four of them became infected with Dutch elm disease and had to be cut down. The state of each tree is as shown, with A representing alive, and D representing dead:

A A A A D D D D A A A A A A A

His family told him that an epidemic had killed large numbers of elm trees in the town. He decided to define an epidemic operationally as the death of four adjacent trees.

a) Specify a hypothesis stating that the outcome is due to chance.

b) Specify the alternative of interest.

Probabilistic and Statistical Concepts Necessary for Nonparametric and Distribution-Free Procedures

c) How many possible outcomes are there for the proposed definition of an epidemic?

d) How many of these outcomes are compatible with the definition?

e) What is the probability of an epidemic?

f) Is the observed outcome indicative of an epidemic?

*3. The brother of Mr. Adams of Exercise 2, who is a graduate student in the local School of Forestry, thinks that the operational definition of an epidemic is too stringent, in that it is a conditional definition, i.e., it is based upon the knowledge that four trees have died. He wants to define an epidemic as the death of any two or more adjacent trees. Answer the questions of Exercise 2, if this definition of an epidemic is used.

*4. Mr. Adams' sister, who is a registered nurse in the local county hospital, thinks that her two brothers are somewhat naive about how epidemics spread, since their models contain implicit assumptions of statistical independence and equally likely outcomes. She believes that the probabilities change and increase upon exposure, so that differential probabilities exist and dependence of events must be considered. What do you think of her analysis? Why?

*5. Consider the set of seven consecutive integers: $\{1, 2, 3, 4, 5, 6, 7\}$:

a) In how many ways can one permute the integers?

b) In how many ways can one select four of the integers and then permute them?

c) For the permutations of (b), let $T = r_1 + r_2 + r_3 + r_4$, so that T represents the sum of the four ranks for any permutation. What is the set of possible values for T?

d) How many groups of four integers can be generated from the group of seven integers?

e) What are the possible values of T across all of the groups of (d)?

f) Is T a function of permutations or combinations? Explain.

*6. For the variable T of Exercise 5, find:

a) $P(T = 10)$ and $P(T = 22)$.

b) $P(T = 11)$ and $P(T = 21)$.

c) $P(T = 12)$ and $P(T = 20)$.

d) $P(T = 13)$ and $P(T = 19)$.

e) If one were to select four numbers at random from the set of seven integers of Exercise 5 and if the numbers were to be $\{1, 2, 4, 5\}$, with total given by $T = 1 + 2 + 4 + 5 = 12$, should one be surprised? Why?

*7. When 34 public colleges in Michigan are classified by 1966 enrollment (under 12,000; 12,000 or more) and type (two-year; four-year), the following table results:

Enrollment	Four-year (B)	Two-year ($\overline{B}$)	Total
Under 12,000 (A)	7	22	29
12,000 or more ($\overline{A}$)	5	0	5
Total	12	22	34

Consider selecting one college at random from the 34. Represent symbolically and compute the probability of selection of:

a) A college with enrollment under 12,000.

b) A four-year college.

c) A four-year college with enrollment under 12,000.

d) A two-year college with enrollment of 12,000 or more.

e) A college that is *either* a school with enrollment under 12,000 or a four-year college.

f) A college with enrollment under 12,000, given that the college is a four-year college.

*8. The following data are reported for the performance of 100 students on two items of a test:

Item 1 \ Item 2	Pass (B)	Fail ($\overline{B}$)	Total
Pass (A)	40	20	60
Fail ($\overline{A}$)	10	30	40
Total	50	50	100

If a single student is selected at random, what is the probability that the student will:

a) Pass Item 1 and Item 2?

b) Pass Item 1, but fail Item 2?

c) Pass Item 1 or Item 2 ($A \cup B$)?

d) Pass Item 2 if the student has passed Item 1?

e) Is performance on the two items independent?

f) If five students are chosen at random, what is the probability that each of them will fail at least one item?

*9. Assume that two objective test questions will be answered on the basis of guessing. Question 1 is a four-option multiple-choice question that will be scored "1" if the correct option is chosen and "0" if not. Question 2 requires the selection of the "best" and "worst" options among three specified options. It will be scored "2" if both the best and the worst options are correctly chosen, "1" if only one of these options is correctly chosen, and "0" if neither is correctly chosen. Let X denote the score on question 1 and Y denote the score on question 2.

a) Identify $P(X = x)$ and $P(Y = y)$ for each possible outcome.

b) Display the joint probability distribution of X and Y in a 2×3 table.

c) What is the conditional probability of $Y = 2$, if $X = 1$?

d) How does the conditional probability in (c) compare with the unconditional (marginal) probability of $Y = 2$? Explain.

e) Compute:

$$E(X), \quad E(Y), \quad \mathrm{Var}(X), \quad \mathrm{Var}(Y), \quad \mathrm{Cov}(XY), \quad \text{and} \quad \rho_{XY}$$

f) Are X and Y independent?

*10. Mr. Brown and Mr. Clark were matching pennies. In one sequence of 10 tosses, Mr. Brown had 10 heads. Mr. Clark accused him of cheating.

a) Was he justified? Use the questions of Exercise 2 in making your decision.

b) What would you have concluded if 10 tails had occurred?

c) What would you have concluded if the sequence of outcomes had been {T H H H H H H H H T}?

*11. Consider the data of Table 2–2. Let:

A refer to the 5 rats above the median.

B refer to the 5 rats below the median.

C refer to the 5 rats in the control group.

E refer to the 5 rats of the experimental group.

If one rat is selected at random from the group of ten rats, find the following probabilities:

a) $P(A)$ b) $P(A \text{ and } C)$ c) $P(A \text{ or } C)$

d) $P(A|C)$ e) $P(A|E)$

f) Is performance independent of group?

If two rats are selected at random from the group of ten rats, find the following probabilities:

g) $P(2 \text{ are in the control group})$

h) $P(\text{Only one is in the control group})$

i) $P(\text{Both are } A \cap C)$

j) $P(\text{Second one selected is } A \cap E)$

k) $P(\text{One is } A \cap C \text{ and one is } B \cap E)$

If three rats are selected at random from the group of ten rats, find the following probabilities:

l) $P(\text{All three are } E)$

m) $P(\text{Last one is } E)$

n) $P(\text{All three are } E \text{ or all three are } C)$

o) $P(\text{All three are } A \text{ or all three are } C)$

p) $P(\text{One is } A \cap C, \text{ one is } B \cap C, \text{ and one is } E \cap B)$

*12. If X has a distribution that is $N(100, 16^2)$, find:

a) $P(X \geq 116)$

b) $P(80 \leq X \leq 120)$

*13. If two observations are selected at random from the distribution of Exercise 12, find:

a) $P(X_1 + X_2 \geq 232)$

b) $P\left[\dfrac{X_1 + X_2}{2} > 105\right]$

*14. If a sample mean based on $N = 25$ observations were selected from the distribution of Exercise 12 and were found to equal $\overline{X} = 95$, would one reject the hypothesis $H_0: \mu = 100$, in favor of the alternative $H_1: \mu < 100$ with a Type I error rate of $\alpha = 0.05$?

a) Answer the question if the number of subjects in the universe is unlimited.

b) Answer the question if the universe is finite and contains exactly 100 people.

The Binomial and Sign Tests: One-Sample Procedures for Dichotomous Variables

3–1. One-Sample Procedures for Dichotomous Variables

Many superficially different statistical tests and confidence intervals are introduced in this chapter. Although they are appropriate for differing research designs and varying population characteristics, they are the progeny of one statistical test, the sign test. The sign test, with its exact sampling distribution and its large-sample normal-curve approximation, is presented initially. Then the progeny are introduced, beginning with the sign test used to determine differences in location in a matched-pairs or repeated-measures design. The matched-pairs sign test is followed by the one-sample sign test used to estimate location in terms of the sample median or to test a hypothesis that the population has a specified median value. The results of individual sign tests are combined to enable the researcher to form an overall assessment of the outcomes of a number of independent replications of a study testing a directional hypothesis. Lastly, the questions with respect to population location are replaced by questions about association between two variables in the population. A special type of association—the presence of a trend over time, testing sequence, or other ordering of one variable—is examined through the use of the Cox–Stuart sign test for trend.

3–2. Introduction to the Sign Test

The prototype of all nonparametric and parametric tests is a test called the *sign test*. This test, based upon elementary binomial-distribution theory was first applied by Dr. John Arbuthnott (1710) to the birth-registration statistics of the City of London, to test the hypothesis that the proportion of males born in the city exceeded the proportion of females born during the same time periods. To help understand the logic behind this frequently performed statistical test, consider the following hypothetical study.

EXAMPLE 3–2.1. A researcher has designed a study to test whether or not a transfer of learning takes place between simple and complex tasks of related form if subjects are given sufficient training in solving problems of simple form before being given the more complex task to learn. As part of his design, he tests each subject individually on five trials with tasks low in a predesigned hierarchy of complexity. On the sixth trial, he gives each subject the more complex task that presumably is easier to learn, provided that the earlier problems were solved with understanding. Following the sixth trial with the more complex task, each subject is asked, "Was this last problem easier or harder to solve than the five problems given before it?" The possible response choices given to the subjects were:

{It was easier.   It was harder.}

If a subject reported that it was of *equal* difficulty, he was then questioned until a decision was made by the subject that the task was, indeed, easier or harder. The responses for the first ten students tested were as shown in Table 3–1. On the basis of the indicated responses, the researcher would like to know whether or not transfer of learning had taken place.

TABLE 3–1. *Response to the question: Was this problem easier or harder to solve than the five problems given before it?*

Subject	Response
Alice	Harder
Bob	Easier
Carol	Easier
Dianne	Easier
Eleanor	Harder
Francine	Easier
Grace	Easier
Harold	Harder
Inez	Easier
Joseph	Easier

Note that, if transfer of learning did not take place, then chance factors determine whether the sixth problem is easier or harder, so that, over the set of response choices, $P(\text{Harder}) = P(\text{Easier}) = \frac{1}{2}$. However, if transfer of learning *does* take place, then it would follow that, over the response choices, $P(\text{Harder}) < \frac{1}{2}$, while $P(\text{Easier}) > \frac{1}{2}$.

In either case, it is not unreasonable to assume that the probability of the response choice {Harder} is constant across all students and is given by $\frac{1}{2}$ if no learning occurs and by some number less than $\frac{1}{2}$ if learning does occur.

Furthermore, there is no reason to believe that the response choices of any student or group of students affect the response choice of any other student since, as is recalled, the researcher has taken extra precautions to ensure that each student performs on the six problems independently of the other students. If these conditions of independence and constant probability hold across all students, then the total number of students who report the test as being {Harder} represents an observation of a discrete random variable whose probability distribution is exactly binomial. Under this model, the researcher can establish a decision rule with preselected probability of a Type I error, which can be used to test the hypothesis of transfer of learning from simple tasks to more complex tasks. The derivation of this test follows.

3–3. The Binomial Distribution

Consider a study that consists of n independent repeated trials of the same experiment, where each trial results in one or the other of two complementary or mutually exclusive and exhaustive possible outcomes, A and $\overline{A}$. If the probability of A is constant across the n trials, then T, the number of occurrences of A in n trials, is a random variable that has a binomial distribution. This distribution is discrete, since the variable defined by the total number of occurrences of A can take on only the finite set of values $\{0, 1, \ldots, n\}$.

EXAMPLE 3–3.1.   For the hypothetical study of Example 3–2.1, A corresponds to the response choice {Harder} while $\overline{A}$ corresponds to the response choice {Easier}. The variable T corresponds to the number of subjects who report that the task is {Harder}. For the data of Table 3–1, $T = 3$ and $P(A) = P(\text{Harder}) = \frac{1}{2}$, provided that no transfer of learning occurs. If learning does take place, $P(\text{Harder}) < \frac{1}{2}$.

EXAMPLE 3–3.2.   As another example of a random variable that possesses a binomial distribution, consider an experiment that consists of tossing a loaded coin four times, where the probability of a head occurring on any one toss is equal to $\frac{1}{3}$. Each toss represents a trial in the experiment. The outcome of a single toss must be either heads or tails, provided one rules out the possibility of the coin landing on its edge. The two possible outcomes are, therefore, mutually exclusive and exhaustive. Further, the outcome of each toss is not affected by the outcome of any other toss, so that the trials are independent. If T represents the total number of heads in the four tosses, then T has a binomial distribution.

The derivation of the binomial distribution can be arrived at with ease by first considering a single trial of the total experiment. On this single trial, denote the probability of outcome A as p and probability of $\overline{A}$ as q. Typically, A is called a *success* and $\overline{A}$ is called a *failure*. Under this notation,

$$P(A) = p$$
$$\underline{P(\overline{A}) = q}$$
$$P(A) + P(\overline{A}) = p + q = 1$$

For a single trial, the *sample space*, or set of possible outcomes, is denoted:

$$S: \{A, \overline{A}\}$$

Let T denote the number of successes A, for the sample space of a single trial. The possible values for T are given by the following set of values:

$$T: \{1, 0\}$$

Since $P(T = 1) = P(A) = p$, and $P(T = 0) = P(\overline{A}) = q$, the probability distribution of T is given by:

$$P(T = 1) = p$$
$$\underline{P(T = 0) = q}$$
$$P(T = 1) + P(T = 0) = p + q = 1$$

A random variable that possesses this specific probability distribution is called a *Bernoulli* variable. The binomial distribution is generated from this distribution.

Now consider n independent trials and let $T = t$ equal the number of successes in these n trials. In the sample space of this experiment, every possible outcome consists of a listing of A's and $\overline{A}$'s, with the number of A's in any one sample extending from $0, 1, \ldots, t, \ldots, n$. Within this sample space, consider those outcomes that consist of t A's and $(n - t)$ $\overline{A}$'s. One such outcome is:

$$\underline{A\,A \cdots A} \qquad \underline{\overline{A}\,\overline{A} \cdots \overline{A}}$$

This represents the outcome in which the A's occur on the first t trials and the $\overline{A}$'s appear on the last $(n - t)$ trials. Since the events are independent, the probability of this specific outcome is, according to Probability Rule Five of Section 2–5, given by:

$$P(A\,A\,A \cdots A\,\overline{A}\,\overline{A} \cdots \overline{A}) = P(A)P(A) \cdots P(A)P(\overline{A})P(\overline{A}) \cdots P(\overline{A})$$
$$= P(A)^t P(\overline{A})^{n-t}$$
$$= p^t q^{n-t}$$

However, there are other outcomes in the sample space that consist of t A's and $(n - t)$ $\overline{A}$'s. If one could determine the number of outcomes that have this property, then one would know the probability of obtaining t successes in n trials.

If the outcomes on each trial were completely different from one another, then the total number of different orderings or arrangements of the outcomes would be given by Rule Three of Section 2–2, so that the total number of permutations would be given by $n(n - 1)(n - 2) \cdots (3)(2)(1)$, or $n!$. However, t of the outcomes are identical A's, while the remaining $(n - t)$ outcomes are identical $\overline{A}$'s. Because of this, the total number of unique arrangements of t A's and $(n - t)$ $\overline{A}$'s is given by $n!/(t!(n - t)!)$, as specified by Rule Six of Section 2–2. Thus, the probability that $T = t$ is given by:

$$P(T = t) = \frac{n!}{t!(n - t)!} p^t q^{n-t}$$

This resulting probability is referred to as a *binomial* probability, since it represents the $(t + 1)$th term in the binomial expansion of $(p + q)^n$. It is customary to denote $n!/(t!(n - t)!)$ by the shortened symbol $\left[{n \atop t}\right]$. Under this model, this symbol represents the number of arrangements or permutations of n objects in which t objects possess identical properties and in which the remaining $(n - t)$ objects possess a common, but different, property. In this form, these constants are called binomial coefficients. A table of these coefficients is presented in Table A–6 of the Appendix. As inspection of Table A–6 shows, $\left[{n \atop 0}\right]$ and $\left[{n \atop n}\right]$ are both equal to 1. This reduction to unity arises since 0! is defined to equal unity.

EXAMPLE 3–3.3. As an illustration of the use of the binomial formula, consider again the experiment of tossing a loaded coin four times, where the probability of a head on any given toss equals $\frac{1}{3}$. Again letting T equal the number of heads, it is possible to give the distribution of T, as reported in Table 3–2. The probability of getting exactly one head is 32/81. The probability of getting at least one head is equal to 1 minus the probability of getting zero heads since the sum of the probabilities must equal 1. Thus:

$$P(\text{At least one head}) = 1 - P(T = 0)$$
$$= 1 - \frac{16}{81} = \frac{65}{81}$$

A graphic representation of this probability distribution is shown in Figure 3–1.

TABLE 3–2. *The binomial distribution with $n = 4$, $p = \frac{1}{3}$, and $q = \frac{2}{3}$.*

Number of heads observed $T = t$	Probability by the binomial formula $\left[{4 \atop t}\right]\left[\frac{1}{3}\right]^t\left[\frac{2}{3}\right]^{4-t}$	Computed probability $P(T = t)$
0	$\left[{4 \atop 0}\right]\left[\frac{1}{3}\right]^0\left[\frac{2}{3}\right]^4 = \frac{16}{81}$	0.1975
1	$\left[{4 \atop 1}\right]\left[\frac{1}{3}\right]^1\left[\frac{2}{3}\right]^3 = \frac{32}{81}$	0.3951
2	$\left[{4 \atop 2}\right]\left[\frac{1}{3}\right]^2\left[\frac{2}{3}\right]^2 = \frac{24}{81}$	0.2963
3	$\left[{4 \atop 3}\right]\left[\frac{1}{3}\right]^3\left[\frac{2}{3}\right]^1 = \frac{8}{81}$	0.0988
4	$\left[{4 \atop 4}\right]\left[\frac{1}{3}\right]^4\left[\frac{2}{3}\right]^0 = \frac{1}{81}$	0.0123
Total	$\sum_{t=0}^{4}\left[{4 \atop t}\right]\left[\frac{1}{3}\right]^t\left[\frac{2}{3}\right]^{4-t}$	1.0000

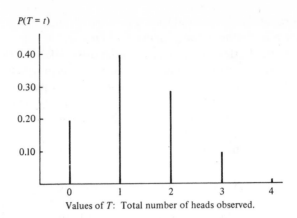

P(T = t)

Values of T: Total number of heads observed.

FIGURE 3–1. The binomial probability distribution with $p = \frac{1}{3}$, $q = \frac{2}{3}$, and $n = 4$.

3–4. The Binomial Test of $H_0 : p = p_0$ Versus $H_1 : p \neq p_0$

The binomial model is encountered frequently in behavioral research. This is illustrated in the following example.

EXAMPLE 3–4.1.   In a certain community, bond issues pass only if 65% or more of the electorate vote in favor of the issue. To test the community's attitudes toward the bond issue, 12 people were interviewed and asked whether they would vote for the bond issue. $T = 10$ people said they would vote for the issue. On the basis of this evidence, would it be reasonable to predict that the bond issue will pass if it is assumed that attitudes will not change between the survey and election time? This question can be answered by testing:

$$H_0: p = 0.65$$

against

$$H_1: p > 0.65$$

The set of outcomes compatible with H_1, in order of magnitude, are $\{12, 11, 10, \ldots\}$. If H_0 is true, the probabilities of the outcomes compatible with H_1 are given by:

$$P(T = 12) = \begin{bmatrix} 12 \\ 12 \end{bmatrix}(0.65)^{12}(0.35)^0 = 0.007$$

$$P(T = 11) = \begin{bmatrix} 12 \\ 11 \end{bmatrix}(0.65)^{11}(0.35)^1 = 0.037$$

$$P(T = 10) = \begin{bmatrix} 12 \\ 10 \end{bmatrix}(0.65)^{10}(0.35)^2 = 0.109$$

$$\vdots \qquad \vdots \qquad \vdots$$

For these three extreme outcomes, $\alpha = 0.007 + 0.037 + 0.109 = 0.153$, so that there is little reason to predict that the bond issue will pass.

If α were to be controlled so that $\alpha \leq .05$, then the *decision rule* for rejecting H_0 is given by:

$$\text{D.R.: Reject } H_0 \text{ if } T \text{ is 11 or 12.}$$

With this rule, $\alpha = 0.044$, so that the test is conservative relative to the rejection of H_0 when it is true.

3–5. The Sign Test: A Special Case of the One-Sample Binomial Test

A little reflection will show that the probability model described by the binomial distribution has application to the studies described in Section 3–2.

EXAMPLE 3–5.1. For the transfer-of-learning study, the criterion variable, T = number of subjects who report the task as harder, represents a binomial random variable with $n = 10$ and $p = \frac{1}{2}$, provided that the hypothesis of *no* transfer of learning is true. Under this model, the probabilities for the various values of T are as reported in Table 3–3. A graphic representation of this distribution is shown in Figure 3–2.

On the basis of the probabilities reported in Table 3–3, a statistical test of the hypothesis that transfer of learning occurs can be made by testing the hypothesis that learning does *not* occur. In statistical form, the tested hypothesis and its alternative are:

$$H_0: P(\text{Harder}) = \tfrac{1}{2}$$
$$H_1: P(\text{Harder}) < \tfrac{1}{2}$$

To determine the critical or rejection region of the test, consider the outcomes that are compatible with the alternative hypothesis. These outcomes are given by small numerical values of T. Referring to the probabilities of Table 3–3 and Figure 3–2, we see that possible critical regions, with their corresponding probabilities of a Type I error, are given by:

Critical region	Probability of a Type I error
$T = \{0\}$	$\alpha = 0.001$
$T = \{0, 1\}$	$\alpha = 0.011$
$T = \{0, 1, 2\}$	$\alpha = 0.055$
$T = \{0, 1, 2, 3\}$	$\alpha = 0.172$

The last region, $T: \{0, 1, 2, 3\}$, is too large, since the probability of a Type I error for this region is much too large. The probability of the region $T: \{0, 1, 2\}$ is slightly larger than 0.05, while the probability of the region $T: \{0, 1\}$ is considerably smaller than 0.05. Unfortunately, it is not possible to derive a statistical test for which $\alpha = 0.05$ unless randomization is used in the decision rule. Thus, a compromise must be made. Suppose it is decided to use the rejection region $T: \{0, 1, 2\}$ with $\alpha = 0.055$.

TABLE 3–3. *Probability distribution of number of subjects who reported that Task Six was harder than the five previous tasks, if $p = \frac{1}{2}$.*

Number of students who reported Task Six was harder. $(T = t)$	Probability by the binomial formula $\begin{bmatrix} 10 \\ t \end{bmatrix} \begin{bmatrix} \frac{1}{2} \end{bmatrix}^t \begin{bmatrix} \frac{1}{2} \end{bmatrix}^{10-t}$	Computed probability $P(T = t)$
0	$\begin{bmatrix} 10 \\ 0 \end{bmatrix} \begin{bmatrix} \frac{1}{2} \end{bmatrix}^0 \begin{bmatrix} \frac{1}{2} \end{bmatrix}^{10} = \dfrac{1}{1024}$	0.001
1	$\begin{bmatrix} 10 \\ 1 \end{bmatrix} \begin{bmatrix} \frac{1}{2} \end{bmatrix}^1 \begin{bmatrix} \frac{1}{2} \end{bmatrix}^9 = \dfrac{10}{1024}$	0.010
2	$\begin{bmatrix} 10 \\ 2 \end{bmatrix} \begin{bmatrix} \frac{1}{2} \end{bmatrix}^2 \begin{bmatrix} \frac{1}{2} \end{bmatrix}^8 = \dfrac{45}{1024}$	0.044
3	$\begin{bmatrix} 10 \\ 3 \end{bmatrix} \begin{bmatrix} \frac{1}{2} \end{bmatrix}^3 \begin{bmatrix} \frac{1}{2} \end{bmatrix}^7 = \dfrac{120}{1024}$	0.117
4	$\begin{bmatrix} 10 \\ 4 \end{bmatrix} \begin{bmatrix} \frac{1}{2} \end{bmatrix}^4 \begin{bmatrix} \frac{1}{2} \end{bmatrix}^6 = \dfrac{210}{1024}$	0.205
5	$\begin{bmatrix} 10 \\ 5 \end{bmatrix} \begin{bmatrix} \frac{1}{2} \end{bmatrix}^5 \begin{bmatrix} \frac{1}{2} \end{bmatrix}^5 = \dfrac{252}{1024}$	0.246
6	$\begin{bmatrix} 10 \\ 6 \end{bmatrix} \begin{bmatrix} \frac{1}{2} \end{bmatrix}^6 \begin{bmatrix} \frac{1}{2} \end{bmatrix}^4 = \dfrac{210}{1024}$	0.205
7	$\begin{bmatrix} 10 \\ 7 \end{bmatrix} \begin{bmatrix} \frac{1}{2} \end{bmatrix}^7 \begin{bmatrix} \frac{1}{2} \end{bmatrix}^3 = \dfrac{120}{1024}$	0.117
8	$\begin{bmatrix} 10 \\ 8 \end{bmatrix} \begin{bmatrix} \frac{1}{2} \end{bmatrix}^8 \begin{bmatrix} \frac{1}{2} \end{bmatrix}^2 = \dfrac{45}{1024}$	0.044
9	$\begin{bmatrix} 10 \\ 9 \end{bmatrix} \begin{bmatrix} \frac{1}{2} \end{bmatrix}^9 \begin{bmatrix} \frac{1}{2} \end{bmatrix}^1 = \dfrac{10}{1024}$	0.010
10	$\begin{bmatrix} 10 \\ 10 \end{bmatrix} \begin{bmatrix} \frac{1}{2} \end{bmatrix}^{10} \begin{bmatrix} \frac{1}{2} \end{bmatrix}^0 = \dfrac{1}{1024}$	0.001
Total	$\displaystyle\sum_{t=0}^{10} \begin{bmatrix} 10 \\ t \end{bmatrix} \begin{bmatrix} \frac{1}{2} \end{bmatrix}^t \begin{bmatrix} \frac{1}{2} \end{bmatrix}^{10-t}$	1.000

The hypothesis of no transfer of learning cannot be rejected since, for the observed set of outcomes, $T = 3$.

The transfer-of-learning study represents an example of the use of the sign test. The response {Harder} refers to a positive statement of difficulty. Thus, the hypothesis $H_0 : P(\text{Harder}) = \frac{1}{2}$ is identical to the hypothesis $H_0 : P(+) = \frac{1}{2}$.

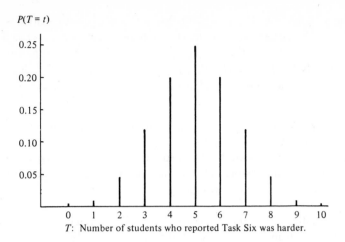

$P(T = t)$

T: Number of students who reported Task Six was harder.

FIGURE 3–2. *Probability distribution of number of subjects who reported that Task Six was harder than the five previous tasks if $p = \frac{1}{2}$.*

3–6. The Large-Sample Form of the Binomial Test

When n becomes large, the probability computations associated with the binomial probabilities are laborious. Fortunately, because of the Central-Limit theorem, a good large-sample normal approximation to the binomial distribution is available. The excellence of the approximation is directly related to the values of np and nq, the expected number of successes and failures. When both exceed 5, the approximation is adequate for the answering of most behavioral research hypotheses that depend upon binomial distribution theory.

EXAMPLE 3–6.1. Suppose, in the study of Section 3–5, that $n = 110$ people were surveyed to test:

$$H_0: p = 0.65$$

against

$$H_1: p > 0.65$$

The critical region for this test would have to be determined by finding the value of j such that:

$$T = \sum_{t=j}^{110} \binom{110}{t}(0.65)^t(0.35)^{110-t} \leq 0.05$$

In practice, this could be a considerable chore, but, with the large-sample approximation, the problem is really quite simple. For the large-sample approximation, one uses either T, the number of A's in the sample, or $\hat{p} = T/n$, the proportion of A's in the sample, by means of the following test statistics:

$$Z = \frac{T - E(T)}{\sqrt{\mathrm{Var}(T)}} \quad \text{or} \quad Z = \frac{\hat{p} - E(\hat{p})}{\sqrt{\mathrm{Var}(\hat{p})}}$$

When H_0 is true, the sampling distribution of these statistics is approximately $N(0, 1)$. With either test statistic, H_0 would be rejected at $\alpha = 0.05$ if $Z > 1.645$, the 95th-percentile value of the $N(0, 1)$ distribution. To apply this approximation, all that one needs to do is verify that $np > 5$, $nq > 5$, and then determine exact values of $E(T)$ and $\text{Var}(T)$ or of $E(\hat{p})$ and $\text{Var}(\hat{p})$.

One way of deriving the mean and variance of a binomial distribution is to note that a variable with a binomial distribution is the sum of n independent Bernoulli variables with a common value for the probability of success. Once the mean and variance of a Bernoulli variable are known, the mean and variance of a binomial variable can also be determined by making use of the theorems presented in Sections 2–6 and 2–7.

Consider the Bernoulli distribution as defined in Section 3–3. According to the definition of Section 2–6, the expected value is given by:

$$E(T) = \sum_{i=1}^{I} t_i P(T = t_i) = (1)(p) + (0)(q) = p$$

and the variance is defined as:

$$\text{Var}(T) = \sum_{i=1}^{I} [t_i - E(t)]^2 P(T = t_i) = (1 - p)^2 p + (0 - p)^2 q$$
$$= q^2 p + p^2 q = pq(q + p) = pq$$

Note that these results hold for all values of i. Thus, for T, a binomial variable that is the sum of n independent Bernoulli variables with a common probability of success, the expected value and variance are given by:

$$E(T) = \sum_{i=1}^{n} \mu_i = \sum_{i=1}^{n} p = np$$

and

$$\text{Var}(T) = \sum_{i=1}^{n} \sigma_i^2 = \sum_{i=1}^{n} pq = npq$$

If $\hat{p} = T/n$, then:

$$E(\hat{p}) = E\left(\frac{T}{n}\right) = \frac{1}{n}E(T) = \frac{1}{n}np = p$$

and

$$\text{Var}(\hat{p}) = \text{Var}\left(\frac{T}{n}\right) = \frac{1}{n^2}\text{Var}(T) = \frac{1}{n^2}npq = \frac{pq}{n}$$

Since T and $\hat{p}$ are on a discrete scale, one can correct for continuity on these statistics, as described in Section 2–4. With these corrections:

$$Z = \frac{(T \pm \frac{1}{2}) - np}{\sqrt{npq}} \quad \text{or} \quad Z = \frac{(\hat{p} \pm 1/(2n)) - p}{\sqrt{pq/n}}$$

If the value of $T < np$, one adds, but if the value of $T > np$, then one subtracts.

EXAMPLE 3–6.2. Suppose that 83 people reported that they would support the bond issue of Example 3–6.1. For this outcome, $83 > 110(0.65) = 71.5$, so that the correction is made to reduce the value of Z by subtracting 0.5 from 83. Thus:

$$Z = \frac{(T \pm \frac{1}{2}) - np}{\sqrt{npq}} = \frac{(83 - 0.5) - 110(0.65)}{\sqrt{110(.65)(.35)}} = 2.20$$

Since $Z = 2.20 > 1.645$, there is reason to believe that the bond issue will pass.

Another, but less frequently used, large-sample approximation to the binomial test is available through the chi-square distribution in a test form attributed to Karl Pearson. In this form, one first determines the expected values of the events A and $\overline{A}$, and then computes:

$$X^2 = \frac{(T_1 - np)^2}{np} + \frac{(T_2 - nq)^2}{nq}$$

$$= \sum_{j=1}^{2} \frac{[T_j - E(T_j)]^2}{E(T_j)}$$

The resulting value is then related to the chi-square distribution with one degree of freedom. Because the individual T values are binomial, $E(T_1) = np$ and $E(T_2) = nq$. If n is small, then a correction for continuity can be applied. This will make the test conservative to the committing of a Type I error, since the corrected X^2 will always be smaller in value than the uncorrected X^2. With the correction for continuity:

$$X^2 = \frac{(T_1 \pm \frac{1}{2} - np)^2}{np} + \frac{(T_2 \pm \frac{1}{2} - nq)^2}{nq}$$

If the value of $T_1 < np$, $\frac{1}{2}$ is added to T_1 and subtracted from T_2, but if the value of $T_1 > np$, $\frac{1}{2}$ is subtracted from T_1 and added to T_2.

EXAMPLE 3–6.3. Without the correction for continuity, the Karl Pearson test for the data of Example 3–6.2 is:

$$X^2 = \frac{(83 - 71.5)^2}{71.5} + \frac{(27 - 38.5)^2}{38.5} = 1.85 + 3.43 = 5.28$$

With $v = 1$, H_0 is rejected since $X^2 = 5.28 > X^2_{1 \cdot 0.95} = 3.84$. Computations with the correction for continuity are summarized in Table 3–4. Since $4.83 > 3.84$, there is reason to believe that $p \neq 0.65$ and that the bond issue will pass.

TABLE 3–4. Computations for the Karl Pearson approximation to the binomial test corrected for continuity

Response	T_j	Corrected T_j	$E(T_j)$	$T_j - E(T_j)$	$\frac{(T_j - E(T_j))^2}{E(T_j)}$
Support bond	83	82.5	71.5	11	1.69
Do not support bond	27	27.5	38.5	-11	3.14
Total	110	110	110	0	4.83

Note that for the two statistics corrected for continuity, $Z^2 = (2.2)^2 = 4.84 = X^2$. This always occurs when $v = 1$, for it is easily shown that $Z^2 = X^2$. This relationship also exists if Z and X^2 are not corrected for continuity. For this reason, the Karl Pearson form of this test may be used if so desired.

3–7. Large-Sample Confidence Interval for the Parameter of the Binomial Distribution

In the examples of Section 3–6, there was reason to believe that the bond issue would pass. As a result, an estimate of the minimum proportion supporting the bond issue would be of interest. This value would be identified by the lower limit of the corresponding confidence interval. In this case, the $(1 - \alpha)$-percent approximate confidence interval for p is given by:

$$p > \hat{p} + Z_\alpha \sqrt{\frac{\hat{p}\hat{q}}{n}}$$

For an upper bound on an unknown proportion, the upper limit of the confidence interval defined by:

$$p < \hat{p} + Z_{(1-\alpha)} \sqrt{\frac{\hat{p}\hat{q}}{n}}$$

would be utilized.

EXAMPLE 3–7.1. For the data of Example 3–6.2, with $\alpha = 0.05$:

$$p > \hat{p} - 1.645 \sqrt{\frac{\hat{p}\hat{q}}{n}}$$

$$> \frac{83}{110} - 1.645 \sqrt{\frac{1}{110} \left(\frac{83}{110}\right)\left(\frac{27}{110}\right)}$$

$$> 0.754 - 0.067$$

$$> 0.687$$

Note that $p = 0.65$ is not in the interval. This is to be expected, since H_0 has been rejected in favor of H_1, which states that $p > 0.65$. According to these computations, it can be concluded that at least 68 percent of the voters will support the bond issue, provided that their attitudes do not change between the time of the survey and election time.

For a two-sided confidence interval, associated with a two-sided test of hypothesis, the $(1 - \alpha)$-percent confidence interval for p is given by:

$$\hat{p} - Z_{1-\alpha/2} \sqrt{\frac{\hat{p}\hat{q}}{n}} < p < \hat{p} + Z_{1-\alpha/2} \sqrt{\frac{\hat{p}\hat{q}}{n}}$$

where $Z_{1-\alpha/2}$ corresponds to the $1 - \alpha/2$ percentile of the $N(0, 1)$ distribution.

3–8. The Sign Test for the Matched-Pairs Design

In the investigation on differential birth rates by sex, as made by Arbuthnott, paired observations (p_M, p_F) were made across n different years of data collection.

In theory, the variables p_M and p_F possess continuous probability distributions. In the most general case, one can consider two continuous variables Y_1 and Y_2 that are observed across n sample elements. Let the n ordered pairs be denoted by

$$\{(y_{11}, y_{21}), (y_{12}, y_{22}), \ldots, (y_{1j}, y_{2j}), \ldots, (y_{1n}, y_{2n})\}$$

and let their differences be denoted by:

$$d_1 = (y_{11} - y_{21}), d_2 = (y_{12} - y_{22}), \ldots, d_j = (y_{1j} - y_{2j}), \ldots, d_n = (y_{1n} - y_{2n})$$

The individual paired observations (y_{1j}, y_{2j}) may refer to different observations on the same subjects, or to similar observations made on matched subjects who have received different treatments. Under the classical model, where it is assumed that the underlying variables are normally distributed or near normal in form, and where the paired observations are statistically independent the hypothesis of no treatment difference would relate to the matched-pair t test. If the normality assumption is invalid, the sign test described in Section 3–4 can be used.

If there is no temporal difference in the performance of the n subjects, or if there is no treatment effect for the n pairs of subjects, then $P(d_j > 0) = P(d_j < 0) = \frac{1}{2}$. Note that this statement precludes the occurrence of tied observations. If Y_1 and Y_2 are continuous, then tied observations are impossible, suggesting that the test depends upon the implicit assumption of continuity. Furthermore, in the case of matched subjects, it is generally assumed that there is no interaction between the treatment effect and any other variables that could be responsible for producing nonzero differences between y_{1j} and y_{2j}.

The null hypothesis of no treatment effect is, under this model, actually a statement that the differences have been drawn from a population having a median of zero. The statistical statement of this hypothesis and its two-directional alternative is:

$$H_0: P(d_j > 0) = P(d_j < 0)$$
$$H_1: H_0 \text{ is false}$$

or, in terms of the median difference, M_d:

$$H_0: M_d = 0$$
$$H_1: M_d \neq 0$$

Under this model, the assumptions necessary for the valid use of this test are:

1. Continuity of the underlying distribution of differences so that $P(d_j = 0)$.
2. Independence between the pairs of observations. If, in addition, it is assumed that:
3. The population of differences is symmetrically distributed,

then the statement that the median of differences equals zero is equivalent to the statement that the mean of the differences equals zero because, under symmetry, the population mean and median are equal. For equal sample sizes, as would be used in all matched-pair designs, $\bar{d} = \bar{Y}_1 - \bar{Y}_2$. Thus, statements about the mean of the differences, $\bar{d}$, also apply to the difference of the means, $\bar{Y}_1 - \bar{Y}_2$. Similar statements cannot be made about the medians. It is not generally true that $\hat{M}_d = \hat{M}_1 - \hat{M}_2$. Thus, under the more restrictive assumption of symmetry of the population of differences, an investigator may assert that the $M_d = 0$ implies not only that half of the y_{1j}'s are numerically larger than the y_{2j}'s, but also that the mean numerical superiority of the y_{1j}'s to the y_{2j}'s is as great as the mean numerical superiority of the y_{2j}'s over the y_{1j}'s. In other words, the assumption of symmetry permits an investigator to draw inferences about the relative magnitude as well as the direction of the differences. Without this assumption, the investigator is restricted to inferences about the direction of the median difference, but not the magnitude of the differences.

The introduction of the binomial-distribution theory is facilitated by letting:

$$x_j = 1, \quad \text{if } d_j > 0$$

or

$$x_j = 0, \quad \text{if } d_j < 0$$

Variables of this nature are often called *indicator* variables. The number 1 is used to indicate presence of the condition and the number 0 is used to indicate absence of the condition. As defined, x_j is a Bernoulli-distributed random variable with $P(x_j = 1) = \frac{1}{2}$ and $P(x_j = 0) = \frac{1}{2}$. If the n pairs of subjects constitute a random sample from a population of such pairs, then the $x_j, j = 1, 2, \ldots, n$, represent n independent Bernoulli random variables. Thus:

$$T = \sum_{j=1}^{n} x_j = \text{Number of positive deviations or plus signs}$$

is a binomial random variable with n trials and probability $p = \frac{1}{2}$. The computation of the test statistic for the sign test is as illustrated with the data in the example in Table 3–5.

EXAMPLE 3–8.1. In this study, an investigator matched ten normal-speaking elementary-school children with ten children identified as having functional articulation defects. The children were matched on the basis of their age, sex, grade, and IQ test scores. All children were given the same test of auditory discrimination. High test scores are associated with poor auditory discrimination.

The investigator wished to test the hypothesis of no difference in auditory discrimination between normal children and children having functional articulation defects. The experimental hypothesis asserts that the children having functional articulation defects also have poorer auditory discrimination (i.e., higher scores on the auditory discrimination test) than normal-speaking children. Because of the

TABLE 3–5. Test scores on an auditory discrimination test for matched pairs of children having functional articulation defects (Y_1), and normal-speaking children (Y_2).

Pair	Y_{1j}	Y_{2j}	Difference: $d_j = Y_{1j} - Y_{2j}$	Sign of d_j	Value of X_j
1	33	28	5	+	1
2	46	6	40	+	1
3	41	30	11	+	1
4	7	10	−3	−	0
5	22	37	−15	−	0
6	43	27	16	+	1
7	21	9	12	+	1
8	45	9	36	+	1
9	14	15	−1	−	0
10	16	8	8	+	1

two extreme paired difference values of 40 and 36, an indiscriminate use of the matched-pair t-test is questionable. It is quite clear that normality of difference values is not valid. As a result, it was decided to test:

H_0: Median difference of the matched pairs is equal to zero

against the alternative:

H_1: Median difference of the matched pairs is greater than zero

Under H_0, T is binomial with $n = 10$ and $p = \frac{1}{2}$, so that the probabilities of Table 3–3 are applicable. Ordered outcomes compatible with H_1 are $\{10, 9, 8, \ldots\}$. For a one-tailed test with $\alpha \leq 0.05$, the appropriate decision rule is given by:

$$\text{D.R.: Reject } H_0 \quad \text{if } T = 9 \text{ or } 10$$

since

$$P[(T = 9) \cup (T = 10)] = P(T = 9) + P(T = 10)$$
$$= \begin{bmatrix} 10 \\ 9 \end{bmatrix} \left(\frac{1}{2}\right)^9 \left(\frac{1}{2}\right)^1 + \begin{bmatrix} 10 \\ 10 \end{bmatrix} \left(\frac{1}{2}\right)^{10} \left(\frac{1}{2}\right)^0$$
$$= 0.010 + .001$$
$$= 0.011$$

while

$$P[(T = 8) \cup (T = 9) \cup (T = 10)] = 0.044 + 0.010 + 0.001$$
$$= 0.055$$

which is greater than $\alpha \leq 0.05$. Since $\alpha = 0.011$, it is said that this test is conservative with respect to the desired probability of a Type I error of $\alpha = 0.05$. Furthermore, since $T = 7$, the hypothesis is not rejected. It cannot be concluded that the median difference of the matched-pair test scores exceeds zero, although the sample median $\hat{M}_d = 11.5$. The reason for this is that the sign test has relatively low power and might not be the best substitute for the matched-pair t test. In Chapter 13, a more powerful test of this same hypothesis will be made by means of a test called the Wilcoxon matched-pair test. The hypothesis that children having articulation defects score higher than normal-speaking children will, indeed, be supported with this more powerful test.

It should be noted that if H_0 had been rejected, it could not be concluded that the median scores in the population of scores differed. The sign test has tested the hypothesis that the median difference is zero and not that the difference of the medians is zero. For these data, the median of the differences is given by $\hat{M}_d = \frac{1}{2}(11 + 12) = 11.5$. The median of the Y_1 values is given by $\hat{M}_1 = \frac{1}{2}(22 + 33) = 27.5$, while the median of the Y_2 values is given by $\hat{M}_2 = \frac{1}{2}(10 + 15) = 12.5$. Clearly:

$$\hat{M}_1 - \hat{M}_2 = 27.5 - 12.5 = 15 \neq 11.5 = \hat{M}_d$$

3–9. Tables of the Binomial for $p = \frac{1}{2}$

Extensive tabling of the binomial distribution for $p = \frac{1}{2}$ makes the determination of the exact null distribution of the sign test an easy matter even for large values of n. A shortened version of these tables is presented in Table A–7. These tables report the conservative 0.5th, 2.5th, 5th, and 12.5th percentile of the corresponding binomial distributions. Since the binomial distribution is symmetric when $p = \frac{1}{2}$, these same tables can be used to determine the 87.5th-, 95th-, 97.5th-, and 99th-percentile values.

For the auditory discrimination study, the $\alpha = .011$ critical region was determined as T: {10, 9}. In Table A–7, with $n = 10$, the 0.5th-percentile value is given by $T = 0$, while the 2.5th-percentile value is given by $T = 1$. Because of symmetry, these values relate $T = 10 - 1 = 9$, and $T = 10 - 0 = 10$, to the 97.5th- and 99.5th-percentile values. Thus, the exact test at $\alpha = 0.011$ with T: {10, 9} corresponds to the conservative test of $\alpha = 0.025$.

When $n > 50$, the exact probabilities of Table A–7 can be employed; however, most researchers employ the large-sample normal approximation. This large-sample approximation is derived in Section 3–10.

3–10. The Large-Sample Approximation to the Sign Test

If a large-sample approximation is desired, the familiar normal approximation to the binomial may be employed to obtain such a test. When $P(x_j = 1) = P(x_j = 0) = \frac{1}{2}$, the statistic:

$$T = \sum_{j=1}^{n} x_j$$

has the following properties:

1. $E(T) = E\left(\sum_{j=1}^{n} x_j\right) = np = n\left(\frac{1}{2}\right) = \frac{n}{2}$

2. $\text{Var}(T) = \text{Var}\left(\sum_{j=1}^{n} x_j\right) = npq = n\left(\frac{1}{2}\right)\left(\frac{1}{2}\right) = \frac{n}{4}$

and

$$Z = \frac{T - E(T)}{\sqrt{\text{Var}(T)}} = \frac{T - n/2}{\sqrt{n/4}}$$

is asymptotically normal with $E(Z) = 0$ and $\text{Var}(Z) = 1$. A correction for continuity (± 0.5) is frequently advocated to improve the fit of the continuous normal distribution to the discrete binomial distribution. The quality of this approximation improves as n and α increase; however, the differences between the corrected and uncorrected normal-curve approximation to the binomial diminish as n increases.

EXAMPLE 3–10.1. The values of $P(T \geq t)$ for $t = 1, 2, \ldots, 10$ are given in Table 3–6 for the exact binomial distribution, the normal approximation to the binomial, and the normal approximation corrected for continuity. Similar computations for $n = 100$ would show much smaller differences between the two normal approximations, as well as between each normal approximation and the exact binomial probability.

TABLE 3–6. $P(T \geq t)$ for the exact binomial, normal approximation, and normal approximation corrected for continuity.

$T \geq t$	Exact binomial probability	Normal uncorrected approximation	Normal corrected approximation
0	1.000	0.999	1.000
1	0.999	0.994	0.999
2	0.989	0.971	0.987
3	0.945	0.897	0.943
4	0.828	0.736	0.829
5	0.623	0.500	0.624
6	0.377	0.264	0.376
7	0.172	0.103	0.171
8	0.055	0.029	0.057
9	0.011	0.006	0.014
10	0.001	0.001	0.002

3–11. The Sign Test in the One-Sample Location Problem

The sign test can also be used as a test of location in the single-sample problem. If the observations Y_j constitute an independent random sample from a continuous distribution, then a test of hypothesis that the population median, M, equals some specified value, M_0, is given by determining the number $(y_j - M_0 > 0)$. The null hypothesis asserts:

$$H_0: M = M_0$$

while a nondirectional alternative claims:

$$H_1: M \neq M_0$$

Once again, let the indicator variable x_j be introduced. Let:

$$x_j = 1 \quad \text{if } d_j = y_j - M_0 > 0$$

and

$$x_j = 0 \quad \text{if } d_j = y_j - M_0 < 0$$

Under the null hypothesis:

1. $P(x_j = 1) = P(x_j = 0) = \frac{1}{2}.$ 2. $T = \sum_{j=1}^{n} x_j$ is binomial $\left(n, \frac{1}{2}\right)$:

Thus, an exact test of the hypothesis that the population median equals M_0 against the alternative that $M \neq M_0$ is given by the decision rule:

D.R.: Reject H_0 if $T \leq t_1$ or   if $T \geq n - t_1$

For large samples, a normal-curve test can be substituted for the exact test. With the correction for continuity:

$$Z = \frac{(T \pm \frac{1}{2}) - n/2}{\sqrt{n/4}}$$

The Binomial and Sign Tests: One-Sample Procedures for Dichotomous Variables

55

The decision rule based on the large-sample approximation is given by:

$$\text{D.R.: Reject } H_0 \text{ if } Z < Z_{\alpha/2} \quad \text{or} \quad \text{if } Z > Z_{(1-\alpha/2)}$$

An example of the use of the one-sample sign test is given from a hypothetical survey.

EXAMPLE 3–11.1. In a survey of adult attitudes toward the proposed creation of a junior-college district, a random sample of 50 adult residents of the community was taken. Data from a survey questionnaire item were used to determine the educational level of each respondent. Two subjects had not completed the eighth grade while three subjects had more than four years of college. For these five subjects, exact years of schooling were unknown. Results are shown in Table 3–7. The investigator believed that the first wave of survey respondents overrepresented the upper educational levels of the target community. To test this hypothesis, an estimate of the median educational level of the adult residents was made from census-tract data, which showed $M_0 = 12.8$ years.

TABLE 3–7. *Number of years of completed education reported by the first wave of respondents to a mail questionnaire. Responses have been rank ordered.*

Subject	Y_j	Subject	Y_j
1	Less than 8	26	12
2	Less than 8	27	12
3	8	28	13
4	8	29	13
5	8	30	14
6	8	31	14
7	8	32	14
8	9	33	14
9	9	34	14
10	10	35	14
11	10	36	15
12	10	37	16
13	10	38	16
14	10	39	16
15	10	40	16
16	11	41	16
17	11	42	16
18	11	43	16
19	11	44	16
20	11	45	16
21	12	46	16
22	12	47	16
23	12	48	More than 16
24	12	49	More than 16
25	12	50	More than 16

The hypothesis to be tested was given by $H_0: M = 12.8$ against the alternative $H_1: M > 12.8$. The data are reported as years of schooling for the 50 respondents to the mailed questionnaire. Note that, even though exact information is missing for five of the respondents, one can still test H_0. For these data:

$$T = \sum_{j=1}^{50} x_j = 23.$$

If H_0 is true:

$$E(T) = \frac{n}{2} = \frac{50}{2} = 25 \quad \text{and} \quad \text{Var}(T) = \frac{n}{4} = \frac{50}{4} = 12.5$$

A large-sample test of this hypothesis at $\alpha = .05$ is given by rejecting H_0 when $Z > 1.645$. For these data, the Z test corrected for continuity is:

$$Z = \frac{(23 + 0.5) - 25}{\sqrt{12.5}} = \frac{-1.5}{3.53} = -0.42$$

The investigator concludes that the median educational level of the respondents in the first wave of responses is no more than 12.8 years of schooling, the median reported by census data for the entire community.

If the investigator were willing to assume that the deviations $d_j = (y_j - 12.8)$ are symmetrically distributed about 12.8, then 12.8 is identical to the mean number of years of education and the inference about the median is also an inference about the mean value. These conclusions might not be a warranted for the education data since it is known that "completed years of education" does not possess a symmetrical distribution. However, if a researcher has reason to believe that a variable is symmetrically distributed about its center, then it follows that the hypothesis tested by the sign test in the one-sample location problem is, in reality, a test of μ, the expected value or mean value, of the underlying distribution. Under these conditions, this form of the sign test serves as an assumption-freer competitor to the classical one-sample t test.

3–12. Tied Observations in the Sign Test

One of the assumptions implicit in the use of the sign test, as illustrated in Example 3–11.1, is that the underlying variable is continuous in its universe. Although the variable "amount of schooling" is continuous, the measurement process leading to the data in Table 3–7 results in a discrete manifest variable. Amount of schooling is reported as the number of years completed. The distinction between a continuous underlying variable and a discrete manifest variable causes no difficulties with the sign test, if all the differences are nonzero values.

If zero differences occur, the researcher may assign the tied data values to the test statistic so as to make rejection of the null hypothesis more difficult. This will tend to make the statistical test more conservative, in that the probability of a Type I error will be smaller than specified and, as a result, the test will lose power in its ability to reject the null hypothesis if it is false.

While this strategy does possess a number of weaknesses, which are discussed in Section 2–4, it is the strategy used throughout this book to achieve uniformity. It should be well understood that this position is not defended on theoretical grounds; instead, it is used for reasons of expediency and simplicity of presentation. Therefore, the researcher is urged to study Section 2–4 and then use the strategy deemed to be optimum for the situation at hand. In all cases, it might be wise to consult a professional statistician if the decisions to be made on the basis of the resulting statistical test are important.

3–13. One-Sample Confidence Interval for the Population Median and Median Difference

It will be recalled that, in testing:

$$H_0: M = M_0$$

versus

$$H_1: M \neq M_0,$$

the appropriate decision rule was given by:

D.R.: Reject H_0 if $T \leq t_1$ or   if $T \geq n - t_1 = t_2$

where the values t_1 and $n - t_1 = t_2$ were symmetric points of the binomial $(n, \frac{1}{2})$ distribution. A confidence interval for the population median M may be constructed on the basis of t_1 and $t_2 = n - t_1$ and used to test the hypothesis $H_0: M = M_0$, or the interval may be used to estimate M following the rejection of the hypothesis. Specifically, it can be shown that, if the n observations are ranked in order of increasing magnitude, as follows:

$$Y^{(1)}, Y^{(2)}, \ldots, Y^{(t_1)}, Y^{(t_1+1)}, \ldots, Y^{(t_2)}, \ldots, Y^{(n)},$$

then the lower and upper limits of an approximate $(1 - \alpha)$-percent confidence interval are given by $Y^{(t_1+1)}$ and $Y^{(t_2)}$, respectively. In symbolic terms:

$$P(Y^{(t_1+1)} \leq M \leq Y^{(t_2)}) \geq 1 - \alpha$$

Once t_1 and t_2 are determined, the interval of interest is then given by:

$$Y^{(t_1+1)} \leq M \leq Y^{(t_2)}$$

EXAMPLE 3–13.1. An example of the use of the binomial distribution to obtain an approximate $(1 - \alpha)$-percent confidence interval for the population median is based on the hypothetical data reported in Table 3–8.

In a study of reading, measurements were obtained on the number of eye fixations per line of print for a random sample of 25 first-grade children. The investigator wanted to establish a 95-percent confidence interval for the median number of eye fixations per line of print for the population of first-graders from which these subjects were chosen. The sample values were determined on the basis of repeated measurements (on different reading materials) for the 25 subjects. The observations are reported in increasing rank order. Note that classical procedures cannot be used since two of the subjects have an average exceeding 40 eye fixations per line. If one were to attempt the *t* test by discarding the two unknown values, a clear bias would occur, since the sample mean would be too small, as would also the sample standard deviation. In cases like this, the sign test can be justified since it makes no assumption about the nature of the underlying variable except the theoretical one of continuity, which has been discussed in Section 3–12.

TABLE 3–8. Number of eye fixations per line for 25 first-grade reading students. (Data have been rank ordered.)

Subject	Number of fixations	Rank
Alice	8.7	1
Bob	8.9	2
Carol	11.0	3
Donald	11.1	4
Elmer	11.3	5
Frank	14.3	6
George	14.8	7
Hannah	16.5	8
Inez	16.8	9
Joseph	17.4	10
Katherine	20.5	11
Larry	21.5	12
Marie	21.8	13
Ned	22.2	14
Oliver	23.0	15
Patricia	24.3	16
Quentin	24.4	17
Ralph	25.2	18
Sally	26.8	19
Theresa	30.6	20
Ursula	30.7	21
Veronica	31.6	22
Welton	33.2	23
Xavier	More than 40	24
Yolanda	More than 40	25

For $n = 25$, and $\alpha = 0.05$, it is seen in Table A–7 that $t_1 = 7$. Thus, $t_1 + 1 = 7 + 1 = 8$. Since the distribution of T is symmetrical, $t_2 = n - t_1 = 25 - 7 = 18$. Thus, the approximate 95-percent confidence interval for M is given by:

$$Y^{(8)} \leq M \leq Y^{(18)}$$

From Table 3–8 it is seen that $Y^{(8)} = 16.5$ and $Y^{(18)} = 25.2$, so the 95-percent confidence interval is given by:

$$16.5 \leq M \leq 25.2$$

In a similar fashion, the large-sample confidence interval for the median can be derived by noting that:

$$P\left[\frac{(t_1 + \frac{1}{2}) - n/2}{\sqrt{n/4}} < Z < \frac{(t_2 - \frac{1}{2}) - n/2}{\sqrt{n/4}} \right] \geq 1 - \alpha$$

Under normality, the above interval has a probability of inclusion of $(1 - \alpha)$. Solving the respective inequalities for t_1 and t_2, it follows that:

$$t_1 = \left(\frac{n}{2} - \frac{1}{2}\right) - Z_{1-\alpha/2}\sqrt{\frac{n}{4}}$$

and

$$t_2 = \left(\frac{n}{2} + \frac{1}{2}\right) + Z_{1-\alpha/2}\sqrt{\frac{n}{4}}$$

Since the binomial is discrete, one is advised to round t_1 down and t_2 up to the nearest integer so as to keep $\alpha \le 0.05$. Thus, when $n = 25$, a 95-percent confidence interval could be computed directly by solving for t_1 and t_2:

$$t_1 = (12.5 - 0.5) - 1.96\sqrt{25/4} = 12.0 - 4.9 = 7.1 \cong 7$$

and

$$t_2 = (12.5 + 0.5) + 1.96\sqrt{25/4} = 13.0 + 4.9 = 17.9 \cong 18$$

and identifying the appropriate ordered observations $Y^{(t_1+1)}$ and $Y^{(t_2)}$. Thus, the interval of interest is given by:

$$Y^{(t_1+1)} \le M \le Y^{(t_2)}$$

or

$$Y^{(8)} \le M \le Y^{(18)}$$
$$16.5 \le M \le 25.2$$

It should be noted that the procedure of this section also applies to the determination of a $(1 - \alpha)$-percent confidence interval for the median difference. This is illustrated in Example 3–13.2.

EXAMPLE 3–13.2. Consider the data of Table 3–5, for which the median difference has been estimated as $\hat{M}_d = 11.5$. For a two-sided test with $\alpha \le 0.05$ and $n = 10$, one reads in Table A–7 that H_0 should be rejected if $t \le 1$ or $t \ge 9$. Thus, the approximate 95-percent confidence interval for M_d is given by:

$$d^{(2)} \le M_d \le d^{(9)}$$

or

$$-3 \le M_d \le 36$$

The techniques presented in this section may be applied to percentiles other than the fiftieth (or median) by making the appropriate changes in the statement of the binomial probability.

3–14. The Power Curve for the Sign Test

The power function of the sign test is more easily computed for directional than nondirectional hypothesis tests. Its computation will be illustrated for the transfer-learning study of Section 3–2.

EXAMPLE 3–14.1. In this study, $H_0: P(+) = p_0 = \frac{1}{2}$ is tested against the alternative $H_1: P(+) = p_1 < \frac{1}{2}$. Let the decision rule for rejecting H_0 with $\alpha \leq 0.055$ be given by:

D.R.: Reject H_0 if $T = 0, 1,$ or 2

Since power is the probability of rejecting H_0 when H_1 is true, it follows that:

$$\text{Power} = P\left[(T = 0) \cup (T = 1) \cup (T = 2) | P(+) < \tfrac{1}{2}\right]$$
$$= \begin{bmatrix} 10 \\ 0 \end{bmatrix} p_1^0 q_1^{10} + \begin{bmatrix} 10 \\ 1 \end{bmatrix} p_1^1 q_1^9 + \begin{bmatrix} 10 \\ 2 \end{bmatrix} p_1^2 q_1^8$$

Since the exact values of p_1 and q_1 are unspecified by the alternatives, one can determine the entire power function by selecting a few values of p_1 to use to evaluate the power, and then graphically portray the power curve for the complete set of alternatives. In most cases this is satisfactory.

TABLE 3–9. Power-curve calculations for the sign test for $n = 10$, $\alpha = 0.055$, $H_0: P(+) = \frac{1}{2}$, and $H_1: P(+) < \frac{1}{2}$.

Value of p_1	$\text{Power} = \begin{bmatrix}10\\0\end{bmatrix}p_1^0 q_1^{10} + \begin{bmatrix}10\\1\end{bmatrix}p_1^1 q_1^9 + \begin{bmatrix}10\\2\end{bmatrix}p_1^2 q_1^8 = (1 - \beta)$
0.5	$\begin{bmatrix}10\\0\end{bmatrix}(0.5)^0(0.5)^{10} + \begin{bmatrix}10\\1\end{bmatrix}(0.5)^1(0.5)^9 + \begin{bmatrix}10\\2\end{bmatrix}(0.5)^2(0.5)^8 = 0.055$
0.4	$\begin{bmatrix}10\\0\end{bmatrix}(0.4)^0(0.6)^{10} + \begin{bmatrix}10\\1\end{bmatrix}(0.4)^1(0.6)^9 + \begin{bmatrix}10\\2\end{bmatrix}(0.4)^2(0.6)^8 = 0.167$
0.3	$\begin{bmatrix}10\\0\end{bmatrix}(0.3)^0(0.7)^{10} + \begin{bmatrix}10\\1\end{bmatrix}(0.3)^1(0.7)^9 + \begin{bmatrix}10\\2\end{bmatrix}(0.3)^2(0.7)^8 = 0.383$
0.2	$\begin{bmatrix}10\\0\end{bmatrix}(0.2)^0(0.8)^{10} + \begin{bmatrix}10\\1\end{bmatrix}(0.2)^1(0.8)^9 + \begin{bmatrix}10\\2\end{bmatrix}(0.2)^2(0.8)^8 = 0.678$
0.1	$\begin{bmatrix}10\\0\end{bmatrix}(0.1)^0(0.9)^{10} + \begin{bmatrix}10\\1\end{bmatrix}(0.1)^1(0.9)^9 + \begin{bmatrix}10\\2\end{bmatrix}(0.1)^2(0.9)^8 = 0.930$

Computations for certain selected values of p_1 are shown in Table 3–9, and the entire power curve is shown in Figure 3–3. As can be seen, the power is quite low unless $p_1 = P(+) < 0.25$, as inspection of the total curve suggests that the power is less than 0.5 for $p_1 \geq .25$. If the researcher thinks that the probability of rejecting H_0 is too small, then he should consider increasing the sample size to achieve an increase in power.

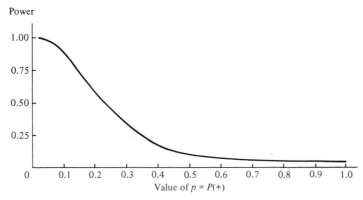

FIGURE 3–3. Power curve for the sign test for $n = 10$, $\alpha = 0.055$, $H_0: P(+) = \frac{1}{2}$ and $H_1: P(+) < \frac{1}{2}$.

The Binomial and Sign Tests: One-Sample Procedures for Dichotomous Variables

When the normal approximation can be justified, one can estimate the power curve for testing $H_0: p = p_0$ versus $H_1: p = p_1$ as follows. By definition:

$$\text{Power} = P[\text{Test statistic is in the critical region}|H_1 \text{ is true}]$$
$$= P[Z < Z_{\alpha/2} \quad \text{or} \quad Z > Z_{1-\alpha/2}|H_1 \text{ is true}]$$
$$= P\left[Z < \frac{p_0 - p_1}{\sqrt{\hat{p}_1 q_1/n}} + Z_{\alpha/2}\sqrt{\frac{p_0 q_0}{p_1 q_1}}\right] + P\left[Z > \frac{p_0 - p_1}{\sqrt{p_1 q_1/n}} + Z_{1-\alpha/2}\sqrt{\frac{p_0 q_0}{p_1 q_1}}\right]$$

EXAMPLE 3–14.2. As an example of the use of this result, find the point on the power curve for testing $H_0: p = 0.5$ against $H_1: p = 0.8$, with $n = 25$ and $\alpha = 0.05$. Making the appropriate substitutions, we have:

$$\text{Power} = P\left[Z < \frac{0.5 - 0.8}{\sqrt{(0.8)(0.2)/25}} - 1.96\sqrt{\frac{(0.5)(0.5)}{(0.8)(0.2)}}\right]$$
$$+ P\left[Z > \frac{0.5 - 0.8}{\sqrt{(0.8)(0.2)/25}} + 1.96\sqrt{\frac{(0.5)(0.5)}{(0.8)(0.2)}}\right]$$
$$= P[Z < -6.20] + P[Z > -1.30]$$
$$= 0.0000 + 0.9032$$
$$= 0.9032$$

Thus, with $n = 25$ and $\alpha = 0.05$, the power is exceptionally high for rejecting $p = 0.5$ if p actually is equal to 0.8. The rest of the power curve can be determined by substituting other values for p.

For a one-tailed test of $H_0: p = p_0$ against $H_1: p > p_0$, the normal approximation is given by:

$$\text{Power} = P\left[Z > \frac{p_0 - p_1}{\sqrt{p_1 q_1/n}} + Z_{1-\alpha/2}\sqrt{\frac{p_0 q_0}{p_1 q_1}}\right]$$

For the alternative of $H_1: p < p_0$, one replaces $Z_{1-\alpha}$ by Z_α and changes the inequality sign from $>$ to $<$.

EXAMPLE 3–14.3. For $H_0: p = 0.5$ tested against $H_1: p = 0.8$, as a one-tailed test with $n = 25$ and $\alpha = 0.05$:

$$\text{Power} = P\left[Z > \frac{0.5 - 0.8}{\sqrt{(0.8)(0.2)/25}} + 1.645\sqrt{\frac{(0.5)(0.5)}{(0.8)(0.2)}}\right] = 0.9515$$

Note that the power for the one-tailed alternative is larger than the corresponding power for a two-tailed alternative.

3–15. Combined Sign Tests

A useful property of the sign test and related binomial tests is that results from independent experiments or groups may be combined to give a test of greater

TABLE 3–10. *Performance on Skill Two, given that Skill One was mastered, for four groups of students.*

Grade	Knowledge of skill two		Value of Z
	Yes	No	
2	13	6	1.61
5	11	6	1.21
8	15	10	1.00
11	18	11	1.30

statistical power than is encountered for each of the separate tests. Three simple variants of this procedure are presented for the data summarized in Table 3–10. As will become apparent, the procedures are valid only when H_1 is one-sided.

EXAMPLE 3–15.1. In a study on reading-skill hierarchies, an attempt was being made to determine which of two reading skills preceded the other in language development. From previous studies there was reason to believe that Skill One was necessary before Skill Two could be mastered. To test this hypothesis, subjects were tested on the mastery of Skill One. If they possessed this skill, they were then tested for mastery of Skill Two. The testing extended over the second, fifth, eighth, and eleventh grades. None of the individual grade comparisons is significant, even though all are in the predicted direction of $p_0 > \frac{1}{2}$.

Procedure One. The first combining procedure is based on the additive property of binomial variables. According to this property, if $X_1, X_2, \ldots, X_K$ are independent binomial variables $B_k(n_k, p_0)$ with common p_0 value, then

$$T = X_1 + X_2 + \cdots + X_K$$

is also binomial with $n = n_1 + n_2 + \cdots + n_K$ and $p = p_0$. Thus, for the data of Table 3–10,

$$T = 13 + 11 + 15 + 18 = 57$$
$$n = 19 + 17 + 25 + 29 = 90$$

and

$$p_0 = \frac{1}{2},$$

provided H_0 is true. Thus, the hypothesis $H_0: p_0 = \frac{1}{2}$ versus $H_1: p_0 > \frac{1}{2}$ is rejected at $\alpha = 0.05$ if:

$$Z = \frac{(T \pm \frac{1}{2}) - n/2}{\sqrt{n/4}} > 1.645$$

For these data:

$$Z = \frac{(57 - \frac{1}{2}) - 45}{\sqrt{22.5}} = \frac{11.5}{4.74} = 2.43$$

so that H_0 is rejected.

Procedure Two. The second procedure is based on the additive property of $N(0, 1)$ variables. According to this property, if $Z_1, Z_2, \ldots, Z_K$ are independent $N(0, 1)$, then

$$T = Z_1 + Z_2 + \cdots + Z_K \quad \text{is } N(0, K).$$

If H_0 is true, then each Z_k is approximately $N(0, 1)$ and:

$$E(T) = E\left[\sum_{k=1}^{K} Z_k\right] = 0$$

and

$$\text{Var}(T) = \text{Var}\left[\sum_{k=1}^{K} Z_k\right] = K$$

Thus, the hypothesis H_0: $p_0 = \frac{1}{2}$, tested against H_1: $p_0 > \frac{1}{2}$, is rejected at $\alpha = 0.05$ if:

$$Z = \frac{T - E(T)}{\sqrt{\text{Var}(T)}} = \frac{T}{\sqrt{K}} > 1.645$$

For these data, $T = 1.61 + 1.21 + 1.00 + 1.30 = 5.12$, so that:

$$Z = \frac{T}{\sqrt{K}} = \frac{5.12}{\sqrt{4}} = 2.56$$

so that H_0 is rejected.

Procedure Three. The third procedure is based on distribution theory attributed to Karl Pearson, and is called Pearson's lambda criterion. According to this procedure, if $p_1, p_2, \ldots, p_K$ are independent values of $P(Z > Z_{1-\alpha})$, then

$$\lambda = -2\left[\log_e p_1 + \log_e p_2 + \cdots + \log_e p_K\right]$$

is distributed as X^2 with $v = 2K$. The λ criterion based on logarithms to the more widely tabled base 10 is given by:

$$\lambda = -4.605\left[\log_{10} p_1 + \log_{10} p_2 + \cdots + \log_{10} p_K\right]$$

For the data of Table 3–10:

$$p_1 = P(Z > 1.61) = 0.0538$$
$$p_2 = P(Z > 1.21) = 0.1132$$
$$p_3 = P(Z > 1.00) = 0.1587$$
$$p_4 = P(Z > 1.30) = 0.0968$$

Thus, the hypothesis H_0: $p_0 = \frac{1}{2}$ versus H_1: $p_0 > \frac{1}{2}$ is rejected at $\alpha = 0.05$ if:

$$\lambda > X^2_{8:.95} = 15.51$$

For these data,

$$\lambda = -4.605\left[(8.73078 - 10) + (9.04385 - 10) \right.$$
$$\left. + (9.20058 - 10) + (8.98588 - 10)\right]$$
$$= 18.60$$

so that H_0 is rejected.

In general, all three procedures lead to the same conclusion. Of the three, Pearson's lambda criterion is the most difficult to compute, but it is also the one with the greatest flexibility. It can be used with many testing models, since all one needs to know are the values of the individual p_k for the directional tests. Other examples of these procedures are provided in Section 5–9.

3–16. The Cox–Stuart Test for Trend

The sign test has employed the binomial distribution to test hypotheses of identical distributions against shifts in location or centers. It is possible to create other binomially distributed variables to test hypotheses about randomness against trend alternatives. Such tests would serve as nonparametric analogs to the linear regression tests of $\beta = 0$ on the model $Y = \alpha + \beta X$. The statement $\beta = 0$ asserts that the slope of the regression line is equal to zero. The Cox–Stuart statistic depends on binomially distributed random variables to test for trend in location or dispersion.

While the classical test of $H_0: \beta = 0$ versus $H_1: \beta \neq 0$ tests for the absence versus the presence of a linear relationship between the underlying variables, the Cox–Stuart test for trend is not so restricted, since the model tests H_0: No trend versus H_1: Monotonic trend. A trend is said to be *monotonic* if the dependent variable increases as the independent variable increases, or if the dependent variable decreases as the independent variable increases. In the former case, the trend is said to be monotonically increasing, while in the latter case it is said to be monotonically decreasing.

Examples of monotonic and nonmonotonic trends are illustrated in Figure 3–4. Example 1 illustrates a relationship that always increases in an orderly fashion.

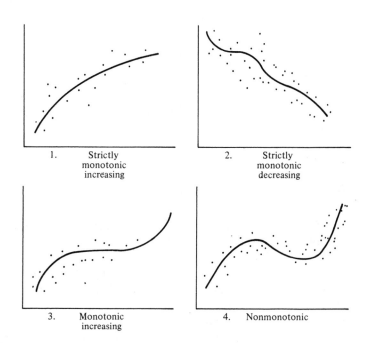

1. Strictly monotonic increasing
2. Strictly monotonic decreasing
3. Monotonic increasing
4. Nonmonotonic

FIGURE 3–4. Examples of monotonic and nonmonotonic trends.

It is said to be *strictly* monotonic increasing. The trend of Example 2 decreases in a strictly monotonic form. The regression of Example 3 is mainly increasing, but it does level off over a portion of the independent variable and is therefore not *strictly* monotonic increasing. Example 4 is mainly increasing but is not monotonic because it does decrease over a portion of the domain of the independent variable.

To test the hypothesis of randomness, or no trend, against trend, consider the observations $y_1, y_2, \ldots, y_N$. If the values of the y_j are randomly distributed over the sequence, then

$$P(y_j - y_{j'} < 0) = P(y_j - y_{j'} > 0) = \tfrac{1}{2}, \qquad j \neq j'.$$

On the other hand, if the y_j increase or decrease monotonically as j increases, then $P(y_j - y_{j'} > 0)$ is not equal to $P(y_j - y_{j'} < 0)$. The Cox–Stuart test for trend examines the relationships of $y_j, y_{j'}$ for various portions of the sequence $j = 1, 2, \ldots, N$.

In particular, for N even, so that $N = 2n$ can be converted to n pairs, a test for trend can be obtained by comparing the values of y_j and y_{n+j}. The comparison of y_j and y_{n+j} is preferable to the comparison of y_j and y_{j+1} because the former comparison is less subject to momentary fluctuations in the sequence than is the latter. If the sequence is random, then:

$$P(y_j - y_{n+j} > 0) = P(y_j - y_{n+j} < 0) = \tfrac{1}{2}$$

Once again an indicator variable,

$$x_j = 1 \quad \text{if } y_j - y_{n+j} > 0 \qquad \text{or} \qquad x_j = 0 \quad \text{if } y_j - y_{n+j} < 0$$

is useful in defining the test statistic. Under the hypothesis of randomness, $P(x_j = 1) = P(x_j = 0) = \tfrac{1}{2}$ and the statistic

$$S = \sum_{j=1}^{n} x_j$$

is binomially distributed with parameters n and $\tfrac{1}{2}$. Large values of S suggest a monotonic decreasing trend for increasing j, while small values of S suggest a monotonic increasing trend. The comparable large-sample test statistic corrected for continuity is given by:

$$Z = \frac{(S \pm \tfrac{1}{2}) - n/2}{\sqrt{n/4}}$$

which, when H_0 is true, is approximately $N(0, 1)$.

EXAMPLE 3–16.1. As an example of the use of this test, consider a coordinator of a house-to-house survey who noticed that the refusal rates of persons to be interviewed appeared to vary over time and, in fact, appeared to be decreasing. He wanted to determine whether the fluctuations that he noted were merely chance fluctuations or whether they reflected the presence of a systematic factor affecting a decline in the refusal rate on various days. The discovery of a systematic factor in the refusal rates could lead the coordinator to modify the training, assignment, and supervision of interviewers. The refusal rates were obtained over an 18-day period of interviewing, and are as shown in Table 3–11.

Day	Refusal rate	Day	Refusal rate	Computations for S	
				$y_j - y_{n+j}$	x_j
1	7.4	10	6.2	7.4 − 6.2	1
2	5.2	11	5.0	5.2 − 5.0	1
3	6.6	12	5.1	6.6 − 5.1	1
4	7.9	13	4.9	7.9 − 4.9	1
5	7.8	14	4.2	7.8 − 4.2	1
6	7.2	15	7.7	7.2 − 7.7	0
7	6.8	16	5.4	6.8 − 5.4	1
8	6.7	17	5.3	6.7 − 5.3	1
9	6.5	18	5.1	6.5 − 5.1	1

$$S = \sum x_j = 8$$

For S, a test of the hypothesis of randomness against either monotonic increasing or monotonic decreasing trend can be made using the binomial distribution with $p = \frac{1}{2}$ and $n = 9$. Entering Table A–7 with $\alpha = 0.05$ and $n = 9$, the decision rule for rejecting H_0 is given by:

D.R.: Reject H_0 if $S \leq 1$ or ≥ 8

This decision rule would be used for a conservative test at the 0.05 level, since the exact probability of a Type I error is given by:

$$P(S \leq 1 \text{ or } \geq 8) = 0.0390$$

In either case, H_0 is rejected. Refusal rates *are* changing. Note that a two-tailed test was performed and not a one-tailed test. It must be recalled that post hoc inspection of the data cannot be used to select the alternative hypothesis.

EXAMPLE 3–16.2.   The use of the large-sample form of the S test is demonstrated in Table 3–12. In this study, an experimenter carrying out a concept-formation study was apprehensive that discussion of the experiment by previous and prospective subjects would affect the later subjects' performance. He suspected that because of the sequential testing of the subjects, later subjects would tend to perform better than earlier subjects. This suspicion appears to be satisfied in the data shown in Figure 3–5, which is based on the scores of the 50 subjects and their ordinal position in the testing schedule.

For the data of Table 3–12, $S = 4$, so that, with the correction for continuity:

$$Z = \frac{(S + \frac{1}{2}) - n/2}{\sqrt{n/4}} = \frac{(4 + \frac{1}{2}) - 25/2}{\sqrt{25/4}} = -3.2$$

Since $Z < -1.645$, the hypothesis of randomness is rejected and the experimenter's suspicion appears to have been justified.

The Cox–Stuart test for trend demands independent observations from a

TABLE 3–12. Scores made by 50 students on a concept-formation study. Scores are ordered by subject over time.

Subject	Score	Subject	Score	Value of x_j
1	81	26	113	0
2	84	27	122	0
3	105	28	106	0
4	74	29	124	0
5	103	30	84	1
6	104	31	109	0
7	92	32	118	0
8	90	33	119	0
9	78	34	133	0
10	79	35	103	0
11	72	36	109	0
12	93	37	104	0
13	108	38	118	0
14	119	39	81	1
15	121	40	115	1
16	116	41	107	1
17	116	42	145	0
18	108	43	147	0
19	115	44	128	0
20	103	45	135	0
21	86	46	112	0
22	115	47	128	0
23	100	48	120	0
24	107	49	132	0
25	86	50	117	0

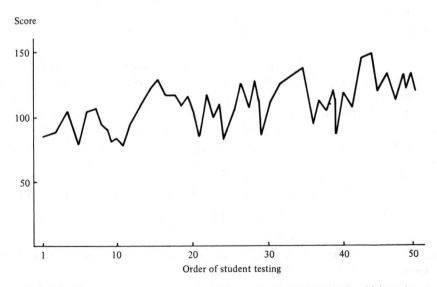

FIGURE 3–5. Scores on the concept-formation study, shown by order in which student was tested.

continuously distributed population. Under these conditions, the test is sensitive only to monotonic trends in location. The ability of the test to detect a cyclic pattern in the data would depend on the periodicity of the cycle as well as on the particular test used. Thus, alternative procedures such as Noether's binomial test for cyclic trend (Noether, 1956) would be preferred if periodicity of the observations was suspected.

The Cox–Stuart test can be modified to test for trend in dispersion about a regression line. In this way, the omnibus test of homoscedasticity:

$$H_0: \sigma^2_{y \cdot x_1} = \sigma^2_{y \cdot x_2} = \ldots = \sigma^2_{y \cdot x_J}$$

versus

$$H_1: H_0 \text{ is false}$$

can be replaced by a test with a trend alternative in the conditional variances:

$$H_1: \sigma^2_{y \cdot x_1} < \sigma^2_{y \cdot x_2} < \cdots < \sigma^2_{y \cdot x_J}$$

or

$$H_1: \sigma^2_{y \cdot x_1} > \sigma^2_{y \cdot x_2} > \cdots > \sigma^2_{y \cdot x_J}$$

References to this modification of the Cox–Stuart test can be found in Bradley (1968) as well as in the Cox and Stuart (1955) paper. Directions for the use of this test are presented in Exercise 3–13.

Finally, it should be noted that the Cox–Stuart test is suspect for *time series* data, if it is believed that adjacent and neighboring observations are correlated. One way to remove the correlation is to pair the first half of the time series to the second half by using a table of random numbers. To obtain the pairing, list the first half of the time series in the temporal order in which measurements were taken. Next, pair the second half of the series to the first half by using a table of random numbers. Upon completion of the pairing, perform the Cox–Stuart test, as illustrated in Examples 3–16.1 and 3–16.2.

Summary

In this chapter, a number of very simple statistical tests based on binomial-distribution theory were presented. These tests included the classical binomial test, the sign test and its extensions to the one-sample median test, the two-sample matched-pair test, and the Cox–Stuart test for monotonic trend and relationship. As stated, a variable T is said to possess a binomial probability distribution if:

1. On repeated trials of the same experiment, only two outcomes, A and $\overline{A}$, are possible.
2. The trials are statistically independent.
3. The probability of the event A remains equal to the fixed constant p over all trials.

When these three conditions are satisfied, the probability that $T = t$ is given by:

$$P(T = t) = \begin{bmatrix} n \\ t \end{bmatrix} p^t q^{n-t}$$

Thus, to test the hypothesis that $H_0: p = p_0$ against the alternative $H_1: p \neq p_0$ with the probability of a Type I error controlled at α, one need only determine t_1 and t_2 such that:

$$\alpha = \sum_{t=0}^{t_1} \begin{bmatrix} n \\ t \end{bmatrix} p^t q^{n-t} + \sum_{t=t_2}^{n} \begin{bmatrix} n \\ t \end{bmatrix} p^t q^{n-t}$$

If the observed value of T is equal to any of the discrete set of values $\{0, 1, \ldots, t_1\}$ or $\{t_2, \ldots, n - 1, n\}$, the hypothesis under test is rejected.

An alternative way to test the same hypothesis is to determine the $(1 - \alpha)\%$ confidence interval for p and then check to see whether $p = p_0$ is included in the interval. If it is not, the hypothesis under test is rejected.

When the sample sizes are large, a normal-curve approximation may be used to test the hypothesis and to set up confidence intervals for p. The large-sample approximation is based upon the simple substitution of $E(T) = np$ and $\text{Var}(T) = npq$ into the standardizing statistic. If a correction for continuity is employed, the resulting test statistic is given by:

$$Z = \frac{(T \pm \frac{1}{2}) - np}{\sqrt{npq}}$$

Since $\hat{p} = T/n$, one can also make use of the following relationships, $E(\hat{p}) = p$ and $\text{Var}(\hat{p}) = pq/n$, to obtain:

$$Z = \frac{(\hat{p} \pm 1/(2n)) - p}{\sqrt{pq/n}}$$

as the corresponding test statistic.

The latter form is customarily used to determine the large-sample confidence interval for p. In this form, the $(1 - \alpha)\%$ confidence interval for p is given by:

$$\hat{p} - Z_{1-\alpha/2} \sqrt{\frac{\hat{p}\hat{q}}{n}} < p < \hat{p} + Z_{1-\alpha/2} \sqrt{\frac{\hat{p}\hat{q}}{n}}$$

Since the quality of the normal approximation depends on the size of n, p, and q, one is advised to verify that $np > 5$ and $nq > 5$ before making use of the large-sample test, since the approximation may be poor when these expected values are less than 5.

For the simple form of the sign test, a variable is observed that indicates direction but not necessarily magnitude of change. For example, in the testing of a drug that is believed to have the ability to produce relaxed sleep among hospital patients, one could, in a controlled study, administer the drug to a group of patients and ask them to report, on waking, whether their sleep was more relaxing than it was the night before. If the response choice "Same" is not permitted, then the remaining response choices of "Less" or "More" are seen to indicate only direction but not magnitude. Thus, if the drug is of no value in producing relaxed sleep, then it should follow that $P(\text{Less}) = P(\text{More}) = \frac{1}{2}$. Since experiences between individuals are independent, then the variable T = number who report "More" is a binomial variable and, therefore, its set of values may be related to the binomial distribution. Thus, with a probability of a Type I error controlled at alpha, the hypothesis tested against a two-sided alternative would be rejected if $T \leq t_1$ or $T \geq t_2$, where t_1 and

t_2 are defined by:

$$\alpha = \sum_{t=0}^{t_1} \begin{bmatrix} n \\ t \end{bmatrix} \left(\frac{1}{2}\right)^t \left(\frac{1}{2}\right)^{n-t} + \sum_{t=t_2}^{n} \begin{bmatrix} n \\ t \end{bmatrix} \left(\frac{1}{2}\right)^t \left(\frac{1}{2}\right)^{n-t}$$

If the sample size is sufficiently large, the large-sample approximation is given by:

$$Z = \frac{(T \pm \frac{1}{2}) - n/2}{\sqrt{n/4}}$$

and the hypothesis of no effectiveness is rejected if $Z < Z_{\alpha/2}$ or $Z > Z_{1-\alpha/2}$.

For the matched-pair form of the sign test, two measures are observed on the same subject, such as a pre- and a post-test, or subjects are matched prior to experimentation and then a single characteristic is observed on both members of the pair. If (y_{1j}, y_{2j}) refers to the observations on each pair, then $d_j = y_{1j} - y_{2j}$ is a simple measure of the difference between the two sets of paired observations. When H_0 is true,

$$P(d_j > 0) = P(d_j < 0) = \tfrac{1}{2}.$$

Thus, the sign test can be used to test H_0: The median value of the difference is zero. Under H_0 and statistical independence between pairs, it follows that the variable $T = \{$Number of pairs for which the difference is positive$\}$ is indeed binomially distributed with $p = \frac{1}{2}$ and n. The decision procedure described for the sign test may now be used to test H_0: $M_d = 0$.

For the one-sample location problem, a researcher hypothesizes that the population median $M = M_0$. When the hypothesis being tested is true, the variable $T = \{$Number of observations that are larger than the hypothesized population median$\}$ is binomial, provided that the original observations are statistically independent. Under these conditions, the variable T has a binomial distribution with parameters $p = \frac{1}{2}$ and n, so that the test can be carried out directly. If the distribution of the differences is symmetrical, then the test of $M = M_0$ is identical to the hypothesis $\mu = \mu_0$.

The Cox–Stuart test for monotonic trend is also referred to the binomial distribution by ordering the observations on one variable, usually time or testing sequence, and then pairing them on the remaining variable to create $N/2 = n$ matched pairs, which are then compared. For the S test, the comparisons are made by means of $d_j = y_j - y_{j+n}$. Under independence of pairs and monotonic relationship, the statistic $S = \{$Number of pairs for which d_j is positive$\}$ possesses a binomial distribution with parameters $p = \frac{1}{2}$ and n, so that the test can be performed in exactly the same manner as described for the simple sign test.

Finally, the power of the sign test can be determined if the researcher has a reasonable estimate of p_1, the value of p, when the hypothesis is false. If the critical region for the test is given by

$$T: \{0, 1, 2, \ldots, t_1, \ldots, t_2, \ldots, n - 1, n\}$$

then the exact power is given by:

$$\text{Power} = 1 - \beta = \sum_{t=0}^{t_1} \begin{bmatrix} n \\ t \end{bmatrix} p_1^t q_1^{n-t} + \sum_{t=t_2}^{n} \begin{bmatrix} n \\ t \end{bmatrix} p_1^t q_1^{n-t}$$

For large samples:

$$\text{Power} = P\left[Z < \frac{p_0 - p_1}{\sqrt{p_1 q_1/n}} + Z_{\alpha/2}\sqrt{\frac{p_0 q_0}{p_1 q_1}}\right]$$

$$+ P\left[Z > \frac{p_0 - p_1}{\sqrt{p_1 q_1/n}} + Z_{1-\alpha/2}\sqrt{\frac{p_0 q_0}{p_1 q_1}}\right]$$

Exercises

*1. In a study in which the effectiveness of a drug to induce relaxed sleep was being examined, 16 patients were identified who reported that their sleep for the previous three nights was very disturbed and not at all relaxing. These 16 patients were given the drug and, upon awaking the next morning, were asked how their sleep was when compared to the previous three nights. Their responses were as follows: 1. Better, 2. Better, 3. Better, 4. Worse, 5. The same, 6. Better, 7. Better, 8. Worse, 9. Better, 10. The same, 11. Better, 12. The same, 13. Worse, 14. Better, 15. Better, 16. The same.

   a) Analyze the data by discarding "The same" responses.
   b) Analyze the data by assigning "The same" responses to "Better" and "Worse" so as to make rejection of the hypothesis more difficult.
   c) Use a coin to assign "The same" responses to the choices "Better" and "Worse," and then analyze the data.
   d) Of the three methods, which do you prefer? What are the advantages and disadvantages in the use of these three methods to break tied observations?

*2. For the data of Exercise 1, set up the 90-percent confidence interval for p if the data are analyzed by method (b).

*3. Determine the 80-percent confidence interval for the median difference examined in Table 3–5. Estimate M_d.

*4. As part of a reading study, 26 children were rank-ordered on the basis of a reading-readiness test. They were then paired. By means of a flip of a coin, one member of each

Pair	Score under traditional program	Score under innovative program
1	25	24
2	23	25
3	19	23
4	22	18
5	12	17
6	18	20
7	19	16
8	6	14
9	11	13
10	4	10
11	7	8
12	10	12
13	6	15

pair was assigned either to a traditional reading program or to a new innovative program. Following five weeks of training the students were tested on a 25-item test. The results are shown in the table on page 72. Perform the Cox–Stuart test on these data. What do you conclude? If observations between pairs are correlated, the Cox–Stuart test is suspect. Repeat the analysis, using the model described in the last paragraph of Section 3–16. What do you conclude? Which model is most reasonable? Why?

*5. Determine the 90-percent confidence interval for the median difference for the data of Exercise 4.

*6. According to published norms, the median score of the test of Exercise 4 is given by $M = 13$.
   a) Does this population value apply to the students trained with the traditional program?
   b) Does it apply to the new program?
   c) What differences are there in the method of analysis for Exercises 5 and 6? Which method do you prefer? Why?

7. Over five years of teaching, an instructor noted that 75% of her students select the wrong answer to a specific true–false question that she believes has high discrimination power. In her most recent class, she has noted that 35 of her 97 students selected the correct answer. Does this evidence suggest that this class is different from her previous classes?

*8. In a study in which two methods for the teaching of fractions were being tested, two different tests were used in two different schools to evaluate the methods. Scores are shown in the table below for a preassigned matched pair. Use the three procedures of Section 3–15 to test for treatment effects. Of the three procedures, which do you prefer? Why?

School One				School Two			
Classroom one		Classroom two		Classroom three		Classroom four	
Old	New	Old	New	Old	New	Old	New
7	10	6	8	23	30	40	49
7	9	7	10	40	42	55	55
4	8	10	10	51	56	39	40
8	7	9	10	40	63	58	57
9	8	9	10	39	50	40	55
7	10	10	9	41	40	60	59
		8	7			55	64
		9	10				

*9. The data of Exercise 8 can also be analyzed by treating the four classrooms as one large sample containing 27 pairs.
   a) Why can the sign test be justified for this combining of data into one large sample?
   b) Analyze the data in this fashion and compare the results with those obtained in Exercise 8.

*10. In a study in which the effects of diet upon maze-running were being evaluated, the following statistics were generated. The dependent variable is the number of trials it takes a rat to make five consecutive successful runs. No rat was given more than 20 trials. Previous studies had suggested that Diet Two produced greater learning than Diet One.

Litter	Diet One	Diet Two
1	7	8
2	8	9
3	12	10
4	20	12
5	15	14
6	9	10
7	20	18
8	13	10
9	20	15
10	9	9
11	14	13
12	20	20
13	16	14
14	20	18
15	14	6
16	13	12
17	20	14
18	20	13

a) Do these data support this observation?

b) Determine the 90-percent confidence interval for the median difference.

c) Can one justify the use of the matched-pair t test for these data? Why?

*11. The study described in Section 3–6 and summarized in Table 3–12 was continued. The remaining results are as shown in the following table. Perform the Cox–Stuart test on these data. What do you conclude?

Subject	Score	Subject	Score
51	121	58	112
52	118	59	99
53	99	60	111
54	128	61	143
55	140	62	142
56	117	63	99
57	113	64	106

*12. Could the sign test be applied to the data of Exercise 2 of Chapter 2? Why?

*13. The Cox–Stuart test can be used to test for monotonic changes in variability, a condition often encountered in growth studies. This modification of the S test is achieved by computing the ranges in each $k \leq 5$ consecutive observations. Choose k so that the number of ranges exceeds 15. For the data of Table 3–12 and for $k = 2$, the 25 ranges are given by

$$R_1 = 84 - 81 = 3, \quad R_2 = 105 - 74 = 31, \quad \ldots, \quad R_{25} = 132 - 117 = 15.$$

If H_0 is true, the ranges should fluctuate in a random manner, but if H_0 is false, the ranges should increase or decrease.

a) Apply the S test to the 25 ranges to determine whether or not a change in variability occurs over time.

b) Repeat the analysis with $k = 4$ for the complete set of 64 subjects as reported in Table 3–12 and Exercise 11.

*14. The sign test can be used to test that the median difference is some number other than zero. The test of H_0: $M_{(Y_2-Y_1)} = C$ against the alternative H_1: $M_{(Y_2-Y_1)} \neq C$ is performed by subtracting C from each observation in Sample 2 and then following through with the ordinary matched-pair sign test. In a study in which a new reading program was being compared to an old program, it was predicted that students given the new training would score, on the average, ten points higher on a standardized test than would the students not given the special training. Data are given in the accompanying table.

Matched pairs according to sex and IQ	Old Y_1	New Y_2	Matched pairs according to sex and IQ	Old Y_1	New Y_2
1	23	28	11	35	42
2	20	22	12	36	42
3	17	35	13	40	45
4	32	27	14	38	47
5	21	32	15	45	40
6	28	25	16	50	48
7	26	30	17	39	42
8	32	40	18	47	48
9	37	39	19	48	47
10	28	36	20	47	46

a) Do the data support this directional claim?
b) What assumption must you make to test H_0: $\mu_2 - \mu_1 = 10$ against H_1: $\mu_2 - \mu_1 > 10$?
c) Determine the one-tailed 95-percent confidence interval for $M_{(Y_2-C-Y_1)}$.
d) Determine the one-tailed 95% confidence interval for $M_{(Y_2-Y_1)}$.
e) Compare (c) and (d).

*15. In the study of Exercise 14, it was decided to adopt the new program if the average increase amounted to $P = 20\% = 0.20$. This can be tested by the sign test by multiplying each Y_1 value by $(1 + P)$ before subtracting the matched-pair scores.
a) Do the data support the hypothesis that $M_{(Y_2-Y_1)} = PM_{Y_1}$?
b) What assumption must you make to test H_0: $\mu_2 - 1.20\mu_1 = 0$ against H_1: $\mu_2 - 1.20\mu_1 > 0$?
c) Determine the one-tailed 95% confidence interval for $M_{(Y_2-1.20Y_1)}$.

*16. The sign test can be used when different measuring instruments are used on independent groups of subjects. The study of Table 3–5 was repeated on a different group of eight matched pairs, but a different instrument was used to test the subjects. The results are as shown in the table below. Combine these results with those of Table 3–5.

Pair	Y_{1j}	Y_{2j}	Pair	Y_{1j}	Y_{2j}
1	10.3	11.7	5	10.8	13.9
2	8.3	9.6	6	8.6	9.7
3	17.2	12.1	7	12.3	11.9
4	10.6	12.7	8	14.1	16.2

a) Perform the corresponding sign test on the $n = 10 + 8 = 18$ pairs.

b) What assumptions have you made?

c) Why can data measured by different instruments be combined to justify the use of the sign test?

*17. Complete the power curve of Example 3–14.2 by finding the power for $p = 0.6$ and $p = 0.9$ and drawing the curve through the points defined by

$$p = 0, \quad p = 0.1, \quad p = 0.2, \quad p = 0.4, \quad p = 0.5, \quad p = 0.6, \quad p = 0.8, \quad p = 0.9,$$
$$\text{and} \quad p = 1.0.$$

Note that:

Power $(p = 0) =$ Power $(p = 1) = 1.0000$,
Power $(p = 0.1) =$ Power $(p = 0.9)$,
Power $(p = 0.2) =$ Power $(p = 0.8) = 0.9032$,
Power $(p = 0.4) =$ Power $(p = 0.6)$,

and

Power $(p = 0.5) = \alpha = 0.0550$.

Statistical Efficiencies
of Nonparametric
and Distribution-Free Tests

4–1. Introduction to Efficiency Comparisons

In Section 3–8, the sign test for the matched-pair design was proposed as a substitute for the matched-pair t test if the assumption of normality could not be justified. The immediate question is what gain or loss is incurred if the sign test is adopted when the classical matched-pair t test is justified. In this section, a comparison of the two procedures is made under the condition that Y_1 and Y_2 are each normally distributed with known variances and known correlation coefficient. While these assumptions are more restrictive than required for the matched-pair t-test model, the basic ideas are illustrated, and tables of the normal-distribution function can be used to make the necessary power calculations.

EXAMPLE 4–1.1. *Power computations in the matched-pair model.* Consider a test of $H_0: \mu_1 - \mu_2 = 0$ against $H_1: \mu_1 - \mu_2 > 0$, where

$$\sigma_1 = 20, \sigma_2 = 15, \qquad \rho_{12} = \tfrac{1}{4}, \qquad n = 25, \qquad \text{and} \qquad \alpha = 0.05$$

Under these conditions, when H_0 is true, the sampling distribution of $\overline{d} = \overline{Y}_1 - \overline{Y}_2$ is normal, with

$$E(\overline{d}\,|\,H_0) = E(\overline{Y}_1 - \overline{Y}_2) = \mu_1 - \mu_2 = 0$$

and

$$\text{Var}(\overline{d}\,|\,H_0) = \text{Var}(\overline{Y}_1 - \overline{Y}_2) = \frac{\sigma_1^2}{n} + \frac{\sigma_2^2}{n} - 2\rho_{12}\frac{\sigma_1\sigma_2}{n}$$

$$= \frac{400}{25} + \frac{225}{25} - 2\left[\frac{1}{4}\right]\frac{(20)(15)}{25}$$

$$= \frac{475}{25} = 19$$

Assume that $\mu_1 - \mu_2 = 8$ is one specific case in which H_1 is true. Then, for this case,

$$E(\overline{d}\,|\,H_1) = 8$$
$$\text{Var}(\overline{d}\,|\,H_1) = 19.$$

The same type of algebra used in Section 3–14 to obtain the power function for the binomial can be used here to show that:

$$\text{Power} = P\left[Z > \frac{E(\overline{d}\,|\,H_0) - E(\overline{d}\,|\,H_1)}{\sqrt{\text{Var}(\overline{d})}} + Z_{(1-\alpha)}\right]$$

For the specified numbers,

$$\text{Power} = P\left[Z > \frac{0 - 8}{\sqrt{19}} + 1.65\right] = 0.5714$$

If the sign test were substituted for this model, the distribution of the individual deviations $d = Y_1 - Y_2$ would be normal, with:

$$\text{Var}(d) = \text{Var}(Y_1 - Y_2) = \sigma_1^2 + \sigma_2^2 - 2\rho_{12}\sigma_1\sigma_2$$

$$= 400 + 225 - 2\left[\frac{1}{4}\right](20)(15) = 475$$

for both H_0 and H_1. When H_0 is true, $E(d\,|\,H_0) = 0$, while when H_1 is true, $E(d\,|\,H_1)$ may assume any positive value. The special case of $E(d\,|\,H_1) = 8$ is illustrated. When $E(d)$ and $\text{Var}(d)$ are used to obtain the corresponding binomial-distribution values, it follows that the probability of a positive deviation is given by:

$$p_0 = P[d > 0\,|\,H_0] = P\left[Z > \frac{d - E(d\,|\,H_0)}{\sqrt{\text{Var}(d)}}\right]$$

$$= P\left[Z > \frac{0 - 0}{\sqrt{475}}\right] = 0.5000$$

while

$$p_1 = P[d > 0\,|\,H_1] = P\left[Z > \frac{d - E(d\,|\,H_1)}{\sqrt{\text{Var}(d)}}\right]$$

$$= P\left[Z > \frac{0 - 8}{\sqrt{475}}\right] = 0.6443$$

This means that the normal-curve model of H_0: $\mu_1 - \mu_2 = 0$ tested against H_1: $\mu_1 - \mu_2 > 0$ for the special case of $\mu_1 - \mu_2 = 8$ is equivalent to the binomial sign test model of H_0: $p_0 = 0.5$ versus H_1: $p_1 > 0.5$ for the special case of $p_1 = 0.6443$. Thus, according to the power-function equation of Section 3–14:

$$\text{Power} = P\left[Z > \frac{\sqrt{n}\,(p_0 - p_1) + Z_{(1-\alpha)}\sqrt{p_0 q_0}}{\sqrt{p_1 q_1}}\right]$$

$$= P\left[Z > \frac{\sqrt{25}\,(0.5 - 0.6443) + 1.65\,\sqrt{(0.5)(0.5)}}{\sqrt{(0.6443)(0.3557)}}\right] = 0.4129$$

Thus, power is reduced from 0.5714 for the normal-curve test to 0.4129 for the sign test. The power of the sign test relative to the corresponding normal-curve test for the matched-pair design is

$$E_{S,N} = \frac{0.4129}{0.5714} = 0.7226$$

when a directional test is performed with $\alpha = 0.05$, $n = 25$, and $\mu_1 - \mu_2 = 8$. In order for the two tests to have equal power for the specified H_0 and H_1, the sign test should be performed with

$$n_S = \frac{n_N}{E_{S,N}} = \frac{25}{0.7226} \cong 35 \text{ pairs}$$

This suggests that

$$E_{S,N} = \frac{n_N}{n_S},$$

the ratio of the sample sizes required to provide equal power for testing H_0 against H_1 with the probability of a Type I error for each test controlled at α. The Type I errors for the two tests are equated, and the power for the two tests is determined for the same alternative. After this, the ratio of the two powers is determined, with the test having the greater power usually employed as the reference test. In these situations the ratio E will be less than one in value. The ratio E can typically be interpreted as the ratio of sample sizes required to give the tests equal power, even when E is determined by different but analogous methods. For Example 4–1.1,

$$E_{S,N} = 0.7226 \cong \frac{25}{35} = \frac{n_N}{n_S}$$

can be interpreted to read that a sign test based on 35 observations has approximately the same power as a normal-curve test based on 25 observations.

The remaining sections of the chapter expand the material illustrated by this example. The term *relative efficiency* is used in two contexts in statistics. It is used to denote a characteristic of two unbiased estimators of the same parameter, and, as illustrated in this section, to describe the comparison of two test statistics used to test the same hypothesis. Relative efficiency used in the first context is termed *estimate efficiency*, while in the second case it is identified as *test efficiency*. In dealing with nonparametric tests, most interest centers on test efficiency; however, the more familiar estimate efficiency is reviewed here to clarify the difference in usage.

4–2. Estimate Efficiency

Since the numerical values of μ and σ^2 are usually unknown, they must be estimated from data based on a random sample of the underlying population. If the sample values are denoted by $(X_1, X_2, \ldots, X_n)$, then the most commonly employed estimators of these parameters are the sample mean (or average) and the sample variance, defined as:

$$\overline{X} = \frac{1}{n} \sum_{i=1}^{n} X_i \quad \text{and} \quad S^2 = \frac{1}{n-1} \sum_{i=1}^{n} (X_i - \overline{X})^2$$

While other estimators exist for these two parameters, the sample mean and sample variance are generally the preferred estimators because they are unbiased. This means that the expected value of their sampling distributions is exactly equal to the respective population parameter; that is, $E(\overline{X}) = \mu$ and $E(S^2) = \sigma^2$.

For a normally distributed variable, it is also true that the sample median $\hat{M}$ is an unbiased estimator of μ, since the expected value of its sampling distribution is also equal to μ. However, the sample mean $\overline{X}$ is still preferred to the sample median, $\hat{M}$, as an estimator of μ, because the sampling distribution of $\overline{X}$ is more compact about μ than is the sampling distribution of $\hat{M}$. This means that $\overline{X}$ is more efficient as an estimator of μ than is $\hat{M}$. In fact, it can be shown that, among the set of unbiased estimators of μ, the estimator $\overline{X}$ has the smallest variance and is therefore the most efficient estimator.

A competing estimator of σ^2 is given by $\tilde{S}^2 = \sum_{i=1}^{n} (X_i - \overline{X})^2 / n$; however, it is biased, since

$$E(\tilde{S}^2) = \left[\frac{n-1}{n}\right] \sigma^2$$

Even so, it is also true that $\text{Var}(\tilde{S}^2) < \text{Var}(S^2)$. Although S^2 is an unbiased estimator of σ^2, it is not true that the *square root* of this estimator provides an unbiased estimator of σ, the population standard deviation. However, S is a *consistent* estimator of σ, since the bias approaches zero as the sample size increases.

A comparison of the estimators for μ, σ^2, and σ discussed in this section is shown in Table 4–1. As can be seen, the sample mean is definitely preferable to the sample median, and the variance and standard deviation estimators based on $(n-1)$ are definitely preferable to the estimators based on n, whenever the sample size is small. It should be noted that, if the underlying distribution is not normal, these relationships may not hold. Because of this, they should be used mainly as guidelines, since other estimators may be preferable for different probability distributions. When the efficiency of one unbiased estimator of a population parameter, relative to another unbiased estimator, is reported, the value may be given as either a ratio of the sample sizes necessary to achieve equal sampling variability or a ratio of the variances of the estimators for equal sample sizes.

TABLE 4–1. *Properties of $\overline{X}$ and $\hat{M}$ as estimators of μ, of S^2 and $\tilde{S}^2$ as estimators of σ^2, and of S and $\tilde{S}$ as estimators of σ. (Infinite populations assumed.)*

Sample size	$E(\overline{X})$	$E(\hat{M})$	$\mathrm{Var}(\overline{X})$	$\mathrm{Var}(\hat{M})$	$\dfrac{\mathrm{Var}(\overline{X})}{\mathrm{Var}(\hat{M})}$	$E(S^2)$	$E(\tilde{S}^2)$	$E(S)$	$E(\tilde{S})$
2	μ	μ	$0.500\sigma^2$	$0.500\sigma^2$	1.	σ^2	$0.500\sigma^2$	0.798σ	0.564σ
3	μ	μ	$0.333\sigma^2$	$0.449\sigma^2$	0.743	σ^2	$0.667\sigma^2$	0.887σ	0.734σ
4	μ	μ	$0.250\sigma^2$	$0.298\sigma^2$	0.838	σ^2	$0.750\sigma^2$	0.922σ	0.798σ
5	μ	μ	$0.200\sigma^2$	$0.287\sigma^2$	0.697	σ^2	$0.800\sigma^2$	0.940σ	0.840σ
6	μ	μ	$0.167\sigma^2$	$0.215\sigma^2$	0.776	σ^2	$0.833\sigma^2$	0.951σ	0.868σ
7	μ	μ	$0.143\sigma^2$	$0.210\sigma^2$	0.679	σ^2	$0.857\sigma^2$	0.960σ	0.889σ
8	μ	μ	$0.125\sigma^2$	$0.168\sigma^2$	0.743	σ^2	$0.875\sigma^2$	0.966σ	0.904σ
9	μ	μ	$0.111\sigma^2$	$0.166\sigma^2$	0.669	σ^2	$0.889\sigma^2$	0.968σ	0.913σ
10	μ	μ	$0.100\sigma^2$	$0.133\sigma^2$	0.723	σ^2	$0.900\sigma^2$	0.973σ	0.923σ

EXAMPLE 4–2.1. Efficiency of the mean relative to the median. The efficiency of the sample mean, $\overline{X}$, relative to the sample median, $\hat{M}$, as estimators of the population mean, μ, of a symmetric population can be identified as either:

$$E_{\overline{X},\hat{M}} = \frac{\text{Sample size to determine } \hat{M}}{\text{Sample size to determine } \overline{X}} = \frac{n_{\hat{M}}}{n_{\hat{X}}}$$

such that the sampling variability of $\hat{M}$ equals that of $\overline{X}$; or as

$$E_{\overline{X},\hat{M}} = \frac{\text{Variance of } \hat{M}}{\text{Variance of } \overline{X}} = \frac{\mathrm{Var}(\hat{M})}{\mathrm{Var}(\overline{X})}$$

for the sampling distributions of the two estimators based on the same sample sizes. If very large samples are drawn from a normally distributed population, the variance of the sample median equals

$$\mathrm{Var}(\hat{M}) = \left[\frac{\pi}{2}\right]\left[\frac{\sigma^2}{n}\right]$$

while that for the sample mean equals

$$\mathrm{Var}(\overline{X}) = \frac{\sigma^2}{n}$$

Thus, the efficiency of the sample mean relative to the sample median as estimators of μ, for large samples drawn from a normally distributed population, is given by:

$$E_{\overline{X},\hat{M}} = \frac{(\pi/2)(\sigma^2/n)}{\sigma^2/n} = \frac{\pi}{2} = 1.57$$

This implies that the variance of the sampling distribution of $\hat{M}$ is approximately 1.57 times that of the variance of the sampling distribution of $\overline{X}$, when simple random samples of the same size are chosen from a normal distribution. It also implies that approximately 157 observations would be needed to yield an estimate of the population mean μ based on the sample median that would have the same sampling variability as a sample mean based on 100 observations. Conversely, the use of the sample median in place of the sample mean as the estimator of μ in a normal population has the effect of throwing away $(1 - E_{\hat{M},\overline{X}})(100\%) = 36.3\%$ of the observations.

Statistical Efficiencies of Nonparametric and Distribution-Free Tests

81

4–3. Test Efficiency

The efficiency of test statistic A relative to test statistic B is defined as the ratio of sample sizes, n_B/n_A, such that the two tests have the same power against the same alternative hypothesis at the same alpha level. According to this definition,

$$E_{A,B} = \frac{n_B}{n_A}$$

EXAMPLE 4–3.1. Efficiency of the sign test relative to the Wilcoxon test. In Example 4–1.1, 35 pairs of observations were required by the sign test to equal the power of 25 pairs of observations for the matched-pair normal-curve test for the same alternative and the same probability of a Type I error. If we were to compare two tests for matched pairs, one based strictly on the signs of the intra-pair differences and the other based on the signs and relative magnitudes of the differences, the efficiency of the first relative to the second would be:

$$E_{S,W} = \frac{n_W}{n_S} = \frac{2}{3} = 0.67$$

if the population distribution of differences were normal. The first of these tests is the sign test described in Chapter 3, while the second test is the Wilcoxon matched-pair test described in greater detail in Chapter 13. The relative efficiency figure of $E_{S,W} = \frac{2}{3}$ implies that 150 observations would be needed to make the sign test as sensitive to differences in location as the Wilcoxon matched-pair test based on 100 observations, if both tests were performed at the same alpha level and if differences had been randomly selected from a normally distributed population.

Specification of what is meant by two tests having the same power has resulted in the identification of several types of test efficiency. Among these are *power efficiency*, *local relative efficiency*, and *asymptotic relative efficiency* (*ARE*). To determine the power efficiency of a test, assume that a researcher wishes to test the null hypothesis:

$$H_0: \theta = \theta_0$$

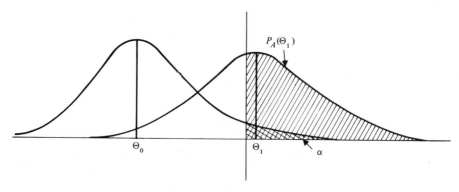

FIGURE 4–1. Sampling distribution of Test A for $\theta = \theta_0$ and $\theta = \theta_1$.

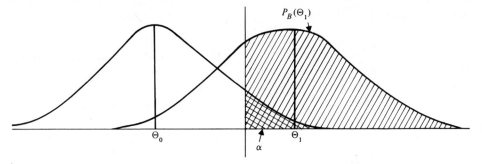

FIGURE 4–2. *Sampling distribution of Test B for $\theta = \theta_0$ and $\theta = \theta_1$.*

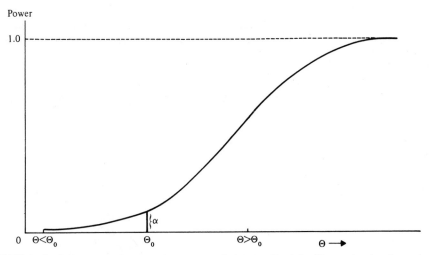

FIGURE 4–3. *Power curve for a consistent one-tailed test at fixed significance level and sample size.*

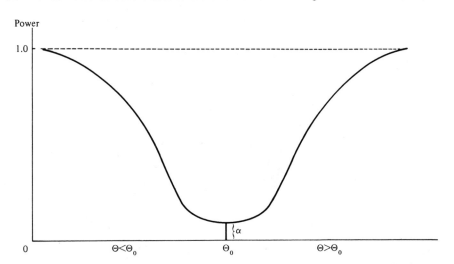

FIGURE 4–4. *Power curve for a two-tailed test at fixed significance level and sample size.*

against the alternative hypothesis

$$H_1: \theta = \theta_1$$

at significance level α. Let $P_A(\theta)$ denote the probability of rejecting H_0 with test A when the true parameter is θ, and let $P_B(\theta)$ be the corresponding probability for test B. The power of test A for θ, the significance level α, and the probability of occurrence of a Type II error (failure to reject H_0 when $\theta = \theta_1$) are represented diagrammatically in Figure 4–1, under the assumption that the sampling distribution for test A is asymptotically normal. A corresponding pictorial representation is given for test B in Figure 4–2. The power curve for a consistent, one-tailed test, at a fixed sample size n and significance level α, can be represented as a function of θ and displayed pictorially as in Figure 4–3, while the corresponding power curve for a two-tailed test can be depicted by Figure 4–4.

In either case, the power efficiency of test A relative to test B is defined as the reciprocal of the ratio of the sample sizes, such that the proportion of times $P_A(\theta) > P_B(\theta)$ equals the proportion of times $P_A(\theta) < P_B(\theta)$. Thus:

$$E_{A,B} = \frac{n_B}{n_A}$$

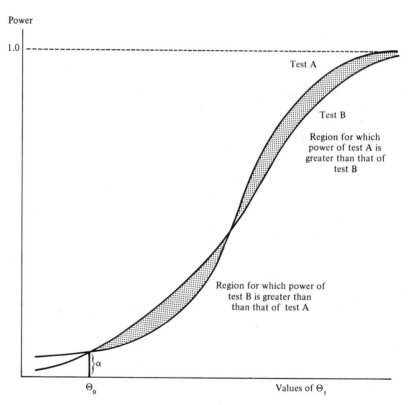

FIGURE 4–5. *Power curves equated for area to assess power efficiency for a one-tailed test.*

is determined so that:
$$\text{Prob}\big[P_A(\theta) > P_B(\theta)\big] = \text{Prob}\big[P_A(\theta) < P_B(\theta)\big].$$
The relationship of the power curves for a one-tailed test can be represented pictorially by Figure 4–5, and for a two-tailed test by Figure 4–6.

Although the term *power efficiency* was used extensively by Siegel (1956) and by Festinger and Katz (1953), it has been supplanted by *local relative efficiency* and *asymptotic relative efficiency* in more recent theoretical and applied works on nonparametric statistics. The local relative efficiency of one test to another is defined for the detection of a specified alternative at a designated significance level. Thus, the local relative efficiency of test *A* to test *B*,

$$E_{A,B}(\theta, \alpha, n_A) = \frac{n_B}{n_A}$$

is not interpretable unless the significance level, the alternative hypothesis, the region of rejection, and the test statistics of interest are reported. Since local relative efficiencies are situation-specific and not easily obtained for many nonparametric tests, they

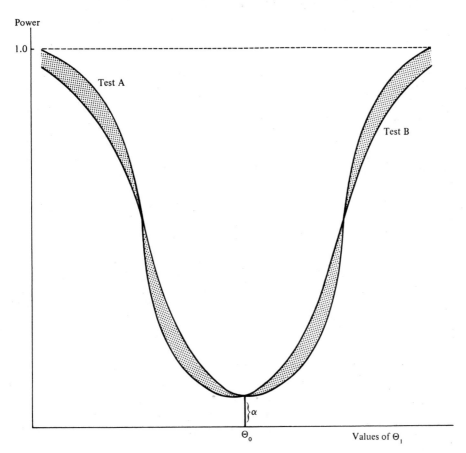

FIGURE 4–6. *Power curves equated for areas to assess power efficiency for a two-tailed test.*

are infrequently used as evidence supporting the choice of one test in preference to another. The illustration of Section 4–1 is an example of the local relative efficiency of the sign test compared to the normal-curve test for a specific α, H_0, and H_1.

On the other hand, asymptotic relative efficiencies are generally constant, regardless of the significance levels and parameter values (θ) considered, so that they facilitate comparisons among tests of the same hypothesis. Moreover, asymptotic relative efficiency can be determined theoretically for various population distributions of the variables of interest, and has been found to correspond closely to local relative efficiency when such comparisons have been made.

If the null and alternative hypotheses are represented by:

$$H_0: \theta = \theta_0$$

and

$$H_1: \theta = \theta_1 = \theta_0 + \frac{k}{\sqrt{n}}$$

respectively, where k is an arbitrary constant, and if, as n_A increases without limit so that θ_1 tends to θ_0, then:

$$E_{A,B} = \text{limit}\left[\frac{n_B}{n_A}\right]$$

defines the asymptotic efficiency of test A relative to test B for samples from some specified distribution. Once the test statistics meet certain mathematical regularity conditions, such as the power of the test approaching *one* as the sample size becomes arbitrarily large, and the population distribution of the observations is known (for example, normal, uniform, logistic, or double-exponential) the asymptotic efficiency of one test relative to another can be determined mathematically. Furthermore, the minimum value of asymptotic relative efficiency for certain classes of tests has been determined. For most of the rank tests examined in Chapters 11, 12, 13, 14, and 15, the ARE of the rank tests relative to their parametric counterparts is at least .864, regardless of the population distribution that is sampled. For most normal-scores tests examined in these chapters, the corresponding lowest ARE, relative to the parametric counterparts, is at least 1.00. Asymptotic relative efficiencies apply most directly to empirical data based on large-sample sizes and nearby alternatives ($\theta_1 \to \theta_0$). Empirical and mathematical studies of relative efficiency for various small-sample sizes have shown the ARE of one test relative to another to be in close agreement with the small-sample or local relative efficiency of the same tests. Consequently, the asymptotic relative efficiencies cited for various pairs of tests will be useful to the practitioner attempting to choose the more powerful of two tests for a fixed, often small, sample size.

The asymptotic relative efficiencies of some frequently used nonparametric tests relative to their parametric analogs are cited in Table 4–2. Although the values of ARE do not depend on sample size or parameter values, they are specific to the population distribution sampled. The values of ARE under the column for the normal distribution represent the ARE of the nonparametric test relative to its parametric analog when the assumptions for the latter are completely warranted. Even in these

TABLE 4–2. Asymptotic relative efficiency of some common nonparametric tests of location relative to their parametric analogs. Samples are assumed to have been chosen from the normal, uniform, logistic, and double-exponential distributions, respectively.

Design	Test	Distribution				
		Normal	Uniform	Logistic	Double exponential	Limiting (lower limit)
One-sample						
	Sign test	$\frac{2}{\pi} = 0.637$	0.333	0.750	2.000	0.333
	Wilcoxon matched-pair	$\frac{3}{\pi} = 0.955$	1.000	1.047	1.500	0.864
Two-sample (independent)						
	Median test	$\frac{2}{\pi} = 0.637$	0.333	0.750	2.000	0.333
	Mann–Whitney	$\frac{3}{\pi} = 0.955$	1.000	1.047	1.500	0.864
	Normal scores	1.000			$\frac{4}{\pi} = 1.273$	1.000
Many-sample (independent)						
	Median test	$\frac{2}{\pi} = 0.637$	0.333	0.750	2.000	0.333
	Kruskal–Wallis	$\frac{3}{\pi} = 0.955$	1.000	1.047	1.500	0.864
	Normal scores	1.000			$\frac{4}{\pi} = 1.273$	1.000

instances, the efficiency of rank and normal-scores nonparametric tests is generally high, and the effective loss of data relative to the parametric tests, as measured by $(1 - E_{NP,P})(100\%)$, is low.

4–4. Theoretical Distributions Used in Efficiency Determinations

In this section, four symmetrical theoretical distributions are examined: the uniform, the normal, the logistic, and the double-exponential. These distributions play a major role in the efficiency comparisons of nonparametric statistical tests. The form of these distributions is illustrated in Figure 4–7 for the special case in which $\mu = 500$ and $\sigma = 10$.

As can be seen, the double-exponential distribution is extremely peaked (leptokurtic), while the uniform distribution represents an extreme in flatness (platykurtic). The logistic distribution, while similar in form to the normal, is slightly more dense in the center than is the corresponding normal distribution. It is this

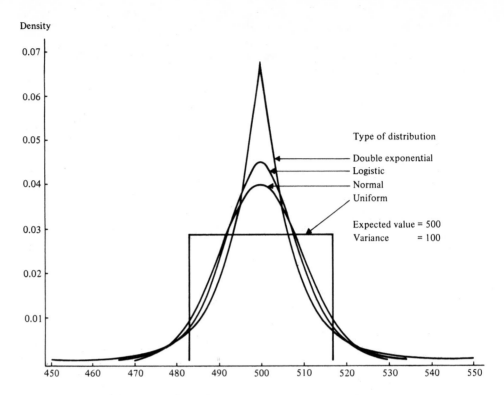

FIGURE 4–7. Four distributions used for efficiency comparisons.

differential in central densities that accounts for the differences in the statistical power of the various nonparametric tests. For the normal distribution,

$$P(\mu - \sigma < X < \mu + \sigma) = 0.68$$

while, for the double-exponential, logistic, and uniform distributions, the corresponding values are 0.75, 0.72, and 0.57, respectively. As might be expected, this also affects the size of the tails and the probabilities of Type I error. For the normal distribution,

$$P(X > \mu + 2\sigma) = 0.023$$

while, for the double-exponential, logistic, and uniform distributions, the corresponding values are equal to 0.030, 0.027, and 0.000, respectively. With respect to the normal distribution, it is said that the tails of the double exponential and logistic are *heavy*, while the tails of the uniform are *light*. This terminology is used in the power and efficiency comparisons provided later in this book.

4–5. Robustness

The asymptotic relative efficiencies reported in Table 4–2 probably seem incongruous to the practitioner who views nonparametric tests as tending to discard data and thereby losing power. Perhaps more surprising is Klotz's (1963) preference for the routine use of rank tests:

> Because of the extremely high efficiency of the nonparametric tests relative to the
> *t* in the region of interest, it is the author's opinion that the nonparametric tests
> would be preferred to the *t* in almost all practical situations. The exactness of the null
> distribution, good power for a wide class of shift alternatives, and the negligible loss
> in efficiency on the home ground of the *t* test support this conclusion.

A critic of Klotz's statement might reasonably object that the robustness of
the parametric procedures to violations of their distributional assumptions has not
been considered. Glass, Peckham, and Sanders' (1972) extensive review of the robustness of parametric tests for ANOVA and ANCOVA reports slight effects of nonnormal skewness and kurtosis, and heterogeneous variances on actual α, when the
tests are two-tailed and the sample sizes are equal. However, the effects on both the
true significance level and the power may be substantial when sample sizes are unequal and nonnormal kurtosis and/or heterogeneity of variance occurs. In the latter
case, the theoretical power is not defined, so comparisons of empirical and true
power are not possible.

Glass, Peckham, and Sanders' review of robustness studies, limited excl-
clusively to parametric procedures, may answer their question, "How important are
the inevitable violations of normal-theory ANOVA assumptions (for parametric
procedures)?" but it fails to ask the equally relevant question, "Are the violations of
these assumptions more serious for parametric than for nonparametric procedures?"
Empirical studies of the relative robustness of both parametric and nonparametric
procedures to skewness, nonnormal kurtosis, the presence of gross errors in the
observations, or heterogeneity of variance, have typically found the rank and
normal-scores tests somewhat less affected than the parametric procedures. Thus,
Ury's term "assumption-freer statistics" may be a more appropriate descriptor than
either nonparametric or distribution-free statistics.

4–6. Other Characteristics of Nonparametric Procedures

Although the high asymptotic relative efficiency and the assumption-freer
characteristics of the rank and normal-scores tests, relative to the parametric tests,
are presently cited as the major theoretical advantages of nonparametric procedures,
several other characteristics of nonparametric tests may appeal to practitioners. In
some cases, nonparametric procedures are the only available data-analytic procedures. For example, if a researcher is able to report only positive or negative gains
for the subjects in an experiment, without any indication of the relative or actual
magnitude of the gains, the sign test will determine whether the gain across subjects
is significantly different from zero.

The structural simplicity of the nonparametric test statistics, and the ease
with which the exact null distributions of the statistics can be obtained, are also cited
as advantages of nonparametric statistics. The development of the exact sampling
distribution of the number of positive differences for the sign test, as shown in
Section 3–3, illustrates the conceptual and computational ease of development of the

null distribution. The same conceptual simplicity applies to multisample statistics such as the Kruskal–Wallis test described in Chapter 12; however, the computational tediousness and the expense of developing a restricted permutation distribution of ranks limit the tabular presentation of the exact null distribution to small-sample sizes. In the case of complex multisample designs, computational time in permuting a restricted distribution of ranks makes the tabulation of the exact null distribution prohibitively expensive, and forces the use of asymptotic distributions as approximations to the exact sampling distributions of the statistics. Although the conceptual simplicity of many nonparametric test statistics and their associated null distributions probably encouraged the development and use of many nonparametric procedures in the 1940s and 1950s, the increasing conceptual and computational complexity of the statistics and their permutation distributions has not prompted the development of similar quick, user-oriented statistics in the 1960s and 1970s. Instead, the recent development of nonparametric statistics by mathematical statisticians such as Puri and Sen (1971) has concentrated heavily on highly efficient, large-sample procedures for complex analyses. In some cases, the methodological advances, such as those by Koch and Sen (1968) and Koch (1969), have been accompanied by computer software to facilitate computation of the statistics.

Summary

The theoretical material presented in this chapter is a digression from the mainstream of the general applied procedures that constitute the core of this book. However, the reader who wants to understand the reasons for designating a particular test as optimal for a given problem needs to understand the concept of relative efficiency. The researcher who is restricted by funds or sample-size limitations may wish to exploit information about the relative efficiencies of competing tests of the same hypothesis, in order to select the most cost-efficient of these test statistics.

There are many types of test efficiency, of which only a few have been described in this chapter. These procedures have been based, in one form or another, on the following general procedure:

> Given two statistical tests for the same hypothesis, the efficiency of test statistic A relative to test statistic B is defined as the ratio of sample sizes $E_{A,B} = n_B/n_A$, such that the two tests have the same power against the same alternative hypothesis at the same alpha level.

The example at the beginning of the chapter was based upon this procedure for determining *local relative efficiency*. The example is academic because it requires a complete statement of the alternative hypothesis with respect to the parameter values, the significance level, and the form of the distribution. For this reason, more general forms of test efficiency are required.

A mathematically more rigorous definition of efficiency is given by *power efficiency*. Consider a test of the null hypothesis $H_0: \theta = \theta_0$ against the alternative hypothesis $H_1: \theta = \theta_1$ at significance level α. Let $P_A(\theta)$ denote the probability of rejecting H_0 with test A when the true parameter is θ. Let $P_B(\theta)$ denote the corresponding probability with test B. The power efficiency of test A to test B is defined as the reciprocal of the ratio of the sample sizes, such that the proportion of times $P_A(\theta) > P_B(\theta)$ equals the proportion of times $P_A(\theta) < P_B(\theta)$.

Asymptotic relative efficiency is defined so that it is specific only to the statistical distribution examined, and not to the significance level of the test or the particular parameter θ. If the alternative hypothesis is denoted as:

$$H_1: \theta_1 = \theta_0 + \frac{k}{\sqrt{n}},$$

where k is an arbitrary constant, then, as n_A is allowed to increase without limit so that θ_1 approaches θ_0, the limit of the ratio n_B/n_A defines the asymptotic efficiency of test A relative to test B for samples from some specified distribution.

Because advanced mathematical procedures are required to determine power efficiency and asymptotic relative efficiency, no computational examples are provided for these measures of efficiency. Most of the efficiency figures cited in this and subsequent chapters are ARE figures. They suggest that most nonparametric tests based on ranks or normal scores are theoretically sound competitors of the classical t and F tests commonly used by researchers in the behavioral sciences. The ARE of many of the common rank tests to the classical tests never falls below 0.864, regardless of the population sampled. For most normal-scores tests, the lower bound never falls below one, indicating that normal-scores tests are strong competitors of the classical t and F tests.

Additional support is given to the choice of nonparametric procedures over classical normal-curve procedures on the basis of many empirical studies of the relative robustness of both parametric and nonparametric procedures to distribution differences such as skewness, nonnormal kurtosis, the existence of gross errors in the observations, or the lack of homogeneity of variance. Many of these studies suggest that the rank and normal-scores tests are as robust as, or more robust than, the more familiar parametric procedures. Since studies in the behavioral sciences are frequently based on small samples for which the nature of the underlying variable is in doubt, the demonstrated robustness of many of the nonparametric tests can be very reassuring. For this reason, Ury's term *assumption-freer* statistics may be a more appropriate descriptor than either nonparametric or distribution-free statistics.

Exercises

*1. Find the local relative efficiency of the sign test to the matched-pair normal-curve test for the example of Section 4–1, but with $\alpha = 0.10$ and $\alpha = 0.01$. What do the three efficiency measures suggest about the effect of changing alpha values on the efficiency comparisons?

*2. Find the local relative efficiency of the sign test to the matched-pair normal-curve test for the example of Section 4–1 for $\alpha = 0.05$, but with $\mu_1 - \mu_2 = 6$ and 10, respectively. What do the three efficiency measures suggest about the effect of the alternative hypothesis on efficiency comparisons?

3. Compare and contrast:
   a) local relative efficiency,
   b) power efficiency,
   c) asymptotic relative efficiency.

4. Explain what is meant by estimate efficiency.

*5. The estimate efficiency figures of Table 4–1 for comparing $\overline{X}$ and $\hat{M}$ as estimates of μ from normal populations apply directly to the test efficiency of the one-sample normal-curve test. Note that the efficiency measure converges upon $E = 2/\pi = 0.637$. How many observations should a researcher take to obtain a median test that has the same power as a normal curve test of $H_0: \mu = \mu_0$ against $H_1: \mu = \mu_1$, if the normal-curve test is based on 50 observations?

*6. On the basis of the efficiency measures reported in Table 4–1 for comparing $\overline{X}$ and $\hat{M}$ as estimates of μ, why are the estimate efficiency measures larger for even-sized samples?

*7. If a researcher were to replace the normal-curve test with the median test of Section 3–11, should he select a sample with an even or an odd number of observations? (See Exercise 6.)

*8. In Exercise 1 of Chapter 3, the underlying variable was binomially distributed. Sixteen subjects were asked how their sleep was, when compared to the previous three nights. Response choices were: {Better, Worse}. On the basis of the discussion in this chapter, how could the test efficiency of the experiment be increased? How many subjects would be needed in order for this modification to equal the power for the 16 subjects of the original study?

Part II

Statistical Methods
for Qualitative Variables:
Contingency Table
Hypotheses of Homogeneity
and Correlation
for Independent
and Related Samples

Chapter 5 presents a detailed discussion of the Irwin–Fisher test, which is used to choose between H_0: $p_1 = p_2$ or H_1: $p_1 \neq p_2$, where p_1 and p_2 are probabilities of success for two independent binomially-distributed variables. This test, in its small-sample form, is based on the hypergeometric distribution. The large-sample form of this test is based on the normal or chi-square distribution. Under this model, the large-sample form of the confidence interval for $\Delta = p_1 - p_2$ is illustrated. Finally, the two-sample median test is presented along with its special application to testing that the slope of a regression line is given by $\beta = 0$ or $\beta \neq 0$.

Chapter 6 presents an extensive discussion of Karl Pearson's chi-square test of homogeneity or identity of K independent populations that are defined by I mutually exclusive and exhaustive classes. The median test, which is a special case of this general omnibus test, is illustrated, along with the binomial model, in which $I = 2$ and $K > 2$. Post hoc and planned confidence intervals for contrasts in the multinomial and binomial models are discussed and illustrated for both small and large samples.

Chapter 7 presents basic statistical procedures for testing equality of proportions for samples in which the observations are correlated. The prototype of these tests is the McNemar test of change. The Bowker, Stuart, and Cochran extensions of this familiar test are presented. Planned and post hoc procedures for these tests are also discussed.

Chapter 8 continues the discussion of nonparametric correlation introduced in Chapter 7, but for models in which the correlation itself and its strength of association are of major concern. In particular, the Karl Pearson chi-square test of independence is examined for 2×2 and $R \times C$ contingency tables. Two commonly encountered measures of association, Cramer's ϕ^2 and Goodman's γ, are introduced and illustrated. In addition, planned and post hoc procedures are described for Goodman's γ. Many researchers confuse the methods of Chapter 6 and Chapter 8 and often interchange them without justification. The differences between tests of homogeneity of proportions and tests of statistical independence of two qualitative variables are described and explained in sufficient detail.

Chapter 9 extends the methods of Chapters 6 and 8 to multisample or multidimensional contingency tables. The extensions are illustrated under two different models described by Lancaster and Bartlett. The Bartlett model, expanded upon by Goodman, leads to simultaneous confidence intervals for multiple-factor interaction measures.

Chapter 10 closes the discussion on contingency tables with illustrations of the Karl Pearson goodness-of-fit test. Finally, the Kolmogorov, the Lilliefors, and the Kolmogorov–Smirnov tests complete the presentation of tests for qualitative variables and at the same time introduce procedures for quantitative variables that appear in Part III. In this sense, Chapter 10 serves as a bridge between the procedures of Part II and those of Part III.

The Irwin-Fisher Test: Two-Sample Procedures for Dichotomous Variables

5–1. Introduction to the Irwin–Fisher Test

Extension of the one-sample binomial test of Section 3–4 to two independent samples leads to a test based on the hypergeometric distribution, which is referred to as the Irwin–Fisher exact test of significance. The Irwin–Fisher procedure tests the hypothesis of equality of population proportions:

$$H_0: p_1 = p_2$$

for two independent groups that are classified dichotomously on an outcome measure. Extensions of the Irwin–Fisher test permit comparison of more than two independent populations with respect to two or more outcome categories. Although the Irwin–Fisher exact test is valid for multiple samples and multiple outcome categories, easier-to-compute large-sample approximations are often preferred to the exact test. A typical example of the type of study using the Irwin–Fisher test is provided by the following hypothetical investigation.

EXAMPLE 5–1.1. Nineteen third-grade slow readers were assigned at random to a control and an experimental treatment for a study in which a new method designed to help slow readers improve their reading skills was being tested. When the experiment was completed all children were given the same reading-achievement test. In the evaluation of the experimental method against the control method, each student was classified as being either below or above grade level. The results were as shown in Table 5–1.

TABLE 5–1. Reading levels of children in the control and experimental group.

Reading skill level	Control group (Treatment 1)	Experimental group (Treatment 2)	Total
Below grade level	6	3	9
Above grade level	2	8	10
Total	8	11	19

For the control group, the proportion below grade level is given by:

$$\hat{p}_1 = \frac{t_1}{n_1} = \frac{6}{8} = 0.75$$

For the experimental group, the corresponding proportion is:

$$\hat{p}_2 = \frac{t_2}{n_2} = \frac{3}{11} = 0.27$$

Visual inspection of the data suggests that the experimental method (Treatment 2) is the more effective of the two methods. This observation can be put to an exact statistical test by means of the Irwin–Fisher test. For this test, the null hypothesis:

$$H_0: p_1 = p_2$$

is tested against the alternative hypothesis:

$$H_1: p_1 \neq p_2$$

The theoretical basis underlying this test is presented in Section 5–3, following a general discussion of the hypergeometric distribution in Section 5–2.

5–2. The Hypergeometric Distribution

Although the hypergeometric distribution will ultimately be used in testing the equality of two population proportions, the distribution itself is presented in terms of a single population. Consider a finite population of size N, which is partitioned into two mutually exclusive and exhaustive subsets C_1 and C_2, having N_1 and N_2 elements, respectively. Select a simple random sample of n elements from the N elements. Let the random variables T_1 and T_2 represent the number of sample members of subsets C_1 and C_2, respectively. Let t_1 and t_2 denote the observed number of elements in these respective subsets. In any sample, $t_1 + t_2 = n$.

The random variables T_1 and T_2 have discrete probability distributions, and they are perfectly correlated in the negative direction for fixed n; that is, $\rho_{T_1 T_2} = -1$. Their "seemingly joint probability distribution" may be determined from elementary probability theory and counting principles.

By the use of counting Rule Five of Section 2–2, the total number of different samples of size n that may be generated from a universe of N elements is given by $\begin{bmatrix} N \\ n \end{bmatrix}$. Some of these samples have outcomes corresponding to t_1 elements in category C_1 and t_2 elements in category C_2. More formally, this may be denoted as $T_1 = t_1$ and $T_2 = t_2$. To establish the total number of different samples that may be generated with $T_1 = t_1$, consider the subset C_1. This subset consists of N_1 elements that must be sampled to give $T_1 = t_1$. The total number of different ways available for selecting t_1 elements from N_1 elements is given by $\begin{bmatrix} N_1 \\ t_1 \end{bmatrix}$. In a like manner, the total number of ways available for selecting t_2 elements from N_2 elements is given by $\begin{bmatrix} N_2 \\ t_2 \end{bmatrix}$. According to Rule One, if action E_1 may be accomplished in n_1 ways and if action E_2 may occur in n_2 ways, then their joint or ordered occurrence may happen in $n_1 n_2$ ways. Thus, it follows that the total number of ways available for selecting a sample of size n in which $T_1 = t_1$ and $T_2 = t_2$ is given by $\begin{bmatrix} N_1 \\ t_1 \end{bmatrix}\begin{bmatrix} N_2 \\ t_2 \end{bmatrix}$. As a result, the probability of interest is given by:

$$P[(T_1 = t_1) \cap (T_2 = t_2)] = \frac{\begin{bmatrix} N_1 \\ t_1 \end{bmatrix}\begin{bmatrix} N_2 \\ t_2 \end{bmatrix}}{\begin{bmatrix} N_1 + N_2 \\ t_1 + t_2 \end{bmatrix}}$$

According to this form, it appears that the probabilities are stated in terms of both t_1 and t_2. Since T_1 and T_2 are perfectly correlated, knowing one variable provides complete information on the other variable. As a result, the last probability statement can be indicated in terms of either t_1 or t_2. Since $N_2 = N - N_1$ and $t_2 = n - t_1$:

$$P(T_1 = t_1) = \frac{\begin{bmatrix} N_1 \\ t_1 \end{bmatrix}\begin{bmatrix} N - N_1 \\ n - t_1 \end{bmatrix}}{\begin{bmatrix} N \\ n \end{bmatrix}}$$

In a like manner,

$$P(T_2 = t_2) = \frac{\begin{bmatrix} N_2 \\ t_2 \end{bmatrix}\begin{bmatrix} N - N_2 \\ n - t_2 \end{bmatrix}}{\begin{bmatrix} N \\ n \end{bmatrix}}$$

If T_1 is treated as the random variable, then the parameters of the distribution are N, N_1, and n. If T_2 is the random variable, the parameters are N, N_2, and n. To simplify the presentation and discussion, T_1 will be treated as the variable for the hypergeometric distribution.

The probability of the subset C_1 is given by $N_1/N = p$, while the probability of the subset C_2 is given by

$$\frac{N_2}{N} = \frac{N - N_1}{N} = 1 - p = q$$

With this "reparametrization," it appears that the hypergeometric distribution has as its parameters p and n, the same parameters as the binomial distribution. In fact, $E(T_1) = np$ for both the binomial and hypergeometric distributions, but for the binomial distribution, $\text{Var}(T_1) = npq$, while for the hypergeometric distribution:

$$\text{Var}(T_1) = npq\left[\frac{N - n}{N - 1}\right]$$

The use of the finite population correction $(N - n)/(N - 1)$ in evaluating $\text{Var}(T_1)$ for the hypergeometric distribution is based on the fact that sampling has been *without* replacement from a finite population. This was discussed in Section 2–12.

EXAMPLE 5–2.1.   Consider a finite universe of $N = 100$ college sophomores enrolled in a beginning psychology course. Let C_1 represent the set of males in the universe and C_2 represent the set of females. Furthermore, suppose $N_1 = 70$ and $N_2 = 30$, and suppose that a simple random sample of size $n = 8$ is to be drawn without replacement from the universe, to participate in a psychological study. Let T_1 represent the number of males in the sample. The only possible values for T_1 are $\{0, 1, 2, 3, 4, 5, 6, 7, 8\}$. The probabilities associated with these outcomes are listed in Table 5–2. The probability distribution of T_1 is illustrated in Figure 5–1.

TABLE 5–2. Hypergeometric probabilities for $N = 100$, $N_1 = 70$, $N_2 = 30$, and $n = 8$.

Value of T_1	$\begin{bmatrix}70\\t_1\end{bmatrix}\begin{bmatrix}30\\t_2\end{bmatrix}\Big/\begin{bmatrix}100\\8\end{bmatrix}$	$P(T_1 = t_1)$
0	$\begin{bmatrix}70\\0\end{bmatrix}\begin{bmatrix}30\\8\end{bmatrix}\Big/\begin{bmatrix}100\\8\end{bmatrix}$	.000
1	$\begin{bmatrix}70\\1\end{bmatrix}\begin{bmatrix}30\\7\end{bmatrix}\Big/\begin{bmatrix}100\\8\end{bmatrix}$	.000
2	$\begin{bmatrix}70\\2\end{bmatrix}\begin{bmatrix}30\\6\end{bmatrix}\Big/\begin{bmatrix}100\\8\end{bmatrix}$	.001
3	$\begin{bmatrix}70\\3\end{bmatrix}\begin{bmatrix}30\\5\end{bmatrix}\Big/\begin{bmatrix}100\\8\end{bmatrix}$	.042
4	$\begin{bmatrix}70\\4\end{bmatrix}\begin{bmatrix}30\\4\end{bmatrix}\Big/\begin{bmatrix}100\\8\end{bmatrix}$	.135
5	$\begin{bmatrix}70\\5\end{bmatrix}\begin{bmatrix}30\\3\end{bmatrix}\Big/\begin{bmatrix}100\\8\end{bmatrix}$	.272
6	$\begin{bmatrix}70\\6\end{bmatrix}\begin{bmatrix}30\\2\end{bmatrix}\Big/\begin{bmatrix}100\\8\end{bmatrix}$	.307
7	$\begin{bmatrix}70\\7\end{bmatrix}\begin{bmatrix}30\\1\end{bmatrix}\Big/\begin{bmatrix}100\\8\end{bmatrix}$	.193
8	$\begin{bmatrix}70\\8\end{bmatrix}\begin{bmatrix}30\\0\end{bmatrix}\Big/\begin{bmatrix}100\\8\end{bmatrix}$	.050

The Irwin—
Fisher Test:
Two-Sample
Procedures for
Dichotomous
Variables

99

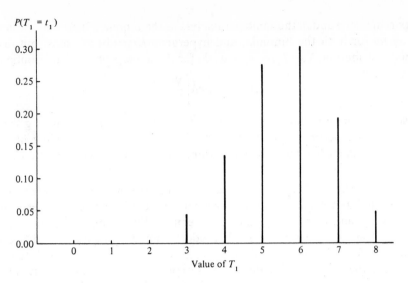

$P(T_1 = t_1)$

Value of T_1

FIGURE 5-1. Hypergeometric distribution with $N_1 = 70$, $N = 100$, and $n = 8$.

5-3. The Irwin–Fisher Exact Test of Significance of $H_0 : p_1 = p_2$

Consider two random samples of predetermined size, n_1 and n_2, selected from two independent populations. Let the variable to be observed on each element of the samples be the appearance of the qualitative characteristic A or its complement $\overline{A}$. Let p_1 be the probability of A in Population 1 and let p_2 be the probability of A in Population 2. Let T_1 be the number of observed A's in sample 1 and let T_2 be the number of A's observed in sample 2. T_1 and T_2 are independent random variables, and each is binomially distributed; T_1 is $B(n_1, p_1)$ and T_2 is $B(n_2, p_2)$. On the basis of the observed outcomes, $T_1 = t_1$ and $T_2 = t_2$, consider the test of the hypothesis:

$$H_0 : p_1 = p_2 = p_0$$

versus the alternative:

$$H_1 : p_1 \neq p_2$$

where p_0 is the common parameter value. To simplify the discussion, let the outcome of the experiment be summarized as shown in Table 5–3.

There are many derivations of this test, with varying degrees of rigor and intuitive appeal. The following derivation, while not rigorous, possesses an intuitive

TABLE 5–3. Outcomes of the experiment in which T_1 and T_2 are independent and where T_1 is $B(n_1, p_1)$ and T_2 is $B(n_2, p_2)$.

Property	Sample 1	Sample 2	Total
$\dfrac{A}{\overline{A}}$	t_1	t_2	t
	$n_1 - t_1$	$n_2 - t_2$	$n - t$
Total	n_1	n_2	n

appeal and serves as one possible derivation of this important test. For this derivation, assume in advance that t elements are *foreordained* to have characteristic A, and $(n - t)$ or $(n_1 + n_2) - (t_1 + t_2)$ are *destined* to have characteristic $\bar{A}$. Under this model, the marginal totals $t = t_1 + t_2$ and $(n - t) = (n_1 + n_2) - (t_1 + t_2)$ are preset.

Although t elements of n are known to possess characteristic A, it is not known in advance how many of these elements belong to sample 1 and how many to sample 2. Instead, the investigator reasons that any n_1 of n elements could be chosen to constitute sample 1. Once these elements have been chosen, the remaining n_2 elements would automatically constitute sample 2. Thus, the number of ways of partitioning n elements, such that n_1 are assigned to sample 1 and n_2 are assigned to sample 2, is the same as the number of partitions of n elements such that n_1 belong to sample 1 and n_2 belong to sample 2. By counting Rules One and Five, this number is given by:

$$\begin{bmatrix} n \\ n_1 \end{bmatrix}\begin{bmatrix} n - n_1 \\ n_2 \end{bmatrix} = \begin{bmatrix} n \\ n_1 \end{bmatrix}\begin{bmatrix} n_2 \\ n_2 \end{bmatrix} = \begin{bmatrix} n \\ n_1 \end{bmatrix}$$

Similar reasoning can be used to argue that if t_1 of the t elements having property A can be assigned to sample 1 in $\begin{bmatrix} t \\ t_1 \end{bmatrix}$ ways, then the remaining $t - t_1 = t_2$ elements are necessarily assigned to sample 2 in $\begin{bmatrix} t - t_1 \\ t_2 \end{bmatrix}$ ways. Therefore the total number of ways of assigning the T elements having property A to samples 1 and 2 is given by:

$$\begin{bmatrix} t \\ t_1 \end{bmatrix}\begin{bmatrix} t - t_1 \\ t_2 \end{bmatrix} = \begin{bmatrix} t \\ t_1 \end{bmatrix}\begin{bmatrix} t_2 \\ t_2 \end{bmatrix} = \begin{bmatrix} t \\ t_1 \end{bmatrix}$$

Similarly, the total number of ways of assigning the $(n - t)$ elements that have property $\bar{A}$, such that $(n_1 - t_1)$ belong to sample 1 and $(n_2 - t_2)$ belong to sample 2, is given by:

$$\begin{bmatrix} n - t \\ n_1 - t_1 \end{bmatrix}\begin{bmatrix} n - t - (n_1 - t_1) \\ n_2 - t_2 \end{bmatrix} = \begin{bmatrix} n - t \\ n_1 - t_1 \end{bmatrix}\begin{bmatrix} n_2 - t_2 \\ n_2 - t_2 \end{bmatrix} = \begin{bmatrix} n - t \\ n_1 - t_1 \end{bmatrix}$$

Thus, by the fundamental principle of counting, the total number of ways for assigning the A's and $\bar{A}$'s to the two samples is given by:

$$\begin{bmatrix} t \\ t_1 \end{bmatrix}\begin{bmatrix} n - t \\ n_1 - t_1 \end{bmatrix}$$

so that the probability of the frequencies reported in Table 5–3 is given by:

$$P(T_1 = t_1) = \frac{\begin{bmatrix} t \\ t_1 \end{bmatrix}\begin{bmatrix} n - t \\ n_1 - t_1 \end{bmatrix}}{\begin{bmatrix} n \\ n_1 \end{bmatrix}}$$

While this appears to be a different result from that dictated by the derivation of the hypergeometric distribution, it is not, as is now shown:

$$P(T_1 = t_1) = \frac{\begin{bmatrix} t \\ t_1 \end{bmatrix}\begin{bmatrix} n - t \\ n_1 - t_1 \end{bmatrix}}{\begin{bmatrix} n \\ n_1 \end{bmatrix}}$$

*The Irwin—
Fisher Test:
Two-Sample
Procedures for
Dichotomous
Variables*

101

$$= \frac{(t_1 + t_2)!}{t_1! t_2!} \frac{(n_1 + n_2 - t_1 - t_2)!}{(n_1 - t_1)!(n_2 - t_2)!} \frac{n_1! n_2!}{n!}$$

$$= \frac{n_1!}{t_1!(n_1 - t_1)!} \frac{n_2!}{t_2!(n_2 - t_2)!} \frac{(t_1 + t_2)!(n_1 + n_2 - t_1 - t_2)!}{n!}$$

$$= \frac{\begin{bmatrix} n_1 \\ t_1 \end{bmatrix} \begin{bmatrix} n_2 \\ t_2 \end{bmatrix}}{\begin{bmatrix} n \\ t_1 + t_2 \end{bmatrix}} = \frac{\begin{bmatrix} n_1 \\ t_1 \end{bmatrix} \begin{bmatrix} n_2 \\ t_2 \end{bmatrix}}{\begin{bmatrix} n_1 + n_2 \\ t_1 + t_2 \end{bmatrix}}$$

EXAMPLE 5–3.1. Table 5–1 indicates that $t_1 + t_2 = 9$, so the analysis of these data can be restricted to the subset of outcomes for which $t_1 + t_2 = 9$. For this analysis it is necessary to determine an appropriate critical region and to reject $H_0: p_1 = p_2 = p_0$ if the observed outcome is in the critical region.

Since success with the new method could not be guaranteed in advance, it is necessary to test H_0 versus $H_1: p_1 \neq p_2$. This means that the probability of a Type I error must be distributed between the two tails of the appropriate probability distribution. The critical region is defined in terms of those points, (t_1, t_2), most indicative of a departure from H_0, subject to the restriction $t_1 + t_2 = 9$. To aid in identifying the most extreme points, the criterion measure:

$$\hat{\Delta} = \hat{p}_1 - \hat{p}_2 = \frac{t_1}{n_1} - \frac{t_2}{n_2}$$

is used. When $H_0: p_1 = p_2 = p_0$ is true, $\Delta = p_1 - p_2 = 0$; otherwise $\Delta \neq 0$. Since $\hat{\Delta}$ is determined by t_1 and t_2, the probability distribution of $\hat{\Delta}$ is exactly the same as that of t_1 or t_2.

The values of $\hat{\Delta}$ are computed first, to aid in determining the critical region for the test. Since $t_1 + t_2 = 9$, $n_1 = 8$, and $n_2 = 11$, certain outcomes are not possible. The values of $\hat{\Delta}$ are summarized in Table 5–4. The outcomes compatible with H_0 are near the center of the range of $\hat{\Delta}$, while the outcomes compatible with H_1 are at the extremes. The outcome most compatible with H_1 occurs when $t_1 = 8$ and $t_2 = 1$. For this outcome, $\hat{\Delta} = 0.910$. Following it in compatibility with H_1 are: $\hat{\Delta} = -0.818$,

TABLE 5–4. *Possible values of* $\hat{\Delta}$ *for* $t_1 + t_2 = 9$, $n_1 = 8$, *and* $n_2 = 11$.

Value of t_1	Value of t_2	Value of $\hat{p}_1$	Value of $\hat{p}_2$	Value of $\hat{\Delta}$
0	9	0.000	0.818	−0.818
1	8	0.125	0.727	−0.602
2	7	0.250	0.637	−0.387
3	6	0.375	0.545	−0.170
4	5	0.500	0.454	0.046
5	4	0.625	0.363	0.262
6	3	0.750	0.272	0.478
7	2	0.875	0.181	0.694
8	1	1.000	0.090	0.910

occurring when $t_1 = 0$ and $t_2 = 9$; $\hat{\Delta} = 0.694$, occurring when $t_1 = 7$ and $t_2 = 2$; $\hat{\Delta} = -0.602$, occurring when $t_1 = 1$ and $t_2 = 8$; and so on. The probabilities of these outcomes are listed in Table 5–5.

On the basis of the computations summarized in Table 5–5, a critical region with $\alpha \leq 0.05$ can be defined. To determine this critical region, start with the outcome least compatible with H_0, determining its probability, and continue to include outcomes in the critical region until $\alpha \leq 0.05$. For this investigation, possible critical regions with increasing size are given in the following tabulation:

TABLE 5–5. Probabilities of the outcomes for $t_1 + t_2 = 9$, $n_1 = 8$, $n_2 = 11$, assuming H_0 is true.

Value of t_1	Value of $\hat{\Delta}$	$\begin{bmatrix} 8 \\ t_1 \end{bmatrix} \begin{bmatrix} 11 \\ t_2 \end{bmatrix} / \begin{bmatrix} 19 \\ 9 \end{bmatrix}$	$P(T_1 = t_1)$	Cumulative probabilities
8	0.910	$\begin{bmatrix} 8 \\ 8 \end{bmatrix} \begin{bmatrix} 11 \\ 1 \end{bmatrix} / \begin{bmatrix} 19 \\ 9 \end{bmatrix}$	0.000119	0.000119
0	−0.818	$\begin{bmatrix} 8 \\ 0 \end{bmatrix} \begin{bmatrix} 11 \\ 9 \end{bmatrix} / \begin{bmatrix} 19 \\ 9 \end{bmatrix}$	0.000595	0.000714
7	0.694	$\begin{bmatrix} 8 \\ 7 \end{bmatrix} \begin{bmatrix} 11 \\ 2 \end{bmatrix} / \begin{bmatrix} 19 \\ 9 \end{bmatrix}$	0.004763	0.005477
1	−0.602	$\begin{bmatrix} 8 \\ 1 \end{bmatrix} \begin{bmatrix} 11 \\ 8 \end{bmatrix} / \begin{bmatrix} 19 \\ 9 \end{bmatrix}$	0.014289	0.019766
6	0.478	$\begin{bmatrix} 8 \\ 6 \end{bmatrix} \begin{bmatrix} 11 \\ 3 \end{bmatrix} / \begin{bmatrix} 19 \\ 9 \end{bmatrix}$	0.050012	0.069778
2	−0.387	$\begin{bmatrix} 8 \\ 2 \end{bmatrix} \begin{bmatrix} 11 \\ 7 \end{bmatrix} / \begin{bmatrix} 19 \\ 9 \end{bmatrix}$	0.100023	0.169801
5	0.262	$\begin{bmatrix} 8 \\ 5 \end{bmatrix} \begin{bmatrix} 11 \\ 4 \end{bmatrix} / \begin{bmatrix} 19 \\ 9 \end{bmatrix}$	0.200046	0.369847
3	−0.170	$\begin{bmatrix} 8 \\ 3 \end{bmatrix} \begin{bmatrix} 11 \\ 6 \end{bmatrix} / \begin{bmatrix} 19 \\ 9 \end{bmatrix}$	0.280064	0.649911
4	0.046	$\begin{bmatrix} 8 \\ 4 \end{bmatrix} \begin{bmatrix} 11 \\ 5 \end{bmatrix} / \begin{bmatrix} 19 \\ 9 \end{bmatrix}$	0.350081	0.999992

Critical Region	Size of α
{0.910}	0.000119
{0.910, −0.818}	0.000714
{0.910, −0.818, 0.694}	0.005477
{0.910, −0.818, 0.694, −0.602}	0.019766
{0.910, −0.818, 0.694, −0.602, 0.478}	0.069778

The last critical region is too large, since $\alpha = 0.069778 > 0.05$. Therefore, the appropriate critical region for this test is the one for which $\alpha = 0.019766$.

The observed outcome has $t_1 = 6$ and $t_2 = 3$ with $\hat{\Delta} = 0.478$. Since $\hat{\Delta} = 0.478$ is not an element of the critical region, there is no reason to doubt H_0. Thus no difference in the effectiveness of the experimental and control methods has been found.

The best estimate of the presumed common parameter value, p_0, is given by:

$$\hat{p}_0 = \frac{t_1 + t_2}{n_1 + n_2} = \frac{9}{19} = 0.474$$

Since $n\hat{p}_0 > 5$ and $n\hat{q}_0 > 5$, the approximate 95% confidence interval for p_0 is given by:

$$\hat{p}_0 - 1.96\sqrt{\frac{\hat{p}_0\hat{q}_0}{n}} < p_0 < \hat{p}_0 + 1.96\sqrt{\frac{\hat{p}_0\hat{q}_0}{n}}$$

$$0.474 - 1.96\sqrt{\frac{(0.474)(0.526)}{19}} < p_0 < 0.474 + 1.96\sqrt{\frac{(0.474)(0.526)}{19}}$$

$$0.250 < p_0 < 0.698$$

Thus, for all practical purposes, a reasonable range for the proportion of children who read below grade level for either teaching method is anywhere from 25 to 70%.

In Section 5–2 it was noted that hypergeometric probabilities can be specified completely in terms of t_1 or t_2, since $\rho_{T_1 T_2} = -1$. This means that the number of truly independent variables is only *one*. Therefore, T_1 could be used as a criterion measure. If T_1 is the statistic used, then the $\alpha = 0.019766$ rejection rule would be to reject H_0 if T_1 is $\{0, 1, 7, 8\}$. Since $T_1 = 6$, the hypothesis is not rejected.

The equivalent distributions of $\hat{\Delta}$ and T_1 are shown in Figures 5–2 and 5–3. It goes without saying that T_2 can also be used as a test statistic. With T_2 as a criterion measure, H_0 would be rejected if T_2 is $\{1, 2, 8, 9\}$. Since $T_2 = 3$, the hypothesis is not rejected.

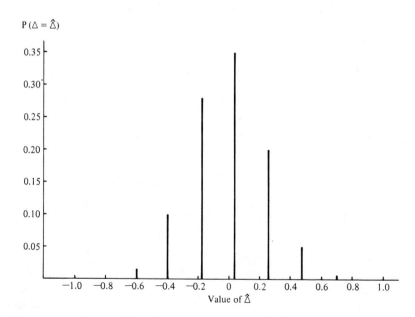

FIGURE 5–2. Probability distribution for the Fisher exact test criterion when $t_1 + t_2 = 9$, $n_1 = 8$, and $n_2 = 11$, and test criterion $\hat{\Delta} = \hat{p}_1 - \hat{p}_2$.

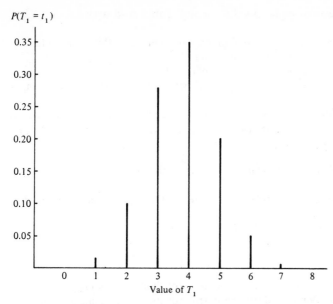

FIGURE 5–3. *Probability distribution for the Fisher exact test criterion when $t_1 + t_2 = 9$, $n_1 = 8$, and $n_2 = 11$, and test criterion T_1.*

5–4. Significance Tables for the Irwin–Fisher Test

In practice, the computations required for the use of the Irwin–Fisher Exact Test of Significance can be ignored if $n_1 + n_2 \leq 15$, since tables are available for testing H_0: $p_1 = p_2$. These tables appear in Appendix A–8 and are entered simply in terms of four numerical values determined from the observed data. The use of the table is illustrated for the data of Table 5–6.

EXAMPLE 5–4.1. Thirteen language teachers were rated as to their ability to teach high-school French according to the length of time lived in France. To test

TABLE 5–6. *Ability of teachers to teach high-school French according to the length of time lived in France.*

Rating	Number of months in France		
	Less than 6	More than 6	Total
Successful	5	4	9
Unsuccessful	3	1	4
Total	8	5	13

the hypothesis of equal p values, enter Table A–8 with (N, S_1, S_2, X), where

1. $N = n_1 + n_2 = $ Total number of elements in the two samples.
2. $S_1 = $ Smallest marginal total.
3. $S_2 = $ Next smallest marginal total.
4. $X = $ Frequency in the cell defined by the cell corresponding to S_1 and S_2.

For these data, $N = 8 + 5 = 13$, $S_1 = 4$, $S_2 = 5$, and $X = 1$. When $(N, S_1, S_2, X) = $ (13, 4, 5, 1), Table A–8 yields the triplet of numbers (0.490, 0.119, 0.608). These numbers represent the probabilities of:

1. A deviation as large, or larger, in the observed direction. (In this case, $X = 1$ or 0.)
2. A deviation as large, or larger, in the opposite direction. (In this case, $X = 3$ or 4.)
3. The total probabilities.

Thus, for these data:

1. 0.490 refers to the one-tailed probability for testing $p_1 > p_2$.
2. 0.119 refers to the one-tailed probability for testing $p_1 < p_2$.
3. 0.608 refers to the two-tailed probability for testing $p_1 \neq p_2$.

Thus, for the two-tailed test of H_0: $p_1 = p_2$ versus H_1: $p_1 \neq p_2$, the hypothesis of equality is not rejected.

5–5. The Large–Sample Approximation of the Normal Distribution to the Hypergeometric Distribution

Just as the binomial distribution tends to the normal distribution as n becomes large, so does the hypergeometric. However, the approach to normality is conditional upon the fact that n/N remains relatively small. The normal approximation to the hypergeometric distribution is expressed in the usual $N(0, 1)$-form, where

$$E(T_1) = np \quad \text{and} \quad \text{Var}(T_1) = npq \left[\frac{N - n}{N - 1} \right]$$

Use of the correction for continuity yields:

$$Z = \frac{(T_1 \pm \frac{1}{2}) - np}{\sqrt{npq \left[\frac{N - n}{N - 1} \right]}}$$

If $T_1 > np$, $\frac{1}{2}$ is subtracted, but if $T_1 < np$, $\frac{1}{2}$ is added.

EXAMPLE 5–5.1. For the normal approximation for the data of Example 5–2.1, $N = 100$, $N_1 = 70$, $N_2 = 30$, $n = 8$, $p = N_1/N = 70/100 = 0.7$, and $q = N_2/N = 30/100 = 0.3$, so that:

$$E(T_1) = np = 8(0.7) = 5.6$$

and

$$\text{Var}(T_1) = npq \left[\frac{N-n}{N-1} \right] = 8(0.7)(0.3) \left[\frac{100-8}{100-1} \right] = 1.5612$$

Thus, the normal approximation, corrected for continuity, is given by:

$$Z = \frac{(T_1 \pm \frac{1}{2}) - 5.6}{\sqrt{1.5612}} = \frac{(T_1 \pm 0.5) - 5.6}{1.249}$$

The computations required for the approximation are summarized in Table 5–7. Their agreement with the exact values is quite good. The maximum deviation between the exact and approximate probabilities is 0.03 at $T_1 = 5$. When $np > 5$, $nq > 5$, and $n/N < 10\%$, the approximation is quite good and is therefore recommended.

TABLE 5–7. Normal approximation to the hypergeometric with $N = 100$, $N_1 = 70$, $N_2 = 30$, and $n = 8$.

Value of T_1	$T_1 + 0.5$	Value of Z	$P(Z \le Z_0)$	$P(T_1 = t_1)$	Exact probability
0	0.5	−4.08	0.000	0.000	0.000
1	1.5	−3.28	0.001	0.001	0.001
2	2.5	−2.48	0.007	0.006	0.010
3	3.5	−1.68	0.046	0.039	0.047
4	4.5	−0.88	0.185	0.139	0.136
5	5.5	−0.08	0.469	0.284	0.254
6	6.5	0.72	0.764	0.295	0.296
7	7.5	1.52	0.936	0.172	0.198
8	8.5	2.32	0.990	0.054	0.058

5–6. The Large-Sample Approximation to the Irwin–Fisher Exact Test

When the sample sizes for the Irwin–Fisher test become large, the amount of work required to compute exact probabilities increases beyond all practical limits. For this reason, approximate methods are needed. Two methods that are particularly good when sample sizes are sufficiently large will be developed and illustrated in this section.

Approximation One (Based on the Normal Distribution). Using the theory developed for finite populations, as applied to the Irwin–Fisher Table 5–3, under the hypothesis that $p_1 = p_2 = p_0$, it follows that:

$$E(T_1) = n_1 p_0$$

and

$$\text{Var}(T_1) = n_1 p_0 q_0 \left[\frac{n-n_1}{n-1} \right] = \frac{n_1 n_2}{n-1}(p_0 q_0)$$

where $n_2 = n - n_1$. If the continuity correction is ignored:

$$Z = \frac{T_1 - E(T_1)}{\sqrt{\text{Var}(T_1)}} = \frac{T_1 - n_1 p_0}{\sqrt{[n_1 n_2/(n - 1)] p_0 q_0}}$$

Let

$$\hat{p}_0 = \frac{t_1 + t_2}{n_1 + n_2} = \frac{n_1 \hat{p}_1 + n_2 \hat{p}_2}{n_1 + n_2}$$

be an estimate of the common proportion p_0. Substituting this estimated value into the normalizing equation, it follows that:

$$Z = \sqrt{\frac{n - 1}{n}} \left[\frac{(\hat{p}_1 - \hat{p}_2)}{\sqrt{\hat{p}_0 \hat{q}_0 [(1/n_1) + (1/n_2)]}} \right]$$

As $n \to \infty$, $(n - 1)/n \to 1$, so that:

$$Z \to \frac{(\hat{p}_1 - \hat{p}_2)}{\sqrt{\hat{p}_0 \hat{q}_0 [(1/n_1) + (1/n_2)]}} = \frac{(\hat{p}_1 - \hat{p}_2)}{\sqrt{(\hat{p}_0 \hat{q}_0/n_1) + (\hat{p}_0 \hat{q}_0/n_2)}}$$

is the large-sample statistic for testing $H_0: p_1 = p_2$, which is discussed in most elementary statistics textbooks. Use of the large-sample approximation will be illustrated by an example.

EXAMPLE 5–6.1. In a community survey, males over the age of 18 were asked whether they believed that the local junior college should create a two-year associates' degree program in computer programming. The results are shown in

TABLE 5–8. Attitudes of males over age 18 toward the creation of a two-year degree in computer programming.

Response	White	Black	Total
Agree	55	21	76
Disagree	20	2	22
Total	75	23	98

Table 5–8, broken down by race. Among the Whites, 73 percent agreed, while among the Blacks, 91 percent agreed. Let p_1 equal the proportion of Whites in the population that agree and let p_2 equal the proportion of Blacks that agree. The hypothesis to be tested is $H_0: p_1 = p_2 = p_0$ against the alternative $H_1: p_1 \neq p_2$. The large-sample test statistic is given by

$$Z = \frac{\hat{p}_1 - \hat{p}_2}{\sqrt{(\hat{p}_0 \hat{q}_0/n_1) + (\hat{p}_0 \hat{q}_0/n_2)}}$$

The computations needed to evaluate the test statistic are

$$\hat{p}_1 = \frac{t_1}{n_1} = \frac{55}{75} = 0.73,$$

$$\hat{p}_2 = \frac{t_2}{n_2} = \frac{21}{23} = 0.91,$$

$$\hat{p}_0 = \frac{t_1 + t_2}{n_1 + n_2} = \frac{55 + 21}{75 + 23} = 0.78,$$

$$Z = \frac{0.73 - 0.91}{\sqrt{[(0.78)(0.22)/75] + [(0.78)(0.22)/23]}} = \frac{-0.18}{0.099} = -1.82.$$

The decision rule for $\alpha = 0.05$ states that H_0 should be rejected when $Z < Z_{0.025} = -1.96$, or if $Z > Z_{0.975} = 1.96$. Thus, H_0 is not rejected. There is no statistical difference between the preference of Whites and Blacks on this question.

Note that the assumptions required for this test are the usual Irwin–Fisher test assumptions of equal probability and independence. Since the total sample size is large, the exact Irwin–Fisher probabilities can be reasonably approximated by the normal distribution.

For this test, large sample size is based on the following rule of thumb for deciding when the normal approximation is acceptable. Determine $n_1 \hat{p}_0$, $n_2 \hat{p}_0$, $n_1 \hat{q}_0$, and $n_2 \hat{q}_0$. If each of these products exceeds five, the approximation will be satisfactory. If at least one does not exceed five, the approximation might be poor, and the exact hypergeometric probabilities should be computed.

Approximation Two (Based on the chi-square distribution with one degree of freedom). In order to facilitate the explanation of this second approximate procedure, it will first be necessary to change the notation that was introduced for the derivation of the Irwin–Fisher exact test. Let t_1 be replaced by X_{11}, t_2 by X_{21}, $(n_1 - t_1)$ by X_{12}, and $(n_2 - t_2)$ by X_{22}. With this new notation, X_{11} represents the observed number of elements of sample 1 that possess property A. The other X_{ij}'s are described in a similar fashion. Let $\hat{E}(X_{11})$ represent the estimated expected frequency for the elements of sample 1 that possess property A, with corresponding meanings for $\hat{E}(X_{21})$, $\hat{E}(X_{12})$, and $\hat{E}(X_{22})$. With this notation, an easy-to-compute test statistic is given by the Karl Pearson chi-square statistic:

$$X^2 = \sum_{i=1}^{2} \sum_{j=1}^{2} \frac{[X_{ij} - \hat{E}(X_{ij})]^2}{\hat{E}(X_{ij})}$$

When $X_{ij} \neq \hat{E}(X_{ij})$, this measure will be large, and when $X_{ij} = \hat{E}(X_{ij})$, the value of the test statistic will be zero. This implies that large values of X^2 are compatible with the alternative hypothesis and, as a result, an $\alpha = 0.05$ decision rule for rejecting H_0 is given by:

D.R.: Reject H_0 if $X^2 > X^2_{1:0.95} = 3.84$

The previous example of the attitudes of Blacks and Whites to a computer-programming degree will illustrate the procedure.

EXAMPLE 5–6.2. The data of Table 5–8 are used to illustrate the large-sample approximation. The expected cell frequency of Whites who agree to the question is found by multiplying the total number of Whites in the sample by the proportion agreeing in the population, that is, $E(X_{11}) = n_1 p_0$. Similarly, $E(X_{12}) =$

$n_1 q_0$, $E(X_{21}) = n_2 p_0$, and $E(X_{22}) = n_2 q_0$. Unfortunately, p_0 is unknown and must be estimated from the data. The best estimate of p_0 is given by:

$$\hat{p}_0 = \frac{X_{11} + X_{21}}{n_1 + n_2} = \frac{55 + 21}{75 + 23} = \frac{76}{98} = 0.78$$

Using this estimate of p_0, the estimated expected frequencies are as shown in Table 5–9.

TABLE 5–9. Estimated expected frequencies for the data of Table 5–8.

Response	White	Black	Total
Agree	58.2	17.8	76
Disagree	16.8	5.2	22
Total	75	23	98

Thus, the value of the test statistic is given by:

$$X^2 = \frac{(55 - 58.2)^2}{58.2} + \frac{(20 - 16.8)^2}{16.8} + \frac{(21 - 17.8)^2}{17.8} + \frac{(2 - 5.2)^2}{5.2}$$
$$= 3.33$$

Since $3.33 < 3.84$, H_0 is not rejected. Note that $3.33 = (-1.82)^2$. This last result holds, since $X^2 = Z^2$. As with the normal approximation, the assumptions that must be satisfied in order to ensure valid use of the chi-square approximation to the Irwin–Fisher test are:

1. Independence of observations within each sample.
2. The probability of the qualitative variable of interest is constant for each subject.
3. The expected frequencies are all greater than five.

5–7   Large-Sample Confidence Interval for $\Delta = p_1 - p_2$

When n_1 and n_2 are large, so that $n_1 \hat{p}_1 > 5$, $n_1 \hat{q}_1 > 5$, $n_2 \hat{p}_2 > 5$, and $n_2 \hat{q}_2 > 5$, large-sample normal-curve theory can be used to determine the confidence interval for $\Delta = p_1 - p_2$. Under usual binomial assumptions, the large-sample $(1 - \alpha)\%$ confidence interval for $\Delta = p_1 - p_2$ is given by:

$$(\hat{p}_1 - \hat{p}_2) - Z_{1-\alpha/2}\sqrt{\frac{\hat{p}_1 \hat{q}_1}{n_1} + \frac{\hat{p}_2 \hat{q}_2}{n_2}} < p_1 - p_2 < (\hat{p}_1 - \hat{p}_2) + Z_{1-\alpha/2}\sqrt{\frac{\hat{p}_1 \hat{q}_1}{n_1} + \frac{\hat{p}_2 \hat{q}_2}{n_2}}$$

$$\hat{\Delta} - Z_{1-\alpha/2}SE_{\hat{\Delta}} < \Delta < \hat{\Delta} + Z_{1-\alpha/2}SE_{\hat{\Delta}}$$

EXAMPLE 5–7.1.   For the data of Table 5–8, $\hat{p}_1 = 0.73$ and $\hat{p}_2 = 0.91$, so that $\hat{\Delta} = \hat{p}_1 - \hat{p}_2 = 0.73 - 0.91 = -0.18$. Also:

$$SE_{\hat{\Delta}}^2 = \frac{(0.73)(0.27)}{75} + \frac{(0.91)(0.09)}{23} = 0.00262 + 0.00350 = 0.00618,$$

so that the approximate 95% confidence interval is given by:

$$-0.18 - 1.96 \sqrt{0.00618} < p_1 - p_2 < -0.18 + 1.96 \sqrt{0.00618}$$
$$-0.33 < p_1 - p_2 < -0.03$$

Note that $n_2 \hat{q}_2 = 23(0.09) = 2.07 < 5$, suggesting that the approximation may not be adequate. It is worth noting that, while it is recommended that all expected values exceed 5, recent investigations suggest that this rule of thumb can be relaxed. However, since a conservative point of view is maintained throughout this book, expected values exceeding 5 are recommended.

The Irwin–Fisher test can be extended in two directions: to more than two populations and to more than two response categories. In each case, determination of the probabilities of the observed tables is time-consuming, but even more tedious is the determination of the appropriate critical region. If sample sizes are not large enough to warrant the use of the X^2 statistic, the reader is urged to consult Maxwell (1961) for a relatively expedient method of defining the critical region for designs having multiple response categories and/or multiple populations.

5-8. Power of the Irwin–Fisher Exact Test

The Irwin–Fisher exact test has no statistical competitors. It is the most powerful test available for testing

$$H_0 : p_1 = p_2 \qquad \text{versus} \qquad H_1 : H_0 \text{ is false}$$

The large-sample normal-curve approximation is used to find

Power = $1 - \beta$

$$= P \left[Z \le \frac{Z_{\alpha/2} \sqrt{(p_0 q_0/n_1) + (p_0 q_0/n_2)} - (p_1 - p_2)}{\sqrt{(p_1 q_1/n_1) + (p_2 q_2/n_2)}} \right]$$

$$+ P \left[Z \ge \frac{Z_{(1-\alpha/2)} \sqrt{(p_0 q_0/n_1) + (p_0 q_0/n_2)} - (p_1 - p_2)}{\sqrt{(p_1 q_1/n_1) + (p_2 q_2/n_2)}} \right]$$

EXAMPLE 5–8.1. Assume that a researcher wants to test $H_0 : p_1 = p_2$ against $H_1 : p_1 = 0.40$ and $p_2 = 0.60$, with $\alpha = 0.05$, and $n_1 = n_2 = 50$ observations. Under these conditions:

$$p_0 = \frac{n_1 p_1 + n_2 p_2}{n_1 + n_2} = \frac{50(0.40) + 50(0.60)}{50 + 50} = 0.50,$$

$$Z_{0.025} = -1.96 \qquad \text{and} \qquad Z_{0.975} = 1.96,$$

so that:

$$\text{Power} = P \left[Z \le \frac{-1.96 \sqrt{[(0.50)(0.50)/50] + [(0.50)(0.50)/50]} - (0.40 - 0.60)}{\sqrt{[(0.40)(0.60)/50] + [(0.40)(0.60)/50]}} \right.$$

The Irwin–
Fisher Test:
Two-Sample
Procedures for
Dichotomous
Variables

111

$$+ P \left[Z \geq \frac{+1.96\sqrt{[(0.50)(0.50)/50] + [(0.50)(0.50)/50]} - (0.40 - 0.60)}{\sqrt{[(0.40)(0.60)/50] + [(0.40)(0.60)/50]}} \right]$$

$$= 0.52$$

With $n_1 = n_2 = 50$, $p_1 = 0.4$, and $p_2 = 0.6$, the power is only slightly better than 0.50. In this case, the researcher might think seriously of either abandoning the study or increasing the sample size to increase the probability of detecting a difference of $\Delta = -0.2$ when it exists.

5–9. Combining Irwin-Fisher Tables

The procedures for combining sign-test analyses described in Section 3–15 can also be used for combining data from independent Irwin–Fisher tables, provided the alternative hypothesis is *directional* (Maxwell, 1961). Each of these procedures is outlined briefly and is illustrated with the data in Table 5–10.

TABLE 5–10. Irwin–Fisher tables for four groups of students in which it was predicted that girls have greater success than boys.

Grade	Outcome	Boys	Girls	Chi-square
2	Success	3	10	4.33
	Failure	12	8	
	Total	15	18	
5	Success	5	10	2.79
	Failure	5	2	
	Total	10	12	
8	Success	6	8	2.71
	Failure	7	2	
	Total	13	10	
11	Success	7	16	0.83
	Failure	5	3	
	Total	12	19	

Procedure 1. If Z_k are independent, identically-distributed standard-normal variables, $N(0, 1)$, then the sum of K such variables is normally distributed with a mean of zero and a variance of K. When H_0 is true, the Karl Pearson X^2 statistic for a 2×2 table is distributed approximately as X_1^2 and the square root of the Pearson statistic is approximately standard normal. Therefore, it follows that, if the hypothesis of no difference between populations is true for all K (2×2) tables, then:

$$T = \sum_{k=1}^{K} \sqrt{X_k^2}$$

is distributed as $N(0, K)$. A test statistic can be formed by standardizing T and referring the statistic to the standard-normal distribution:

$$Z = \frac{T - 0}{\sqrt{\mathrm{Var}(T)}} = \frac{T}{\sqrt{K}}$$

EXAMPLE 5–9.1.   In a study that was replicated over grade levels 2, 5, 8, and 11, it was hypothesized that girls would be more successful than boys at the task of interest. Visual inspection of the data in Table 5–10 supports this assertion for all four groups. For these data:

$$T = \sqrt{4.33} + \sqrt{2.79} + \sqrt{2.71} + \sqrt{0.83}$$
$$= 2.08 + 1.67 + 1.64 + 0.91 = 6.30$$

$$\sigma_T = \sqrt{\mathrm{Var}(T)} = \sqrt{4} = 2$$

and

$$Z = \frac{T - 0}{\sigma_T} = \frac{T}{\sqrt{K}} = \frac{6.30}{\sqrt{4}} = \frac{6.30}{2} = 3.15$$

Since $Z = 3.15 > Z_{(0.95)} = 1.645$, H_0 is rejected. It is concluded that girls have greater success than boys.

Procedure 2.   Independent hypergeometric variables can be added if their success probabilities are equal. Thus, if each X_k is hypergeometric n_k, N_k, p_0, then $T = X_1 + X_2 + \ldots + X_K$ is also hypergeometric with parameters $n = n_1 + n_2 + \ldots + n_K$, $N = N_1 + N_2 + \ldots N_K$, p_0.

TABLE 5–11. Irwin–Fisher table generated from the data of Table 5–10.

Outcome	Boys	Girls	Total
Success	21	44	65
Failure	29	15	44
Total	50	59	109

EXAMPLE 5–9.2.   The data of Table 5–10 can be combined to form the single 2 × 2 array of Table 5–11. For these data,

$$T = 3 + 5 + 6 + 7 = 21$$
$$n = 15 + 10 + 13 + 12 = 50$$

and

$$N = 33 + 22 + 23 + 31 = 109$$

and $X^2 = 11.94$. Since the distribution of X_1^2 is always positive, an adjustment in the critical region is required for a directional alternative. In terms of the normal distribution, $Z = \sqrt{11.94} = 3.45$. The one-sided $\alpha = 0.05$ critical region for Z is given by $Z > Z_{0.95} = 1.645$. Thus, the appropriate $\alpha = 0.05$ directional critical region

The Irwin–
Fisher Test:
Two-Sample
Procedures for
Dichotomous
Variables

113

for X^2 is defined by $X^2_{1:0.90} = 1.645^2 = 2.71$. Since $X^2 = 11.94 > 2.71$, H_0 is rejected and, once again, it is concluded that girls have greater success than boys on the task of interest.

    Procedure 3. Cochran (1954) proposed a method of combining the data from independent (2 by 2) tables that is especially efficient when the sample sizes of the individual tables differ greatly. The Cochran statistic is given by:

$$Z = \frac{\bar{d}}{SE_{\bar{d}}}$$

where $\bar{d}$ is a weighted sum of the paired differences in proportions, each weighted by the sum of the reciprocals of their sample sizes. In particular,

$$d_k = \hat{p}_{1k} - \hat{p}_{2k}$$

$$\hat{W}_k = \frac{n_{1k}n_{2k}}{n_{1k} + n_{2k}}$$

$$\bar{d} = \frac{\sum_{k=1}^{K} \hat{W}_k d_k}{\sum_{k=1}^{K} \hat{W}_k}$$

$$\hat{p}_k = \frac{T_k}{n_k},$$

$$SE^2_{\bar{d}} = \frac{\sum_{k=1}^{K} \hat{W}_k \hat{p}_k \hat{q}_k}{\left[\sum_{k=1}^{K} \hat{W}_k\right]^2}$$

The resulting Z statistic is referred to the $N(0, 1)$ distribution.

    EXAMPLE 5–9.3. The computations for the Cochran procedure are as shown:

$$d_1 = \frac{10}{18} - \frac{3}{15} = 0.3556, \quad \hat{p}_1 = \frac{13}{33} = 0.3939, \quad w_1 = \frac{(15)(18)}{15 + 18} = 8.1818$$

$$d_2 = \frac{10}{12} - \frac{5}{10} = 0.3333, \quad \hat{p}_2 = \frac{15}{22} = 0.6818, \quad w_2 = \frac{(10)(12)}{10 + 12} = 5.4545$$

$$d_3 = \frac{8}{10} - \frac{6}{13} = 0.3385, \quad \hat{p}_3 = \frac{14}{23} = 0.6087, \quad w_3 = \frac{(13)(10)}{13 + 10} = 5.6522$$

$$d_4 = \frac{16}{19} - \frac{7}{12} = 0.2588, \quad \hat{p}_4 = \frac{23}{31} = 0.7419, \quad w_4 = \frac{(12)(19)}{12 + 19} = 7.3548$$

With these statistics,

$$\bar{d} = \frac{8.1818(0.3556) + \ldots + 7.3548(0.2588)}{8.1818 + \ldots + 7.3548} = 0.3207$$

$$SE^2_{\bar{d}} = \frac{8.1818(0.3939)(0.6061) + \ldots + 7.3548(0.7419)(0.2581)}{(8.1818 + \ldots + 7.3548)^2} = 0.0078$$

so that:

$$Z = \frac{\bar{d}}{SE_{\bar{d}}} = \frac{0.3207}{\sqrt{0.0078}} = 3.62$$

Since $Z = 3.62 > 1.645$, H_0 is rejected. As with the other combining procedures, it is concluded that girls have greater success than boys.

Note that the Z values for Procedures 1, 2, and 3 are given, respectively, by 3.15, 3.45, and 3.62, suggesting that, for these data, the Cochran procedure has more power. It should also be noted that the Cochran procedure can be used for nondirectional alternatives, since the numerator can assume both positive and negative values. While the computations for the Cochran test are more extensive, it is probably a better test because of apparent higher power and amenability to two-tailed alternatives.

Procedure 4. Pearson's Lambda Criterion, based on the significance probabilities of the individual tests for 2×2 tables, can be used as described in Section 3–15. For 2×2 tables, one determines, for each k:

$$p_k = P[X_1^2 > \text{computed } X_{(k)}^2]$$

and then computes:

$$\lambda = -4.605 \sum_{k=1}^{K} \log_{10} p_k$$

which is related to the chi-square distribution with $v = 2K$.

EXAMPLE 5–9.4. For the data of Table 5–10;
$$p_1 = P[\chi_1^2 > 4.33] = 0.0188$$
$$p_2 = P[\chi_1^2 > 2.79] = 0.0475$$
$$p_3 = P[\chi_1^2 > 2.71] = 0.0505$$
$$p_4 = P[\chi_1^2 > 0.83] = 0.1814$$

so that:
$$\lambda = -4.605[\log_{10}(0.0188) + \log_{10}(0.0475) + \log_{10}(0.0505) + \log_{10}(0.1814)]$$
$$= -4.605[(8.2742 - 10) + (8.6767 - 10) + (8.7033 - 10) + (9.2587 - 10)]$$
$$= 23.43$$

Since $K = 4$, λ is referred to the chi-square distribution with $v = 2K = (2)(4) = 8$; thus $\chi_{8:0.95}^2 = 15.51$. Again, H_0 is rejected; girls have greater success than the boys.

5–10. Correction for Continuity in 2×2 Irwin–Fisher Tables

Both the large-sample normal-curve approximation to the Irwin–Fisher test and the Karl Pearson X^2 approximation to the Irwin–Fisher test employ statistics that are referred to continuous null distributions. On the other hand, the sampling distribution of the random variable of interest in the Irwin–Fisher test is the discrete hypergeometric distribution. Consequently, the researcher may wish to apply a correction for continuity to the discretely distributed observed outcomes when a continuous distribution will be used as the reference null distribution. If the normal-curve test is employed, the correction for continuity described in Section 5–5 may be used. If Karl Pearson's X^2 statistic is used for the large-sample approximation,

The Irwin–
Fisher Test:
Two-Sample
Procedures for
Dichotomous
Variables

115

the statistic corrected for continuity is

$$X_c^2 = \sum_i \sum_j \frac{[X_{ij} \pm \frac{1}{2} - \hat{E}(X_{ij})]^2}{\hat{E}(X_{ij})}$$

with the $\frac{1}{2}$ being added or subtracted so as to make the rejection of H_0 more difficult.

EXAMPLE 5–10.1. For the data of Tables 5–8 and 5–9, the chi-square statistic, corrected for continuity, is given by:

$$X^2 = \frac{(55 + 0.5 - 58.2)^2}{58.2} + \frac{(21 - 0.5 - 17.8)^2}{17.8} + \frac{(20 - 0.5 - 16.8)^2}{16.8}$$

$$+ \frac{(2 + 0.5 - 5.2)^2}{5.2} = 2.52$$

This value is considerably smaller than the uncorrected statistic, $X^2 = 3.33$.

Statisticians dispute the utility of the correction for continuity. Grizzle (1967) argued against its use, noting that it tends to make the test overly conservative. Mantel and Greenhouse (1968) were more favorable to retention of the continuity correction, emphasizing its utility as a device for adjusting for the discreteness of the variable of interest.

5–11. The Two-Sample Median Test, A Special Case of the Irwin–Fisher Test

The Irwin–Fisher two-sample test is the most powerful test of equality of two proportions if the random variable of interest is qualitative and dichotomous. Often, the nature of the study dictates this condition. Examples of this occur when A and $\overline{A}$ are {Passed, Failed}, {Lived, Died}, {Above median, Below median}, and so on. However, if a variable can be measured on a quantitative scale, most researchers want to use the scale of measurement in testing hypotheses about equal proportions in the population. A statistical test that uses minimal information about the scale of measurement is the two-sample median test.

The rationale for the two-sample median test is as follows. Let n_1 random quantitative observations be obtained from Population 1 and let n_2 similar observations be obtained from Population 2. If $\hat{M}_1$ and $\hat{M}_2$ denote the medians for the first and second sample, respectively, then the difference between the sample medians can be used to make an inference about a difference in the population values. Thus, one can test the hypothesis:

$$H_0: M_1 = M_2 = M_0$$

against the alternative:

$$H_1: M_1 \neq M_2$$

Under H_0 it is hypothesized that there is no statistical difference between the medians of the two populations from which the samples are drawn. As a result, the two samples can be combined into one sample. For the combined observations, it is possible to find the common median, $\hat{M}_0$, determine the number of observations in each sample that are above and below the common median, and then test the hypothesis $H_0: M_1 = M_2$. This hypothesis can also be viewed in terms of probabilities associated with binomial random variables. For this, let X_1 be the number of observations above $\hat{M}_0$ in sample 1 and X_2 be the number of observations above $\hat{M}_0$ in sample 2. If $P(X_1 > \hat{M}_0)$ is denoted by p_1 and $P(X_2 > \hat{M}_0)$ is denoted by p_2, then the hypothesis can be written as:

$$H_0: p_1 = p_2 = \tfrac{1}{2}$$

versus the alternative:

$$H_1: p_1 \neq p_2$$

In other words, H_0 reduces to a hypothesis that states that the parameters of two binomial variables are equal to $\tfrac{1}{2}$, while a nondirectional alternative states that p_1 and p_2 are not both equal to $\tfrac{1}{2}$.

EXAMPLE 5–11.1. As an illustration of this test, reconsider the problem of Section 5–1. The dependent variable of the study is a qualitative measure of grade level of students on a reading test. While performance was merely classified as above or below grade level, the exact values shown in Table 5–12 could be used. Visual inspection of the data suggests that the test had a ceiling effect for the experimental subjects. Therefore, the classical t test, which would normally be used in this case, is definitely not appropriate.

TABLE 5–12. *Reading-test grade levels of students in the control and experimental conditions.*

Control	Experimental
1.2	2.4
1.7	2.6
1.7	2.9
1.9	3.2
2.2	3.7
2.3	4.1
3.2	4.8
3.7	4.8
	4.9
	4.9
	4.9

If H_0 is true, then both samples come from populations with a common median value. Since n is odd, the best estimate of M_0 is given by the $[(n + 1)/2]$th ordered observation $= (19 + 1)/2 = 10$th ordered observation, which in this case is $\hat{M}_0 = X^{(10)} = 3.2$. Note that two observations are tied at the median value of 3.2. One is added to the control group above the median cell and the other to the experimental group below the median cell. Distributing the data in this manner reduces the probability of rejecting H_0.

The Irwin—
Fisher Test:
Two-Sample
Procedures for
Dichotomous
Variables

117

Grade level	Control treatment 1	Experimental treatment 2	Total
Below median	6	4	10
Above median	2	7	9
Total	8	11	19

The categorical representation of the data in Table 5–13 produces an Irwin–Fisher table. Thus, the Irwin–Fisher exact test can be performed on the data with:

$$n_1 = 8, \qquad n_2 = 11, \qquad X_1 + X_2 = 10.$$

Possible outcomes for control (X_1) and experimental (X_2) at the "Below median" grade level, and their probabilities, are summarized in Table 5–14. When these probabilities are used, the decision rule for $\alpha = 0.0198$ is to reject H_0 if $X_1 = \{0, 1, 7, 8\}$. Since $X_1 = 6$ does not lie in the rejection region, there is no reason to doubt the assertion of equality of the population medians, $H_0: M_1 = M_2 = M_0$.

TABLE 5–14. Hypergeometric probabilities for the median test based on data of Table 5–13.

Value of X_1	Value of X_2	Probability
0	10	$\begin{bmatrix}8\\0\end{bmatrix} \begin{bmatrix}11\\10\end{bmatrix} \Big/ \begin{bmatrix}19\\10\end{bmatrix} = .0001$
1	9	$\begin{bmatrix}8\\1\end{bmatrix} \begin{bmatrix}11\\9\end{bmatrix} \Big/ \begin{bmatrix}19\\10\end{bmatrix} = .0048$
2	8	$\begin{bmatrix}8\\2\end{bmatrix} \begin{bmatrix}11\\8\end{bmatrix} \Big/ \begin{bmatrix}19\\10\end{bmatrix} = .0500$
3	7	$\begin{bmatrix}8\\3\end{bmatrix} \begin{bmatrix}11\\7\end{bmatrix} \Big/ \begin{bmatrix}19\\10\end{bmatrix} = .2000$
4	6	$\begin{bmatrix}8\\4\end{bmatrix} \begin{bmatrix}11\\6\end{bmatrix} \Big/ \begin{bmatrix}19\\10\end{bmatrix} = .3501$
5	5	$\begin{bmatrix}8\\5\end{bmatrix} \begin{bmatrix}11\\5\end{bmatrix} \Big/ \begin{bmatrix}19\\10\end{bmatrix} = .2801$
6	4	$\begin{bmatrix}8\\6\end{bmatrix} \begin{bmatrix}11\\4\end{bmatrix} \Big/ \begin{bmatrix}19\\10\end{bmatrix} = .1000$
7	3	$\begin{bmatrix}8\\7\end{bmatrix} \begin{bmatrix}11\\3\end{bmatrix} \Big/ \begin{bmatrix}19\\10\end{bmatrix} = .0143$
8	2	$\begin{bmatrix}8\\8\end{bmatrix} \begin{bmatrix}11\\2\end{bmatrix} \Big/ \begin{bmatrix}19\\10\end{bmatrix} = .0006$

The median test provides a test of the hypothesis $H_0: M_1 = M_2 = M_0$ only when $\hat{M}_0$ is exactly equal to M_0; otherwise the hypothesis reduces to $H_0: P(X_1 > \hat{M}_0) = P(X_2 > \hat{M}_0) = p_0$, where p_0 is an unknown population value. Since $\hat{M}_0$ is almost certain not to equal M_0, the test actually tests the hypothesis that the proportion of cases above $\hat{M}_0$ is the same for both populations. If this hypothesis is rejected, there is good reason to believe that $M_1 \neq M_2$. On the other hand, if $H_0: P(X_1 > \hat{M}_0) =$

$P(X_2 > \hat{M}_0)$ is not rejected, this does not necessarily imply that $M_1 = M_2$. If $\hat{M}_0$ is a reasonably close estimate of M_0 and if the probability distributions of X_1 and X_2 are symmetrical, then the test of the hypothesis $H_0: M_1 = M_2 = M_0$ is actually a test of $H_0: E(X_1) = E(X_2) = \mu_0$.

The two-sample parametric test used most frequently to test hypotheses about measures of central tendency is the t test. When the conditions for the t test are valid, the asymptotic efficiency of the median test relative to the t test is found to be $2/\pi$, or 64%. In essence, this can be interpreted as follows: A median test based upon 100 observations has the same probability of rejecting $H_0: E(X_1) = E(X_2) = \mu_0$ as a t test based upon 64 observations, when the t test is a valid test. Two-sample tests exist that have higher efficiency than the median test. For this reason, the median test is not usually recommended as an alternative to the t test or to the Welch–Aspin analog to the t test. However, if the distribution of the underlying variable has long tails and is peaked about the center, then the median test is an excellent competitor to the two-sample t test. If, in particular, the underlying variable has a double-exponential distribution, the median test is known to be optimum. For this distribution, $E = 2$, when compared to the t test.

Finally, it should be noted that the two-sample median test can be used as a test for trend on data collected over time. For this extension, find the median of the total sample and divide the total sample into two equal halves. The first half consists of the first $n/2$ observations, while the second half consists of the last $n/2$ observations. In each subsample, determine the number of observations above and below the total sample median. This produces a 2×2 table, which is then analyzed as an Irwin–Fisher table. If this test is performed as a substitute for $H_0: \beta = 0$ against the alternative $H_1: \beta \neq 0$ when the assumptions of normality and common variance are satisfied, a small loss in power is observed relative to the t test for $H_0: \beta = 0$. The asymptotic efficiency of the Irwin–Fisher test for trend relative to the classical t test, when the latter is valid, is given by $E = 0.78$.

Summary

In this chapter, one of the most frequently performed statistical tests of behavioral research was presented. This test, proposed by R. A. Fisher and independently by J. Irwin, is frequently referred to as the Irwin–Fisher Exact Test of Significance. The test is used to determine whether the probability parameters of two independent binomially-distributed random variables are equal. In the most general model, two independent random samples of size n_1 and n_2 are selected from two populations that are known to be $B(n_1, p_1)$ and $B(n_2, p_2)$. On each sample, the number of elements having characteristics A and $\bar{A}$ are determined. If T_1 and T_2 represent the numbers of A's in each sample, then the probability distribution of T_1 and T_2 is known to be hypergeometric with the individual probability values given by:

$$P\left[(T_1 = t_1) \cap (T_2 = t_2)\right] = \frac{\begin{bmatrix} n_1 \\ t_1 \end{bmatrix} \begin{bmatrix} n_2 \\ t_2 \end{bmatrix}}{\begin{bmatrix} n_1 + n_2 \\ t_1 + t_2 \end{bmatrix}}$$

The Irwin–
Fisher Test:
Two-Sample
Procedures for
Dichotomous
Variables

119

Since $t_1 + t_2 = t$, it follows that t_1 and t_2 are perfectly negatively correlated for fixed t, so that T_1 or T_2 can be called a hypergeometric variable. Because of this, the $P[(T_1 = t_1) \cap (T_2 = t_2)]$ is identical to:

$$P(T_1 = t_1 | t_1 + t_2 = t) = \frac{\begin{bmatrix} n_1 \\ t_1 \end{bmatrix} \begin{bmatrix} n - n_1 \\ t - t_1 \end{bmatrix}}{\begin{bmatrix} n \\ t \end{bmatrix}}$$

or to:

$$P(T_2 = t_2 | t_1 + t_2 = t) = \frac{\begin{bmatrix} n_2 \\ t_2 \end{bmatrix} \begin{bmatrix} n - n_2 \\ t - t_2 \end{bmatrix}}{\begin{bmatrix} n \\ t \end{bmatrix}}$$

Thus, if the hypothesis H_0: $p_1 = p_2$ is tested against the nondirectional alternative H_1: $p_1 \neq p_2$, with the probability of a Type I error controlled at $\alpha = \alpha_0$, then the hypothesis is rejected if T_1 or T_2 is too large, with largeness being defined in terms of the probabilities of T_1 and T_2, given that the hypothesis under test is true.

Since the large-sample approximation to this test usually employs the criterion variable

$$\hat{\Delta} = \frac{t_1}{n_1} - \frac{t_2}{n_2} = \hat{p}_1 - \hat{p}_2$$

it is possible to define the critical region as the set of $\hat{\Delta}$ values that are most compatible with the alternative hypothesis. For a two-tailed test, this gives rise to the decision rule:

D.R.: Reject H_0 if $\hat{\Delta} < \hat{\Delta}_L$ and if $\hat{\Delta} > \hat{\Delta}_U$, where $\hat{\Delta}_L$ is the lower $\alpha/2$-percentile value of the hypergeometric distribution and $\hat{\Delta}_U$ is the upper $(1 - \alpha/2)$-percentile value of the hypergeometric distribution.

For the large-sample test, the usual test statistic is given by:

$$Z = \frac{\hat{p}_1 - \hat{p}_2}{\sqrt{(\hat{p}_0 \hat{q}_0 / n_1) + (\hat{p}_0 \hat{q}_0 / n_2)}}$$

where

$$\hat{p}_1 = \frac{t_1}{n_1}, \qquad \hat{p}_2 = \frac{t_2}{n_2}, \qquad \text{and} \qquad \hat{p}_0 = \frac{t_1 + t_2}{n_1 + n_2}$$

A second large-sample approximation is given by the Karl Pearson statistic

$$X^2 = \sum_{i=1}^{2} \sum_{j=1}^{2} \frac{[X_{ij} - \hat{E}(X_{ij})]^2}{\hat{E}(X_{ij})}$$

which is approximately X_1^2. The observed frequencies X_{ij} can be expressed in terms of t as:

$$X_{11} = t_1, \qquad X_{21} = t_2, \qquad X_{12} = n_1 - t_1, \qquad \text{and} \qquad X_{22} = n_2 - t_2$$

If H_0 is rejected, confidence intervals for $\Delta = p_1 - p_2$ may be determined by direct probability calculations or by the large-sample approximation to the distribution of $\hat{\Delta}$. Since the small-sample confidence interval is almost never determined, attention generally focuses on the large-sample interval, which is given by:

$$\hat{\Delta} - Z_{1-\alpha/2}SE_{\hat{\Delta}} < \Delta < \hat{\Delta} + Z_{1-\alpha/2}SE_{\hat{\Delta}}$$

or:

$$(\hat{p}_1 - \hat{p}_2) - Z_{1-\alpha/2}\sqrt{\frac{\hat{p}_1\hat{q}_1}{n_1} + \frac{\hat{p}_2\hat{q}_2}{n_2}} < p_1 - p_2 < (\hat{p}_1 - \hat{p}_2) + Z_{1-\alpha/2}\sqrt{\frac{\hat{p}_1\hat{q}_1}{n_1} + \frac{\hat{p}_2\hat{q}_2}{n_2}}$$

As with all large-sample approximations of the normal to the binomial, it is necessary that

$$n_1\hat{p}_1 > 5, \qquad n_2\hat{p}_2 > 5, \qquad n_1\hat{q}_1 > 5, \qquad \text{and} \qquad n_2\hat{q}_2 > 5;$$

otherwise, the approximation will not be adequate.

In most cases, the power of this test is ignored. As a general rule of thumb, one can feel confident that H_0 will be rejected if n_1 and n_2 are both greater than 50 and $\Delta = p_1 - p_2$ exceeds 0.20. With alpha equal to 0.05, the power for this outcome exceeds 0.50 and approaches *one* in numerical value as Δ increases.

The extension of the Irwin–Fisher test to more than two populations or to more than two possible outcomes runs into two major problems when the sample sizes are small. Computations become involved, and the determination of the rejection region becomes exceedingly complex. If attention can be focused on pairwise differences in the parameters, then a compromise procedure can be used to test the basic research hypothesis. This compromise is based upon Bonferroni confidence intervals. If Q pairwise differences are of interest, then each is tested at $\alpha_0 \leqq \alpha_T/Q$, where α_T equals the probability of at least one Type I error over the entire set of Q intervals. If any one test leads to a rejection of equality for the pair of parameters being compared, then the overall hypothesis is also rejected.

The two-sample Irwin–Fisher test can be modified to serve as a competitor to the classical two-sample t test. In this form, it is called the two-sample median test and is based on two independent samples of quantitative observations. The median $\hat{M}_0$ of the joint sample is determined, and the observations in each sample are classified as being above or below $\hat{M}_0$. The resulting 2×2 table is then analyzed as an Irwin–Fisher table. This procedure is not recommended if the underlying variable is close to normal in form, since the asymptotic efficiency relative to the t test is only $E = 0.64$. However, if the distribution is sharply peaked, then the median test is clearly recommended.

Finally, the median test can be modified to serve as a test for trend over time, by finding the median of the total sample and splitting the sample in half. Observations from each half are classified as being above or below the median, and the resulting 2×2 table is analyzed as an Irwin–Fisher table. In this form, the test is a fair competitor to the t test for $\beta = 0$ and to the Cox–Stuart test for trend discussed in Section 3–16.

Exercises

*1. In a pilot study, 12 cats were trained to walk a maze and obtain food behind a door with a catch that they had to learn to open. When the cats had learned the task, six were subjected to a brain operation in which nerves were severed that connected parts of the brain believed to control memory functions. Following the operation and recovery, all 12 cats were tested in the maze to see how well they remembered the maze solution. Results were as shown in the table below. What is the hypothesis under test and what is the decision with $\alpha \leq 0.05$?

Observation	Operation	No operation	Total
Remembered	1	6	7
Did not remember	5	0	5
Total	6	6	12

*2. The study of Exercise 1 was repeated, but with 22 cats. This time, a one-tailed test was adopted. Results are as shown in the accompanying table. What is the hypothesis under test and what is the decision with $\alpha \leq 0.05$?

Observation	Operation	No operation	Total
Remembered	1	11	12
Did not remember	9	1	10
Total	10	12	22

*3. In a factory that employs $N = 900$ men, of which 75% belong to a union, what is the probability that, in a random selection of $n = 40$ men,
a) more than 35 belong to the union?
b) exactly 30 belong to the union?

*4. If, in the selection of $n = 40$ men in the factory of Exercise 3, it were found that only 25 men belonged to the union, should one be surprised? Why?

*5. If, in the study of Exercises 3 and 4, the 40 men were asked:
Has the union improved working conditions in the factory?
Yes_____ No_____

Response	Union member	Not a union member	Total
Yes	20	4	24
No	5	11	16
Total	25	15	40

and if the results were as shown in the accompanying table, what would this indicate about the beliefs of union and non-union members at $\alpha \leq 0.05$?

a) Answer the question by means of a statistical test.
b) Answer the question by means of a confidence interval.

*6. In a large sample of registered voters in a large California city, 273 people were asked: Are you satisfied with the way the President is handling his job?

$$Yes\text{\_\_\_\_\_} \quad No\text{\_\_\_\_\_} \quad Don't\ know\text{\_\_\_\_\_}$$

If the respondents were separated on the basis of political party affiliation and if the "Don't know" responses were eliminated, results were as shown in the following table. On the basis of this evidence, is there a difference in attitude between Democrats and Republicans at $\alpha \leq 0.05$? Determine the 95% confidence interval for the difference in the two proportions of "Yes" responses.

Response	Democrats	Republicans	Total
Yes	47	41	88
No	94	12	106
Total	141	53	194

*7. For the example of Section 5–8, find the power for $n_1 = n_2 = 75$. Repeat the power computations for $n_1 = n_2 = 100$. How large should n_1 and n_2 be, to obtain a power of 0.80?

*8. One hundred sixty adults were stopped on a busy street corner in San Francisco on a mid-week noon hour and were asked to read a petition, which was actually the first amendment to the U.S. Constitution. They were then asked to sign the petition supporting the ideas of the amendement. Among those people who did not know that the petition was a word-by-word copy of the amendment, their decision to sign or not, along with religious preference, is shown in the table. Use the methods of this chapter to analyze these data.

Religion	Would sign	Would not sign	Total
Catholic	18	27	45
Jewish	12	2	14
Protestant	21	17	38
No religion	14	6	20
Total	65	52	117

*The Irwin—
Fisher Test:
Two-Sample
Procedures for
Dichotomous
Variables*

123

*9. In the study of Exercise 8, among the adults who did not recognize the amendment, they also were asked if they were regular church-goers. Results are as shown in the accompanying table. Use Procedures 1, 2, 3, and 4, of Section 5–9 to analyze these data. What is the specific hypothesis under test?

Religion	Decision	Church attendance Yes	No	Total
Catholic	Would sign	8	10	18
	Would not sign	21	6	27
	Total	29	16	45
Protestant	Would sign	9	12	21
	Would not sign	12	5	17
	Total	21	17	38
Other	Would sign	8	18	26
	Would not sign	5	3	8
	Total	13	21	34

*10. In the study of Exercises 8 and 9, subjects were also asked about the number of completed years of education they had. Results are shown for the Protestants, in the table below. Use the median test in the analysis of these data.

Would sign	Would not sign	Would sign	Would not sign
6	8	12	12
8	8	12	12
8	10	14	13
10	10	14	14
11	11	16	14
12	11	16	More than 16
12	11	More than 16	
12	12	More than 16	
12	12	More than 16	
12	12	More than 16	
12	12		

*11. In the study of Exercises 8, 9, and 10, subjects were asked to estimate the percentage of adult Americans who would support the petition. In the accompanying table, results are shown for the Protestants who would sign the petition, according to years of education. Is there any reason to believe that the subjective-probability assignments are correlated with completed years of education? Apply the median test to these data. What is the specific hypothesis under test? Is the median test a good test for these data? Why?

Years of education	Percent	Years of education	Percent
6	80	12	75
8	75	12	80
8	60	14	100
10	70	14	90
11	50	16	100
12	60	16	75
12	50	More than 16	20
12	80	More than 16	60
12	85	More than 16	100
12	100	More than 16	100
12	70		

*12. Apply the median test for trend to the data of Table 3–11, and compare the results to the Cox–Stuart S test.

*13. Apply the median test for trend to the data of Table 3–12 and compare the results to the Cox–Stuart S test.

*14. The accompanying table shows the findings of a study of reading ability and syntactical mediation in paired-associate learning. Do these data suggest that good readers are more likely to mediate spontaneously than poor readers? Use $\alpha \leq 0.05$ in responding to this question.

Syntactical rating	Good readers	Poor readers	Total
Mediators	5	1	6
Nonmediators	3	7	10
Total	8	8	16

*15. A researcher wants to determine whether, in a certain company, the promotion of males and females to first-level supervisory positions is equally likely. The hypothetical data are as shown in the following table. Carry out the indicated test at $\alpha \leq 0.05$. What are your conclusions? If there is a sex difference in proportion promoted, how large is the difference?

Promotion Status	Sex of employee		Total
	Male	Female	
Promoted	25	10	35
Not promoted	155	150	305
Total	180	160	340

*16. The researcher of Exercise 15 also wants to know whether sex differences in job promotion are absent from the following civil service job classifications: rank and file, first-level supervisory, and second-level supervisory. The hypothetical data are as shown in the accompanying table. Use as many of the procedures 1 through 4 of Section 5–9 as you consider appropriate to analyze these data. What are your conclusions?

	Rank-and-file			First-level supervisory			Second-level supervisory		
	Male	Female	Total	Male	Female	Total	Male	Female	Total
Promoted	38	12	50	25	10	35	30	35	65
Not promoted	102	148	250	155	150	305	130	125	255
Total	140	160	300	180	160	340	160	160	320

The Irwin–Fisher Test: Two-Sample Procedures for Dichotomous Variables

*17. A counselor wants to analyze the following data obtained from *a single subject*. The data consist of the number of interactions with peers before and after the introduction

125

of a treatment designed to increase peer interaction. The number of interactions was recorded at each of 20 observation times, 8 pretreatment and 12 posttreatment. The results were dichotomized at the median, and the observations at each time were classified as above or below the median. Is any statistical test studied in this chapter appropriate for the analysis of these data? Explain.

Interaction with peers	Pretreatment observations	Posttreatment observations	Total
Number above the median	2	8	10
Number below the median	6	4	10
Total	8	12	20

*18. The following relative-frequency distributions were recorded in a study of the TV viewing habits of 100 five-year-olds and 100 seven-year-olds. Do five- and seven-year-olds differ in the amount of time they typically spend viewing TV? Defend your choice of test statistic to answer this question. Use $\alpha = 0.05$ in carrying out the test you have chosen.

Hours of TV watched per day	Age of child	
	Five	Seven
Less than 2	0.17	0.33
2	0.28	0.22
3	0.25	0.40
4	0.18	0.05
5	0.05	0.00
6 or more	0.07	0.00

Chi-Square Tests
of Homogeneity of Proportions
for Qualitative Variables
in Multiple Independent
Samples

6-1. Extension of the Median Test to More than Two Populations

There are times when an experimenter wishes to test a hypothesis that involves more than two populations. In the classical model, the one-way analysis of variance serves as a prototype. The simplest nonparametric competitor to it is the extended median test. Table 6-1 shows the layout for such an extension. In this form:

X_{1K} = Number of observations that exceed $\hat{M}_0$, the common median for all K samples,

X_{2K} = Number of observations that are less than $\hat{M}_0$.

If the median of the combined samples, $\hat{M}_0$, is a good estimate of M_0, then the hypothesis H_0: $M_1 = M_2 = \ldots = M_K = M_0$ may be tested against the alternative H_1: H_0 is false. In this sense, the null form of the hypothesis states that

TABLE 6-1. Data table for the median test for K populations.

	Sample 1	Sample 2	...	Sample K	Total
Above median	X_{11}	X_{12}	...	X_{1K}	$X_1.$
Below median	X_{21}	X_{22}	...	X_{2K}	$X_2.$
Total	$n_{.1}$	$n_{.2}$	...	$n_{.K}$	n

127

the medians across the K populations are not statistically different. If the dependent variable is denoted by Y, a more general hypothesis would be $H_0: P(Y_1 > \hat{M}_0) = P(Y_2 > \hat{M}_0) = \ldots = P(Y_K > \hat{M}_0) = p_0$, where p_0 is some unspecified parameter value. The alternative hypothesis would still be $H_1: H_0$ is false. This is a more general model in that it implies that the proportion of cases lying above $\hat{M}_0$ is the same for all populations and is, therefore, a simple extension of the two-sample binomial or Irwin–Fisher test. The constant proportion may or may not be $\frac{1}{2}$. If $\hat{M}_0$ is a good estimate of M_0, then $P(Y_k > \hat{M}_0) = \frac{1}{2}$ might well be a true statement. Whether or not $p_0 = \frac{1}{2}$ is of no importance for the valid use of this test.

If the sample sizes are sufficiently large, H_0 can be tested by use of the large-sample Karl Pearson statistic:

$$X^2 = \sum_{i=1}^{2} \sum_{k=1}^{K} \frac{\left[X_{ik} - \hat{E}(X_{ik}) \right]^2}{\hat{E}(X_{ik})}$$

which can be computed simply as:

$$X^2 = \sum_{i=1}^{2} \sum_{k=1}^{K} \frac{X_{ik}^2}{\hat{E}(X_{ik})} - n$$

or, in terms of the cell and marginal frequencies, by:

$$X^2 = \left[\sum_{i=1}^{2} \sum_{k=1}^{K} \frac{X_{ik}^2}{X_{i.} X_{.k}} - 1 \right] n$$

This latter form is well suited for use with hand calculators that have a memory.

If the cell frequencies in the expected frequency table are all greater than 5, then X^2 can be approximated by a chi-square variable with $v = (K - 1)$ degrees of freedom. The approximation is illustrated in Section 10–1 for $n = 10$ and $K = 3$.

When the original data are available, the method for assigning observed frequencies to cells is similar to the method explained for the two-sample problem. The general procedure requires the combining of all data into one sample and then determining the common median, $\hat{M}_0$. For each sample, the number of observations lying above and below $\hat{M}_0$ are counted. If ties exist at $\hat{M}_0$, the option of (1) eliminating these scores or (2) assigning them to cells in a manner which ensures a more conservative test is left to the discretion of the experimenter. With the resulting $2 \times K$ frequency table, Karl Pearson's chi-square is computed and evaluated. The test is illustrated by an example.

EXAMPLE 6–1.1. In a study in which heroin addicts were being rehabilitated, four experimental conditions were being investigated. They are as follows:

1. Daily doses of methadone were given to confirmed heroin addicts, who were required to attend twice-a-week encounter sessions with other addicts also undergoing treatment of some kind.
2. Daily doses of methadone were given to experimental subjects but attendance at encounter sessions was voluntary.
3. Methadone was given to subjects on request, but attendance at twice weekly group encounter sessions was mandatory.

4. Methadone was given to subjects on request, but attendance at group encounter sessions was voluntary.

TABLE 6–2. *Number of days confirmed heroin addicts remained off heroin, according to the kind of treatment received.*

Condition 1	Condition 2	Condition 3	Condition 4
3	6	12	6
17	18	19	9
34	22	27	11
34	26	27	11
More than 35	35	33	13
More than 35	35	33	26
More than 35	More than 35	35	29
More than 35	More than 35	More than 35	32
More than 35	More than 35	More than 35	32
More than 35	More than 35	More than 35	33
	More than 35		More than 35
			More than 35
			More than 35

The dependent variable was the number of days the subject remained off heroin in a period of 60 days. Results were as shown in Table 6–2. As can be seen, 17 of the 44 experimental subjects stayed off heroin for more than 35 days, or five continuous weeks. Since exact numerical values are not available for these 17 subjects, the classical F test cannot be performed, to test H_0: $\mu_1 = \mu_2 = \mu_3 = \mu_4$. However, the extended median test is eminently viable for these data. Across the 44 subjects,

$$\hat{M}_0 = \tfrac{1}{2}(Y^{(22)} + Y^{(23)})$$

where

$$Y^{(22)} = \text{22nd ordered observation}$$

and

$$Y^{(23)} = \text{23rd ordered observation}$$

For the ordered observations, the median is given by

$$\hat{M}_0 = \tfrac{1}{2}(33 + 34) = 33.5$$

The number of subjects who exceeded or did not exceed 33.5 days off heroin is reported in Table 6–3. Under binomial distribution theory, $E(X_{ik}) = n_{.k}p_0$, where

TABLE 6–3. *Distribution of confirmed heroin addicts according to the combined sample median value.*

Condition	1	2	3	4	Total
Above median	8	7	4	3	22
Below median	2	4	6	10	22
Total	10	11	10	13	44

n_k is the number of subjects tested under condition k and p_0 is the value of the unknown probability. Since p_0 is unknown, it is estimated from the data as:

$$\hat{p}_0 = \frac{X_{11} + X_{12} + \ldots + X_{1K}}{n_{.1} + n_{.2} + \ldots + n_{.K}} = \frac{X_{1.}}{n}$$

Thus, for the two cells of column 1, the estimated expected frequencies are given by

$$\hat{E}(X_{11}) = \hat{E}(X_{21}) = n_{.1}\frac{X_{1.}}{n} = 10\left(\frac{22}{44}\right) = 5$$

for column 2,

$$\hat{E}(X_{12}) = \hat{E}(X_{22}) = n_{.2}\frac{X_{1.}}{n} = 11\left(\frac{22}{44}\right) = 5.5$$

for column 3,

$$\hat{E}(X_{13}) = \hat{E}(X_{23}) = n_{.3}\frac{X_{1.}}{n} = 10\left(\frac{22}{44}\right) = 5$$

and for column 4,

$$\hat{E}(X_{14}) = \hat{E}(X_{24}) = n_{.4}\frac{X_{1.}}{n} = 13\left(\frac{22}{44}\right) = 6.5$$

For these data, Karl Pearson's statistic is given by the definitional formula as:

$$X^2 = \frac{(8-5)^2}{5} + \frac{(2-5)^2}{5} + \frac{(7-5.5)^2}{5.5} + \frac{(4-5.5)^2}{5.5}$$
$$+ \frac{(4-5)^2}{5} + \frac{(6-5)^2}{5} + \frac{(3-6.5)^2}{6.5} + \frac{(10-6.5)^2}{6.5}$$
$$= 8.59.$$

With the computational formula, using frequencies and estimated expected frequencies,

$$X^2 = \frac{8^2}{5} + \frac{2^2}{5} + \frac{7^2}{5.5} + \frac{4^2}{5.5} + \frac{4^2}{5} + \frac{6^2}{5} + \frac{3^2}{6.5} + \frac{10^2}{6.5} - 44$$
$$8.59$$

or with the form using cell and marginal frequencies,

$$X^2 = \left[\frac{8^2}{10(22)} + \frac{7^2}{11(22)} + \frac{4^2}{10(22)} + \frac{3^2}{13(22)} + \frac{2^2}{10(22)} + \frac{4^2}{11(22)} + \frac{6^2}{10(22)}\right.$$
$$\left. + \frac{10^2}{13(22)} - 1\right]44$$
$$= 8.59$$

With $\alpha \leq 0.05$, the hypothesis of equal population medians is rejected, since $X^2 = 8.59 > 7.82$, the 95-percentile value of the chi-square distribution with $v = K - 1 = 4 - 1 = 3$ degrees of freedom. Across the four samples, the sample medians are:

$$\hat{M}_1 = \text{more than } 35; \qquad \hat{M}_2 = 35; \qquad \hat{M}_3 = 33; \qquad \text{and} \qquad \hat{M}_4 = 27.5$$

At this point it is customary to ask which treatment medians are statistically different from one another. One way to answer this question is to perform all possible two-sample median tests with $\hat{M} = 33.5$, and determine which hypotheses are rejected; but, to do this correctly, particular attention must be paid to the possible increased risks of Type I errors in the set of possible comparisons. One way to control the probability of Type I errors is to count the number of tests to be made, divide the resulting number into the overall probability of a Type I error of particular interest, and then perform each test at the resulting alpha level. For this study, the number of pairwise comparisons is given by

$$Q = \begin{bmatrix} 4 \\ 2 \end{bmatrix} = 6$$

If the total alpha is to be controlled at $\alpha_T = 0.05$, then each test should be done at

$$\alpha = \frac{\alpha_T}{Q} = \frac{0.05}{6} = 0.0083$$

While the method is not illustrated, it is easy to carry out and is left as an exercise for the reader. See Section 2–8 for further discussion on this subject.

In Section 6–5, another procedure will be illustrated to identify significant differences in medians. As will be seen, the method does not focus on the actual problem of interest, in that confidence intervals for $(M_k - M_{k'})$ are not obtained. Instead, confidence intervals for $(p_k - p_{k'})$ are produced. For the observed data, the proportions of cases that exceed the median are given by:

$$\hat{p}_1 = \frac{8}{10}, \qquad \hat{p}_2 = \frac{7}{11}, \qquad \hat{p}_3 = \frac{4}{10}, \qquad \text{and} \qquad \hat{p}_4 = \frac{3}{13}$$

The method described in Section 6–5 will enable one to determine which of these proportions are statistically different from one another. While this does not produce intervals on the original metric, it is reasonable to assume that significant differences in proportions are correlated with significant differences in medians, and in that sense, the resulting intervals can be used to make decisions about median values. Thus, if it is concluded that $p_k - p_{k'} \neq 0$, it follows that $M_k - M_{k'} \neq 0$.

6–2. The K-Sample Binomial Test for Equal Proportions

As indicated in Section 6–1, the extended median test is actually a special case of the test of $H_0: p_1 = p_2 = \ldots = p_K = p_0$ against the alternative $H_1: H_0$ is false, where the individual p_k are the parameters of K independent binomially distributed random variables, but for which it is hypothesized that $p_0 = \frac{1}{2}$. For the general case, one need not specify that $p_0 = \frac{1}{2}$. Thus, if in Table 6–1, $X_{11}, X_{12}, \ldots,$ X_{1K} represent independent observations on K independent binomially distributed random variables, then the Karl Pearson statistic,

$$X^2 = \sum_{i=1}^{2} \sum_{k=1}^{K} \frac{[X_{ik} - \hat{E}(X_{ik})]^2}{\hat{E}(X_{ik})}$$

can be used to test H_0 against H_1.

Chi-Square Tests
of Homogeneity
of Proportions for
Qualitative
Variables in
Multiple
Independent
Samples

EXAMPLE 6–2.1. As an illustration of this test, consider a study in which four different experimental methods for the treatment of schizophrenic patients were being investigated. Suppose the methods under investigation are as follows:

1. Weekly shock treatments.
2. Weekly treatments with carbon dioxide inhalation.
3. Biweekly shock treatments alternated with biweekly carbon dioxide inhalation.
4. Administration of proven drug tranquilizers.

Suppose that the dependent variable, measured four weeks following initial treatment, consists of subjective judgments of improvement or no improvement by ward nurses and orderlies, concerning psychological and emotional stability in the patients. Under this model, the dependent variable corresponds to a Bernoulli outcome for each subject, in that a dichotomous variable $Y: \{1, 0\}$, where

1. Improved
0. Not improved

is applied to each patient. For expository purposes, let it also be assumed that ward nurses and orderlies made their judgments in ignorance of the actual treatment performed on each patient. In reality, this assumption is difficult to justify and is a

TABLE 6–4. *Status of schizophrenic patients as rated by ward nurses and orderlies following four weeks of specialized treatment.*

Status of patient	Treatment				
	One	Two	Three	Four	Total
Improved	12	19	13	21	65
Not improved	6	11	3	24	44
Total	18	30	16	45	109

constant problem in these kinds of investigations. Let the results of the ratings be as shown in Table 6–4. With these data, it is possible to test:

$$H_0: p_1 = p_2 = p_3 = p_4$$

against the alternative:

$$H_1: H_0 \text{ is false}$$

with the Karl Pearson statistic if it can be assumed that:

1. Ratings within a treatment classification are independently made on each subject.
2. Ratings between treatment classifications are made independently.
3. Probability of improvement within each treatment classification is constant across all subjects receiving a specific treatment.
4. The expected frequencies in each cell exceed five in number.

Actually, there is some evidence that assumptions 3 and 4 can be weakened without violating the integrity of the Karl Pearson form of the test. However, extreme violations of the assumptions cannot be tolerated.

Under the assumption that H_0 is true, the best unbiased estimate of the common probability value is given by:

$$\hat{p}_0 = \frac{X_{11} + X_{12} + X_{13} + X_{14}}{n_{.1} + n_{.2} + n_{.3} + n_{.4}} = \frac{X_{1.}}{n} = \frac{65}{109} = 0.5963$$

As a result, $\hat{q}_0 = 1 - \hat{p}_0 = 0.4037$. With these estimates, the estimated expected values are computed as $\hat{E}(X_{1k}) = n_{.k}\hat{p}_0$ and $\hat{E}(X_{2k}) = n_{.k}\hat{q}_0$. These values are reported in Table 6–5.

TABLE 6–5. Estimated expected values for the data of Table 6–4.

Status of patient	Treatment				
	One	Two	Three	Four	Total
Improved	10.73	17.89	9.54	26.83	65
Not improved	7.27	12.11	6.46	18.17	44
Total	18	30	16	45	109

There are a number of things to note about the figures in Table 6–5. While one can estimate $\hat{E}(X_{ik})$ by multiplying $n_{.k}$ by $\hat{p}_0$, it is customary to multiply the marginal totals associated with a particular cell and then divide the resulting product by the grand total. Thus, for example,

$$\hat{E}(X_{13}) = \frac{16(65)}{109} = 9.54.$$

It should be noted that the row totals and column totals of the estimated expected table are identical to the row totals and column totals of the observed table. If, when setting up the expected table, these common totals are not generated, then one should recompute the estimated expected frequencies, since it is almost certain that computational errors have been made. Finally, it should be noted that estimated expected frequencies are determined to two decimal points. This is recommended as a means of reducing rounding errors, which can accumulate to a sizable quantity under the approximation.

For the observed data:

$$X^2 = \frac{(12 - 10.73)^2}{10.73} + \frac{(19 - 17.89)^2}{17.89} + \cdots + \frac{(24 - 18.17)^2}{18.17}$$
$$= 6.79.$$

With $\alpha \leq 0.05$, the hypothesis of equal probabilities of improvement across the four treatments is not rejected, since $X^2 = 6.79 < 7.82$, the 95th-percentile value of the chi-square distribution with $v = 4 - 1 = 3$ degrees of freedom. Since the evidence leads to a decision of no differences in the population proportions, the best point estimate of p_0 is given by $\hat{p}_0 = 0.5943$ with a 95-percent confidence interval for p given by:

$$p_0 = \hat{p}_0 \pm 1.96 \sqrt{\hat{p}_0 \hat{q}_0/n}$$

$$= (0.5943) \pm 1.96\sqrt{(0.5943)(0.4037)/109}$$
$$= 0.59 \pm 0.09$$

Thus, across all four tested treatments, about 59 percent of the patients show some improvement in psychological and emotional stability. If the experiment were to be repeated, one would expect the proportion of improvement to be some number between 50 percent and 68 percent.

6–3. Karl Pearson's Chi-Square Test of Homogeneity of Distributions

An important extension of the K-sample binomial test for equal proportions to the case in which the individual populations are partitioned into more than two mutually exclusive and exhaustive subclasses is available through the extension of Karl Pearson's chi-square statistic. This extension is referred to as the chi-square test of homogeneity for equal proportions.

For this test, consider K populations from which random samples of size $n_{.1}, n_{.2}, \ldots, n_{.K}$ are selected. Let the data be as represented in Table 6–6. In this table the lower marginal totals are fixed constants $n_{.1}, n_{.2}, \ldots, n_{.k}, \ldots, n_{.K}$, whereas the vertical marginal totals are random variables $X_{1.}, X_{2.}, \ldots, X_{i.}, \ldots, X_{I.}$, as are all frequencies, $X_{11}, X_{12}, \ldots, X_{ik}, \ldots, X_{IK}$ in each of the cells.

TABLE 6–6. A typical $I \times K$ homogeneity table.

Response variable	Condition				
	B_1	B_2	$\ldots$	B_K	Total
A_1	X_{11}	X_{12}	$\ldots$	X_{1K}	$X_{1.}$
A_2	X_{21}	X_{22}	$\ldots$	X_{2K}	$X_{2.}$
.	.	.	$\ldots$	.	.
.	.	.	$\ldots$	.	.
.	.	.	$\ldots$	.	.
A_I	X_{I1}	X_{I2}	$\ldots$	X_{IK}	$X_{I.}$
Total	$n_{.1}$	$n_{.2}$	$\ldots$	$n_{.K}$	n

After the samples are obtained, let each individual element be assigned to one and only one of the following sets of mutually exclusive and exhaustive subsets $A_1, A_2, \ldots, A_I$. The hypothesis to be tested is that the probability distributions of each of the populations are identical or homogeneous. Stated in statistical form,

$$
H_0: \begin{bmatrix} P(A_1|B_1) \\ P(A_2|B_1) \\ \cdot \\ \cdot \\ \cdot \\ P(A_I|B_1) \end{bmatrix} = \begin{bmatrix} P(A_1|B_2) \\ P(A_2|B_2) \\ \cdot \\ \cdot \\ \cdot \\ P(A_I|B_2) \end{bmatrix} = \ldots = \begin{bmatrix} P(A_1|B_K) \\ P(A_2|B_K) \\ \cdot \\ \cdot \\ \cdot \\ P(A_I|B_K) \end{bmatrix} = \begin{bmatrix} P(A_1) \\ P(A_2) \\ \cdot \\ \cdot \\ \cdot \\ P(A_I) \end{bmatrix}.
$$

The alternative hypothesis is:

$$H_1: H_0 \text{ is false}$$

This means that the alternative hypothesis is really a catch-all or *omnibus* alternative. Anything that will make H_0 false is included in the set of alternative hypotheses. Thus, the rejection of H_0 does not yield direct information as to the reason for the rejection.

The test statistic for this test is given by:

$$
X^2 = \sum_{k=1}^{K} \sum_{i=1}^{I} \frac{\left[X_{ik} - \hat{E}(X_{ik})\right]^2}{\hat{E}(X_{ik})}
$$

which, when H_0 is true, has an approximate chi-square distribution with $v = (K - 1)(I - 1)$ degrees of freedom. While it is impossible to prove, with the materials developed thus far, that X^2 is approximately chi-square, it is easy to show that the degrees of freedom for the test are, indeed, given by $v = (K - 1)(I - 1)$. Since the estimated expected frequencies of sample 1 must add to $n_{.1}$, it follows that the number of degrees of freedom available for the frequencies of sample 1 is given by $(I - 1)$. Thus, for K samples, it appears that the total number of degrees of freedom available for the test is $K(I - 1)$. But since $p_1, p_2, \ldots, p_I$ are unknown, they must be estimated from the data, and since these estimates must satisfy the relation $p_1 + p_2 + \ldots + p_I = 1$, it follows that $(I - 1)$ degrees of freedom are utilized in their estimation. Thus, $v = K(I - 1) - (I - 1) = (I - 1)(K - 1)$. The use of this test is illustrated in the following example.

EXAMPLE 6–3.1. As part of a concept-formation study in learning, 150 eighth-grade students were randomly assigned to four different experimental conditions. The subjects assigned to condition 1 were given 20 practice trials, subjects in condition 2 were given 15 practice trials, subjects in condition 3 were given 10 practice trials, and subjects in condition 4 were given no training. At the final testing period, each student was given a 30-item test, which contained 15 items similar to the items on the practice trials. After the testing, each subject was asked to rate the test according to difficulty. Possible choices for the responses were:

1. Very easy;   2. Average;   3. Very hard.

The responses to the question are summarized in Table 6–7. Although both sets of variables are defined on an ordered scale, it should not be assumed that this test *requires* that the sets be ordered. Very frequently the categories are similar

TABLE 6-7. Responses to the question concerning difficulty of a concept-learning test.

Treatment condition

Response variable	20 pretrials	15 pretrials	10 pretrials	0 pretrials	Total
Very easy	28	20	5	0	53
Average	6	9	17	10	42
Very hard	1	9	18	27	55
Total	35	38	40	37	150

to the following partition used for race:

{Caucasian, Oriental, Negro, Other}.

Clearly such sets cannot be ordered. In most applications of this test, neither the response classes nor the treatment conditions are ordered. When there is ordering, this test is not recommended, since better tests are available. These better tests are illustrated in Sections 8–5 and 16–10.

The experimental hypothesis of this example is that the perceived difficulty level of the test is related to the degree to which the original task has been learned by the students. At one level, it seems reasonable to assume that students who were given no previous training would experience the greatest difficulty, while at the other extreme it would be assumed that students with the most training would find the test the easiest. Visual inspection of the data supports these assumptions.

The hypothesis of the study to be tested is that the four trinomial probability distributions generated by the responses to the question are identical or that they are homogeneous. In statistical terms this reduces to:

$$H_0: \begin{vmatrix} P(A_1|B_0) \\ P(A_2|B_0) \\ P(A_3|B_0) \end{vmatrix} = \begin{vmatrix} P(A_1|B_{10}) \\ P(A_2|B_{10}) \\ P(A_3|B_{10}) \end{vmatrix} = \begin{vmatrix} P(A_1|B_{15}) \\ P(A_2|B_{15}) \\ P(A_3|B_{15}) \end{vmatrix} = \begin{vmatrix} P(A_1|B_{20}) \\ P(A_2|B_{20}) \\ P(A_3|B_{20}) \end{vmatrix} = \begin{vmatrix} P(A_1) \\ P(A_2) \\ P(A_3) \end{vmatrix}$$

Unfortunately, H_0 can be tested only against an *omnibus* alternative:

$$H_1: H_0 \text{ is false.}$$

Anything that will deny the truth of the hypothesis under test is considered as an appropriate alternative. Even though it is reasonable to expect certain ordered relations among the parameters as the manipulated experimental conditions vary, it is impossible to identify them with this test. For example, if H_0 is false, it is reasonable to assume that the parameters could satisfy the following sets of inequalities:

$$P(A_1|B_0) < P(A_1|B_{10}) < P(A_1|B_{15}) < P(A_1|B_{20})$$

or

$$P(A_3|B_0) > P(A_3|B_{10}) > P(A_3|B_{15}) > P(A_3|B_{20})$$

Unfortunately, H_0 could be rejected even if these relationships did *not* hold, because this test is *insensitive* to orderings on the variables.

If H_0 is true, then the best estimates of the common parameter values are:

$$\hat{p}_1 = \frac{28 + 20 + 5 + 0}{35 + 38 + 40 + 37} = \frac{53}{150} = 0.353,$$

$$\hat{p}_2 = \frac{6 + 9 + 17 + 10}{35 + 38 + 40 + 37} = \frac{42}{150} = 0.280,$$

$$\hat{p}_3 = \frac{1 + 9 + 18 + 27}{35 + 38 + 40 + 37} = \frac{55}{150} = 0.367.$$

The estimated expected frequencies are found by multiplying these relative frequencies by the three different sample sizes. The estimated expected frequencies are summarized in Table 6–8. Once the table is determined, it should be inspected

TABLE 6–8. The estimated expected frequencies for the data of Table 6–7.

Response variable	Treatment condition				Total
	20 pretrials	15 pretrials	10 pretrials	0 pretrials	
Very easy	12.37	13.43	14.13	13.07	53
Average	9.80	10.64	11.20	10.36	42
Very hard	12.83	13.93	14.67	13.57	55
Total	35	38	40	37	150

to ensure that all expected marginal frequencies equal those of the observed frequency table. Also, the estimated expected frequencies should be checked to see that they are greater than 5. Even if all expected frequencies do not exceed 5, there is evidence that one can still proceed with the test if less than 20 percent of the cells have estimated expected frequencies less than 5. In this case, all expected frequencies are greater than 5, so that one should reject H_0 with $\alpha = 0.05$ if $X^2 > X^2_{6;095} = 12.59$. In this case:

$$X^2 = \sum_{k=1}^{4} \sum_{i=1}^{3} \frac{\left[X_{ik} - \hat{E}(X_{ik})\right]^2}{\hat{E}(X_{ik})}$$

$$= \frac{(28 - 12.37)^2}{12.37} + \frac{(6 - 9.80)^2}{9.80} + \ldots + \frac{(27 - 13.57)^2}{13.57}$$

$$= 73.37$$

Since $X^2 = 73.37 > 12.59$, there is reason to doubt the truth of H_0. One can say that the probability distributions for the four experimental conditions are not the same.

For emphasis, it is worth repeating that the test of homogeneity described in this section is not dependent on an ordering of either the treatment or response variable. When they are not ordered, the test is optimum; however, when both variables are ordered, the test is not optimum. Instead, the tests described in Sections 8–5 or 16–10 are preferred. The reason for this is that the Karl Pearson statistic is

TABLE 6–9. *Homogeneity table generated from Table 6–7 by interchanging columns 2 and 3 and rows 1 and 2.*

	B_1	B_2	B_3	B_4	Total
A_1	6	17	9	10	42
A_2	28	5	20	0	53
A_3	1	18	9	27	55
Total	35	40	38	37	150

insensitive to permutations of frequencies across the rows and columns. For example, if the frequencies of columns 2 and 3 of Table 6–7 are interchanged and then if the frequencies of rows 1 and 2 of the resulting table are interchanged, one obtains the figures shown in Table 6–9. The value of chi-square for this table is also equal to $X^2 = 73.37$, although the interpretation of the findings is very different.

6–4. Partitioning of Chi-Square in Tests of Homogeneity

One of the important properties of variables whose sampling distribution is chi-square with v degrees of freedom is that of additiveness. For example, if two variables U_1 and U_2 are independently distributed as $X_{v_1}^2$ and $X_{v_2}^2$, respectively, then the sampling distribution of $U = U_1 + U_2$ is also chi-square, with $v = v_1 + v_2$. Surprisingly, there exists a converse to this statement, which essentially states that if U is chi-square with v degrees of freedom, then U can be partitioned into two independent components U_1 and U_2 that are each chi-square-distributed with v_1 and v_2 degrees of freedom if $v_1 + v_2 = v$. Together these statements convey the idea stated in Cochran's theorem, which incidentally gives the analysis of variance its nature. For completeness:

Cochran's Theorem. Suppose $U = U_1 + U_2 + \ldots + U_Q$ represents a partition of:

$$U = \sum_{k=1}^{K} Z_k^2$$

where each Z_k is independent $N(0, 1)$; then a necessary and sufficient condition that ensures independent distribution of each U_q such that U_1 is distributed as $X_{v_1}^2$, U_2 is distributed as $X_{v_2}^2, \ldots, U_Q$ is distributed as $X_{v_Q}^2$ is that $v_1 + v_2 + \ldots + v_Q = v_K$.

In theory, it is possible to take a variable that is distributed as chi-square with v degrees of freedom and partition it so as to produce v separate chi-square components, each of which are distributed as chi-square variables with one degree of freedom. While this partitioning is theoretically possible, it is, in practice, difficult to achieve. In this section, one possible approach will be illustrated for $2 \times K$ homogeneity tables. It is based on methods described by Maxwell (1961).

Reconsider the data matrix of Table 6–1. This represents a $2 \times K$ test of homogeneity with $v = K - 1$. Tables of this form can be decomposed so that the total X^2 can be partitioned into three components with degrees of freedom given by

$$v_1 = 1, \qquad v_2 = K_1 - 1, \qquad \text{and} \qquad v_3 = K_2 - 1$$

where $K = K_1 + K_2$. For this sort of partitioning, an analysis-of-chi-square table could be prepared as illustrated in Table 6–10. For this partitioning, one begins

TABLE 6–10. Analysis of chi-square for $2 \times K$ tests of homogeneity.

Source of variance	df	X^2
Difference between p_1 and p_2 of Group 1 and Group 2	1	X_1^2
Difference between proportions in Group 1	$K_1 - 1$	$X_{K_1-1}^2$
Difference between proportions in Group 2	$K_2 - 1$	$X_{K_2-1}^2$
Total	$K - 1$	X_{K-1}^2

by dividing the K columns into two groups on some rational basis suggested by the researcher, and forming a 2×2 Irwin–Fisher table. This gives rise to two two-column homogeneity tables. Within the resulting homogeneity tables, a test of homogeneity is performed across the columns that define each group of the 2×2 Irwin–Fisher table. If, in addition, the two resulting homogeneity tables can be partitioned, a researcher may do so, provided that the splits are reasonable and interpretable. In any case, the easiest way to present the method is by an example. For this reason, no formulas are presented and no derivation is provided.

EXAMPLE 6–4.1. As an example of partitioning of chi-square for a $2 \times K$ frequency table, consider the data of Table 6–3, for which $\hat{p}_0 = \frac{22}{44} = 0.5$ and $\hat{q}_0 = \frac{22}{44} = 0.5$. For these data, partitioning can be accomplished only for $K_1 = 2$ and $K_2 = 2$, since $K = K_1 + K_2 = 4$. The partitionings are shown in Tables 6–11, 6–12, and 6–13. As reported by Maxwell, the chi-square for each of these

TABLE 6–11. Comparison of required and requested doses of methadone by 44 test subjects, according to number of days they remained off heroin.

Days	Required doses	Requested doses	Total
Above median	15	7	22
Below median	6	16	22
Total	21	23	44

TABLE 6–12. *Comparison of required and voluntary encounter-group attendance in the 21 subjects required to take daily doses of methadone.*

Days	Required attendance	Voluntary attendance	Total
Above median	8	7	15
Below median	2	4	6
Total	10	11	21

tables can be computed as:

$$X_1^2 = \frac{1}{0.5(0.5)}\left[\frac{15^2}{21} + \frac{7^2}{23}\right] - \frac{22^2}{44} = 7.38$$

$$X_2^2 = \frac{1}{0.5(0.5)}\left[\frac{8^2}{10} + \frac{7^2}{11}\right] - \frac{15^2}{21} = 0.56$$

and

$$X_3^2 = \frac{1}{0.5(0.5)}\left[\frac{4^2}{10} + \frac{3^2}{13}\right] - \frac{7^2}{23} = 0.65$$

As indicated, the X^2 values are determined entirely from the first row of the resulting summary tables and the values of $\hat{p}_0$ and $\hat{q}_0$. In most applications, $\hat{p}_0$ and $\hat{q}_0$ will be different from 0.5. They are equal to 0.5 in this example only because of the nature of the median test.

TABLE 6–13. *Comparison of required and voluntary encounter-group attendance in the 23 subjects who take methadone on request.*

Days	Required attendance	Voluntary attendance	Total
Above median	4	3	7
Below median	6	10	16
Total	10	13	23

For these data, it is concluded that a significant difference exists between subjects who request methadone and those required to take the drug on a daily basis, since $X^2 = 7.39 > 3.84$, the 95th percentile value of X_1^2. The remaining two comparisons are not significant at $\alpha = 0.05$. With each test performed at $\alpha = 0.05$, the total error rate for the three tests is given by $\alpha_T \leq 0.15$. An alternative Type I error control is presented in Section 6–7. However, the important point of this presentation is that:

$$X_{Total}^2 = X_1^2 + X_2^2 + X_3^2$$

or, in terms of the observed data:

$$7.38 + 0.56 + 0.65 = 8.59$$

These results are summarized in an analysis of chi-square table, similar to Table 6–14.

TABLE 6–14. Analysis of chi-square for the data of Table 6–3.

Source of variance	df	Chi-square	Decision
Between required and requested doses of methadone	1	7.38	Sig.
Between required and voluntary attendance at encounter sessions for subjects on daily doses of methadone	1	0.56	N.S.
Between required and voluntary attendance at encounter sessions for subjects who receive methadone on request	1	0.65	N.S.
Total	3	8.59	

Other methods exist for the partitioning of chi-square. However, many of the methods require that the researcher examine components that, if proved to be significant, would be hard to interpret in a rational fashion. Fortunately, other methods based on the familiar theory of linear contrasts and planned and post hoc comparisons, be they orthogonal or nonorthogonal, exist. These methods are illustrated and discussed in Section 6–5.

6–5. Post Hoc Multiple Comparisons in Sample Proportions for Tests of Homogeneity

So far, tests for equality of proportions and medians have been presented as exact tests or as large-sample approximations to the exact statistics. Furthermore, it has been noted that the hypothesis tests are not limited to just two populations but extend to $K > 2$ independent populations. In the case of just two populations, rejection of the hypothesis of equality of the proportions or medians implies that the two populations sampled differ with respect to these parameters. The conclusions are less specific for the more-than-two-sample case, in which the hypothesis of equality of proportions or medians is tested against the omnibus alternative that the null hypothesis is false. In the former situation, planned confidence intervals can be used to estimate the magnitude of the difference between the two parameters. In the latter case, post hoc procedures are used, not merely to *estimate* the relevant differences but, primarily, to *identify* the causes for rejection of the null hypothesis. In Section 6–7 planned comparison methods similar to Dunn's method for parametric tests are examined.

The estimation procedures associated with the chi-square and median tests are multiple-comparison procedures analogous to Scheffé's and Tukey's multiple-comparison procedures for parametric tests. Although the Scheffé procedure has been described in Section 2–8, several terms will be introduced here to clarify the use of these procedures for the described tests of homogeneity. If the hypothesis of equal proportions or medians has been rejected, the relevant values to be estimated are the differences among the corresponding population proportions (or among the proportions exceeding the median). A statement of these differences may be written in summation form as:

$$\psi = (+1)p_1 + (-1)p_2$$

or

$$\psi = (+1)p_1 + (+1)p_2 + (-2)p_3$$

in which the resulting expression is a weighted sum of the population values of interest. Such a weighted sum, termed a *contrast*, is a combination of population values, subject to the restriction that the weights must add to zero. For each of the contrasts given as examples, this restriction is satisfied, since:

$$(+1) + (-1) = 0 \quad \text{and} \quad (+1) + (+1) + (-2) = 0$$

More generally, a contrast in the proportions may be written as:

$$\psi = a_1 p_1 + a_2 p_2 + \ldots + a_K p_K = \sum_{k=1}^{K} a_k p_k$$

where p_k denotes the population proportions, a_k denotes the weights, and

$$a_1 + a_2 + \ldots + a_K = \sum_{k=1}^{K} a_k = 0$$

To estimate the value of such a contrast, one substitutes the sample proportions for the unknown population proportions. Under this substitution:

$$\hat{\psi} = a_1 \hat{p}_1 + a_2 \hat{p}_2 + \ldots + a_K \hat{p}_K = \sum_{k=1}^{K} a_k \hat{p}_k$$

is the sample estimate of ψ.

The variance of a contrast, $\hat{\psi}$, is given by:

$$\text{Var}(\hat{\psi}) = \text{Var}\left[\sum_{k=1}^{K} a_k \hat{p}_k\right] = \sum_{k=1}^{K} a_k^2 \text{Var}(\hat{p}_k) = \sum_{k=1}^{K} a_k^2 \frac{p_k q_k}{n_k}$$

In most cases, the p_k are unknown and must be estimated from the data. When this occurs, $\text{Var}(\hat{\psi})$ is estimated by:

$$SE_{\hat{\psi}}^2 = \sum_{k=1}^{K} a_k^2 \frac{\hat{p}_k \hat{q}_k}{n_k}$$

Thus, for the contrasts used as examples, the squared standard error of:

$$\hat{\psi}_1 = \hat{p}_1 - \hat{p}_2 = (+1)\hat{p}_1 + (-1)\hat{p}_2$$

is given by:

$$SE_{\hat{\psi}_1}^2 = \sum_{k=1}^{K} a_k^2 \hat{V}\text{ar}(\hat{p}_k) = (+1)^2 \hat{V}\text{ar}(\hat{p}_1) + (-1)^2 \hat{V}\text{ar}(\hat{p}_2)$$

$$= \frac{\hat{p}_1 \hat{q}_1}{n_1} + \frac{\hat{p}_2 \hat{q}_2}{n_2}$$

For:

$$\hat{\psi}_2 = \hat{p}_1 + \hat{p}_2 - 2\hat{p}_3 = (+1)\hat{p}_1 + (+1)\hat{p}_2 + (-2)\hat{p}_3$$

the squared standard error is given by:

$$SE^2_{\hat{\phi}_2} = (+1)^2 \, \hat{V}ar(\hat{p}_1) + (+1)^2 \, \hat{V}ar(\hat{p}_2) + (-2)^2 \, \hat{V}ar(\hat{p}_3)$$

$$= \frac{\hat{p}_1 \hat{q}_1}{n_1} + \frac{\hat{p}_2 \hat{q}_2}{n_2} + 4\left(\frac{\hat{p}_3 \hat{q}_3}{n_3}\right)$$

Since the sample estimators of the population parameters are approximately normally distributed by application of the Central Limit theorem to large-sample estimators, the following theorem can be used to generate a set of confidence intervals for the contrasts, ψ:

Theorem. In the limit the probability is $(1 - \alpha)$ that, simultaneously for all contrasts, ψ:

$$\hat{\psi} - \sqrt{X^2_{K-1:(1-\alpha)}} \sqrt{SE^2_{\hat{\phi}}} < \psi < \hat{\psi} + \sqrt{X^2_{K-1:(1-\alpha)}} \sqrt{SE^2_{\hat{\phi}}}.$$

This theorem is used to generate multiple confidence intervals for the various contrasts of interest, such that the probability of one or more confidence intervals being significant when $H_0 : p_1 = p_2 = \ldots = p_K$ is true is no more than alpha. Because the probability of a Type I error is determined for the entire set of confidence intervals that could be set up, rather than for each separate confidence interval, the investigator is free to consider as many confidence intervals as are of interest, without suffering the penalty of an extremely high probability of some falsely significant results.

When the hypothesis $H_0 : p_1 = p_2 = \ldots = p_K$ has been rejected by a chi-square test of homogeneity, an investigator will ordinarily wish to determine the relationships among the $p_k(k = 1, 2, \ldots, K)$ that have led to its rejection. If he unwisely chooses to compare all of the sample proportions in a pairwise fashion by multiple Z or chi-square tests with $\alpha \leq \alpha_0$, the overall probability that one or more of these comparisons will be falsely significant is some indeterminate value between:

$$1 - (1 - \alpha_0)^{\binom{K}{2}} \quad \text{and} \quad \binom{K}{2} \alpha_0$$

When, for example, six different populations are studied, then the testing of each possible pair comparison at $\alpha = 0.05$ would result in the overall probability of at least one Type I error falling between $1 - (0.95)^{15} = 0.54$ and $15(0.05) = 0.75$. If the simultaneous confidence-interval procedure based on $\sqrt{X^2}$ is used, in place of multiple Z or X^2 tests, the overall probability of a Type I error can be fixed at 0.05 for the entire set of confidence intervals. In doing this the investigator sacrifices the shorter confidence intervals or more powerful tests of the multiple Z or X^2 procedure in exchange for the smaller probability of a Type I error to be gained from the use of the simultaneous $\sqrt{X^2}$ procedure. The simultaneous confidence-interval procedure based on $\sqrt{X^2}$ has a second advantage that also distinguishes it from multiple Z or X^2 tests. If the null hypothesis, $H_0 : p_1 = p_2 = \ldots = p_K$, is rejected at the alpha level by a chi-square test of homogeneity, then at least one confidence interval based on a weighted sum of the $p_1, p_2, \ldots, p_K$ will be statistically significant at the alpha level. This property of the simultaneous confidence interval procedure does not guarantee that the investigator will find a statistically significant pair comparison or that a significant confidence interval, when found, will be experimentally meaningful. On the other hand, it does assure the investigator that he has rejected the null hypothesis for cause, in that there is at least one nonzero contrast among the population proportions although it is not necessarily a simple one. The method of post hoc multiple comparisons is illustrated by an example.

EXAMPLE 6–5.1. In a study designed to measure the relationship between the number of learning trials and success in learning a list of 15 nonsense syllables, 180 subjects were assigned at random to one of six experimental conditions. Subjects in group 1 were given five trials in which to learn the list, subjects in group 2 were given ten trials, those in group 3, 15 trials, and so on. Several subjects who had been assigned to treatment groups failed to participate in the experiment, so that the actual sample consisted of 177 rather than 180 subjects. Resulting statistics are shown in Table 6–15.

TABLE 6–15. Statistics for the learning study of Example 6–5.1.

Sample values	Number of trials						Total
	5	10	15	20	25	30	
Number learning list	2	10	11	23	22	22	90
Number not learning list	28	20	18	7	8	6	87
Total	30	30	29	30	30	28	177
Proportion learning	0.067	0.333	0.379	0.767	0.733	0.786	
Square SE of proportion	0.00207	0.00741	0.00812	0.00596	0.00652	0.00601	

The investigator was interested in determining whether the number of trials had an effect on the subject's success in learning the list and, if there were an effect, whether it could be expressed mathematically in the form of a first- or second-degree equation representing a linear or quadratic trend over trials. The hypothesis of interest, $H_0: p_1 = p_2 = \ldots = p_6$, may be tested by the chi-square test of homogeneity presented in Section 6–2. For these data, X^2 is asymptotically distributed as chi-square with $K - 1 = 5$ degrees of freedom when the hypothesis of equal population proportions is true. A test at $\alpha = 0.05$ employs the decision rule:

D.R.: Reject H_0 if $X^2 > 11.07$

In this case, $X^2 = 51.28$ leads to rejection of the hypothesis of equal population proportions. Consequently, at least two of the parameters are statistically different from one another, or at least one of the contrasts of the parameters, $p_1, p_2, \ldots, p_6$ is significantly different from zero.

For this example, both simple pair comparisons and contrasts testing for the presence of linear and quadratic trend would probably be of interest to the investigator. If simple pair comparisons are considered, the contrasts will have the form $p_k - p_{k'} (k, k' = 1, 2, \ldots, K; k \neq k')$ and their variances will be estimated by:

$$SE_{\hat{\phi}}^2 = \frac{\hat{p}_k \hat{q}_k}{n_k} + \frac{\hat{p}_{k'} \hat{q}_{k'}}{n_{k'}}$$

The general form of the $(1 - \alpha)$ percent set of simultaneous confidence intervals about the contrasts will be given by:

$$\psi = (p_k - p_{k'}) = (\hat{p}_k - \hat{p}_{k'}) \pm \sqrt{X_{K-1:1-\alpha}^2} \sqrt{\frac{\hat{p}_k \hat{q}_k}{n_k} + \frac{\hat{p}_{k'} \hat{q}_{k'}}{n_{k'}}}$$

In this example:

$$S^* = \sqrt{X_{K-1:1-\alpha}^2} = \sqrt{3.33} = \sqrt{11.07} = 3.33$$

The fifteen simple contrasts of this example and their confidence limits are summarized in Table 6–16. Values marked by an asterisk signify that the corresponding confidence intervals are statistically significant at the 0.05 level and that the respective contrasts $\psi = p_k - p_{k'}$ are nonzero in value.

TABLE 6–16. Confidence intervals for the simple contrasts of Table 6–15.

Contrast ψ	Estimate $\hat{\phi}$	Estimated variance $SE_{\hat{Q}}^2$	Lower limit	Upper limit
$p_1 - p_2$	−0.266	0.00948	−0.590	0.058
$p_1 - p_3$	−0.312	0.01019	−0.648	0.024
$p_1 - p_4$	−0.700*	0.00803	−0.998	−0.402
$p_1 - p_5$	−0.666*	0.00859	−0.975	−0.347
$p_1 - p_6$	−0.719*	0.00808	−1.018	−0.420
$p_2 - p_3$	−0.046	0.01553	−0.462	0.370
$p_2 - p_4$	−0.434*	0.01337	−0.820	−0.048
$p_2 - p_5$	−0.400*	0.01393	−0.793	−0.007
$p_2 - p_6$	−0.453*	0.01342	−0.839	−0.057
$p_3 - p_4$	−0.388	0.01408	−0.784	0.008
$p_3 - p_5$	−0.354	0.01464	−0.757	0.049
$p_3 - p_6$	−0.407*	0.01413	−0.803	−0.011
$p_4 - p_5$	0.034	0.01248	−0.339	0.407
$p_4 - p_6$	−0.019	0.01197	−0.382	0.344
$p_5 - p_6$	−0.053	0.01253	−0.426	0.320

*Significant at $\alpha_T \leqq 0.05$.

Inspection of the confidence intervals indicates that the performance of subjects who have either five or 10 practice trials differs from the performance of subjects who have either 20, 25, or 30 practice trials. In addition, the performance of subjects who have 15 trials differs from the performance of subjects who have 30 trials.

An investigator interested in the nature of the relationship between the number of trials and success in learning might hypothesize that proportions of success have a linear or quadratic relationship with the number of practice trials. Under these hypotheses, a linear relationship between the number of practice trials and the proportion of success would be represented by the equation

$$p_k = \alpha + \beta X_k$$

while a quadratic relation would be given by

$$p_k = \beta_0 + \beta_1 X_k + \beta_2 X_k^2$$

These equations suggest that the investigator should consider regression theory in order to test his hypothesis that there is a linear or a quadratic relationship between number of practice trials and proportion of successes. Fortunately, the tests can also be performed within the context of multiple confidence intervals. In order to do so, it will be necessary to define the appropriate contrasts that should be used to test the null hypothesis that there are no linear and no quadratic relationships. The "weights" (a_k) to be used in the contrasts,

$$\psi_{\text{linear}} = a_1 p_1 + a_2 p_2 + \ldots + a_K p_K$$

and

$$\psi_{\text{quadratic}} = a_{1'} p_1 + a_{2'} p_2 + \ldots + a_{K'} p_K$$

are presented in Table A–9 for the case in which the K levels of the independent variable are equally spaced and where equal-sized samples have been taken at all levels. For example, if the independent variable has six equally spaced levels and one is interested in testing the hypothesis of no linear relationship, the coefficients as defined in Table A–9 show that:

$$\psi = -5p_1 - 3p_2 - 1p_3 + 1p_4 + 3p_5 + 5p_6$$

so that:

$$a_1 = -5, \qquad a_2 = -3, \qquad a_3 = -1, \qquad a_4 = 1, \qquad a_5 = 3, \qquad \text{and} \qquad a_6 = 5$$

EXAMPLE 6–5.2. The data of Table 6–15 satisfy the first requirement for the use of the tabled coefficients, equally spaced intervals of the independent variable, but not the second requirement, equal sample sizes. Although there are special techniques that permit the investigator to derive the correct orthogonal polynomials when the sample sizes differ, the departures from $n_k = 30$ are so slight in this illustration that the tabled values of the orthogonal polynomials will be used without correction.

The hypothesis of no linear trend can be tested by determining whether the contrast:

$$\psi_{\text{linear}} = -5p_1 - 3p_2 - 1p_3 + 1p_4 + 3p_5 + 5p_6$$

is significantly different from zero. A similar test of the hypothesis of quadratic trend is made by determining whether:

$$\psi_{\text{quadratic}} = 5p_1 - 1p_2 - 4p_3 - 4p_4 - 1p_5 + 5p_6$$

is significant. The estimated variances of these contrasts, $\hat{\psi}$, are given by:

$$SE_{\hat{\phi}}^2 = \sum_{k=1}^{6} a_k^2 \hat{V}ar(\hat{p}_k)$$

where the a_k are the orthogonal polynomials. Thus:

$$\hat{\psi}_{\text{linear}} = -5(0.067) - 3(0.333) - 1(0.379) + 1(0.767) + 3(0.733) + 5(0.786)$$
$$= 5.183$$

and

$$SE^2_{\hat{\phi}_L} = (-5)^2(0.00207) + (-3)^2(0.00741) + (-1)^2(0.00812) + 1^2(0.00596) +$$
$$3^2(0.00652) + 5^2(0.00601)$$
$$= 0.34145$$

while

$$\hat{\psi}_{\text{quadratic}} = 5(0.067) - 1(0.333) - 4(0.379) - 4(0.767) - 1(0.733) + 5(0.786)$$
$$= -1.385$$

and

$$SE^2_{\hat{\phi}_Q} = 5^2(0.00207) + (-1)^2(0.00741) + (-4)^2(0.00812) + (-4)^2(0.00596)$$
$$+ (-1)^2(0.00652) + 5^2(0.00601)$$
$$= 0.44121$$

The corresponding intervals are given by:

$$5.813 - 3.33\sqrt{0.34145} < \psi_{\text{linear}} < 5.813 - 3.33\sqrt{0.34145},$$
$$3.238 < \psi_{\text{linear}} < 7.128$$

and

$$-1.385 - 3.33\sqrt{0.44121} < \psi_{\text{quadratic}} < -1.385 + 3.33\sqrt{0.44121},$$
$$-3.496 < \psi_{\text{quadratic}} < 0.826$$

Since the interval for the linear contrast does not cross zero, a linear relationship for the proportions of success does exist. The interval for the quadratic component is not significant at the 0.05 level, so the investigator must conclude that no quadratic component is superimposed on the linear trend. Higher-order components could be studied in the same manner, although the interpretive difficulties that they may present diminish their practical value. Results are summarized graphically in Figure 6–1.

6–6. Multiple Comparisons for Proportions Based on the Arcsine Transformation

The use of the multiple-comparison procedures based on the chi-square distribution requires that the sample estimates, $\hat{p}_1, \ldots, \hat{p}_K$, be approximately normally distributed. Approximate normality of these estimators is ordinarily a consequence of large sample sizes, since as n_k becomes large the discrete binomial distribution is well approximated by the continuous normal distribution.

The researcher will sometimes be faced with the problem of comparing K different populations when at least some of the sample proportions have been based on small samples. Since approximate normality of the statistic $\hat{p}_k$ cannot be guaranteed in this case, a transformation of the $\hat{p}_k$ to variables that are approximately normally

Chi-Square Tests
of Homogeneity
of Proportions for
Qualitative
Variables in
Multiple
Independent
Samples

147

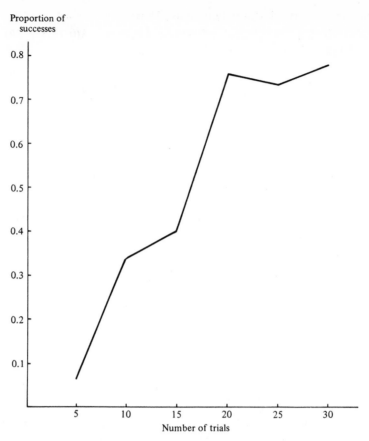

FIGURE 6–1. Relationship between number of trials and proportion of successes in learning 15 nonsense syllables.

distributed is desirable. The arcsine transformation,

$$\hat{\phi}_k = 2 \arcsin \sqrt{\hat{p}_k} \qquad \text{for } 0 < \hat{p}_k < 1,$$

$$= 2 \arcsin \sqrt{1/(4n_k)} \qquad \text{for } \hat{p}_k = 0$$

$$= \pi - 2 \arcsin \sqrt{1/(4n_k)} \qquad \text{for } \hat{p}_k = 1$$

is approximately normally distributed for small sample sizes, and its approximate variance,

$$\text{Var}(\hat{\phi}_k) \cong \frac{1}{n_k}$$

is independent of the unknown parameters ϕ_k and p_k. In addition, the estimated variance of $\hat{\phi}_k$ is nonzero even when $\hat{p}_k = 0$ or 1, while the estimated variance of the original variable, $\hat{p}_k$, is zero for these values.

Cohen (1967) suggested that the arcsine transformation be used in place of

$\hat{p}_k$ in the hypothesis test and interval-estimation procedures associated with the hypothesis $H_0: p_1 = p_2 = \ldots = p_K$. Because the transformation $\hat{\phi}_k = 2 \arcsin \sqrt{\hat{p}_k}$ is a one-to-one transformation and is approximately linear over the range of values $0.25 < \hat{p}_k < 0.75$ and over small intervals beyond this range, statements about the relationships among the ϕ_k will generally be comparable to statements about the original proportions. The values of $\hat{\phi}_k$ for $0 \le \hat{p}_k \le 1$ are found in Table A–10.

The appropriate test statistic for the hypothesis

$$H_0: p_1 = p_2 = \cdots = p_K \qquad \text{or, analogously,} \qquad H_0: \phi_1 = \phi_2 = \cdots = \phi_K = \phi_0$$

can be obtained by using a weighted least-squares procedure, as described in Section 2–10. The test statistic may seem more reasonable if one considers that:

$$Z_k = \frac{\hat{\phi}_k - \phi_0}{\sqrt{\text{Var}(\hat{\phi}_k)}}$$

is approximately $N(0, 1)$ if $\hat{\phi}_k$ is approximately normal. As a result,

$$Z_k^2 = \frac{(\hat{\phi}_k - \phi_0)^2}{\text{Var}(\hat{\phi}_k)}$$

is approximately X_1^2, so that, under the model of Section 2–10,

$$U = \sum_{k=1}^{K} Z_k^2 = \sum_{k=1}^{K} \frac{(\hat{\phi}_k - \phi_0)^2}{\text{Var}(\hat{\phi}_k)}$$

is approximately X_K^2. Since ϕ_0 is unknown, a single degree of freedom is used to estimate the unknown common ϕ_0 from the sample values. The weighted estimate is given by:

$$\hat{\phi}_0 = \frac{\sum_{k=1}^{K} w_k \hat{\phi}_k}{\sum_{k=1}^{K} w_k} = \frac{\sum_{k=1}^{K} \hat{\phi}_k / \text{Var}(\hat{\phi}_k)}{\sum_{k=1}^{K} 1 / \text{Var}(\hat{\phi}_k)} = \frac{\sum_{k=1}^{K} n_k \hat{\phi}_k}{\sum_{k=1}^{K} n_k}$$

With this substitution, the test statistic becomes:

$$U = \sum_{k=1}^{K} \frac{(\hat{\phi}_k - \hat{\phi}_0)^2}{\text{Var}(\hat{\phi}_k)} = \sum_{k=1}^{K} n_k (\hat{\phi}_k - \hat{\phi}_0)^2$$

Under H_0, U is distributed as Chi-square with $v = K - 1$ degrees of freedom.

EXAMPLE 6–6.1. As an example of the use of this test, consider the data of Table 6–17. On the basis of these data, the estimated common value ϕ_0 is given

TABLE 6–17. Data for central city students on percent of students representing a general cross section of the community.

Sample statistic	Region			
	Northeast	Great Lakes	Plains	Far West
Proportion, $\hat{p}_k$	0.550	0.675	0.228	0.929
Number of schools, n_k	36	21	6	12
$\hat{\phi}_k = 2 \arcsin \sqrt{\hat{p}_k}$	1.6710	1.9284	0.9956	2.6022
$\text{Var}(\hat{\phi}_k) = 1/n_k$	0.02778	0.04762	0.16667	0.08333

by:

$$\hat{\phi}_0 = \frac{\sum_{k=1}^{K} n_k \hat{\phi}_k}{\sum_{k=1}^{K} n_k}$$

$$= \frac{36(1.6710) + 21(1.9284) + 6(0.9956) + 12(2.6022)}{75}$$

$$= 1.8380.$$

The value of the test statistic is given by:

$$U = \sum_{k=1}^{K} n_k (\hat{\phi}_k - \hat{\phi}_0)^2$$

$$= 36(1.6710 - 1.8380)^2 + 21(1.9284 - 1.8380)^2$$
$$+ 6(0.9956 - 1.8380)^2 + 12(2.6022 - 1.8380)^2$$

$$= 12.44$$

The hypothesis of equal proportions of children from a "general cross section of the community" across the regions is rejected at the 0.05 level because the obtained test statistic, 12.44, exceeds 7.82, the chi-square value with three degrees of freedom at the 0.05 level.

Inspection of the data suggests that differences between the Plains and Far West, and perhaps between the Northeast and Great Lakes, combined versus each other region may account for the rejection of the null hypothesis. To check this conjecture, the investigator can apply the theorem on contrasts to the transformed variables, rather than to proportions.

For simple pair comparisons, the contrasts of interest would be:

$$\hat{\psi} = \hat{\phi}_k - \hat{\phi}_{k'} = (+1)\hat{\phi}_k + (-1)\hat{\phi}_{k'}, \qquad k \neq k'.$$

In this case, their variances can be determined directly as:

$$\text{Var}(\hat{\psi}) = (+1)^2 \text{Var}(\hat{\phi}_k) + (-1)^2 \text{Var}(\hat{\phi}_{k'}) = \frac{1}{n_k} + \frac{1}{n_{k'}}$$

and

$$S^* = \sqrt{X_{K-1:(1-\alpha)}^2} = \sqrt{X_{3:0.95}^2} = \sqrt{7.82} = 2.796$$

The summary data for the contrasts $\hat{\psi} = \hat{\phi}_k - \hat{\phi}_{k'}$ appear in Table 6–18.

TABLE 6–18. Confidence intervals for the pairwise contrasts of Table 6–17.

Pairwise contrast	Estimate	Estimated variance	Lower limit	Upper limit
$\psi_1 = \phi_1 - \phi_2$	−0.2574	0.07540	−1.0263	0.5115
$\psi_2 = \phi_1 - \phi_3$	0.6754	0.19445	−0.5576	1.9084
$\psi_3 = \phi_1 - \phi_4$	−0.9312*	0.11111	−1.8623	−0.0001
$\psi_4 = \phi_2 - \phi_3$	0.9328	0.21429	−0.3617	2.2273
$\psi_5 = \phi_2 - \phi_4$	−0.6738	0.13095	−1.6860	0.3384
$\psi_6 = \phi_3 - \phi_4$	−1.6066*	0.25000	−3.0046	−0.2086

*Significant at $\alpha \leq 0.05$.

A regional difference in the percentage of central-city students classified as from a "general cross section of the community" exists for the Northeast and Far West and for the Plains and Far West. No other pairwise comparisons are significant at the 0.05 level. Complex contrasts combining the results for the Northeast and Great Lakes regions would have the form:

$$\hat{\psi}_7 = (+1)\hat{\phi}_1 + (+1)\hat{\phi}_2 + (-2)\hat{\phi}_3$$
$$= (+1)(1.6710) + (1)(1.9284) + (-2)(0.9956) = 1.6082$$

and

$$\hat{\psi}_8 = (+1)\hat{\phi}_1 + (+1)\hat{\phi}_2 + (-2)\hat{\phi}_4$$
$$= (+1)(1.6710) + (+1)(1.9284) + (-2)(2.6022) = -1.6050$$

Their respective variances are given by:

$$\text{Var}(\hat{\psi}) = \sum_{k=1}^{K} a_k^2 \text{Var}(\hat{\phi}_k) = \sum_{k=1}^{K} \frac{a_k^2}{n_k},$$

so that the variances are:

$$\text{Var}(\hat{\psi}_7) = \frac{1}{n_1} + \frac{1}{n_2} + \frac{4}{n_3} = \frac{1}{36} + \frac{1}{21} + \frac{4}{6} = 0.74207$$

and

$$\text{Var}(\hat{\psi}_8) = \frac{1}{n_1} + \frac{1}{n_2} + \frac{4}{n_4} = \frac{1}{36} + \frac{1}{21} + \frac{4}{12} = 0.40873$$

Then the confidence intervals are:

$$\psi_7 = 1.6082 \pm 2.80\sqrt{0.74207}$$
$$= 1.6082 \pm 2.4122$$

and

$$\psi_8 = -1.6050 \pm 2.80\sqrt{0.40873}$$
$$= -1.6050 \pm 1.7899$$

neither of which is statistically significant.

6–7. Planned Multiple Comparisons in Sample Proportions for Tests of Homogeneity

Since the sample sizes $n_1, n_2, \ldots, n_K$, are fixed constants, the chi-square test of homogeneity is analogous to the classical F test of the analysis of variance. In essence, both tests examine equality of distribution. Because of this commonality, one might expect that the method of planned comparisons could be used in the analysis of homogeneity in the qualitative model. Such is the fact for $2 \times K$ tables as illustrated in the following example. As will be seen, a planned analysis differs from a post hoc analysis, in that the squared standard errors of the various contrasts are estimated under H_0 and not under H_1. This means that $\hat{p}_0$ and $\hat{q}_0$ are used for unknown parameters in the computations of the individual standard errors. This is analogous to the two-sample test of $p_1 = p_2$ and the corresponding confidence-interval procedure. In the test, $\hat{p}_0$ is used, but in the confidence intervals, $\hat{p}_1$ and $\hat{p}_2$ are employed.

EXAMPLE 6–7.1. Reconsider the data of Table 6–3 in the same way that it was examined in Table 6–14. The three one-degree-of-freedom partitions of the total X^2 correspond to the following three contrasts:

$$\psi_1 = \frac{n_1 p_1 + n_2 p_2}{n_1 + n_2} - \frac{n_3 p_3 + n_4 p_4}{n_3 + n_4}$$

$$\psi_2 = p_1 - p_2$$

$$\psi_3 = p_3 - p_4$$

which are estimated in the samples by:

$$\hat{\psi}_1 = \frac{8 + 7}{10 + 11} - \frac{4 + 3}{10 + 13} = \frac{15}{21} - \frac{7}{23} = 0.4099$$

$$\hat{\psi}_2 = \frac{8}{10} - \frac{7}{11} = 0.1636$$

$$\hat{\psi}_3 = \frac{4}{10} - \frac{3}{13} = 0.1692$$

The squared standard errors of these contrasts under H_0 are given by:

$$SE^2_{\hat{\psi}_1} = \left[\frac{n_1}{n_1 + n_2}\right]^2 \frac{\hat{p}_0 \hat{q}_0}{n_1} + \left[\frac{n_2}{n_1 + n_2}\right]^2 \frac{\hat{p}_0 \hat{q}_0}{n_2}$$

$$+ \left[\frac{-n_3}{n_3 + n_4}\right]^2 \frac{\hat{p}_0 \hat{q}_0}{n_3} + \left[\frac{-n_4}{n_3 + n_4}\right]^2 \frac{\hat{p}_0 \hat{q}_0}{n_4}$$

$$= \hat{p}_0 \hat{q}_0 \left[\frac{1}{n_1 + n_2} + \frac{1}{n_3 + n_4}\right]$$

$$= (0.5)(0.5)\left[\frac{1}{21} + \frac{1}{23}\right] = 0.0228,$$

$$SE^2_{\hat{\psi}_2} = \frac{\hat{p}_0 \hat{q}_0}{n_1} + \frac{\hat{p}_0 \hat{q}_0}{n_2} = \hat{p}_0 \hat{q}_0 \left[\frac{1}{n_1} + \frac{1}{n_2}\right]$$

$$= (0.5)(0.5)\left[\frac{1}{10} + \frac{1}{11}\right] = 0.0477,$$

$$SE^2_{\hat{\psi}_3} = \frac{\hat{p}_0 \hat{q}_0}{n_3} + \frac{\hat{p}_0 \hat{q}_0}{n_4} = \hat{p}_0 \hat{q}_0 \left[\frac{1}{n_3} + \frac{1}{n_4}\right]$$

$$= (0.5)(0.5)\left[\frac{1}{10} + \frac{1}{13}\right] = 0.0442$$

Under large-sample theory, it is known that any statistic of the form:

$$Z = \frac{\hat{\psi} - 0}{SE_{\hat{\psi}}}$$

is distributed as an $N(0, 1)$ variate. Thus,

$$Z^2 = \frac{\hat{\psi}^2}{SE^2_{\hat{\psi}}}$$

tends to approximate a chi-square variable with $\nu = 1$. For these three contrasts,

$$X_{\phi_1}^2 = \frac{0.4099^2}{0.0228} = 7.38$$

$$X_{\phi_2}^2 = \frac{0.1636^2}{0.0477} = 0.56$$

$$X_{\phi_3}^2 = \frac{0.1692^2}{0.0442} = 0.65$$

As might be expected,, these three values are identical to the values reported in Table 6–14.

In this case, the critical value for each of the one-degree-of-freedom tests can be determined from Table A–1. With three contrasts, the Dunn–Bonferroni value read from the right-hand column is given by $Z = 2.39$, so that any contrast that produces a X^2 value greater than $Z^2 = (2.39)^2 = 5.71$ is statistically significant. In this case, $\phi_1 \neq 0$.

6–8. Contrasts in the $I \times K$ Test of Homogeneity

Post hoc analysis of $I \times K$ tests of homogeneity is considerably more involved than the analysis of $2 \times K$ tables. For $I \times K$ tables, the critical value is defined as:

$$S^* = \sqrt{X_{(I-1)(K-1):1-\alpha}^2}$$

and for any (i, k)-cell,

$$\hat{p}_{ik} = \frac{X_{ik}}{n_{.k}}$$

produces an unbiased estimate of p_{ik}. Furthermore, the squared standard error of $\hat{p}_{ik}$ is given by:

$$SE_{\hat{p}_{ik}}^2 = \frac{\hat{p}_{ik}\hat{q}_{ik}}{n_{ik}}$$

where

$$\hat{q}_{ik} = 1 - \hat{p}_{ik}$$

These estimates are used in exactly the same fashion as for $I = 2$. The method is illustrated for the data of Table 6–7. In Section 8–10, a second method is illustrated that may also be used for post hoc investigations when null hypotheses are rejected.

EXAMPLE 6–8.1. If one focuses attention on the response category {Very Easy}, sample proportions are given by:

$$\hat{p}_{20} = \frac{28}{35} = 0.80, \quad \hat{p}_{15} = \frac{20}{38} = 0.53, \quad \hat{p}_{10} = \frac{5}{40} = 0.125$$

and

$$\hat{p}_0 = \frac{0}{37} = 0.00$$

with squared standard errors given by:

$$SE^2_{\hat{p}_{20}} = \frac{1}{35}\left[\frac{28}{35}\right]\left[\frac{7}{35}\right] = 0.0046$$

$$SE^2_{\hat{p}_{15}} = \frac{1}{38}\left[\frac{20}{38}\right]\left[\frac{18}{38}\right] = 0.0066$$

$$SE^2_{\hat{p}_{10}} = \frac{1}{40}\left[\frac{5}{40}\right]\left[\frac{35}{40}\right] = 0.0027$$

$$SE^2_{\hat{p}_{0}} = \frac{1}{37}\left[\frac{0}{37}\right]\left[\frac{37}{37}\right] = 0.0000$$

The confidence interval for $\psi_1 = p_{20} - p_{15}$ is given by:

$$\psi_1 = (\hat{p}_{20} - \hat{p}_{15}) \pm \sqrt{X^2_{(I-1)(K-1):(1-\alpha)}} \sqrt{SE^2_{\hat{p}_{20}} + SE^2_{\hat{p}_{15}}}$$

For the observed data:

$$S^* = \sqrt{X^2_{6:0.95}} = \sqrt{12.59} = 3.55$$

$$\psi_1 = (0.80 - 0.53) \pm 3.55 \sqrt{0.0046 + 0.0066}$$
$$= 0.27 \pm 3.55(0.1058)$$
$$= 0.27 \pm 0.38$$

indicating that the difference is not significant.

While one might like to test for a linear trend in the proportions, one soon learns that it cannot be done using orthogonal coefficients, since the spaces between the treatments are not of equal width. In addition, the squared standard error is not estimable since $\hat{p}_0 = 0.00$. In any case, a researcher can examine as many contrasts of interest as he wishes, by defining the probabilities of success in any specific row and then using the frequencies in the remaining rows to define the probabilities of failure. Finally, the multiplier for all resulting standard errors is given by $\sqrt{X^2_{(I-1)(K-1):(1-\alpha)}}$, the square root of the $(1 - \alpha)$-percentile value of the chi-square distribution with $v = (I - 1)(K - 1)$.

6–9. Explained Variance in Tests of Homogeneity

In recent years, behavioral scientists have tended to extend the notion of explained variability of classical correlation theory, as measured by the square of the sample correlation coefficients, to analysis-of-variance designs. Naturally, similar measures are of considerable interest in the qualitative sphere, but until now such measures have not been available or, if available, not always appropriate. Light and Margolin (1971) have proposed a measure that is appropriate, easily interpreted, and not difficult to compute. Their measure is described and examined in this section.

The method is based on a little-known formula for calculating the sample variance. For this method, let $Y_1, Y_2, \ldots, Y_n$ represent n observations from some population of interest. Let the difference between any two observations be denoted by $d_{jj'} = Y_j - Y_{j'}$. In terms of these differences, the sample variance is given by:

$$S^2 = \frac{SS}{n-1} = \frac{1/2n \sum_{j=1}^{n} \sum_{j'=1}^{n} d_{jj'}^2}{n-1} = \frac{\sum_{j=1}^{n} \sum_{j'=1}^{n} d_{jj'}^2}{2n(n-1)}.$$

EXAMPLE 6–9.1.   As an example of the use of this formula, let the ordered observed values of a sample be given by 3, 7, 11, 16, 23. By the definitional formula of a sample variance:

$$S^2 = \frac{(3-12)^2 + (7-12)^2 + (11-12)^2 + (16-12)^2 + (23-12)^2}{5-1}$$

$$= \frac{244}{4} = 61$$

In terms of the formula based on paired differences,

$$
\begin{aligned}
S^2 = \{&(3-7)^2 + (3-11)^2 + (3-16)^2 + (3-23)^2 + (7-3)^2 \\
+ &(7-11)^2 + (7-16)^2 + (7-23)^2 + (11-3)^2 + (11-7)^2 \\
+ &(11-16)^2 + (11-23)^2 + (16-3)^2 + (16-7)^2 + (16-11)^2 \\
+ &(16-23)^2 + (23-3)^2 + (23-7)^2 + (23-11)^2 \\
+ &(23-16)^2\}/[(2)(5)(5-1)]
\end{aligned}
$$

$$= \frac{2440}{40} = 61$$

This formula can be extended to cover qualitative data. For this extension, let A be a variable that can be partitioned into a set of mutually exclusive and exhaustive subsets $\{A_1, A_2, \ldots, A_I\}$, and let $Y_1, Y_2, \ldots, Y_n$ be elements of A. Consider two elements, Y_j and $Y_{j'}$. Clearly, if Y_j and $Y_{j'}$ are members of the same set, then their difference $d_{jj'} = 0$. If Y_j and $Y_{j'}$ are members of different sets, let their difference be quantified as $d_{jj'} = 1$. With this formulation,

$$SS = \frac{1}{2n} \sum_{j=1}^{n} \sum_{j'=1}^{n} d_{jj'}^2$$

$$= \frac{1}{2n} \sum_{j=1}^{n} \sum_{j'=1}^{n} d_{jj'}$$

since $d_{jj'}^2 = d_{jj'}$.

Consider the data matrix of Table 6–6. With the notation of this table:

$$n = X_{1.} + X_{2.} + \ldots + X_{I.}$$

where $X_{i.}$ equals the number of Y_j that are elements of A_j. Consider the $X_{1.}$ objects that have property A_1. Each of these objects is different from the remaining $X_{2.} + X_{3.} + \ldots + X_{I.}$ objects. Thus, when any given object of A_1 is paired with an object that is not in A_1, it contributes $(X_{2.} + X_{3.} + \ldots + X_{I.})$ units to $\sum_{j=1}^{n}\sum_{j'=1}^{n} d_{jj'}$, so that the entire collection of $X_{i.}$ objects that are elements of A_1 contribute $X_{1.}(X_{2.} +$

$X_{3.} + \ldots + X_{I.}$) units to the $\sum_{j=1}^{n} \sum_{j'=1}^{n} d_{jj'}$. Repeating this argument for each row total, it then follows that:

$$\sum_{j=1}^{n} \sum_{j'=1}^{n} d_{jj'} = X_{1.}(X_{2.} + X_{3.} + \ldots + X_{I.})$$
$$+ X_{2.}(X_{1.} + X_{3.} + \ldots + X_{I.}) + \ldots$$
$$+ X_{I.}(X_{1.} + X_{2.} + \ldots + X_{I-1})$$
$$= n^2 - \sum_{i=1}^{I} X_{i.}^2$$

so that

$$\sum_{i=1}^{I} \sum_{i'=1}^{I} X_{i.} X_{i'.} = n^2 - \sum_{i=1}^{I} X_{i.}^2$$

Thus, for the marginal totals,

$$SST = \frac{1}{2n}\left[n^2 - \sum_{i=1}^{I} X_{i.}^2\right] = \frac{n}{2} - \frac{1}{2n} \sum_{i=1}^{I} X_{i.}^2$$

Consider column 1 of Table 6–6. For this column, the above formula is given by:

$$SS_1 = \frac{n_{.1}}{2} - \frac{1}{2n_{.1}} \sum_{i=1}^{I} X_{1k}^2$$

Hence, across the K columns,

$$SS_1 + SS_2 + \ldots + SS_K = SSW$$

corresponds to the sum of squares within groups of a classical one-way analysis of variance for quantitative variables. In terms of the notation of Table 6–6,

$$SSW = \sum_{k=1}^{K} \frac{n_{.k}}{2} - \sum_{k=1}^{K} \frac{1}{2n_{.k}} \sum_{i=1}^{I} X_{ik}^2$$

$$= \frac{n}{2} - \frac{1}{2} \sum_{k=1}^{K} \frac{1}{n_{.k}} \sum_{i=1}^{I} X_{ik}^2$$

Continuing with the correspondence to the classical ANOVA model, it follows that:

$$SSB = SST - SSW$$

$$= \left[\frac{n}{2} - \frac{1}{2n} \sum_{i=1}^{I} X_{i.}^2\right] - \left[\frac{n}{2} - \frac{1}{2} \sum_{k=1}^{K} \frac{1}{n_{.k}} \sum_{i=1}^{I} X_{ik}^2\right]$$

$$= \frac{1}{2} \sum_{k=1}^{K} \frac{1}{n_{.k}} \sum_{i=1}^{I} X_{ik}^2 - \frac{1}{2n} \sum_{i=1}^{I} X_{i.}^2$$

Finally, the Light–Margolin measure of explained variance is given simply as:

$$\hat{R}_{LM}^2 = \frac{SSB}{SST}$$

the same equation used to define the correlation ratio of regression and analysis-of-variance designs.

As shown by Light and Margolin, $R^2 = 0$ when the hypothesis of homogeneity is true and $R^2 = 1$ when all the frequencies in a given column are localized in the cells of one row. They also showed that:

$$X_{LM}^2 = (n - 1)(I - 1)\hat{R}_{LM}^2$$

is asymptotically chi-square with $v = (I - 1)(K - 1)$.

EXAMPLE 6–9.2. The use of the Light and Margolin statistic is illustrated for the data of Table 6–7. For these data,

$$SST = \frac{150}{2} - \frac{1}{2(150)}(53^2 + 42^2 + 55^2) = 49.6733$$

$$SSW = \frac{150}{2} - \frac{1}{2}\left[\frac{28^2 + 6^2 + 1^2}{35} + \cdots + \frac{0^2 + 10^2 + 27^2}{37}\right] = 36.6990$$

$$SSB = 49.6733 - 36.6990 = 12.9743$$

$$\hat{R}^2_{LM} = \frac{12.9743}{49.6733} = 0.2612$$

and

$$X^2_{LM} = (150 - 1)(3 - 1)(0.2612) = 77.84$$

which, with $v = (3 - 1)(4 - 1) = 6$, leads to a rejection of $H_0 : R^2_{LM} = 0$ at $\alpha \leq 0.05$. Following the Light and Margolin model, results can be summarized in a categorical analysis-of-variance table as shown in Table 6–19.

TABLE 6–19. The categorial analysis-of-variance table for the data of Table 6–7.

Source	SS	$\hat{R}^2_{LM}$	X^2_{LM}
Between pretrials	12.97	0.26	77.84
Within pretrials	36.70		
Total	49.67		

Finally, it should be noted that the Light–Margolin statistic $X^2_{LM} = 77.84$ is larger than the Karl Pearson statistic $X^2 = 73.77$. In an empirical sampling study, Light and Margolin have shown that X^2_{LM} tends to exceeds X^2, indicating that their method of analysis is more powerful than the traditional test of homogeneity and is therefore strongly recommended.

Summary

In this chapter, a detailed discussion of tests of homogeneity for qualitative variables was presented. If the data matrix is as portrayed in Table 6–6, the hypothesis of identity of distribution for the categories $A_1, A_2, \ldots, A_I$, across the K populations $B_1, B_2, \ldots, B_K$, should be rejected if the Karl Pearson statistic,

$$X^2 = \sum_{k=1}^{K}\sum_{i=1}^{I}\frac{[X_{ik} - \hat{E}(X_{ik})]^2}{\hat{E}(X_{ik})},$$

exceeds the $(1 - \alpha)$-percentile point of the chi-square distribution with $v = (K - 1)(I - 1)$.

If H_0 is rejected, a post hoc analysis of the data can be performed by means of contrasts of the form

$$\psi = a_1 p_{i1} + a_2 p_{i2} + \cdots + a_K p_{iK}$$

where $a_1 + a_2 + \cdots + a_K = 0$, with

$$\hat{\psi} = a_1 \hat{p}_{i1} + a_2 \hat{p}_{i2} + \cdots + a_K \hat{p}_{iK}$$

and

$$SE_{\hat{\psi}}^2 = a_1^2 \frac{\hat{p}_{i1} \hat{q}_{i1}}{n_{.1}} + a_2^2 \frac{\hat{p}_{i2} \hat{q}_{i2}}{n_{.2}} + \cdots + a_k^2 \frac{\hat{p}_{iK} \hat{q}_{iK}}{n_{.K}}$$

If the confidence interval for ψ:

$$\psi = \hat{\psi} \pm \sqrt{X^2_{(K-1)(I-1):1-\alpha}}\, SE_{\hat{\psi}}$$

covers zero, it is concluded that $\psi = 0$; otherwise, it is concluded that $\psi \neq 0$.

One frequently encountered special case of this model occurs when $I = 2$. Under this model, the dependent variable is binomially distributed, so that the test reduces to the K-sample analog of the two-sample Irwin–Fisher test. Furthermore, in this form, the test can be used to test the hypothesis that K populations have equal medians. If the combined median of the K samples is denoted by $\hat{M}_0$, the test that all $P(Y_k > \hat{M}_0)$ are equal to a common value serves as a test that all populations have identical medians, provided that $\hat{M}_0$ is identical to or close to the population median value. In this form, the median test can be viewed as a competitor to the classical one-way analysis of variance.

If the hypothesis of identical medians is rejected, one can perform a post hoc analysis on the data that indirectly focuses on contrasts in the medians. In particular, one can examine pairwise contrasts in the probabilities of exceeding $\hat{M}_0$, to determine differences in medians. If

$$\psi = (\hat{p}_k - \hat{p}_{k'}) \pm \sqrt{X^2_{K-1:1-\alpha}} \sqrt{\frac{\hat{p}_k \hat{q}_k}{n_k} + \frac{\hat{p}_{k'} \hat{q}_{k'}}{n_{k'}}}$$

fails to cover zero, it can be concluded that $M_k \neq M_{k'}$. In almost all cases, this decision will be correct.

The choice of the sample median as the basis for subdividing each of the K groups into mutually exclusive and exhaustive subgroups is arbitrary. Any percentiles or quantiles of interest to the researcher can be used to categorize the K groups into equal numbers of mutually exclusive and exhaustive subgroups. One common choice is to use the sample quantiles to form the four subgroups:

$$Y > \hat{Q}_3, \qquad \hat{Q}_2 < Y < \hat{Q}_3, \qquad \hat{Q}_1 < Y < \hat{Q}_2, \qquad Y < \hat{Q}_1$$

and create a $4 \times K$ homogeneity table. If the sample estimates of the quantiles $\hat{Q}_3$, $\hat{Q}_2$, and $\hat{Q}_1$ are equal to their respective population values Q_3, Q_2, and Q_1, then the resulting test of homogeneity is a test of equal quantiles. This quantile test is a special case of the chi-square test of homogeneity, and can be viewed as a more sensitive test of homogeneity than the median test. As expected, the sensitivity of the percentile-type tests increases as the number of intervals increases. In the limit, intervals reduce to original observations, and at that point, the percentile tests are identical to the test of Kolmogorov and Smirnov, discussed in Sections 10–3 and 10–4, which is optimum.

If $I = 2$ and the sample sizes are small, then the Karl Pearson statistic is not recommended because it is known that the approximation to the exact distribution will not be adequate if the $\hat{E}(X_{1k})$ and $\hat{E}(X_{2k})$ are less than 5 in numerical value. If this should occur, one can use the Cohen model based on the theory of Section 6–6 to achieve a transformation to a computable test statistic. For this model, each $\hat{p}_k$ is transformed by the equation:

$$\hat{\phi}_k = 2 \arcsin \sqrt{\hat{p}_k}$$

and the hypothesis of identical p values is rejected if:

$$U = \sum_{k=1}^{K} n_k (\hat{\phi}_k - \hat{\phi}_0)^2$$

exceeds $X^2_{K-1:1-\alpha}$, the $(1 - \alpha)$-percentile point of the X^2 distribution, with $v = K - 1$. In this case, one must first compute $\hat{\phi}_0$, the best estimate of the common $\hat{\phi}_0$ as:

$$\hat{\phi}_0 = \frac{\sum_{k=1}^{K} n_k \hat{\phi}_k}{\sum_{k=1}^{K} n_k}$$

before U can be evaluated. If the hypothesis of equal ϕ_k values is rejected, one can identify reasons for the rejection by examining contrasts in the ϕ_k with:

$$\hat{\psi} = a_1 \hat{\phi}_1 + a_2 \hat{\phi}_2 + \ldots + a_K \hat{\phi}_K$$

$$\mathrm{Var}(\hat{\psi}) = \frac{a_1^2}{n_1} + \frac{a_2^2}{n_2} + \ldots + \frac{a_K^2}{n_K}$$

and

$$S^* = \sqrt{X^2_{K-1:1-\alpha}}$$

For the special case in which $I = 2$, one can achieve a partition of X^2 into three components, with degrees of freedom given by $v_1 = 1$, $v_2 = K_1 - 1$, and $v_3 = K_2 - 1$, where $K = K_1 + K_2$. This method, developed by Maxwell, is extremely versatile and can be applied repeatedly to v_2 and v_3 to obtain a series of one-degree-of-freedom tests of homogeneity that are actually simple 2×2 Irwin–Fisher tests of equal binomial probabilities.

Finally, the Light and Margolin measure of explained variance for tests of homogeneity was presented. This statistic, based on the notion of variance for qualitative variables, is computed simply as:

$$\hat{R}^2_{\mathrm{LM}} = \frac{SSB}{SST}$$

where

$$SSB = \frac{1}{2} \sum_{k=1}^{K} \frac{1}{n_{.k}} \sum_{i=1}^{I} X_{ik}^2 - \frac{1}{2n} \sum_{i=1}^{K} X_i^2.$$

and

$$SST = \frac{n}{2} - \frac{1}{2n} \sum_{i=1}^{I} X_i^2.$$

As shown by Light and Margolin, one can test the hypothesis of homogeneity by referring:

$$X_{LM}^2 = (n - 1)(I - 1)\hat{R}_{LM}^2$$

to the chi-square distribution with $v = (K - 1)(I - 1)$. If $X_{LM}^2 > X_{(K-1)(I-1):1-\alpha}^2$, then the hypothesis of identical distributions is rejected.

Exercises

*1. A group of 100 workers and 30 managers was studied in a Kibbutz with respect to the reward that authority over other persons gave them. The 130 subjects of the study were asked:

How much personal reward and satisfaction do you gain or derive from having authority over other people?

    1. Very little 2. Little 3. A medium amount 4. Much 5. Very much

Responses are as shown in the accompanying table.

Reward	Worker	Manager
Very much	4	6
Much	15	12
A medium amount	33	9
Little	24	2
Very Little	24	1
Total	100	30

Use the methods of this chapter to analyze these data.
a) What are H_0 and H_1?
b) If H_0 is rejected, do a post hoc analysis on the data.
c) What assumptions have you made? Are they reasonable? Explain.
d) Determine the Light and Margolin measure of explained variance. What does it say about the variables under study?

*2. Note that the analysis of Exercise 1 could be achieved through five planned comparisons within each response category. Do this planned analysis and compare the results to the post hoc procedure of Exercise 1. Which method is more powerful? What evidence is there to support your claim?

*3. The response variable of Exercise 1 is ordered from "very little" to "very much". How does the chi-square test of homogeneity take this order effect into account? Explain this in terms of the study of Exercise 1.

*4. In a study of productivity and recognition, the names of 75 researchers who had published in journals read by psychologists were obtained. The 75 researchers were classified according to the number of journal articles they had published. The classification is as follows:

    Few   0 to 10
    Many   11 to 30
    Very many 31 or more

Two names were selected from each group in a preassigned manner and then the list of six

Number of publications

Contribution	0 to 10	11 to 30	31 or more	Total
Low	140	62	7	209
Medium	15	112	49	176
High	45	26	144	215
Total	200	200	200	600

names was given to a random sample of 100 psychologists at an annual convention. The psychologists were asked to rate each researcher on the list according to the contribution made to psychology. Ratings were to be Low, Medium, and High. Results are as shown below.

a) Test the hypothesis of homogeneity by means of the Karl Pearson statistic.

b) What assumptions have you made? Are they reasonable? Explain.

*5. Determine the Light and Margolin measure of explained variance for the data of Exercise 4. Test H_0: $R^2_{LM} = 0$ against H_1: $R^2_{LM} > 0$. Compare the Karl Pearson statistic, X^2, of Exercise 4 to the Light and Margolin X^2_{LM}. Which test is more powerful? Why?

*6. In a study of manager mobility in a large industrial plant, managers were divided by age into two groups: {Under 35, Over 35}. Each manager was classified by his supervisors as: {Upward bound, Stationary, Downward bound}. Later, each manager was asked:

Is your job and work the main interest of your life?

Yes _____ No _____ .

Results are as shown in the accompanying table.

a) Use the method of Section 6–2 to analyze these data.

b) Analyze the pairwise difference by a post hoc and by a planned analysis. Are there any differences in the decisions reached by the two methods? Which method would you recommend? Why?

Age

Mobility response	Under 35			Over 35		
	Up	Stat.	Down	Up	Stat.	Down
Yes	26	13	12	45	12	15
No	12	14	23	15	38	36
Total	38	27	35	60	50	51

*7. Each age category of Exercise 6 represents a 2 × 3 test of homogeneity, in which one of the variables is ordered.

a) For each age category, perform the test for trend described in Section 6–5.

b) What are the hypotheses under test? (See Section 3–16.)

*8. Analyze the data of Exercise 4 according to the procedures outlined in Section 6–5.

*9. In the partition of chi-square as defined in Section 6–4, perform a trend analysis on each of the subsets of Exercise 6, defined by "Under 35" and "Over 35". Compare the methods of Exercises 6, 7, and 8, with that of this exercise. Which method would you recommend? Why?

*10. For the data of Exercise 6, compute:

a) $\hat{\psi} = \hat{\psi}_{\text{linear}}^{\text{under 35}} - \hat{\psi}_{\text{linear}}^{\text{over 35}}$

b) $SE_{\hat{\psi}}^2 = SE_{\hat{\psi}\,\text{linear}}^2 \, \text{under 35} + SE_{\hat{\psi}\,\text{linear}}^2 \, \text{over 35}$

c) $X^2 = \dfrac{\hat{\psi}^2}{SE_{\hat{\psi}}^2}$

d) What is H_0 and what do the results indicate?

*11. Determine the Light and Margolin measure of explained variance for the data of Exercise 6.

*12. Determine the three Light and Margolin measures of explained variance for the partitioned chi-squares generated in the analysis of Exercise 9. Does the sum of the three Light and Margolin measures have any relationship to the Light and Margolin measure determined in Exercise 11?

*13. In a study in which college students' perceptions of the Watts riots as a statement of social protest were being investigated, the more than 800 students enrolled in a large freshman chemistry class were given an inventory to determine their attitudes toward Blacks. Students were classified as having favorable, neutral, or unfavorable attitudes. Among the two extreme groups, 40 males and 40 females were selected at random and asked:

Is protest a legitimate means of expressing displeasure over discrimination?
Yes _____   No _____

Results are as shown in the table.
Use the partitioned chi-square method of Section 6 to analyze these data.

Attitude toward Blacks

Endorsement of protest	Favorable		Unfavorable	
	Males	Females	Males	Females
Yes	33	26	19	9
No	7	14	21	31
Total	40	40	40	40

*14. In the study of Exercise 13, 40 males and 40 females who were neutral were also asked their opinion. Results are as shown below. Use the methods of this chapter to analyze these data.

Sex

Attitude	Male			Female		
	Favorable	Neutral	Unfavorable	Favorable	Neutral	Unfavorable
Yes	33	32	19	26	22	9
No	7	8	21	14	18	31
Total	40	40	40	40	40	40

*15. Apply the median test to X_3: (paragraph meaning scores) across the three social classes represented in the table of data for Exercise 10 of Chapter 10. If H_0 is rejected, perform a post hoc analysis to determine which medians differ. Compare the analysis to the classical F test and post hoc procedure. Explain what you observe in this comparison.

*16. Use the Cohen procedure of Section 6–7 to analyze the data of Table 5–10.

*17. Use the methods of this chapter to analyze the data of Exercise 8 in Chapter 5. Compare the methods of this chapter to those used in the previous analysis. Which method would you recommend? Why?

*18. Use the methods of Section 6–4 to test for differences among the three religious groups of Exercise 9 in Chapter 5, according to the two categories of church attendance.

*19. The data in the accompanying table are based on the running of 72 maze-dull rats through a maze. Twenty-four of the rats had been deprived of food and water for two days; another 24 had been deprived for one day, and the remaining 24 had all the food and water they wanted. The dependent variable, Y, is the total number of wrong turns each rat took over 10 trials in reaching the goal box. Determine $\hat{Q}_1$, $\hat{Q}_2$, $\hat{Q}_3$ and classify each rat according to the categories $X < \hat{Q}_1, \hat{Q}_1 \leq X < \hat{Q}_2, \hat{Q}_2 \leq X < \hat{Q}_3$, and $X \geq \hat{Q}_3$. Perform a three-group quartile test on the resulting 4×3 table of frequencies. What are H_0 and H_1? Which pairwise contrasts are significant at $\alpha \leq 0.05$? Compare these results with those of the classical F test applied to the same data.

Group 1	Group 2	Group 3
2 Days' deprivation	1 Day's deprivation	0 Day's deprivation
6	2	0
6	2	0
7	3	1
7	7	1
8	7	1
12	12	1
13	12	2
14	12	7
15	13	8
20	16	8
26	17	9
27	18	10
28	19	12
28	19	13
29	19	16
30	21	18
35	23	26
38	26	27
40	29	27
47	30	27
50	35	28
56	36	29
57	40	30
69	43	34

Chi-Square Tests of Homogeneity of Proportions for Qualitative Variables in Multiple Independent Samples

Chi-Square Tests of Homogeneity of Proportions for Qualitative Variables in Correlated Samples

7–1. Correlated Proportions

The methods presented in the previous chapters have been based, for the most part, on the assumption that observations between and within samples are statistically independent. Frequently, studies are encountered where one or both of these assumptions are not satisfied. A simple way to illustrate the violation of these assumptions and the appearance of statistical dependence between observations is to consider the following three examples, which serve as prototypes for the methods described in this chapter. As will be apparent, these models are often encountered in attitude-change studies, investigations of organizational stability, problems in psychometrics, and other types of studies. Since these methods are not well known, procedures described in the previous chapters are often erroneously used to attack the research questions examined in this chapter. These errors are unnecessary and unfortunate. Furthermore, a number of the methods described in this chapter are the most powerful available for specific hypotheses, and in many cases are without viable competition. For that reason, they are worth knowing and using.

EXAMPLE 7–1.1. Consider an investigator who was interested in studying the changes in an audience's attitude toward the position espoused by a low-credibility communicator. Measures of agreement or disagreement were obtained for a random sample of 78 high-school seniors following a talk by the school principal, a low-credibility speaker, on regular VD checkups. Results are shown in Table

TABLE 7–1. Frequency of agreement with a low-credibility speaker at times 1 and 2.

Time 1 \ Time 2	Agree	Disagree	Total
Agree	30	6	36
Disagree	18	24	42
Total	48	30	78

7–1 for observations made immediately after the talk and after a one-month delay. Specifically, the experimenter predicted that over time there would be a greater probability of change toward agreement with the low-credibility speaker than toward disagreement. This prediction was made because it was believed that failure to identify the topic with the school principal over a period of time would result in increased acceptance of the views of the communicator.

EXAMPLE 7–1.2. Sponsorship and organizational stability in a national probability sample of Boy Scout troops were studied in a longitudinal study covering the period from 1958 to 1966. It was hypothesized that any changes in the sponsorship of the scout troops over the eight-year period would favor national rather than local sponsorship, since the former was assumed to be a more stable affiliation than the latter. The data for level of troop sponsorship in 1958 and in 1966 are given in Table 7–2.

EXAMPLE 7–1.3. Students participating in an experiment dealing with response latency were presented with booklets consisting of four problems. The problems were arranged in all possible permutations of four, and each student worked all four problems. No overall practice effects were found for the problems. The investigator wished to determine whether the problems differed in difficulty as

TABLE 7–2. Frequency of sponsorship states of Boy Scout troops at two different time periods.

1958 \ 1966	National organization	Local school	Local nonschool	Total
National organization	48	4	5	57
Local school	2	9	2	13
Local nonschool	20	3	29	52
Total	70	16	36	122

TABLE 7–3. Frequency of correct solutions to each of four problems by 39 subjects.

Subject number	Problem number				Total for all four problems
	1	2	3	4	
1	0	0	0	1	1
2	1	0	1	1	3
3	0	1	1	0	2
4	0	0	1	1	2
5	0	0	1	1	2
6	0	0	0	1	1
7	0	0	1	1	2
8	0	1	1	1	3
9	0	0	1	0	1
10	0	0	0	0	0
11	1	0	1	1	3
12	0	0	0	1	1
13	0	0	0	1	1
14	0	0	0	0	0
15	1	1	1	1	4
16	0	0	1	1	2
17	1	0	1	1	3
18	1	1	1	1	4
19	0	0	1	1	2
20	0	0	0	0	0
21	0	0	0	1	1
22	0	0	1	1	2
23	1	0	1	0	2
24	1	0	1	1	3
25	1	0	1	1	3
26	1	0	0	0	1
27	0	0	0	0	0
28	0	0	1	1	2
29	1	0	1	1	3
30	0	0	0	1	1
31	0	0	0	0	0
32	0	0	0	1	1
33	0	1	0	1	2
34	0	0	1	1	2
35	0	0	0	1	1
36	1	0	0	0	1
37	1	1	1	1	4
38	0	1	0	1	2
39	0	1	0	1	2
Total	12	8	21	29	70

measured by the proportion of students solving each problem correctly. For these data, shown in Table 7–3, a "1" denotes a correct solution and a "0" an incorrect solution.

In each of these examples, the use of a chi-square test of homogeneity of the proportions would be open to serious question because the proportions are correlated. Instead of assuming that responses to the individual items come from independent, univariate distributions, it must be assumed that the responses are observations from a multivariate distribution of categorical variables. The task is to determine whether the corresponding marginal probabilities for these distributions are equal.

7–2. The McNemar Test For 2 × 2 Tables

In the case of a 2 × 2 table, an exact test of equality of the proportions can be found by using the binomial distribution. A large-sample approximate test can be used based on the chi-square distribution or on the standard-normal distribution (McNemar, 1947).

The attitude consistency problem of Example 7–1.1 is used to illustrate the nature of the McNemar test. In this study, the investigator wishes to determine whether the proportion agreeing with the low-credibility speaker will be greater after a one-month delay than immediately after the communication. For a general model, the data of Table 7–1 can be represented by the contingency table, shown as Table 7–4, where X_{ij} refers to the number of subjects falling in the ith category at Time 1 and the jth category at Time 2. The number of subjects agreeing at Time 1 is represented by $X_{1.}$ and the number agreeing at Time 2 by $X_{.1}$. The total number of subjects, n, equals the sum of those agreeing and disagreeing at either point in time. Thus:

$$X_{1.} + X_{2.} = n$$

and

$$X_{.1} + X_{.2} = n$$

The corresponding population probability model indicates the probability p_{ij} that any

TABLE 7–4. Contingency table for the data of Table 7–1.

Time 1 \ Time 2	Agree	Disagree	Total
Agree	X_{11}	X_{12}	$X_{1.}$
Disagree	X_{21}	X_{22}	$X_{2.}$
Total	$X_{.1}$	$X_{.2}$	n

TABLE 7–5. Probability table for the data of Table 7–1.

Time 1 \ Time 2	Agree	Disagree	Total
Agree	p_{11}	p_{12}	$p_{1.}$
Disagree	p_{21}	p_{22}	$p_{2.}$
Total	$p_{.1}$	$p_{.2}$	1

subject falls in the ith category at Time 1 and the jth category at Time 2, and is as shown in Table 7–5. The marginal probabilities of agreement and disagreement at either point in time sum to unity. Thus:

$$p_{1.} + p_{2.} = 1$$

and

$$p_{.1} + p_{.2} = 1$$

Under this model, one can test the hypothesis of equality of the marginal probability distributions, $p_{i.} = p_{.i}$, for $i = 1, 2$. However, in order to study change in attitude, a researcher may be more interested in restricting the study to a consideration of the joint probabilities, p_{ij}, where $i \neq j$. Under this model, one can test the hypothesis of symmetry, stated in terms of the joint probabilities as H_0: $p_{ij} = p_{ji}$, for all $i \neq j$.

In the special case of a two-by-two table, equality of marginal probabilities implies equality of the off-diagonal joint probabilities, since, if $p_{.1} = p_{1.}$, then it follows that $p_{11} + p_{21} = p_{11} + p_{12}$, so that $p_{21} = p_{12}$. For this reason, the null hypothesis of the McNemar test could be written as a test of equality of correlated proportions:

$$H_0: p_{.1} = p_{1.}$$

or as a test of symmetry of the joint probabilities:

$$H_0: p_{21} = p_{12}$$

For a 2 × 2 table, these hypotheses and their test statistics are equivalent and identical. Yet one should note that the null hypothesis of symmetry states that, *among those scores that change*, the probability of change to a more favorable position equals the probability of change to a less favorable position. Thus, the $X_{21} + X_{12}$ subjects in the symmetrically located *change cells* can be thought of as $m = X_{21} + X_{12}$ independent trials for which the probability of change from initial disagreement to later agreement equals the probability of change from initial agreement to subsequent disagreement equals one-half. Under the null hypothesis, the frequency in each of the change cells, X_{21} and X_{12}, is binomially distributed over m trials, with probability $\frac{1}{2}$ of change in a given direction. Symbolically:

$$X_{21} \text{ is } B(m, \tfrac{1}{2}) \quad \text{and} \quad X_{12} \text{ is } B(m, \tfrac{1}{2})$$

A one-sided test of H_0: $p_{21} = p_{12}$ against the alternative H_1: $p_{21} > p_{12}$, or of H_0: $p_{.1} = p_{1.}$ against the alternative H_1: $p_{.1} > p_{1.}$, can be performed at the alpha level of significance by rejecting H_0 if:

$$P(X_{21} \geq x) = \sum_{X=x_{21}}^{m} \begin{bmatrix} m \\ x \end{bmatrix} \begin{bmatrix} 1 \\ 2 \end{bmatrix}^x \begin{bmatrix} 1 \\ 2 \end{bmatrix}^{m-x} = \sum_{X=x_{21}}^{m} \begin{bmatrix} m \\ x \end{bmatrix} \begin{bmatrix} 1 \\ 2 \end{bmatrix}^m \leq \alpha$$

EXAMPLE 7–2.1. For the data of Table 7–1, X_{21} is $B(24, \frac{1}{2})$. For a one-tailed test of $H_0: p_{21} = p_{12}$ against $H_1: p_{21} > p_{12}$, one can use Table A–7 to determine an $\alpha \leq 0.05$ decision rule. For $m = 24$, one reads, for the fifth percentile value of X_{21} in Table A–7, the number $X_{21} = 7$. Thus, for the one-tailed alternative $p_{.1} > p_{1.}$, H_0 is rejected if $X_{21} \geq 24 - 7 = 17$. In the case, $X_{21} = 18$, so it would be concluded that the probability of changing toward agreement with the low-credibility speaker after a one-month delay is greater than the probability of changing toward dis-agreement.

7–3. Large-Sample Approximations to the McNemar Test

X_{21} is $B(m, \frac{1}{2})$ under the null hypothesis of symmetry; then under the same conditions:

$E(X_{21})$ = Number of trials × probability of change in a given direction,
$m(\frac{1}{2})$ = $(\frac{1}{2})(X_{21} + X_{12})$,
$\text{Var}(X_{21})$ = Number of trials × product of probabilities of change in each direction,
$m(\frac{1}{2})(\frac{1}{2})$ = $(\frac{1}{4})(X_{21} + X_{12})$.

Large-sample tests can be based on either the normal approximation to the binomial distribution or the chi-square test of goodness of fit to the binomial distribution. Under normal curve theory,

$$Z = \frac{X_{21} - E(X_{21})}{\sqrt{\text{Var}(X_{21})}} = \frac{X_{21} - \frac{1}{2}(X_{21} + X_{12})}{\sqrt{(\frac{1}{4})(X_{21} + X_{12})}} = \frac{X_{21} - X_{12}}{\sqrt{X_{21} + X_{12}}}$$

has a standard $N(0, 1)$ distribution. If a correction for continuity is applied, the test statistic becomes:

$$Z = \frac{X_{21} - X_{12} \pm 1}{\sqrt{X_{21} + X_{12}}}$$

In keeping with the statistical convention of favoring a conservative rather than a liberal test, the sign on the correction is chosen to minimize the distance between X_{21} and X_{12}. Thus, if $X_{21} > X_{12}$, the negative sign is used, while if $X_{21} < X_{12}$, the positive sign is chosen. In the chi-square form, the large-sample test statistic leads to rejection of the hypothesis of symmetry if

$$X^2 = \frac{(X_{21} - X_{12} \pm 1)^2}{X_{21} + X_{12}}$$

Chi-Square Tests
of Homogeneity
of Proportions for
Qualitative
Variables in
Correlated
Samples

169

exceeds the tabled chi-square value with one degree of freedom. The use of the test is illustrated in the following example, where H_1 is a one-tailed alternative.

EXAMPLE 7–3.1.   When the data of Example 7–1.1 are analyzed by means of the large-sample approximations with continuity corrections,

$$Z = \frac{X_{21} - X_{12} \pm 1}{\sqrt{X_{21} + X_{12}}} = \frac{18 - 6 - 1}{\sqrt{18 + 6}} = 2.245$$

and

$$X^2 = \frac{(X_{21} - X_{12} \pm 1)^2}{X_{21} + X_{12}} = \frac{(18 - 6 - 1)^2}{18 + 6} = 5.04 = (2.245)^2 = Z^2$$

A one-tailed test at $\alpha = 0.05$ leads to rejection of the hypothesis of correlated proportions in favor of the alternative $p_{21} > p_{12}$ or, equivalently, $p_{.1} > p_{1.}$, because $Z = 2.245 > Z_{0.95} = 1.645$ for the Z test, or because $X^2 = 5.04 > X^2_{1:0.90} = 2.71$ for the X^2 test. In this example, $X^2_{1:0.90}$ is used for the one-tailed alternative tested by means of the chi-square distribution, since $X^2_{1:1-2\alpha} = Z^2_{1-\alpha}$, where α is the probability of a Type I error under the normal curve test.

EXAMPLE 7–3.2.   As might be expected, the large-sample approximation is quite good since

$$E(X_{21}) = E(X_{12}) = m(\tfrac{1}{2}) = 24(\tfrac{1}{2}) = 12 > 5$$

Under the large-sample theory with a correction for continuity,

$$\begin{aligned} P(X \geq 18) &= P(X_{21} \geq 17.5 | p_{21} = p_{12}) \\ &= P(Z > 2.245) \\ &= P(X^2 > 5.04) \\ &= 0.0122 \end{aligned}$$

while the value obtained for the exact binominal probability is:

$$P(X_{21} \geq 18 | p_{21} = p_{12}) = \sum_{x=18}^{24} \begin{bmatrix} 24 \\ x \end{bmatrix} \left(\frac{1}{2}\right)^{24} = 0.0113$$

The McNemar test of symmetry for two dichotomous variables can be extended to include multisample, multivariable, and multilevel designs. The multilevel extension of the McNemar test, called the Bowker and Stuart tests, are described in Sections 7–5 and 7–6, while the multivariable, multisample extension of the McNemar test, called the Cochran Q test, is described in Section 7–7.

7–4. Confidence Interval for $\psi = p_{.1} - p_{1.}$ of the McNemar Test

A large-sample confidence interval for the difference in marginal probabilities, $\psi = p_{.1} - p_{1.}$, can be formed using the standard normal distribution. Under the model described in Section 7–3, the $(1 - \alpha)\%$ confidence interval for $p_1 - p_1$ is given

by:

$$\hat{\psi} - Z_{1-\alpha/2}SE_{\hat{\psi}} < \psi < \hat{\psi} + Z_{1-\alpha/2}SE_{\hat{\psi}}$$

where

$$\hat{\psi} = \hat{p}_{.1} - \hat{p}_{1.}$$

and

$$SE_{\hat{\psi}}^2 = \frac{\hat{p}_{.1}\hat{p}_{.2}}{n} + \frac{\hat{p}_{1.}\hat{p}_{2.}}{n} - 2\frac{(\hat{p}_{11} - \hat{p}_{.1}\hat{p}_{1.})}{n}$$

The use of this confidence interval is illustrated for the one-sided alternative $\psi = p_{.1} - p_{1.} > 0$. This one-sided confidence interval agrees with the one-sided test performed in Example 7–3.1.

> **EXAMPLE 7–4.1.** For the data of Table 7–1,
>
> $$\hat{\psi} = \hat{p}_{.1} - \hat{p}_{1.} = \frac{48}{78} - \frac{36}{78} = 0.6154 - 0.4615 = 0.1539$$
>
> and
>
> $$SE_{\hat{\psi}}^2 = \frac{1}{n}\left[\hat{p}_{.1}\hat{p}_{.2} + \hat{p}_{1.}\hat{p}_{2.} - 2\hat{p}_{11} + 2\hat{p}_{.1}\hat{p}_{1.}\right]$$
>
> $$= \frac{1}{78}\left[0.6154(0.3846) + 0.4615(0.5385) - 2(0.3846) + 2(0.6154)(0.4615)\right]$$
>
> $$= 0.003641$$
>
> so that:
>
> $$\psi = (p_{.1} - p_{1.}) > (\hat{p}_{.1} - \hat{p}_{1.}) - Z_{1-\alpha}SE_{(\hat{p}_{.1} - \hat{p}_{1.})}$$
>
> $$> 0.1539 - 1.645\sqrt{0.003641}$$
>
> $$> 0.0546$$

Thus, the proportion of persons who agree, or the probability of agreeing, with the low-credibility speaker is greater at Time 2 than at Time 1 by at least 0.0546.

7–5. The Bowker Extension of the McNemar Test to a Test of Symmetry in a Square Contingency Table

The McNemar test for a 2×2 table was identified as a test of equality of correlated marginal probabilities:

$$H_0: p_{.1} = p_{1.} \quad \text{or} \quad H_0: p_{.2} = p_{2.}$$

or as a test of symmetry of the "change" probabilities:

$$H_0: p_{21} = p_{12}$$

The extension of this second model is called Bowker's test (Bowker, 1948). In particular, the Bowker test is used to test:

$$H_0: p_{ij} = p_{ji} \quad \text{for } i > j$$

TABLE 7–6. Population probability model for an $I \times J$ table with $I = J$.

	Levels	Time 2						Total
		1	2	...	j	...	J	
	1	p_{11}	p_{12}	...	p_{1j}	...	p_{1J}	$p_{1.}$
	2	p_{21}	p_{22}	...	p_{2j}	...	p_{2J}	$p_{2.}$
	.	.	.	...	.	...	.	.
	.	.	.	...	.	...	.	.
Time 1	i	p_{i1}	p_{i2}	...	p_{ij}	...	p_{iJ}	$p_{i.}$
	.	.	.	...	.	...	.	.
	.	.	.	...	.	...	.	.
	I	p_{I1}	p_{I2}	...	p_{Ij}	...	p_{IJ}	$p_{I.}$
	Total	$p_{.1}$	$p_{.2}$	...	$p_{.j}$	...	$p_{.J}$	1

against the alternative:

H_1: At least one pair of symmetric probabilities is unequal.

The population probability model for the $I \times J$ table, where $I = J$, is shown in Table 7–6. The square contingency table for the multilevel $I \times J$ model can be represented as shown in Table 7–7. With this model, Bowker's extension of the McNemar test uses the statistic:

$$X^2 = \sum_{\substack{i=1 \\ i \neq j}}^{I} \sum_{j=1}^{J} \frac{[X_{ij} - E(X_{ij})]^2}{E(X_{ij})} = \sum_{\substack{i=1 \\ i \neq j}}^{I} \sum_{j=1}^{J} \frac{(X_{ij} - np_{ij})^2}{np_{ij}}$$

to test the hypothesis of symmetry of the off-diagonal probabilities. Since the

TABLE 7–7. Frequency table for the population model of Table 7–6.

	Levels	Time 2						Total
		1	2	...	j	...	J	
	1	X_{11}	X_{12}	...	X_{1j}	...	X_{1J}	$X_{1.}$
	2	X_{21}	X_{22}	...	X_{2j}	...	X_{2J}	$X_{2.}$
	.	.	.	...	.	...	.	.
	.	.	.	...	.	...	.	.
Time 1	i	X_{i1}	X_{i2}	...	X_{ij}	...	X_{iJ}	$X_{i.}$
	.	.	.	...	.	...	.	.
	.	.	.	...	.	...	.	.
	I	X_{I1}	X_{I2}	...	X_{Ij}	...	X_{IJ}	$X_{I.}$
	Total	$X_{.1}$	$X_{.2}$	...	$X_{.j}$	...	$X_{.J}$	n

p_{ij} are unknown, Bowker recommends that the estimators

$$\hat{p}_{ij} = \frac{(X_{ij} + X_{ji})}{2n}$$

be substituted for the unknown parameters p_{ij}. With these substitutions, the test statistic becomes:

$$X^2 = \sum_{i=1}^{I} \sum_{j=1}^{J} \frac{(X_{ij} - X_{ji})^2}{X_{ij} + X_{ji}}, \quad i > j$$

The resulting test statistic has the chi-square distribution with $v = \left[\begin{smallmatrix}I\\2\end{smallmatrix}\right] = \left[\begin{smallmatrix}J\\2\end{smallmatrix}\right]$ degrees of freedom as its asymptotic null distribution. For the special case, $I = J = 2$, the Bowker statistic is identical to the uncorrected McNemar chi-square test of goodness of fit to the binomial.

EXAMPLE 7–5.1. The hypothesis of interest in Example 7–1.2 strongly suggests that a test of symmetry of the joint probabilities would be appropriate. It was predicted that any changes in the sponsorship of Boy Scout troops will favor affiliations with the presumably more stable national groups in preference to local affiliations. Stated symbolically, the experimental hypothesis is the directional assertion:

$$H_1: p_{ij} > p_{ji}, \quad i > j$$

The corresponding null hypothesis asserts:

$$H_0: p_{ij} = p_{ji}$$

Note that, although the alternative hypothesis is directional, the Bowker test permits only a test of H_0 being false. Inspection of the 3×3 table of Example 7–1.2 reveals that there are $\left[\begin{smallmatrix}I\\2\end{smallmatrix}\right] = \left[\begin{smallmatrix}3\\2\end{smallmatrix}\right] = 3$ pairs of off-diagonal cells for which most of the estimated expected values are less than 5. The value of the Bowker statistic for these data is given by:

$$X^2 = \frac{(2 - 4)^2}{6} + \frac{(20 - 5)^2}{25} + \frac{(3 - 2)^2}{5} = 9.87$$

and leads to rejection of the hypothesis of symmetric changes in organizational sponsorship, since for $\alpha = 0.05$:

$$X^2 = 9.87 > X^2_{3:0.95} = 7.82$$

An investigator might reasonably protest against the use of a nondirectional test when a directional prediction of results has been proposed as H_1. The solution of doubling the alpha level when using the chi-square distribution for a directional test of size alpha is not possible when the degrees of freedom exceed one. Another objection to the use of the Bowker test for these data might be based on the observation that the estimated cell frequencies, $E(X_{ij}) = np_{ij}$, are small. The empirical results of Cochran (1952, 1954), Lewontin and Felsenstein (1965), and Slakter (1966) suggest that the presence of small expected cell frequencies will not impair the quality of the approximation to the chi-square distribution if the degrees of freedom are relatively large.

The Bowker statistic used in the previous example tests the hypothesis that

Chi-Square Tests
of Homogeneity
of Proportions for
Qualitative
Variables in
Correlated
Samples

173

changes in categorization over time are essentially random and do not reflect a directional preference. If the null hypothesis of symmetry is true:

$$H_0: p_{ij} = p_{ji}, \quad i > j$$

the corresponding marginal probability distributions for Time 1 and Time 2 will be identical:

$$p_{.i} = p_{i.}$$

The converse is not necessarily true. Two distributions may have the same marginal characteristics while differing in their respective conditional distributions. A test of symmetry would detect such a difference, but a test of equality of the correlated proportions would be insensitive to it.

7–6. The Stuart Extension of the McNemar Test to a Test of Equality of Correlated Marginal Probabilities in a Square Contingency Table

When an investigator is more interested in comparing marginal probability distributions than in studying patterns of change in a joint distribution, the Stuart test of equality of marginals may be appropriate (Stuart, 1955, 1957). This test serves as the extension of the 2×2 table hypothesis $H_0: p_{.1} = p_{1.}$, to the $I \times J$ table hypothesis $H_0: p_{.i} = p_{i.}$.

EXAMPLE 7–6.1. Consider a study of school desegregation in which the racial composition of a city's schools shortly after the 1954 Supreme Court decision (1955) was to be compared to the racial composition over a decade later (1965). In particular, consider the data for the city schools as reported in Table 7–8. Changes in the racial composition of the schools after ten years would be tested by the hypothesis:

$$H_0: \begin{bmatrix} P_{SB(1955)} \\ P_{D(1955)} \\ P_{SW(1955)} \end{bmatrix} = \begin{bmatrix} P_{SB(1965)} \\ P_{D(1965)} \\ P_{SW1965)} \end{bmatrix}$$

TABLE 7–8. *Racial composition of 124 city schools in 1955 and 1965.*

1955 \ 1965	Segregated 90–100% Black	Desegregated 11–89% Black/White	Segregated 90–100% White	Total
Segregated Black	50	9	10	69
Desegregated	2	6	29	37
Segregated White	0	0	18	18
Total	52	15	57	124

Although the null hypothesis is a statement of homogeneity of proportions, the chi-square test of homogeneity is inappropriate. Recategorization of the same schools at two points in time has introduced a positive correlation between the marginal probability distributions. As a result, statistical independence of the marginal probabilities cannot be assumed, and the chi-square test of homogeneity is clearly incorrect in the face of violation of this assumption. The Stuart test is an appropriate test of homogeneity for bivariate distributions that do not have independent marginals. This test employs the differences of the corresponding marginal probabilities in both the null hypothesis and the test statistic. The null hypothesis of homogeneity of the marginal probability distributions can be stated as:

$$H_0: \Delta_i = p_{.i} - p_{i.} = 0 \qquad \text{for all } i = 1, 2, \ldots, I$$

Since

$$\sum_{i=1}^{I} p_{.i} = \sum_{i=1}^{I} p_{i.} = 1$$

and

$$\sum_{i=1}^{I} \hat{p}_{.i} = \sum_{i=1}^{I} \hat{p}_{i.} = 1$$

it follows that:

$$\sum_{i=1}^{I} \Delta_i = 0$$

and that any $(I - 1)$ of the Δ_i determine the value of the remaining Δ_i. Because the values of Δ_i are completely determined by the knowledge of any $(I - 1)$ of them, the Stuart test is based on a chi-square distribution with $\nu = I - 1$.

Stuart verified that the null sampling distribution of the differences in the marginal relative frequencies

$$\hat{\Delta}_i = \hat{p}_{.i} - \hat{p}_{i.}$$

is multivariate normal, with a clearly defined function that involves the inversion of an $(I - 1)$-by-$(I - 1)$ variance–covariance matrix. Since matrix inversion is not required for the use of the methods in this book, the test statistic is not presented. Furthermore, if H_0 is rejected, a post hoc analysis on the differences in the marginal probabilities becomes necessary in order to identify reasons for the rejection. For this reason, the post hoc procedure is presented. The only disadvantage in this approach is that if H_0 is not rejected, the computations involved with the post hoc procedure are wasteful of a researcher's time, but if, as stated, H_0 is rejected, the post hoc analysis is mandatory.

For a post hoc multiple-comparisons procedure, the large-sample confidence intervals introduced in Section 7–4 can be adopted if the critical value for the confidence intervals is replaced with:

$$\underline{S}^* = \sqrt{X^2_{I-1:1-\alpha}}$$

For paired comparisons:

$$\hat{\Delta} = \hat{p}_{.i} - \hat{p}_{i.}$$

and

$$SE^2(\hat{\Delta}) = \frac{\hat{p}_{.i}(1 - \hat{p}_{.i})}{n} + \frac{\hat{p}_{i.}(1 - \hat{p}_{i.})}{n} - 2\frac{\hat{p}_{ii} - \hat{p}_{i}\hat{p}_{i.}}{n}$$

Chi-Square Tests
of Homogeneity
of Proportions for
Qualitative
Variables in
Correlated
Samples

175

The corresponding confidence intervals are given by:

$$\Delta = \hat{\Delta} \pm \underline{S}^* SE(\hat{\Delta})$$

EXAMPLE 7–6.2. For the data of Example 7–6.1, $I = 3$, so that three contrasts

$$\Delta_1 = p_{.1} - p_{1.}, \qquad \Delta_2 = p_{.2} - p_{2.}, \qquad \text{and} \qquad \Delta_3 = p_{.3} - p_{3.}$$

are of interest. For the data of Table 7–8, these are:

$$\hat{\Delta}_1 = \hat{p}_{.1} - \hat{p}_{1.} = \frac{-17}{124} = -0.1371$$

$$\hat{\Delta}_2 = \hat{p}_{.2} - \hat{p}_{2.} = \frac{-22}{124} = -0.1774$$

$$\hat{\Delta}_3 = \hat{p}_{.3} - \hat{p}_{3.} = \frac{39}{124} = 0.3145$$

Then

$$SE^2(\hat{\Delta}_i) = \frac{1}{n^3}\left[X_{.i}(n - X_{.i}) + X_{i.}(n - X_{i.}) - 2nX_{ii} + 2X_{.i}X_{i.} \right]$$

$$SE^2(\hat{\Delta}_1) = \frac{1}{124^3}\left[52(72) + 69(55) - 2(124)(50) + 2(52)(69) \right]$$
$$= 0.001214$$

$$SE^2(\hat{\Delta}_2) = \frac{1}{124^3}\left[15(109) + 37(87) - 2(124)(6) + 2(15)(37) \right]$$
$$= 0.002348$$

$$SE^2(\hat{\Delta}_3) = \frac{1}{124^3}\left[57(67) + 18(106) - 2(124)(18) + 2(57)(18) \right]$$
$$= 0.001739$$

The confidence intervals with $\underline{S}^* = \sqrt{X^2_{I-1:1-\alpha}} = \sqrt{5.99} = 2.45$ are:

$$\Delta_1 = -0.1371 \pm 0.0853$$
$$\Delta_2 = -0.1774 \pm 0.1186$$
$$\Delta_3 = 0.3145 \pm 0.1021$$

The proportions of schools in all three racial classifications, segregated Black, integrated, and segregated White, differ in 1955 and 1965. The relative incidence of racially segregated schools with a predominantly White enrollment is greater in 1965 than in 1955, while the relative incidence of racially integrated or predominantly Black schools is less in 1965 than in 1955.

7–7. The Cochran Q Test

Several multilevel extensions of the McNemar test, the tests of Bowker and Stuart, have been considered in detail. The multivariable extension of the McNemar test, Cochran's Q test (Cochran, 1950), is used more frequently than either of the preceding tests. The Cochran test, which extends the McNemar test to a multivariate distribution of dichotomous variables, often appears in a correlated-observations design.

In the Cochran model, each of n individuals is tested under K conditions. An indicator variable $X_{ik} = 1$ if the observation on the ith subject under the kth condition can be termed a "success" and $X_{ik} = 0$ if the observation is a "failure." The term "success" is arbitrarily applied to the outcome of interest. Let

$$T_{i.} = \sum_{k=1}^{K} X_{ik}$$

denote the number of successes for the ith subject; let

$$T_{.k} = \sum_{i=1}^{n} X_{ik}$$

represent the number of successes under the kth condition, and

$$T_{..} = \sum_{i=1}^{n} \sum_{k=1}^{K} X_{ik}$$

symbolize the total number of successes. $T_{i.}$, the number of successes for the ith subject, is assumed to be fixed. Let:

$$\overline{T}_{..} = \frac{1}{K} \sum_{i=1}^{n} \sum_{k=1}^{K} X_{ik} = \frac{1}{K} \sum_{k=1}^{K} T_{.k}$$

Table 7–9 summarizes the various T values. Under these conditions:

$$E(X_{ik}) = \frac{T_{i.}}{K}$$

$$\mathrm{Var}(X_{ik}) = \left(\frac{T_{i.}}{K}\right)\left(1 - \frac{T_{i.}}{K}\right)$$

$$\mathrm{Cov}(X_{ik}X_{ik'}) = -\left[\frac{1}{K-1}\right]\left[\frac{T_{i.}}{K}\right]\left[1 - \frac{T_{i.}}{K}\right] \qquad (k \neq k')$$

TABLE 7–9. Data matrix for the Cochran Q test.

Conditions (treatments)

Subjects	1	2	...	k	...	K	Totals
1	X_{11}	X_{12}	...	X_{1k}	...	X_{1K}	$T_{1.}$
2	X_{21}	X_{22}	...	X_{2k}	...	X_{2K}	$T_{2.}$
.	.	.	...	.	...	.	.
.	.	.	...	.	...	.	.
i	X_{i1}	X_{i2}	...	X_{ik}	...	X_{ik}	$T_{i.}$
.	.	.	...	.	...	.	.
.	.	.	...	.	...	.	.
n	X_{n1}	X_{n2}	...	X_{nk}	...	X_{nK}	$T_{n.}$
Total	$T_{.1}$	$T_{.2}$	...	$T_{.k}$	...	$T_{.K}$	
Means	$\overline{T}_{.1}$	$\overline{T}_{.2}$	...	$\overline{T}_{.k}$	...	$\overline{T}_{.K}$	

as can be shown by using the methods presented in Section 2–10. When $T_{.k}$ is expressed as the sum of the indicator variables:

$$T_{.k} = \sum_{i=1}^{n} X_{ik}$$

and when there are no treatment effects, it follows that:

1. $E(T_{.k}) = \sum_{i=1}^{n} \left(\frac{T_{i.}}{K} \right) = \overline{T}_{..}$

2. $\text{Var}(T_{.k}) = \sum_{i=1}^{n} \left(\frac{T_{i.}}{K} \right) \left[1 - \left(\frac{T_{i.}}{K} \right) \right]$

3. $\underset{k \neq k'}{\text{Cov}(T_{.k}T_{.k'})} = - \left[\frac{1}{K-1} \right] \sum_{i=1}^{n} \left(\frac{T_{i.}}{K} \right) \left[1 - \left(\frac{T_{i.}}{K} \right) \right]$

so that

4. $\rho_{T_{.k}T_{.k'}} = - \frac{1}{K-1} = \rho$

Under the model of Section 2–10 with $\hat{\theta}_k = T_{.k}$:

$$Q = \frac{1}{1-\rho} \sum_{k=1}^{K} \frac{\left[T_{.k} - E(T_{.k}) \right]^2}{\text{Var}(T_{.k})}$$

has a distribution that is approximately X^2 with $v = K - 1$ degrees of freedom. With the corresponding substitutions:

$$Q = \frac{K(K-1) \sum_{k=1}^{K} (T_{.k} - \overline{T}_{..})^2}{K \sum_{i=1}^{n} T_{i.} - \sum_{i=1}^{n} T_{i.}^2}$$

A test of the hypothesis that the proportions of success are the same for all treatments, or that treatment effects are absent, can be made by rejecting H_0 if:

$$Q > X^2_{K-1:1-\alpha}.$$

An exact permutation distribution for Q can be generated under the assumptions that there are no treatment effects and that each row total, $T_{i.}$, is fixed. If the number of successes for each subject, $T_{i.}$, is fixed, then the absence of treatment effects implies that all permutations of the X_{ik} ($k = 1, 2, \ldots, K$) for a given subject are equally likely. For example, if a subject is exposed to four treatments (or measured under four conditions) and obtains three successes, then the absence of treatment effects implies that all of the following permutations of the subject's score are equally probable:

$$
\begin{aligned}
p &= P(X_{i1} = 1, \quad X_{i2} = 1, \quad X_{i3} = 1, \quad X_{i4} = 0) \\
&= P(X_{i1} = 1, \quad X_{i2} = 1, \quad X_{i3} = 0, \quad X_{i4} = 1) \\
&= P(X_{i1} = 1, \quad X_{i2} = 0, \quad X_{i3} = 1, \quad X_{i4} = 1) \\
&= P(X_{i1} = 0, \quad X_{i2} = 1, \quad X_{i3} = 1, \quad X_{i4} = 1).
\end{aligned}
$$

This statement is termed the *interchangeability* hypothesis. Interchangeability implies homogeneity, so that the null hypothesis for the Cochran Q test is usually written in one of the simpler forms cited earlier:

$$P(X_{i1} = 1) = P(X_{i2} = 1) = \ldots = P(X_{ik} = 1) = \ldots = P(X_{iK} = 1)$$

or, if the absence of subject-by-treatment interaction is assumed,

$$E(\overline{T}_{.1}) = E(\overline{T}_{.2}) = \ldots = E(\overline{T}_{.k}) = \ldots = E(\overline{T}_{.K})$$

If there are $T_{i.}$ successes in row i, then they may be allocated across the K treatment conditions in any of $\left[\begin{smallmatrix} K \\ T_{i.} \end{smallmatrix}\right]$ equally likely ways under H_0. Since the n rows are independent and Q is insensitive to row order, there are:

$$Q = \prod_{i=1}^{n} \begin{bmatrix} K \\ T_{i.} \end{bmatrix}$$

possible ways to arrange the successes, given H_0 true and the $T_{i.}$ fixed. The significance probability of an observed Q can be assessed by determining the relative incidence of permuted successes that would yield values of Q as extreme as or more extreme than the observed value. This permutation approach is practical only if the number of permuted successes is relatively small; however, its consideration is informative, since the approach emphasizes that rows for which $T_{i.} = 0$ or $T_{i.} = K$ yield no information concerning the truth of H_0 since, for these outcomes:

$$\begin{bmatrix} K \\ 0 \end{bmatrix} = \begin{bmatrix} K \\ K \end{bmatrix} = 1$$

As was true with the McNemar test, the Bowker test, and the Stuart test, information is obtained only from those cells that exhibit inconsistency within the subject and, therefore, satisfy the inequality $0 < T_{i.} < K$.

The tediousness of the permutation approach and the relatively good fit of the chi-square distribution to the sampling distribution of Q when the number of permuted successes is large make the use of a large-sample approximation to the distribution of Q feasible.

Cochran compared the chi-square approximation to the permutation distribution of Q and noted a relatively good fit, with average errors of 14% on the estimated actual alpha at the 0.05 level, for values from $K = 3$, $n = 10$ to $K = 5$, $n = 8$. In Cochran's study, only the *informative* rows that satisfied the inequality $0 < T_{i.} < K$ were used. Tate and Brown (1970) noted that a good fit of Q by the chi-square distribution is obtained with 24 or more informative observations distributed over $n \geq 4$ rows. Lunney (1970) and D'Agostino (1971) debated the merits of the use of an ANOVA F test versus Cochran's Q test for dichotomous data.

EXAMPLE 7–7.1. An illustration of the use of the Cochran Q test is based on the data of Table 7–3. The hypothesis to be tested is that the four problems do not differ in difficulty. When difficulty of the problem is measured in terms of the number of correct solutions, the hypothesis may be written as:

$$H_0: E(\overline{T}_{.1}) = E(\overline{T}_{.2}) = E(\overline{T}_{.3}) = E(\overline{T}_{.4}).$$

In this case, the hypothesis of equal difficulty of the four problems will be rejected if, after deletion of the noninformative rows,

$$Q = \frac{K(K - 1) \sum_{k=1}^{K} (T_{.k} - \overline{T}_{..})^2}{K \sum_{i=1}^{n} T_{i.} - \sum_{i=1}^{n} T_{i.}^2} > X_{K-1:1-\alpha}^2 = X_{3:0.95}^2 = 7.81$$

For the informative rows of Table 7–3, $T_{.1} = 9$, $T_{.2} = 5$, $T_{.3} = 18$, $T_{.4} = 26$, and $T_{..} =$

58, so that:

$$Q = \frac{4(3)\left[(9 - 14.5)^2 + (5 - 14.5)^2 + (18 - 14.5)^2 + (26 - 14.5)^2\right]}{4(58) - 126}$$

$$= 30.00$$

The hypothesis of no problem effects is rejected.

7–8. Post Hoc Procedures for the Cochran Test

On the basis of the hypothesis test in Section 7–7, the investigator would conclude that the problems differed in difficulty; however, he would not be able to judge the magnitude or the direction of the differences in difficulty among problems on the basis of the tests alone. Post hoc multiple comparisons of the treatment means can be used to examine the differences among problems more carefully.

If a contrast is written in the treatment means as:

$$\hat{\psi} = \sum_{k=1}^{K} a_k \overline{T}_{.k} = \sum_{i=1}^{n} \sum_{k=1}^{K} \frac{a_k X_{ik}}{n}$$

it can be shown, on the basis of knowledge of $E(X_{ik})$, $\text{Var}(X_{ik})$, and $\text{Cov}(X_{ik} X_{ik'})$, that, under the model of Section 2–7:

$$\text{Var}(\hat{\psi}) = \frac{K \sum_{i=1}^{n} T_{i.} - \sum_{i=1}^{n} T_{i.}^2}{nK(K - 1)} \left[\frac{\sum_{k=1}^{K} a_k^2}{n}\right]$$

If the investigator is interested in simple pairwise comparisons of the $\overline{T}_{.k}$, use of the Dunn–Bonferroni inequality will give narrower confidence intervals than will the Scheffé technique.

EXAMPLE 7–8.1. For the 39 subjects of Table 7–3, the variance of contrasts on the treatment means or proportions simplifies to:

$$\text{Var}(\hat{\psi}) = \frac{4(70) - 174}{(39)(4)(3)} \left[\frac{\sum_{k=1}^{K} a_k^2}{39}\right] = 0.0058 \sum_{k=1}^{K} a_k^2$$

For $K = 4$, there are $\begin{bmatrix} 4 \\ 2 \end{bmatrix} = 6$ pair comparisons of the form $\overline{T}_{.k} - \overline{T}_{.k'}$. To control $\alpha \leq 0.05$, one reads the Dunn–Bonferroni values of Table A–1 as $Z_{6:0.025} = -2.64$ and $Z_{6:0.975} = 2.64$ for the critical value in the confidence interval. Thus:

$$\psi = \hat{\psi} \pm 2.64\sqrt{\text{Var}(\hat{\psi})}$$

If

$$\hat{\psi} = \overline{T}_{.k} - \overline{T}_{.k'}$$

then

$$\text{Var}(\hat{\psi}) = 0.0058 \sum_{k=1}^{K} a_k^2 = 0.0058(2) = 0.0116$$

and

$$\psi = \hat{\psi} \pm 2.64\sqrt{0.0116} = \hat{\psi} \pm 0.2843$$

As reported in Table 7–10, Problem 4 differs in difficulty from Problems 1 and 2. Also, Problems 2 and 3 differ in difficulty.

If the chi-square analog to Scheffé's theorem is used to generate confidence intervals, with an experiment error rate of $\alpha = 0.05$, the appropriate critical value is:

$$S^* = \sqrt{X^2_{K-1:1-\alpha}} = \sqrt{7.81} = 2.80$$

The limits of the corresponding confidence intervals are given by:

$$\psi = \hat{\psi} \pm \sqrt{X^2_{K-1:1-\alpha}} \sqrt{\mathrm{Var}(\hat{\psi})} = \hat{\psi} \pm 2.80\sqrt{0.0116} = \hat{\psi} \pm 0.3016$$

Once again, Problem 4 differs from 1 and 2 in difficulty, and 2 and 3 differ. As expected, the confidence intervals using the Dunn–Bonferroni values are narrower than those using $\sqrt{X^2_{K-1:1-\alpha}}$. The relationship between $Z_{\alpha/2Q}$ and $\sqrt{X^2_{K-1:1-\alpha}}$ observed in this problem, $Z_{1-\alpha/2Q} < \sqrt{X^2_{K-1:1-\alpha}}$, will generally hold when the number of comparisons studied, Q, is small and the degrees of freedom $(K - 1)$ are large. The reverse will be true for large Q and small $(K - 1)$; however, the specific point at which $Z > \sqrt{X^2}$ is a function of α as well as of Q and $(K - 1)$.

Summary

In this chapter, methods for correlated dichotomous variables were presented. The most frequently encountered test in the behavioral sciences based on correlated dichotomous variables is called the McNemar test. This test can be used to test the hypothesis that two correlated proportions are identical, or that, among observations that involve a two-state change, the probability of change from status one to status two is identical to the probability of change from status two to status one. As an example, suppose 50 people are given an attitude inventory that measures their attitude toward the teaching in a high-school science class about the story of the creation of the world as presented in the Bible. On the basis of the inventory, each member of the sample can be classified as positive or negative in attitude. Suppose

TABLE 7–10. The six pairwise contrasts for the data of Table 7–3.

ψ	$\hat{\psi}$
$E(\overline{T}_{.1}) - E(\overline{T}_{.2})$	$12/39 - 8/39 = -0.1026$
$E(\overline{T}_{.1}) - E(\overline{T}_{.3})$	$12/39 - 21/39 = -0.2308$
$E(\overline{T}_{.1}) - E(\overline{T}_{.4})$	$12/39 - 29/39 = -0.4359$
$E(\overline{T}_{.2}) - E(\overline{T}_{.3})$	$8/39 - 21/39 = -0.3334$
$E(\overline{T}_{.2}) - E(\overline{T}_{.4})$	$8/39 - 29/39 = -0.5385$
$E(\overline{T}_{.3}) - E(\overline{T}_{.4})$	$21/39 - 29/39 = -0.2052$

that the group of 50 people are shown a film in which evidence opposing the biblical account is presented, and then, after the film showing, the same inventory is administered, and the people are again classified as positive or negative in their attitude. For this example, the McNemar form of the null hypothesis can be stated as:

$$H_{01}: P(\text{negative at time one and positive at time two})$$
$$= P(\text{positive at time one and negative at time two})$$

or as:

$$H_{02}: P(\text{positive at time one}) = P(\text{positive at time two})$$

If

$$m = \text{Number who change}$$
$$= X_{21} + X_{12},$$

where

$$X_{21} = \text{Number who change from negative to positive}$$

and

$$X_{12} = \text{Number who change from positive to negative},$$

it is easy to show that X_{21} and X_{12} are each binomially distributed with parameters m and $p = \frac{1}{2}$. Under this model, H_0 can be rejected by referring X_{21} and X_{12} to the appropriate tail of the corresponding binomial distribution, or for the values of α specified in Table A–7 to the related rejection region defined in this table.

If m is large, one can use tables of the $N(0, 1)$ distribution or X_1^2 in the decision-making process. For a two-tailed alternative, H_0 is rejected at the specified alpha level if

$$Z < Z_{\alpha/2} \qquad \text{or if} \qquad Z > Z_{1-\alpha/2}$$

where Z, corrected for continuity, is defined as:

$$Z = \frac{X_{21} - X_{12} \pm 1}{\sqrt{X_{21} + X_{12}}}$$

or if

$$X^2 > X_{1:1-\alpha}^2$$

where X^2, corrected for continuity, is defined as:

$$X^2 = \frac{(X_{21} - X_{12} \pm 1)^2}{X_{21} + X_{12}}$$

If H_0 is rejected, the two-sided $(1 - \alpha)\%$ confidence interval for $\psi = p_{.1} - p_{1.}$ is given by:

$$\psi = \hat{\psi} \pm Z_{1-\alpha/2} \, SE\hat{\psi}$$

where

$$\hat{\psi} = \hat{p}_{.1} - \hat{p}_{1.} = \frac{X_{.1}}{n} - \frac{X_{1.}}{n}$$

and

$$SE_{\hat{\psi}}^2 = \frac{\hat{p}_{.1}\hat{p}_{.2}}{n} + \frac{\hat{p}_{1.}\hat{p}_{2.}}{n} - \frac{2(\hat{p}_{11} - \hat{p}_{.1}\hat{p}_{1.})}{n}$$

A number of extensions of the one-sample McNemar test have been proposed. Three of these extensions, called the Bowker test, the Stuart test, and the Cochran Q test, are described in this chapter. Both the Bowker and the Stuart tests are based upon an extension of the number of states or categories observed at each time period from $I = 2$ to $I > 2$. The Bowker test serves as an extension of the H_{01} hypothesis of the McNemar test, while the Stuart test serves as an extension of the H_{02} hypothesis of the McNemar test.

In particular, the Bowker hypothesis is:

$$H_0 : p_{ij} = p_{ji} \quad \text{for } i > j$$

It is referred to as a test of symmetry, since it states that the probabilities of change are identical with respect to the diagonal cells of the square contingency table illustrated in Tables 7–6 and 7–7. It says, in essence, that among those observations where change is observed, the probability of change from state i to state j is identical to the probability of change from state j to state i. The test statistic, uncorrected for continuity, is given by:

$$X^2 = \sum_{i=1}^{I} \sum_{j=1}^{J} \frac{(X_{ij} - X_{ji})^2}{X_{ij} + X_{ji}}, \quad i > j$$

which, under large-sample theory, is asymptotically chi-square with $v = \begin{bmatrix} I \\ 2 \end{bmatrix} = \begin{bmatrix} J \\ 2 \end{bmatrix}$ degrees of freedom. Thus, the hypothesis of symmetry is rejected at α if X^2 exceeds the $X^2_{v:1-\alpha}$ tabled value. Since no simultaneous confidence-interval procedure has been proposed for this test, a rejected hypothesis has to be evaluated in terms of the contributions to X^2 from the symmetrically located cells.

The Stuart test, on the other hand, has a simple simultaneous confidence-interval procedure but a difficult-to-evaluate test statistic, which involves the inversion of a matrix. Because of this, the test statistic has not been presented. The Stuart hypothesis is simply stated as:

$$H_{02} : p_{i.} = p_{.i} \quad \text{for all } i = 1, 2, \ldots, I$$

and is seen to be the simple extension of H_{02} of the dichotomous McNemar test.

The $(1 - \alpha)\%$ simultaneous confidence intervals for $\Delta_i = p_{i.} - p_{.i}$ are given by:

$$\Delta_i = \hat{\Delta}_i \pm \sqrt{X^2_{I-1:1-\alpha}} \; SE_{\hat{\Delta}}$$

where

$$\hat{\Delta}_i = \hat{p}_{.i} - \hat{p}_{i.} = \frac{X_{.i}}{n} - \frac{X_{i.}}{n}$$

$$SE^2_{\hat{\Delta}_i} = \frac{\hat{p}_{.i}(1 - \hat{p}_{.i})}{n} + \frac{\hat{p}_{i.}(1 - \hat{p}_{i.})}{n} - \frac{2(\hat{p}_{ii} - \hat{p}_{.i}\hat{p}_{i.})}{n}$$

When $I = 2$, the set of I intervals reduces to the one interval associated with the McNemar test.

The large-sample assumptions for the McNemar, Bowker, and Stuart tests are independence of observations between subjects but not within subjects, and sufficiently large n so that the expected cell frequencies exceed 5. As indicated, there is some evidence that a few of the cells may have expected values less than 5 and still produce a reasonable approximation to the corresponding continuous chi-square distribution. However, it is recommended that the number of such cells be kept small.

For the Cochran extension of the McNemar test, the response variable remains dichotomous but the number of observations per subject or block is permitted to increase. For K conditions, the Cochran hypothesis can be written as:

$$H_0: E(\overline{T}_{.1}) = E(\overline{T}_{.2}) = \ldots = E(\overline{T}_{.K})$$

or as:

$$H_0: P(X_{i1} = 1) = P(X_{i2} = 1) = \ldots = P(X_{iK} = 1)$$

for all $i = 1, 2, \ldots, n$.

If K refers to the number of treatments or conditions observed on each of the n subjects or blocks, and if the treatments do not interact with the subjects, the hypothesis of no treatment effect is rejected at alpha if:

$$Q = \frac{K(K - 1)\sum_{k=1}^{K}(T_{.k} - \overline{T}_{..})^2}{K\sum_{i=1}^{n} T_{i.} - \sum_{i=1}^{n} T_{i.}^2}$$

exceeds $X^2_{K-1:1-\alpha}$.

If $\psi = a_1 E(\overline{T}_{.1}) + a_2 E(\overline{T}_{.2}) + \ldots + a_K E(\overline{T}_{.K})$ is a contrast in the $E(\overline{T}_{.k})$, the $(1 - \alpha)\%$ set of simultaneous confidence intervals in the ψ is given by:

$$\psi = \hat{\psi} \pm \sqrt{X^2_{K-1:1-\alpha}}\sqrt{\text{Var}(\hat{\psi})}$$

where

$$\hat{\psi} = \sum_{k=1}^{K} a_k \overline{T}_{.k}$$

and

$$\text{Var}(\hat{\psi}) = \frac{K\sum_{i=1}^{n} T_{i.} - \sum_{i=1}^{n} T_{i.}^2}{nK(K - 1)} \sum_{k=1}^{K} \frac{a_k^2}{n}$$

The designs considered in this chapter have been treated within the context of a general linear-models approach to categorical data (Grizzle, Starmer, and Koch, 1969; Koch and Reinfurt, 1971; and Koch, Freeman, Freeman, and Lehnen, 1974). The reader who has some knowledge of matrix algebra and multiple regression will find that the general linear-models approach to repeated-measures problems offers a comprehensive solution to design and analysis problems that have been treated with a multiplicity of separate tests in this chapter. Other statisticians (e.g., Kullback, 1968, 1971; Bishop, Fienberg, and Holland, 1975) have used maximum-likelihood estimation and iterative procedures to deal with the analysis of complex contingency tables. These approaches are also well beyond the level of statistical sophistication expected of most users of this text.

Exercises

*1. In the study of Example 7–1.1, another sample of 83 high-school seniors was given the same message by a Public Health officer whose area of specialization was venereal disease among high-school students. Results for the two testing periods are as shown in the table. Has there been a change of attitude over the two testing periods?

Time 1 \ Time 2	Agree	Disagree	Total
Agree	56	15	71
Disagree	7	5	12
Total	63	20	83

*2. According to the confidence-interval procedure of Section 7–4, the contrast for the low-credibility speaker, the school principal, is given by:

$$\hat{\psi}_1 = \hat{p}_{.1} - \hat{p}_{1.} = \frac{48}{72} - \frac{36}{72},$$

while for the Public Health officer of Exercise 1, the contrast is given by:

$$\hat{\psi}_2 = \hat{p}_{.1} - \hat{p}_{1.} = \frac{63}{83} - \frac{71}{83}.$$

Is there any reason to believe that $\psi_1 = \psi_2$? If $H_0: \psi_1 = \psi_2$ were to be rejected, what would it mean?

*3. In a study of job mobility, 196 workers in a large industrial plant were followed to see how they changed jobs or progressed along the job hierarchy in the factory. People who were not employed at both of the two time periods were not included in the study. The accompanying table sets forth the findings.
   a) Among those people who remained in the factory over the two time periods, has there been a shift to higher status and higher paying jobs?
   b) Is the test you performed the Bowker or Stuart test?
   c) What is the hypothesis of the test?

Job status, Time 1 \ Job status, Time 2	Low	Medium	High	Total
Low	40	18	29	87
Medium	6	37	29	72
High	0	11	26	37
Total	46	66	84	196

Chi-Square Tests of Homogeneity of Proportions for Qualitative Variables in Correlated Samples

*4. For the data of Exercise 3, should one conclude that the distribution of jobs according to status has remained constant over the two time periods? What is the name of the test you have performed?

*5. Combining the results of Exercises 3 and 4, what should one conclude?

*6. In the study of Example 7–1.3, 30 other students were tested with the same problems, but during the testing period, 5-minute rests were interpolated between problems. Results are as shown in the accompanying table. Use Cochran's test to analyze these data. What is H_0 and what is the decision? If H_0 is rejected, make a post hoc investigation of the differences.

Subject number	Problem number 1	2	3	4	Total for all problems
1	0	0	1	1	2
2	0	0	1	1	2
3	1	1	1	1	4
4	1	0	0	1	2
5	0	0	1	1	2
6	1	0	1	0	2
7	0	0	0	1	1
8	0	1	1	1	3
9	1	0	1	0	2
10	1	1	1	1	4
11	1	1	1	1	4
12	1	0	1	1	3
13	1	1	1	0	3
14	1	1	1	1	4
15	0	0	0	1	1
16	0	0	1	1	2
17	0	0	1	1	2
18	0	0	1	1	2
19	0	1	0	0	1
20	1	1	1	1	4
21	1	1	1	1	4
22	0	0	0	0	0
23	1	0	0	1	2
24	1	0	1	1	3
25	0	1	1	1	3
26	1	0	0	1	2
27	1	0	0	1	2
28	1	0	0	1	2
29	1	0	1	1	3
30	1	1	1	0	3
Total	18	11	21	24	74

*7. Since the data of Exercise 6 is independent of the data of Table 7–3, one can make pairwise comparisons across the two sets of data using contrasts. For example, for Problem One:

$$\hat{\psi}_1 = \overline{T}_{.1}^{(1)} - \overline{T}_{.1}^{(2)} = \frac{12}{39} - \frac{18}{30}.$$

Determine the $SE_{\hat{\psi}_1}^2$ and surround it with a confidence interval at $\alpha = 0.05$. What specific hypothesis are you testing under this procedure?

*8. For the model of Exercise 7, four planned contrasts are of interest. Use the Dunn–

Bonferroni model to determine four confidence intervals for ψ_1, ψ_2, ψ_3, and ψ_4. What do you conclude on the basis of these four intervals?

*9. Verify the $SE_{\hat{\psi}}^2$ formula of Section 7–4.

*10. Use the methods of Section 2–10 to show that:

$$\rho_{T_{.k},T_{.k'}} = -\frac{1}{K-1}$$

*11. Include the (0, 0, 0, 0) and (1, 1, 1, 1) rows of Table 7–3 and compute Q. What effect does their elimination have upon the value of Q?

*12. Show how Q is developed from U of Section 2–10.

*13. Apply the McNemar test to the data of Exercise 8 of Chapter 2. What is the hypothesis under test? What is the decision?

*14. Analyze the data of Table 8–2 in terms of the models presented in this chapter.

*15. Use the methods of this chapter to analyze the data of Exercise 11 of Chapter 8.

Chi-Square Tests
of Homogeneity
of Proportions for
Qualitative
Variables in
Correlated
Samples

187

One-Sample Chi-Square Tests of Independence and Correlation and Measures of Association for Qualitative Variables

8–1. Exact Test of Independence for Two Dichotomous Variables

Assume that a *single random sample* of size n has been selected from a universe of interest. On each element of the sample, let measurements be simultaneously recorded relative to *two* dichotomous variables. Let the two variables be denoted by Y_1 and Y_2, respectively. Furthermore, denote the characteristics associated with Y_1 by A and $\bar{A}$, respectively, and those associated with Y_2 by B and $\bar{B}$. The four sets generated by the intersection of the Y_1 and Y_2 variables are mutually exclusive. Furthermore, since two variables are being observed, this is referred to as a bivariate problem, and the test is called a bivariate test of hypothesis. The results from such a study can be cast in the form of a 2×2 table, as shown in Table 8–1. While this

TABLE 8–1. A typical 2×2 contingency table.

Variables		Y_2 B	$\bar{B}$	Total
Y_1	A	X_{11}	X_{12}	$X_{1.}$
	$\bar{A}$	X_{21}	X_{22}	$X_{2.}$
Total		$X_{.1}$	$X_{.2}$	n

table resembles an Irwin–Fisher 2 × 2 table, it differs from the Irwin–Fisher tables on a number of dimensions. They are:

1. The Irwin–Fisher table represents the outcomes on two independent samples, while the 2 × 2 contingency table represents the outcomes on only one sample.
2. The Irwin–Fisher table is used to represent the outcomes on *one* random variable observed on two independent samples, while the 2 × 2 contingency table represents the joint outcomes on *two* random variables observed on the single sample.
3. The Irwin–Fisher table is generated to test the hypothesis that the parameters, p_1 and p_2, of two independent binomial variables are equal, while the 2 × 2 contingency table is generated to test the hypothesis that the correlation coefficient between two dichotomous variables is equal to zero.

In the notation of the 2 × 2 contingency tables, X_{11} represents the observed number of elements of the sample that possess both properties A and B; $X_{12}, X_{21},$ and X_{22} are defined in a similar fashion. For this table, only the sample size, n, is known ahead of time. All other marginals and cell frequencies are allowed to vary freely.

The hypothesis to be tested with the data in a 2 × 2 contingency table is that the variables Y_1 and Y_2 are statistically independent. Such a statement can be viewed in two ways when true. Independence between Y_1 and Y_2 requires that:

$$P(A|B) = P(A|\bar{B}) = P(A)$$

or that:

$$P(A \cap B) = P(A)P(B)$$

For a 2 × 2 contingency table, it is easier to work with the latter statement of independence. If this hypothesis is true, then it is also true that

$$P(A \cap \bar{B}) = P(A)P(\bar{B}), \qquad P(\bar{A} \cap B) = P(\bar{A})P(B),$$

and

$$P(\bar{A} \cap \bar{B}) = P(\bar{A})P(\bar{B})$$

These relationships can be used to determine the probability distribution of the various values of $X_{11}, X_{12}, X_{21},$ and $X_{22},$ so that a decision rule can be generated to indicate when the hypothesis of independence should be rejected. To simplify the derivation, let:

$$p_{11} = P(A \cap B), \qquad p_{12} = P(A \cap \bar{B}), \qquad p_{21} = P(\bar{A} \cap B),$$

and

$$p_{22} = P(\bar{A} \cap \bar{B})$$

With this notation, the probability of a 2 × 2 contingency table is given, according to Rule Seven of Section 2–2, as:

$$P[(X_{11} = x_{11}) \cap (X_{12} = x_{12}) \cap (X_{21} = x_{21}) \cap (X_{22} = x_{22})]$$

$$= \begin{bmatrix} n \\ x_{11}\ x_{12}\ x_{21}\ x_{22} \end{bmatrix} x_{11}\ x_{12}\ x_{21}\ x_{22} \ p_{11}\ p_{12}\ p_{21}\ p_{22}$$

If the hypothesis of independence is true, it follows that:

$$p_{11} = p_{1.}p_{.1}, \qquad p_{12} = p_{1.}p_{.2}, \qquad p_{21} = p_{2.}p_{.1}, \qquad \text{and} \qquad p_{22} = p_{2.}p_{.2}$$

where

$$p_{1.} = P(A), \qquad p_{2.} = P(\bar{A}), \qquad p_{.1} = P(B), \qquad \text{and} \qquad p_{.2} = P(\bar{B})$$

so that:

$$P[(X_{11} = x_{11}) \cap (X_{12} = x_{12}) \cap (X_{21} = x_{21}) \cap (X_{22} = x_{22})]$$

$$= \begin{bmatrix} n \\ x_{11}\ x_{12}\ x_{21}\ x_{22} \end{bmatrix} \frac{x_{11}\ x_{11}\ x_{12}\ x_{12}\ x_{21}\ x_{21}\ x_{22}\ x_{22}}{p_{1.}\ p_{.1}\ p_{1.}\ p_{.2}\ p_{2.}\ p_{.1}\ p_{2.}\ p_{.2}}$$

$$= \begin{bmatrix} n \\ x_{11}\ x_{12}\ x_{21}\ x_{22} \end{bmatrix} \frac{x_{1.}\ x_{.1}\ x_{2.}\ x_{.2}}{p_{.1}\ p_{.1}\ p_{2.}\ p_{.2}}$$

If a conditional probability model is assumed for this test, the undesirable nuisance parameters $p_{1.}, p_{2.}, p_{.1},$ and $p_{.2}$ can be eliminated. The elimination is possible if the probabilities are measured relative to the fixing of both margins. Since the probabilities of the margins are given by:

$$P[(X_{1.} = x_{1.}) \cap (X_{2.} = x_{2.})] = \begin{bmatrix} n \\ x_{1.}\ x_{2.} \end{bmatrix} \frac{x_{1.}\ x_{2.}}{p_{1.}\ p_{2.}}$$

and

$$P[(X_{.1} = x_{.1}) \cap (X_{.2} = x_{.2})] = \begin{bmatrix} n \\ x_{.1}\ x_{.2} \end{bmatrix} \frac{x_{.1}\ x_{.2}}{p_{.1}\ p_{.2}}$$

it follows that:

$$P\left[(X_{11} = x_{11}) \cap (X_{12} = x_{12}) \cap (X_{21} = x_{21}) \cap (X_{22} = x_{22}) \middle| \begin{matrix} X_{1.} = x_{1.}\ X_{.1} = x_{.1} \\ X_{2.} = x_{2.}\ X_{.2} = x_{.2} \end{matrix} \right]$$

$$= \frac{\begin{bmatrix} n \\ x_{11}\ x_{12}\ x_{21}\ x_{22} \end{bmatrix} \dfrac{x_{1.}\ x_{.1}\ x_{2.}\ x_{.2}}{p_{1.}\ p_{.1}\ p_{2.}\ p_{.2}}}{\begin{bmatrix} n \\ x_{1.}\ x_{2.} \end{bmatrix} \dfrac{x_{1.}\ x_{2.}}{p_{1.}\ p_{2.}} \begin{bmatrix} n \\ x_{.1}\ x_{.2} \end{bmatrix} \dfrac{x_{.1}\ x_{.2}}{p_{.1}\ p_{.2}}} = \frac{\begin{bmatrix} x_{1.} \\ x_{11} \end{bmatrix}\begin{bmatrix} x_{2.} \\ x_{22} \end{bmatrix}}{\begin{bmatrix} n \\ x_{.1} \end{bmatrix}}$$

which is immediately recognized as the hypergeometric probability formula. Thus, if $n \leq 15$, Table A–8 can be used to test for independence. When $n \geq 15$, exact probabilities or a Karl Pearson approximation to chi-square can be used for testing, the choice depending upon the degree of accuracy desired.

EXAMPLE 8–1.1. As an example of the use of the exact test, consider the data of Table 8–2, which were generated by the joint responses to the following two questions asked of graduating White middle-class seniors in a newly integrated school.

1. Have you invited any Black classmate to your home during the past year for a party or other social event?   Yes_____   No_____
2. Do you consider yourself to be a regular churchgoer?   Yes_____   No_____

On the basis of these data, one would like to know whether social acceptance of

TABLE 8–2. *Responses to questions concerning invitation of Blacks to social events in own home and regularity of church attendance, by White graduating seniors.*

	Question 2		
Question 1	Yes	No	Total
Yes	5	1	6
No	5	6	11
Total	10	7	17

Blacks, as measured by invitations to home, is independent of religious commitment as measured by church attendance. The hypothesis under test is:

H_0: Social acceptance of Blacks is independent of church attendance. The alternative hypothesis

$$H_1: H_0 \text{ is false.}$$

Since $n = 17$ is greater than 15, exact probabilities must be calculated by the hypergeometric formula, and since a nondirectional statement of correlation is offered as an alternative, both tails of the hypergeometric distribution must be investigated. If X_{11} = number who say "Yes" to both questions, possible values for X_{11} are: {0, 1, 2, 3, 4, 5, 6}. The probabilities for those values of X_{11}, conditional on the observed margins, are given in Table 8–3.

TABLE 8–3. *Probabilities for X_{11}, when $n = 17$ and $X_{1.} = 6$ and $X_{.1} = 10$.*

Values of X_{11}	$\begin{bmatrix}6\\x_{11}\end{bmatrix} \begin{bmatrix}11\\10-x_{11}\end{bmatrix} / \begin{bmatrix}17\\10\end{bmatrix}$	$P(X_{11} = x_{11})$
0	$\begin{bmatrix}6\\0\end{bmatrix}\begin{bmatrix}11\\10\end{bmatrix}/\begin{bmatrix}17\\10\end{bmatrix}$	0.00056
1	$\begin{bmatrix}6\\1\end{bmatrix}\begin{bmatrix}11\\9\end{bmatrix}/\begin{bmatrix}17\\10\end{bmatrix}$	0.01696
2	$\begin{bmatrix}6\\2\end{bmatrix}\begin{bmatrix}11\\8\end{bmatrix}/\begin{bmatrix}17\\10\end{bmatrix}$	0.12726
3	$\begin{bmatrix}6\\3\end{bmatrix}\begin{bmatrix}11\\7\end{bmatrix}/\begin{bmatrix}17\\10\end{bmatrix}$	0.33936
4	$\begin{bmatrix}6\\4\end{bmatrix}\begin{bmatrix}11\\6\end{bmatrix}/\begin{bmatrix}17\\10\end{bmatrix}$	0.35633
5	$\begin{bmatrix}6\\5\end{bmatrix}\begin{bmatrix}11\\5\end{bmatrix}/\begin{bmatrix}17\\10\end{bmatrix}$	0.14253
6	$\begin{bmatrix}6\\6\end{bmatrix}\begin{bmatrix}11\\4\end{bmatrix}/\begin{bmatrix}17\\10\end{bmatrix}$	0.01699
Total	$\sum_{x_{11}=0}^{6} \begin{bmatrix}6\\x_{11}\end{bmatrix}\begin{bmatrix}11\\10-x_{11}\end{bmatrix}/\begin{bmatrix}17\\10\end{bmatrix}$	0.99999

From the distribution of Table 8–3, it is seen that the $\alpha \leq 0.05$ critical region is given by X_{11}: $\{0, 1, 6\}$. Since $X_{11} = 5$, the hypothesis of independence is not rejected. Failure to reject H_0 for these data occurred either because the two variables were independent in the population of White graduating seniors, or because the small sample size and small set of X_{11} values available to define the critical region prevented detection of the relationship between the variables.

Like the Irwin–Fisher test, this test is the most powerful for the hypothesis being tested. Although it is also based on hypergeometric probabilities, it is not, strictly speaking, the Irwin–Fisher test. The Irwin–Fisher test is a *two*-sample test, while this test of independence is a *one*-sample test relating two variables to one another via a correlation model. This is apparent in the special case of the test described in Section 8–2.

8–2. Blomqvist's Double-Median Test for Association

Blomqvist's double-median test (Blomqvist, 1951) is used to test the hypothesis that two quantitative variables are statistically independent. It is an assumption-freer competitor to normal-curve tests for Pearson product-moment correlation coefficients. The test is based on the distribution-free test of independence described in Section 8–1. It is performed on a 2×2 contingency table created by partitioning the two dependent measures at their respective sample medians. If the variables are independent, equal or near-equal frequencies would be expected in each of the four cells of the resulting 2×2 table. If the frequencies deviate significantly from $\frac{1}{4}n$, then the hypothesis of independence is suspect. The test is illustrated in the following example.

EXAMPLE 8–2.1. Consider the data of Table 3–5 which were used to test the hypothesis that no difference in auditory discrimination existed between normal children and children having functional articulation defects. Since the children were matched, their auditory discrimination scores can be seen as a sample of 10 pairs of values from a bivariate distribution. We can determine whether the discrimination scores of the normal children and those having articulation defects are correlated by partitioning the two sets of data at their median values and testing the resulting 2×2 table for independence. For these data, $\hat{M}_1 = 27.5$ and $\hat{M}_2 = 12.5$. The resulting 2×2 contingency table is as shown in Table 8–4.

Note that, if the scores were correlated, most of the frequencies would probably be centered in the diagonal cells, so that the table of perfect positive correlation would have $X_{11} = 0$ with the next highest correlational table given by $X_{11} = 1$. On this basis, it is reasonable to conclude that the observed table, with $X_{11} = 2$, is indicative of *no* correlation. That this is, indeed, true is easy to show by referring to the one-tailed hypergeometric probabilities of Table A–8. For these data, the table is entered with:

$$N = 10, \quad S_1 = 5, \quad S_2 = 5, \quad \text{and} \quad X = 2.$$

For these values, it is seen that:

$$P_{Obs} = 0.500 \quad \text{and} \quad P_{Other} = 0.500,$$

so that the one-tailed alternative is not supported.

This exact test of independence is the nonparametric analog to the classical test, where it is assumed that ρ, the correlation coefficient, measures the association between two variables Y_1 and Y_2, which are known to be bivariate normal. If the assumption of bivariate normality is in question because of lack of normality in the marginal distributions, because one or both of the regressions are not linear, or because homoscedasticity is not satisfied, then recourse can be had to the test of independence presented in this example. The assumptions for this form of the test of independence are minimal. In addition to independence between pairs of observations, the only requirement for the test is that the underlying variables be continuous, so that no values are tied at $\hat{M}_1$ and $\hat{M}_2$. If tied values do occur as a consequence of the crudeness of the measuring instrument used, they can be assigned to the four cells of the table so as to minimize the chances of rejection of H_0. This convention lessens the chance of the occurrence of a type I error as an artifact of the assignment of tied observations to the cells.

When data are given in the form of a 2×2 table with a double dichotomy at the median, Blomqvist's test is best. However, if the original scores on the continuous variables or their ranks are available, several more powerful analyses exist. As will be seen in Chapter 16, Pitman's rho, Spearman's rank measure of correlation, and Kendall's tau are more efficient, and are generally preferred to Blomqvist's test under these conditions. If Y_1 and Y_2 are known to be bivariate normal, the classical t test based on Pearson's r is far more efficient than the Blomqvist test. The efficiency of the Blomqvist test relative to the t test is only 0.405.

It should be noted that the Blomqvist test can be extended to more than 2×2 tables. For a 3×3 table, partitions on the Y_1 and Y_2 variables would be made at the $33\frac{1}{3}$ and $66\frac{2}{3}$ percentile values. Since *more* information is being retained, the power of the test is increased, so that $E > 0.405$. In fact, as the number of partition values increases, the efficiency of the test increases to 1.00, provided the assumption of bivariate normality is valid. Of course, it is understood that, if bivariate normality can be assumed, then classical procedures would be used.

TABLE 8–4. 2×2 contingency table for the match pair data of Table 3–5.

Variables Y_1	Y_2		
	Score below 12.5	Score above 12.5	Total
Score above 27.5	2	3	5
Score below 27.5	3	2	5
Total	5	5	10

8–3. The Large-Sample Form of the Karl Pearson One-Sample Test of Independence, or Lack of Correlation Between Two Dichotomous Variables

When n is large, a Karl Pearson chi-square statistic can be used to approximate the exact hypergeometric probabilities. If:

$$H_0: P(A \cap B) = P(A)P(B)$$

is true, it follows that:

$$P(A \cap \bar{B}) = P(A)P(\bar{B}), \qquad P(\bar{A} \cap B) = P(\bar{A})P(B),$$

and

$$P(\bar{A} \cap \bar{B}) = P(\bar{A})P(\bar{B})$$

Given these probabilities, it is possible to determine expected frequencies, since it would be true that $E(X_{11}) = nP(A)P(B)$, with corresponding expected frequencies for the remaining cells. Since these probabilities are unknown, they can be estimated from the observed data and then used to approximate the expected cell frequencies under the assumption that the hypothesis of independence is true. This would produce a table of estimated expected frequencies which, when taken along with the observed table of frequencies, could be used to compute a chi-square statistic in the Karl Pearson form. The test statistic is given by:

$$X^2 = \sum_{i=1}^{2} \sum_{j=1}^{2} \frac{[X_{ij} - \hat{E}(X_{ij})]^2}{\hat{E}(X_{ij})}$$

The hypothesis of independence is rejected if this statistic exceeds the $(1 - \alpha)$-percentile of the chi-square distribution with one degree of freedom.

Since there are four cell frequencies to be computed, it appears that the test will utilize four degrees of freedom. However, the chi-square test of independence is a one-sample test with only the total sample size n known ahead of time. Thus, given three cells, the fourth cell is automatically determined by subtracting the sum of the elements in three cells from n. This reduces the number of degrees of freedom to an apparent three. However, in order to compute the estimated expected frequency table, it is necessary to estimate $P(A)$ and $P(B)$ from the data, as $\hat{P}(A)$ and $\hat{P}(B)$. Once these are computed,

$$\hat{P}(\bar{A}) = 1 - \hat{P}(A) \qquad \text{and} \qquad \hat{P}(\bar{B}) = 1 - \hat{P}(B)$$

are determined. With these four parameter estimates, the estimated expected cell frequencies, $\hat{E}(X_{11})$, $\hat{E}(X_{21})$, $\hat{E}(X_{12})$, and $\hat{E}(X_{22})$, can now be computed. As indicated, one degree of freedom is "utilized" to estimate $P(A)$ and one is "used" to estimate $P(B)$, so that the apparent three degrees of freedom are reduced by two, to a value of one. The test will now be illustrated by an example.

EXAMPLE 8–3.1. In a survey of adult residents of Berkeley, California, it was found that attitudes toward ability grouping in junior-high-school classes were not independent of amount of education possessed by the respondents. This decision was based on joint responses given to the following two edited questions.

TABLE 8–5. *Joint responses to two questions concerning the use of ability groupings in junior high school classes and level of education attained by the respondents to the questionnaire.*

	Question 2		
Question 1	B: Yes	$\bar{B}$: No	Total
A: High school graduate or less	109	129	238
$\bar{A}$: Some college	334	188	522
Total	443	317	760

1. How much education have you had?
   High-school graduate or less —— Some college ——
2. Should junior-high-schools be divided by ability grouping tracks?
   Yes —— No ——

The joint responses to these two questions are summarized in Table 8–5.

For these data, the estimates of the unknown parameters are given by:

$$\hat{P}(A) = \frac{238}{760} = 0.313, \qquad \hat{P}(\bar{A}) = \frac{522}{760} = 0.687$$

$$\hat{P}(B) = \frac{443}{760} = 0.583, \qquad \hat{P}(\bar{B}) = \frac{317}{760} = 0.417$$

The estimated expected frequencies are given by:

$$\hat{E}(X_{11}) = 760(.313)(.583) = 138.69$$
$$\hat{E}(X_{12}) = 760(.313)(.417) = \ \ 99.20$$
$$\hat{E}(X_{21}) = 760(.687)(.583) = 304.40$$
$$\hat{E}(X_{22}) = 760(.687)(.417) = 217.72$$

These frequencies are summarized in Table 8–6.

The value of the test statistic is:

$$X^2 = \frac{(109 - 138.69)^2}{138.69} + \frac{(129 - 99.20)^2}{99.20} + \frac{(334 - 304.40)^2}{304.40} + \frac{(188 - 217.72)^2}{217.72}$$
$$= 22.27.$$

TABLE 8–6. *Estimated Expected Frequencies for the data of Table 8–5.*

	Question 2		
Question 1	B: Yes	$\bar{B}$: No	Total
A: High school graduate or less	138.69	99.20	238
$\bar{A}$: Some college	304.40	217.72	522
Total	443	317	760

The hypothesis of statistical independence should be rejected if $X^2 > X^2_{1:0.95} = 3.84$. Since 22.27 is greater than 3.84, there is reason to doubt the hypothesis of independence. It is concluded that attitude toward ability grouping is not independent of amount of schooling of the respondents. Individuals who have had a high school education or less tend to be almost equally divided on the issue of ability grouping, while people who have had some college training support ability grouping. In the sample, the estimates of these probabilities are given by:

$$\hat{P}(B|A) = \frac{109}{238} = 0.46 \quad \text{and} \quad \hat{P}(B|\overline{A}) = \frac{334}{522} = 0.64$$

8–4. Chi-Square Test of Independence for an R × C Contingency Table

In the previous sections, 2×2 contingency tables were examined in sufficient detail for most behavioral research. As might be expected, the large-sample test of independence can be extended to cover the situation where there are R rows and C columns. Let the variable Y_1 be partitioned into R mutually exclusive and exhaustive subsets $A_1, A_2, \ldots, A_R$ and the variable Y_2 into C mutually exclusive and exhaustive subsets $B_1, B_2, \ldots, B_C$. The configuration for such a layout is as shown in Table 8–7.

The data from such a table can be used to test the hypothesis that variables Y_1 and Y_2 are independent. The Karl Pearson test statistic is given by:

$$X^2 = \sum_{i=1}^{R} \sum_{j=1}^{C} \frac{\left[X_{ij} - \hat{E}(X_{ij})\right]^2}{\hat{E}(X_{ij})}$$

where

$$\hat{E}(X_{ij}) = n\hat{P}(A_i)\hat{P}(B_j) \quad \text{for } i = 1, 2, \ldots, R \text{ and } j = 1, 2, \ldots, C.$$

The distribution of X^2 is approximately chi-square with $v = (R-1)(C-1)$ degrees of freedom. If only the sample size, n, is known ahead of time, the number of independent cell frequencies is given by $(RC - 1)$. The number of independent parameters, $P(A_i)$, to be estimated for the Y_1 variable is $(R - 1)$. Since the sum of the

TABLE 8–7. A typical R × C contingency table.

Variables		B_1	B_2	$\ldots$	B_C	Total
				Y_2		
	A_1	X_{11}	X_{12}	$\ldots$	X_{1C}	$X_{1.}$
	A_2	X_{21}	X_{22}	$\ldots$	X_{2C}	$X_{2.}$
Y_1	.	.	.	$\ldots$	.	.
	.	.	.	$\ldots$	.	.
	.	.	.	$\ldots$	.	.
	A_R	X_{R1}	X_{R2}	$\ldots$	X_{RC}	$X_{R.}$
Total		$X_{.1}$	$X_{.2}$	$\ldots$	$X_{.C}$	n

marginal probabilities must add to 1, knowledge of $(R - 1)$ of the probabilities determines the Rth probability. Similarly, the number of independent parameters, $P(B_j)$, to be estimated for the Y_2 variable is $(C - 1)$. Thus, the number of degrees of freedom for the test statistic is given by:

$$v = (RC - 1) - (R - 1) - (C - 1)$$
$$= RC - R - C + 1$$
$$= (R - 1)(C - 1)$$

The following example illustrates the large-sample form of the chi-square test of independence.

EXAMPLE 8–4.1. In a study on school integration, 158 graduating seniors were asked the following question:

The word *integration* often has a different meaning for different people. Here are several possible meanings for the word:

1. Integration is the free association of people of different races on the basis of mutual or like interests.
2. Integration is the forced mixing of people of different races.
3. Integration is the open acceptance of another person and his racial and cultural heritage.
4. Integration is all people having equal social value (may marry outside of their own races, join social clubs, etc.), and receiving equal justice under the law.

Which one of these meanings comes *closest* to your own?

The distribution of the responses according to race of the student is as shown in Table 8–8. The hypothesis to be tested is that the meaning of the word "integration" is independent of race of the students interrogated. As a statistical hypothesis, this reduces to H_0: $P(A_i \cap B_j) = P(A_i)P(B_j)$, where $i = 1, 2, 3, 4$ corresponds to definitions 1, 2, 3, and 4, while $j = 1, 2, 3$ corresponds to Asian, Black, and White, respectively. The alternative hypothesis is H_1: H_0 is false.

The test statistic for this test is:

$$X^2 = \sum_{i=1}^{4} \sum_{j=1}^{3} \frac{[X_{ij} - \hat{E}(X_{ij})]^2}{\hat{E}(X_{ij})}$$

TABLE 8–8. Meaning of the word "integration" according to the responses made by 158 students who were Asian, Black, or White.

Definition	Asian	Black	White	Total
One	7	14	39	60
Two	8	5	8	21
Three	9	7	29	45
Four	5	12	15	32
Total	29	38	91	158

TABLE 8–9. Estimated expected frequencies for the data of Table 8–8.

Definition	Asian	Black	White	Total
One	11.01	14.43	34.56	60
Two	3.86	5.05	12.09	21
Three	8.26	10.82	25.92	45
Four	5.87	7.70	18.43	32
Total	29	38	91	158

TABLE 8–10. Contributions to the total chi-square for the data of Table 8–8.

Definition	Asian	Black	White	Total
One	1.46	0.01	0.57	2.04
Two	4.44	0.00	1.38	5.82
Three	0.07	1.35	0.37	1.79
Four	0.13	2.40	0.64	3.17
Total	6.10	3.76	2.96	12.82

Since $v = (R - 1)(C - 1) = (4 - 1)(3 - 1) = (3)(2) = 6$, the hypothesis of statistical independence should be rejected if $X^2 > X^2_{6:.95} = 12.59$. The estimated expected frequencies under the hypothesis of statistical independence are summarized in Table 8–9. The value of the test statistic is given by:

$$X^2 = \frac{(7 - 11.01)^2}{11.01} + \frac{(8 - 3.86)^2}{3.86} + \cdots + \frac{(15 - 18.43)^2}{18.43} = 12.82$$

with the individual contributions to X^2 summarized in Table 8–10. Since 12.82 is larger than 12.59, H_0 is rejected. It is concluded that the responses to the question are not independent of race. Inspection of the chi-square contributions reported in Table 8–10 suggests that more Asian students than expected think that integration is the forced mixing of people of different races.

8–5. Tests for Trend in Contingency Tables

The chi-square test of independence is frequently applied to $R \times C$ contingency tables in which the categories $A_1, A_2, \ldots, A_R$ or $B_1, B_2, \ldots, B_C$, or both, are ordered. While the test may be used for the analysis of data in which the categories define an ordered scale or relationship, it is not recommended since better tests are available. These tests are discussed in Sections 12–8 and 16–10, and one other form is presented in this section. For the data of Table 8–8, neither the column nor row characteristic is ordered. This means that the frequencies can be permuted by rows or by columns without influencing the value of X^2 or the interpretation of the final data. This is not true for the data to be examined in Table 8–11. If the columns of

TABLE 8–11. Joint responses to the questionnaire on the pre- and posttest of the 76 adult citizens in the study.

Y_2 / Y_1	First quartile	Second quartile	Third quartile	Fourth quartile	Total
Lower third	12	6	5	2	25
Middle third	6	9	7	4	26
Upper third	1	4	7	13	25
Total	19	19	19	19	76

Table 8–11 are permuted in any way, the value of X^2 is left invariant, but the alteration of the ordering of the column or row classes makes the interpretation of the data somewhat fuzzy. This insensitivity of the chi-square test of independence to ordering on Y_1 or Y_2 reduces the statistical power of the test for ordinal data.

The procedure described in this section is adapted from methods described by Maxwell (1961) for ordered contingency tables. However, the methods are also valid for tests of homogeneity where both the response variable and the treatment variable are ordered. When this occurs, it is possible to quantify the variables and then use classical methods to test for linear trend in mean response across the treatment conditions. In this form, the test serves as an assumption-freer competitor to bivariate normal-curve models.

EXAMPLE 8–5.1. In a study on attitudes of adults in a small city in western New York State, 76 parents of medium family-income level were asked to respond to a questionnaire in which they were asked about their attitudes toward their school administration, certain school programs, and general school problems. The questionnaires were administered to the parents prior to instituting an experimental reading program in which their children were to participate.

During the program, parents were informed about how well their children were doing, and general information was given to them about the school and its objectives. After the completion of the program, the parents were given the same questionnaire and asked to report their attitudes on the same questions answered at the beginning of the study. On both tests, high scores represented positive attitudes.

The researcher of this study would like to know whether there is a relationship between the two sets of responses. That is, did parents with favorable responses maintain their positive attitudes and those with negative attitudes retain their negative views? Thus, one is asking whether the responses on the two testings are correlated in some fashion. If the two sets of scores approximate a bivariate normal distribution, use can be made of classical correlation models.

The research question is evaluated by dividing the scores on the pretest at the lower, middle, and upper third scores and then checking to see whether scores on the posttest maintain the relative positions as defined by the first, second, third, and fourth quartiles. Pretest scores were divided into thirds to ensure that no cell would have an expected value less than 5. The joint frequency table for the pre- and post-test scores is shown in Table 8–11.

The hypothesis tested by the method of Section 8–5 is that the responses to the two administrations of the questionnaire are unrelated, or statistically independent. As a statistical hypothesis, this reduces to $H_0: P(A_i \cap B_j) = P(A_i)P(B_j)$, where i = lower, middle, and upper on the pretest and j = first, second, third, and fourth quartile on the posttest. The alternative hypothesis is $H_1: H_0$ is false.

The test statistic for this test is:

$$X^2 = \sum_{i=1}^{3} \sum_{j=1}^{4} \frac{[X_{ij} - \hat{E}(X_{ij})]^2}{\hat{E}(X_{ij})}$$

The hypothesis of statistical independence is rejected if:

$$X^2 > X^2_{6;0.95} = 12.59$$

The estimated expected frequencies under the hypothesis of statistical independence are summarized in Table 8–12. The value of the test statistic is given by:

$$X^2 = \frac{(12 - 6.25)^2}{6.25} + \frac{(6 - 6.25)^2}{6.25} + \cdots + \frac{(13 - 6.25)^2}{6.25} = 23.04$$

Since 23.04 is larger than 12.59, H_0 is rejected. It is concluded that the responses to the questionnaire on two testings are not independent. One would like to conclude that parents with negative attitudes maintain their negative attitudes, while parents with positive attitudes continue to have positive attitudes; however, such a conclusion is not justified under the model. Unfortunately, the alternative hypothesis of actual interest has not been tested by this specific test. Instead, the alternative of interest states that the scores on the two tests increase together. In statistical terms, this means that a linear, or even curvilinear, component of trend is observed in the test scores. Classical quantitative regression methods can be used to test this ordered hypothesis on qualitative data. The method of analysis to be described is taken from Maxwell (1961).

The regression model requires that both variables, Y_1 and Y_2, be defined by ordered classes. Thus, if Y_1 is ordered and Y_2 is not, then the methods described in Chapter 16 can be employed. To initiate the computations, the ordered classes are quantified by any ordered sequence of numbers of interest. Surprisingly, the final results are essentially independent of the numerical values assigned to the ordered

TABLE 8–12. The estimated expected frequencies for the data of Table 8–11.

Pretest / Posttest	First quartile	Second quartile	Third quartile	Fourth quartile	Total
Lower third	6.25	6.25	6.25	6.25	25
Middle third	6.50	6.50	6.50	6.50	26
Upper third	6.25	6.25	6.25	6.25	25
Total	19	19	19	19	76

classes, but, as recommended by Maxwell, one should select the numerical values so as to keep the arithmetic simple. This can be achieved with ease by using the coefficients associated with the linear component from the standard table of orthogonal polynomials.

EXAMPLE 8–5.2. According to the figures of Table A–9, the linear coefficients for $K = 3$ are $-1, 0, +1$, while for $K = 4$ the linear coefficients are $-3, -1, +1, +3$. With these scaled values and the frequencies of Table 8–11:

1. $\Sigma\ y_1 = 25(-1) + 26(0) + 25(+1) = 0$
2. $\Sigma\ y_1^2 = 25(-1)^2 + 26(0)^2 + 25(+1)^2 = 50$
3. $\Sigma\ y_2 = 19(-3) + 19(-1) + 19(+1) + 19(+3) = 0$
4. $\Sigma\ y_2^2 = 19(-3)^2 + 19(-1)^2 + 19(+1)^2 + 19(+3)^2 = 380$
5. $\Sigma\ y_1 y_2 = 12(-1)(-3) + 6(0)(-3) + 1(+1)(-3)$
   $\quad + 6(-1)(-1) + 9(0)(-1) + 4(+1)(-1)$
   $\quad + 5(-1)(+1) + 7(0)(+1) + 7(+1)(+1)$
   $\quad + 2(-1)(+3) + 4(0)(+3) + 13(+1)(+3) = 70$

With standard linear regression theory, the slope of a regression line can be computed as:

6. $\hat{\beta} = \dfrac{N(\Sigma\ y_1 y_2) - (\Sigma\ y_1)(\Sigma\ y_2)}{N(\Sigma\ y_1^2) - (\Sigma\ y_1)^2} = \dfrac{76(70) - (0)(0)}{76(50) - (0)^2} = 1.4000$

At this point, the nonparametric test departs from the classical procedure, in that:

$$S^2_{Y_2 \cdot Y_1} = \frac{N-1}{N-2}\left[S^2_{Y_2} - \hat{\beta}^2 S^2_{Y_1}\right]$$

is not used to compute $SE^2_{\hat{\beta}}$, since the determination of the partitioned chi-square component is made under the assumption that $\beta = 0$. When $\beta = 0$, it follows that $S^2_{Y_2 \cdot Y_1} = S^2_{Y_2}$, so that:

$$SE^2_{(\beta=0)} = \frac{S^2_{Y_2}}{(N-1)S^2_{Y_1}}$$

For the observed data:

7. $S^2_{Y_1} = \dfrac{76(50) - 0^2}{76(75)} = 0.6667$

8. $S^2_{Y_2} = \dfrac{76(380) - 0^2}{76(75)} = 5.0667$

9. $SE^2_{(\beta=0)} = \dfrac{5.0667}{(76-1)(0.6667)} = 0.1013$

Under large-sample theory, $Z = \hat{\beta}/SE_{(\beta=0)}$ has a sampling distribution that is approximately $N(0, 1)$, so that $Z^2 = \hat{\beta}^2/SE^2_{(\beta=0)}$ is approximately X^2 with $v = 1$ degrees of freedom. Thus, for the observed results:

$$10. \; X^2 \;=\; \frac{\hat{\beta}^2}{SE^2_{(\beta=0)}} \;=\; \frac{(1.4)^2}{0.1013} \;=\; \frac{1.96}{0.1013} \;=\; 19.35$$

Since $X^2 = 19.35 > 3.84$, the 95% point of the X_1^2, it is neconcluded that the relation between the scores has a linear component. Final results are summarized in Table 8–13. As indicated, the departure from linearity is not significant, since $X^2 = 3.69 < 11.10$, the 95% point of X_5^2.

One advantage of this method is that the one-degree-of-freedom test for linearity may be significant, even when the total chi-square is not significant. This is a result of the higher power of the one-degree-of-freedom test when compared to the omnibus test of independence. Also, it should be noted that this method is symmetrical in Y_1 and Y_2. This means that the computed value of chi-square is independent of whether Y_1 or Y_2 is selected as the dependent variable. In this case, Y_1 was selected as the independent variable. If one were to repeat the analysis with Y_1 as the dependent variable, the resulting value of chi-square would be found to equal 19.35. As in standard regression theory, the positive algebraic sign of the regression slope is interpreted to mean that scores on the posttest increase as scores on the pretest increase.

Finally, it should be noted that the test of this section tests for linear relationships, provided the categories are equally spaced; otherwise the test is one of monotonicity of relationship, as described in Section 3–16. Since, in general, the exact nature of an ordered qualitative variable is unknown, it may be more prudent to state H_0 and H_1 as:

H_0: Relationship is not monotonic
H_1: Relationship is monotonic

8–6. Computing Formula for Chi-Square

A relatively simple computing formula is available for the Karl Pearson X^2 statistic. It was used repeatedly in Chapter 6, but it was not developed earlier since

TABLE 8–13. Analysis of chi-square table for the test of linear trend in the ordered contingency Table 8–11.

Source of variation	$\frac{d}{f}$	Value of X^2
Due to linear regression	1	19.35
Departure from regression*	5	3.69
Total	6	23.04

*Found by subtraction.

it was hoped that an intuitive feeling for the test statistic could be developed by doing the computations according to the defining formulas of Pearson. The computing formula is best suited for most modern desk or hand calculators and is, of course, recommended. Using this procedure, an experienced person can carry out the computations for most X^2 tests in five minutes or less. The computing formula is given by:

$$X^2 = \sum_{i=1}^{R} \sum_{j=1}^{C} \frac{X_{ij}^2}{\hat{E}(X_{ij})} - n$$

If the estimated expected frequencies are not computed, another computing formula is given by:

$$X^2 = n\left(\sum_{i=1}^{R} \sum_{j=1}^{C} \frac{X_{ij}^2}{X_{i.}X_{.j}} - 1 \right)$$

This latter formula is the easiest one to use.

8-7. The Mean Square Contingency Coefficient

If the hypothesis H_0: $P(A_i \cap B_j) = P(A_i)P(B_j)$ is rejected, then it is concluded that the two variables, Y_1 and Y_2, are not independent, or that they are correlated with each other. As in the classical correlation model, it is desirable to estimate the strength of the association between the two variables. In the classical model, the Pearson product-moment correlation coefficient is typically employed to describe the strength of the association between two variables that have a joint bivariate normal distribution. A corresponding measure for an R by C contingency table is the *mean square contingency coefficient*. This measure is defined as:

$$\phi^2 = \sum_{i=1}^{R} \sum_{j=1}^{C} \frac{[P(A_i \cap B_j)]^2}{P(A_i)P(B_j)} - 1$$

and is estimated in the sample by:

$$\hat{\phi}^2 = \sum_{i=1}^{R} \sum_{j=1}^{C} \frac{X_{ij}^2}{X_{i.}X_{.j}} - 1$$

In terms of the second computing formula for X^2, introduced in Section 8–6, it is seen that this estimate reduces to $\hat{\phi}^2 = (1/n)X^2$, a very simple function of the Karl Pearson statistic.

When the two variables Y_1 and Y_2 are independent, $X^2 = 0$, so that:

$$\hat{\phi}^2 = \frac{1}{n} X^2 = \frac{1}{n}(0) = 0$$

When the variables are not independent, $\hat{\phi}^2 > 0$. It can be shown that, when the variables are perfectly correlated:

$$\hat{\phi}^2_{max} = \min\{R - 1, C - 1\} = q$$

Since most researchers are used to thinking of correlation coefficients on a scale ranging from -1 to $+1$, or from 0 to $+1$, it is customary to redefine $\hat{\phi}^2$ as:

$$\hat{\phi}'^2 = \frac{\hat{\phi}^2}{\hat{\phi}^2_{max}} = \frac{X^2}{nq}$$

With this modification, the mean square contingency coefficient is often referred to as Cramer's measure of association (Cramer, 1946). Also with this modification, $\hat{\phi}'^2$ is similar to the Light and Margolin measure of explained variance for $I \times K$ tests of homogeneity (Light and Margolin, 1971; Margolin and Light, 1974). If it is noted that SST of the Light and Margolin statistic is the maximum value that SSB can attain, then the Light and Margolin statistic can be thought of as $\hat{R}^2_{LM} = SS_{observed}/SS_{maximum}$ and is like

$$\hat{\phi}'^2 = \frac{\hat{\phi}^2_{observed}}{\hat{\phi}^2_{maximum}}$$

EXAMPLE 8–7.1. For the data of Table 8–8, $X^2 = 12.82$. Thus:

$$\hat{\psi}'^2 = \frac{12.82}{158(\min \{3, 2\})} = \frac{12.82}{158(2)} = \frac{12.82}{316} = 0.0406$$

suggests an extremely weak but statistically significant association between race and type of definition of integration.

Note that even though the association between Y_1 and Y_2 is statistically significant, it is of such a small magnitude as to be worthy of little discussion. This example illustrates a very important rule of behavioral research. Statistical significance does not mean practical or real-world significance. Statistical significance means only that the relationship is not a chance or random relationship. It does not signify that the relationship is large enough to deserve further comment or analysis. For this reason, measures like $\hat{\phi}'^2$ and $\hat{R}^2_{LM}$ are extremely valuable. No chi-square test of independence or homogeneity should stop with the computation of X^2. Its value does not convey any practical information to a researcher, since it is a direct function of sample size. It is possible to increase n, and thereby increase X^2, but not increase $\hat{\phi}'^2$ or $\hat{R}^2_{LM}$. This is easily shown for $\hat{\phi}'^2$. For a sample of size n:

$$X^2_{(n)} = \sum_{i=1}^{R} \sum_{j=1}^{C} \frac{X^2_{ij}}{\hat{E}(X_{ij})} - n$$

Suppose the sample is increased by a factor of K. This means that, under H_0, each X_{ij} increases on the average to KX_{ij} and each $\hat{E}(X_{ij})$ is increased to $K\hat{E}(X_{ij})$. Thus:

$$X^2_{(Kn)} = \sum_{i=1}^{R} \sum_{j=1}^{C} \frac{(KX_{ij})^2}{K\hat{E}(X_{ij})} - Kn$$

$$= K\left(\sum_{i=1}^{R} \sum_{j=1}^{C} \frac{X^2_{ij}}{\hat{E}(X_{ij})} - n \right)$$

$$= KX^2_{(n)}$$

but

$$\hat{\phi}'^2_{(Kn)} = \frac{1}{q}\frac{X^2_{(Kn)}}{Kn} = \frac{1}{q}\frac{KX^2_{(n)}}{Kn} = \frac{1}{q}\frac{X^2_{(n)}}{n} = \hat{\phi}'^2_{(n)}$$

TABLE 8–14. *Observed frequencies for 100 teachers according to whether they held office in school and whether they were successful as teachers.*

Variables		Teacher performance		
		Successful	Unsuccessful	Total
Held offices	Yes	50	20	70
	No	10	20	30
Total		60	40	100

EXAMPLE 8–7.2. For data in Table 8–8, if $n = 158$ were increased to $n = (4)158 = 632$, the value of X^2 would also be increased to a value near $(4)(12.82) = 51.28$, but $\hat{\phi}'^2$ would remain equal to:

$$\hat{\phi}'^2 = \frac{51.28}{632(\min\{3, 2\})} = 0.0406,$$

the same value as found for $n = 158$.

In the case of the 2 × 2 contingency table, $\hat{\phi}'^2 = \hat{\phi}^2$, since $(R - 1) = (C - 1) = (2 - 1) = 1$. It is then customary to compute $\hat{\phi}$, the *phi coefficient*, as a measure of association.

8–8. The Phi Coefficient for 2 × 2 Contingency Tables

EXAMPLE 8–8.1. As an example of the determination of $\hat{\phi}$ for a 2 × 2 contingency table, consider the data of Table 8–14. These data represent the results of a study in which 100 teachers were randomly selected to take part in a teacher-efficiency experiment. Of these 100 teachers, 60 were judged to be "successful" by a panel of their superiors. Forty were placed in the "unsuccessful" category. Fifty of the successful teachers had held an elected office as a student in high school or college, while only 20 of the unsuccessful teachers had held such offices. With these data, one would like to determine whether a relationship exists between teacher performance and participation in the governing of school activities while a student. The estimated expected frequencies for the data of Table 8–14 are shown in Table 8–15.

In terms of the computing formula:

$$X^2 = \sum_{i=1}^{2} \sum_{j=1}^{2} \frac{X_{ij}^2}{\hat{E}(X_{ij})} - n$$

$$= \left(\frac{(50)^2}{42} + \frac{(10)^2}{18} + \frac{(20)^2}{28} + \frac{(20)^2}{12} \right) - 100$$

$$= 12.70$$

Since $X^2 = 12.70$ is greater than 3.84, it is concluded that a correlation between

TABLE 8–15. Estimated expected frequencies for the data of Table 8–14.

Variables		Teacher performance		Total
		Successful	Unsuccessful	
Held offices	Yes	42	28	70
	No	18	12	30
Total		60	40	100

teacher performance and offices held as a high-school or college student is significant at the 0.05 level. The strength of association is estimated by making the appropriate substitution with $q = \min\{1, 1\} = 1$:

$$\hat{\phi}'^2 = \left(\frac{1}{q}\right)\frac{X^2}{n} = \frac{1}{100}(12.70) = 0.127$$

and the correlation is:

$$\hat{\phi}' = \sqrt{0.127} = 0.36$$

This last example suggests that a test of H_0: $\phi = 0$ versus H_1: $\phi \neq 0$ is identical to a test of the hypotheses H_0: $P(A \cap B) = P(A)P(B)$ versus H_1: H_0 is false. Thus, one can state that a statistical test of independence is identical to the statement that $\phi = 0$. The only assumption required to justify the test is that the n pairs (Y_{1i}, Y_{2i}) are statistically independent. If the estimated expected frequencies exceed 5, then the Karl Pearson statistic may be used as a test statistic. If $X^2 > X^2_{v:1-\alpha}$, then the hypothesis of independence is rejected. If the estimated expected frequencies are less than 5, then the probabilities of Table A–8 may be used when making the decision to reject or retain H_0.

In classical theory, the Pearson product-moment correlation coefficient is used to determine whether two variables that have a bivariate normal distribution are statistically independent. It may be a surprise to some readers that the phi coefficient is computationally identical to the Pearson product-moment correlation coefficient. This equivalence is demonstrated in the following exposition.

TABLE 8–16. 2 × 2 contingency table in which A and B are scored with a numerical value of 1, while Ā and B̄ are scored 0.

Variable		Y_2		Total
		1	0	
Y_1	1	X_{11}	X_{12}	$X_{1.}$
	0	X_{21}	X_{22}	$X_{2.}$
Total		$X_{.1}$	$X_{.2}$	n

If, for a 2×2 table, the variables are rescored so that A is scored 1, $\bar{A}$ is scored 0, B is scored 1, and $\bar{B}$ is scored 0, then Table 8–1 can be written as Table 8–16.

The most frequently employed computing formula for the Pearson product-moment correlation coefficient is:

$$r = \frac{n\sum_{i=1}^{n} Y_{1i}Y_{2i} - \sum_{i=1}^{n} Y_{1i}\sum_{i=1}^{n} Y_{2i}}{\sqrt{n\sum_{i=1}^{n} Y_{1i}^2 - (\sum_{i=1}^{n} Y_{1i})^2} \ \sqrt{n\sum_{i=1}^{n} Y_{2i}^2 - (\sum_{i=1}^{n} Y_{2i})^2}}$$

Since the variables have been quantified,

$$\sum_{i=1}^{n} Y_{1i} = (1)X_{1.} + (0)X_{2.} = X_{1.}$$

$$\sum_{i=1}^{n} Y_{1i}^2 = (1^2)X_{1.} + (0^2)X_{2.} = X_{1.}$$

$$\sum_{i=1}^{n} Y_{2i} = (1)X_{.1} + (0)X_{.2} = X_{.1}$$

$$\sum_{i=1}^{n} Y_{2i}^2 = (1^2)X_{.1} + (0^2)X_{.2} = X_{.1}$$

$$\sum_{i=1}^{n} Y_{1i}Y_{2i} = (1)(1)X_{11} + (1)(0)X_{21} + (0)(1)X_{12} + (0)(0)X_{22} = X_{11}$$

so that:

$$r = \frac{nX_{11} - X_{1.}X_{.1}}{\sqrt{nX_{1.} - X_{1.}^2}\sqrt{nX_{.1} - X_{.1}^2}}$$

With a little algebra, it is easy to show that the latter result reduces to:

$$r = \frac{X_{11}X_{22} - X_{12}X_{21}}{\sqrt{X_{1.}X_{2.}X_{.1}X_{.2}}}$$

EXAMPLE 8–8.2. For the data of Table 8–14,

$$r = \frac{(50)(20) - (20)(10)}{\sqrt{(60)(40)(70)(30)}} = 0.36 = \hat{\phi}$$

the exact value found by computing $\hat{\phi}^2 = (1/n)X^2$.

8–9. Goodman's $\hat{\gamma}$ as a Measure of Association on a 2×2 Table

In addition to the phi coefficient as a measure of association for 2 by 2 tables, the following measure is also used. It was ascribed to R. A. Fisher by Goodman (1964). The measure is defined as:

$$g = \frac{P_{11}P_{22}}{P_{12}P_{21}}$$

If the variables being studied are statistically independent, it follows that:

$$g = \frac{P_{1.}P_{.1}P_{2.}P_{.2}}{P_{1.}P_{.2}P_{2.}P_{.1}} = 1$$

Since most researchers prefer to have statistical independence associated with a measure equal to zero, consider:

$$\gamma = \log_e g$$
$$= \log_e p_{11} + \log_e p_{22} - \log_e p_{12} - \log_e p_{21}$$

where $\log_e g$ is the natural logarithm of g. This is used as an alternative measure of correlation since, when the variables are independent, $\gamma = \log_e 1 = 0$. When the correlation is positive, $\gamma > 0$, while, if the correlation is negative, $\gamma < 0$. Goodman has shown that γ can be estimated as:

$$\hat{\gamma} = (\log_e X_{11} + \log_e X_{22}) - (\log_e X_{12} + \log_e X_{21})$$
$$= \log_e \left(\frac{X_{11}X_{22}}{X_{12}X_{21}} \right)$$

and that its variance is given by:

$$\text{Var}(\hat{\gamma}) = \frac{1}{X_{11}} + \frac{1}{X_{22}} + \frac{1}{X_{12}} + \frac{1}{X_{21}}$$

In practice, one computes $\hat{\gamma}$ not in terms of logarithms to the base e, but in terms of logarithms to the base 10. With this transformation:

$$\hat{\gamma} = 2.3026 \log_{10} \hat{\gamma} = 2.3026 \log_{10} \left(\frac{X_{11}X_{22}}{X_{12}X_{21}} \right)$$

EXAMPLE 8–9.1.   For the data of Table 8–14

$$\hat{g} = \frac{X_{11}X_{22}}{X_{12}X_{21}} = \frac{(50)(20)}{(20)(10)} = 5$$

so that:

$$\hat{\gamma} = 2.3026 \log_{10} 5 = 2.3026(0.6990) = 1.6095$$

while

$$\text{Var}(\hat{\gamma}) = \frac{1}{50} + \frac{1}{20} + \frac{1}{20} + \frac{1}{10} = 0.22$$

For large samples, $\hat{\gamma}$ tends to be $N(\gamma, \text{Var}[\hat{\gamma}])$. Thus, to test the hypothesis H_0: $\gamma = 0$ versus H_1: $\gamma \neq 0$ at $\alpha = 0.05$, one uses:

$$Z = \frac{\hat{\gamma} - 0}{\sigma_{\hat{\gamma}}}$$

as the test statistic and rejects H_0 if $Z < -1.96$, or if $Z > 1.96$. For these data:

$$Z = \frac{1.6095 - 0}{\sqrt{0.22}} = 3.43$$

Thus, H_0 is rejected. This agrees with the decision made for the test of H_0: $\phi = 0$ versus H_1: $\phi \neq 0$.

The 95% confidence interval for γ is given by:

$$\gamma = \hat{\gamma} \pm 1.96\sqrt{\mathrm{Var}(\hat{\gamma})}$$
$$= 1.6095 \pm 1.96\sqrt{0.22}$$
$$= 1.6095 \pm 0.9192$$

In confidence-interval form, this reduces to:

$$0.69 < \gamma < 2.53$$

Since $\gamma = 0$ is not included in the interval, it follows that Y_1 and Y_2 are correlated.

Since the sampling distribution of $\hat{\gamma}$ tends to be normal and its standard deviation is easy to compute, this measure of correlation has a number of advantages over $\hat{\phi}^2$ as a measure of association. Statistical tests and confidence intervals for γ are easy to establish. Also, one can test H_0: $\gamma_1 = \gamma_2$ by relating:

$$Z = \frac{\hat{\gamma}_1 - \hat{\gamma}_2}{\sqrt{\mathrm{Var}(\hat{\gamma}_1) + \mathrm{Var}(\hat{\gamma}_2)}}$$

to the standard $N(0, 1)$ distribution, provided observations between and within samples are independent. In addition, a confidence interval for $\theta = \gamma_1 - \gamma_2$ is given simply as:

$$\theta = (\gamma_1 - \gamma_2) = (\hat{\gamma}_1 - \hat{\gamma}_2) \pm Z_{1-\alpha/2}\sqrt{\mathrm{Var}(\hat{\gamma}_1) + \mathrm{Var}(\hat{\gamma}_2)}$$

Finally, one can test the hypothesis that K two-by-two contingency tables have equal correlation measures by means of the individual γ measures, but not through the corresponding ϕ measures. This procedure is described in Section 9–4.

8–10. Goodman's Simultaneous Confidence-Interval Procedure for R × C Contingency Tables Using Cross-Product Ratios

The coefficient $g = p_{11}p_{22}/p_{12}p_{21}$ defined in Section 8–9 is often called the cross-product ratio for a 2×2 contingency table. It equals 1 when the variables Y_1 and Y_2 are independent. The transformed measure $\gamma = \log_e g$ is called a first-order interaction component. Its similarity to an interaction term of a 2×2 analysis-of-variance model is apparent in the equation:

$$\gamma = \log_e p_{11} + \log_e p_{22} - \log_e p_{12} - \log_e p_{21}$$

Goodman (1964) has described a procedure that permits an in-depth analysis of the hypothesis of independence by means of contrasts in the g values or in terms of their transformed values defined as $\gamma = \log_e g$. The procedure is surprisingly easy to execute and efficient in its identification of reasons for rejecting the hypothesis of independence. For the procedure, a researcher examines contrasts in the individual γ values of the corresponding $R \times C$ frequency table. For a post hoc analysis, the constant value for each confidence interval is defined by:

$$\underline{S^*} = \sqrt{X^2_{(R-1)(C-1):1-\alpha}}$$

For planned analysis, one simply counts the contrasts of interest and then selects the critical value from the last column of the Dunn table of significant values reported in Table A–1 of the appendix. Since the contrast method is independent of conditions placed on the margins of a two-factor frequency table, the Goodman procedure may also be used for post hoc investigations of rejected hypotheses of homogeneity, as described in Chapter 6. Although the theory behind the procedure is easy to understand, it is not developed here, mainly because the corresponding test statistic requires the inversion of a fairly large variance–covariance matrix. Although it has not been verified, it is probably safe to conclude that the Goodman procedure can be used as a post hoc procedure for the Karl Pearson tests described in Sections 6–5 and 8–4. In any case, the method is best explained by an example.

EXAMPLE 8–10.1.   In the example of Section 8–4, it was concluded that the preferred definition of integration by high-school students was not independent of their race and, by inspection of the contributions to the Karl Pearson statistic, it was suggested that perhaps the major reason for the rejection was that Asian students selected definition 2 more frequently than chance selection would predict. This can be studied in greater detail by examining the contrasts in the individual γ associated with the $Q = \left[\begin{smallmatrix} R \\ 2 \end{smallmatrix}\right]\left[\begin{smallmatrix} C \\ 2 \end{smallmatrix}\right]$ 2 × 2 frequency tables. For the data of Table 8–8, $Q = \left[\begin{smallmatrix} 4 \\ 2 \end{smallmatrix}\right]\left[\begin{smallmatrix} 3 \\ 2 \end{smallmatrix}\right] = 18$. These tables are summarized in Table 8–17. Also reported are the individual $\hat{g}$, $\hat{\gamma}$, $\sigma_{\hat{\gamma}}$, and the confidence limits for each γ. For these data:

$$\underline{S^*} = \sqrt{X^2_{6:.95}} = \sqrt{12.59} = 3.55$$

As can be seen, none of the interaction components are statistically different from zero, but since the hypothesis of independence has been rejected, it is known that some contrast in the first-order interactions is different from zero.

This example demonstrates that the Goodman contrast procedure for tests of independence is similar to the contrast procedure of Scheffé for tests of equal centers in the classical ANOVA model. Rejection of H_0 does not guarantee that a meaningful contrast will necessarily be identified as statistically significant. An identified significant contrast may have no reasonable interpretation within the confines of the study even though it may be the reason for the rejection of H_0. In this example, it is not surprising that no γ was identified as being different from zero since the Karl Pearson statistic for the data, $X^2 = 12.82$, is just slightly larger than $X^2_{6:0.95} = 12.59$. Furthermore, $\hat{\phi}^2 = 0.041$ is essentially zero in value.

It is worth noting that each $\hat{\gamma}$ is a linear contrast in the $\log_e X_{ij}$. In fact, Goodman shows that all contrasts of the form:

$$\hat{\psi} = \sum_{i=1}^{R} \sum_{j=1}^{C} a_{ij} \log_e X_{ij}$$

are first-order interaction components with variances defined by:

$$\mathrm{Var}(\hat{\psi}) = \sum_{i=1}^{R} \sum_{j=1}^{C} \frac{a_{ij}^2}{X_{ij}}$$

TABLE 8–17. Confidence intervals for the 18 Goodman first-order interaction measures associated with the data of Table 8–8.

Table	Definition	Race	$\hat{g}$	$\hat{\gamma}$	$\sigma_{\hat{\gamma}}$	$\pm 3.55_{\hat{\gamma}}$	Decision
7 14 8 5	1 2	Asian Black	0.313	−1.1633	0.7343	2.6068	N.S.
7 39 8 8	1 2	Asian White	0.179	−1.7203	0.6469	2.2965	N.S.
14 39 5 8	1 2	Black White	0.574	−0.5551	0.6496	2.3061	N.S.
7 14 9 7	1 3	Asian Black	0.389	−0.9443	0.6843	2.4293	N.S.
7 39 9 29	1 3	Asian White	0.578	−0.5482	0.5604	1.9894	N.S.
14 39 7 29	1 3	Black White	1.487	0.3970	0.5238	1.8595	N.S.
7 14 5 12	1 4	Asian Black	1.200	0.1824	0.7054	2.5042	N.S.
7 39 5 15	1 4	Asian White	0.538	−0.6199	0.6597	2.3419	N.S.
14 39 12 15	1 4	Black White	0.449	−0.8008	0.4971	1.7647	N.S.
8 5 9 7	2 3	Asian Black	1.244	0.2183	0.7609	2.7012	N.S.
8 8 9 29	2 3	Asian White	3.222	1.1702	0.6289	2.2326	N.S.
5 8 7 29	2 3	Black White	2.590	0.9517	0.7088	2.5162	N.S.
8 5 5 12	2 4	Asian Black	3.840	1.3454	0.7800	2.7689	N.S.
8 8 5 15	2 4	Asian White	3.000	1.0986	0.7187	2.5514	N.S.
5 8 12 15	2 4	Black White	0.781	−0.2471	0.6892	2.4467	N.S.
9 7 5 12	3 4	Asian Black	3.086	1.1269	0.7330	2.6022	N.S.
9 29 5 15	3 4	Asian White	0.931	−0.0716	0.6420	2.2791	N.S.
7 29 12 15	3 4	Black White	0.302	−1.1973	0.5721	2.0310	N.S.

provided

$$\sum_{i=1}^{r} a_{ij} = 0 \qquad \text{for each value of } j$$

and

$$\sum_{j=1}^{c} a_{ij} = 0 \qquad \text{for each value of } i$$

This means that a researcher need not restrict his data-snooping to $\hat{\gamma}$ values only.

   EXAMPLE 8–10.2.   As an example, consider the second and fourth rows of Table 8–8, in which Asians are compared to Blacks and Whites for definitions 2 and 4. The coefficients for this contrast are shown in Table 8–18. In terms of these coefficients:

$$\hat{\psi} = (2 \log_e X_{21} + \log_e X_{42} + \log_e X_{43}) \\ - (2 \log_e X_{41} + \log_e X_{22} + \log_e X_{23})$$

so that, in terms of logarithms to the base 10:

$$\hat{\psi} = 2.3026(2 \log_{10} 8 + \log_{10} 12 + \log_{10} 15) - (2 \log_{10} 5 + \log_{10} 5 + \log_{10} 8) \\ = 2.4442.$$

For this contrast:

$$\text{Var}(\hat{\psi}) = \frac{2^2}{8} + \frac{1^2}{12} + \frac{1^2}{15} + \frac{(-2)^2}{5} + \frac{(-1)^2}{5} + \frac{(-1)^2}{8} \\ = 1.7750$$

so that the post hoc confidence interval for ψ is given by:

$$\psi = \hat{\psi} \pm \sqrt{X^2_{(R-1)(C-1):1-\alpha}} \; \sigma_{\hat{\gamma}}$$

$$= 2.4442 \pm 3.55\sqrt{1.7750}$$

$$= 2.4442 \pm 4.7297$$

Since zero is in the interval, the post hoc hypothesis is not supported.

8–11. Combining Data from Independent $R \times C$ Contingency Tables

The procedures of Sections 3–15 and 5–9 can be used to combine $K(R \times C)$

TABLE 8–18. Coefficients for the contrasts of Example 8–10.2.

Row \ Column	1	2	3	Total
2	+2	−1	−1	0
4	−2	+1	+1	0
Total	0	0	0	0

contingency tables if:

1. Individual hypotheses associated with each table are identical.
2. The alternative hypotheses are identical and directional.
3. The tables are of the same dimensions.

If the K tables are not 2×2, then procedures one, two, and three of Section 5–9 cannot be used. However, Pearson's lambda criterion can be used. This procedure is illustrated for the data of Table 8–19. For these three tables $X_L^2 = 4.92, X_M^2 = 5.71$, and $X_H^2 = 9.59$. Only the table associated with the high-income group is significant at $\alpha = 0.05$. However, visual inspection of the data suggests that the three tables are essentially the same, so that it makes sense to combine the tables as suggested by the λ criterion. For these data:

$$P_1 = P(X_2^2 > 4.92) = 0.0895$$
$$P_2 = P(X_2^2 > 5.71) = 0.0598$$
$$P_3 = P(X_2^2 > 9.59) = 0.0086$$

so that:

$$\lambda = -4.605 \sum_{k=1}^{3} \log_{10} P_k$$

$$= -4.605\left[\log_{10}(0.0895) + \log_{10}(0.0598) + \log_{10}(0.0086)\right]$$
$$= -4.605\left[(8.9518 - 10) + (8.7767 - 10) + (7.9345 - 10)\right]$$
$$= 19.97$$

TABLE 8–19. Experience with marijuana according to income of father and grade-point ratio of college sophomores.

Variable	Yearly income of father								
Experience w. Marijuana	Low			Medium			High		
	Yes	No	Tot.	Yes	No	Tot.	Yes	No	Tot.
Grade point ratio in freshman year									
3.0 more	8	10	18	10	10	20	10	12	22
2.0 to 3.0	4	23	27	5	23	28	5	22	27
Under 2.0	3	7	10	5	8	13	6	2	8
Total	15	40	55	20	41	61	21	36	57
Value of X^2		4.92			5.71			9.59	
Value of $\hat{\phi}^2$		0.090			0.094			0.168	

One-Sample Chi-Square Tests of Independence and Correlation and Measures of Association for Qualitative Variables

213

Since $K = 3$, $v = 2K = 6$, and the 95% decision rule is to reject H_0 if $\lambda > X^2_{6:0.95} = 12.59$. Thus, H_0 is rejected. It is concluded that the use of marijuana is not independent of grade-point ratio.

It should be noted that the additive property of chi-square can also be used in combining data from independent contingency tables. Under H_0, each $\phi^2_k = 0$, so that each X^2_k is distributed as $X^2_{v_k}$. Thus, $T = X^2_1 + X^2_2 + \cdots + X^2_k$ is approximately X^2 with $v = v_1 + v_2 + \cdots + v_K$. For these data:

$$T = 4.92 + 5.71 + 9.59 = 20.22$$
$$v = 2 + 2 + 2 = 6$$

so that H_0: $\phi^2 = 0$ is rejected, since $T = 20.22 > X^2_{6:0.95} = 12.59$. Thus, the final decision is the same as that made using Pearson's lambda criterion. Note that the Pearson $\lambda = 19.97$ is quite close in numerical value to $T = 20.22$. When the underlying variables are themselves distributed as X^2, this agreement should not be unexpected. This agreement would not be observed if the three tables had been combined into a single table and tested for independence. If this were done, it would be seen that $X^2 = 16.67$. Since this value would be related to the chi-square distribution with $v = 2$ degrees of freedom, it would appear that a spurious gain in statistical power has been achieved. In any case, it is suggested that the Pearson lambda criterion or the additive property of chi-square be used, since they are based on sound statistical theory.

Summary

Contingency-table analysis represents one of the oldest nonparametric procedures used by behavioral scientists. Introduced by Karl Pearson at the turn of the century, this method of analysis has essentially remained unchanged over time. In its most general form, a researcher has two variables, Y_1 and Y_2, which are partitioned respectively into R and C mutually exclusive and exhaustive subsets. For Y_1, the sets may be denoted by A_1, A_2, ..., A_R, and for Y_2 the sets may be denoted by B_1, B_2, ..., B_C. The hypothesis to be tested is that the two variables are statistically independent. In its statistical form, this hypothesis reduces to:

$$H_0: P(A_i \cap B_j) = P(A_i)P(B_j) \qquad \text{for all } i \text{ and } j.$$

The alternative hypothesis is generally denoted by:

$$H_1: H_0 \text{ is false.}$$

Thus, the statistical test is omnibus in nature. If H_0 is rejected, exact reasons for the rejection may not be known with any assurance. The test statistic used for deciding between H_0 and H_1 is given by the Karl Pearson statistic:

$$X^2 = \sum_{i=1}^{R} \sum_{j=1}^{C} \frac{[X_{ij} - \hat{E}(X_{ij})]^2}{\hat{E}(X_{ij})}$$

where $\hat{E}(X_{ij}) = n\hat{P}(A_i)\hat{P}(B_j)$. If each $\hat{E}(X_{ij}) \geq 5$, or if 20 percent of the cells fail to satisfy this condition, then one can reject H_0 with a Type I error of size α, if $X^2 > X^2_{v:1-\alpha}$, where $v = (R - 1)(C - 1)$.

In an alternative method of analysis, the hypotheses of independence can be stated in a qualitative correlational model. In this model, it is stated that the mean-square contingency, a measure of bivariate association, is zero. By definition, the sample mean-square contingency is given by:

$$\hat{\phi}'^2 = \frac{1}{q}\left[\sum_{i=1}^{R}\sum_{j=1}^{c}\frac{X_{ij}^2}{X_{i.}X_{.j}} - 1\right]$$

With $q = \min\{(R-1),(C-1)\}$, and where X_{ij}, $X_{i.}$, and $X_{.j}$ are as defined in Table 8–7, the estimate is quickly computed as:

$$\hat{\phi}'^2 = \frac{X^2}{nq}$$

where X^2 is the Karl Pearson statistic. With this model, H_0, as stated above, is equivalent to:

$$H_0: \phi'^2 = 0$$

with the alternative given by:

$$H_1: \phi'^2 > 0$$

When $I = J = 2$, the mean-square contingency reduces to the Pearson product-moment correlation and is simply computed as:

$$\hat{\phi} = r = \frac{X_{11}X_{22} - X_{12}X_{21}}{\sqrt{X_{1.}X_{2.}X_{.1}X_{.2}}}$$

where X_{11}, X_{22}, X_{12}, X_{21}, $X_{1.}$, $X_{2.}$, $X_{.1}$, and $X_{.2}$ are as defined in Table 8–1.

When sample sizes are small and $I = J = 2$, exact probabilities can be computed from the hypergeometric probability model, or Table A–8 can be used if $n \leq 15$. Use of the exact probability values should be considered if any expected value is less than 5. When this occurs, exact probabilities are given by:

$$P = \frac{\begin{bmatrix}X_{1.}\\X_{11}\end{bmatrix}\begin{bmatrix}X_{2.}\\X_{22}\end{bmatrix}}{\begin{bmatrix}X_{1.}+X_{2.}\\X_{11}+X_{22}\end{bmatrix}}$$

where $X_{1.}$, $X_{2.}$, X_{11}, X_{22}, n, and $X_{.1}$ are as defined in Table 8–1.

A special case of the 2×2 contingency table can be used to test the hypothesis that two continuous variables are statistically independent. In the literature, this test is called Blomqvist's double-median test for association. For this test, one first computes $\hat{M}_1$ and $\hat{M}_2$, the median values for each variable, and then determines the number of cases that are members of the four resulting sets defined by the partitioning values of $\hat{M}_1$ and $\hat{M}_2$. In general, the test is not recommended if the exact observation values are known, since the efficiency of the test, when compared to its parametric alternative for bivariate normal data, is equal to $E = (2/\pi)^2 = 0.405$. If, however, only scoring above or below the median is provided, then the efficiency of this test is *one*, since no competitors exist in this specific case. If the expected values are below 5, then the use of exact hypergeometric probabilities should be considered; otherwise, the Karl Pearson statistic can be computed.

While large-sample computations can be performed by means of the Karl Pearson definitional formula, many researchers prefer simpler computational methods which are given by:

$$X^2 = \sum_{i=1}^{R} \sum_{j=1}^{C} \frac{X_{ij}^2}{\hat{E}(X_{ij})} - n \quad \text{or} \quad X^2 = n \left[\sum_{i=1}^{R} \sum_{j=1}^{C} \frac{X_{ij}^2}{X_{i.}X_{.j}} - 1 \right]$$

where $\hat{E}(X_{ij}) = n\hat{P}(A_i)\hat{P}(B_j) = (1/n)X_{i.}X_{.j}$.

One of the disadvantages encountered in the use of $\hat{\phi}'^2$ as a measure of correlation for 2×2 tables is that the sampling distribution of $\hat{\phi}'^2$, when H_0 is false, is complex. Another measure of correlation that does not suffer from this disadvantage is the first-order interaction measure called gamma, which is defined as:

$$\gamma = \log_e g = 2.3026 \log_{10} g$$

where $g = p_{11}p_{22}/p_{12}p_{21}$. When $\phi = 0$, $g = 1$, and $\gamma = 0$; when $\phi < 0$, $g < 1$, and $\gamma < 0$; when $\phi > 0$, $g > 1$, and $\gamma > 0$; however, the range of γ is given as $-\infty < \gamma < +\infty$. This range is not easily interpretable.

The advantage that γ has over ϕ as a measure of 2×2 association is that the sampling distribution of γ is normal with:

$$E(\hat{\gamma}) = \gamma$$

$$\text{Var}(\hat{\gamma}) = \frac{1}{X_{11}} + \frac{1}{X_{22}} + \frac{1}{X_{12}} + \frac{1}{X_{21}}$$

where X_{11}, X_{22}, X_{12}, and X_{21} are as defined in Table 8–1. While confidence intervals for ϕ are not simple in form, $(1 - \alpha)$-percent confidence intervals for γ are given simply as:

$$\hat{\gamma} - Z_{1-\alpha/2} \sqrt{\text{Var}(\hat{\gamma})} < \gamma < \hat{\gamma} + Z_{1-\alpha/2} \sqrt{\text{Var}(\hat{\gamma})}$$

where $\hat{\gamma} = (\log_e X_{11} + \log_e X_{22}) - (\log_e X_{12} + \log_e X_{21})$. To test $H_0: \gamma_1 = \gamma_2$ versus $H_1: H_0$ is false, the appropriate test statistic is given by:

$$Z = \frac{\hat{\gamma}_1 - \hat{\gamma}_2}{\sqrt{\text{Var}(\hat{\gamma}_1) + \text{Var}(\hat{\gamma}_2)}}$$

which, when H_0 is true, is $N(0, 1)$. The $(1 - \alpha)\%$ confidence interval for $\gamma_1 - \gamma_2$ is given by:

$$(\gamma_1 - \gamma_2) = (\hat{\gamma}_1 - \hat{\gamma}_2) \pm Z_{1-\alpha/2} \sqrt{\text{Var}(\hat{\gamma}_1) + \text{Var}(\hat{\gamma}_2)}$$

In any $R \times C$ contingency table there exist $Q = \left[{R \atop 2} \right]\left[{C \atop 2} \right]$ first-order interaction measures. Thus, a post hoc or planned comparison analysis can be performed for any $R \times C$ contingency table or homogeneity table in terms of contrasts in the individual γ's of the model. Moreover, it has been shown by Goodman that:

$$\hat{\psi} = \sum_{i=1}^{R} \sum_{j=1}^{C} a_{ij} \log_e X_{ij}$$

where

$$\sum_{i=1}^{R} a_{ij} = 0 \quad \text{for } j = 1, 2, \ldots, C$$

and

$$\sum_{j=1}^{C} a_{ij} = 0 \quad \text{for } i = 1, 2, \ldots, R$$

are contrasts in the first-order interaction components with:

$$\text{Var}(\hat{\psi}) = \sum_{i=1}^{R} \sum_{j=1}^{C} \frac{a_{ij}^2}{X_{ij}}$$

These contrasts can be tested simultaneously for significance at $1 - \alpha$, by examining:

$$\hat{\psi} - \sqrt{X^2_{(R-1)(C-1):1-\alpha}}\; \sigma_{\hat{\psi}} < \psi < \hat{\psi} + \sqrt{X^2_{(R-1)(C-1):1-\alpha}}\; \sigma_{\hat{\psi}}$$

for the inclusion of zero. If zero is in the interval, it is concluded that $\psi = 0$; otherwise it is concluded that $\psi \neq 0$. For the special case in which $\hat{\psi}$ is defined by only 2 rows and 2 columns, $\hat{\psi}$ is reduced to the corresponding $\hat{\gamma}$ so that the γ are included in the set of contrasts investigated by the Goodman procedure.

Finally, the dependence of X^2 upon sample size should be understood. As the sample size increases, the value of X^2 increases. In fact, if for a sample of size n, the value of the Karl Pearson statistic is equal to $X^2_{(n)}$, it is then known that, if the sample size is increased to Kn, then the value of the Karl Pearson statistic is increased to $KX^2_{(n)}$. Even though the Karl Pearson statistic is inflated, the value of $\hat{\phi}'^2$ or $\hat{\gamma}$ is not, and for this reason, they should be determined and evaluated for *practical significance*. Just because a difference or correlation is statistically significant, it should not be concluded that a finding is of practical or scientific significance. Statistical significance means that the observed relationship cannot be attributed to chance; it means this, and *only* this. Practical significance is a value judgment of the researcher; it is not a statistical decision and should *never* be construed to represent such a point of view.

Exercises

1. Are the paragraph-meaning test scores independent of mental age for the three different social classes represented in the data of Exercise 10 of Chapter 10? Since three tests of independence are being examined, use $\alpha_0 = \alpha_T/3 = 0.05/3 = 0.0167$ for each test. Also, note that negative correlations are not generally observed for these kinds of variables, so that one-tailed tests are easy to justify.

2. A study of teachers' perceptions of the causes of school failure reported the data shown

Teacher Grade Levels (percentages)

Perceived cause of school failure	Elementary teachers	Secondary teachers	Vocational-technical teachers
Student characteristics	54%	65%	64%
Family and/or social conditions	62%	44%	34%
Work and methods of school	27%	63%	57%
Other causes	15%	8%	27%
Number of teachers	300	90	70

One-Sample Chi-Square Tests of Independence and Correlation and Measures of Association for Qualitative Variables

in the table for a sample of 460 teachers who were classified by level taught. Can the chi-square test of independence be used, validly, to determine whether teachers' perceptions of the causes of school failure are related to the level taught? Explain why, or why not.

*3. A group of 219 college sophomores were randomly selected from campus registration rolls by 18 students enrolled in a class of Physiological Psychology. The 219 students were asked their sex and whether or not they had red-green colorblindness. Results are as shown in the accompanying table. On the basis of this evidence, would one conclude that red-green colorblindness is independent of sex? Use the large-sample Karl Pearson test to answer the question. Estimate ϕ^2 from the data.

Variable	Male	Female	Total
Colorblind	11	1	12
Not colorblind	107	100	207
Total	118	101	219

*4. Analyze the data of Exercise 3 in terms of the Goodman first-order interaction measure, γ, of Section 8–9. What relationship exists between the Karl Pearson statistic of Exercise 3 and $Z^2 = \hat{\gamma}^2/\text{Var}(\hat{\gamma})$? Which test seems to have more power? Why?

*5. A group of 302 White sophomore males were randomly selected from campus registration rolls and examined with respect to hair and eye color. Results are as shown in the table. On the basis of these data, should one conclude that hair color and eye color are independent genetic traits? Estimate ϕ'^2 for these data.

Eye color	Hair color				Total
	Black	Brown	Red	Blonde	
Brown	38	61	13	4	116
Blue	10	43	8	51	112
Other	9	40	13	12	74
Total	57	144	34	67	302

*6. The hypothesis of independence of Exercise 5 was rejected. Perform a post hoc investigation on the frequencies, using the Goodman procedures of Section 8–10.

*7. With respect to color pigmentation, the hair colors of Exercise 5 can be ordered as black > brown > red > blonde. This suggests that the test for trend procedure described in Section 8–5 can be used in the analysis of the tabled data. Since the eye color cannot be ordered, remove the 74 males who were classified as "Other" and do a test for trend on the resulting 4 × 2 contingency table. What is the specific hypothesis under test? What do you conclude?

*8. The analysis of Exercise 7 can be performed by examining the linear contrast defined by the coefficients of Table A–9 for ($K = 4$). For these data:

$$\hat{\psi} = -3\hat{p}_{black} - 1\hat{p}_{brown} + 1\hat{p}_{red} + 3\hat{p}_{blonde}$$

Compute:

$$Z^2 = \frac{\hat{\psi}^2}{SE_{\hat{\psi}}^2}$$

and compare it to X_1^2 of Exercise 7. What does this suggest to you about the two methods being compared?

*9. Repeat the analysis of Example 8–5.2, but switch the roles of Y_1 and Y_2. Let Y_1 serve as the independent variable and Y_2 as the dependent variable.

*10. Perform a post hoc analysis of the data of Table 8–11 in terms of the Goodman first-order interaction components.

*11. 120 college sophomores were given a 15-item questionnaire designed to assess their attitude toward the Nazi atrocities against the Jews before and during the Second World War. High scores represented unfavorable attitudes. The score distribution was

Pretest → Posttest ↓	Group 1 Strong critical message			
	Low	Medium	High	
	0 to 8	9 to 13	14 to 15	Total
High, 14 to 15	12	15	18	45
Medium, 9 to 13	6	4	1	11
Low, 0 to 8	2	1	1	4
Total	20	20	20	60

Pretest → Posttest ↓	Group 2 Weak critical message			
	Low	Medium	High	
	0 to 8	9 to 13	14 to 15	Total
High, 14 to 15	1	3	19	23
Medium, 9 to 13	6	15	0	21
Low, 0 to 8	13	2	1	16
Total	20	20	20	60

divided into thirds, and half of the members of each third were assigned to one of two different persuasion conditions. Group 1 was given a strongly worded essay critical of the Nazi atrocities, while Group 2 was given an essay that did not condemn the Nazi cruelties. The students were posttested two weeks later on the same instrument that had been used as a pretest instrument. Results are as shown in tables herewith. Analyze these two tables by using the methods of Section 8–5. What are the specific hypotheses under test? For the code values use:

a) $\{-1\ 0\ +1\}$, the coefficients of the linear contrast for $K = 3$, and

b) $\{3.5\ 11\ 14.5\}$, the midscores for each score category

What are the effects of these two coding schemes on the test statistics and the decisions?

12. A researcher wanted to determine whether there was a relationship between musical knowledge, measured by a paper-and-pencil test, and musical performance rated by judges. Twenty advanced piano students were given the paper-and-pencil test of musical knowledge, and a tape-recording of each student's performance of the same selections was rated by expert judges. The data were reported in contingency-table form, as shown. Identify several tests of relationship that can be used for 2×2 tables and defend your choice of the "best" test. Carry out your chosen test at $\alpha = 0.05$.

| | Musical knowledge | | |
Musical performance	Above median	Below median	Total
Above median	7	3	10
Below median	3	7	10
Total	10	10	20

13. Use the Goodman post hoc procedures for the frequencies of Table 6–7.

*14. Use the Goodman post hoc procedure for the data of Exercise 4 of Chapter 6.

15. A sociometric study carried out in a small college asked each of the 165 faculty members to "Name the colleague at the college, regardless of field, whom you regard most highly for teaching skills." The 165 choices were classified on a number of dimensions, including age. Assume that the data were as shown in the accompanying

| | Age of person chosen | | | | |
Age of chooser	Under 30	30–39	40–49	50 plus	Total
Under 30	27	19	8	6	60
30–39	12	16	11	5	44
40–49	15	5	12	4	36
50 plus	6	4	5	10	25
Total	60	44	36	25	165

table. The person conducting the study wants to determine whether the age of the person chosen is independent of the age of the chooser. In what ways(s) does the design of this study differ from designs used in this chapter? Is use of the chi-square test of independence for these data warranted? Why?

*16. A study similar to that in Exercise 15 was carried out in a large teachers' college. A sample of 165 faculty members was randomly chosen from the very large faculty and the question of Exercise 15 was put to each person. Their choices were limited to the faculty of the college, but not to the 165 members of the sample. Assume that the data were as shown in the table herewith. How would you test the hypothesis that the age of the person chosen is independent of the age of the chooser? If you arbitrarily interchanged both the first and second rows and the first and second columns of the data, would your test statistic and/or measure of association be affected? Explain. If your answer is that the measures would be unaffected, propose another test or measure of association that is sensitive to the order in the data.

Age of chooser	Age of person chosen				Total
	Under 30	30–39	40–49	50 plus	
Under 30	27	19	8	6	60
30–39	7	16	7	14	44
40–49	5	9	12	10	36
50 plus	4	5	6	10	25
Total	43	49	33	40	165

17. Assume that five chi-square tests of independence are performed at $\alpha = 0.01, 0.05, 0.05$, 0.01, and 0.01, respectively. What is the probability of making at least one Type I error in the set of five tests? What have you assumed in responding?

18. In $n = 100$, how large would the computed chi-square for a 3×2 contingency table have to be so that $\hat{\phi}' \geq 0.05$? What is the probability of obtaining a chi-square value this large or larger if the null hypothesis of $\hat{\phi}'^2 = 0$ is really true? To what value of $\hat{\phi}'$ would a computed chi-square of 6.00 correspond? (Assume $n = 100$, and a 3×2 table.)

19. A researcher reported the following percentage distributions of responses to questions asked in a survey of a low-income community.
Question 1: Can you think of any families around here that are poor?
Question 2: What is your yearly family income?

Question 2	Question 1	
	Yes	No
$0–$3600	43%	57%
$3601–$6400	43%	57%
$6401–$9200	54%	46%

Use these data to determine whether there is a nonzero relationship between the respondent's family income and his/her perception of poverty. Use $\alpha = 0.05$ and assume

$n = 300$, with 100 respondents in each of the three income categories. Would your conclusions regarding the relationship of respondent's family income and perception of poverty be the same if $n = 1200$, with 400 respondents in each of the three income categories?

20. What extra information would one obtain if the chi-square test of independence were to be applied to the data of Exercise 3 of Chapter 7? Do the test and determine $\hat{\phi}'$. Does this analysis help in the interpretation of Exercise 3(a) of Chapter 7? Provide an explanation to defend your position.

21. Determine the phi coefficient of Table 7–1. What bearing does this have on the hypothesis of the McNemar test? Why?

22. Use the method of Section 8–5 to analyze the data of Table 6–7.

23. Use the method of Section 8–5 to analyze the data of Exercise 4 in Chapter 6.

24. Use the method of Section 8–5 to analyze the data of Example 6–5.1. Compare the X_1^2 value of the method of Section 8–5 to the X_1^2 of Example 6–5.1, which is defined as $\hat{\psi}_{linear}^2 / SE_{linear}^2$.

Chi-Square Tests
of Independence in Contingency
Tables for Three or More
Variables

9–1. Interaction Hypotheses in Multidimensional Contingency Tables

Interaction hypotheses involving qualitative variables are relatively common in social-science research; however, until the early 1960s, only a few statistical tests were available for such data-analysis problems. Recent work by Goodman (1963a, 1963b, 1964a, 1964b, 1969, 1970), Grizzle, Starmer, and Koch (1969), Lewis (1962), and Mosteller (1968) has focused attention on the analysis of interaction in multiple-factor contingency tables.

This chapter considers some of the newer analytic procedures for multi-factor contingency tables. Chapters 6 and 8 distinguished between tests of equality for proportions across independent samples and tests of statistical independence between variables in two-factor contingency tables. A similar distinction is maintained in this chapter, as two additional factors are included in the basic two-factor tables of Chapters 6 and 8.

9–2. Nonparametric Interaction Analysis of K Two-Sample Binomial Tables

To simplify the presentation of this method, consider the following example from an evaluation of the effectiveness of a junior-high-school reorganization program designed to integrate the *de facto* segregated public schools of a northern urban community.

EXAMPLE 9–2.1. As part of the reorganization program, two *de facto* segregated schools, one primarily White and the other primarily Black, had their school boundaries altered so that the proportion of White and Black students in the two schools reflected the general racial composition of the community. A third school, which was essentially racially balanced, was not included in the reorganization. Because of the boundary changes, about one-half of the students at the predominantly White school were transferred during the reorganization year to the school that had been primarily Black. At the same time, about half of the students from the predominantly Black school were sent to the White school.

After one year of operation of the reorganization plan, random samples of Black and White students were selected from each school and given a 25-item questionnaire designed to measure their attitudes toward the reorganization program. One of the questions asked of the students was:

How well do you get along with your classmates this year

(as compared to last year)? Better _____ Worse _____

While differences in attitudes were expected between schools because of the inequalities in school facilities and the resulting mixing of students from very different cultural strata, there was interest in determining whether the attitudes differed within the schools by race. It was felt that each racial group would resent the "intrusion" of the newcomers of a different race at "their school." No difference in attitudes between the races was expected at the school not involved in the reorganization. Let P_{Wk} represent the proportion of White students at school k who report they got along "better," and let P_{Bk} represent the corresponding proportion for Black students at the same school. Let the difference in these proportions be represented by $\Delta_k = P_{Wk} - P_{Bk}$. The responses by school and race and the estimates of the parameters are shown in Tables 9–1 and 9–2, respectively.

The evaluator's hypothesis can be restated as the more general question, "Do school and race interact to produce differences in attitudes?" In statistical terms, the null hypothesis is:

$$H_0: \Delta_1 = \Delta_2 = \Delta_3 = \Delta_0$$

TABLE 9–1. *Frequency of responses to questionnaire item, by race and school.*

School	School 1		School 2		School 3	
Race	White	Black	White	Black	White	Black
Attitude						
Better	76	107	91	73	96	59
Worse	37	25	39	49	43	36
Total	113	132	130	122	139	95

TABLE 9–2. *Proportions or estimates of the binomial probabilities of responses for the data of Table 9–1.*

School	School 1		School 2		School 3	
Race	White	Black	White	Black	White	Black
Attitude						
Better	0.6726	0.8106	0.7000	0.5984	0.6906	0.6211
Worse	0.3274	0.1894	0.3000	0.4016	0.3094	0.3789
$\hat{\Delta}$	-0.1380		0.1016		0.0695	

versus the alternative hypothesis:

$$H_1 : H_0 \text{ is false.}$$

This represents a test of *no interaction* effects, since it asserts that racial differences in attitude are consistent across schools. Consider the equivalent contrast if only two schools are studied:

$$\psi = \Delta_1 - \Delta_2 = (p_{11} - p_{21}) - (p_{12} - p_{22})$$
$$= (p_{11} + p_{22}) - (p_{21} + p_{12})$$

As can be seen, this contrast has exactly the same form as an ANOVA contrast of interaction. The only difference is that proportions are substituted for means.

To develop a test statistic for this hypothesis, consider the model presented in Table 9–3. For this model, there are K different conditions or treatments that characterize or are applied to the two subpopulations. For each condition, random samples from each of the two different universes are selected. Each element from each sample is scored for the presence, A, or absence, $\overline{A}$, of the attribute or qualitative variable.

To specify the model more fully, let the K conditions of Table 9–3 be observed on two independent random samples selected from two binomial populations and let:

n_{1k} = Number of elements selected from binomial population *one* under condition k

n_{2k} = Number of elements selected from binomial population *two* under condition k

TABLE 9–3. *Mathematical notation for interaction hypotheses involved for K sets of two independent binomial samples.*

Attribute	Condition one		Condition two		...	Condition K	
	Pop. 1	Pop. 2	Pop. 1	Pop. 2	...	Pop. 1	Pop. 2
A	X_{11}	X_{21}	X_{12}	X_{22}	...	X_{1K}	X_{2K}
$\overline{A}$	$n_{11} - X_{11}$	$n_{21} - X_{21}$	$n_{12} - X_{12}$	$n_{22} - X_{22}$	...	$n_{1K} - X_{1K}$	$n_{2K} - X_{2K}$
Total	n_{11}	n_{21}	n_{12}	n_{22}	...	n_{1K}	n_{2K}

X_{1k} = Number of elements in sample 1 under condition k that possess attribute A

X_{2k} = Number of elements in sample 2 under condition k that possess attribute A

$\hat{p}_{1k} = \dfrac{X_{1k}}{n_{1k}}$ = Proportion of A's in sample 1 under condition k

$\hat{p}_{2k} = \dfrac{X_{2k}}{n_{2k}}$ = Proportion of A's in sample 2 under condition k

Under the model being considered, the sample sizes are fixed in advance, so that each 2 by 2 table defined for a fixed level of k corresponds to a 2 by 2 Irwin–Fisher table.

For large samples it is known that:

$$\hat{\Delta}_k = \hat{p}_{1k} - \hat{p}_{2k}$$

is approximately normally distributed with:

$$E(\hat{\Delta}_k) = E(\hat{p}_{1k} - \hat{p}_{2k}) = p_{1k} - p_{2k} = \Delta_k$$

and

$$\mathrm{Var}(\hat{\Delta}_k) = \mathrm{Var}(\hat{p}_{1k}) + \mathrm{Var}(\hat{p}_{2k}) = \frac{p_{1k}q_{1k}}{n_{1k}} + \frac{p_{2k}q_{2k}}{n_{2k}}$$

so that for each k,

$$Z_k = \frac{\hat{\Delta}_k - \Delta_k}{\sqrt{\mathrm{Var}(\hat{\Delta}_k)}}$$

is approximately $N(0, 1)$. Furthermore,

$$Z_k^2 = \frac{(\hat{\Delta}_k - \Delta_k)^2}{\mathrm{Var}(\hat{\Delta}_k)}$$

is approximately X^2 with $v = 1$ degrees of freedom. According to the model of Section 2–10, one tests $H_0\colon \Delta_1 = \Delta_2 = \ldots = \Delta_K = \Delta_0$ by computing:

$$U = \sum_{k=1}^{K} \frac{(\hat{\Delta}_k - \Delta_0)^2}{\mathrm{Var}(\hat{\Delta}_k)}$$

and rejecting H_0 if $U > X^2_{K:1-\alpha}$. However, Δ_0 and the $\mathrm{Var}(\hat{\Delta}_k)$ are unknown and must be estimated from the data. Under classical binomial theory, the estimate of $\mathrm{Var}(\hat{\Delta}_k)$ is given by:

$$SE^2_{\hat{\Delta}_k} = \frac{\hat{p}_{1k}\hat{q}_{1k}}{n_{1k}} + \frac{\hat{p}_{2k}\hat{q}_{2k}}{n_{2k}}$$

Since the sample sizes are assumed to be large and the $SE^2_{\hat{\Delta}_k}$ are consistent estimators of the $\mathrm{Var}(\hat{\Delta}_k)$, the $SE^2_{\hat{\Delta}_k}$ should be relatively close in value to the unknown $\mathrm{Var}(\hat{\Delta}_k)$. Under the model of Section 2–10, with $\hat{\theta}_k = \hat{\Delta}_k$ and $\hat{W}_k = 1/SE^2_{\hat{\Delta}_k}$, Δ_0 is estimated as:

$$\hat{\Delta}_0 = \frac{\sum_{k=1}^{K} \dfrac{1}{SE^2_{\hat{\Delta}_k}} \hat{\Delta}_k}{\sum_{k=1}^{K} \dfrac{1}{SE^2_{\hat{\Delta}_k}}} = \frac{\sum_{k=1}^{K} \hat{W}_k \hat{\Delta}_k}{\sum_{k=1}^{K} \hat{W}_k}$$

With this estimate, the final test statistic for the interaction hypothesis is given

by:

$$U'_0 = \sum_{k=1}^{K} \frac{(\hat{\Delta}_k - \hat{\Delta}_0)^2}{SE^2_{\hat{\Delta}_k}} = \sum_{k=1}^{K} \hat{W}_k(\hat{\Delta}_k - \hat{\Delta}_0)^2,$$

which has an approximate chi-square distribution with $v = K - 1$ degrees of freedom. Thus, the hypothesis of equal Δ_k is rejected if $U'_0 > X^2_{K-1:1-\alpha}$.

If the null hypothesis is rejected, one can define contrasts in the parameters and determine the simultaneous confidence intervals to identify the reasons for the rejection. Those intervals that do not include zero give clues as to why H_0 was rejected.

The contrasts for this model are given by:

$$\psi = a_1\Delta_1 + a_2\Delta_2 + \ldots + a_K\Delta_K,$$

with $a_1 + a_2 + \ldots + a_K = 0$. Unbiased estimates of the contrasts are given by:

$$\hat{\psi} = a_1\hat{\Delta}_1 + a_2\hat{\Delta}_2 + \ldots + a_K\hat{\Delta}_K,$$

while the squared standard errors of the contrasts are given by:

$$SE^2_{\hat{\Delta}} = a_1^2 SE^2_{\hat{\Delta}_1} + a_2^2 SE^2_{\hat{\Delta}_2} + \ldots + a_K^2 SE^2_{\hat{\Delta}_K}$$

If $\underline{S}^* = \sqrt{X^2_{K-1:1-\alpha}}$, the $(1 - \alpha)$-percent set of simultaneous confidence intervals for the ψ is given by:

$$\hat{\psi} - \underline{S}^*(SE_{\hat{\psi}}) < \psi < \hat{\psi} + \underline{S}^*(SE_{\hat{\psi}}).$$

If q, the number of contrasts in the Δ_k, is small, a researcher can make a more powerful analysis by replacing $\underline{S}^* = \sqrt{X^2_{K-1:1-\alpha}}$ by the normal-curve value $Z_{1-\alpha/2Q}$, which is read from the last column of Table A–1 of the appendix.

$$SE^2_{\hat{\Delta}_1} = \frac{\hat{p}_{11}\hat{q}_{11}}{n_{11}} + \frac{\hat{p}_{21}\hat{q}_{21}}{n_{21}} = \frac{0.6726(0.3274)}{113} + \frac{0.8106(0.1894)}{132} = 0.00311;$$

$$SE^2_{\hat{\Delta}_2} = \frac{\hat{p}_{12}\hat{q}_{12}}{n_{12}} + \frac{\hat{p}_{22}\hat{q}_{22}}{n_{22}} = \frac{0.7000(0.3000)}{130} + \frac{0.5984(0.4016)}{122} = 0.00357;$$

$$SE^2_{\hat{\Delta}_3} = \frac{\hat{p}_{13}\hat{q}_{13}}{n_{13}} + \frac{\hat{p}_{23}\hat{q}_{23}}{n_{23}} = \frac{0.6906(0.3094)}{139} + \frac{0.6211(0.3789)}{95} = 0.00401;$$

$$\hat{\Delta}_0 = \frac{\sum_{k=1}^{K} \frac{1}{SE^2_{\hat{\Delta}_k}}\hat{\Delta}_k}{\sum_{k=1}^{K} \frac{1}{SE^2_{\hat{\Delta}_k}}}$$

$$= \frac{(-0.1380/0.00311) + (0.1016/0.00357) + (0.0695/0.00401)}{(1/0.00311) + (1/0.00357) + (1/0.00401)} = 0.0017$$

$$U'_0 = \sum_{k=1}^{K} \hat{W}_k(\hat{\Delta}_k - \hat{\Delta}_0)^2$$

$$= \frac{(-0.1380 - 0.0017)^2}{0.00311} + \frac{(0.1016 - 0.0017)^2}{0.00357} + \frac{(0.0695 - 0.0017)^2}{0.00401}$$

$$= 10.21$$

Since 10.21 > 5.99, the hypothesis is rejected. Thus, it is concluded that racial differences in attitude are not equal across the three schools.

The $\begin{bmatrix} 3 \\ 2 \end{bmatrix} = 3$ simple pairwise contrasts for this study are:

$$\hat{\psi}_1 = \hat{\Delta}_1 - \hat{\Delta}_2 = -0.1380 - 0.1016 = -0.2396$$
$$\hat{\psi}_2 = \hat{\Delta}_1 - \hat{\Delta}_3 = -0.1380 - 0.0695 = -0.2075$$
$$\hat{\psi}_3 = \hat{\Delta}_2 - \hat{\Delta}_3 = 0.1016 - 0.0695 = 0.0321$$

for which the squared standard errors are equal to:

$$SE^2_{\hat{\psi}_1} = SE^2_{\hat{\Delta}_1} + SE^2_{\hat{\Delta}_2} = 0.00311 + 0.00357 = 0.00668$$
$$SE^2_{\hat{\psi}_2} = SE^2_{\hat{\Delta}_1} + SE^2_{\hat{\Delta}_3} = 0.00311 + 0.00401 = 0.00712$$
$$SE^2_{\hat{\psi}_3} = SE^2_{\hat{\Delta}_2} + SE^2_{\hat{\Delta}_3} = 0.00357 + 0.00401 = 0.00758$$

Since $X^2_{2:0.95} = 5.99$, the three simultaneous confidence intervals for the three simple pairwise contrasts are given by:

$$\psi_1 = 0.2396 \pm \sqrt{5.99}\sqrt{0.00668} = -0.2396 \pm 0.2000$$
$$\psi_2 = -0.2075 \pm \sqrt{5.99}\sqrt{0.00712} = -0.2075 \pm 0.2065$$
$$\psi_3 = 0.0321 \pm \sqrt{5.99}\sqrt{0.00758} = 0.0321 \pm 0.2131$$

The confidence intervals for ψ_1 and ψ_2 are statistically significant, while that for ψ_3 is not. Thus, race and school have an interactive effect on attitudes when Blacks and Whites in school 1 are compared with their peers in schools 2 and 3. Visual inspection of the data and the statistical significance of ψ_1 and ψ_2 suggests that the parameter differences, Δ_k, are alike for schools 2 and 3 and jointly different from that of school 1. This assertion can be tested by the following contrast:

$$\psi_4 = \Delta_1 - \tfrac{1}{2}(\Delta_2 + \Delta_3)$$

which is estimated by:

$$\hat{\psi}_4 = \hat{\Delta}_1 - \tfrac{1}{2}(\hat{\Delta}_2 + \hat{\Delta}_3) = -0.1380 - \tfrac{1}{2}(0.1016 + 0.0695)$$
$$= -0.2236$$

The squared standard error for this contrast is equal to:

$$SE^2_{\hat{\Delta}_4} = SE^2_{\hat{\Delta}_1} + \tfrac{1}{4}SE^2_{\hat{\Delta}_2} + \tfrac{1}{4}SE^2_{\hat{\Delta}_3}$$
$$= 0.00311 + \tfrac{1}{4}(0.00357) + \tfrac{1}{4}(0.00401)$$
$$= 0.00500$$

so that the corresponding confidence interval is given by:

$$\psi_4 = -0.2236 \pm \sqrt{5.99}\sqrt{0.00500} = -0.2236 \pm 0.1731$$

Since zero is not included in this interval, it is concluded that $\psi_4 \neq 0$.

Finally, three individual large-sample Irwin–Fisher tests of H_0: $\Delta_k = p_{1k} - p_{2k} = 0$ can be performed to determine if there are racial differences in attitude at each school. For this example:

$$Z_1 = \frac{\hat{\Delta}_1 - 0}{SE_{\hat{\Delta}_1}} = \frac{-0.1380}{\sqrt{0.00311}} = \frac{-0.1380}{0.0558} = -2.47$$

$$Z_2 = \frac{\hat{\Delta}_2 - 0}{SE_{\hat{\Delta}_2}} = \frac{0.1016}{\sqrt{0.0357}} = \frac{0.1016}{0.0597} = 1.70$$

$$Z_3 = \frac{\hat{\Delta}_3 - 0}{SE_{\hat{\Delta}_3}} = \frac{0.0695}{\sqrt{0.00401}} = \frac{0.0695}{0.0633} = 1.10$$

In terms of the critical values reported in the last column of Table A–1 for $Q = 3$ and $\alpha_T \leq 0.05$, individual hypotheses of no difference should be rejected if $Z < -2.39$ or if $Z > 2.39$. Thus, it is concluded that a significant racial difference in attitude exists at school 1.

The assumptions required for the preceding test are samples large enough so that the $\hat{\Delta}_k$ will be approximately normally distributed and independent binomial distributions for the populations within each condition.

The perennial question of how large a sample size is "large enough" is no more easily answered in this context than in that of the two-variable contingency-table design. A conservative rule of thumb suggests that all n_{ik} be large enough so that all:

$$n_{ik}p_{ik} \geq 5 \quad \text{and} \quad n_{ik}q_{ik} \geq 5$$

In this study, the independence assumptions are somewhat questionable. The Black and White students within a school had many opportunities to interact in classes, the cafeteria, library, and halls of the schools. Both casual and deliberate encounters could influence the attitudes of students of both races. Although the assumption of independence is probably violated, the magnitude of the effects of this violation upon the null distribution of the test statistic and the corresponding post hoc procedures is unknown.

9–3. Tests for First- and Second-Order Interactions

In the test for independence in the two-variable contingency table of Chapter 8, the null hypothesis stated that the product of the marginal probabilities of variables A and B equaled the joint probability of A and B:

$$H_0: P(A_i \cap B_j) = P(A_i)P(B_j) \quad \text{for all } i, j$$

One can extend this definition to include a three-dimensional or higher-dimensional contingency table. Thus, if all three variables are independent, their joint probability equals the product of their marginal probabilities:

$$H_0: P(A_i \cap B_j \cap C_k) = P(A_i)P(B_j)P(C_k) \quad \text{for all } i, j, k$$

This null hypothesis is not simply a statement of no second-order interaction; it is a statement of the joint independence of all three variables. Thus the null hypothesis implies:

1. $P(A_i \cap B_j) = P(A_i)P(B_j)$
2. $P(A_i \cap C_k) = P(A_i)P(C_k)$
3. $P(B_j \cap C_k) = P(B_j)P(C_k)$

That is, if the three variables are jointly independent, then they are independent in a pairwise fashion as well. Thus, the joint independence of all three variables implies no first-order interaction when the variables are considered in pairs by summing over the third variable; however, the simple absence of first-order interaction does not necessarily imply joint independence.

If H_0: $P(A_i \cap B_j \cap C_k) = P(A_i)P(B_j)P(C_k)$ states that the three variables are jointly independent; and if:

$$H_0: P(A_i \cap B_j) = P(A_i)P(B_j)$$
$$H_0: P(A_i \cap C_k) = P(A_i)P(C_k)$$
$$H_0: P(B_j \cap C_k) = P(B_j)P(C_k)$$

state the absence of first-order interaction, how is the absence of second-order interaction expressed? Several different answers have been given to this question. We will consider two such answers and the statistical procedures associated with one of the others. Historically, the first answer to the question of expressing *absence of second-order interaction* was Bartlett's (1935). This solution is based on the cross-product ratio defined in Section 8–9 for $I = 2$, $J = 2$, and $K = 1$. Bartlett's definition of no second-order interaction is conceptually simple and is symmetric; that is, no second-order interaction of A and B among the levels of C implies no second-order interaction of A and C among the levels of B. If P_{ijk} denotes the joint probability $P(A_i \cap B_j \cap C_k)$, then Bartlett's formulation of no second-order interaction is given as a statement of equality of all cross-product ratios:

$$H_0: \frac{P_{ijk}P_{i'j'k}}{P_{i'jk}P_{ij'k}} = \frac{P_{ijk'}P_{i'j'k'}}{P_{i'jk'}P_{ij'k'}} \qquad \begin{array}{l} \text{all } i \neq i', \text{ all } j \neq j', \\ \text{and all } k \neq k' \end{array}$$

The Bartlett hypothesis of no second-order interaction corresponds to the statement that all first-order interactions, as measured by the complete set of cross-product ratios defined in Section 8–9, are equal. Thus, if all cross-product ratios in an $I \times J \times K$ contingency table are equal, then the three factors do not have a second-order interaction.

Despite the simplicity of statement, the computational procedures associated with Bartlett's definition are quite tedious. The Bartlett model was used by Goodman (1964a) in the procedure illustrated in Section 9–5. Lancaster (1951) proposed a partition of an $I \times J \times K$ contingency table that tests the hypotheses of joint independence of all three variables and pairwise independence of A and B, A and C, and B and C, simply and directly. However, Lancaster's procedure tests second-order interaction as the *residual* of joint association of all three variables *less* all the pairwise associations. This results in an asymmetric and almost uninterpretable test of second-order interaction. Although Lancaster's procedure is computationally straightforward, an extensive discussion of the procedure is not given here because its artificial conceptualization of second-order interaction makes it less usable to the researcher than the computationally more complex procedures of Goodman (1964a) and Grizzle, Starmer, and Koch (1969).

9–4. Tests of Equality of Association Over K Independent Populations

In Sections 8–7, 8–8, and 8–9, several measures of association for contingency tables were introduced. The most commonly used such measure:

$$\hat{\phi}^2 = \frac{X^2}{n}$$

ranges from *zero* for statistical independence to the minimum of $(I - 1)$ and $(J - 1)$ for perfect association. Attempts to develop a coefficient with a range from 0 to 1 resulted in the mean-square contingency coefficient:

$$\hat{\phi}'^2 = \frac{\hat{\phi}^2}{q}$$

where $q = \min\{(I - 1), (J - 1)\}$. The logarithm of the cross-product ratio defined in Section 8–9 as:

$$\hat{\gamma} = \log_e\left[\frac{\hat{P}_{11}\hat{P}_{22}}{\hat{P}_{12}\hat{P}_{21}}\right] = 2.3026 \log_{10}\left[\frac{\hat{P}_{11}\hat{P}_{22}}{\hat{P}_{12}\hat{P}_{21}}\right]$$

does not have the desired range, $0 \le |\hat{\gamma}| \le 1$. However, $\hat{\gamma}$ can be used to test equality of association across independent groups and it can be extended to measure partial association in complex contingency tables. It should be noted that $\hat{\gamma}$ written as:

$$\hat{\gamma} = (\log_e \hat{p}_{11} + \log_e \hat{p}_{22}) - (\log_e \hat{p}_{12} + \log_e \hat{p}_{21})$$
$$= (\log_e X_{11} + \log_e X_{22}) - (\log_e X_{12} + \log_e X_{21})$$

has the form of the interaction contrast of the classical 2×2 ANOVA design and is therefore a measure of the two-factor interaction.

If K independent random samples are chosen and dichotomized on the basis of each of two random variables, the data table symbolized by Table 9–4 would be generated. For this data paradigm, in which the $2K$-column sample sizes are not chosen in advance but where the individual table sample sizes $n_1, n_2, \ldots, n_k$ are known in advance, the following notation is used:

X_{11k} = Number of elements in condition k that possess both A and B
X_{12k} = Number of elements in condition k that possess A and $\overline{B}$
X_{21k} = Number of elements in condition k that possess $\overline{A}$ and B
X_{22k} = Number of elements in condition k that possess $\overline{A}$ and $\overline{B}$

In the kth data table, the association between variables A and B is denoted by:

$$\hat{\gamma}_k = (\log_e X_{11k} + \log_e X_{22k}) - (\log_e X_{12k} + \log_e X_{21k})$$

The hypothesis of equality of association, or no difference in interaction, across the K tables is given by:

$$H_0: \gamma_1 = \gamma_2 = \ldots = \gamma_K = \gamma_0$$

with the alternative being $H_1: H_0$ is false.

Since, for large samples, the $\hat{\gamma}_k$ are approximately normal with:

$$E(\hat{\gamma}_k) = \gamma_k$$

and

$$\text{Var}(\hat{\gamma}_k) = \frac{1}{X_{11k}} + \frac{1}{X_{22k}} + \frac{1}{X_{12k}} + \frac{1}{X_{21k}},$$

Variables	Sample 1		Sample 2		. . .	Sample K		Total
	B	$\overline{B}$	B	$\overline{B}$	. . .	B	$\overline{B}$	
A	X_{111}	X_{121}	X_{112}	X_{122}	. . .	X_{11K}	X_{12K}	$X_{1..}$
$\overline{A}$	X_{211}	X_{221}	X_{212}	X_{222}	. . .	X_{21K}	X_{22K}	$X_{2..}$
Total	$X_{.11}$	$X_{.21}$	$X_{.12}$	$X_{.22}$	. . .	$X_{.1K}$	$X_{.2K}$	N

it follows that each

$$Z_k = \frac{(\hat{\gamma}_k - \gamma_k)}{\sqrt{\text{Var}(\hat{\gamma}_k)}}$$

is approximately $N(0, 1)$. Furthermore, each

$$Z_k^2 = \frac{(\hat{\gamma}_k - \gamma_k)^2}{\text{Var}(\hat{\gamma}_k)}$$

is approximately X_1^2. Thus, under the model of Section 2–10:

$$U = \sum_{k=1}^{K} \left[\frac{(\hat{\gamma}_k - \gamma_0)^2}{\text{Var}(\hat{\gamma}_k)} \right] = \sum_{k=1}^{K} W_k(\hat{\gamma}_k - \gamma_0)^2,$$

where

$$W_k = \frac{1}{\text{Var}(\hat{\gamma}_k)}$$

Since the variances of the estimates are known exactly, the W's do not have to be estimated. However, γ_0 is not specified by the hypothesis and, as a result, it is estimated from the data as:

$$\hat{\gamma}_0 = \frac{\sum_{k=1}^{K} \left[1/\text{Var}(\hat{\gamma}_k) \right] \hat{\gamma}_k}{\sum_{k=1}^{K} \left[1/\text{Var}(\hat{\gamma}_k) \right]} = \frac{\sum_{k=1}^{K} W_k \hat{\gamma}_k}{\sum_{k=1}^{K} W_k}.$$

With this value of $\hat{\gamma}_0$, the final test statistic is given by:

$$U_0' = \sum_{k=1}^{K} W_k(\hat{\gamma}_k - \hat{\gamma}_0)^2$$

Under the model of Section 2–10, U_0' is approximately chi-square with $(K - 1)$ degrees of freedom, provided the sample sizes in the individual contingency tables are relatively large.

If H_0 is rejected, a post hoc investigation of the γ_k is in order. For this post hoc analysis, contrasts in the γ_k are surrounded by confidence intervals. If zero is covered by an interval, it is concluded that the hypothesis associated with the contrast is not significantly different from zero. As shown by Goodman (1964c), the set of $(1 - \alpha)\%$ simultaneous confidence intervals for ψ is given by:

$$\psi = \hat{\psi} \pm \underline{S}\sigma_{\hat{\psi}}$$

where

1. $\underline{S} = \sqrt{X^2_{K-1:1-\alpha}}$
2. $\psi = a_1 \gamma_1 + a_2 \gamma_2 + \ldots + a_K \gamma_K$
3. $a_1 + a_2 + \ldots + a_K = 0$
4. $\hat{\psi} = a_1 \hat{\gamma}_1 + a_2 \hat{\gamma}_2 + \ldots + a_K \hat{\gamma}_K$

and

5. $\sigma^2_{\hat{\psi}} = a_1^2 \mathrm{Var}(\hat{\gamma}_1) + a_2^2 \mathrm{Var}(\hat{\gamma}_2) + \ldots + a_K^2 \mathrm{Var}(\hat{\gamma}_K)$.

If K is large and only Q planned contrasts in the individual γ_k are desired, then a researcher is well advised to replace $\underline{S} = \sqrt{X^2_{K-1:1-\alpha}}$ by the normal-curve value $Z_{1-\alpha/2Q}$ reported in the last column of Table A–1.

EXAMPLE 9–4.1. The test of equality of association across independent populations will be illustrated with a hypothetical study of employment status and occupational orientation in various delinquent and nondelinquent male adolescents. Assume that three groups of male adolescents, nondelinquents, first offenders, and repeat offenders, were selected and that each boy was classified with respect to his employment status and orientation toward occupational stability. The boy was classified as "employed" if he held a part- or full-time job on a regular basis, and "unemployed" if he held no job or was working only on a sporadic basis. Scores on an attitude measure of orientation toward occupational stability were used to classify the boys as "high" or "low" on occupational orientation. A test of equality of the γ_k's will determine whether employment status and occupational orientation are equally related for nondelinquents, first offenders, and repeat offenders. The data are reported in Table 9–5.

For these data and with logarithms to base 10:

$$\hat{\gamma}_1 = 2.3026 \log_{10} \left[\frac{135(12)}{25(35)} \right] = 0.6159$$

$$\hat{\gamma}_2 = 2.3026 \log_{10} \left[\frac{102(9)}{75(108)} \right] = -2.1778$$

$$\hat{\gamma}_3 = 2.3026 \log_{10} \left[\frac{59(8)}{139(40)} \right] = -2.4663$$

and

$$\mathrm{Var}(\hat{\gamma}_1) = \frac{1}{135} + \frac{1}{25} + \frac{1}{12} + \frac{1}{35} = 0.1593$$

$$\mathrm{Var}(\hat{\gamma}_2) = \frac{1}{102} + \frac{1}{9} + \frac{1}{108} + \frac{1}{75} = 0.1435$$

$$\mathrm{Var}(\hat{\gamma}_3) = \frac{1}{59} + \frac{1}{8} + \frac{1}{139} + \frac{1}{40} = 0.1741$$

TABLE 9–5. Occupational orientation, employment status for nondelinquents, first offender delinquents, and repeat offender delinquents.

Orientation toward occupational stability	Nondelinquents		First offenders		Repeat offenders	
Employment status	Employed	Unemployed	Employed	Unemployed	Employed	Unemployed
Low	135	25	102	75	59	40
High	35	12	108	9	139	8
Total	170	37	210	84	198	48

The estimate of the common measure of association across groups, $\hat{\gamma}_0$, is given by:

$$\hat{\gamma}_0 = \frac{(0.6159/0.1593) + (-2.1778/0.1435) + (-2.4663/0.1741)}{(1/0.1593) + (1/0.1435) + (1/0.1741)} = -1.3416$$

The test statistic is:

$$U_0' = \frac{(0.6159 + 1.3416)^2}{0.1593} + \frac{(-2.1778 + 1.3416)^2}{0.1435} + \frac{(-2.4663 + 1.3416)^2}{0.1741}$$
$$= 36.19$$

For $K = 3$, the hypothesis of equal measures of association should be rejected, since $X^2_{2:0.95} = 5.99$.

The pair comparisons of interest in this study are given by:

$$\hat{\psi}_1 = \hat{\gamma}_1 - \hat{\gamma}_2 = 0.6159 - (-2.1778) = 2.7937$$
$$\hat{\psi}_2 = \hat{\gamma}_1 - \hat{\gamma}_3 = 0.6159 - (-2.4663) = 3.0822$$
$$\hat{\psi}_3 = \hat{\gamma}_2 - \hat{\gamma}_3 = -2.1778 - (-2.4663) = 0.2885$$

with:

$$\text{Var}(\hat{\psi}_1) = \text{Var}(\hat{\gamma}_1) + \text{Var}(\hat{\gamma}_2) = 0.1593 + 0.1435 = 0.3028$$
$$\text{Var}(\hat{\psi}_2) = \text{Var}(\hat{\gamma}_1) + \text{Var}(\hat{\gamma}_3) = 0.1593 + 0.1741 = 0.3334$$
$$\text{Var}(\hat{\psi}_3) = \text{Var}(\hat{\gamma}_2) + \text{Var}(\hat{\gamma}_3) = 0.1435 + 0.1741 = 0.3176$$

so that the simultaneous confidence intervals with $\alpha = 0.05$ are given by:

$$\psi_1 = 2.7937 \pm \sqrt{5.99}\sqrt{0.3028} = 2.7937 \pm 1.3468$$

$$\psi_2 = 3.0822 \pm \sqrt{5.99}\sqrt{0.3334} = 3.0822 \pm 1.4132$$

$$\psi_3 = 0.2885 \pm \sqrt{5.99}\sqrt{0.3176} = 0.2885 \pm 1.3793$$

The measure of association for the nondelinquent group, γ_1, differs from those of both delinquent groups, the first offenders and the repeat offenders. Furthermore, γ_1 for the nondelinquents is indistinguishable from zero at the 0.05 level:

$$Z_1 = \frac{\hat{\gamma}_1 - 0}{\sqrt{\text{Var}(\hat{\gamma}_1)}} = \frac{0.6159}{\sqrt{0.1593}} = 1.54$$

while both γ_2 and γ_3 exhibit a nonzero relationship between employment status and orientation toward occupational stability:

$$Z_2 = \frac{\hat{\gamma}_2 - 0}{\sqrt{\text{Var}(\hat{\gamma}_2)}} = \frac{-2.1778}{\sqrt{0.1435}} = -5.75$$

$$Z_3 = \frac{\hat{\gamma}_3 - 0}{\sqrt{\text{Var}(\hat{\gamma}_3)}} = \frac{-2.4663}{\sqrt{0.1741}} = -5.91$$

For both groups of delinquents, boys who are classified as "high" in orientation toward occupational stability are more likely to be employed than are boys who are classified as "low" on the same scale.

9–5. Tests of Second-Order Interactions in $I \times J \times K$ Contingency Tables

In this section, the Bartlett model of no second-order interactions,

$$H_0: \frac{P_{ijk} P_{i'j'k}}{P_{i'jk} P_{ij'k}} = \frac{P_{ijk'} P_{i'j'k'}}{P_{i'jk'} P_{ij'k'}} \qquad \begin{array}{l} \text{all } i \neq i', \quad \text{all } j \neq j', \\ \text{and all } k \neq k' \end{array}$$

is presented in the form described by Goodman (1964c). This procedure is the simple extension of the model presented in Section 8–10. Goodman derived a test statistic which, under large-sample theory, has a chi-square distribution with degrees of freedom given by:

$$v = (I - 1)(J - 1)(K - 1)$$

An example of a three-dimensional contingency table is illustrated in Figure 9–1 for $I = 2, J = 3$, and $K = 2$. The Bartlett model of no second-order interaction implies that:

1. The two 2×3 contingency tables defined by the two rows and three columns are identical; or,
2. The three 2×2 contingency tables defined by the two rows and two levels are identical; or,
3. The two 2×3 contingency tables defined by the two levels and three columns are identical.

This means that a researcher has great flexibility of choice in performing the analysis of an $I \times J \times K$ contingency table. This flexibility is apparent in the example presented in this section, in which one of three possible interpretations of no second-order interaction is investigated. Furthermore, Goodman indicates that the model is valid for:

1. One sample partitioned on the three dimensions of rows, columns, and levels;
2. K samples partitioned on the two dimensions of rows and columns; and
3. KJ samples partitioned on the one dimension of rows.

The first model is similar to the Lancaster model. The second model is the extension of the procedure described in Section 9–4. Finally, the third model is the extension of

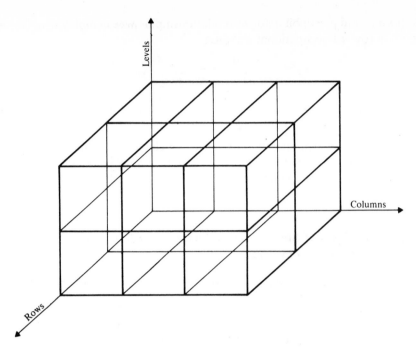

FIGURE 9–1. Three-dimensional contingency table.

the procedure described in Section 9–2 for $I = 2$ and $J = 2$. The Goodman procedure is illustrated for the first of these models.

In his writings, Goodman has presented a test statistic for testing the hypothesis of no second-order interactions. Since the test requires the inversion of a relatively large matrix of variances and covariances, it is intentionally not presented in this book. While the test statistic is difficult to compute, the contrasts defined by the post hoc procedure are not. As shown by Goodman, a researcher can set up contrasts in the row-and-column, the row-and-level, or the column-and-level γ's, and surround them with confidence intervals. If the confidence interval for any one contrast covers zero, it is concluded that the population contrast is not significantly different from zero. For the post hoc procedure, confidence intervals are determined with:

$$\underline{S}^* = \sqrt{X^2_{(I-1)(J-1)(K-1):1-\alpha}}$$

For planned analysis with Q contrasts, values of $Z_{1-\alpha/2Q}$ are read from the last column of Table A–1. For expository purposes only, contrasts will be defined in terms of the row-by-column γ's, though the row-by-level γ's and column-by-level γ's can be used. In any case, a researcher can define the variables so that contrasts of interest are defined in terms of the row-by-column γ's.

In terms of the row and column probabilities for the kth table, the $\gamma_{(ii')(jj')k}$, defined as shown in Table 9–6, are:

TABLE 9–6. $\gamma_{(ii')(jj')k}$ for a 2 $\times$ 2 table defined for rows (i, i'), columns (j, j'), and level k.

Row	Column j	j'
i	P_{ijk}	$P_{ij'k}$
i'	$P_{i'jk}$	$P_{i'j'k}$

$$\gamma_{(ii')(jj')k} = \log_e \frac{P_{(ij)k}P_{(i'j')k}}{P_{(i'j)k}P_{(ij')k}} = 2.3026 \log_{10} \frac{P_{(ij)k}P_{(i'j')k}}{P_{(i'j)k}P_{(ij')k}}$$

which are estimated in the sample as:

$$\hat{\gamma}_{(ii')(jj')k} = \log_e \frac{X_{(ij)k}X_{(i'j')k}}{X_{(i'j)k}X_{(ij')k}} = 2.3026 \log_{10} \frac{X_{(ij)k}X_{(i'j')k}}{X_{(i'j)k}X_{(ij')k}}$$

Across the K levels, a typical contrast is estimated as:

$$\hat{\psi} = \sum_{k=1}^{K} \sum_{i=1}^{I} \sum_{i'=1}^{I} \sum_{j=1}^{J} \sum_{j'=1}^{J} a_{(ii')(jj')k}\, \hat{\gamma}_{(ii')(jj')k}$$
$$_{i \neq i', \quad j \neq j'}$$

where

$$\sum_{k=1}^{K} \sum_{i=1}^{I} \sum_{i'=1}^{I} \sum_{j=1}^{J} \sum_{j'=1}^{J} a_{(ii')(jj')k} = 0$$
$$_{i \neq i', \quad j \neq j'}$$

and

$$\mathrm{Var}(\hat{\psi}) = \sum_{k=1}^{K} \sum_{i=1}^{I} \sum_{i'=1}^{I} \sum_{j=1}^{J} \sum_{j'=1}^{J} a^2_{(ii')(jj')k}\, \mathrm{Var}(\hat{\gamma}_{(ii')(jj')k})$$
$$_{i \neq i', \quad j \neq j'}$$

with

$$\mathrm{Var}(\hat{\gamma}_{(ii')(jj')k}) = \frac{1}{X_{(ij)k}} + \frac{1}{X_{(ij')k}} + \frac{1}{X_{(i'j)k}} + \frac{1}{X_{(i'j')k}}$$

The method is illustrated for the data of Table 9–7.

EXAMPLE 9–5.1. Data from junior-high-school questionnaires were categorized according to the race of the student (Black or White), the number of new friends made from the other race (Many, Some, or None), and the perceived amount of social mixing of students of different races (Often, Sometimes, or Hardly ever). The investigators were interested in determining whether racial differences and degree of integration, as measured by the number of interracial friendships, influenced the perception of interracial socialization on the part of other classmates.

TABLE 9–7. *Perceived social mixing of black and white students according to the race of the perceiver and the number of new friends from the other race made by the perceiver.*

Race of perceiver	Perceived social mixing	Number of new friends from other race		
		Many	Some	None
White	Often	230	246	9
	Sometimes	130	478	47
	Hardly ever	15	83	54
Black	Often	244	191	19
	Sometimes	109	259	49
	Hardly ever	12	59	37

They obtained the data reported in Table 9–7, for the total sample of 2271 junior-high-school students. Second-order interaction terms are investigated in a post hoc fashion with $I = 3$, $J = 3$, and $K = 2$, so that:

$$\underline{S}^* = \sqrt{X^2_{(I-1)(J-1)(K-1):1-\alpha}} = \sqrt{X^2_{4:0.95}} = \sqrt{9.49} = 3.08$$

For these data, the number of three-factor pairwise interaction contrasts is given by:

$$Q = \begin{bmatrix} I \\ 2 \end{bmatrix} \begin{bmatrix} J \\ 2 \end{bmatrix} \begin{bmatrix} K \\ 2 \end{bmatrix} = \begin{bmatrix} 3 \\ 2 \end{bmatrix} \begin{bmatrix} 3 \\ 2 \end{bmatrix} \begin{bmatrix} 2 \\ 2 \end{bmatrix} = 9$$

The nine contrasts are reported in Table 9–8 in terms of the frequencies defined in Table 9–7. For the contrasts defined by:

1. Perceived social mixing: {Often, Sometimes}, and
2. Number of new friends: {Many, Some},

$$\hat{\psi}_1 = 2.3026 \log_{10} \frac{230(478)}{130(246)} - 2.3026 \log_{10} \frac{244(259)}{109(191)} = 0.1245$$

The variance of this contrast is given by:

$$\text{Var}(\hat{\psi}_1) = \frac{1}{230} + \frac{1}{478} + \frac{1}{130} + \frac{1}{246} + \frac{1}{244} + \frac{1}{259} + \frac{1}{109} + \frac{1}{191} = 0.0405$$

so that:

$$\sigma_{\hat{\psi}_1} = 0.2010$$

The 95% confidence interval for ψ is given by

$$\psi_1 = \hat{\psi}_1 \pm S^* \sigma_{\hat{\psi}_1} = 0.1245 \pm 3.08(0.2010) = 0.1245 \pm 0.6191$$

Since zero is in the interval, H_0 is not rejected for this hypothesis. In terms of a statistical test,

$$Z_1 = \frac{\hat{\psi}_1 - 0}{\sigma_{\hat{\psi}_1}} = \frac{0.1245}{0.2010} = 0.62$$

TABLE 9–8. The $Q = \begin{bmatrix} I \\ 2 \end{bmatrix}\begin{bmatrix} J \\ 2 \end{bmatrix}\begin{bmatrix} K \\ 2 \end{bmatrix} = \begin{bmatrix} 3 \\ 2 \end{bmatrix}\begin{bmatrix} 3 \\ 2 \end{bmatrix}\begin{bmatrix} 2 \\ 2 \end{bmatrix} = 9$ pairwise comparisons for the $I \times J \times K$ Table 9–7.

Variable	Category	$\hat{\psi} = (\hat{\gamma}\text{ in White group}) - (\hat{\gamma}\text{ in Black group})$	$\sigma_{\hat{\psi}}$	Z	Decision
Perceived social mixing	Number of new friends				
Often Sometimes	Many Some	$\log_e\left[\dfrac{230(478)}{130(246)}\right] - \log_e\left[\dfrac{244(259)}{109(191)}\right] = 0.1245$	0.2010	0.62	N. S.
Often Sometimes	Many None	$\log_e\left[\dfrac{230(47)}{130(9)}\right] - \log_e\left[\dfrac{244(49)}{109(19)}\right] = -0.4700$	0.4803	−0.98	N. S.
Often Sometimes	Some None	$\log_e\left[\dfrac{246(47)}{478(9)}\right] - \log_e\left[\dfrac{191(49)}{259(19)}\right] = 0.3456$	0.4698	0.74	N. S.
Often Hardly ever	Many Some	$\log_e\left[\dfrac{230(83)}{15(246)}\right] - \log_e\left[\dfrac{244(59)}{12(191)}\right] = -0.1941$	0.4435	−0.44	N. S.
Often Hardly ever	Many None	$\log_e\left[\dfrac{230(54)}{15(9)}\right] - \log_e\left[\dfrac{244(37)}{12(19)}\right] = 0.8430$	0.6069	−1.39	N. S.
Often Hardly ever	Some None	$\log_e\left[\dfrac{246(54)}{83(9)}\right] - \log_e\left[\dfrac{191(37)}{59(19)}\right] = 1.0332$	0.4975	2.08	N. S.
Sometimes Hardly ever	Many Some	$\log_e\left[\dfrac{130(83)}{15(478)}\right] - \log_e\left[\dfrac{109(59)}{12(259)}\right] = 0.3185$	0.4492	0.71	N. S.
Sometimes Hardly ever	Many None	$\log_e\left[\dfrac{130(54)}{15(47)}\right] - \log_e\left[\dfrac{109(37)}{12(49)}\right] = 0.3730$	0.5040	0.74	N. S.
Sometimes Hardly ever	Some None	$\log_e\left[\dfrac{478(54)}{83(47)}\right] - \log_e\left[\dfrac{259(37)}{59(49)}\right] = 0.6930$	0.3494	1.98	N. S.

Thus, $\psi_1 = 0$ is not rejected since Z is not in the critical region defined by $Z < -3.08$ or $Z > 3.08$. The remaining eight tests are summarized in Table 9–8. None of the pairwise first-order interaction components are different from one another across the populations of Whites and Blacks.

Finally, with these $Q = 9$ contrasts considered as planned comparisons, the same decisions are reached, since none of the Z values is in the critical region $Z < -2.77$ or $Z > 2.77$, as read from Table A–1 of the appendix for $\alpha \leq 0.05$.

Summary

In this chapter, nonparametric tests of interaction were presented. These models can be used for any $I \times J \times K$ contingency table that arises from:

1. One sample partitioned on the three dimensions of rows, columns, and levels;
2. K samples partitioned on the two dimensions of rows and columns; and
3. KJ samples partitioned on the one dimension of rows.

The first of these models is like the Lancaster model, but Goodman's procedure uses a more satisfactory definition of second-order interaction. The second model, with $I = 2$ and $J = 2$, was illustrated in Section 9–4; while the third model, with $I = 2$ and $J = 2$, was illustrated in Section 9–2 in a slightly different fashion. For the latter form, contrasts are defined in terms of:

$$\Delta_k = p_{1k} - p_{2k}$$

which are estimated in the K samples as:

$$\hat{\Delta}_k = \hat{p}_{1k} - \hat{p}_{2k}$$

with

$$SE^2_{\hat{\Delta}_k} = \frac{\hat{p}_{1k}\hat{q}_{1k}}{n_{1k}} + \frac{\hat{p}_{2k}\hat{q}_{2k}}{n_{2k}}$$

Under this formulation, each

$$\psi = \sum_{k=1}^{K} a_k \Delta_k$$

is surrounded by a confidence interval with

$$\hat{\psi} = \sum_{k=1}^{K} a_k \hat{\Delta}_k,$$
$$SE^2_{\hat{\psi}} = \sum_{k=1}^{K} a_k^2 SE^2_{\hat{\Delta}_k}$$

and

$$\underline{S}^* = \sqrt{X^2_{K-1:1-\alpha}}$$

If $\psi = 0$ is not included in the interval, it is concluded, at probability level α, that $\psi \neq 0$.

Goodman's post hoc procedures can be used with the first model to determine whether any meaningful second-order interactions exist. Consider the $I \times J \times K$ contingency table, and focus on the set of 2×2 contingency tables that can be generated for each level of k. The general form of these tables is represented in

Table 9–6. A contrast in the cross-product ratios can be defined as:

$$\psi = \sum_{k=1}^{K} \sum_{i=1}^{I} \sum_{i'=1}^{I} \sum_{j=1}^{J} \sum_{j'=1}^{J} a_{(ii')(jj')k} \gamma_{(ii')(jj')k}$$

where

$$\gamma_{(ii')(jj')k} = \log_e \left[\frac{P_{(ij)k} P_{(i'j')k}}{P_{(ij')k} P_{(i'j)k}} \right] = 2.3026 \log_{10} \left[\frac{P_{(ij)k} P_{(i'j')k}}{P_{(ij')k} P_{(i'j)k}} \right]$$

is estimated in the sample by:

$$\hat{\gamma}_{(ii')(jj')k} = \log_e \left[\frac{X_{(ij)k} X_{(i'j')k}}{X_{(ij')k} X_{(i'j)k}} \right] = 2.3026 \log_{10} \left[\frac{X_{(ij)k} X_{(i'j')k}}{X_{(ij')k} X_{(i'j)k}} \right]$$

with

$$\mathrm{Var}(\hat{\gamma}_{(ii')(jj')k}) = \frac{1}{X_{(ij)k}} + \frac{1}{X_{(ij')k}} + \frac{1}{X_{(i'j)k}} + \frac{1}{X_{(i'j')k}}$$

If one then places confidence intervals about the individual ψ of interest, with:

$$\underline{S}^* = \sqrt{\chi^2_{(I-1)(J-1)(K-1):1-\alpha}}$$

and if $\psi = 0$ is not included in the interval, it can be concluded, at probability level α, that $\psi \neq 0$.

All of the methods of this chapter assume that all observations are statistically independent. Furthermore, since the tests of this chapter are all based on chi-square approximations, a researcher should ensure that each expected value exceeds 5, or that very few cell frequencies are less than 5.

Exercises

*1. The data of Table 9–1 can be analyzed in terms of the cross-product ratio method illustrated for the data of Table 9–7. Perform this analysis and compare the results of the two methods. What does this suggest to you about the two methods? Note, however, that the data of Table 9–7 cannot be analyzed according to the method used for Table 9–1. Can you tell why the two methods cannot be used in a reciprocal relationship?

*2. The two 3×3 contingency tables of Table 9–7 have both their variables categorized on an ordered scale. Use the methods of Section 8–5 to test:
$$H_{01}: \beta_W = 0$$
$$H_{02}: \beta_B = 0$$

*3. Use the method of Section 9–2 to analyze the data of Table 5–10. Compare this result to those reported in Section 5–9. What do the results suggest about the various procedures?

*4. Use the method of Section 9–5 to analyze the data of Exercise 9 in Chapter 5. Compare the results to the four procedures examined in Exercise 9 of Chapter 5. What do the results suggest about the various procedures? Are the hypotheses under test the same?

*5. Can the Goodman method of Section 9–5 be applied to the data of Exercise 11 of Chapter 8? Why?

*6. In a nationwide survey of the American public's attitude towards abortion, the statistics in the accompanying table were generated from answers to the question:

Does a woman have the right to decide whether an unwanted birth can be terminated during the first three months of pregnancy? Yes_____ No_____ No opinion_____

If the "No opinion" responses are ignored, a planned analysis for pairwise differences in the first-order interactions can be made for $A = \begin{bmatrix} 2 \\ 2 \end{bmatrix}\begin{bmatrix} 4 \\ 2 \end{bmatrix}\begin{bmatrix} 2 \\ 2 \end{bmatrix} = 6$ contrasts. Examine these six contrasts at $\alpha \le 0.05$ for the existence of second-order interaction components. What do the findings suggest?

Sex			Males		
Religion / Response	Catholic	Protestant	Jewish	Other	Total
Yes	76	115	41	77	309
No	64	82	8	12	166
No opinion	11	6	2	6	25
Total	151	203	51	95	500

	Females				
	Catholic	Protestant	Jewish	Other	Total
	61	117	63	71	312
	146	126	3	14	289
	9	12	8	10	39
	216	255	74	95	640

*7. Use the method of Section 8–10 to analyse the data for the males of Exercise 6. Repeat the analysis for the females. Compare the results to those of Exercise 6. Do the results make sense? Explain what you mean.

*8. The females of Exercise 7 were also asked their age. Results are as shown in the table herewith. Use the methods of Section 9–5 and Section 8–5 to analyze these data. Compare the two methods.

Religion	Catholic				Protestant			
Age / Response	Under 30	30 to 45	45 and over	Total	Under 30	30 to 45	45 and over	Total
Yes	39	17	5	61	61	35	21	117
No	28	64	54	146	10	61	55	126
Total	67	81	59	207	71	96	76	243

Tests of Goodness of Fit

10–1. The Approximation of X_ν^2 by X_ν^2

In Section 3–6, a large-sample approximation to the sign test, achieved through the Karl Pearson statistic, was introduced. Also, the Karl Pearson statistic was used as a test of H_0: $p = p_0$ against the alternative H_1: $p \neq p_0$. In Section 5–6, the use of the Karl Pearson statistic as a test of the Irwin–Fisher hypothesis H_0: $p_1 = p_2$ against the alternative H_1: $p_1 \neq p_2$ was presented. In Section 6–3, the Karl Pearson statistic was again presented as a test of H_0: K populations are homogeneous across the categories $A_1, A_2, \ldots, A_K$, against the omnibus alternative H_1: H_0 is false. In none of these developments was an attempt made to justify this general model for these situations. For the sign test and the Irwin–Fisher model, examples were presented to show that tests based on the $N(0, 1)$ distribution lead to the same decision as tests based on X_1^2. In these cases, the agreement is easily understood since $Z^2 = X_1^2$. In this section, an example is presented to demonstrate the closeness of the X_ν^2 approximation to the exact probabilities associated with X_ν^2, for the special case of $\nu = 2$.

EXAMPLE 10–1.1. As an example, consider the multinomial distribution defined by the following set of probabilities:

$$P = P\left[(X_1 = x_1) \cap (X_2 = x_2) \cap (X_3 = x_3)\right]$$

$$= \begin{bmatrix} 8 \\ x_1 \ x_2 \ x_3 \end{bmatrix} \left[\frac{1}{8}\right]^{x_1} \left[\frac{3}{8}\right]^{x_2} \left[\frac{4}{8}\right]^{x_3}$$

TABLE 10–1. Value of P and X^2 for the trinomial variable with $n = 8$, $p_1 = \frac{1}{8}$, $p_2 = \frac{3}{8}$, and $p_3 = \frac{4}{8}$.

Value of x_1	x_2	x_3	P	X^2
0	0	8	0.0039	8.00
0	1	7	0.0234	5.33
0	2	6	0.0615	2.33
0	3	5	0.0922	1.25
0	4	4	0.0865	1.33
0	5	3	0.0519	2.58
0	6	2	0.0194	5.00
0	7	1	0.0041	6.42
0	8	0	0.0003	13.33
1	0	7	0.0078	5.25
1	1	6	0.0410	2.33
1	2	5	0.0922	0.58
1	3	4	0.1153	0.00
1	4	3	0.0865	0.58
1	5	2	0.0389	2.33
1	6	1	0.0097	5.25
1	7	0	0.0010	9.33
2	0	6	0.0068	5.00
2	1	5	0.0307	2.58
2	2	4	0.0576	1.33
2	3	3	0.0576	1.25
2	4	2	0.0324	2.33
2	5	1	0.0097	4.58
2	6	0	0.0012	8.00
3	0	5	0.0034	7.25
3	1	4	0.0128	5.33
3	2	3	0.0192	4.58
3	3	2	0.0144	5.00
3	4	1	0.0054	7.42
3	5	0	0.0008	9.33
4	0	4	0.0010	12.00
4	1	3	0.0032	10.58
4	2	2	0.0036	10.33
4	3	1	0.0018	11.25
4	4	0	0.0003	13.33
5	0	3	0.0002	19.25
5	1	2	0.0004	18.67
5	2	1	0.0003	18.58
5	3	0	0.0000	20.00
6	0	2	0.0000	29.00
6	1	1	0.0000	28.58
6	2	0	0.0000	29.33
7	0	1	0.0000	41.25
7	1	0	0.0000	41.33
8	0	0	0.0000	56.00

The exact probabilities of this particular trinomial can be approximated by the chi-square distribution with $v = 2$ and, moreover, the probabilities of the general multinomial distribution with probabilities defined by:

$$P = P[(X_1 = x_1) \cap (X_2 = x_2) \cap \ldots \cap (X_K = x_K)]$$

$$= \begin{bmatrix} n \\ x_1 \, x_2 \ldots x_K \end{bmatrix} p_1^{x_1} p_2^{x_2} \ldots p_K^{x_K}$$

can be approximated by a chi-square variable with $v = (K - 1)$ degrees of freedom.

In Table 10–1 are presented the complete set of values that x_1, x_2, and x_3 can assume if $x_1 + x_2 + x_3 = 8$. Also reported are the exact probabilities that $X_1 = x_1$, $X_2 = x_2$, and $X_3 = x_3$, along with the corresponding values of the Karl Pearson statistic:

$$X^2 = \sum_{i=1}^{3} \frac{[X_i - E(X_i)]^2}{E(X_i)}$$

For this specific trinomial distribution, all expected values are less than 5. In particular:

$$E(x_1) = np_1 = 8(\tfrac{1}{8}) = 1,$$
$$E(x_2) = np_2 = 8(\tfrac{3}{8}) = 3,$$
$$E(x_3) = np_3 = 8(\tfrac{4}{8}) = 4,$$

so that the Karl Pearson statistic reduces to:

$$X^2 = \frac{(x_1 - 1)^2}{1} + \frac{(x_2 - 3)^2}{3} + \frac{(x_3 - 4)^2}{4}$$

As can be seen by examining the probabilities of Table 10–1, the outcome with greatest probability has $x_1 = 1$, $x_2 = 3$, and $x_3 = 4$. For this modal outcome, $P = 0.1153$ and $X^2 = 0$.

Exact cumulative probabilities for this distribution are presented in Table 10–2 for common percentile values determined from the theoretical chi-square distribution with $v = 2$. For example, the 80th percentile value of the X_2^2 distribution is defined by $P_{80} = 3.22$. For the trinomial distribution, $X^2 = 3.22$ corresponds to the 84th percentile value. The agreement between the exact X_2^2 and approximate X_2^2 is visually displayed in Figure 10–1. When it is recalled that the chi-square approximation to the Karl Pearson statistic is suspect if the expected values are less than 5, it would have to be concluded that the approximation is impressive, even though all expected values are less than 5.

In general, the agreement between the distribution of X_v^2 and X_v^2 is not very close unless the expected values of the underlying variables exceed 5, even though situations exist in which the agreement is excellent. In any case, the agreement steadily improves as n increases in value. This is not surprising since the Karl Pearson statistic can be written as the exponent or quadratic form of the corresponding multivariate normal distribution with rank $v = K - 1$, which can be shown to be distributed as X_v^2.

TABLE 10–2. *Exact and approximate chi-square cumulative probabilities for the trinomial distribution with parameters* $n = 8$, $p_1 = \frac{1}{8}$, $p_2 = \frac{3}{8}$, *and* $p_3 = \frac{4}{8}$.

Value of X_2^2	Cumulative probability	Cumulative probability of multinomial
0.01	0.0050	0.1153
0.02	0.0100	0.1153
0.05	0.0250	0.1153
0.10	0.0500	0.1153
0.21	0.1000	0.1153
0.45	0.2000	0.1153
0.71	0.3000	0.2940
1.00	0.4000	0.2940
1.39	0.5000	0.5879
1.80	0.6000	0.5879
2.41	0.7000	0.7617
3.22	0.8000	0.8443
4.61	0.9000	0.8732
5.99	0.9500	0.9675
7.38	0.9750	0.9750
9.21	0.9900	0.9855
10.60	0.9950	0.9941

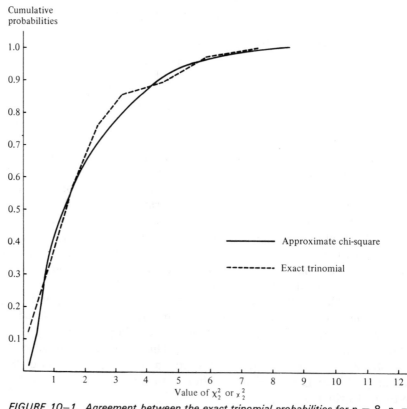

FIGURE 10–1. *Agreement between the exact trinomial probabilities for* $n = 8$, $p_1 = \frac{1}{8}$, $p_2 = \frac{3}{8}$, *and* $p_3 = \frac{4}{8}$, *and the theoretical chi-square probabilities with* $v = 2$.

10–2. The Karl Pearson Goodness-of-Fit Test

The Karl Pearson statistic can be used to test how well an observed frequency distribution agrees with a theoretical probability distribution defined by I mutually exclusive categories. If p_i represents the theoretical probabilities and X_i the observed frequencies, the hypothesis of agreement is rejected if:

$$X^2 = \sum_{i=1}^{I} \frac{[X_i - E(X_i)]^2}{E(X_i)} = \sum_{i=1}^{I} \frac{(X_i - np_i)^2}{np_i}$$

exceeds $X^2_{v:1-\alpha}$ where $v = (I - 1)$. The test is illustrated by an example.

EXAMPLE 10–2.1. Thirty students in a beginning statistics class were given a loaded die and each was asked to roll the die 10 times and record the results, which are shown in Table 10–3. If the die were fair, the probability of any outcome would by given by $p_i = \frac{1}{6}$. Thus, one can test the hypothesis:

$$H_0: p_1 = p_2 = p_3 = p_4 = p_5 = p_6 = \tfrac{1}{6}$$

against the alternative:

$$H_1: H_0 \text{ is false}$$

by means of the Karl Pearson statistic, and reject H_0 if

$$X^2 > X^2_{5:0.95} = 11.07.$$

For these data, $E(X_i) = np_i = 300(\frac{1}{6}) = 50$, so that:

$$X^2 = \frac{(43 - 50)^2}{50} + \frac{(30 - 50)^2}{50} + \frac{(52 - 50)^2}{50} + \frac{(47 - 50)^2}{50}$$

$$+ \frac{(73 - 50)^2}{50} + \frac{(55 - 50)^2}{50}$$

$$= 20.32.$$

The hypothesis of equally likely outcomes is rejected, since $X^2 = 20.32 > 11.07$.

If the goodness-of-fit hypothesis is rejected, a post hoc analysis can be performed on the unknown probabilities with the Scheffé-type coefficient defined by $S^* = \sqrt{X^2_{v:1-\alpha}}$. The method is illustrated for the data of Example 10–2.1.

EXAMPLE 10–2.2. For the data of Example 10–2.1, the critical value for

TABLE 10–3. Results for the tosses of a loaded die by 30 students in a beginning statistics class.

Value of x_i	X_i	$\hat{p}_i$	Confidence interval for p_i		Decision
			Lower limit	Upper limit	
1	43	0.143	0.076	0.210	N. S.
2	30	0.100	0.042	0.158	Significant
3	52	0.173	0.100	0.246	N. S.
4	47	0.157	0.087	0.227	N. S.
5	73	0.243	0.161	0.325	N. S.
6	55	0.183	0.109	0.257	N. S.

the post hoc confidence interval is given by $\underline{S}^* = \sqrt{11.07} = 3.33$. Thus, any confidence interval of the form:

$$p_i = \hat{p}_i \pm 3.33 \sqrt{\frac{\hat{p}_i \hat{q}_i}{n}}$$

that does not cross $p = \frac{1}{6}$ represents a statistically significant source of variance. The limits of the confidence intervals are reported in Table 10–3. As can be seen, all cross $p = \frac{1}{6}$ except the confidence interval for p_2. Because of the way dice are numbered, the too frequent appearance of 5 is associated with the too infrequent appearance of 2.

    Like most post hoc procedures, the model illustrated spreads the probability of a Type I error over all conditions in the p values. Since only six specific contrasts are of interest, thought should be given to a planned comparison procedure. If this were to be done, the value of $\underline{S}^* = 3.33$ would be replaced by the corresponding Dunn critical value read from Table A–1. For six planned comparisons, $Z = 2.64$.

    A simple modification of the Karl Pearson goodness-of-fit test is required if the exact values of p_i cannot be specified because of dependency upon other population parameters. For example, if the underlying variable has a normal distribution with unknown μ and σ^2, the researcher must first estimate these parameters from the data before the test can be performed. If the expected frequencies are estimated from $\overline{X}$ and S, then two restrictions are forced upon the $\hat{E}(X_i)$ that do not exist for the $E(X_i)$. To compensate for these added restrictions, the degrees of freedom of the test are reduced by 2, to a new value of $v = I - 3$. In a like manner, if the underlying variable is binomially distributed and if the parameter, p, of the binomial is estimated from the data, v is reduced to $I - 2$. In general, if q parameters are estimated from the data, the degrees of freedom of the Karl Pearson goodness-of-fit test are given by $v = I - q - 1$.

    The assumptions for the Karl Pearson goodness-of-fit test are minimal. The observations must be independent and the expected number in each cell should exceed 5 in number. If the latter condition cannot be achieved, then a researcher should consider the test of Section 10–3, which is, in fact, more powerful than the Karl Pearson test. However, it has the disadvantage that post hoc data-snooping cannot be conducted if the goodness-of-fit hypothesis is rejected.

10–3. The Kolmogorov Goodness-of-Fit Test

    The Kolmogorov goodness-of-fit test (Massey, 1951) can be used whenever the Karl Pearson test is justified and even when it is not. Since the theory of the test is beyond the requirements of this book, the test is simply illustrated. To use the test, the researcher must specify the probability distribution of the underlying variable. Then, for each value of the variable, the cumulative probabilities $P(X < x_i)$ must be determined for $i = 1, 2, \ldots, n$. These cumulative probabilities are then compared to the corresponding cumulative relative frequencies $\hat{P}(X < x_i)$ in the sample. The hypothesis that the underlying variable is distributed according to the probability distribution defined by $P(X < x_i)$ is rejected if:

$$K = \max|P(X < x_i) - \hat{P}(X < x_i)|$$

exceeds the $K_{n:1-\alpha}$ point of the K distribution. The test is illustrated for the data of Table 10–3.

EXAMPLE 10–3.1. If the die of Example 10–2.1 were a fair die, the probabilities of each outcome would be given by $p_i = \frac{1}{6}$. Under this model, the cumulative probabilities and the cumulative relative frequencies are as reported in Table 10–4. For these data, the maximum absolute difference in $P(X < x_i)$ and $\hat{P}(X < x_i)$ is found to be given by $K = 0.094$. To determine the critical value for this test, one enters Table A–11 with n, the sample size, and α, the probability of a Type I error. For $n = 300$ and $\alpha = 0.05$, the hypothesis of uniform distribution should be rejected if

$$K > \frac{1.36}{\sqrt{n}} = \frac{1.36}{\sqrt{300}} = 0.079$$

In this case, the hypothesis of uniform distribution is rejected, and it is concluded that the die is loaded.

The assumption for this test is that the theoretical probability distribution is continuous, so that tied observations are not encountered. However, with behavioral data, ties are the rule and not the exception. Thus, this assumption is generally relaxed. If ties in the data occur, corrections can be made, but if they are not, then the actual probability of a Type I error is less than the nominal value selected for the test. In this sense, the test becomes conservative.

Finally, efficiency comparisons with the Karl Pearson goodness-of-fit test indicate that the Kolmogorov test is the more powerful of the two procedures.

10–4. The Lilliefors Test

The Kolmogorov test has been modified by Lilliefors (1967) to serve as a test of normality when μ and σ^2 are unknown. For this modification, rank-order the n

TABLE 10–4. Computations for the Kolmogorov test.

Value of X	Cumulative probability $P(X \leq x_i)$	Cumulative relative frequency $\hat{P}(X \leq x_i)$	Absolute value of the difference
1	1/6 = 0.167	43/300 = 0.143	0.024
2	2/6 = 0.333	73/300 = 0.243	0.090
3	3/6 = 0.500	125/300 = 0.416	0.084
4	4/6 = 0.667	172/300 = 0.573	0.094
5	5/6 = 0.833	245/300 = 0.816	0.017
6	6/6 = 1.000	300/300 = 1.000	0.000

observations $\{X^{(1)}, X^{(2)}, \ldots, X^{(n)}\}$ and standardize them as $Z^{(i)} = (X^{(i)} - \overline{X})/S$. These normalized values are then compared to the $N(0, 1)$ distribution by means of a Kolmogorov-type statistic defined as:

$$L = \max|P(Z < Z_i) - \hat{P}(Z < Z_i)|$$

H_0 is rejected if L exceeds $L_{n:1-\alpha}$. The test is illustrated in the following example.

EXAMPLE 10–4.1. According to test theory, the mental ages of the 18 girls listed in Table 10–5 should be normally distributed. For these girls, $\overline{X} = 99.22$ and $S = 10.44$. On the basis of these statistics, Z scores have been computed and are rank-ordered in Table 10–5. Also reported are the cumulative relative frequencies for the sample and the corresponding normal-curve probabilities, read from Table A–2. For these data,

$$L = \max|P(Z < Z_i) - \hat{P}(Z < Z_i)| = 0.155$$

To determine the critical value for this test, enter Table A–12 with n, the sample size, and α, the probability of a Type I error. With $n = 18$ and $\alpha = 0.05$, the hypothesis of normality should be rejected if $L > L_{18:0.95} = 0.200$. Since $L = 0.155 < 0.200$, the hypothesis of normality is retained.

10–5. The Kolmogorov–Smirnov Test

The Kolmogorov test has been modified by Smirnov to serve as a competitor to classical two-sample tests. The Kolmogorov–Smirnov test is used to test the

TABLE 10–5. Mental ages of 18 girls rank-ordered to test for normality of distribution.

Name	Mental age	Z Score	Cumulative relative frequencies $\hat{P}(Z < Z_i)$	Exact normal cumulative probability $P(Z < Z_i)$	Absolute value of the difference
Dorabella	81	−1.75	0.056	0.041	0.015
Helen	87	−1.17	0.111	0.121	0.010
Ophelia	87	−1.17	0.167	0.121	0.046
Jolanda	89	−0.98	0.222	0.164	0.058
Alicia	93	−0.60	0.278	0.274	0.004
Barbara	93	−0.60	0.333	0.274	0.059
Marguerite	93	−0.60	0.389	0.274	0.115
Letitia	95	−0.40	0.444	0.345	0.099
Ruth	95	−0.40	0.500	0.345	0.155
Irene	99	−0.02	0.556	0.492	0.064
Norma	100	+0.07	0.611	0.528	0.083
Querida	106	+0.65	0.667	0.742	0.075
Carola	108	+0.84	0.722	0.800	0.078
Frances	108	+0.84	0.778	0.800	0.022
Patsy	111	+1.13	0.833	0.871	0.038
Elise	113	+1.32	0.889	0.907	0.018
Gertrude	114	+1.41	0.944	0.921	0.023
Katerina	114	+1.44	1.000	0.921	0.079

hypothesis that two samples come from identical populations, versus the alternative that the distributions are different. The test is given simply as:

$$KS = \max |\hat{P}(X_1 < x) - \hat{P}(X_2 < x)|$$

where

$$\hat{P}(X_1 < x) = \text{Cumulative probability of sample 1}$$

and

$$\hat{P}(X_2 < x) = \text{Cumulative probability of sample 2}$$

The null hypothesis of this test states that the distributions are identical. If this hypothesis is rejected, it could be that the location parameters, the scale parameters, the skewness, or even the kurtosis parameters differ. In other words, the alternative hypothesis is very broad in nature; however, the test is a good competitor to the two-sample t test for testing equal centers.

The assumptions for the test are minimal. The test assumes that the observations between and within samples are independently drawn from continuous distributions. The assumption of continuity is required, in order to eliminate ties. If corrections are not made, ties render the test conservative with respect to the probability of a Type I error. The test is illustrated for the data of Table 10–6.

EXAMPLE 10–5.1. In this example, one would like to test H_0: $\mu_1 = \mu_2$ against the alternative H_1: $\mu_1 \neq \mu_2$. This can be determined indirectly by testing the hypothesis that both samples come from identical populations. If H_0 is rejected, it is concluded that $\mu_1 \neq \mu_2$. To do the test, rank-order the data as shown in Table 10–6. Next, determine the cumulative relative frequencies for each sample, and then subtract them term by term. The value of KS corresponds to the largest difference. For these data:

$$KS = 0.689$$

The critical value for the test is read from Table A–13, which is entered with $n_1 = 15$ and $n_2 = 18$. In this case, the large-sample approximation must be used. Thus, H_0 is rejected if:

$$KS_{n_1, n_2 : .95} > 1.36 \sqrt{\frac{n_1 + n_2}{n_1 n_2}} = 1.36 \sqrt{\frac{15 + 18}{15(18)}} = 0.476$$

Since $KS = 0.689 > KS_{15, 18 : 0.95} = 0.476$, H_0 is rejected. The two distributions are not identical and their expected values are believed to be different.

Summary

In this chapter, four goodness-of-fit tests were presented. The oldest of these tests was introduced by Karl Pearson at the turn of the century. To perform the test, the researcher must specify the exact probabilities of the distribution in terms of I mutually exclusive and exhaustive categories. If the probabilities are denoted as p_i and frequencies by X_i, the Karl Pearson statistic is defined as:

$$X^2 = \sum_{i=1}^{I} \frac{(X_i - np_i)^2}{np_i}$$

Condition 1	Condition 2	$\hat{P}(X_1 < x)$	$\hat{P}(X_2 < x)$	Absolute Value of difference
	0	0.000	0.056	0.056
	0	0.000	0.111	0.111
	11	0.000	0.167	0.167
	12	0.000	0.222	0.222
	16	0.000	0.278	0.278
	16	0.000	0.333	0.333
20	20	0.067	0.389	0.322
20		0.133	0.389	0.256
	21	0.133	0.444	0.311
23	23	0.200	0.500	0.300
	24	0.200	0.556	0.356
	26	0.200	0.611	0.411
	27	0.200	0.667	0.467
	27	0.200	0.722	0.522
	28	0.200	0.778	0.578
	28	0.200	0.833	0.633
	30	0.200	0.889	0.689
31		0.267	0.889	0.622
35		0.333	0.889	0.556
36	36	0.400	0.944	0.544
	36	0.400	1.000	0.600
39		0.467	1.000	0.533
46		0.533	1.000	0.467
49		0.600	1.000	0.400
50		0.667	1.000	0.333
50		0.733	1.000	0.267
53		0.800	1.000	0.200
58		0.867	1.000	0.133
58		0.933	1.000	0.067
60		1.000	1.000	0.000

The hypothesis under test is rejected if X^2 exceeds $X^2_{I-1:1-\alpha}$. The assumptions for the test are that the n observations are statistically independent and that each $E(X_i) = np_i > 5$.

The Kolmogorov test is a useful competitor to the Karl Pearson test because it does not require grouped frequency data with category counts exceeding 5. It can be used with small samples. The assumptions for the test are continuity in the underlying variable and independence of observations. If ties occur in the data, the test becomes conservative, in that the true alpha of the test is less than the tabled alpha. The test statistic is defined by:

$$K = \max|P(X < x_i) - \hat{P}(X < x_i)|$$

where

$P(X < x_i) = $ Cumulative probability for the theoretical distribution

and

$$\hat{P}(X < x_i) = \text{Cumulative relative frequency for the observed distribution}$$

The goodness-of-fit hypothesis is rejected if K is too large, as determined from the sampling distribution of K.

While the rejected hypothesis of the Karl Pearson test can be investigated by means of post hoc or planned confidence intervals of the form:

$$p_i = \hat{p}_i \pm \sqrt{X^2_{I-1:1-\alpha}} \sqrt{\frac{\hat{p}_i \hat{q}_i}{n}}$$

or

$$p_i = \hat{p}_i \pm Z_{1-\alpha/2I} \sqrt{\frac{\hat{p}_i \hat{q}_i}{n}}$$

the same hypothesis rejected by the Kolmogorov test cannot. This may be the only major disadvantage in the use of the Kolmogorov test. In general, it is more powerful than the Karl Pearson test and it can be performed on small samples.

The Lilliefors test is a simple modification of the Kolmogorov test, which can be used to test the hypothesis that a random variable with unknown mean and standard deviation is normal. To perform this test, a researcher need only rank-order the data as $X^{(1)}, X^{(2)}, \ldots, X^{(n)}$, and compute the ordered $Z^{(i)} = (X^{(i)} - \overline{X})/S$, where $\overline{X}$ and S are estimated from the data. The Lilliefors statistic is defined as:

$$L = \max | P(Z < Z_i) - \hat{P}(Z < Z_i) |$$

The hypothesis of normality is rejected if L is larger than the tabled $(1 - \alpha)$ point of the sampling distribution of L.

The Kolmogorov–Smirnov test is used to determine whether or not two distributions are identical. If $\hat{P}_1(X < x)$ and $\hat{P}_2(X < x)$ represent the cumulative relative frequency distributions of the two samples, the hypothesis of identity of distributions is rejected if:

$$KS = \max | \hat{P}(X_1 < x) - \hat{P}(X_2 < x) |$$

exceeds the tabled $KS_{n_1, n_2:1-\alpha}$ value. This test assumes that the observations between and within the samples are independent and that the underlying variable is continuous. Ties render the test conservative, provided that a correction for ties is not instituted.

Except for the Lilliefors test, which is based on a $N(0, 1)$ variable, the tests of this section are distribution-free. The assumptions are minimal. However, this does not mean that these tests are highly recommended. If H_0 is rejected by these tests, a researcher may still wonder whether the rejection is due to shifts in centers or differences in scales. Simple rejection of H_0 provides no clue as to the reason for rejection.

Exercises

*1. Thirty students enrolled in a beginning statistics class each selected at random 10 samples of size 5 for which it was known that the underlying variable was $N(50, 10^2)$.

On each sample, $\overline{X}$ and $\hat{M}$ were determined. The pooled results are shown as follows:
Theory stated that the sampling distribution of $\overline{X}$ is $N(50, 10^2/5)$, and the sampling distribution of $\hat{M}$ is $N[50, (\pi/2)(10^2/5)]$. Do these data support the theory?

Interval	Number of means	Number of medians
36.5–39.5	1	8
39.5–42.5	17	22
42.5–45.5	32	31
45.5–48.5	64	57
48.5–51.5	86	67
51.5–54.5	65	62
54.5–57.5	22	37
57.5–60.5	10	11
60.5–63.5	3	2
63.5–66.5	0	3
Total	300	300

a) Use the Karl Pearson statistic in defending your answer.
b) Repeat the analysis with the Lilliefors test and the Kolmogorov test.
c) Compare the three tests. Which would you recommend? Why?

*2. Use the Kolmogorov–Smirnov test to determine whether or not the distributions of the means and medians of Exercise 1 are identical. If H_0 were to be rejected, what would be the reason? Would it be differences in centers or differences in scales?

*3. Apply the Karl Pearson test of homogeneity to answer Exercise 2. Compare these results to those of the Kolmogorov–Smirnov test. Which method would you recommend? Why?

*4. If H_0 is rejected in Exercise 3, which intervals account for the difference? Why would this be the case?

*5. The analyses of Exercises 2, 3, and 4 required independence between and within samples. Are the assumptions justified for these data? Explain. A second class repeated the study and the distributions of $\overline{X}$ and $\hat{M}$ were almost identical to those reported in Exercise 1. If the distribution of $\hat{M}$ for the first class were to be replaced by the distribution of $\hat{M}$ for the second class, how would it influence your response? Explain.

*6. Use the Lilliefors test to determine whether the difference score of Table 3–5 is normally distributed.

*7. Are the differences of Exercise 10 in Chapter 3 normally distributed?

*8. Use the Kolmogorov–Smirnov test to investigate the data of Table 5–12.

*9. Are the distributions of Exercise 8 normal in form?

*10. Consider the set of data given in the accompanying table. The eight tabled variables are social class, sex, experimental condition, mental age, vocabulary score, paragraph-meaning score, arithmetic-reasoning score, and arithmetic-computation score. In particular:

SES	Sex	Condition	X_1	X_2	X_3	X_4	X_5
High	Male	Old	112	19	6	22	15
H	M	O	117	21	10	23	12
H	M	O	130	22	11	22	15
H	M	New	128	25	15	22	14
H	M	N	109	23	15	22	12
H	M	N	131	25	11	25	12
Middle	M	Old	107	15	6	19	10
M	M	O	84	14	5	10	7
M	M	O	115	17	8	18	9
M	M	New	99	19	10	15	12
M	M	N	85	18	11	19	8
M	M	N	112	21	13	23	13
Low	M	Old	90	9	11	18	10
L	M	O	75	7	4	15	6
L	M	O	83	6	4	16	9
L	M	New	106	13	7	23	15
L	M	N	114	15	10	23	14
L	M	N	82	12	7	20	13
High	Female	Old	115	21	11	22	15
H	F	O	132	24	11	25	15
H	F	O	118	23	9	22	14
H	F	New	112	25	15	25	14
H	F	N	112	25	15	25	14
H	F	N	116	25	14	21	15
Middle	F	Old	92	17	8	16	10
M	F	O	122	19	9	19	12
M	F	O	97	16	8	10	6
M	F	New	113	23	14	20	15
M	F	N	85	21	13	17	12
M	F	N	101	20	13	12	14
Low	F	Old	76	9	2	2	2
L	F	O	120	11	5	17	5
L	F	O	85	8	1	10	1
L	F	New	96	16	9	11	9
L	F	N	101	18	10	16	10
L	F	N	99	15	11	16	11

1. Social class is defined in terms of the 1970 census-tract data based on student addresses.
2. Sex is taken from school records.
3. Experimental conditions consisted of an old method and a new method for teaching reading.
4. X_1: Mental age is obtained from third-grade performance on the Stanford-Binet test.
5. X_2: Vocabulary scores are determined from a 25-item teacher-made test administered five weeks after the new method was in operation.
6. X_3: Paragraph-meaning scores are determined from a 15-item teacher-made test administered five weeks after training with the new method.
7. X_4: Arithmetic-reasoning scores are determined from a 25-item teacher-made test administered at the time of the paragraph-meaning test.

8. X_s: Arithmetic-computation scores are determined from a 15-item teacher-made test administered at the time of the paragraph-meaning test.

Use the Kolmogorov–Smirnov test to investigate the paragraph-meaning scores across the three social classes. Do each test at $\alpha_0 = 0.02$, so that the $\alpha_T \le 0.06$.

*11. Many genetic traits appear in large populations according to the Hardy–Weinberg Law, which is based on the binomial expansion $(p + q)^2 = p^2 + 2pq + q^2$. The law is illustrated for the so-called M–N blood types associated with human populations. Three phenotypes have been identified. They are described as follows, according to genotype and probability of occurrence.

Phenotype	Genotype	Probability defined by the Hardy–Weinberg Law
M antigen only	$M \times M$	p^2
Both $M + N$ antigen	$M \times N$	$2pq$
N antigen only	$N \times N$	q^2

People whose phenotype is M receive an M allele from their father and an M allele from their mother; their blood contains the M antigen only. People phenotypic for N receive an N allele from their father and an N allele from their mother; their blood contains the N antigen only. People who are $M \times M$ and $N \times N$ are referred to as *homozygotes* with respect to their alleles. People who are $M \times N$ are referred to as *heterozygotes*. They receive an M allele from one parent and an N allele from the other parent; their blood carries both the M antigen and the N antigen.

Studies have shown that in the United States, the probabilities of these antigens in White populations are given by:

$$p = P(M) = 0.54 \quad \text{and} \quad q = P(N) = 0.46$$

In a sample of 200 White college freshmen, a study generated the statistics shown in the accompanying table.

Phenotype	Number
M	63
M–N	105
N	32
Total	200

a) Does the Hardy–Weinberg Law serve as a satisfactory model for these data?
b) What is the value of v for the test of this goodness-of-fit hypothesis?

*12. A sample of 200 American Indians living on reservations in the vicinity of Gallup, New Mexico, had their blood tested. For this sample, the results are as shown herewith. Does the Hardy–Weinberg Law with $p = 0.54$ and $q = 0.46$ describe the blood-antigen distribution of this population of American Indians? Use data of Exercise 13.

*13. In Exercise 12, the goodness-of-fit hypothesis was rejected, either because the Hardy–Weinberg Law was invalid or because $p \ne 0.54$ and $q \ne 0.46$. One can test the last assumption by estimating $P(M)$ and $P(N)$ in the population of American Indians from the sample data. Each M phenotype carries two alleles for M and each M–N phenotype carries one allele for N. Therefore:

$$\hat{p} = \frac{\text{Number of } M \text{ alleles}}{\text{Number of alleles}} = \frac{2X_{MM} + X_{MN}}{2n}$$

where

$$X_{MM} = \text{Number of } M \text{ phenotypes}$$
$$X_{MN} = \text{Number of } M\text{-}N \text{ phenotypes}$$

For these data:

$$\hat{p} = \frac{2(122) + 71}{2(200)} = \frac{315}{400} = 0.7875,$$

$$\hat{q} = 1 - \hat{p} = 1 - 0.7875 = 0.2125$$

a) Does the Hardy-Weinberg Law serve as a satisfactory model for these data?
b) What is the value of v for this goodness-of-fit hypothesis?

Phenotype	Number
M	122
M-N	71
N	7
Total	200

*14. The Rh-positive and -negative blood factor appears to follow the same model as the M-N-antigen blood types, but in this case the heterozygotes have external appearances similar to the Rh-positive homozygotes who inherit the allele for the production of the positive Rh blood factor from both parents. When the heterozygote is like the homozygote, it is said that the trait is dominant, while its complement is recessive. If Rh refers to the dominant allele and rh to the recessive allele, phenotypes, genotypes, and probabilities, as defined by the Hardy–Weinberg Law, are as follows:

Phenotype	Genotype	Probability defined by the Hardy–Weinberg Law
Rh	Rh × Rh or Rh × rh	$p^2 + 2pq$
rh	rh × rh	q^2

In the general United States White population, about 16% of the public is of the rh phenotype. Thus, $q^2 = 0.16$, so that $q = 0.40$ and $p = 1 - q = 0.60$. Thus, about 16% of all women contain the blood antigen that could result in erythroblastosis fetalis.

In a sample of 200 college freshmen, 41 were identified as rh × rh.

a) Does the Hardy–Weinberg Law serve as a satisfactory model for these data?
b) What is the value of v for this goodness-of-fit hypothesis?

*15. A sample of 200 Black college freshmen was tested for the presence of the Rh factor. Eighteen were identified as rh × rh.
a) Does the Hardy–Weinberg Law with $p = 0.6$ and $q = 0.4$ describe the blood antigen distribution for this population of American Blacks?

b) If the answer to (a) is "No," estimate q from the data and repeat the analysis.

c) What is the value of v for part (b)?

*16. The probability distribution of the O, A, and B blood antigens can be determined from the terms of the following trinomial expansion:

$$(p_O + p_A + p_B)^2 = p_O^2 + p_A^2 + p_B^2 + 2p_O p_A + 2p_O p_B + 2p_A p_B$$

where

$$p_O = P(O) = \text{probability of the } O \text{ allele}$$
$$p_A = P(A) = \text{probability of the } A \text{ allele}$$
$$p_B = P(B) = \text{probability of the } B \text{ allele}$$

For these antigens, A and B are both dominant with respect to O but not to each other. Thus, there are four phenotypes, O, A, B, and AB. The genotypes and probabilities for these phenotypes are as follows:

Phenotype	Genotype	Probability
O	$O \times O$	p_O^2
A	$A \times A$ or $A \times O$	$p_A^2 + 2p_A p_O$
B	$B \times B$ or $B \times O$	$p_B^2 + 2p_B p_O$
AB	$A \times B$	$2p_A p_B$

For the United States White population, approximate probabilities for these alleles are given by:

$$p_O = 0.675, \qquad p_A = 0.250, \qquad \text{and} \qquad p_B = 0.075.$$

In a sample of 200 college freshmen, the following number of phenotypes were identified:

Phenotype	Number
O	95
A	78
B	23
AB	8
	200

a) Does the trinomial form of the Hardy–Weinberg Law hold for these data?

b) What is the value of v for the goodness-of-fit test?

*17. In a sample of 200 Japanese living in San Francisco, California, the following number of phenotypes were identified:

Phenotype	Number
O	59
A	85
B	38
AB	18
	200

Does the trinomial form of the Hardy–Weinberg Law hold for $p_O = 0.675$, $p_A = 0.250$, and $p_B = 0.075$?

*18. The goodness-of-fit hypothesis of Exerices 17 was rejected, either because the Hardy–Weinberg Law was invalid or because the values of p_O, p_A, and p_B were incorrect. One can test the last assumption by making estimates from the data. Since the number of O individuals is given by $n_O = 59$,

$$\hat{p}_O^2 = \frac{n_O}{n} = \frac{59}{200} = 0.2950$$

so that $\hat{p}_O = \sqrt{0.2950} = 0.543$. Since:

$$\frac{n_O + n_A}{n} = \hat{p}_O^2 + 2\hat{p}_A\hat{p}_O + \hat{p}_A^2 = (\hat{p}_O + \hat{p}_A)^2$$

it follows that:

$$\hat{p}_O + \hat{p}_A = \sqrt{\frac{n_O + n_A}{n}} = \sqrt{\frac{59 + 85}{200}} = \sqrt{0.72} = 0.849$$

so that:

$$\hat{p}_A = 0.849 - \hat{p}_O = 0.849 - 0.543 = 0.306$$

Finally, $\hat{p}_B = 1 - \hat{p}_O - \hat{p}_A = 1 - 0.543 - 0.306 = 0.151$, or, since

$$\frac{n_O + n_B}{n} = \hat{p}_O^2 + 2\hat{p}_B\hat{p}_O + \hat{p}_B^2 = (\hat{p}_O + \hat{p}_B)^2$$

it follows that:

$$\hat{p}_O + \hat{p}_B = \sqrt{\frac{n_O + n_B}{n}} = \sqrt{\frac{59 + 38}{200}} = \sqrt{0.485} = 0.697$$

so that:

$$\hat{p}_B = 0.697 - 0.543 = 0.154$$

a) Does the trinomial form of the Hardy–Weinberg Law hold for $\hat{p}_O = 0.54$, $\hat{p}_A = 0.31$, and $\hat{p}_B = 0.15$?

b) What is the value of v for this goodness-of-fit test?

*19. Analyze the data of Exercise 1 of Chapter 6, in terms of the Kolmogorov–Smirnov test. Compare the two sets of results. Which of these two methods would you recommend? Why?

Part III

Statistical Methods for Quantitative Variables. Tests and Confidence-Interval Procedures for Nonparametric Analysis-of-Variance Designs for Independent and Related Samples

Chapter 11 consists of a presentation of two-sample tests for equal central values and equal variances, utilizing ranks and normal scores. In particular, Fisher's permutation test, the two-sample Wilcoxon–Mann–Whitney test, the Terry–Hoeffding, the Van der Waerden, and the Bell–Doksum tests for equal centers are illustrated. The Siegel–Tukey test, the Mood test, and the Klotz test for equal scale parameters are also illustrated. Finally, the Wilcoxon test is used to describe a test of equal slope for two independent regression lines.

Chapter 12 extends the methods of Chapter 11 to the one-way layout or one-way analysis of variance. Tests based on normal scores are illustrated and compared to the familiar Kruskal–Wallis test. Post hoc and planned-contrast procedures are illustrated, as well as the partitioning of the Kruskal–Wallis H statistic into one-degree-of-freedom chi-square tests. Finally, Hodges–Lehmann estimators are illustrated for the one-way analysis of variance. While more difficult to conduct, their method has the advantage of returning the researcher from rank values to the original metric.

Chapter 13 presents methods for one- and two-sample matched pair designs in which the underlying variable is quantitative. The prototype for these designs is the Fisher randomization or permutation test. Since different researchers could reach different decisions with the same set of data, two alternatives to this test, the Wilcoxon matched-pair test and the matched-pair normal scores, are presented. Confidence-interval procedures for the Wilcoxon test are illustrated, and their extension to a median test and a test of zero slope in regression analysis is demonstrated.

Chapter 14 extends the methods of Chapter 13 to K treatments observed on n subjects. This test, called the Friedman test, corresponds to the K treatment repeated-measures design of classical ANOVA procedures. Planned and post hoc procedures for this test are illustrated. The Page test for ordered relationship is also presented, and the Durbin test for incomplete designs is illustrated.

Chapter 15 contains distribution-free tests for randomized blocks based on alignment of the original observations so as to remove the effects of extraneous variables. This model, based upon work by Hodges and Lehmann, is extended to tests of two-factor interactions in fully crossed designs. Planned and post hoc comparisons are illustrated for tests based on ranks or normal scores.

Chapter 16 presents an extensive discussion of nonparametric correlation theory, with an emphasis on Kendall's tau. Spearman's rank correlation and Pitman's measure of correlation are also investigated. Kendall's coefficient of concordance for repeated-measures designs and Goodman's and Kruskal's gamma are presented.

Two-Sample Methods
for Quantitative Variables
Based on Ranks
and Normal Scores

11–1. Fisher's Randomization Two-Sample t Test

The most commonly performed test of the hypothesis that two distributions have the same or equal-valued centers is the classical two-sample Student's t test given by:

$$t = \frac{\overline{X}_1 - \overline{X}_2}{\sqrt{(S_p^2/n_1) + (S_p^2/n_2)}} = \frac{\overline{X}_1 - \overline{X}_2}{\sqrt{MSW[(1/n_1) + (1/n_2)]}}$$

The assumptions for this test are:

1. Independence of observations within each sample;
2. Independence of observations between each sample;
3. Equality of population variances; and
4. Normality of underlying error distributions.

If these four conditions can be satisfied, the Student test is optimum with respect to both Type I and Type II errors. If only assumptions 1 and 2 are known to be satisfied, the t test may not be acceptable, whereas the test to be described here is always justified. In some respects, it is the most powerful test for testing H_0: $\mu_1 = \mu_2$ against the alternative H_1: H_0 is false. It is called the Fisher randomization t test, and is best illustrated by an example.

EXAMPLE 11–1.1. Consider a study in which ten maze-bright rats were randomly divided into two groups. One group served as the experimental group and the other as the control group. Following a training period, in which the rats learned the correct path of a complex maze, the rats in the experimental group were prevented from sleeping for 24 continuous hours. After this period of sleep deprivation, both the control rats and the experimental rats were re-run on the known maze path. The number of seconds to run the maze was determined for each rat. The times are reported in Table 11–1.

The hypothesis to be tested is that the average number of seconds to run the maze required by the rats in the control condition is equal to the average number of seconds taken by the rats in the experimental condition. The alternative hypothesis states that this hypothesis is false. In statistical terms, this reduces to:

$$H_0: \mu_1 = \mu_2$$
$$H_1: H_0 \text{ is false}$$

To generate the Fisher test for the observed data, assume that the time values for the group of ten rats have been predetermined so that the finite population of values to be observed is given by the ordered values:

$$P: \{17, 36, 39, 40, 42, 48, 54, 55, 61, 64\}$$

If H_0 is true, then all assignments of these ten times to the rats are equally likely. The total number of assignments of ten numbers to groups of size four and six is given by Rules Two and Five of Section 2–2, as:

$$T = \begin{bmatrix} 10 \\ 4 \end{bmatrix} \begin{bmatrix} 10 - 4 \\ 6 \end{bmatrix} = \begin{bmatrix} 10 \\ 6 \end{bmatrix} \begin{bmatrix} 10 - 6 \\ 4 \end{bmatrix} = 210$$

With each assignment, one could compute the resulting two-sample t statistic and thereby obtain the entire distribution over the ten observed scores. On this distribution, one could find the rejection region consisting of the $\alpha\%$ extreme t statistics and then reject H_0 if the observed t was a member of the set of t values that define the rejection region. This procedure produces the most powerful test of H_0. In this case, at $\alpha \leq 0.05$, the number of extreme t values is given by:

$$K = \alpha \begin{bmatrix} n_1 + n_2 \\ n_1 \end{bmatrix} = (0.05) \begin{bmatrix} 10 \\ 4 \end{bmatrix} = (0.05)(210)$$
$$= 10.50$$

TABLE 11–1. *Number of seconds to run a known maze path by two groups of rats.*

1. Control rats	2. Experimental rats
36	39
42	55
17	48
40	61
	54
	64

or, when rounded down to the nearest even integer, by:

$$K = 10$$

Since a two-tailed test of hypothesis is being made, the number of extreme t values in each tail of the resulting distribution is given by $\frac{1}{2}(10) = 5$. Thus, in practice, one need consider only the five extreme values that agree in sign with the observed t value.

On the surface, one might think that the arithmetic associated with this procedure is truly gargantuan, but such is not the case when n_1 and n_2 are small.

Consider the formula or equation of the t test statistic. Its denominator is *always* positive, so that the magnitude of t is directly determined by the magnitude of $\overline{d} = \overline{X}_1 - \overline{X}_2$. In this test, t is maximum when $\overline{d}$ is maximum; t is minimum when $\overline{d}$ is minimum; and $t = 0$ when $\overline{d} = 0$. Thus, instead of t as a test statistic, one could use $\overline{d}$, since $\overline{d}$ is monotonically related to t. Within the observed sample values:

$$n_1\overline{X}_1 + n_2\overline{X}_2 = \sum_{k=1}^{2} \sum_{i=1}^{n_k} X_{ik} = \text{Constant} = C$$

This means that $\overline{d}$ is a function of $\overline{X}_1$ or $\overline{X}_2$ alone. Thus, one can use $\overline{X}_1$ or $\overline{X}_2$ as the test statistic. Customarily, the mean associated with the smaller sample is chosen. Thus, if n_1 is the smaller of n_1 and n_2, then:

$$\overline{X}_1 = \frac{X_{11} + X_{12} + \cdots + X_{1n_1}}{n_1} = \frac{1}{n_1} T_1$$

is suggested as the test statistic. Yet one might ask, "Why is $\overline{X}_1$ used when T_1 itself could be used as the test statistic?" In practice this is what generally *is* used, as illustrated in Table 11–2, where the 10 extreme values of T_1 are listed.

EXAMPLE 11–1.2. Since the observed total in Example 11–1.1, given by:

$$T_1 = 17 + 36 + 40 + 42 = 135$$

is among the extreme T_1 values that define the $\alpha = 10/210 = 0.0476 < 0.05$ rejection region, the hypothesis of equal centers is rejected. It is worth emphasizing that this decision is based simply on the assumption that the observations within each sample and between each sample are independent. No assumption of normality or common variance is required. If those assumptions are satisfied and if this test is still performed, no penalty accrues, since the efficiency of the Fisher randomization t test to the classical Student's t test is unity, when the assumptions of Student's test are valid.

Tied values are a potential problem for this test because:

$$T = \begin{bmatrix} n_1 + n_2 \\ n_1 \end{bmatrix} = \begin{bmatrix} n_1 + n_2 \\ n_2 \end{bmatrix}$$

assumes that each object in the permutation set is different. If tied values occur, adjustments can be made by subscripting the tied values.

EXAMPLE 11–1.3. Suppose the following data had been generated from a two-sample study:

$$P: \{2, 3, 3, 7, 7, 7, 12, 14, 15, 16, 16\}$$

TABLE 11–2. *The rejection region for the Fisher randomization test for the data of Table 11–1.*

Values of X assigned to the samller sample				Value of T_1
17	36	39	40	132
17	36	39	42	134
17	36	40	42	135
17	39	40	42	138
17	36	39	48	140
.	.	.	.	.
.	.	.	.	.
.	.	.	.	.
48	54	55	61	218
42	55	61	64	222
48	54	61	64	227
48	55	61	64	228
54	55	61	64	234

One can break the ties by denoting the scores as follows:

$$2, \quad 3_1, \quad 3_2, \quad 7_1, \quad 7_2, \quad 7_3, \quad 12, \quad 14, \quad 15, \quad 16_1, \quad 16_2$$

so that if the smaller sample consists of four subjects, the following permutations represent different assignments:

$$2, \quad 3_1, \quad 3_2, \quad 7_1$$
$$2, \quad 3_1, \quad 3_2, \quad 7_2$$
$$2, \quad 3_1, \quad 3_2, \quad 7_3$$

Often, one reads that the underlying variable for the Fisher randomization t test must be continuous. This assumption is made to avoid tied values, but if the tied values are treated as different scores, the assumption can be relaxed. Finally, since the distribution of T_1 is discrete, exact tests of 0.05 or 0.01 are not usually possible. In these cases, one defines the rejection region so that $\alpha < 0.05$ or $\alpha < 0.01$. As might be expected, the large-sample form of the Fisher randomization t test is the Student's t test with $v = n_1 + n_2 - 2$.

Some questionable criticism has been leveled against the use of the Fisher test since the rejection region is conditional upon, or determined from, the observed sample values. If one requires random samples from the parent populations, the criticism is of academic interest only, for, under repeated random sampling, all possible assignments of values are observed and, over the full randomization, the total critical region is of size alpha, the probability of a Type I error selected by the researcher.

11–2. The Wilcoxon–(Mann–Whitney) Two-Sample Test

Probably the most frequently employed two-sample test when the assumptions of the t test cannot be satisfied is the Wilcoxon test (1949). Various forms of this test are available, one of which is the Mann–Whitney U test developed inde-

Two-Sample
Methods for
Quantitative
Variables Based
on Ranks and
Normal Scores

267

pendently in 1947 (Mann and Whitney, 1947). Compared to the t test, this test has an asymptotic efficiency of $3/\pi = 95.5\%$, when the assumptions for t can be satisfied. Under some situations, the efficiency, when compared to the t test, is even greater than unity, such as for the double exponental, where $E = 1.5$. This test is illustrated by means of the example used in Section 11–1.

The Wilcoxon test is performed in the same manner used for the Fisher randomization t test, except that ranks are substituted for the observed values. To perform the Wilcoxon test, one first combines the observations from both samples and ranks them as a unit. Once the appropriate ranks are assigned to the respective samples, the test statistic is taken as the sum of the ranks attached to the smaller sample. Since the sum of N ranks equals:

$$1 + 2 + 3 + \cdots + N = \frac{N(N + 1)}{2}$$

it follows that once the sum of the ranks of the smaller group is computed, the sum of the ranks of the larger group is automatically determined. If H_0 is true, then it must also be true that the expected average rank for the two groups is equal. Thus, a logical consequence of H_0 and H_1 are the two hypotheses:

$$H_0: E(\overline{R}_1) = E(\overline{R}_2)$$
$$H_1: H_0 \text{ is false}$$

where $E(\overline{R}_1)$ equals the expected average rank for group one and $E(\overline{R}_2)$ equals the expected average rank for group two. The test is illustrated in the following example.

EXAMPLE 11–2.1. If the hypothesis of Example 11–1.1 is true, then the total number of different assignments of ranks to the sample of four rats and six rats, respectively, is given by:

$$T = \begin{bmatrix} 10 \\ 4 \end{bmatrix}\begin{bmatrix} 10 - 4 \\ 6 \end{bmatrix} = \begin{bmatrix} 10 \\ 6 \end{bmatrix}\begin{bmatrix} 10 - 6 \\ 4 \end{bmatrix} = 210$$

The rank assignments to the smaller sample, along with the rank totals, are summarized in Table 11–3.

If T_1 equals the sum of the ranks for the smaller sample, then possible values for T_1 are (10, 11, 12, 13, . . . , 31, 32, 33, 34).

Since there are 210 possible values, a test with $\alpha = 0.05$ requires a listing of the most extreme 5% or 210(0.05) = 10.5, or 10 values. Totals of 10, 11, 12, 32, 33, and 34 account for the eight most extreme values. Since there are six assignments that give a total of 13 or 31, it is not possible to isolate two of them, which, when added to those previously obtained, would make the total number of extreme values equal to 10. Instead, only the eight most extreme values are utilized. The probability associated with these outcomes is $\alpha = 8/210 = 0.038 < 0.05$. For the example, $T_1 = 12$. Since this value is in the critical region, the hypothesis of equal expected average ranks is rejected. This agrees with the decision reached by means of the Fisher randomization t test.

Since the Wilcoxon test tests equality of average ranks, it is not necessarily

TABLE 11–3. The rejection region for the two-sample Wilcoxon test for the
data of Table 11–1.

Ranks assigned to the smaller sample	Value of T_1
1 2 3 4	10
1 2 3 5	11
1 2 3 6	12
1 2 4 5	12
. . . .	.
. . . .	.
. . . .	.
6 7 9 10	32
5 8 9 10	32
6 8 9 10	33
7 8 9 10	34

true that reliable differences in the means of the original variables exist when H_0 is rejected. It can only be concluded that the two distributions are not identical. In the example, one can conclude that the distributions of times it takes to run the maze for the control and experimental conditions are not equal. Visual inspection of the observed data suggests that the experimental rats took more time to run the maze than did the control rats. If the researcher knows that the distributions of times are symmetrical, then the statement of population differences can be equated to a statement of mean differences.

It is worth emphasizing that the final decision is based upon minimal assumptions. All that must be assumed is that the number of seconds used by any one rat is independent of the time used by any of the other rats, regardless of whether they are in the control or experimental group. In most behavioral studies that do not involve repeated measures, this assumption is easily justified.

EXAMPLE 11–2.2.   Tables of T_1 are given in the Appendix as Table A–14. The use of this table is straightforward, as is now illustrated for the rat and maze example. One enters the table with $(n_1, n_2) = (4, 6)$. Since the reported probabilities are one-tailed, $P(T_1 \leq 10) = 0.005$, $P(T_1 \leq 11) = 0.010$, $P(T_1 \leq 12) = 0.019$, and so on. A two-tailed test with $\alpha \leq 0.05$ is given by $T_1 \leq 12$ and $T_1 \geq 32$. These values define the two-tailed rejection region for the test. In this case, the $\alpha \leq 0.05$ decision rule is given by:

D.R.: Reject H_0 if $T_1 \leq 12$ or   if $T_1 \geq 32$

In this case, $T_1 = 12$, so H_0 is rejected.

One-tailed tests can also be constructed in a direct manner. Suppose the alternative states that $\mu_1 < \mu_2$. If this alternative were true, then the one-tailed decision rule for $\alpha \leq 0.05$ is given by:

D.R.: Reject H_0 if $T_1 \leq 13$ for which $\alpha = 0.033 \leq 0.05$

Two-Sample
Methods for
Quantitative
Variables Based
on Ranks and
Normal Scores

269

Another form of this test was developed by Mann and Whitney and is often reported in the literature. To understand this second model, consider the following sequence of numbers: (4, 3, 2, 1, 5). In this sequence it is quite clear that the first ordered pair of numbers, 4 and 3, is inverted. That is, they do not appear in their normal numerical order. The total set of inverted pairs in this sequence is {(4, 3), (4, 2), (4, 1), (3, 2), (3, 1), (2, 1)}. The correctly ordered pairs are {(4, 5), (3, 5), (2, 5), (1, 5)}. Of the 10 ordered pairs, a total of $I = 6$ are inverted.

EXAMPLE 11–2.3. With the inversion model in mind, consider outcomes on the two samples of Example 11–1.1, and list them with the smallest-sized sample being listed first. In the listing, order the outcomes within each sample and then rank the total set of data. The listing and ranking are shown in Table 11–4.

For the ranked values, the total number of inversions is equal to two. The inverted ranks are (4, 3) and (5, 3). If the hypothesis being tested is false, then one would expect the number of inversions to be close to either zero or the maximum value, $n_1 n_2$. In this example, the maximum number of inversions possible is $(4)(6) = 24$. If the hypothesis is true, then the number of inversions should be somewhere between these two extremes at:

$$E(I) = (\tfrac{1}{2})(n_1 n_2) = (\tfrac{1}{2})(24) = 12$$

It is somewhat surprising, but it can be shown that the number of inversions (I) is directly related to T_1 or T_2 of the Wilcoxon test. To see this connection, let n_1 equal the number of observations in the smaller sample, n_2 equal the number of observations in the larger sample, T_1 equal the sum of the ranks of the smaller sample, and T_2 equal the sum of the ranks of the larger sample. If the ordered observations of the smaller sample are listed first, then the number of inversions is:

$$I_1 = n_1 n_2 + \frac{n_2(n_2 + 1)}{2} - T_2$$

On the other hand, if the larger sample is listed first, then the number of inversions is:

$$I_2 = n_1 n_2 + \frac{n_1(n_1 + 1)}{2} - T_1$$

For simplicity in the construction of tables of the critical values, it is customary to use the minimum of the two values I_1 and I_2. This minimum value is known as U. Thus, the relationship between the sum of the ranks (T_1, T_2) for the two samples

TABLE 11–4. *Table of ordered rankings for the data of Table 11–1.*

	1. Control				2. Experimental					
Outcomes	17	36	40	42	39	48	54	55	61	64
Ranks	1	2	4	5	3	6	7	8	9	10

and the number of inversions (I_1, I_2) is given by:

$$U = \text{minimum} \begin{bmatrix} n_1 n_2 + \dfrac{n_1(n_1 + 1)}{2} - T_1 \\ n_1 n_2 + \dfrac{n_2(n_2 + 1)}{2} - T_2 \end{bmatrix}$$

As an example, consider the data ranked as shown in Table 11–5.

EXAMPLE 11–2.4. Let the elements of the control group of Example 11–1.1 be denoted by the letter X and those of the experimental group by the letter Y. The number of inversions, I, is equal to the number of times a Y value precedes an X value. In this case, the Y value, 39, precedes the X values of 40 and 42. Thus, the number of times a Y precedes an X is given by 2.

Under the Mann–Whitney model, the decision rule for rejecting H_0 is found as follows. For the Wilcoxon test, it was seen that H_0 is rejected if $T_1 \leq 12$ or if $T_1 \geq 32$. Focusing on T_1 only, the value of U is given by:

$$U = n_1 n_2 + \frac{n_1(n_1 + 1)}{2} - T_1$$

It follows that, for $T_1 = 12$:

$$U = 4(6) + \frac{4(5)}{2} - 12 = 22$$

and for $T_1 = 32$:

$$U = 4(6) + \frac{4(5)}{2} - 32 = 2$$

From these computations, it is seen that the decision rule is to reject H_0 if $U \leq 2$ or if $U \geq 22$. Thus, H_0 is rejected, just as it was for the Wilcoxon model.

The relationship between U and T_1, T_2 is easy to obtain. For the ordered values, let the first X have a rank of r_1. There are $(r_1 - 1)$ Y's that are smaller than the first X. If the rank of the second X is denoted by r_2, then there are $(r_2 - 1)$ rank values smaller than this rank, one of which is the rank associated with the first X. Therefore, there are $(r_2 - 2)$ Y's smaller than the second X. Continuing in a similar fashion, there are $(r_3 - 3)$ Y's smaller than the third X, etc. The total number of Y's

TABLE 11–5. Rank order of the data of Table 11–1.

Time (in sec.)

	17	36	39	40	42	48	54	55	61	64
Sample letter	X	X	Y	X	X	Y	Y	Y	Y	Y
Ranks	1	2	3	4	5	6	7	8	9	10

preceding X's is denoted by I_1 as:

$$I_1 = (r_1 - 1) + (r_2 - 2) + \ldots + (r_{n_1} - n_1)$$
$$= \sum_{i=1}^{n_1} (r_i - i) = \sum_{i=1}^{n_1} r_i - \sum_{i=1}^{n_1} i$$
$$= T_1 - \frac{n_1(n_1 + 1)}{2}$$

Similarly, the total number of X's preceding Y's can be denoted by I_2 as:

$$I_2 = T_2 - \frac{n_2(n_2 + 1)}{2}.$$

Since

$$T_1 + T_2 = \frac{N(N + 1)}{2},$$

where $N = (n_1 + n_2)$, it follows that:

$$T_1 = \frac{N(N + 1)}{2} - T_2$$

and

$$T_2 = \frac{N(N + 1)}{2} - T_1$$

Substituting these values into I_1 and I_2, we obtain:

$$U = \min \begin{bmatrix} n_1 n_2 + \dfrac{n_1(n_1 + 1)}{2} - T_1 \\[2ex] n_1 n_2 + \dfrac{n_2(n_2 + 1)}{2} - T_2 \end{bmatrix}$$

Since $I_1 + I_2 = n_1 n_2$, it is only necessary to work with the minimum of I_1 and I_2.

EXAMPLE 11–2.5. In general, it is easier to assign ranks to the data than it is to count the number of inversions. However, if one wants to count the inversions, the following simple counting procedure can be employed. Rank the observations for the larger sample and list them across the top of a two-dimensional matrix. Along the lefthand margin of the matrix, list the ordered values for the smaller sample. Finally, compute all the *ordered differences*, as shown in Table 11–6. The number of inversions equals the number of negative differences; that is, $U = 2$. Thus, the test can be performed by counting the number of ordered pairs that produce a negative difference.

The possible values for the number of inversions extend from a minimal value of $U = 0$ to a maximum value of $U = n_1 n_2$. By definition, the Mann–Whitney U statistic is the number of times an element of sample 2 is less than an element in sample 1. Thus, if X refers to an element of population 2, and Y refers to an element of population 1, an unbiased estimate of $P(X > Y)$ is given by:

$$\hat{p} = \frac{\text{observed } U}{\text{maximum } U} = \frac{U}{n_1 n_2}.$$

		Control sample $n_2 = 6$					
		39	48	54	55	61	64
Experimental	17	22	31	37	38	44	47
sample	36	3	12	18	19	25	28
$n_1 = 4$	40	−1	8	14	15	21	24
	42	−3	6	12	13	19	22

If H_0 is true, $E(U) = n_1 n_2/2$, so that $E(\hat{p}) = \frac{1}{2}$. Thus, the hypothesis that the two distributions are identical is equivalent to the hypothesis:

$$H_0: P(X < Y) = P(X > Y) = \tfrac{1}{2}.$$

EXAMPLE 11–2.6.   For Example 11–1.1,

$$\hat{p} = \frac{U}{n_1 n_2} = \frac{2}{46} = 0.0833.$$

It should be noted that the sampling distribution of $\hat{p}$ is known when H_0 is false but, since it depends upon three unknown parameters, it is not presented.

11–3. Point and Interval Estimates for the Median Difference

Use can be made of the table of ordered differences to determine point and interval estimates for the median difference or the mean difference, provided that the sample sizes are equal or the distribution of differences is symmetrical. These estimates are obtained under the Mann–Whitney model. The statistical theory that justifies the procedures is not presented. Instead, an example illustrating the basis of the model is presented.

EXAMPLE 11–3.1.   Table 11–6 can be used to estimate the median difference. Since there are 24 difference scores, the median lies halfway between the 12th and 13th ordered difference. Both these differences are equal to 19; therefore, the median difference is given by:

$$\hat{M} = (\tfrac{1}{2})(D^{(12)} + D^{(13)}) = (\tfrac{1}{2})(19 + 19) = 19$$

If the distribution of these differences is symmetrical or if $n_1 = n_2$, then the median difference is an unbiased estimate of $\mu_C - \mu_E$. Since the sample sizes of this example are almost equal, it follows that, for all practical purposes, rats with normal sleep will, on the average, take 19 seconds less time to run the maze.

EXAMPLE 11–3.2.   For an $\alpha = 0.038$ two-tailed test on the data of Example 11–1.1, the hypothesis H_0 would be rejected if the number of negative differences is (0, 1, 2, 22, 23, 24). With this region of rejection, one can proceed simultaneously from both ends to establish bounds on the median difference, M_d. The number 2 in the decision rule corresponds to the third ordered difference from the lower end. The number 22 corresponds to the third ordered difference from the upper end. A confidence interval with $\alpha = 0.038$ will be given as:

$$D^{(3)} \leq M_d \leq D^{(22)}$$
$$3 \leq M_d \leq 38$$

As would be expected, zero is not included in this interval. If the alpha level is increased to $\alpha = 2(0.057) = 0.114$, then the 5th and 20th ordered differences would be used as bounds. For the example, the interval extends from 8 seconds to 31 seconds.

11–4. Large-Sample Approximation for the Wilcoxon Test and Mann–Whitney Test

When n_1 and n_2 are both greater than 10, a normal-approximation procedure is available for the Wilcoxon and Mann–Whitney tests. The expected value and variance of T_1 are:

$$E(T_1) = \frac{n_1(n_1 + n_2 + 1)}{2}$$

$$\mathrm{Var}(T_1) = \frac{n_1 n_2}{12}(n_1 + n_2 + 1)$$

so that the normal approximation for the Wilcoxon statistic T_1 is given by:

$$Z = \frac{T_1 - E(T_1)}{\sqrt{\mathrm{Var}(T_1)}} = \frac{T_1 - \left[n_1(n_1 + n_2 + 1)/2\right]}{\sqrt{(n_1 n_2/12)(n_1 + n_2 + 1)}}$$

For the two-sample Mann–Whitney U statistic, the expected value and variance of U are given by:

$$E(U) = \frac{n_1 n_2}{2}$$

$$\mathrm{Var}(U) = \frac{n_1 n_2}{12}(n_1 + n_2 + 1)$$

so that the normal approximation for the Mann–Whitney U statistic is given by:

$$Z = \frac{U - E(U)}{\sqrt{\mathrm{Var}(U)}} = \frac{U - (n_1 n_2/2)}{\sqrt{(n_1 n_2/12)(n_1 + n_2 + 1)}}$$

The derivation of these large-sample forms follows from first principles and from two basic sums, shown in most elementary algebra texts as:

$$1 + 2 + 3 + \ldots + N = \frac{N(N + 1)}{2}$$

and

$$1^2 + 2^2 + 3^2 + \ldots + N^2 = \frac{N(N + 1)(2N + 1)}{6}$$

Because of these properties on the integers 1, 2, ..., N, large-sample formulas for the Wilcoxon and Mann–Whitney tests are easily obtained.

The large-sample test is based on the distribution of ranks $1, 2, \ldots, r_i, \ldots, N$, which are assumed to be equally likely, so that $P[r = r_i] = 1/N$. Under this model:

$$E(r) = \sum_{i=1}^{N} r_i P[r = r_i] = \frac{N + 1}{2}$$

and

$$\text{Var}(r) = \sum_{i=1}^{N} [r_i - E(r)]^2 P[r = r_i] = \frac{N^2 - 1}{12}$$

The expected value of T_1 is:

$$E(T_1) = E(r_1 + r_2 + \ldots + r_{n_1}).$$

Since the expected value of any particular rank r_i is given by $E(r)$, it follows that:

$$E(T_1) = n_1 E(r) = n_1 \left[\frac{N + 1}{2} \right] = n_1 \left[\frac{n_1 + n_2 + 1}{2} \right]$$

The ranks 1 through N define a finite population, so it follows from the model of Section 2–12 that:

$$\text{Var}(T_1) = n_1 \left[\frac{N - n_1}{N - 1} \right] \text{Var}(r) = \frac{n_1 n_2}{N - 1} \left[\frac{N^2 - 1}{12} \right] = \frac{n_1 n_2}{12} (n_1 + n_2 + 1)$$

In a similar fashion,

$$E(T_2) = n_2 \left[\frac{n_1 + n_2 + 1}{2} \right]$$

and

$$\text{Var}(T_2) = \frac{n_1 n_2}{12} (n_1 + n_2 + 1)$$

For the Mann–Whitney statistic,

$$E(U) = E(I_1) = E(I_2) = \frac{n_1 n_2}{2}$$

and

$$\text{Var}(U) = \text{Var}(T_1) = \text{Var}(T_2) = \frac{n_1 n_2}{12} (n_1 + n_2 + 1)$$

Thus, the large-sample forms of the test are as shown.

Since the distributions of T_1 and U are discrete, with unit intervals between the values, one can make a correction of continuity of $\pm \frac{1}{2}$ to improve the approximation to the normal distribution. In general, most practitioners do not bother with the correction unless the computed Z value is close in numerical value to the critical Z value that defines the rejection region of the test.

Ties are a problem with this test, since, in its development, all ranks from 1, 2, ..., N are assigned. Furthermore, it is assumed that the underlying variable is continuous. Even if the underlying variable *is* continuous, measurement itself may produce tied values. To handle this problem, one can break ties by assigning mid-ranks, and using:

$$\text{Var}(T_1) = \text{Var}(U) = \frac{n_1 n_2}{12}(n_1 + n_2 + 1)\left[1 - \sum_{s=1}^{S} \frac{t_s^3 - t_s}{N^3 - N}\right]$$

where $t_1, t_2, \ldots, t_s$ are numbers of observations tied at specific rank values.

Also, if $n_1 = n_2$, or if the distributions are symmetrical, the hypothesis of identical distributions is identical to H_0: $\mu_1 = \mu_2$, with the alternative being H_1: H_0 is false. Of course, there is no requirement that the underlying variables be normally distributed.

EXAMPLE 11–4.1.   As an example of the use of the Mann–Whitney form of the large-sample test, consider the following study, in which 16 boys and 11 girls were shown a 20-minute movie on the role of sex in certain occupations. Following the film, subjects were asked to rate 10 jobs on a scale from 0 to 5 as to whether the jobs were male-oriented (0) to female-oriented (5). The dependent variable is the *total rankings* given to the 10 jobs. A rank total of 25 would indicate that jobs were viewed as neither male nor female in nature. The data suggest that most of the boys found the jobs highly masculine, while the girls found them more toward the center but still masculine in nature. The hypothesis to be tested is that average scores for the students shown the film are unrelated to their sex. The alternative is that this hypothesis is false. The scores are summarized in Table 11–7. Inspection of the data

TABLE 11–7. Total ranks on the rating of 10 jobs by the boys and girls of Example 11–4.1.

Boys		Girls	
Total ranks	Rank	Total ranks	Rank
0	3	0	3
0	3	5	10.5
0	3	6	12
0	3	7	14
1	6	12	17.5
3	7	13	19
4	8.5	19	21
4	8.5	20	22
5	10.5	21	23
7	14	22	24.5
7	14	30	26
10	16		
12	17.5		
18	20		
22	24.5		
39	27		
$T_1 = 185.5$		$T_2 = 192.5$	

shows that the normality assumption has not been justified: scores cluster near zero. Thus, the Wilcoxon or Mann–Whitney test is clearly justified.

Tied scores are a problem for this test since the process of ranking assumes that each score occupies a unique position in the ranks from 1 to N. One procedure to use in breaking tied values is to assign midranks to the tied values. In Table 11–7, tied scores are given midranks. As a check on the computations, note that:

$$T_1 + T_2 = \frac{N(N + 1)}{2} = \frac{27(28)}{2} = 378$$

For these data,

$$U = \min \begin{bmatrix} 16(11) + \dfrac{16(17)}{2} - 185.5 \\ 16(11) + \dfrac{11(12)}{2} - 192.5 \end{bmatrix} = \begin{bmatrix} 126.5 \\ 49.5 \end{bmatrix} = 49.5$$

$$E(U) = \frac{16(11)}{2} = 88$$

$$\mathrm{Var}(U) = \frac{16(11)}{12}(16 + 11 + 1) = 410.7$$

and Z, corrected for continuity, is given by:

$$Z = \frac{\left[(49.5 + 0.5) - 88\right]}{\sqrt{410.7}} = \frac{-38}{20.27} = -1.87$$

With the correction for ties, note that $t_1 = 5$ values are tied at 0, $t_2 = 2$ values are tied at 4, $t_3 = 2$ values are tied at 5, $t_4 = 3$ values are tied at 7, $t_5 = 2$ values are tied at 12, and $t_6 = 2$ values are tied at 22. With these ties:

$\mathrm{Var}(U) =$

$$410.7\left[1 - \frac{\left[(5^3 - 5) + (2^3 - 2) + (2^3 - 2) + (3^3 - 3) + (2^3 - 2) + (2^3 - 2)\right]}{(27^3 - 27)}\right]$$

$$= 410.7(1 - 0.0085)$$
$$= 410.7(0.9915)$$
$$= 407.21$$

With the correction for ties,

$$Z = \frac{(49.5 + 0.5) - 88}{\sqrt{407.21}} = \frac{-38}{20.18} = -1.88$$

Since the computed Z is greater than -1.96, H_0 is not rejected at the 0.05 level. The evidence does not support the conclusions that a sex difference exists relative to performance on the ratings.

In the next example, a large-sample confidence interval for the median difference is illustrated. While a justification for the method is not provided, it is hoped that the detail in the example will facilitate the use of the method for the behavioral scientist. In any case, it must be recalled that a confidence interval for the median difference does not correspond to a confidence interval for $\mu_1 - \mu_2$, unless $n_1 = n_2$ or the underlying distributions are symmetrical.

EXAMPLE 11–4.2 An approximate 90-percent confidence interval for the median difference in ratings for the data of Example 11–4.1 is determined. As before, one sets up the matrix of difference, as shown in Table 11–8. Since $n_1 > 10$ and $n_2 > 10$, $U_{0.05}$ and $U_{0.95}$ must be approximated from the normal approximation. Letting $\alpha = 0.10$, then $Z_{0.05} = -1.645$ and $Z_{0.95} = 1.645$. Thus, the lower cutoff point for the confidence interval is determined from:

$$U_{0.05} = E(U) + Z_{0.05} \sqrt{\mathrm{Var}(U)} = 88 + 1.645(20.27) = 55$$

The lower limit for the confidence interval is the difference associated with $U_L + 1$. In the matrix, the 56th lowest difference is equal to -13. The upper limit is the difference associated with:

$$U_{0.95} = E(U) + Z_{0.95} \sqrt{\mathrm{Var}(U)} = 88 + 1.645(20.27) = 121.$$

The total number of differences is $n_1 n_2 = 16(11) = 176$. Thus, the $176 - 121 + 1 = 56$th greatest difference is found in the matrix to be -1. Thus, the 90% confidence interval for $\Delta = M_d$ is

$$-13 \le M_d \le -1.$$

Girls rated the jobs as more feminine from 1 to 13 more points than the boys. A 95% confidence interval would be defined by:

$$U_{0.025} = 88 - 1.96(20.27) = 48$$

and

$$U_{0.975} = 88 + 1.96(20.27) = 128$$

For these limits, $D^{(48+1)} = D^{(49)} = -15$ and $D^{(128)} = 0$ so that

$$-15 \le M_d \le 0$$

Since H_0 was not rejected, it is reasonable to expect zero to appear in the interval. Since the distribution of differences is not symmetrical, inference cannot be made to $\mu_B - \mu_G$. The best point estimate of M_d is $\hat{M}_d = -7$, the mean of $D^{(88)}$ and $D^{(89)}$.

11–5. The Two-Sample Tests Based on Normal Scores

The Wilcoxon test of Section 11–2 is basically a variation on the Fisher randomization two-sample t test, in that the original observations are replaced by ranks. Other variables may be substituted for original observations besides their ordinary ranks. Three such substitutions are considered in the following sections. Collectively, these tests are referred to as normal-scores tests, since the transformation variables are associated with various characteristics of the normal distribution.

TABLE 11–8. Computations for the median difference for the data of Example 11–4.1.

										Data for boys							
Data for girls	0	0	0	0	0	1	3	4	4	5	7	7	10	12	18	22	39
0	0	0	0	0	0	1	3	4	4	5	7	7	10	12	18	22	39
5	−5	−5	−5	−5	−5	−4	−2	−1	−1	0	2	2	5	7	13	17	34
6	−6	−6	−6	−6	−6	−5	−3	−2	−2	−1	1	1	4	6	12	16	33
7	−7	−7	−7	−7	−7	−6	−4	−3	−3	−2	0	0	3	5	11	15	32
12	−12	−12	−12	−12	−12	−11	−9	−8	−8	−7	−5	−5	−2	0	6	10	27
13	−13	−13	−13	−13	−13	−12	−10	−9	−9	−8	−6	−6	−3	−1	5	9	26
19	−19	−19	−19	−19	−19	−18	−16	−15	−15	−14	−12	−12	−9	−7	−1	3	20
20	−20	−20	−20	−20	−20	−19	−17	−16	−16	−15	−13	−13	−10	−8	−2	2	19
21	−21	−21	−21	−21	−21	−20	−18	−17	−17	−16	−14	−14	−11	−9	−3	1	18
22	−22	−22	−22	−22	−22	−21	−19	−18	−18	−17	−15	−15	−12	−10	−4	0	17
30	−30	−30	−30	−30	−30	−29	−27	−26	−26	−25	−23	−23	−20	−18	−12	−8	9

Two-Sample
Methods for
Quantitative
Variables Based
on Ranks and
Normal Scores

279

In the technical literature they are referred to as:

1. The Terry–Hoeffding normal-scores test (Terry, 1952);
2. The Van der Waerden normal-scores test (Van der Waerden, 1953); and,
3. The Bell–Doksum normal-scores test (Bell and Doksum, 1965).

These nonparametric tests, like the Wilcoxon test, replace the original variable with monotonically related variables. With tests of this nature, the shape or form of the parent distribution from which the original scores·are drawn is of minor relevance. Thus, the term *distribution-free statistics* is attached to tests of this nature. Upon making these substitutions, information is generally lost; however, procedures that minimize the loss of information when comparable values are substituted for the original observations are frequently judged to be good tests. These tests preserve much of the original information, but in a different form.

As indicated in Section 4–3, the goodness of a test can also be analyzed in terms of its efficiency. Since efficiency represents a relative measure of the ability to reject the hypothesis under test, H_0, when it is false, the normal-scores tests should appeal to behavioral scientists, because their asymptotic efficiency relative to the t test is 1 when the t test is appropriate and greater than 1 when the t test is not appropriate. Since the efficiency of the Wilcoxon–Mann–Whitney U test relative to the t test is equal to $3/\pi = 95.5\%$, under the same circumstances it follows that the efficiency of the normal-scores test is greater than that of the corresponding rank test.

The Wilcoxon–Mann–Whitney U test requires that ranks be substituted in place of the original set of scores. For the three forms of the normal-scores test, three different score substitutions are required. In each case, the new scores are derived from the normal distribution. The Terry–Hoeffding test replaces the original data with the *expected values* of the corresponding normal-order statistic; the Van der Waerden test utilizes the *inverse-normal* scores; and the Bell–Doksum test substitutes *random normal deviates*. In all cases, the asymptotic efficiency relative to the t test is 1, when the assumptions under the t test are satisfied.

When n_1 and n_2 are large, and tables are not available, one can use the familiar tables of the $N(0, 1)$ distribution to generate the appropriate values for the Van der Waerden inverse-normal scores. For the Terry–Hoeffding form, other tables are always necessary. With the Bell–Doksum test, it is quite possible that different researchers may select, on the basis of chance, different Z values and thereby come to different decisions. This is certain to make the researcher uneasy and is therefore a point against the general use of this form of the normal-scores test.

11–6. The Terry–Hoeffding Normal-Scores Test

For this test, assume that the original scores have been lost and only the corresponding ranks are available. Now, attempt to reconstruct the original scores from the given ranks. The *best guess* as to the value of the original score is given by the expected normal order statistic, $E(V^{(i)})$, corresponding to the rank of that score. If $V^{(i)}$ is the ith ranked score in the combined sample of size $N = n_1 + n_2$, then $E(V^{(i)})$ is the expected value of the score in the ith position. The $E(V^{(i)})$ acts as a distance measure in much the same way that Z scores express relative distance in a normal distribution. High ranks will have a large positive $E(V^{(i)})$ and low ranks will have a large negative $E(V^{(i)})$. Those ranks toward the middle of the distribution will have an $E(V^{(i)})$ close to zero. Also, for a given N, the sum of the $E(V^{(i)})$ will be zero. As an illustration of the use of this test, consider the data of Table 11–1.

EXAMPLE 11–6.1. For the data of Table 11–1, replace each observation by its expected normal order statistic, $E(V^{(i)})$, as listed in Table A–15. The results of this substitution are shown in Table 11–9. Note that the sum of T_1 and T_2 is zero. Under H_0, $E(\overline{T}_1) = E(\overline{T}_2) = 0$. If there is no central-tendency difference between the two populations from which the samples are drawn, one would expect that the difference between $\overline{T}_1$ and $\overline{T}_2$ would be close to zero. Since $T_1 = -T_2$, one need only use:

$$T_1 = \sum_{i=1}^{n_1} E(V^{(i)})$$

as the test statistic, where T_1 is associated with the group containing the lesser number of observations. Tables for determining a decision rule are available, but it is very easy to determine the decision rule when the number of scores in each sample is small. The procedure is exactly the same as that used for the Fisher randomization two-sample t test and the two-sample Wilcoxon test.

Under H_0, the number of equally likely assignments of four $E(V^{(i)})$ to sample 1 and six $E(V^{(i)})$ to sample 2 is given by:

$$T = \begin{bmatrix} 10 \\ 4 \end{bmatrix} = \begin{bmatrix} 10 \\ 6 \end{bmatrix} = 210$$

For a two-tailed test with $\alpha \le 0.05$, the number of extreme T_1 values is given by:

$$K = \alpha \begin{bmatrix} n_1 + n_2 \\ n_1 \end{bmatrix} = \alpha \begin{bmatrix} n_1 + n_2 \\ n_2 \end{bmatrix}$$
$$= 0.05(210) = 10.5$$

which, when rounded down to the nearest even integer, gives $K = 10$. The 10 most

TABLE 11–9. Expected normal-order statistics for the data of Table 11–1.

Control group		Experimental group	
Number of seconds	$E(V^{(i)})$	Number of seconds	$E(V^{(i)})$
17	−1.54	39	−0.66
36	−1.00	48	0.12
40	−0.38	54	0.38
42	−0.12	55	0.66
		61	1.00
		64	1.54
$T_1 = -3.04$		$T_2 = 3.04$	

Two-Sample
Methods for
Quantitative
Variables Based
on Ranks and
Normal Scores

281

extreme values of T_1 are shown in Table 11–10. Since the observed T_1 is an element of the rejection set, H_0 is rejected.

For the large-sample test, the values of $E(V^{(i)})$ are assumed to be equally likely under H_0, so that the expected value of $E(V^{(i)})$ is given by:

$$E[E(V^{(i)})] = \frac{1}{N} \sum_{i=1}^{N} E(V^{(i)}) = 0$$

and the variance is given by:

$$\text{Var}[E(V^{(i)})] = \sum_{i=1}^{N} \left[E(V^{(i)}) - E[E(V^{(i)})] \right]^2 \frac{1}{N}$$

$$= \frac{1}{N} \sum_{i=1}^{N} E(V^{(i)})^2$$

By definition,

$$T_1 = \sum_{i=1}^{n_1} E(V^{(i)})$$

so that

$$E(T_1) = n_1 E[E(V^{(i)})] = 0$$

Also, since $n_1 + n_2 = N$ represents a finite population, it follows, under the theory of Section 2–12, that:

$$\text{Var}(T_1) = n_1 \text{Var}[E(V^{(i)})] \frac{N - n_1}{N - 1}$$

$$= \frac{n_1 n_2}{N - 1} \frac{\sum_{i=1}^{N} E(V^{(i)})^2}{N}$$

If the number of subjects in each sample is greater than or equal to 8, the normal approximation is found to give very good results with:

$$Z \doteq \frac{T_1 - E(T_1)}{\sqrt{\text{Var}(T_1)}}$$

The large-sample form of the test is illustrated in Section 11–9.

TABLE 11–10. The rejection region for the Terry–Hoeffding statistic for the data of Table 11–1.

Value of $E(V^{(i)})$ assigned to the smaller sample	Value of T_1
$-1.54 - 1.00 - 0.66 - 0.38$	-3.58
$-1.54 - 1.00 - 0.66 - 0.12$	-3.32
$-1.54 - 1.00 - 0.66 + 0.12$	-3.08
$-1.54 - 1.00 - 0.38 - 0.12$	-3.04
$-1.54 - 1.00 - 0.66 + 0.38$	-2.82
$1.54 + 1.00 + 0.66 - 0.38$	2.82
$1.54 + 1.00 + 0.38 + 0.12$	3.04
$1.54 + 1.00 + 0.66 - 0.12$	3.08
$1.54 + 1.00 + 0.66 + 0.12$	3.32
$1.54 + 1.00 + 0.66 + 0.38$	3.58

11-7. The Van der Waerden Normal-Scores Test

For this form of the normal-scores test, let $r_1, r_2, \ldots, r_N$ correspond to the ranks of the ordered observations. Let:

$$p_i = \frac{r_i}{N+1} = \Phi(Z^{(i)}) \qquad \text{for } i = 1, 2, \ldots, N = n_1 + n_2$$

be the percentile rank associated with the ith ordered normalized observation.

EXAMPLE 11-7.1. Suppose $N = 4$ and $X_1 = 8$, $X_2 = 11$, $X_3 = 15$, and $X_4 = 20$. For these observations, $p_1 = \frac{1}{5} = 0.20$, $p_2 = \frac{2}{5} = 0.40$, $p_3 = \frac{3}{5} = 0.60$, and $p_4 = \frac{4}{5} = 0.80$, for which the inverse-normal scores are given by $Z^{(1)} = -0.84$, $Z^{(2)} = -0.25$, $Z^{(3)} = 0.25$, and $Z^{(4)} = 0.84$, as examination of Tables A-2 and A-16 indicates. As shown:

$$Z^{(i)} = \Phi^{-1}(p_i) = \Phi^{-1}\left[\frac{r_i}{N+1}\right]$$

While most of the technical literature employs this involved notation, one could use $Z^{(i)}$ to denote the same normal-curve characteristic. Let the $Z^{(i)}$ be replaced for the original variables, and let:

$$T_1 = \sum_{i=1}^{n_1} Z^{(i)}$$

correspond to the sum of the inverse-normal scores assigned to the smaller sample. As with the Terry–Hoeffding test, $T_1 + T_2 = 0$, so once again the hypothesis under test, H_0, is that $E(\overline{T}_1) = E(\overline{T}_2) = 0$.

EXAMPLE 11-7.2. The $Z^{(i)}$ corresponding to the data of Table 11.1 are shown in Table 11-11. The 10 extreme values of T_1 are shown in Table 11-12. Since the observed T_1 is in the rejection region, H_0 is rejected.

If the size of both samples is greater than or equal to 8, the normal approxi-

TABLE 11-11. Inverse normal-order statistics for the data of Table 11-1.

Control group		Experimental group	
Number of seconds	$Z^{(i)}$	Number of seconds	$Z^{(i)}$
17	-1.34	39	-0.60
36	-0.91	48	0.11
40	-0.35	54	0.35
42	-0.11	55	0.60
		61	0.91
		64	1.34
$T_1 = -2.71$		$T_2 = 2.71$	

Two-Sample
Methods for
Quantitative
Variables Based
on Ranks and
Normal Scores

283

TABLE 11-12. The rejection region for the Van der Waerden statistic for the data of Table 11-1.

Values of $Z^{(i)}$ assigned to the smaller sample	Value of T_1
$-1.34 - 0.91 - 0.60 - 0.35$	-3.20
$-1.34 - 0.91 - 0.60 - 0.11$	-2.96
$-1.34 - 0.91 - 0.60 + 0.11$	-2.74
$-1.34 - 0.91 - 0.35 - 0.11$	-2.71
$-1.34 - 0.91 - 0.35 + 0.11$	-2.49
$1.34 + 0.91 + 0.35 - 0.11$	2.49
$1.34 + 0.91 + 0.35 + 0.11$	2.71
$1.34 + 0.91 + 0.60 - 0.11$	2.74
$1.34 + 0.91 + 0.60 + 0.11$	2.96
$1.34 + 0.91 + 0.60 + 0.35$	3.20

mation is appropriate. With algebra quite similar to that of Section 11–6, it can be shown that:

$$Z = \frac{T_1 - E(T_1)}{\sqrt{\text{Var}(T_1)}}$$

where

$$E(T_1) = 0$$

and

$$\text{Var}(T_1) = \frac{n_1 n_2}{N - 1} \sum_{i=1}^{N} \frac{(Z^{(i)})^2}{N}$$

The large-sample form of this test is illustrated in Section 11–9.

This form of the normal-scores test should be of considerable interest to psychologists and researchers in education because of their use of standard scores in measurement models, since the Van der Waerden scores are immediately transferable to T scores with a mean of 50 and a standard deviation of 10.

EXAMPLE 11–7.3. For the normal scores of the control group in Table 11–11, the corresponding T scores are 36.6, 40.9, 46.5, and 48.9. The mean T score is:

$$\overline{T}_1 = \frac{1}{4}(36.6 + 40.9 + 46.5 + 48.9) = 43.2$$

The T scores for the experimental group are given by 44.0, 51.1, 53.5, 56.0, 59.1, and 63.4 with a mean value of $\overline{T}_2 = 54.5$. As shown by the normal-scores test, the standardized difference between $\hat{\Delta} = \overline{T}_1 - \overline{T}_2 = 43.2 - 54.5 = -10.2$ is statistically significant, and what is more, the difference is easily interpretable as 1.02 standard deviation units.

11–8. The Bell–Doksum Normal-Scores Test

For this form of the normal-scores test, one selects a sample of size N from a table of random normal deviates, such as Table A–17. The normal deviates are ranked in ascending order and are then substituted in place of the corresponding ranks $r_1, r_2, \ldots, r_N$. This method introduces new randomness into the problem, which may not seem desirable, and for this reason most behavioral scientists would object to this characteristic of the test. After assigning the normal deviates to the ranks associated with each sample, one operates on them in a fashion similar to the two-sample t test. If the sample sizes are small, one generates an exact test in exactly the same fashion used for the Fisher randomization t test, the Wilcoxon test, the Terry–Hoeffding test, and the Van der Waerden test.

EXAMPLE 11–8.1. Data for the Bell–Doksum test of Table 11–1 are shown in Table 11–13. The set of 10 extreme values for this test is shown in Table 11–14. With these values, H_0 is rejected, since T_1 is an element of the rejection set, as shown in Table 11–14.

TABLE 11–13. *Random normal deviates for the data of Table 11–1.*

Control group		Experimental group	
Number of seconds	$Z^{(i)}$	Number of seconds	$Z^{(i)}$
17	−1.94	39	−0.63
36	−0.89	48	−0.24
40	−0.54	54	0.40
42	−0.44	55	0.49
		61	0.53
		64	0.66
$T_1 = -3.81$		$T_2 = 1.21$	

TABLE 11–14. *The rejection region of the Bell–Doksum statistic for the data of Table 11–1.*

Values of $Z^{(i)}$ assigned to the smaller sample	Value of T_1
−1.94 − 0.89 − 0.63 − 0.54	−4.00
−1.94 − 0.89 − 0.63 − 0.44	−3.90
−1.94 − 0.89 − 0.54 − 0.44	−3.81
−1.94 − 0.89 − 0.63 − 0.24	−3.70
−1.94 − 0.89 − 0.54 − 0.24	−3.61
0.53 + 0.49 + 0.40 − 0.24	1.18
0.66 + 0.53 + 0.49 − 0.24	1.24
0.66 + 0.49 + 0.40 − 0.24	1.31
0.66 + 0.53 + 0.40 − 0.24	1.35
0.66 + 0.53 + 0.49 − 0.24	1.44
0.66 + 0.53 + 0.49 + 0.40	2.08

Under H_0, the $E(Z^{(i)}) = 0$ and $\text{Var}(Z^{(i)}) = 1$, so that the large-sample properties of this test are such that:

$$E(\overline{T}_1 - \overline{T}_2) = \frac{T_1}{n_1} - \frac{T_2}{n_2}$$

and

$$\text{Var}(\overline{T}_1 - \overline{T}_2) = \frac{1}{n_1} + \frac{1}{n_2}$$

so that the test statistic

$$Z = \frac{\overline{T}_1 - \overline{T}_2}{\sqrt{(1/n_1) + (1/n_2)}}$$

is approximately $N(0, 1)$. The large-sample form of the test is illustrated in Section 11–9.

Since $T_1 + T_2 \neq 0$ and since the normal random deviates vary over repeated sampling, two researchers given the same data might arrive at different values of T_1 and different conclusions. Thus, even though the test has an efficiency of 1 when compared to the classical t test, it may not be preferred by a researcher.

11–9. The Large-Sample Form of the Normal-Scores Tests

The large-sample forms of the three normal-scores tests of Section 11–6, 11–7, and 11–8 are illustrated by means of the following example.

EXAMPLE 11–9.1. Consider a study in which it was of interest to determine if the order in which questions were presented in a multiple-choice test had an effect on exam grades. In this study, 22 students taking a beginning course in inferential statistics were divided randomly into two groups and given a quiz covering elements of statistical inference. Half the students were presented 20 multiple-choice questions arranged in the same order as the material was presented in the class lectures. The other half took the same test with questions in a scrambled order. The results in terms of number of questions answered correctly are as shown in Table 11–15. One person in the scrambled group failed to take the quiz. Since the original contention was that the students in the ordered group would score higher on the exam than the students in the scrambled group, a one-tailed test is appropriate The results are analyzed by using the t test, the Wilcoxon–Mann–Whitney rank test, and the three forms of the normal-scores test. Ties have been broken by random assignments of ranks and not by midrank assignment. The $E(V^{(i)})$ are taken from Table A–15 with $n_1 + n_2 = 21$, the $\Phi^{-1}[r_i/(N + 1)]$ are taken from Table A–16 with $n_1 + n_2 = 21$, while the Z_i are taken from Table A–17. Note that, if another researcher were to analyze the same data, he would find that the figures of the last column of Table 11–15 would differ from those reported; however, all the other figures would remain the same.

In order for the data to be analyzed using the t test, the following assumptions must hold:

TABLE 11–15. The large-sample forms of the normal-scores test based on the data of Example 11–9.1.

Group	Scores	Rank	$E(V^{(i)})$	$\dfrac{r_i}{N+1}$	$\Phi^{-1}\left[\dfrac{r_i}{N+1}\right]$	Z_i
Ordered	15	19	1.16	0.86	1.10	1.04
	10	8	−0.36	0.36	−0.35	−0.88
	7	3	−1.16	0.14	−1.10	−1.36
	9	5	−0.78	0.23	−0.75	−0.98
	11	9	−0.24	0.41	−0.23	−0.85
	19	21	1.89	0.96	1.69	1.54
	9	7	−0.49	0.32	−0.47	−0.89
	12	13	0.24	0.59	0.23	−0.35
	14	17	0.78	0.77	0.75	0.49
	11	12	0.12	0.54	0.11	−0.37
	17	20	1.43	0.91	1.34	1.14
		134	2.59		2.32	−1.47
Scrambled	3	1	−1.89	0.04	−1.69	−1.66
	11	10	−0.12	0.46	−0.11	−0.72
	11	11	0.00	0.50	0.00	−0.41
	13	16	0.63	0.73	0.60	0.42
	15	18	0.95	0.82	0.91	0.62
	8	4	−0.95	0.18	−0.91	−1.15
	13	14	0.36	0.64	0.35	−0.07
	6	2	−1.43	0.09	−1.34	−1.28
	13	15	0.49	0.68	0.47	0.17
	9	6	−0.63	0.27	−0.60	−0.93
		97	−2.59		−2.32	−5.01

1. Independence within groups.
2. Independence between groups.
3. Normal distributions in the populations from which the subjects are drawn.
4. The same variance in both populations.

For the observed data:

$$t = \frac{\overline{X}_1 - \overline{X}_2}{S_p \sqrt{(1/n_1) + (1/n_2)}} = \frac{12.18 - 10.20}{3.69 \sqrt{\frac{1}{11} + \frac{1}{10}}} = 1.22$$

If the test is conducted at the $\alpha \leq 0.05$ level, the null hypothesis is not rejected since $t = 1.22 < t_{19:0.95} = 1.729$. The scores obtained by students taking the ordered form of the test are not statistically different from the scores of the scrambled group.

The Wilcoxon test values are given by:

$$T_1 = \sum_{i=1}^{n_1} r_i = 134$$

$$E(T_1) = \frac{n_1(n_1 + n_2 + 1)}{2} = \frac{11(11 + 10 + 1)}{2} = 121$$

Two-Sample
Methods for
Quantitative
Variables Based
on Ranks and
Normal Scores

287

and

$$\text{Var}(T_1) = \frac{n_1 n_2}{12}(n_1 + n_2 + 1) = \frac{(11)(10)(22)}{12} = 201.67$$

$$Z = \frac{T_1 - E(T_1)}{\sqrt{\text{Var}(T_1)}} = \frac{134 - 121}{\sqrt{201.67}} = \frac{13}{14.2} = 0.91$$

Since $Z = 0.91 < 1.645$, the 95th percentile of the $N(0, 1)$ distribution, H_0 is not rejected.

For the Terry–Hoeffding form of the normal-scores test:

$$T_1 = \sum_{i=1}^{n_1} E(V^{(i)}) = 2.59$$

$$E(T_1) = 0$$

$$\text{Var}(T_1) = \frac{n_1 n_2}{N - 1} \left[\frac{\sum_{i=1}^{N} E(V^{(i)})^2}{N} \right]$$

$$= \frac{(11)(10)}{21 - 1} \left[\frac{(1.16)^2 + \ldots + (-.63)^2}{21} \right] = 4.8778,$$

$$Z = \frac{T_1 - E(T_1)}{\sqrt{\text{Var}(T_1)}} = \frac{2.59}{\sqrt{4.8778}} = 1.17$$

Since $Z = 1.17 < 1.645$, the 95th percentile of the $N(0, 1)$ distribution, H_0 is not rejected.

For the Van der Waerden form of the normal-scores test:

$$T_1 = \sum_{i=1}^{n_1} \Phi^{-1} \left[\frac{r_i}{N + 1} \right] = 2.32$$

$$E(T_1) = 0$$

$$\text{Var}(T_1) = \frac{n_1 n_2}{N - 1} \left[\frac{\sum_{i=1}^{N} \Phi^{-1} \left[\frac{r_i}{N + 1} \right]^2}{N} \right]$$

$$= \frac{(11)(10)}{20} \left[\frac{(1.10)^2 + \ldots + (-.60)^2}{21} \right] = 4.1916$$

$$Z = \frac{T_1 - E(T_1)}{\sqrt{\text{Var}(T_1)}} = \frac{2.32}{\sqrt{4.1916}} = 1.13$$

Since $Z = 1.13 < 1.645$, the 95th percentile of the $N(0, 1)$ distribution, H_0 is not rejected.

For the Bell–Doksum form of the normal-scores test:

$$Z = \frac{\overline{T}_1 - \overline{T}_2}{\sqrt{(1/n_1) + (1/n_2)}} = \frac{(-1.47/11) - (-5.02/10)}{\sqrt{\frac{1}{11} + \frac{1}{10}}} = 0.84$$

Since $Z = 0.84 < 1.645$, the 95th percentile of the $N(0, 1)$ distribution, H_0 is not rejected.

After computing a number of examples, there would be little doubt in the experimenter's mind that the procedures associated with the normal-scores test are somewhat more difficult to handle than those of the Wilcoxon test. Once learned, however, the normal-scores test will proceed very quickly. Thus, the choice of test will become a matter of power. For scores drawn from distributions with sharp tails, such as the exponential or the normal, the normal-scores test is best. For scores drawn from distributions having heavy tails, such as the uniform, logistic, double-exponential, or Cauchy, the Wilcoxon test proves to be superior.

11–10. The Siegel–Tukey Test for Equal Variability

The Wilcoxon test can be modified to test the hypothesis that two populations have equal variability if it is believed that they already possess equal centers (Siegel and Tukey, 1960). For this test, one assigns a rank of 1 to the smallest value, a rank of 2 to the largest, a rank of 3 to the second largest, a rank of 4 to the second smallest, a rank of 5 to the third smallest, a rank of 6 to the third largest, and so on. If the tested hypothesis of no difference in spread is true, $\overline{T_1}$ and $\overline{T_2}$ should be about equal. If the *smaller* sample is associated with T_1, then $\overline{T_1}$ should be less than $\overline{T_2}$, provided that population 1 has the greater variance, whereas, if population 2 has the greater variability, $\overline{T_1}$ will exceed $\overline{T_2}$. The test is best illustrated by example.

EXAMPLE 11–10.1. Consider the data of Table 11–15 as rank-ordered in Table 11–16. For the *smaller* sample:

$$T_1 = 1 + 4 + 8 + 12 + 20 + 21 + 15 + 14 + 11 + 7 = 113$$

$$E(T_1) = n_1 \left[\frac{n_1 + n_2 + 1}{2} \right] = 10 \left[\frac{22}{2} \right] = 110$$

$$\text{Var}(T_1) = \frac{n_1 n_2}{12}(n_1 + n_2 + 1) = 201.67$$

$$Z = \frac{T_1 - E(T_1)}{\sqrt{\text{Var}(T_1)}} = \frac{113 - 110}{\sqrt{201.67}} = \frac{3}{14.2} = .21$$

so that there is no reason to doubt the hypothesis that the variability in the two populations is identical.

If the populations also differ in centers, the Siegel–Tukey test may not be useful, since rejection of the hypothesis of equal variability may result from differences in center. If it is known that the centers are the same, then rejection implies differences in spread. If it is known that the distributions differ in center, then one can adjust the data by subtracting the appropriate means or medians from

TABLE 11-16. Rank orders of the observations of Table 11-15 for the Siegel–Tukey test.

Ranked scores	Sample	Siegel–Tukey rank
3	S	1
6	S	4
7	O	5
8	S	8
9	O	9
9	S	12
9	O	13
10	O	16
11	O	17
11	S	20
11	S	21
11	O	19
12	O	18
13	S	15
13	S	14
13	S	11
14	O	10
15	S	7
15	O	6
17	O	3
19	O	2

each of the observations. The Siegel–Tukey ranking then is performed on the aligned observations.

If the Siegel–Tukey test is substituted for the classical F test of equal variances when the F test is justified, a considerable drop in power occurs, since the asymptotic relative efficiency is only 0.61. However, if the distribution is double-exponential, then the asymptotic relative efficiency is 0.94.

11-11. The Mood Test for Equal Variances

A test having slightly more power than the Siegel–Tukey test and yet based upon the assignment of ranks to the original observations is the Mood test (Mood, 1954). When compared to the classical F test when it can be justified, the asymptotic relative efficiency of the Mood test is 0.76, which is slightly higher than the Siegel–Tukey efficiency measure of 0.61.

For the Mood test, data are ranked as they are for the two-sample Wilcoxon test. If the population centers are equal, then:

$$M = \sum_{i=1}^{n_1} \left[r_i - E(r_i) \right]^2$$

tends to be large if the variation of sample 1 exceeds the variation of sample 2, or it tends to be small if the opposite situation holds. Thus, two- or one-tailed tests can be performed with M as the test statistic. If n_1 and n_2 are small, the rejection region can be determined in the same manner as used to determine the rejection region of the Fisher randomization test, the Wilcoxon test, or the three forms of the normal-scores test. If n_1 and n_2 are large, a normal approximation may be used, since M tends to a normal form. For the *smaller* sample,

$$E(M) = n_1 \left[\frac{N^2 - 1}{12} \right]$$

$$\text{Var}(M) = \frac{n_1 n_2 (N + 1)(N^2 - 4)}{180}$$

The use of the test is illustrated for the data of Table 11–15.

EXAMPLE 11–11.1. Since it is known that the centers for the data of Table 11–15 are not significantly different from one another, it is not necessary to align the data before the assignment of ranks. For the ranks of Table 11–15,

$$\begin{aligned}
M &= (1 - 11)^2 + (10 - 11)^2 + (11 - 11)^2 + \ldots + (6 - 11)^2 \\
&= (-10)^2 + (-1)^2 + (0)^2 + (5)^2 + (7)^2 + (-7)^2 + (3)^2 + (-9)^2 + (4)^2 \\
&\quad + (-5)^2 \\
&= 355
\end{aligned}$$

$$E(M) = \frac{n_1}{12}(N^2 - 1) = \frac{10}{12}(21^2 - 1) = 366.67$$

$$\text{Var}(M) = \frac{n_1 n_2 (N + 1)(N^2 - 4)}{180} = \frac{(10)(11)(22)(21^2 - 4)}{180}$$

$$= 5875.22$$

$$Z = \frac{M - E(M)}{\sqrt{\text{Var}(M)}} = \frac{355 - 366.67}{\sqrt{5875.22}} = \frac{-11.67}{76.65} = -0.15$$

With $\alpha \leq 0.05$, H_0 is not rejected, since $Z = -0.15$ is in the acceptance region, $-1.96 < Z < 1.96$.

Like the Siegel–Tukey test for equal scale parameters, it must be assumed that the location parameters are equal. If the data suggest to a researcher that the population centers are unequal, then some form of alignment should be imposed before assigning the ranks. If the alignment values are not close in absolute value to the unknown parameter values, then it is possible that rejection of H_0 does not indicate differences in scale. In any case, when the Siegel–Tukey test, the Mood test, or the Klotz test discussed in the next section are used to test for identical population spread, one must be careful in the final interpretation of the data, because of the high dependence of these tests on equal population centers.

11–12. The Klotz Test for Equal Variances

Klotz has developed a test, based on inverse-normal scores, for testing the hypothesis that two distributions have equal variances if it is known that they have equal centers (Klotz, 1962). If the underlying distributions are also symmetrical, the test becomes an excellent competitor to the classical F test. On the home ground of the F test, its asymptotic relative efficiency is one. In many other cases, its efficiency exceeds one. The test statistic is given by:

$$K = \sum_{i=1}^{n_1} \left[\Phi^{-1} \left[\frac{r_i}{N+1} \right] \right]^2$$

where n_1 refers to the *smaller* sample. Klotz has shown that:

$$E(K) = \frac{n_1}{N} \sum_{i=1}^{N} \left[\Phi^{-1} \left[\frac{r_i}{N+1} \right] \right]^2$$

with

$$\text{Var}(K) = \frac{n_1 n_2}{N(N-1)} \sum_{i=1}^{N} \left[\Phi^{-1} \left[\frac{r_i}{N+1} \right] \right]^4 - \frac{n_2 E(K)^2}{n_1(N-1)}$$

and that

$$Z = \frac{K - E(K)}{\sqrt{\text{Var}(K)}}$$

tends to a $N(0, 1)$ form. The test is illustrated for the data of Table 11–15.

EXAMPLE 11–12.1. Since it is known that the centers of the two distributions of Table 11–15 are not statistically different, there is no need to align the data before ranking. However, to illustrate the complete procedure, both samples are aligned in terms of their sample means, $\overline{X}_0 = 12.2$ and $\overline{X}_S = 10.2$. Basic statistics are summarized in Table 11–17. Aligned scores in group 1 are found by subtracting 12.2 from each sample value. In group 2, aligned scores are found by subtracting 10.2 from each sample value. Tied values are broken by averaging the associated inverse-normal statistics. For the *smaller* sample:

$$K = (-1.69)^2 + (-1.10)^2 + \ldots + (1.22)^2 = 7.3440$$

$$E(K) = \frac{10}{21}\left[(-1.34)^2 + (-0.83)^2 + \ldots + (1.22)^2\right] = 7.5449$$

$$\text{Var}(K) = \frac{10(11)}{21(20)}\left[(-1.34)^4 + (-0.83)^4 + \ldots + (1.22)^4\right] - \frac{11(7.5449)^2}{10(20)}$$

$$= 4.0540$$

$$Z = \frac{7.3440 - 7.5449}{\sqrt{4.0540}} = \frac{-.2009}{2.0135} = -0.10$$

With $\alpha \le 0.05$, there is no reason to doubt the hypothesis, since $Z = 0.08$ is within $-1.96 < Z < 1.96$.

When $6 \le n_1 \le 10$ and $6 \le n_2 \le 10$, one can perform the exact test at $\alpha \le 0.05$ or $\alpha \le 0.01$ by referring K to the critical values reported in Table A–18.

TABLE 11–17. Inverse normal-order statistics for the Klotz test of equal variance for the data of Table 11–15.

Group 1	Aligned scores	$\Phi^{-1}\left[\dfrac{r_i}{N+1}\right]$
7	−5.2	−1.34
9	−3.2	−0.83
9	−3.2	−0.83
10	−2.2	−0.54
11	−1.2	−0.23
11	−1.2	−0.23
12	−0.2	0.00
14	1.8	0.35
15	2.8	0.68
17	4.8	1.22
19	6.8	1.69
Group 2		
3	−7.2	−1.69
6	−4.2	−1.10
8	−2.2	−0.54
9	−1.2	−0.23
11	0.8	0.17
11	0.8	0.17
13	2.8	0.68
13	2.8	0.68
13	2.8	0.68
15	4.8	1.22

11–13. Test of Equal Slopes for Two Regression Lines

The two-sample Wilcoxon test can be used to test that two regression lines have equal slopes. This test is based on the fact that the slope of a straight line is determined by two points that lie on the line. If (x_1, y_1) and (x_2, y_2) are two points on the line $Y = \alpha + \beta x$, then the slope, β, is given by:

$$\beta = \frac{y_2 - y_1}{x_2 - x_1}.$$

How the Wilcoxon test can be used to test $H_0 : \beta_1 = \beta_2$ against $H_1 : \beta_1 \neq \beta_2$ is illustrated for the data in Example 11–13.1. As will be seen, the method is based upon estimating the slopes of the regression lines for each group from points that are far apart in Euclidean distance. Slope estimates made under these conditions have high efficiencies.

EXAMPLE 11–13.1. Consider the regression of X_4 on X_1 for the $n_1 = 18$ males and $n_2 = 18$ females of Exercise 10 of Chapter 10. Let the data be rank-ordered on the basis of X_1, as shown in Table 11–18 for each group. From these data one

TABLE 11–18. Data of Exercise 10 of Chapter 10, rank-ordered on the basis of X_1 and used to test $H_0: \beta_M = \beta_F$ against $H_1: \beta_M \neq \beta_F$.

Males		Females	
X_1	X_4	X_1	X_4
75	15	76	2
82	20	85	10
83	16	85	17
84	10	92	16
85	19	96	11
90	18	97	10
99	15	99	16
106	23	101	16
107	19	101	12
109	22	112	25
112	22	112	25
112	23	113	20
114	23	115	22
115	18	116	21
117	23	118	22
128	22	120	17
130	22	122	19
131	25	132	25

obtains, for each group, $n_k/2$ estimates of β by pairing pair 1 with pair $(n_k/2)$, pair 2 with pair $((n_k/2) + 1)$, etc. If n_k is odd, the middle set of values is eliminated before pairing begins. For each pair, one computes β and then applies the two-sample Wilcoxon test on the β values. The slopes are listed in Table 11–19. If the sum of the ranks for the males is taken to represent the test statistic, the two-sided $\alpha \leq 0.05$ decision rule read from Table A–14 is:

$$\text{D.R.: Reject } H_0 \text{ if } T_M \leq 63 \qquad \text{or} \qquad \text{if } T_M \geq 108$$

Since $T_M = 66$, H_0 is not rejected. If desired, the confidence-interval procedure of Section 11–3 can be used to set up a $(1 - \alpha)$-percent confidence interval for the median difference in the beta weights. Point estimators for each regression line are examined in Section 13–11.

Frequently, the X_1 variable is a surrogate for another variable that represents time. Examples are trial number, problem order, day of week, time of day, and so on. Under these conditions, the test of $H_0: \beta_1 = \beta_2$, as presented, is suspect. Measurements between adjacent observations in time are not independent; they are correlated, so that the main assumption of the two-sample Wilcoxon test, namely, independence of observations within each sample, is violated.

One way to remove or reduce the correlation is to consider each sample separately, and use a table of random numbers to achieve a pairing of the first half of the *time series* to the second half of the set of observations. This is achieved by listing, for one sample, the first half of the series in the observed temporal order. The second half is paired to the first half by using a table of random numbers as

β_M for males	Rank	β_F for females	Rank
$\dfrac{22 - 15}{109 - 75} = 0.2059$	8	$\dfrac{25 - 2}{112 - 76} = 0.6111$	18
$\dfrac{22 - 20}{112 - 82} = 0.0667$	4	$\dfrac{25 - 10}{112 - 85} = 0.5556$	16
$\dfrac{23 - 16}{112 - 83} = 0.2414$	9.5	$\dfrac{20 - 17}{113 - 85} = 0.1071$	5
$\dfrac{23 - 10}{114 - 84} = 0.4333$	14	$\dfrac{22 - 16}{115 - 92} = 0.2609$	12
$\dfrac{18 - 19}{115 - 85} = -0.0333$	2	$\dfrac{21 - 11}{116 - 96} = 0.5000$	15
$\dfrac{23 - 18}{117 - 90} = 0.1852$	7	$\dfrac{22 - 10}{118 - 97} = 0.5714$	17
$\dfrac{22 - 15}{128 - 99} = 0.2414$	9.5	$\dfrac{17 - 16}{120 - 99} = 0.0476$	3
$\dfrac{22 - 23}{130 - 106} = -0.0417$	1	$\dfrac{19 - 16}{122 - 101} = 0.1429$	6
$\dfrac{25 - 19}{131 - 107} = 0.2500$	11	$\dfrac{25 - 12}{132 - 101} = 0.4194$	13
Sum of ranks	66		105

permutations. This randomization, or random pairing, is repeated for the remaining sample. With these two randomizations, the two-sample Wilcoxon test is performed, as described, in Example 11–3.1.

A second model has been proposed by Hollander (1970), to eliminate the correlation effects. According to the Hollander model the slope of each regression line is estimated according to the procedure described in Example 11–3.1, but then the estimates in one sample are paired to the estimates in the remaining sample by the use of a table of random numbers. After completion of the pairing, the matched-pair Wilcoxon test is applied to the pairs. This test is described in Section 13–3.

Summary

In this chapter, a number of highly efficient competitors to the classical two-sample Student t test were presented and illustrated. These tests, based on the assignment of ranks or normal scores for the original variables, are known to have efficiencies exceeding 0.864 for the rank tests and 1.00 for the normal-scores tests. For this reason, these nonparameteric tests are highly recommended, if it is known that the distributions of the underlying variables are not normal or have different spreads about their centers.

All of these assumption-freer tests are based on the Fisher randomization procedure, which must be called upon when the sample sizes are small, since good approximations exist only for large samples. For tests based on ranks, sample sizes

Two-Sample Methods for Quantitative Variables Based on Ranks and Normal Scores

are considered large in the two-sample case if each sample exceeds 10 observations. For the normal-scores test, the approximation appears satisfactory if, in the two-sample case, each sample exceeds 8 observations.

For the Fisher randomization two-sample t test, one considers the finite set of observed values, n_1 and n_2, as a finite population of $N = n_1 + n_2$ values. Under the hypothesis of identical distributions, the $T = \begin{bmatrix} N \\ n_1 \end{bmatrix} = \begin{bmatrix} N \\ n_2 \end{bmatrix}$ assignments of observed values are equally likely. Thus, under H_0, the α_T extreme assignments constitute the critical region or rejection outcomes of the test. If N is small, one can actually generate the α_T extreme values with ease, provided that $T_1 = \sum_{i=1}^{n} x_i$, the total of the smaller sample, is used as the test statistic. If N is large, the ordinary two-sample t test can be used as a good approximation to the Fisher randomization test of identical distributions for the two populations.

Even though the Fisher randomization test has an efficiency of 1.00 compared to the t test when it can be justified, the more easily computed Wilcoxon–Mann–Whitney form of the Fisher randomization test is often preferred. This test is performed in exactly the same manner as the Fisher test except that the original observations are replaced by their rank values. If N is small, one can generate the extreme α_T outcomes of $T_1 = \sum_{i=1}^{n_1} r_i$, the sum of the ranks assigned to the smaller sample, or if $N = n_1 + n_2 \le 20$, one can use Table A–14 to determine the rejection region for the test of identical distributions. For large N, one can use the following normal approximation:

$$Z = \frac{T_1 - E(T_1)}{\sqrt{\mathrm{Var}(T_1)}} = \frac{T_1 - \dfrac{n_1(n_1 + n_2 + 1)}{2}}{\sqrt{(n_1 n_2 / 12)(n_1 + n_2 + 1)}}$$

with a $\pm \frac{1}{2}$-unit correction for continuity if desired. If $T_1 > E(T_1)$, $\frac{1}{2}$ is subtracted from T_1, while if $T_1 < E(T_1)$, $\frac{1}{2}$ is added to T_1.

The Mann–Whitney form of the Wilcoxon test is based on counting inversions as the number of times an observation in one sample exceeds a value in the other sample. The Mann–Whitney form of the Wilcoxon test has the advantage in that it leads to a confidence interval for the median difference in the two populations. If the distributions should be symmetric, or if $n_1 = n_2$, then the confidence interval for the median difference reduces to a confidence interval for the mean difference between the populations. This is of considerable practical value, since assumptions of normality are not required.

If the Wilcoxon hypothesis of identical distributions is considered in the Mann–Whitney form:

$$H_0: P(X < Y) = P(X > Y) = \tfrac{1}{2}$$

it is seen that the Mann–Whitney U statistic has a simple interpretation in that:

$$\hat{p} = \frac{U}{n_1 n_2}$$

is an unbiased estimate of the probability that an observation in one population exceeds an observation in the second population.

Even though the efficiency of the rank test relative to the t test is equal to

0.955, one can obtain a test with even greater efficiency by substituting, in place of ranks, numbers based on the normal distribution.

The Terry–Hoeffding test replaces the original data with the expected values of the corresponding normal-order statistic; the Van der Waerden test utilizes the inverse-normal scores; and the Bell–Doksum test substitutes random normal deviates. In all cases, the asymptotic efficiency relative to the t test is 1, when the assumptions under the t test are satisfied. The operation of these tests parallels that of the Fisher randomization test and the Wilcoxon test. For large n_1 and n_2, a good approximation is available through:

$$Z = \frac{T_1 - E(T_1)}{\sqrt{\text{Var}(T_1)}}$$

where

1. For the Terry-Hoeffding test:

$$E(T_1) = 0, \qquad \text{Var}(T_1) = \frac{n_1 n_2}{N - 1} \sum_{i=1}^{N} \frac{E(V^{(i)})^2}{N}$$

2. For the Van der Waerden test:

$$E(T_1) = 0, \qquad \text{Var}(T_1) = \frac{n_1 n_2}{N - 1} \sum_{i=1}^{N} \frac{(Z^{(i)})^2}{N}$$

3. For the Bell–Doksum test, the corresponding test statistic is given by:

$$Z = \frac{\overline{T}_1 - \overline{T}_2}{\sqrt{(1/n_1) + (1/n_2)}}$$

For scores drawn from distributions with large tails, such as the exponential or the normal, the normal-scores test is best. For scores drawn from distributions having small tails, such as the uniform, logistic, double-exponential, or Cauchy, the Wilcoxon test proves to be superior.

Finally, the Siegel–Tukey test, the Mood test, and the Klotz test for equal population variances were presented and illustrated. The Siegel–Tukey test reduces to the Wilcoxon test, so that Table A–14 can be used if $n_1 + n_2 \leq 20$, while the large-sample Wilcoxon test can be used if $n_1 + n_2 \geq 20$. The Mood test requires computations involving fourth powers and can be performed only for large samples. The Klotz test, which is based upon the use of normal scores in place of the ranks, has an advantage over the Mood test in that use of Table A–18 is possible for small samples. It is also preferred since, on the home ground of the two-sample F test, its asymptotic relative efficiency is 1, while the corresponding figures for the Siegel–Tukey test and Mood test are 0.61 and 0.76, respectively. However, all three of these tests are dependent upon equal centers. If the data suggest to a researcher that the population centers are unequal, then some form of alignment should be imposed before assigning the ranks or normal scores.

Exercises

*1. Apply the two-sample Wilcoxon test to the paragraph-meaning scores for the old and new conditions of Exercise 10 of Chapter 10.

*2. Repeat Exercise 1 with:
a) the two-sample t test,
b) the Van der Waerden normal-scores test,
c) the median test.
Of the four tests, which would you recommend? Why?

*3. For the data of Exercise 1, find the confidence interval for the median difference.

*4. a) Apply the Siegel–Tukey test to the data of Exercise 1.
b) Apply the Mood test to the data of Exercise 1.
c) Apply the Klotz test to the data of Exercise 1.
d) Compare (a), (b), and (c) with the classical F test for equal variances. Which test do you prefer? Why?

*5. For the data of Exercise 10 in Chapter 10, is there reason to believe that $\beta_{old} = \beta_{new}$ for the paragraph-meaning scores regressed on mental age? Set up a 95% confidence interval for the median difference in beta weights. Since $n_1 = n_2 = 9$, can the resulting interval be treated as one for $\beta_{old} - \beta_{new}$?

*6. Show that:
a) $1 + 2 + 3 + \cdots + N = \dfrac{N(N+1)}{2}$

b) $1^2 + 2^2 + 3^2 + \cdots + N^2 = \dfrac{N(N+1)(2N+1)}{6}$

*7. Use the Mann–Whitney model based on inversions to analyze the data of Table 11–15. Under the Wilcoxon model, $Z = 0.91$. Compare the two methods.

*8. Analyze the data of Table 10–6 in terms of:
a) the Wilcoxon–Mann–Whitney model.
b) the Terry–Hoeffding model.
c) the Van der Waerden model.
Compare the results to those obtained under the Kolmogorov–Smirnov model.

*9. Analyze the data of Table 5–12 under:
a) the Wilcoxon or Mann–Whitney model.
b) the Van der Waerden normal-scores model.
Compare the results to the median test model of Section 5–11. Which procedure do you prefer? Why?

*10. Use the methods of this chapter to analyze the data of Exercise 10 of Chapter 5. Which methods do you prefer? Why?

*11. How many unique permutations are there of the 11 scores reported in Example 11–1.3?

*12. Analyze the data of Table 11–15 with your own selection of random normal deviates. How does your result compare with those presented in Section 11–9?

*13. Align the observations of Table 11–15 by removing the treatment effects by subtracting the median score from each group. Then perform the Siegel–Tukey test and compare the results to those presented in Section 11–10.

*14. Repeat Exercise 13 for the Mood test of equal variances.

Multiple-Sample Methods for Quantitative Variables Based on Ranks and Normal Scores: The Nonparametric One-Way Analysis of Variance

12–1. The Kruskal–Wallis Test

The classical K-sample test for testing that K populations have equal centers is the F test. Under normal-curve theory, the test statistic is defined as:

$$F = \frac{\text{MSB}}{\text{MSW}} = \frac{\dfrac{1}{K-1} \sum_{k=1}^{K} n_k (\overline{X}_k - \overline{X})^2}{\dfrac{1}{N-K} \sum_{k=1}^{K} \sum_{i=1}^{n_k} (X_{ik} - \overline{X}_k)^2}$$

which is known to be distributed as F with $v_1 = K - 1$ and $v_2 = N - K$ degrees of freedom, if:

1. Observations within each sample are independent;
2. Observations between each sample are independent;
3. Observations are from normally distributed populations; and
4. Variances across the populations are equal and unknown.

If the population variances were known, then:

$$X^2 = \sum_{k=1}^{K} \frac{(\overline{X}_k - \overline{X})^2}{\text{Var}(\overline{X}_k)} = \frac{1}{\sigma^2} \sum_{k=1}^{K} n_k (\overline{X}_k - \overline{X})^2$$

could be used as a test statistic for testing H_0, since it is known that X^2 has a sampling distribution that is chi-square with $v = K - 1$ degrees of freedom. Both the F and X^2 statistics rely on the normality of the parent populations or the approximate normality of the sampling distributions of the $\overline{X}_k$ for the assertion that their respective null distributions are F and X^2.

Kruskal and Wallis constructed a test statistic for the one-way analysis of variance that also has a sampling distribution that tends to be X^2 with $v = K - 1$ degrees of freedom (Kruskal and Wallis, 1952). Their test is based on a substitution of ranks for the original observations. To derive the test, let r_{ik} denote the rank of X_{ik} in the entire set of $N = n_1 + n_2 + \ldots + n_K$ observations. Let:

$$\overline{R}_k = \frac{1}{n_k} \sum_{i=1}^{n_k} r_{ik} = \frac{R_k}{n_k}$$

be the mean rank for the kth sample, and let $E(\overline{R}_k) = \overline{R}$ be the expected mean rank across all N observations under H_0. The test statistic, U, defined in Section 2–10 as:

$$U = Z_1^2 + Z_2^2 + \ldots + Z_K^2 = \sum_{k=1}^{K} \frac{(\overline{R}_k - \overline{R})^2}{\text{Var}(\overline{R}_k)}$$

suggests itself as a reasonable rank analog to chi-square. However, Kruskal and Wallis found that the quality of the approximation to the chi-square distribution with $v = K - 1$ degrees of freedom is improved if:

$$H = \frac{N - n_1}{N} Z_1^2 + \frac{N - n_2}{N} Z_2^2 + \ldots + \frac{N - n_K}{N} Z_K^2$$

$$= \sum_{k=1}^{K} \left[\frac{N - n_k}{N} \right] \frac{(\overline{R}_k - \overline{R})^2}{\text{Var}(\overline{R}_k)}$$

were used in place of U. As shown in Section 11–4,

$$E(r_{ik}) = \frac{N + 1}{2} \quad \text{and} \quad \text{Var}(r_{ik}) = \frac{N^2 - 1}{12}$$

Under H_0:

$$E(\overline{R}_k) = E\left[\frac{1}{n_k} \sum_{i=1}^{n_k} r_{ik} \right] = \frac{1}{n_k} n_k E(r_{ik}) = E(r_{ik}) = \frac{N + 1}{2}$$

Since $\overline{R}_k$ is determined on a finite population of size N, it follows from the model of Section 2–12 that:

$$\text{Var}(\overline{R}_k) = \frac{\text{Var}(r_{ik})}{n_k} \left[\frac{N - n_k}{N - 1} \right] = \frac{1}{n_k} \left[\frac{N^2 - 1}{12} \right] \left[\frac{N - n_k}{N - 1} \right] = \frac{(N + 1)(N - n_k)}{12 n_k}$$

With these substitutions, H reduces to:

$$H = \frac{12}{N(N + 1)} \sum_{k=1}^{K} n_k \left[\overline{R}_k - \frac{N + 1}{2} \right]^2$$

or, as seen in its more traditional computational form:

$$H = \frac{12}{N(N + 1)} \sum_{k=1}^{K} \frac{R_k^2}{n_k} - 3(N + 1)$$

EXAMPLE 12–1.1. As an example of the use of this test consider a study in which sixteen slow readers in the eighth grade of an urban junior high school were given special training in a remedial reading program that also included cultural enrichment trips to a ballet, a professional play, an opera, a college football game, a professional basketball game, a jazz concert, a visit to a planetarium, an art museum, a science museum, and other cultural or entertaining activities. In addition to improvements in reading skills, it was hypothesized that school attendance would increase with an increase in the number of activities attended by the students. To test the effectiveness of the enrichment program, not all students were permitted to attend all enrichment activities. For the experimental design, the sixteen students were assigned at random to one of the following four experimental conditions:

Condition 1.	No enrichment trips.	
Condition 2.	Five enrichment trips.	
Condition 3.	Ten enrichment trips.	
Condition 4.	Fifteen enrichment trips.	

The attendance of the students for the 20 weeks of the program is shown in Table 12–1.

For the data, the rank sums are 49, 47, 23, and 17, respectively, and the sum of all $N = 16$ ranks is $49 + 47 + 23 + 17 = 136$. A check on the accuracy of ranking can be made by showing that:

$$\sum_{k=1}^{K} \sum_{i=1}^{n_k} r_{ik} = \frac{N(N + 1)}{2} = \frac{16(17)}{2} = 136$$

With equal $n_k = 4$, the value of the test statistic for these ranks is given by:

$$H = \frac{12}{N(N + 1)} \sum_{k=1}^{K} \frac{R_k^2}{n} - 3(N + 1)$$

$$= \frac{12}{16(17)} \left[\frac{49^2 + 47^2 + 23^2 + 17^2}{4} \right] - 3(17)$$

$$= 8.87$$

Since $H = 8.87$ exceeds $X_{3;0.95}^2 = 7.82$, the hypothesis of identity of the four populations can be rejected.

The next example illustrates the model for the presence of tied observations in the data. Since the null distribution of the test statistic is based on equal probability of assignment of the ranks 1, 2, ..., N, the presence of tied observations affects the null distribution of H. If a random process is employed to assign ranks to the tied observations, the requirement $P(X_{ik} = r_{ik}) = 1/N$ is satisfied and the distribution theory for the test is unaffected. On the other hand, if midranks are assigned to the tied values, the null distribution for the test is altered. Most users of rank tests prefer the midrank procedure to the random breaking of ties, because the former procedure tends to reduce the value of H, thereby producing a conservative test, while the latter procedure raises the specter of two different analyses of the same data leading to different results. If there are many tied ranks, use of

Multiple-Sample Methods for Quantitative Variables Based on Ranks and Normal Scores: The Nonparametric One-Way Analysis of Variance

301

TABLE 12–1. Number of days absent during the enrichment reading program described in Example 12–1.1. (Also shown are the ranked data.)

	Days absent				Ranked data		
	Condition of the experiment				Condition of the experiment		
One	Two	Three	Four	One	Two	Three	Four
17	14	6	11	12	11	4	9
9	10	8	2	7	8	6	1
35	21	5	4	16	15	3	2
20	18	13	7	14	13	10	5
Total sum of ranks				49	47	23	17

the midranks procedure may produce an extremely conservative test. A correction for ties that depends only on the number and not on the identity of the tied observations can be applied in these circumstances. Let t_s denote the number of observations tied at rank S; then H can be corrected for ties by dividing H by:

$$C = 1 - \frac{1}{N^3 - N} \sum_{s=1}^{d} (t_s^3 - t_s)$$

The test statistic corrected for ties is:

$$H^* = \frac{H}{C}$$

which is also referred to the chi-square distribution with $K - 1$ degrees of freedom. Unless the number of observations tied for any one rank, t_s, is relatively large, the effect of the correction is minimal.

EXAMPLE 12–1.2.   Consider a study in which a random sample of 36 senior high school students (12 sophomores, 12 juniors, and 12 seniors) were given a test designed to measure their attitudes toward working part-time after school in a vocational setting compatible with their own interests. High scores represent positive attitudes. The hypothesis tested by the Kruskal–Wallis test is that the three distributions of scores are identical, while the alternative is that the three distributions have the same forms but their centers are shifted from one another. The data for this study and the ranks are presented in Table 12–2.

Midranks have been used to break the ties for the data of Table 12–2. When the correction for ties is not applied, the value of the test statistic is:

$$H = \frac{12}{N(N + 1)} \sum_{k=1}^{K} \frac{R_k^2}{n} - 3(N + 1)$$

$$= \frac{12}{36(37)} \left[\frac{139^2 + 200^2 + 327^2}{12} \right] - 3(37)$$

$$= 13.81$$

TABLE 12–2. Attitudes toward working part-time in areas similar to vocational interest on the part of senior high school students.

Sophomores		Juniors		Seniors	
Score	Rank	Score	Rank	Score	Rank
6	1	31	34.5	13	10
11	7	7	2	32	36
12	9	9	4	31	34.5
20	19	11	7	30	33
24	23	16	14	28	31
21	20	19	17.5	29	32
18	16	17	15	25	24
15	13	11	7	26	26.5
14	11.5	22	21	26	26.5
10	5	23	22	27	29.5
8	3	27	29.5	26	26.5
14	11.5	26	26.5	19	17.5
$R_1 = 139.0$		$R_2 = 200.0$		$R_3 = 327.0$	

The frequency distribution of tied ranks for the data of Table 12–2 is reported in Table 12–3. The correction for ties is given by:

$$C = 1 - \frac{1}{N^3 - N} \sum_{s=1}^{d} (t_s^3 - t_s)$$

$$= 1 - \frac{1}{36^3 - 36}[(3^3 - 3) + (2^3 - 2) + \ldots + (2^3 - 2)]$$

$$= 1 - \frac{180}{46620}$$

$$= 0.9961$$

and

$$H^* = \frac{H}{C} = \frac{13.81}{0.9961} = 13.86$$

In either case, the null hypothesis is rejected because the computed value of the test statistic exceeds $X^2_{2:0.95} = 5.99$.

TABLE 12–3. Frequency distribution of tied rank values for the data of Table 12–2.

s	Tied rank	Frequency of ties t_s
1	7	3
2	11.5	2
3	17.5	2
4	26.5	4
5	29.5	2
6	34.5	2

Multiple-Sample Methods for Quantitative Variables Based on Ranks and Normal Scores: The Nonparametric One-Way Analysis of Variance

303

The two-sample and K-sample rank tests such as the Wilcoxon and Kruskal–Wallis statistics are designed to test the hypothesis of equality of the underlying distributions. Only when these distributions are identical is it true that all assignments of ranks are equally likely. In the K-sample case, the number of permutations of the N ranks is given by $T = N!$ so that one can determine an exact test of size alpha by finding the αT permutations that produce the largest values of H. Generally, this is not done, because of the great amount of arithmetic involved and because many permutations give rise to the same value of the test statistic. In the general case, the number of ways for ranking the data is given by Rule 7 of Section 2–2 as:

$$T_H = \frac{n!}{n_1! \, n_2! \cdots n_K!} = \left[\begin{array}{c} n \\ n_1 \, n_2 \ldots n_K \end{array} \right]$$

Exact probability tables are available for $K = 3$ and $n_k \leq 5$. These tables are reported in Table A-19. Note that even for $K = 3$ and $n_k = 5$, the total number of permutations is given by:

$$T_H = \frac{15!}{5!5!5!} = 756{,}756$$

If the underlying distributions differ in form or in scale, but not in location, the computed value of H will tend to be small, so that the probability of rejection of the hypothesis of equality of the K distributions will remain close to alpha. Consequently, the Kruskal–Wallis test is rather insensitive to differences in the skewness, kurtosis, or scale of the K distributions. On the other hand, if one or more of the K distributions differ in location, the value of H will tend to be large and the probability of rejecting the hypothesis of equality of the K distributions will be considerably larger than alpha. For these reasons, the Kruskal–Wallis test and its two-sample analog, the Wilcoxon test, are identified primarily as tests of location. In theory, these tests require that the underlying distributions be identical in form.

Since they have low, but nonzero, power in detecting nonlocation alternatives, the assumption of identity of distribution can be relaxed. Their insensitivity to nonlocation alternatives and their high asymptotic efficiency relative to the parametric F test and t test make them excellent nonparametric tests of location. The asymptotic efficiency of each of these rank tests relative to its parametric alternative is 0.955 when the assumptions of normality and common variance for the parametric test are satisfied. If the underlying distributions are nonnormal, the efficiency of the rank test relative to that of the parametric tests is always at least 0.86 and equals or exceeds 1 for some commonly encountered nonnormal distributions, such as the uniform distribution and the exponential distribution.

In Figure 12–1, a number of different situations are exhibited to show the effect differences in form, center, and spread have upon the value of H. The H statistic is designed to test the hypothesis of identical distributions versus shifts in center. This is case I of Figure 12–1. In all the other cases, H_0 is false and yet it is seen, in cases II, III, and IV, that nonrejection of H_0 is expected. Case V is the stated alternative to case I and if it occurs, rejection of H_0 is expected. However, in cases VI, VII, and VIII, rejection of H_0 is also expected, even though the alternative is not of the kind specified by the alternative hypothesis. This means that the Kruskal–Wallis

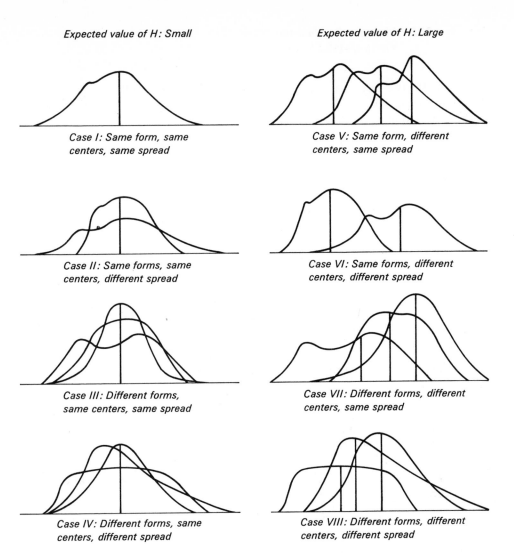

Case I: Same form, same centers, same spread

Case V: Same form, different centers, same spread

Case II: Same forms, same centers, different spread

Case VI: Same forms, different centers, different spread

Case III: Different forms, same centers, same spread

Case VII: Different forms, different centers, same spread

Case IV: Different forms, same centers, different spread

Case VIII: Different forms, different centers, different spread

FIGURE 12–1. Effect of form, center, and spread upon H.

test is not too sensitive to differences in spread and form, but is most sensitive to differences in centers. For this reason, rejection of H_0 via the H statistic is almost certain to be equivalent to differences in mean, median, center, or some other measure of shift.

This statement is supported by Srisukho (1974), who examined the power of the H test when the distributions differed in form as well as location. Under all six models considered, power increased as the location differences among groups increased. Power was not restricted by variation in the shapes of the distributions. The power for three distributions differing in form as well as location corresponded quite favorably to the case when the distributions were all uniform.

Multiple-Sample Methods for Quantitative Variables Based on Ranks and Normal Scores: The Nonparametric One-Way Analysis of Variance

12–2. Multiple Confidence-Interval Procedures for the Kruskal–Wallis Test

In the two examples of Section 12–1, the hypothesis of identical probability distributions was rejected. Since the rejected hypothesis is also a statement of equality of the expected mean ranks:

$$H_0: E(\overline{R}_1) = E(\overline{R}_2) = \ldots = E(\overline{R}_K) = \frac{N+1}{2}$$

it follows that at least one contrast in the expected mean ranks will be significantly different from zero. Thus, the differences among the K populations can be identified by considering all confidence intervals of interest of the form:

$$\hat{\psi} - \sqrt{\chi^2_{K-1:1-\alpha}}\sqrt{\mathrm{Var}(\hat{\psi})} < \psi < \hat{\psi} + \sqrt{\chi^2_{K-1:1-\alpha}}\sqrt{\mathrm{Var}(\hat{\psi})}$$

where

$$\hat{\psi} = a_1\overline{R}_1 + a_2\overline{R}_2 + \ldots + a_K\overline{R}_K$$
$$= \sum_{k=1}^{K} a_k\overline{R}_k$$

and

$$a_1 + a_2 + \ldots + a_K = \sum_{k=1}^{K} a_k = 0$$

The variance of $\hat{\psi}$ is given by:

$$\mathrm{Var}(\hat{\psi}) = \frac{N(N+1)}{12} \sum_{k=1}^{K} \frac{a_k^2}{n_k}$$

The derivation of this variance for the special case of equal sample sizes has been given by Marascuilo and McSweeney (1967).

EXAMPLE 12–2.1. For the data of Table 12–2, the mean ranks of the K samples are:

$$\overline{R}_1 = \frac{139}{12} = 11.38, \qquad \overline{R}_2 = \frac{200}{12} = 16.67, \qquad \text{and} \qquad \overline{R}_3 = \frac{327}{12} = 27.25$$

Simple pairwise contrasts in the mean ranks are given by:

$$\hat{\psi} = (+1)\overline{R}_k + (-1)\overline{R}_{k'} = \overline{R}_k - \overline{R}_{k'}$$

and the corresponding variances by:

$$\mathrm{Var}(\hat{\psi}) = \frac{N(N+1)}{12}\left(\frac{2}{n}\right) = \frac{36(37)(2)}{12(12)} = 18.50$$

With

$$\underline{S}^* = \sqrt{\chi^2_{K-1:1-\alpha}} = \sqrt{\chi^2_{2:0.95}} = \sqrt{5.99} = 2.45$$

the simultaneous post hoc confidence intervals for the pairwise comparisons are given by:

$$\overline{R}_k - \overline{R}_{k'} - 2.45\sqrt{18.50} < E(\overline{R}_k) - E(\overline{R}_{k'}) < \overline{R}_k - \overline{R}_{k'} + 2.45\sqrt{18.50}$$

TABLE 12–4. *Confidence intervals for $E(\overline{R}_k) - E(\overline{R}_{k'})$ for the data of Table 12–2*

Contrast	Estimate	Lower limit	Upper limit
$\overline{R}_1 - \overline{R}_2$	−5.09	−15.62	5.44
$\overline{R}_1 - \overline{R}_3$	−15.67*	−26.20	−5.15
$\overline{R}_2 - \overline{R}_3$	−10.58*	−21.11	−.05

*Significant at $\alpha = 0.05$.

The upper and lower limits for these intervals are reported in Table 12–4, along with the corresponding estimates of the contrasts.

If a researcher wishes to examine only pairwise contrasts, use can be made of Tukey's method for pairwise comparisons, provided that the sample sizes are equal. If this model is adopted, then the critical value $\underline{S}^* = \sqrt{X^2_{k-1:1-\alpha}}$ is replaced by:

$$T = \frac{q^{(\alpha)}_{K:v_2}}{\sqrt{2}}$$

where q is read from Table A-20. For Example 12–2.1, $\underline{S}^* = 2.45$ is replaced by:

$$T = \frac{q^{(.05)}_{3:\infty}}{\sqrt{2}} = \frac{3.31}{\sqrt{2}} = 2.34$$

EXAMPLE 12–2.2. As seen in Example 12–2.1, there are differences in attitudes between sophomores and seniors and between juniors and seniors. Since no differences were found between sophomores and juniors, one might wonder whether:

$$\hat{\psi} = \overline{R}_1 + \overline{R}_2 - 2\overline{R}_3$$

represents a difference between the lower classes and the seniors. For this contrast:

$$\hat{\psi} = \overline{R}_1 + \overline{R}_2 - 2\overline{R}_3 = 11.58 + 16.67 - 2(27.25) = -26.25$$

and

$$\text{Var}(\hat{\psi}) = \frac{N(N+1)}{12} \sum_{k=1}^{K} \frac{a_k^2}{n}$$

$$= \frac{36(37)}{12} \left[\frac{1^2 + 1^2 + (-2)^2}{12} \right] = 55.50$$

The corresponding confidence interval is given by:

$$-26.25 - \sqrt{5.99}\sqrt{55.50} < E(\overline{R}_1) + E(\overline{R}_2) - 2E(\overline{R}_3) < -26.25 + \sqrt{5.99}\sqrt{55.50}$$

or

$$-44.55 < E(\overline{R}_1) + E(\overline{R}_2) - 2E(\overline{R}_3) < -7.95$$

Since the contrast $\psi = E(\overline{R}_1) + E(\overline{R}_2) - 2E(\overline{R}_3)$ is significantly different from zero, it appears that, as a group, the sophomores and juniors differ in attitude from the seniors.

Multiple-Sample Methods for Quantitative Variables Based on Ranks and Normal Scores: The Nonparametric One-Way Analysis of Variance

307

12–3. *Partitioning of Chi-square for the Kruskal–Wallis Test*

As shown in Chapters 6 and 8, chi-square for contingency tables can be partitioned into specific X^2 components under certain conditions. Similar partitioning is permissible for the H test by means of *orthogonal* contrasts. Two contrasts:

$$\psi_1 = \sum_{k=1}^{K} a_k \theta_k \quad \text{and} \quad \psi_2 = \sum_{k=1}^{K} b_k \theta_k$$

are said to be orthogonal if:

$$\sum_{k=1}^{K} a_k b_k = a_1 b_1 + a_2 b_2 + \ldots + a_K b_K = 0$$

Consider the following example, which employs orthogonal contrasts.

EXAMPLE 12–3.1. While the data of the previous two examples have been examined from a post hoc point of view, it should be observed that planned comparisons could be investigated either as orthogonal or nonorthogonal contrasts. Since $v = K - 1 = 3 - 1 = 2$, one could examine two orthogonal contrasts. One set of possibilities is:

$$\psi_1 = E(\overline{R}_1) - E(\overline{R}_2) \quad \text{and} \quad \psi_2 = E(\overline{R}_1) + (\overline{R}_2) - 2E(\overline{R}_3)$$

Contrast ψ_1 compares sophomores and juniors while contrast ψ_2 compares the combined group of sophomores and juniors to the seniors. For these contrasts:

$$\hat{\psi}_1 = -5.09 \qquad \hat{\psi}_2 = -26.25$$
$$\text{Var}(\hat{\psi}_1) = 18.50 \qquad \text{Var}(\hat{\psi}_2) = 55.50$$

$$Z_2^2 = \frac{\hat{\psi}_1^2}{\text{Var}(\hat{\psi}_1)} \qquad\qquad Z_2^2 = \frac{\hat{\psi}_2^2}{\text{Var}(\hat{\psi}_2)}$$

$$= \frac{(-5.09)^2}{18.50} \qquad\qquad = \frac{(-26.25)^2}{55.50}$$

$$= 1.40 \qquad\qquad = 12.41$$

Since these contrasts are orthogonal, it is seen that:

$$Z_1^2 + Z_2^2 = 1.40 + 12.41 = 13.81 = H$$

If each test statistic is compared to:

$$X^2_{1:1-\alpha/2} = X^2_{1:0.975} = 5.02$$

it is concluded that $\psi_1 = 0$ and that $\psi_2 \neq 0$ with $\alpha \leq 0.05$.

As this example shows, the Kruskal–Wallis statistic H can be decomposed into $(K - 1)$ orthogonal components, each having a chi-square distribution with $v = 1$ degrees of freedom. In general:

$$H = \frac{\hat{\psi}_1^2}{\text{Var}(\hat{\psi}_1)} + \frac{\hat{\psi}_2^2}{\text{Var}(\hat{\psi}_2)} + \ldots + \frac{\hat{\psi}_{K-1}^2}{\text{Var}(\hat{\psi}_{K-1})}$$

where $\hat{\psi}_1, \hat{\psi}_2, \ldots, \hat{\psi}_{K-1}$ are orthogonal to one another. If:

$$Z_k^2 = \frac{\hat{\psi}_k^2}{\text{Var}(\hat{\psi}_k)} > X^2_{1:1-\alpha_0/(K-1)}$$

one rejects the hypothesis that $\psi_k = 0$ with an overall probability of at least one Type I error controlled at $\alpha \leq \alpha_0$.

Since the values of $X^2_{1:1-\alpha/(K-1)}$ are not tabled, one can use the last column of Table A-1 with $K - 1$ set equal to Q and determine the critical value as:

$$X^2_{1:1-\alpha/(K-1)} = Z^2_{1-\alpha/[2(K-1)]}$$

Under this model, a researcher can carry out a planned analysis on any number of planned contrasts whether they are orthogonal or not.

As another example in which a planned analysis may be preferred, refer to Example 12–1.1, in which the treatment variable is on an equally-spaced ordered scale of 0, 5, 10, and 15 enrichment trips. For such treatments, a planned trend analysis is clearly called for. This is illustrated in the following example.

EXAMPLE 12–3.2. The contrast for a linear or monotonic relationship in the expected values for four treatments is given by Table A–9 as:

$$\hat{\psi}_{Linear} = -3\overline{R}_1 - 1\overline{R}_2 + 1\overline{R}_3 + 3\overline{R}_4$$

For the data of Table 12–1:

$$\hat{\psi}_{Linear} = -3\left(\frac{49}{4}\right) - 1\left(\frac{47}{4}\right) + 1\left(\frac{23}{4}\right) + 3\left(\frac{17}{4}\right) = -30$$

$$\mathrm{Var}(\hat{\psi}_{Linear}) = \frac{N(N + 1)}{12} \sum_{k=1}^{K} \frac{a_k^2}{n}$$

$$= \frac{16(17)}{12} \left[\frac{(-3)^2 + (-1)^2 + (1)^2 + (3)^2}{4} \right]$$

$$= 113.33$$

so that:

$$X_1^2 = \frac{\hat{\psi}_{Linear}^2}{\mathrm{Var}(\hat{\psi}_{Linear})} = \frac{(-30)^2}{113.33} = 7.94$$

Since $X_1^2 = 7.94 > X^2_{1:0.95} = 3.84$, the hypothesis of no linear trend in the mean ranks is rejected. These results can be summarized in an analysis-of-chi-square table, as shown in Table 12–5. The test for linear trend in the mean ranks corresponds to a test

Multiple-Sample Methods for Quantitative Variables Based on Ranks and Normal Scores: The Nonparametric One-Way Analysis of Variance

309

TABLE 12–5. Partitioning of the Kruskal–Wallis statistic in tests for monotonic trend.

Source	d/f	Value of X^2
Monotonic trend	1	7.94
Residual	2	.93*
Total	3	8.87

*By subtraction.

of monotonic relationship in the original metric. Thus, a monotonic relationship has been found between number of enrichment trips and number of days absent. Inspection of the data indicates that the relationship is monotonically decreasing.

12–4. Hodges–Lehmann Estimators for the Kruskal–Wallis Test

Hodges and Lehmann (1963) proposed point estimators for pairwise contrasts and complex contrasts for the K-sample Kruskal–Wallis test. Unfortunately, the estimators are incompatible, since a comparison between groups 1 and 3 cannot be generated from the comparisons between groups 1 and 2 and groups 2 and 3. For example, in the classical analysis of variance, it follows that $(\overline{X}_3 - \overline{X}_2) = (\overline{X}_3 - \overline{X}_1) - (\overline{X}_2 - \overline{X}_1)$; however, such relationships are not satisfied by the originally proposed Hodges–Lehmann estimators. In 1968, Spjøtvoll corrected the problem (Spjøtvoll, 1968). For expository purposes, the determination of the compatible pairwise contrasts is illustrated in Example 12–4.1 for the data of Table 12–1. While this example uses equal-sized samples, it is given in the general form which is valid for unequal-sized samples as well.

EXAMPLE 12–4.1. The Hodges–Lehmann estimation procedure begins with a determination of all pairwise median difference values as defined in Section 11–3. These estimates are summarized in Table 12–6. The largest median difference is that for the comparison of condition one with condition four. For this comparison, $\hat{M}_D^{14} = -13.0$. The smallest median difference is seen for the comparison of condition three with condition four. For this pairwise comparison, $\hat{M}_D^{34} = -2.0$. As can be seen, these estimates are indeed incompatible. For example, $\hat{M}_D^{32} = 8.0$ cannot be reproduced as $\hat{M}_D^{32} = \hat{M}_D^{31} - \hat{M}_D^{21} = 11.5 - 2.5 = 9.0$. To produce compatible estimates, compute the average median difference for each of the K population groups as:

$$\overline{\hat{\Delta}_k} = \frac{\sum_{k'=1}^{K} n_{k'} \hat{M}_D^{kk'}}{\sum_{k'=1}^{K} n_{k'}}$$

and estimate the compatible median differences as:

$$\hat{M}_D^{kk'} = \hat{\Delta}_k - \hat{\Delta}_{k'}$$

For the observed median differences of Table 12–6:

$$\hat{\Delta}_1 = \frac{4(0) + 4(-2.5) + 4(-11.5) + 4(-13.0)}{4 + 4 + 4 + 4} = -4.75$$

$$\hat{\Delta}_2 = \frac{4(2.5) + 4(0) + 4(-8.0) + 4(-10.0)}{4 + 4 + 4 + 4} = -3.88$$

$$\hat{\Delta}_3 = \frac{4(11.5) + 4(8.0) + 4(0) + 4(-2.0)}{4 + 4 + 4 + 4} = 4.38$$

k \ k'	1	2	3	4
1	—	−2.5	−11.5	−13.0
2	2.5	—	−8.0	−10.0
3	11.5	8.0	—	−2.0
4	13.0	10.0	2.0	—

and

$$\hat{\Delta}_4 = \frac{4(13.0) + 4(10.0) + 4(2.0) + 4(0)}{4 + 4 + 4 + 4} = 6.25$$

In terms of these estimators, the compatible estimators for the median differences are as shown in Table 12–7. For example,

$$\hat{M}_D^{32} = \hat{M}_D^{31} - \hat{M}_D^{21} = 9.13 - 0.87 = 8.26.$$

Unfortunately, those differences that are significantly different from zero are not indicated. If the post hoc procedure of Section 12–2 is applied to the six planned pairwise contrasts in the mean ranks, any difference in mean ranks is significant if:

$$\psi = \overline{R}_k - \overline{R}_{k'} \pm Z_{1-\alpha/2Q} \sqrt{\frac{N(N + 1)}{12}\left[\frac{1}{n_k} + \frac{1}{n_{k'}}\right]}$$

does not contain zero. For the observed data:

$$\psi = \overline{R}_k - \overline{R}_{k'} \pm 2.64 \sqrt{\frac{16(17)}{12}\left[\frac{1}{4} + \frac{1}{4}\right]}$$
$$= \overline{R}_k - \overline{R}_{k'} \pm 8.88$$

Results are shown in Table 12–8. None of the differences is significant. Whether

TABLE 12–7. Compatible median differences for the data of Table 12–1.

Comparison	Median difference		
1 vs. 2	−4.75 − (−3.88)	=	−0.87
1 vs. 3	−4.75 − (4.38)	=	−9.13
1 vs. 4	−4.75 − (6.25)	=	−11.00
2 vs. 3	−3.88 − (4.38)	=	8.26
2 vs. 4	−3.88 − (6.25)	=	−10.13
3 vs. 4	4.38 − (6.25)	=	−1.87

Multiple-Sample Methods for Quantitative Variables Based on Ranks and Normal Scores: The Nonparametric One-Way Analysis of Variance

311

TABLE 12–8. Planned pairwise analysis of mean ranks for the data of Table 12–1 based on the method of Section 12–2.

Comparison	Value of ψ	Decision
1 vs. 2	0.5	N.S.
1 vs. 3	6.5	N.S.
1 vs. 4	8.0	N.S.
2 vs. 3	6.0	N.S.
2 vs. 4	7.5	N.S.
3 vs. 4	1.5	N.S.

this decision based on mean ranks applies to the compatible median differences of Table 12–7 is not clear. That it may is suggested by the finding that the $1 - \alpha/2Q = 1 - 0.05/[2(6)] = 1 - 0.004 = 0.996$ confidence interval for M_{14} does include zero. In fact, under the model of Section 11–3, it can be shown that:

$$-30 \leq M_{14} \leq 4$$

12–5. Pairwise Contrast Based on Multiple Two-Sample Wilcoxon Tests

The major disadvantage of the procedures of Sections 12–2, 12–3, and 12–4 is that confidence intervals on the original scale of the observed variable are not attainable. If a researcher is willing to focus on pairwise comparisons only, a solution has been proposed by Steel (1960). This solution is to perform all $Q = \binom{K}{2}$ two-sample Wilcoxon tests with $\alpha \leq \alpha_T/Q$. This also means that all $Q = \binom{K}{2}$ confidence intervals for the median differences could be examined. Thus, for the data of Table 12–1, six Wilcoxon tests would be performed at $\alpha = 0.05/6 = 0.0083$. Since no decision rule can be obtained for the rank totals listed in Table A–14 for $(n_1, n_2) = (4, 4)$ and $\alpha = 0.0083$, consider the case for $\alpha = 0.014$ and $\alpha_T = Q\alpha = 6(0.014) = 0.084$. For this α, one would reject the hypothesis of zero pairwise differences if any $T_1 \leq 10$ or if any $T_1 \geq 26$. With these values, the lower and upper limits of the ordered difference for the pairwise confidence intervals would be given by:

$$U_{0.007} = n_1 n_2 + \frac{n_1(n_1 + 1)}{2} - T_U + 1 = 4(4) + \frac{4(5)}{2} - 26 + 1 = 1$$

and

$$U_{0.993} = n_1 n_2 + \frac{n_1(n_1 + 1)}{2} - T_L = 4(4) + \frac{4(5)}{2} - 10 = 16$$

With these limits, the procedure of Section 11–3 would be performed six times. If sample sizes had been unequal, then six different decision rules and six different sets of $(U_{0.007}, U_{0.993})$ would have to be determined.

12–6. The Normal-Scores Test for the K-Sample Problem

The Kruskal–Wallis test based on ranks is the most frequent nonparametric substitute for the F test in a one-way analysis of variance. Although the Kruskal–Wallis test has virtually preempted the field of nonparametric one-way analysis of variance, many other K-sample tests based on ranks have been proposed. The K-sample normal-scores test, which exists in three different forms, is one such test. Since the Bell–Doksum form can lead to inconsistencies across researchers analyzing the same data, only the Terry–Hoeffding and the Van der Waerden forms of this test are illustrated in this section.

The test statistics based on

$$E(V^{(ik)}) \qquad \text{and} \qquad \Phi^{-1}\left[\frac{r_{ik}}{N+1}\right]$$

are both asymptotically equivalent and structurally identical; thus, a single statement of the normal-scores test statistic can be made. Let W_{ik} represent the expected normal-order statistic $E(V^{(ik)})$ or the inverse normal-order statistic

$$\Phi^{-1}\left[\frac{r_{ik}}{N+1}\right] = Z^{(ik)}$$

Under both models, the K-sample statistic can be written as:

$$W = \frac{(N-1)\sum_{k=1}^{K}\frac{1}{n_k}\left[\sum_{i=1}^{n_k} W_{ik}\right]^2}{\sum_{k=1}^{K}\sum_{i=1}^{n_k} W_{ik}^2} = \frac{(N-1)\sum_{k=1}^{K} n_k \overline{W}_k^2}{\sum_{k=1}^{K}\sum_{i=1}^{n_k} W_{ik}^2}$$

In analysis-of-variance terminology:

$$W = (N-1)\frac{\text{SSB}}{\text{SST}}$$

It can be shown that W is asymptotically chi-square with $K-1$ degrees of freedom when the null hypothesis of equality of the K populations is true. The algebraic development of the test statistic and the associated post hoc multiple comparisons based on $\sqrt{X^2_{K-1:1-\alpha}}$ is given by McSweeney and Penfield (1969).

In classical ANOVA theory, the correlation ratio is defined as $\hat{\eta} = \text{SSB}/\text{SST}$ and is used as a measure of explained variance. An analogous measure for the normal-scores test is given by $W/(N-1)$.

EXAMPLE 12–6.1. Consider the performance of middle-class girls on a learning task under various reinforcement conditions. The example is taken from a larger study of learning as a function of the nature of the task, the type of reinforcement, and the educational-environment aspects of social class. Four levels of the independent variable, reinforcement condition, are considered:

1. Informative–verbal reinforcement
2. Material reinforcement

Multiple-Sample Methods for Quantitative Variables Based on Ranks and Normal Scores: The Nonparametric One-Way Analysis of Variance

313

3. A combination of informative and material reinforcement
4. Knowledge only (control)

The number of trials to the criterion of 12 correct responses in a row serves as the dependent variable. The failure of some subjects to attain the criterion of a sequence of 12 correct responses in the time allotted for testing produced a truncated distribution of scores.

The hypothesis to be tested is that the performance of middle-class girls on a learning task is unaffected by the nature of the reinforcement: material and/or informative–verbal reinforcement or knowledge of the results alone. The ranks and normal scores for these data are reported in Table 12–9. The Kruskal–Wallis test statistic is:

$$H = \frac{12}{32(33)} \left[\frac{73^2 + 179^2 + 125^2 + 151^2}{8} \right] - 3(33) = 8.66$$

The Terry–Hoeffding normal-scores test is:

$$W = \frac{(32 - 1)}{29.5960} \left[\frac{(-6.18)^2}{8} + \frac{(4.35)^2}{8} + \frac{(-0.59)^2}{8} + \frac{(2.42)^2}{8} \right] = 8.29$$

while for the Van der Waerden form:

$$W = \frac{(32 - 1)}{26.3618} \left[\frac{(-5.86)^2}{8} + \frac{(4.20)^2}{8} + \frac{(-0.56)^2}{8} + \frac{(2.21)^2}{8} \right] = 8.40$$

With $K - 1 = 3$ degrees of freedom, the hypothesis of stochastic equality of the K populations is rejected at the 0.05 level, since $X^2_{3:0.95} = 7.815$.

TABLE 12–9. *Performance on a learning task for four reinforcement conditions: informative–verbal (IV), material (M), combination of IV and M(C), and knowledge of results alone (K).*

Ranks of scores				Expected normal-order statistics				Inverse-normal statistics			
IV	M	C	K	IV	M	C	K	IV	M	C	K
1	6	8	2	−2.07	−0.94	−0.72	−1.65	−1.88	−0.91	−0.70	−1.55
3	13	12	5	−1.40	−0.28	−0.36	−1.07	−1.34	−0.27	−0.35	−1.03
4	24	14	11	−1.22	0.62	−0.20	−0.44	−1.17	0.60	−0.19	−0.43
7	25	15	19	−0.82	0.72	−0.12	0.20	−0.80	0.70	−0.11	0.19
9	26	16	22	−0.62	0.82	−0.04	0.44	−0.60	0.80	−0.04	0.43
10	27	17	29	−0.53	0.94	0.04	1.22	−0.52	0.91	0.04	1.17
18	28	20	31	0.12	1.07	0.28	1.65	0.11	1.03	0.27	1.55
21	30	23	32	0.36	1.40	0.53	2.07	0.35	1.34	0.52	1.88
$\sum W_{ik}$				−6.18	4.35	−0.59	2.42	−5.86	4.20	−0.56	2.21
$\overline{W}_k$				−0.77	0.54	−0.07	0.30	−0.73	0.53	−0.07	0.28
$\sum\sum W_{ik}^2$				29.5960				26.3618			
W				8.29				8.40			

12–7. Multiple Confidence-Interval Procedures for the Normal-Score K-Sample Test

Multiple comparison procedures based on the chi-square distribution can be used to obtain post hoc multiple comparisons for the normal-scores test. Let

$$\hat{\psi} = \sum_{k=1}^{K} a_k \overline{W}_k$$

be any contrast in the mean normal scores. It was shown by McSweeney and Penfield (1969) that:

$$\text{Var}(\hat{\psi}) = \left[\frac{\sum_{k=1}^{K} \sum_{i=1}^{n_k} W_{ik}^2}{N - 1}\right] \sum_{k=1}^{K} \frac{a_k^2}{n_k}$$

Under this model:

$$\psi = \hat{\psi} \pm \sqrt{X_{K-1:1-\alpha}^2} \sqrt{\text{Var}(\hat{\psi})}$$

defines the set of simultaneous $(1 - \alpha)\%$ confidence intervals for contrasts in the mean normal scores. The use of this procedure is illustrated for the data of Table 12–9.

EXAMPLE 12–7.1. Post hoc examination of the simple pairwise contrasts in the means of the expected normal-order statistics at the $\alpha = 0.10$ level reveals that responses obtained under the informative–verbal condition and those obtained under the material reinforcement condition are significantly different. No other pairwise comparisons are significant. Under the Terry–Hoeffding model:

1. $\hat{\psi} = \overline{W}_1 - \overline{W}_2 = -0.77 - 0.54 = -1.31$

2. $\text{Var}(\hat{\psi}) = \left[\dfrac{29.5960}{31}\right]\left[\dfrac{2}{8}\right] = 0.2388$

3. $\sqrt{X_{3:0.90}^2} = \sqrt{6.25} = 2.50$

4. $\psi = -1.31 \pm 2.50\sqrt{0.2388} = -1.31 \pm 1.22$

Post hoc multiple comparisons under the Van der Waerden model identify the same pairwise comparison as significant. For this model:

1. $\hat{\psi} = \overline{W}_1 - \overline{W}_2 = -0.73 - 0.53 = -1.26$

2. $\text{Var}(\hat{\psi}) = \left[\dfrac{26.3618}{31}\right]\left[\dfrac{2}{8}\right] = 0.2126$

3. $\sqrt{X_{3:0.90}^2} = \sqrt{6.25} = 2.50$

4. $\psi = -1.26 \pm 2.50\sqrt{0.2126} = -1.26 \pm 1.15$

12–8. The Kruskal–Wallis Test for Ordered Contingency Tables

An important application of the Kruskal–Wallis test arises in the analysis of contingency tables, where the dependent variable is defined by a set of ordered

Multiple-Sample Methods for Quantitative Variables Based on Ranks and Normal Scores: The Nonparametric One-Way Analysis of Variance

315

mutually exclusive and exhaustive subclasses. An example of this situation is provided in Example 12–8.1. If, in addition, the independent variable is ordered, a planned one-degree-of-freedom test of monotonicity can be performed in the manner of Section 12–3 and Example 12–3.2. Also, the method of Section 8–5 is appropriate for the case in which both variables are ordered.

EXAMPLE 12–8.1. As part of a school desegregation program, a sample of graduating seniors was asked:

"When the school integration program began, did you think it would work?" (Circle your answer.) 1. Definitely yes. 2. Maybe yes. 3. Don't know. 4. Maybe not. 5. Definitely not.

Results are as shown in Table 12–10, by race of respondents. For these data, the Karl Pearson statistic is given by $X^2 = 13.91$. With $v = (3 - 1)(5 - 1) = 8$, the hypothesis of identity of distributions is not rejected at $\alpha \leq 0.05$, since $X^2_{8;0.95} = 15.51$. Yet inspection of the data suggests that Blacks were more inclined to select responses indicating possible failure with the integration program, while Whites were more positive in their responses. Since the Karl Pearson statistic ignores the order on the response variable and since the sample sizes are small, one might question the use of the Karl Pearson test. To take advantage of the ordered response categories, even for small samples, a researcher can use the Kruskal–Wallis test. Since the alternative of interest concerns shifts in centers and not just the global differences in the distributions tested by the Karl Pearson chi-square test of homogeneity, the H test is actually the more appropriate test. For the data of Table 12–10, one assigns ranks in the usual fashion by taking into account the large number of tied values.

Recall that $1 + 2 + 3 + \ldots + N = \frac{1}{2}N(N + 1)$, and assign midranks as follows:

1. The 7 responses *definitely not* are ranked

$$\frac{1}{7}\left[\frac{1}{2}(7)(8)\right] = \frac{1}{7}(28) = 4$$

TABLE 12–10. *Responses by race to a question of opinion on whether school integration would work.*

Response	Asian	Black	White	Total
1. Definitely yes	2	3	7	12
2. Maybe yes	3	3	7	13
3. Didn't know	6	4	3	13
4. Maybe not	3	7	2	12
5. Definitely not	0	5	2	7
Total	14	22	21	57

2. The 12 *maybe not* responses are ranked

$$\frac{1}{12}\left[\frac{1}{2}(19)(20) - \frac{1}{2}(7)(8)\right] = \frac{1}{12}(190 - 29) = \frac{1}{12}(162) = 13.5$$

3. The 13 *didn't know* responses are ranked

$$\frac{1}{13}\left[\frac{1}{2}(32)(33) - \frac{1}{2}(19)(20)\right] = \frac{1}{13}(528 - 190) = \frac{1}{13}(338) = 26$$

4. The 13 *maybe yes* responses are ranked

$$\frac{1}{13}\left[\frac{1}{2}(45)(46) - \frac{1}{2}(31)(32)\right] = \frac{1}{13}(1035 - 528) = \frac{1}{13}(507) = 39$$

5. The 12 *definitely yes* responses are ranked

$$\frac{1}{12}\left[\frac{1}{2}(57)(58) - \frac{1}{2}(45)(46)\right] = \frac{1}{12}(1653 - 1035) = \frac{1}{12}(618) = 51.5$$

As a first computational check on the midrank assignment, note that

$$12(51.5) + 13(39) + 13(26) + 12(13.5) + 7(4) = 1653$$

which is the sum of $1 + 2 + 3 + \ldots + 56 + 57 = \frac{1}{2}(57)(58)$. Thus, with these midrank values:

$$R_1 = 0(4) + 3(13.5) + 6(26) + 3(39) + 2(51.5) = 416.5$$
$$R_2 = 5(4) + 7(13.5) + 4(26) + 3(39) + 3(51.5) = 490.0$$
$$R_3 = 2(4) + 2(13.5) + 3(26) + 7(39) + 7(51.5) = 746.5$$

As a second computation check,

$$R_1 + R_2 + R_3 = \frac{N(N + 1)}{2} = 1653$$

With these rank totals, the uncorrected H is given by:

$$H = \frac{12}{N(N + 1)} \sum_{k=1}^{3} \frac{R_k^2}{n_k} - 3(N + 1)$$
$$= \frac{12}{57(58)}\left[\frac{416.5^2}{14} + \frac{490^2}{22} + \frac{746.5^2}{21}\right] - 3(58) = 6.91$$

With the correction for ties:

$$C = 1 - \frac{1}{N^3 - N} \sum_{s=1}^{d} (t_s^3 - t_s)$$
$$= 1 - \frac{1}{57^3 - 57}\left[(7^3 - 7) + (12^3 - 12) + (13^3 - 13) + (13^3 - 13) + (12^3 - 12)\right]$$
$$= 1 - \frac{8136}{185136} = 1 - 0.0439 = 0.9561$$

so that the corrected H is equal to:

$$H^* = \frac{H}{C} = \frac{6.91}{0.9561} = 7.23$$

Multiple-Sample
Methods for
Quantitative
Variables Based
on Ranks and
Normal Scores:
The
Nonparametric
One-Way Analysis
of Variance

317

The hypothesis of identical distributions is rejected at $\alpha \leq 0.05$ since $X^2_{2;0.95} = 5.99$. It is concluded that distributions are different, and that the difference is most likely a result of different central values.

12–9. The Variance of a Contrast When There Are Many Ties in the Kruskal–Wallis Test

The variance formula for contrasts as given in Section 12–2 assumes that no tied values are observed. When ties occur, the variance of a contrast is given by:

$$\text{Var}(\hat{\phi}) = C\left[\frac{N(N + 1)}{12} \sum_{k=1}^{K} \frac{a_k^2}{n_k}\right]$$

where C is the correction factor for tied values in the Kruskal–Wallis test.

EXAMPLE 12–9.1. In Example 12–8.1, the 95% confidence interval for the comparison of Whites and Blacks is given by:

$$\phi = (\overline{R}_2 - \overline{R}_3) \pm \sqrt{X^2_{K-1;1-\alpha}} \sqrt{C\left[\frac{N(N + 1)}{12}\left[\frac{1}{n_2} + \frac{1}{n_3}\right]\right]}$$

$$= \left[\frac{490.0}{22} - \frac{746.5}{21}\right] \pm \sqrt{5.99} \sqrt{0.9561\left[\frac{57(58)}{12}\left[\frac{1}{22} + \frac{1}{21}\right]\right]}$$

$$= -13.28 \pm 2.45(4.95)$$

$$= -13.28 \pm 12.13$$

indicating that Black and White students had different expectations concerning the success of the integration program.

Summary

The extension of the Wilcoxon two-sample test to the K-sample analog is called the Kruskal–Wallis test. Since tables of this test are not available, except for small sample sizes, it is customary to perform the large-sample test by obtaining the rank totals for each sample, $R_1, R_2, \ldots, R_K$, and then computing

$$H = \frac{12}{N(N + 1)} \sum_{k=1}^{K} \frac{R_k^2}{n_k} - 3(N + 1)$$

The hypothesis of identical distributions is rejected if $H > X^2_{K-1;1-\alpha}$. If H_0 is rejected, one can examine contrasts in the $\overline{R}_k$ to identify possible reasons for the statistically large H statistic. Under this model, contrasts are defined as:

$$\hat{\phi} = a_1\overline{R}_1 + a_2\overline{R}_2 + \ldots + a_K\overline{R}_K$$

with

$$\text{Var}(\hat{\phi}) = \frac{N(N + 1)}{12} \sum_{k=1}^{K} \frac{a_k^2}{n_k}$$

The set of $(1 - \alpha)\%$ simultaneous confidence intervals is given by:

$$\psi = \hat{\psi} \pm \sqrt{X^2_{K-1:1-\alpha}} \sqrt{\text{Var}(\hat{\psi})}$$

Any confidence interval that does not cover zero is said to contribute to the rejection of H_0.

If a researcher can define $(K - 1)$ orthogonal contrasts in the $\overline{R}_k$, then individual tests of $H_0: \psi_k = 0$ can be performed with:

$$X_1^2 = \frac{\hat{\psi}_k^2}{\text{Var}(\hat{\psi}_k)}$$

as a test statistic. To control the overall family error rate to $\alpha \leq 0.05$ or $\alpha \leq 0.01$, the critical values reported in the last column of Table A–1 can be used. Under this model, H_0 should be rejected if $X_1^2 > Z^2_{1-\alpha/[2(K-1)]}$, where $Z_{1-\alpha/[2(K-1)]}$ is read from Table A–1.

Just as the efficiency of the Wilcoxon test can be improved by the substitution of normal scores, so can the efficiency of the Kruskal–Wallis test be improved by the same substitutions. If $W_{ik} = E(V^{(ik)})$ or $Z^{(ik)}$, then the Terry–Hoeffding form and the Van der Waerden form of the K-sample normal-scores test are given by:

$$W = \frac{(N-1)\sum_{k=1}^{K}\frac{1}{n_k}\left[\sum_{i=1}^{n_k} W_{ik}\right]^2}{\sum_{k=1}^{K}\sum_{i=1}^{n_k} W_{ik}^2} = \frac{(N-1)\sum_{k=1}^{K} n_k \overline{W}_k^2}{\sum_{k=1}^{K}\sum_{i=1}^{n_k} W_{ik}^2}$$

In this case, H_0, the hypothesis of identical distributions, is rejected if $W > X^2_{K-1:1-\alpha}$. Under this model, contrasts are defined in terms of the mean normal-order statistics $\overline{W}_1, \overline{W}_2, \ldots, \overline{W}_K$ as:

$$\hat{\psi} = a_1 \overline{W}_1 + a_2 \overline{W}_2 + \ldots + a_K \overline{W}_K$$

with

$$\text{Var}(\hat{\psi}) = \left[\frac{\sum_{k=1}^{K}\sum_{i=1}^{n_k} W_{ik}^2}{N-1}\right]\sum_{k=1}^{K}\frac{a_k^2}{n_k}$$

The set of $(1 - \alpha)\%$ simultaneous confidence intervals is given by:

$$\psi = \hat{\psi} \pm \sqrt{X^2_{K-1:1-\alpha}} \sqrt{\text{Var}(\hat{\psi})}$$

As with the Kruskal–Wallis model, planned contrasts may be examined by selecting the critical value from the last column of Table A–1.

Finally, the point-estimation procedure for comparisons of median differences, as described by Hodges and Lehmann, is suggested as a competitor to the post hoc procedure for differences in mean ranks. Unfortunately, confidence-interval procedures for the method are difficult to execute, so that clear identification of significant differences is difficult to obtain. There is some evidence that significant differences in mean ranks correspond to significant differences in median value. However, this is only conjecture.

An alternative post hoc procedure, which seems to have high statistical power, is one proposed by Steel. For this method, one determines all $Q = \left[\begin{smallmatrix} K \\ 2 \end{smallmatrix}\right]$ pairwise confidence intervals of the two-sample Wilcoxon model with endpoints of

Multiple-Sample Methods for Quantitative Variables Based on Ranks and Normal Scores: The Nonparametric One-Way Analysis of Variance

319

the intervals determined by $\alpha = \alpha_T/Q$, where α_T is the desired family error rate. If any interval does not contain zero, the hypothesis of equal median differences is rejected. If sample sizes are all equal, or if all distributions are symmetrical, it can be concluded that the population means are statistically different from one another.

An important use of the Kruskal–Wallis test for the analysis of a contingency table where one of the variables is ordered was illustrated in this chapter. Since the ranking of the dependent variable maintains the ordered relationship on the categories, the resulting test proves to be more powerful than the usually performed Karl Pearson Chi-square test. For this reason, it is recommended.

Exercises

*1. a) Are there any significant differences detected by the Kruskal–Wallis test across social class for the data of Exercise 10 of Chapter 10 for X_2: Vocabulary scores?
   b) Repeat (a), but with normal scores of the Van der Waerden form.
   c) Compare (a) and (b) with the classical F test.

*2. In a developmental study, infants were tested with a simple Piagetian task on the conservation of matter. Results are as shown in the following table. No child was given more than two minutes to demonstrate knowledge of the task. The dependent variable is number of seconds to reach solution.

Group	One	Two	Three	Four	Five	Six
Sex	Male	Male	Male	Female	Female	Female
Age in months	24	30	36	24	30	36
Number of seconds to complete task	55	38	20	48	30	20
	58	39	30	49	35	30
	60	52	32	55	35	36
	63	55	32	55	39	39
	68	58	41	60	39	45
	75	70	47	63	50	46
	80	71	58	69	52	55
	100	73	70	71	55	60
	112	115	76	80	56	61
	120	120	78	120	58	63

a) Set up five orthogonal contrasts in the mean ranks and then analyze these data in terms of the Dunn–Bonferroni model.
b) Examine the $\binom{K}{2} = \binom{6}{2} = 15$ pairwise differences in mean rank by means of Tukey's method.
c) Repeat (a) and (b) with normal scores of the Van der Waerden form.

*3. Test the data of Exercise 2 by means of the Klotz test applied to a pairing of the samples, with $\alpha_T \leq 0.10$.

*4. Do an analysis of the data of Exercise 2 across the males, using:
   a) The Terry–Hoeffding normal-order statistic.
   b) The Van der Waerden normal scores.
   c) Compare the results for the two kinds of normal scores.

*5. In a study in which two persuasion techniques were being investigated, 48 college sophomores were given a pre- and a posttest concerning their attitude toward the question of whether policemen should carry batons or pistols. One group of students read a five-page paper supporting the use of batons, while the second group attended a 10-minute film in which the script consisted of the same five-page report read by the other students. On the pre- and posttest, students were scored according to the number of responses to a 10-item questionnaire that supported the use of batons over pistols. Results are as shown in the following table for the students who took both tests.

Males				Females			
Report		Film		Report		Film	
Pre	Post	Pre	Post	Pre	Post	Pre	Post
0	4	0	8	2	4	3	8
0	4	1	7	2	4	3	10
0	2	1	10	4	3	3	10
1	2	2	9	5	6	4	7
1	2	2	9	5	6	4	8
5	7	3	10	5	4	4	8
7	8	3	10	5	4	4	10
		4	10	5	8	4	10
		4	10	6	5	6	10
						6	9
						6	10
						6	10

a) Analyze the difference score for these data, using the methods of this chapter.
b) Would you recommend that classical methods be used on these data? Why?
c) Which is more effective for changing attitude, reading or seeing a film?
d) Are there any significant differences between males and females with respect to their persuasability?
e) Is there an interaction of sex with technique?
f) Are questions (c), (d), and (e) orthogonal to one another?

*6. In an experimental study, 20 retarded children of ages 2 to 3 years were divided at

Method			
a	b	c	d
2.9	1.6	2.1	1.1
3.1	1.7	2.8	1.3
3.2	2.4	2.9	1.6
4.6	2.7	3.2	1.8
4.7	2.8	3.9	3.1

Multiple-Sample Methods for Quantitative Variables Based on Ranks and Normal Scores: The Nonparametric One-Way Analysis of Variance

321

random into four groups and each group was trained by a different method in the use of the toilet. The methods are:

a) Mother directed own child, following training by a public health nurse on the reinforcement toilet hygiene habits.
b) Mother directed her own child, but without the advantage of training.
c) Nurse trainee directed the child after training by a public health nurse.
d) Nurse trainee directed the child, but without the advantage of training.

The ratios of postexperiment scores to preexperiment scores on a checklist of self-sufficiency are reported in the accompanying table. Are the differences between methods significant at the 5% level?

*7. Set up three orthogonal contrasts to analyze the data of Exercise 6. Show that the corresponding Z values sum to H.

*8. Use the Terry–Hoeffding model to analyze the data of Exercise 7.

*9. In a study in which the effects of color upon test performance was being studied, the statistics in the following table were obtained. In this study, 40 students were assigned at random to one of four identical rooms, identical except that wall colors were different. Two of the rooms were painted with cool colors, and the other two with warm colors. During the experimental period, students studied a section on French history following the French Revolution and extending up to the accession of Napoleon to the imperial throne. Students were instructed to study only in the assigned study room. The criterion variable is the score on a 60-item multiple-choice test. Did room color have an influence upon test scores?

Color of Walls in Study Room

	Light blue	Light green	Deep yellow	Deep red
	41	46	40	28
	45	47	40	30
	45	49	41	30
Scores	46	49	42	31
on	48	51	43	31
60-item	50	55	44	36
test	56	55	46	39
	56	58	50	41
	57	59	52	42
	57	60	58	44

*10. As in the study of Exercise 7, three orthogonal contrasts are suggested by the data of Exercise 12–9:

a) Comparison of warm colors versus cool colors:

$$\psi_1 = (\mu_B + \mu_G) - (\mu_Y + \mu_R)$$

b) Comparison of cool colors:

$$\psi_2 = (\mu_B - \mu_G)$$

c) Comparison of warm colors:

$$\psi_3 = (\mu_Y - \mu_R)$$

Investigate these three contrasts. Show how they relate to H, the Kruskal–Wallis statistic.

*11. Analyze the contrasts of Exercise 10, using the Van der Waerden model.

*12. Repeat the analysis of Exercise 10, using the Bell–Doksum model.

*13. A group of 30 high-school sophomores were randomly assigned to three groups. Each group participated in a series of meetings designed to modify the students' attitudes toward professional prizefighting. In each of the three groups, a different attitude-modification approach was employed. Below are the scores of the 30 students on an attitude scale administered at the close of the series of meetings. Analyze the data, using the methods of this chapter. The modification methods used were as follows:

Method 1	Method 2	Method 3
38	35	32
37	34	32
37	33	30
36	33	29
36	31	28
34	30	24
34	30	22
33	29	18
33	27	17
29	21	15

Method 1. Use of film narrated by a well-known Hollywood actor.
Method 2. Use of film narrated by a well-known national TV news commentator.
Method 3. Use of film narrated by an unknown speaker.

*14. The following are error scores on a psychomotor test for four groups of subjects tested under four experimental conditions. Use the Kruskal–Wallis model to test the null hypothesis of no mean or median difference in group centers. The four experimental groups are defined by:

Group	Error scores						
I	16	7	19	24	31		
II	24	6	15	25	32	24	29
III	16	15	18	19	6	13	18
IV	25	19	16	17	42	45	

  I. Males walking 10 minutes on treadmill.
 II. Males walking 1 minute on treadmill.
III. Females walking 10 minutes on treadmill.
 IV. Females walking 1 minute on treadmill.

*15. Analyze the data of Exercise 14 by means of three planned contrasts. How do the contrasts relate to H? See Example 12–3.1. What does this indicate about unequal sample sizes with respect to contrasts that appear to be orthogonal?

16. Forty third-grade students reading two years behind grade level were randomly assigned to college students who gave them tutoring in the process of reading. Results are

Multiple-Sample
Methods for
Quantitative
Variables Based
on Ranks and
Normal Scores:
The
Nonparametric
One-Way Analysis
of Variance

323

Test scores after the following hours of tutoring per week			
Zero	Two	Four	Six
10	12	18	16
12	18	18	17
12	18	23	18
13	23	30	18
22	27	31	28
24	32	36	33
26	34	39	40
26	40	40	40
30	40	40	40
31	40	40	40

as shown, on a 40-item reading test given ten weeks after tutoring began. What has happened?

*17. Analyze the data of Table 6–2 in terms of the Kruskal–Wallis test and associated contrast procedures. Compare the results to those reported in Chapter 6. Which procedure would you recommend for these kinds of data? Why? Note that, for the Kruskal–Wallis model, among the tied values, 10 observations are tied at more than 40.

*18. The data of Exercise 1 of Chapter 6 can be analyzed by means of the H test corrected for ties. For this model, the hypothesis under test is the same as that used for the chi-square test of homogeneity; that is, both distributions are identical. However, the alternatives are not operationally the same. What are they for the two models? Do the two analyses, and compare the results. Which method would you recommend? Why?

*19. Apply the H test corrected for ties to the data of Exercise 4 in Chapter 6 and test for monotonic trend as described in Section 12–3. Compare your results to those of the earlier exercise. Which method would you recommend. Why?

*20. Apply the H test corrected for ties to the data of Example 6–3.1 and test for monotonic trend as described in Section 12–3. Compare the results to those of Example 6–3.1. Which method would you recommend? Why?

21. The original data for Example 12–6.1 are as shown in the table below. Repeat the analysis of Example 12–6.1 with the Van der Waerden normal scores, but break the ties by averaging the tied normal scores. Compare the two analyses. Which do you prefer? Why?

IV	M	C	K
15	23	24	18
20	29	29	20
20	37	30	28
24	37	30	35
24	39	30	35
24	40	31	40
35	40	35	40
35	40	36	40

Nonparametric One- and Two-Sample Tests for Repeated Measures and Matched Samples

13–1. Repeated Measures and Correlated Samples

Repeated-measure designs are commonly encountered in behavioral research in the case in which multiple observations are made on each unit or subject of a study. The prototype of all univariate repeated-measures design is the classical matched-pair t test. For this model, a researcher has a sample of n experimental units in which two observations on the same random variable are available. Usually, the measurements are made at two different time periods, once before the application of a treatment and once after the treatment has had its effect. If μ_1 and μ_2 refer to the mean population values for the two sets of observations, the effect of the treatment is assessed by testing the null hypothesis $H_0: \mu_d = \mu_2 - \mu_1 = 0$ against $H_1: \mu_d \neq 0$ by referring $t = \overline{d}/SE_{\overline{D}} = \overline{d}/(S_d/\sqrt{n})$ to the t distribution with $\nu = n - 1$ degrees of freedom, where $\overline{d}$ and S_d refer to the mean difference and standard deviation of the differences of the paired observations. The $(1 - \alpha)\%$ confidence interval for $\mu_1 - \mu_2$ is given by:

$$\mu_1 - \mu_2 = \overline{d} \pm t_{\nu:\alpha/2} \frac{S_d}{\sqrt{n}}$$

Often, the repeated measures are made on two different experimental units that have been paired on the basis of some external criterion variable and randomly assigned to the two conditions of the study. This form is usually referred to as a *randomized block* design, in which there are two observations per block. Even in this form, the matched-pair t test is valid and is often performed. However, tradition has displaced the t test with an analysis-of-variance F test, in which the test statistic is given by:

$$F = \frac{\text{Mean square between treatments}}{\text{Mean-square error}}$$

The reason the F test is preferred over the t test is that it covers designs in which K measurements are made on the same experimental units or upon the elements in an individual block and is therefore not restricted to testing $\mu_1 = \mu_2$.

It should be noted that the oldest nonparametric test, the sign test, can be viewed as a repeated-measures test and is therefore a nonparametric competitor to the matched-pair t test as described in Section 3–8. However, we must repeat that the sign test is not generally recommended for quantitative data, since the corresponding nonparametric tests presented in this chapter generally have greater statistical power. The sign test reduces the data to the form of an algebraic sign for each pair of observations and so disregards the information that some pairs of observations are *more* different than others. Because the sign test ignores information that is typically available, it has low efficiency relative to the corresponding parametric procedures.

Three other nonparametric approaches to test the null hypothesis do not ignore the magnitude of the differences of the paired observations and, as a result, are more efficient than the sign test. These three nonparametric tests are similar in their rationale. They are the Fisher method of randomization for matched pairs, the Wilcoxon matched-pairs test, and the normal-scores matched-pairs tests.

We will begin by illustrating a test that has a simple theoretical basis but is somewhat difficult to perform in practice. This is Fisher's exact test for the matched-pair design. It is nearly an ideal test; its efficiency is *exactly one* whenever it is used in place of a valid classical t test. In all other cases, it also performs well and is therefore highly recommended for the matched-pair problem.

13–2. Fisher's Exact Test in the Matched-Pair Problem

The Fisher matched-pair test is illustrated in the following model. Consider $2n$ subjects that are matched on some basis of interest to a researcher. Let the conditions of the study be denoted as the Experimental and Control conditions.

Let X_{iE} represent the observation in the experimental group for the ith pair and X_{iC} represent the observation in the control group for the ith pair. The differences between the n pairs of observations can be represented for $i = 1, 2, \ldots, n$, by:

$$d_i = X_{iE} - X_{iC}$$

If each member of a matched pair comes from a population identical to the population from which the other member of that pair was taken, it follows that the null hypothesis $H_0 : \mu_d = 0$ is true. As a result, the difference for each of the n pairs of observations is just as likely to be positive as it is to be negative. If each of the pairs of observations results in no zero differences, then there are $N = 2^n$ possible ways that algebraic signs could have been assigned to the $d_i = X_{iE} - X_{iC}$ differences. This follows from Counting Rule Two presented in Section 2–2. If any one of two mutually exclusive and exhaustive events can occur on each of n trials, then there are $N = 2^n$ different sequences that may result from a set of trials. Under the null hypothesis and independence of the n pairs, these $N = 2^n$ sequences of plus or minus algebraic signs are equally likely. This statement is valid even if the null hypothesis is relaxed to read that "the two populations are identical or both are symmetric about the same center."

Thus, if one focuses on the $N = 2^n$ different permutations of plus and minus signs assignable to the n different d_i values, one could compute the classical $t = \overline{d}/(S_d/\sqrt{n})$ for each of the 2^n different outcomes, where S_d^2 is the variance of the difference observations under the assumption that H_0 is true. In the sample of d_i values:

$$S_d^2 = \frac{1}{n-1} \sum_{i=1}^{n} (d_i - \overline{d})^2 = \frac{\sum_{i=1}^{n} d_i^2 - n\overline{d}^2}{n-1}$$

so that

$$t = \frac{\overline{d}\sqrt{n(n-1)}}{\sqrt{\sum_{i=1}^{n} d_i^2 - n\overline{d}^2}}$$

Since n and $\sum_{i=1}^{n} d_i^2 = C$ are constant over all permutations of the d_i, it follows that

$$t = \frac{\overline{d}\sqrt{n(n-1)}}{\sqrt{C - n\overline{d}^2}}$$

is a function of $\overline{d}$ only. As $\overline{d}$ increases, t increases, since an increase in $\overline{d}$ in the numerator produces an increase in t, and an increase of $\overline{d}$ in the denominator also produces an increase in t. Thus, $\overline{d}$ alone can be used as the test statistic. An alpha-level decision rule for the Fisher test can be defined in terms of the sampling distribution of $\overline{d}$. The resulting distribution of $\overline{d}$ is a *conditional* distribution defined by the n differences generated by the original data. The distribution is conditional, since the n observed differences are treated as population values and not as sample observations.

In practice, the numerical determination of 2^n different values of $\overline{d}$ would be a formidable task; however, only tail values of the sampling distribution of $\overline{d}$ are required. If the test is performed with a probability of a Type I error less than or equal to α, it follows that the number of assignments to the critical region is given by:

$$T = 2^n\alpha$$

In general, this produces a nonintegral value of T. For a one-tailed test, T is rounded down to the nearest integer, while for a two-tailed test, T is rounded down to the nearest even integer. In any case, α is reduced in value.

To perform the test, it is necessary to generate only the T most extreme possible values of $\overline{d}$. If the actual sample value of $\overline{d}$ is one of the T values generated, the null hypothesis of equal centers is rejected at the desired level of significance. If $\overline{d}$ is not a member of the set of critical values, the null hypothesis is retained. If a directional alternative hypothesis is investigated, all T of the $\overline{d}$ values are placed in one tail. For a symmetric nondirectional alternative, half of the T critical $\overline{d}$ values

Nonparametric
One- and Two-
Sample Tests for
Repeated
Measures and
Matched Samples

327

must be in one tail and half in the other. For a nondirectional test, T must be an even integer, and so T is rounded down to the nearest even integer. The $T/2$ most extreme values of $\overline{d}$ are generated and given the sign of the observed sample value of $\overline{d}$.

The Fisher randomization matched-pair test is illustrated by the use of the data in Table 13–1.

EXAMPLE 13–2.1. Consider a comparative study in which the effectiveness of traditional and modern mathematics instruction in algebra is being evaluated. In this study, 14 subjects were randomly drawn from the population of interest and seven matched pairs were formed on the basis of IQ scores. The members of each IQ pair were then randomly assigned to a modern instruction group or traditional instruction group. Once the students were assigned, each group received three weeks of instruction. All students took the same final test at the end of the instruction period. The data for the experiment are represented in Table 13–1. The values of the paired differences are in order of pair: $\{-5, 4, 11, 12, -2, 8, 10\}$ and $\overline{d} = 5.43$. If a one-tailed test, with alpha less than or equal to 0.05, is desired, it is seen that:

$$T = 2^n\alpha = (2^7)(0.05) = 6.40$$

Reducing this number to an integer value, we find that the one-tailed critical region is defined by the six largest values of $\overline{d}$. The six extreme values of $\overline{d}$ are reported in Table 13–2. Since $\overline{d} = 5.43$ is in the rejection region, it is concluded that training with the new method produces higher scores than the traditional method, at least as measured by this criterion variable.

For completeness, the entire distribution of 128 possible $\overline{d}$ values is shown in Figure 13–1. As can be seen, the sampling distribution of $\overline{d}$ is symmetrical about zero and, in addition, has the typical bell-shaped normal form. This convergence to the normal form is a property of this test. When n is large, the closeness of the distribution to the normal distribution is striking. Because of this convergence, the

TABLE 13–1. *Achievement scores made by 14 children trained in a modern or traditional program in algebra.*

Pair: IQ level from low to high	Modern group	Traditional group	d_i	Ranks for $+d_i$	Ranks for $-d_i$
1	31	36	−5		3
2	42	38	+4	2	
3	44	33	+11	6	
4	48	36	+12	7	
5	51	53	−2		1
6	57	49	+8	4	
7	62	52	+10	5	

TABLE 13–2. *The six extreme positive values of $\bar{d}$ for the data of Table 13–1.*

	Absolute values of d_i							Value of $\bar{d}$
	2	4	5	8	10	11	12	
Algebraic	+	+	+	+	+	+	+	7.43
sign	−	+	+	+	+	+	+	6.86
of	+	−	+	+	+	+	+	6.29
the	+	+	−	+	+	+	+	6.00
difference	−	−	+	+	+	+	+	5.71
	−	+	−	+	+	+	+	5.43

large-sample form of the Fisher randomization matched-pair t test is the ordinary classical t test for match pairs.

The use of both the magnitude and the direction of the obtained differences in the Fisher randomization statistic produces a test that is more efficient than the sign test. The sign test retains only the sign of each difference; thus, the basic data employed by the sign are merely indications of the direction but not of the magnitude of each difference. For the data of Table 13–1, the sign test replaces the differences by: {−, +, +, +, −, +, +} and produces a test with lower power.

Unfortunately, the randomization test is a conditional test, since its null distribution depends upon the configuration of absolute differences actually ob-

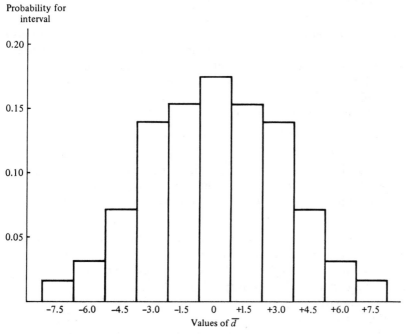

FIGURE 13–1. *The sampling distribution of the Fisher randomization test statistic $\bar{d}$ for the data of Table 13–1.*

tained in the sample, which are treated as representing a finite population of size n. Thus, unlike the sign test, which is unconditional and has an easily tabled null distribution, the randomization test is untabled and requires a separate computation of the significance probability for each use of the test. Furthermore, probability levels ordinarily cannot be equated for different experiments because no two samples of pair differences use the same rejection region even though the samples are identical in size. Although the randomization test uses more of the available sample data and gives a wider selection of probability levels than does the sign test, the restrictions associated with the conditionality of the randomization test make it a less than ideal choice for the matched-pairs problem.

13-3. The Wilcoxon Matched-Pair Test

A test proposed by Wilcoxon is a compromise between the loss of information inherent in the sign test and the tedious computations presented by the conditionality of the randomization test (Wilcoxon, 1949). Wilcoxon's matched-pair signed-ranks test employs both the magnitude and the direction of the differences by ranking the absolute values of the differences, $r_i = \text{rank}|X_{iE} - X_{iC}| = \text{rank}|d_i|$, and attaching to the ranks the signs of the original differences. In this way, all samples of n pairs $d_i = X_{iE} - X_{iC}$ will have the same set of absolute values associated with the differences, i.e., the ranks $(1, 2, \ldots, n)$; however, the signed values of the ranks will differ with the individual samples.

This means that all possible samples of size n that could be generated from the original underlying population are eventually mapped into the one uniform population of rank values: $\{1, 2, \ldots, n\}$. Thus, *all* conditional distributions of the observations become associated with the same discrete distribution of integers extending from 1 to n. Since all conditional distributions transform to the same integral values, the distribution of the Wilcoxon statistic is easy to derive by noting that, under the null hypothesis, a positive or a negative sign is equally likely to be associated with any given rank, so that:

$$P(\text{positive rank}) = P(\text{negative rank}) = \tfrac{1}{2}$$

One way to define the Wilcoxon statistic is to consider only the ranks assigned to the deviations that have positive signs and to define the Wilcoxon statistic as the sum of the ranks associated with the positive deviations and denoted as $T_{(+)}$. The determination of this distribution for $n = 4$ is illustrated in Table 13-3.

EXAMPLE 13-3.1. For $n = 4$, the distribution of plus and minus signs is given by the binomial distribution with $p = \tfrac{1}{2}$. Zero plus signs occur in $\begin{bmatrix} 4 \\ 0 \end{bmatrix} = 1$ way; one plus sign occurs in $\begin{bmatrix} 4 \\ 1 \end{bmatrix} = 4$ ways; two plus signs occur in $\begin{bmatrix} 4 \\ 2 \end{bmatrix} = 6$ ways; three plus signs occur in $\begin{bmatrix} 4 \\ 3 \end{bmatrix} = 4$ ways; and four plus signs occur in $\begin{bmatrix} 4 \\ 4 \end{bmatrix} = 1$ way. These 16 ways are summarized in Table 13-3.

In the first row of the table, all deviations are negative so that $T_{(+)} = 0$. In the second row, the smallest deviation is positive so that $T_{(+)} = 1$. The other sums are similarly defined. The distribution of $T_{(+)}$, summarized in Table 13-4, is seen to

TABLE 13–3. *The Wilcoxon matched-pair statistic* $T_{(+)}$ *for* $n = 4$.

	Rank value				
	1	2	3	4	$T_{(+)}$
Zero plus signs	−	−	−	−	0
One plus sign	+	−	−	−	1
	−	+	−	−	2
	−	−	+	−	3
	−	−	−	+	4
Two plus signs	+	+	−	−	3
	+	−	+	−	4
	+	−	−	+	5
	−	+	+	−	5
	−	+	−	+	6
	−	−	+	+	7
Three plus signs	−	+	+	+	9
	+	−	+	+	8
	+	+	−	+	7
	+	+	+	−	6
Four plus signs	+	+	+	+	10

be symmetric. At this point, it should be noted that for $n = 4$, no two-tailed test of hypothesis is available at alpha equal to 0.05, since

$$P(T_{(+)} = 0) + P(T_{(+)} = 10) = \tfrac{1}{16} + \tfrac{1}{16} = \tfrac{1}{8} = 0.125.$$

In addition to defining the Wilcoxon statistic as the sum of the ranks associated with the positive deviations $T_{(+)}$, one could define the Wilcoxon statistic as the sum of the ranks associated with the negative deviations $T_{(-)}$, or as the mini-

TABLE 13–4. *The distribution of the Wilcoxon matched-pair statistic* $T_{(+)}$ *for* $n = 4$.

Value of $T_{(+)}$	Probability
0	1/16
1	1/16
2	1/16
3	2/16
4	2/16
5	2/16
6	2/16
7	2/16
8	1/16
9	1/16
10	1/16

TABLE 13–5. The five extreme large values of $T_{(+)}$ for the data of Table 13–1.

	Absolute values of r_i							Value of $T_{(+)}$
	1	2	3	4	5	6	7	
Algebraic	+	+	+	+	+	+	+	28
sign	−	+	+	+	+	+	+	27
of	+	−	+	+	+	+	+	26
the	−	−	+	+	+	+	+	25
difference	+	+	−	+	+	+	+	25

mum of $T_{(+)}$ and $T_{(-)}$. These alternative definitions are possible since $T_{(+)} + T_{(-)} = n(n + 1)/2$. For unifying purposes, the first proposed definition, $T_{(+)}$, is used throughout this and subsequent chapters. In terms of the model of Section 13–2 and Example 13–2.1, small values of $T_{(+)}$ are compatible with the alternative that the location parameter of the control group exceeds that of the experimental group, while large values of $T_{(+)}$ are in agreement with the alternative that the center of the experimental group is larger than that of the control group.

EXAMPLE 13–3.2. An application of the Wilcoxon matched-pair test can be illustrated by use of the data in Table 13–1. For a one-tailed test with $\alpha \leq 0.05$, $T = 2^7(0.05) = 6.40$. As a result, the rejection region is defined by the six largest rank assignment totals. These rank totals are given in Table 13–5. As is seen, the rejection region is defined by $T_{(+)}$: {25, 26, 27, 28}, the four most extreme values. If $T_{(+)} = 24$ were added, α would exceed 0.05 in value. To obtain the observed value of $T_{(+)}$, one assigns the ranks {1, 2, ..., 7} to the absolute values of the paired differences and sums ranks for the positive differences. These rank assignments are reported in the last column of Table 13–1. For these rank assignments:

$$T_{(+)} = 2 + 6 + 7 + 4 + 5 = 24$$

Since $T_{(+)} = 24$ is not an element of the rejection region, the hypothesis of identical population centers for the experimental and control condition is not rejected. This does not agree with the decision reached by the Fisher randomization test.

If the decision rule had been stated in terms of $T_{(-)}$, one would have concluded that no central population values differ since:

$$T_{(-)} = 1 + 3 = 4$$

would not be in the rejection region defined by $T_{(-)}$: {0, 1, 2, 3}.

With the Wilcoxon statistic defined as the minimum of $T_{(+)}$ and $T_{(-)}$, the rejection region is defined simply by {0, 1, 2, 3} while the value of the Wilcoxon statistic is defined as the minimum of {4, 24} = 4. Under this definition, H_0 is retained.

As this example shows, all three definitions may be used to test the hypothesis of identical location parameters. Nevertheless, we shall use $T_{(+)}$ for most of the examples that follow.

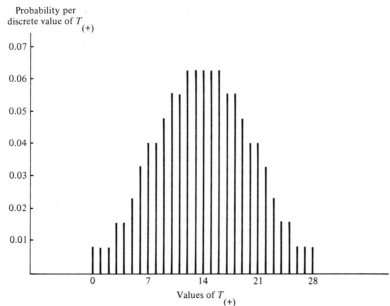

FIGURE 13–2. The sampling distribution of $T_{(+)}$, the test statistic of the Wilcoxon matched-pair test, for n = 7.

For $n = 7$, the entire distribution of $T_{(+)}$ is presented in Figure 13–2. This distribution is found by taking the ranks 1, 2, 3, 4, 5, 6, 7 and affixing a plus or minus sign to each rank and then computing $T_{(+)}$ for each of the 128 equally likely assignments of algebraic signs. As can be seen, the Wilcoxon matched-pair statistic $T_{(+)}$ is symmetrically distributed about its expected value in the usual bell-shaped form. As might be expected, the distribution tends to a normal form as n increases in numerical value. Because of this convergence to a normal form, the large-sample form of the Wilcoxon test is easy to perform.

13–4. Zero and Tied Differences in the Wilcoxon Matched-Pair Test

The discussion of the Wilcoxon matched-pair test has assumed continuity of the distribution of differences, such that $P(d_i = 0) = 0$; however, many applications of this test encounter tied observations. Several options are available when zero differences are encountered. If there are p such differences they may be dropped, reducing the effective sample size to $n - p$ differences. This procedure favors the rejection of the hypothesis of equality of the distributions, by discarding those observations that tend to support the null hypothesis. The increased power obtained is an artifact of the treatment of tied observations. An alternative procedure consists of assigning the midrank, $(p + 1)/2$, to the p zero differences, with half of the zero differences receiving a positive midrank and half a negative midrank. The second procedure, unlike the first, is conservative, in that the use of midranks favors the retention rather than the rejection of the null hypothesis. The principal disadvantage of this method lies in the fact that the ranked differences can no longer be written as $\{\pm 1, \pm 2, \ldots, \pm n\}$. Consequently, the exact null distribution of the Wilcoxon test statistic is no longer unconditional, and exact tables of the distribution are inapplicable. Despite these disadvantages, the midrank procedure is preferable to dropping the zero differences, because the former procedure is conservative while the latter is not.

Similar difficulties arise when two or more differences have the same absolute values. If there are p such differences, the p corresponding ranks may be randomly assigned to these differences, or the midrank of the p differences may be assigned to all of them. The randomization procedure is undesirable because it introduces randomization that is extraneous to the data themselves and, in so doing, it may cause different experimenters analyzing the same data to arrive at different statistical conclusions. On the other hand, randomization does retain the original ranks, so that the test remains an unconditional one. The midrank procedure destroys the un-conditional properties of the Wilcoxon test by requiring a statistic conditioned upon the number of tied differences. Once again, this procedure is conservative relative to the unconditional procedure, and for this reason is the preferred technique.

The problem of tied observations and the disavantages associated with each of the correction procedures are recurrent problems in dealing with rank tests. The midrank procedure is not an ideal solution to the problem; however, it does minimize the potentially misleading effects associated with other adjustment procedures.

The development of the Fisher and the Wilcoxon matched-pair tests is based on two assumptions. First, the assumption was made that the populations are continuously distributed. The assumption was necessary so that there would be 2^n possible values of the test statistic. The second assumption was that sampling is random and pairs are independent. This assumption was necessary so that the 2^n possible values are equally likely.

A third assumption is necessary to define more clearly the alternative hypo-thesis for the two tests. The null hypothesis is that the two populations are identical or that they are symmetric about a common point. The null hypothesis can thus be false because the two populations differ in shape, in means, in medians, or in both means and medians. If an assumption is added that the two populations have identical shapes or are both symmetric, then both methods are tests for a difference of population means and medians.

13–5. Tables of the Wilcoxon Matched-Pair Statistic

Fortunately, a researcher need not generate the sampling distribution of $T_{(+)}$ for each hypothesis tested, since extensive tables have been prepared and are available. In this book, percentile values are reported in Table A–21. Since the Wilcoxon statistic has a discrete probability distribution, exact values are not avail-able over the 0 to 1 probability scale. The use of Table A–21 will be illustrated in terms of the data of Table 13–1.

EXAMPLE 13–5.1. For the data of Table 13–1, $n = 7$, the approximate 0.025 and 0.975 percentile values for the Wilcoxon statistic are read from Table A–21 to be $T_{(+)}(0.023) = 2$ and $T_{(+)}(0.977) = 26$. Thus, the $\alpha \leq 0.05$ decision rule for rejecting the hypothesis of identical distributions or equal centers is given by:

$$\text{D.R.: Reject } H_0 \text{ if } T_{(+)} \leq 2 \quad \text{or} \quad \text{if } T_{(+)} \geq 26$$

For the observed data, $T_{(+)} = 4$, so H_0 is not rejected.

If a one-tailed test were wanted for testing:

$$H_0: \text{Identical distributions}$$

against the alternative:

H_1: The distribution for the modern-mathematics training is displaced above the distribution for the traditional program,

the $\alpha \leq 0.05$ decision rule is given by:

$$\text{D.R.: Reject } H_0 \text{ if } T_{(+)} \geq 25$$

For the observed data, $T_{(+)} = 24$, so the hypothesis is not rejected at $\alpha \leq .039$.

13–6. Confidence Interval for Δ, the Median Difference

The confidence interval for the median difference can be generated in a fashion similar to that used in Section 3–13 for the sign test, but instead of using the binomial distribution to define the critical region, one uses the Wilcoxon matched-pair rank statistic. This is illustrated for the data of Table 13–1, for which the confidence interval for M, based on the sign test, would be given by

$$d^{(1)} \leq M_d \leq d^{(7)} \quad \text{or} \quad -5 \leq M_d \leq 12$$

with $\alpha = 2(0.0078) = 0.0156$.

A statistic as simple in form as the Wilcoxon statistic, $T_{(+)}$, could be expected to arise in many different contexts and from different starting points. One of these different approaches was proposed by Tukey (1949). For this model, one begins by forming all $n(n + 1)/2$ averages of the paired ordered differences

$$\bar{d} = \frac{1}{2}(d^{(i)} + d^{(i')}) \quad \text{for } i \leq i'$$

As shown by Tukey, $T_{(+)}$ is identical to the number of positive averages. In a like manner, $T_{(-)}$ is equal to the number of negative averages. In a more formal algebraic form:

$$T_{(+)} = \sum_i^n \sum_{i'}^n D_{ii'} \quad (i \leq i')$$

where

$$D_{ii'} = \begin{cases} 1, & \text{if } \bar{d} = \frac{1}{2}(d^{(i)} + d^{(i')}) > 0 \\ 0, & \text{if } \bar{d} = \frac{1}{2}(d^{(i)} + d^{(i')}) < 0 \end{cases}$$

In a like manner:

$$T_{(-)} = \sum_i^n \sum_{i'}^n D_{ii'} \qquad (i \leq i')$$

where

$$D_{ii'} = \begin{cases} 1, & \text{if } \bar{d} = \frac{1}{2}(d^{(i)} + d^{(i')}) < 0 \\ 0, & \text{if } \bar{d} = \frac{1}{2}(d^{(i)} + d^{(i')}) > 0 \end{cases}$$

If the $n(n + 1)/2$ averages are rank ordered, and the median value of the averages is found, one has an estimate of the median difference in the population of difference scores. If, in addition, the distribution of difference scores is symmetrical, one has an unbiased estimate of the difference in mean values of the original two sampled populations. Furthermore, from the ordered set of averages, the $(1 - \alpha)\%$ confidence interval for M_d is simply determined.

The interval is found by computing all $n(n + 1)/2$ averages of the paired differences and rank-ordering them. The interval estimate of M_d is bounded by the average values in the $(W + 1)$th position from either end of the ranking, where W denotes the lower critical value of the Wilcoxon test. To aid in the determination of these end values, the procedure illustrated in Table 13–6 is helpful. Rank-order the n differences as shown. Then fill in the average values in the upper part of the resulting matrix. A search is then made for the $(W + 1)$th smallest and the $(W + 1)$th largest difference.

EXAMPLE 13–6.1. For the data of Table 13–1, the $\frac{1}{2}(d^{(i)} + d^{(i')})$ are as shown in Table 13–6. This table is found by rank ordering the d_i values across the top and left-hand margins of the table. The entries to the table are found by averaging the intersecting row and column d_i's, being sure to include the diagonal elements. The number of positive averages is given by $T_{(+)} = 24$ and the number of negative averages is equal to $T_{(-)} = 4$. For $\alpha \leq 0.05$, the decision rule is to reject H_0 if $T_{(+)} \leq 2$ or if $T_{(+)} \geq 26$. Since $T_{(+)} = 24$, the hypothesis of identical distributions is not rejected. Since the lower critical value of $W = 2$, the $(W + 1) = 3$rd smallest and $(W + 1) = 3$rd largest differences are found to be -2 and 11, respectively. Thus, the

TABLE 13–6. Computations leading to the $(1 - \alpha)\%$ confidence interval for the median difference in the population characteristics of the data of Table 13–1.

Values of d_i	−5	−2	4	8	10	11	12
−5	−5	−3.5	−0.5	1.5	2.5	3	3.5
−2		−2	1	3	4	4.5	5
4			4	6	7	7.5	8
8				8	9	9.5	10
10					10	10.5	11
11						11	11.5
12							12

$(1 - \alpha) \geq 0.95$ confidence interval for M_d is:

$$-2 \leq M_d \leq 11$$

Note that this interval covers zero, as it should, since H_0 is not rejected. Also, it is narrower than that obtained with the sign test model.

It should be noted that the confidence interval generated is for the median difference and not the difference in the medians or the difference in the means or mean difference. Of course, these measures are all equal if the null hypothesis of identical distributions is true; otherwise, they will differ from one another to some degree.

EXAMPLE 13–6.2. For the data of Table 13–1, differences in population centers are estimated by the following numerical values:

Measure of difference	Value
1. Median difference	$\hat{M}_d = 8$
2. Difference in medians	$\hat{M}_E - \hat{M}_C = 48 - 38 = 10$
3. Difference in means	$\bar{X}_E - \bar{X}_C = 47.9 - 42.4 = 5.5$
4. Mean difference	$\bar{d} = 5.5$

Note that $\hat{M}_d \neq \hat{M}_E - \hat{M}_C$, although it is true that $\bar{d} = \bar{X}_E - \bar{X}_C$.

13–7. Hodges–Lehmann Estimate of the Median Difference

None of the estimators of Example 13–6.2 is associated with the Wilcoxon matched-pair test. $\hat{M}_d = 8$ is the estimator of the median difference associated with the sign test. Hodges and Lehmann (1963) have shown that the estimator of the median difference is defined as the median value of the $\bar{d}$ generated for the Tukey confidence-interval procedure. If the number of $\bar{d}$ values is odd, the median difference is estimated as the median $\bar{d}$, but if the number of $\bar{d}$ is even, it is estimated as the average of the two middle values.

EXAMPLE 13–7.1. For the data of Table 13–1, the number of $\bar{d}$ values is equal to 28. Thus, the median difference is estimated as:

$$\hat{M}_d = \frac{\bar{d}^{(14)} + \bar{d}^{(15)}}{2}$$

As is seen in Table 13–6, $\bar{d}^{(14)} = 5$, and $\bar{d}^{(15)} = 6$, so that:

$$\hat{M}_d = \frac{5 + 6}{2} = 5.5$$

13–8. Large-Sample Approximation for the Wilcoxon Matched-Pair Test

Since the Wilcoxon matched-pair statistic consists of the sum of the signed ranks, it may be denoted as:

$$T_{(+)} = 1W_1 + 2W_2 + \ldots + rW_r + \ldots + nW_n$$

Nonparametric
One- and Two-
Sample Tests for
Repeated
Measures and
Matched Samples

337

where W_r is a Bernoulli variable that equals 1 if $X_{iE} > X_{iC}$ and 0 if $X_{iE} < X_{iC}$. The coefficients $1, 2, \ldots, r, \ldots, n$ of W_r are the respective ranks. Under the null hypothesis of identity or symmetry,

1. $P(W_r = 1) = P(W_r = 0) = \dfrac{1}{2}$

so that:

2. $E(W_r) = \displaystyle\sum_{w_r} W_r P(W_r) = (1)\left(\dfrac{1}{2}\right) + (0)\left(\dfrac{1}{2}\right) = \dfrac{1}{2}$

3. $\text{Var}(W_r) = E(W_r^2) - E^2(W_r) = \displaystyle\sum_{w_r} W_r^2 P(W_r) - \left(\dfrac{1}{2}\right)^2$

$$= \left[(1^2)\left(\dfrac{1}{2}\right) + (0^2)\left(\dfrac{1}{2}\right)\right] - \left(\dfrac{1}{2}\right)^2 = \dfrac{1}{4}$$

Since it is known that:

4. $\displaystyle\sum_{i=1}^{n} r_i = 1 + 2 + \ldots + n = \dfrac{n(n + 1)}{2}$

and

5. $\displaystyle\sum_{i=1}^{n} r_i^2 = 1^2 + 2^2 + \ldots + n^2 = \dfrac{n(n + 1)(2n + 1)}{6}$

it follows that

6. $E(T_{(+)}) = \displaystyle\sum_{r} rE(W_r) = \sum_{r} r\left(\dfrac{1}{2}\right) = \left(\dfrac{1}{2}\right)\sum_{r} r$

$$= \left(\dfrac{1}{2}\right)\dfrac{n(n + 1)}{2} = \dfrac{n(n + 1)}{4}$$

and

7. $\text{Var}(T_{(+)}) = \displaystyle\sum_{r} r^2 \text{Var}(W_r) = \sum_{r} r^2\left(\dfrac{1}{4}\right) = \left(\dfrac{1}{4}\right)\sum_{r} r^2$

$$= \left(\dfrac{1}{4}\right)\dfrac{n(n + 1)(2n + 1)}{6}$$

$$= \dfrac{n(n + 1)(2n + 1)}{24}$$

For large samples, the null distribution of:

$$Z = \dfrac{T_{(+)} - E(T_{(+)})}{\sqrt{\text{Var}(T_{(+)})}} = \dfrac{T_{(+)} - [n(n + 1)/4]}{\sqrt{n(n + 1)(2n + 1)/24}}$$

approaches the standard normal distribution. The statistic, with or without correction for continuity, can be used to test the hypothesis of equal centers or identical distributions. Illustration of the large-sample approximation to the Wilcoxon test

TABLE 13–7. *Wilcoxon test of no difference in sample and population distribution of sex as measured by percent male in 28 sampled census tracts.*

Census tract	Percent male in sample	Percent male in census	Difference	Sign of difference	Signed rank of difference
1A	35.0	49.6	−14.6	−	−28
1B	37.0	50.7	−13.7	−	−27
2A	46.2	46.7	−0.5	−	−2
2B	52.9	45.9	7.0	+	20
2C	48.6	45.6	3.0	+	12
2D	37.5	46.5	−9.0	−	−22
3A	51.2	47.1	4.1	+	15
3B	54.8	45.3	9.5	+	23.5
3C	38.0	41.9	−3.9	−	−14
3D	40.9	40.2	0.7	+	4
3E	45.0	43.4	1.6	+	6.5
4A	50.0	47.2	2.8	+	11
4B	50.0	46.4	3.6	+	13
4C	45.9	45.3	0.6	+	3
4D	50.0	48.0	2.0	+	9
4E	45.5	47.3	−1.8	−	−8
5A	41.2	53.3	−12.1	−	−26
5BA	55.6	53.0	2.6	+	10
5BB	40.0	50.8	−10.8	−	−25
5BC	50.0	49.6	0.4	+	1
5C	42.2	46.4	−4.2	−	−16
5D	38.2	42.9	−4.7	−	−18
5E	41.9	46.3	−4.4	−	−17
6A	52.2	45.9	6.3	+	19
6B	37.8	45.2	−7.4	−	−21
6C	45.0	45.8	−0.8	−	−5
6D	54.8	45.3	9.5	+	23.5
6E	41.7	43.3	−1.6	−	−6.5

is given for the data of Table 13–7. If the data have a large number of tied values, a correction for ties is recommended. For this test, $\text{Var}(T_{(+)})$ is replaced with:

$$\text{Var}(T_{(+)}) = \frac{n(n+1)(2n+1)}{24} - \frac{1}{48}\sum_{s=1}^{S} t_s(t_s - 1)(t_s + 1)$$

where t_s = number of observations tied at a specific value.

EXAMPLE 13–8.1. In a survey of attitudes toward *de facto* school segregation conducted in Berkeley, California, census tracts were used as the sampling strata. In order to test for sampling bias, a number of comparisons were made between sample results and census data for the same census tracts. The data comparing the sex distribution of the survey informants with the corresponding distribution reported for the 1960 census are given.

The investigator was interested in determining whether the sampled population and the census population were identical with respect to sex distribution in the various census tracts. Ties were broken by assigning midranks to the tied difference scores. The hypothesis to be tested is one of identity of the sampled population and the census population with respect to the percentage of males. For these data:

$$T_{(+)} = 170.5$$

$$E(T_{(+)}) = \frac{n(n+1)}{4} = \frac{28(28+1)}{4} = 203$$

$$\text{Var}(T_{(+)}) = \frac{n(n+1)(2n+1)}{24} = \frac{28(28+1)[2(28)+1]}{24} = 1928.5$$

Making a correction for continuity, we find

$$Z = \frac{(170.5 + 0.5) - 203}{\sqrt{1928.5}} = \frac{171 - 203}{43.91} = -0.73$$

and the hypothesis of identity of the distributions is retained.

13–9. One-Sample Test for the Median

Given n observations from a symmetric population, the Wilcoxon matched-pair test can be used to test whether the population has a median equal to some specified value. The procedure is identical to the one just described except that the difference scores are formed by subtracting the hypothesized value of the median from each of the n sample observations. An illustration of the use of the Wilcoxon statistic to test the hypothesis that the population median is some specified value appears in Table 13–8.

EXAMPLE 13–9.1. The median number of correct responses on a 30-item recall task was 15 items when high-school students were tested. The words used in the recall task bore no apparent relationship to each other. An investigator

TABLE 13–8. Number of correct words recalled by 10 high-school students as compared to a median number of 15 words.

Number correct	Number correct minus median	Signed rank of difference
13	−2	−2
14	−1	−1
20	5	4
28	13	9
21	6	5
24	9	8
23	8	7
11	−4	−3
29	14	10
22	7	6

interested in the effect of categorization of words on their recall used a similar list containing related words scattered at random throughout the list. The scores reported are the number of words recalled on the 30-item list of related words by a random sample of 10 high-school students. The hypothesis to be tested is that the median number of words correctly recalled from the list of partially related words is 15.

The two-tailed $\alpha \leq 0.05$ rejection rule for the test of the hypothesis that the median equals 15 is read from Table A–21 as:

$$\text{D.R.: Reject } H_0 \text{ if } T_{(+)} \leq 8 \quad \text{or} \quad \text{if } T_{(+)} \geq 47$$

For the rank data of Table 13–8, $T_{(+)} = 4 + 9 + 5 + 8 + 7 + 10 + 6 = 49$. Since $T_{(+)} = 49$ is in the critical region, the null hypothesis is rejected at $\alpha \leq 0.05$.

It may be of interest to the investigator to estimate the median of the population as it would be of interest to estimate the population mean in the parametric case. In addition, an interval estimate for the median, M, can be found by computing all $n(n + 1)/2$ averages of the paired scores and rank-ordering them. The interval estimate of M is bounded by the averages in the $(W + 1)$st position from either end of the distribution of averages, where W denotes the lower critical value of the Wilcoxon test. For this illustration, $W = 8$, so that the $(1 - \alpha)\%$ confidence interval for the median is bounded by the $(W + 1) = 9$th smallest value and the $n(n + 1)/2 - W = 47$th largest value of the averaged paired scores. Table 13–9 illustrates the computation required for determining the point and interval estimates for the median based on the data of Table 13–8. Ordered scores $X^{(i)}$ are reported in the margins; averaged pairs of scores, $\overline{X}^{(ii')} = \frac{1}{2}(X^{(i)} + X^{(i')})$, with $i \leq i'$, are reported in the body of the table. To compute an approximate 95% confidence interval for M, the population median, one reads from the table of $\frac{1}{2}(X^{(i)} + X^{(i')})$ the values that are the $(W + 1)$th largest and smallest. From this table the 9th and the 47th values are 16.5 and 25, respectively. Thus, $16.5 \leq M \leq 25$. It is not surprising that the interval estimate for M does not include the value $M = 15$, since the hypothesis of symmetry of the scores about $M = 15$ was rejected.

TABLE 13–9. Computations required to find the 95% confidence interval for the population median of data presented in Table 13–8.

i/i'	11	13	14	20	21	22	23	24	28	29
11	11	12	12.5	15.5	16	16.5	17	17.5	19.5	20
13		13	13.5	16.5	17	17.5	18	18.5	20.5	21
14			14	17	17.5	18	18.5	19	21	21.5
20				20	20.5	21	21.5	22	24	24.5
21					21	21.5	22	22.5	24.5	25
22						22	22.5	23	25	25.5
23							23	23.5	25.5	26
24								24	26	26.5
28									28	28.5
29										29

Nonparametric One- and Two-Sample Tests for Repeated Measures and Matched Samples

While the sign-test estimate of the median is defined as the sample median $\hat{M} = \frac{1}{2}(21 + 22) = 21.5$, the Wilcoxon estimate is defined as the median of the $\overline{X}^{(ii')}$. For the data of Table 13–8, $\hat{M} = \overline{X}^{(28)} = 21$.

The method used to set up the confidence interval for a median can also be used to test hypotheses about medians. This is illustrated in the following example.

EXAMPLE 13–9.2.   The hypothesis H_0: $M = 15$ can be tested by simply counting the number of average values in Table 13–9 that are less than 15. In this case, $T_{(-)} = 6$. Thus, since $W = 6 \leq 8$, the hypothesis is rejected at $\alpha \leq 0.05$. This decision agrees with that made in terms of the confidence-interval procedure and in the usual procedure for computing W.

13–10. Normal Scores in the Matched-Pair Problem

Positive normal scores, as described in Section 11–5, may be used in the same manner as the individual r_i are used in the Wilcoxon matched-pair test. This is illustrated for the Van der Waerden normal scores for the data of Table 13–10. In this case, only the positive normal scores enter the computation of the test statistic. Under this model:

$$T_{(+)} = W_1 Z_1 + W_2 Z_2 + \ldots + W_n Z_n$$

where $Z_1, Z_2, \ldots, Z_n$ are the absolute normal scores and where W_i is a Bernoulli variable with $W_i = 1$ if d_i is positive, $W_i = 0$ if d_i is negative, and

$$P(W_i = 1) = P(W_i = 0) = \tfrac{1}{2}, \quad \text{if } H_0 \text{ is true.}$$

Like the Wilcoxon statistic, the distribution of $T_{(-)}$ is identical to that of $T_{(+)}$. As expected, $T_{(+)}$ differs from $T_{(-)}$ by an interchange of the values that W_i can assume.

EXAMPLE 13–10.1.   For the data of Table 13–10, one considers only the positive normal scores. For n pairs, Table A–16 is entered with parameter $2n + 1 =$

TABLE 13–10. The Van der Waerden normal scores form of the matched-pair problem for the data of Table 13–1.

Value of d_i	Rank of $|d_i|$	$r_i/(n+1)$	Z_i
− 5	3	0.375	0.49
+ 4	2	0.250	0.32
+11	5	0.625	0.89
+12	7	0.875	1.53
− 2	1	0.125	0.16
+ 8	4	0.500	0.67
+10	6	0.750	1.15

$2(7) + 1 = 15$. With this parameter, the seven positive normal deviates are given by:

$$\{0.16, 0.32, 0.49, 0.67, 0.89, 1.15, 1.53\}$$

Then

$$T_{(+)} = W_1 Z_1 + W_2 Z_2 + \ldots + W_n Z_n$$
$$= 0.16 W_1 + 0.32 W_2 + 0.49 W_3 + 0.67 W_4 + 0.89 W_5 + 1.15 W_6 + 1.53 W_7$$

where W_i is a Bernoulli variable with $W_i = 1$ if d_i is positive, $W_i = 0$ if d_i is negative, and

$$P(W_i = 1) = P(W_i = 0) = \tfrac{1}{2}, \quad \text{if } H_0 \text{ is true.}$$

For $\alpha = 0.05$, $T = N\alpha = (2^7)(0.05) = 6$, rounded down to the nearest integer. For a one-tailed alternative, the six largest values of the Wilcoxon-type sum must be examined. Under this model, the six most extreme values are as reported in Table 13–11. The observed total is given by:

$$T_{(+)} = 0.32 + 0.67 + 0.89 + 1.15 + 1.53 = 4.56$$

Since this value is in the rejection region of the test, the hypothesis of identical distributions is rejected.

The complete distributions of 128 positive normal-score values are summarized in Figure 13–3. The distribution of $T_{(+)}$ is symmetric and has the usual bell-shaped form. As n increases, the approximation to the normal distribution improves.

The large-sample form of the test in terms of $T_{(+)}$ is given by the normal-curve statistic:

$$Z = \frac{T_{(+)} - E(T_{(+)})}{\sqrt{\text{Var}(T_{(+)})}}$$

Since $E(W_i) = \tfrac{1}{2}$ and $\text{Var}(W_i) = \tfrac{1}{4}$:

$$E(T_{(+)}) = \sum_{i=1}^{n} Z_i E(W_i) = \sum_{i=1}^{n} Z_i \left(\frac{1}{2}\right) = \left(\frac{1}{2}\right) \sum_{i=1}^{n} Z_i$$

TABLE 13–11. *The one-sided rejection region for testing that the location parameter of the experimental group is larger than the location parameter of the control group for the data of Table 13–1.*

Value of the absolute-normal scores

	0.16	0.32	0.49	0.67	0.89	1.15	1.53	$T_{(+)}$
Algebraic	+	+	+	+	+	+	+	5.21
sign	−	+	+	+	+	+	+	5.05
of	+	−	+	+	+	+	+	4.89
the	−	−	+	+	+	+	+	4.73
difference	+	+	−	+	+	+	+	4.72
	−	+	−	+	+	+	+	4.56

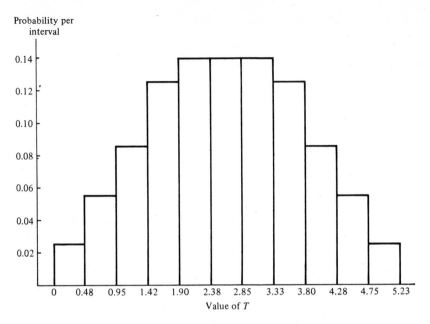

Probability per interval

Value of T

FIGURE 13–3. *The sampling distribution of the absolute normal order statistic for the matched-pair problem with n = 7.*

and

$$\text{Var}(T_{(+)}) = \sum_{i=1}^{n} Z_i^2 \text{ Var}(W_i) = \sum_{i=1}^{n} Z_i^2 \left(\frac{1}{4}\right) = \left(\frac{1}{4}\right) \sum_{i=1}^{n} Z_i^2$$

EXAMPLE 13–10.2. For the data of Table 13–10:

$$T_{(+)} = 0.32 + 0.89 + 1.53 + 0.67 + 1.15 = 4.56$$

$$E(T_{(+)}) = \frac{1}{2}\Sigma Z_i = \frac{1}{2}(5.21) = 2.605$$

and

$$\text{Var}(T_{(+)}) = \frac{1}{4}\Sigma Z_i^2 = \frac{1}{4}(5.2725) = 1.3181$$

so that:

$$Z = \frac{4.56 - 2.605}{\sqrt{1.3181}} = \frac{1.955}{1.148} = 1.70$$

Thus, the hypothesis of identical distributions is rejected since $Z = 1.70 > 1.645$, the 95th percentile of the standard normal variable. In terms of $T_{(-)} = 0.16 + 0.49 = 0.65$:

$$Z = \frac{T_{(-)} - E(T_{(-)})}{\sqrt{\text{Var}(T_{(-)})}} = \frac{0.65 - 2.605}{\sqrt{1.3181}} = -1.70$$

13–11. Power Comparisons of the Matched-Pair Tests

Four different nonparametric tests, the sign test, the Fisher randomization t test, the Wilcoxon test, and the normal-scores test, have been presented to test the hypothesis that two different distributions are identical or that the median value of a single population is equal to some specified value. With so many tests it is easy to understand why the behavioral scientist prefers to use the matched-pair t test in all cases. If the assumptions for the t test are valid, then indeed the t test ought to be preferred. In addition to familiarity, it is easy to explain to others. However, power comparisons indicate that the tests of this chapter should not be excluded, since in some cases, their power matches or exceeds that of the classical t test. On the home ground of the matched-pair t test, the asymptotic efficiencies are given by $E = 2/\pi = 0.637$ for the sign test, $E = 3/\pi = 0.955$ for the Wilcoxon test, $E = 1.000$ for the Fisher test, and $E = 1.000$ for the Van der Waerden test.

Of these tests, only the sign test is decidedly lower in power, and when normality is satisfied, it is not recommended. When the underlying variable has a double-exponential form, the sign test is preferred since in that special case the efficiency of the sign test to the matched-pair t test is given by $E = 2$. An example of a double-exponential distribution is shown in Figure 4–7. Distributions of this sort may seem rare in behavioral research, and the efficiency statement comparing the sign test to the t test in this case may appear to be of academic interest only. However, such is not the case; extreme peakedness is sometimes encountered. If a distribution tends to be peaked with relatively heavy and long tails, it is conceivable that the sign test will be more powerful than the matched-pair t test and is preferable to it.

When normality is not satisfied, the sign test may still turn out to be the best test. For Examples 3–11.1 and 3–13.1, it is the best test, since no measurements are available on some of the test subjects. It is also the only test, and therefore the best test, when only the direction of the difference is known. In this case, the Fisher test based on permutations of the measured observations cannot be performed, nor can the data be ranked for the Wilcoxon or normal-scores tests. When no other test is possible, it is reasonable to assume that the sign test is possible in most cases.

When measurements are taken on all sample members, then the Fisher test is highly recommended. In all cases, its efficiency equals or exceeds 1, relative to other tests, since its critical region is the most powerful one for the hypothesis under test. Although it is an excellent statistical test, the computations required for its use are prohibitive, unless it has been programmed for a high-speed electronic computer. Perhaps the main reason this test has not gained much acceptance by behavioral scientists is that the critical values change under repeated applications of the test, even under identical conditions with equal sample sizes.

It is quite surprising that a test that replaces measurement with ranking should possess properties that make it a near-ideal test, and this is exactly what can be said for the Wilcoxon matched-pair test. The loss in power from 1 to 0.955 when normality holds is negligible and suggests that the Wilcoxon test be used frequently. This is especially true when it is noted that the asymptotic relative efficiency of the Wilcoxon test never falls below $E = 108/125 = 0.864$. Thus, if a researcher plans to perform a matched-pair t test with $n = 10$ subjects, he is relatively likely to equal the power of the t test or even exceed it by using $n' = n/0.864 = 10/0.864 = 11.57 = 12$ subjects and not worry about the assumption of normality. For distributions that show considerable flatness, the Wilcoxon test is suggested. If the distribution of the differences is uniform, and therefore extremely flat, the asymptotic efficiency of the Wilcoxon test to the t test is given by $E = 1.000$. For extreme peakedness, as represented by the double exponential, $E = 1.5$. However, since the efficiency for the sign test is, in this case, given by $E = 2$, the sign test would be preferred for extreme peakedness.

Finally, the normal-scores test is also recommended, even though it requires more computation than the Wilcoxon test. In all cases the asymptotic efficiency of this test to the matched-pair t test has as its lower bound $E = 1.000$.

The conclusion that may be drawn from this discussion is that the matched-pair t test can be disregarded by a researcher who has data that are clearly not normal. If a researcher is not afraid of arithmetic, then the Fisher test or the Van der Waerden test is best, but if the simplest test is desired, then use of the Wilcoxon test is not harmful. If H_0 is rejected, confidence intervals can be determined and the study can be evaluated for the strength and importance of the findings in exactly the same manner a researcher would use in the parametric case.

13–12. The Wilcoxon Matched-Pair Test for Determining whether the Slope of a Regression Line Is Different from Zero

The Wilcoxon matched-pair test can be used to determine whether or not the slope of a regression line is significantly different from zero or from any pre-assigned value without having to assume normality of errors. To perform the test, a researcher obtains n independent estimates of β, the slope of the regression line, and then applies the Wilcoxon matched-pair test to the n deviations, $d_i = \beta_i - \beta_0$, where β_0 is the hypothesis value.

The method is based on forming n estimates of the beta weight from $2n$ observations. The n estimates are made from points that are far apart in Euclidian distance, since it is known that such estimates tend to be more stable than estimates based on observations that are close together. If (x_1, y_1) and (x_2, y_2) are two points on the line $Y = \alpha + \beta x$, then the slope is defined as:

$$\beta = \frac{y_2 - y_1}{x_2 - x_1}$$

The test is illustrated in the following example.

EXAMPLE 13–12.1. Consider the regression of X_s (arithmetic computation score) on X_1 (mental age) for the data reported for Exercise 10 of Chapter 10 and for which it is expected that $\beta > 0$. The scores have been rank-ordered on the basis of mental age and are as reported in Table 13–12. Since there are 36 sets of values, 18 estimates of β can be obtained by pairing set 1 with set 19, set 2 with set

TABLE 13–12. Test of $\beta = 0$ for the regression of X_5 (arithmetic computation score) on X_1 (mental age) for the data of Exercise 10 in Chapter 10.

First half		Second half		Beta weights	Rank
X_1	X_5	X_1	X_5		
75	6				
		109	12	$\dfrac{12 - 6}{109 - 75} = 0.18$	9
76	2				
		112	15	$\dfrac{15 - 2}{112 - 76} = 0.36$	17
82	13				
		112	13	$\dfrac{13 - 13}{112 - 82} = 0.00$	1.5
83	9				
		112	14	$\dfrac{14 - 9}{112 - 83} = 0.17$	7.5
84	7				
		112	14	$\dfrac{14 - 7}{112 - 84} = 0.25$	13.5
85	8				
		113	15	$\dfrac{15 - 8}{113 - 85} = 0.25$	13.5
85	12				
		114	14	$\dfrac{14 - 12}{114 - 85} = 0.07$	4
85	1				
		115	9	$\dfrac{9 - 1}{115 - 85} = 0.28$	15
90	10				
		115	15	$\dfrac{15 - 10}{115 - 90} = 0.20$	10.5
92	10				
		116	15	$\dfrac{15 - 10}{116 - 92} = 0.21$	12
96	9				
		117	12	$\dfrac{12 - 9}{117 - 96} = 0.13$	5.5
97	6				
		118	14	$\dfrac{14 - 6}{118 - 97} = 0.38$	18
99	11				
		120	5	$\dfrac{5 - 11}{120 - 99} = -0.29$	16
99	15				
		122	12	$\dfrac{12 - 15}{122 - 99} = -0.13$	5.5
101	14				
		128	14	$\dfrac{14 - 14}{128 - 101} = 0.00$	1.5
101	10				
		130	15	$\dfrac{15 - 10}{130 - 101} = 0.17$	7.5
106	15				
		131	12	$\dfrac{12 - 15}{131 - 106} = -0.12$	3
107	10				
		132	15	$\dfrac{15 - 10}{132 - 107} = 0.20$	10.5

20, ..., and set 18 with set 36. The pairings and the resulting estimated beta weights are reported in Table 13–12, along with the rank values. Treating one of the 0.00 values as a negative deviation:

$$T_{(+)} = 1.5(0) + 1.5(1) + 3(0) + 4(1) + \ldots + 18(1) = 145$$

Under the large-sample model:

$$E(T_{(+)}) = \frac{n(n + 1)}{4} = \frac{18(19)}{4} = 85.5$$

Nonparametric
One- and Two-
Sample Tests for
Repeated
Measures and
Matched Samples

347

and

$$\text{Var}(T_{(+)}) = \frac{n(n+1)(2n+1)}{24} = \frac{18(19)(37)}{24} = 527.25$$

With a correction for continuity:

$$Z = \frac{\left[T_{(+)} - \frac{1}{2}\right] - E(T_{(+)})}{\sqrt{\text{Var}(T_{(+)})}} = \frac{(145 - 0.5) - 85.5}{\sqrt{527.25}} = 2.57$$

Since $Z = 2.57 > 1.645$, the upper 95% of the $N(0, 1)$ distribution, the hypothesis of zero slope is rejected.

13–13. Point and Interval Estimate of the Slope of a Regression Line

Point estimates and interval estimates of the slope of a regression line are determined according to the model of Section 13–6, which can be used to test $H_0:\beta = 0$ against the alternative $H_1:\beta \neq 0$. The method will be illustrated for the data for the males of Table 11–19.

EXAMPLE 13–13.1. Under the model of Section 13–6, the data matrix for determining the point and interval estimates of β is as shown in Table 13–13. Since the number of average $\overline{\beta}$ values is given by $9\,(10)/2 = 45$, the point estimate of the slope is:

$$\hat{\beta} = \overline{\beta}^{(23)} = 0.195$$

The lower and upper limits are read from Table A–21 as:

$$\overline{\beta}_L = \overline{\beta}^{(T_L + 1)} = \overline{\beta}^{(5 + 1)} = \overline{\beta}^{(6)} = 0.07$$

and

$$\overline{\beta}_U = \overline{\beta}^{(T_U)} = \overline{\beta}^{(40)} = 0.31$$

TABLE 13–13. Data matrix to determine the median beta and 95% confidence interval for beta for the males of Table 11–19.

β_M	−0.04	0.03	0.07	0.19	0.21	0.24	0.24	0.25	0.43
−0.04	−0.04	−0.005	0.015	0.075	0.085	0.10	0.10	0.105	0.195
0.03		0.03	0.05	0.11	0.12	0.135	0.135	0.14	0.23
0.07			0.07	0.13	0.14	0.155	0.155	0.16	0.25
0.19				0.19	0.20	0.215	0.215	0.22	0.31
0.21					0.21	0.225	0.225	0.23	0.32
0.24						0.24	0.24	0.245	0.335
0.24							0.24	0.245	0.335
0.25								0.25	0.34
0.43									0.43

so that the approximate 95% confidence interval for β is given by:

$$0.07 \leq \beta \leq 0.31$$

Since zero is not in the interval, it is concluded that β is significantly different from zero. It should be noted that the assumptions for this model are that the regression is linear and observations are independent. Normality is not required, nor is the assumption of homoscedasticity absolutely essential. Departures from these assumptions can be tolerated.

Finally, it is worth noting that time-series data can be evaluated with this model. Since data collected over time entail a correlation between neighboring observations, a simple modification is required to satisfy the independence between observations. To reduce or eliminate the effects of the correlation, list the observations in the first half of the time series in their observed temporal order. Next, pair the observations in the second half of the time series to those of the first half by a random assignment based on a table of random numbers. Finally, perform the matched-pair Wilcoxon test on the estimated slopes, as illustrated in Example 13–12.1.

Summary

This chapter began with a discussion of the Fisher randomization test for matched-pair designs, which serves as a powerful competitor to the sign test. If ranks are assigned to the paired differences, another test with greater statistical power than the sign test is generated. This test is called the Wilcoxon matched-pair test and is used to test the hypothesis of identical distribution against the alternative hypothesis that the two distributions have different centers. This test is important since its minimum efficiency exceeds 0.864 and its efficiency equals 0.955 when the underlying variable is normally distributed.

The Wilcoxon statistic is usually defined as the sum of the ranks assigned to the positive deviations. Under this form Table A–21 can be used to test for identity of distributions. If n is large, a normal-curve approximation is available with:

$$Z = \frac{T_{(+)} - E(T_{(+)})}{\sqrt{\mathrm{Var}(T_{(+)})}}$$

where

$$E(T_{(+)}) = \frac{n(n + 1)}{4}$$

and

$$\mathrm{Var}(T_{(+)}) = \frac{n(n + 1)(2n + 1)}{24}$$

On the basis of the Wilcoxon model, Tukey proposed a procedure for obtaining a confidence interval for the median difference between two populations. This interval is found by rank-ordering the paired differences and then computing all $n(n + 1)/2$ averages of the paired differences. These averages are then rank-

Nonparametric
One- and Two-
Sample Tests for
Repeated
Measures and
Matched Samples

349

ordered and the endpoints of the confidence interval are read simply as the $(W + 1)$th ordered observations from the extremes of the ordered values. The value of W is read directly from Table A–21.

The Wilcoxon distribution can also be used to obtain a confidence interval for a population median. This interval is obtained by computing all averages of the paired observations and then rank-ordering them. The endpoints of the interval are defined by the $(W + 1)$th ordered observations from either end of the ordered averages. The midaverage is an estimate of the median population difference.

Finally, the Wilcoxon test can be strengthened by substituting normal scores for ranks. This procedure generates a test that has greater power but for which confidence intervals on the original metric are not available.

Exercises

*1. Generate the distribution of the Wilcoxon matched-pair statistic for $n = 5$ and $n = 6$. Compare these distributions graphically to the ones generated by $n = 4$ and $n = 7$ and represented in Table 13–4 and Figure 13–2.

*2. Analyze the data of Table 3–5 by means of the Wilcoxon matched-pair test and normal-scores test of the Van der Waerden form. Compare the results to those obtained for the sign test. Explain what the comparison means.

*3. Find the 95% two-tailed confidence interval for the median difference for the data of Table 3–5 under the Wilcoxon matched-pair model. Compare this interval to the one obtained under the sign test model. Which procedure is more powerful? Why?

*4. Estimate the median difference for the data of Exercise 4 of Chapter 3 under the Wilcoxon matched-pair model. Compare it to the estimate obtained under the sign test model. Which estimate do you prefer? Why?

*5. Answer the questions of Exercises 5 and 6 of Chapter 3 with the methods of this chapter.

*6. Analyze the data of Exercise 4 of Chapter 3 in terms of the Van der Waerden normal-scores model.

*7. Apply the Van der Waerden normal-scores model to the data of Exercise 10 of Chapter 3.

*8. Use the large-sample form of the Wilcoxon matched-pair test to analyze the data of Exercises 14 and 15 of Chapter 3.

*9. Use the Wilcoxon matched-pair test to analyze the data of Exercise 11 of Chapter 3. How do you justify the use of this test in this case? Compare the results of the Cox–Stuart test to that obtained under the Wilcoxon matched-pair test.

*10. Apply the Wilcoxon matched-pair test to the solution of the problem of Exercise 13 in Chapter 3 and compare the two solutions. Which would you recommend? Why?

*11. Estimate the slope of the regression line for the females of Table 11–19. Also, find the 95% confidence interval for β_F.

*12. Estimate the slopes of the regression lines for the old and new methods of Exercise

10 of Chapter 10 for X_3 regressed on X_1. Also, determine the two 97.5% confidence intervals for β_{Old} and β_{New}.

*13. The study reported in Table 13–1 was repeated the following year with 14 new students who were randomly assigned to the control and experimental conditions by a matching on IQ scores. The difference scores were as follows:

$$\{-4, -4, 1, 7, 12, 13, 14\}.$$

Notice that two differences are tied at -4.

a) Find the one-tailed decision rule for the Fisher test. What is the decision?
b) Repeat (a) for the Wilcoxon test.
c) Repeat (a) for the normal-scores test.
d) What effects do tied values have on the numbers of outcomes that define the critical region?

*14. Find the one-tailed confidence interval for β for the data of Table 13–13 where it is believed that $\beta > 0$.

*15. Many studies in psychology and education are based on repeated observations on one subject. One such study is called an A–B design. During the first set of trials, the subject is watched to determine how long he stays on the target task. Then a treatment

Session number	Base-line data	Session number	Training data
One	5.1	Five	1.6
	3.2		1.7
	3.6		3.2
	2.0		1.9
	1.1		3.5
	0.9		3.7
Two	1.4	Six	1.8
	1.6		3.8
	2.0		4.9
	1.1		4.6
	0.8		4.1
	0.7		4.0
Three	2.3	Seven	2.2
	2.1		3.8
	0.9		4.2
	1.6		4.0
	3.1		2.6
	1.9		1.1
Four	1.2	Eight	3.8
	1.2		4.7
	0.1		4.6
	0.6		4.2
	1.7		4.4
	0.9		1.9

Nonparametric One- and Two- Sample Tests for Repeated Measures and Matched Samples

is instituted and the observations are repeated. In training students to use a talking typewriter in the learning of arithmetic, it was noted that subjects failed to attend to the task after a few minutes of exposure. It was decided to institute some behavior-modification principles to induce attention. The conditioning process was performed by a teacher who, at five-minute intervals, asked the subject how he or she was doing with the exercise. Data were observed over five-minute intervals as to the amount of time spent on target. Each typewriter session lasted 30 minutes, so that six observations were obtained at a session. Results are shown in the accompanying table for eight sessions, the first four constituting the base line period, and the last four the training period. Use the methods of Section 13–12 to analyze these data. What is the hypothesis? Are the assumptions satisfied? Explain what you mean.

16. The Bowker test of Section 7–5 is a repeated-measures test for unordered qualitative variables. If it is used for ordered qualitative variables, information concerning directional shifts is ignored or discarded. Consider the following set of data generated from the two questions observed before and after a school integration program was instituted.

<table>
<tr><td></td><td colspan="4" align="center">After</td></tr>
<tr><td>Before</td><td>1. Separate</td><td>2. No effect</td><td>3. Bring together</td><td>Total</td></tr>
<tr><td>1. Separate</td><td>3</td><td>12</td><td>26</td><td>41</td></tr>
<tr><td>2. No effect</td><td>2</td><td>25</td><td>12</td><td>39</td></tr>
<tr><td>3. Bring together</td><td>6</td><td>15</td><td>40</td><td>61</td></tr>
<tr><td>Total</td><td>11</td><td>52</td><td>78</td><td>141</td></tr>
</table>

1. When the school integration program began, I thought it would:
   a) separate   b) have no effect on   c) bring together
   students of different races.
2. Now, after 5 years in the program, I think it
   a) separated   b) had no effect   c) brought together
   students of different races.
   The results for 141 students are as shown in the accompanying table.
a) Analyze the data in terms of the Bowker test.
b) Analyze the data in terms of the Wilcoxon matched-pair test. Assign index scores

Difference scores	Frequency
−2	6
−1	17
0	68
1	24
2	26
Total	141

*This model has been suggested by Dr. Joel Levin of the University of Wisconsin at Madison.

of {1, 2, 3} to the response categories {separate, no effect, bring together} and set up the resulting frequency table. Use midranks to break ties. For the six people with difference scores of -2, the midrank value is 3.5.

Since there are so many tied values, a correction for ties is mandatory.

c) What are the hypotheses for (a) and (b)?
d) What are the assumptions for (a) and (b)?
e) Which method would you recommend? Why?

Nonparametric Tests for Repeated Measures and Matched Samples for Multiple Samples: The Friedman Model

14–1. The K-Matched-Sample Problem

Under normal distribution theory, the matched-pair problem extends to a general randomized block model or a repeated-measures design. Under these models, it is assumed that the underlying variables are normal with common variance and common correlation coefficient between the treatments or conditions of the study. The usual test statistic for testing $H_0 : \mu_1 = \mu_2 = \ldots = \mu_K$ is F.

If normality, common variance, or equal correlation coefficients cannot be assumed, then one of the three nonparametric tests to be presented in this chapter can be considered. These tests are straightforward extensions of the sign test, the Wilcoxon matched-pair test, and the normal-scores test, as illustrated in the Van der Waerden form only. The first of these extensions is the Friedman test or two-way analysis of variance in ranks (Friedman, 1937). The other two tests are nameless and might be called simply the multiple Wilcoxon test and the normal-scores K-matched-sample test. As will be seen, none of these tests is difficult to perform and none is sensitive to non-normality, unequal variances, and inequality of correlation coefficients.

As a passing note, it should be reported that the exact Fisher randomization or permutation test can be performed in much the same manner as the classical F test. If n is large, it is possible to show that the null distribution of the classical F test is *essentially* distribution-free. This extension has been investigated in great detail by Scheffé (1959) for the randomized block design. As might be expected, the one-factor analysis-of-variance discussion is valid even in the K-matched-sample model. However, if n is small, then the reliance upon the F distribution is not meaningful, and the small-sample performance of the Fisher test becomes excessively difficult to obtain. For these reasons, the three tests presented in this chapter are of practical value.

14–2. The Friedman Test

The most frequently performed nonparametric matched-sample test is the Friedman test. In its simplest form, the test is applied to data generated by a study in which a group of n subjects are given K wines, colas, cigarettes, statements, movies, persons, and so on, and are asked to rank the K elements in order of increasing preference or degree of attribute. They are told to assign a rank of 1 to the lowest or least-preferred element of the set, and a rank of K to the largest or most-preferred element of the set. Thus, if a subject is given 5 wines $\{W_A, W_B, W_C, W_D, W_E\}$ to rank according to bouquet, he might think that W_E has the best bouquet, while W_B has the worst, with W_A being second worst, W_D occupying a middle position, and W_C being second-to-best in bouquet. As a result, he would rank the wines $\{2, 1, 4, 3, 5\}$. If there is agreement between the tasters, then it would be reasonable to assume that the average ranks assigned to the wines will show certain ordered patterns, indicating that one or more wines are best or preferred. This decision would be made if the hypothesis $H_0: E(\overline{R}_1) = E(\overline{R}_2) = E(\overline{R}_3) = E(\overline{R}_4) = E(\overline{R}_5)$ were to be rejected, where $E(\overline{R}_k)$ is the expected rank assigned to the kth wine. Under the hypothesis of no difference, $E(\overline{R}_k) = \frac{1}{5}(1 + 2 + 3 + 4 + 5) = 3$.

EXAMPLE 14–2.1. The results of a testing, by four wine-testing experts, of three different California burgundies, from three different wineries, are presented in Table 14–1. Note that if there are no differences among the wines, each taster should give each wine a tied rank value of $\overline{R} = \frac{1}{3}(1 + 2 + 3) = 2$. Thus, across the four tasters, the average total rank should be given by $R = 4\overline{R} = 4(2) = 8$. The observed totals for the data of Table 14–1 are given by $R_A = 6$, $R_B = 6$, and $R_C = 12$. A statistic that measures the variance among the wines is given by:

$$S = (R_A - R)^2 + (R_B - R)^2 + (R_C - R)^2$$
$$= (6 - 8)^2 + (6 - 8)^2 + (12 - 8)^2 = 24$$

TABLE 14–1. *The rank ordering of three California burgundies by four wine experts.*

	Brand A	Brand B	Brand C
Tester 1	2	1	3
Tester 2	2	1	3
Tester 3	1	2	3
Tester 4	1	2	3

When there are no differences, each total is equal to $+8$, so that S is given by:

$$S = (8 - 8)^2 + (8 - 8)^2 + (8 - 8)^2 = 0$$

When there are maximum differences in the wines, the total ranked values can be any one of the six permutations (4, 8, 12), (4, 12, 8), (8, 4, 12), (8, 12, 4), (12, 4, 8), and (12, 8, 4), depending upon which wine is first, second, and third, in rated bouquet. For any of these maximal permutations:

$$S = (4 - 8)^2 + (8 - 8)^2 + (12 - 8)^2 = 32$$

This suggests that, if the distribution of S were to be known, then an $\alpha = 0.05$ decision

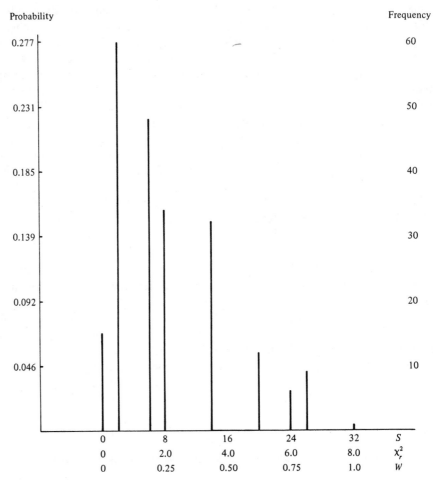

FIGURE 14–1.   Distribution of the Friedman statistic X_r^2, Kendall's S, and Kendall's coefficient of concordance W, for $K = 3$ and $n = 4$.

Scale of S, X_r^2, and W.[1]

[1] Definition of S: see Section 14–2.
  Definition of X_r^2: see Section 14–3.
  Definition of W: see Section 16–17.

rule could be determined for rejecting H_0. In this case, the distribution of S is easy to obtain.

For tester number one, the number of different possible assignments of ranks 1, 2, and 3 is given by $3! = 6$. This is also true for testers two, three, and four. Since they assign ranks independently, it is known, by the fundamental principle of counting, that the total number of different rank assignments is given by $(3!)(3!)$ $(3!)(3!) = 6^4 = 1296$. However, as we have seen, $3! = 6$ different permutations of any total configuration give rise to the same value for S. Thus, the number of really different permutations is given by

$$N = \frac{1296}{6} = 216, \quad \text{or by} \quad (3!)^{4-1}$$

In the general case of K wines and n testers, $N = (K!)^{n-1}$. Since large values of S are compatible with the rejection of H_0, an $\alpha = 0.05$ critical region consists of the $T = 0.05(216) = 10.8 \simeq 10$ most extreme assignments of ranks. However, if the rank assignments are made for all 216 permutations, it is seen that only nine can be used to define a critical region of size $\alpha \leq 0.05$. The entire distribution is shown in Figure 14–1. The $P[S \geq 26] = 9/216 = 0.042$. Thus, the $\alpha = 0.042$ decision rule for rejecting H_0 is given by:

D. R.: Reject H_0 if $S \geq 26$

For the observed data, $S = 24$. Thus, H_0 is not rejected, and it cannot be concluded that any one of the three wines has a better bouquet, at least as judged by the four testers of the study.

This development of the Friedman test was actually based upon Fisher's method of randomization, as applied to the block or subject ranks $\{1, 2, 3\}$. When $n \leq 4$ and $K \leq 4$, the sampling distribution of S is not too difficult to generate; but, as soon as n or K exceeds four, the arithmetic becomes excessive, and so a large-sample procedure is desired. This procedure is described in Section 14–3. Also, tables for $K = 3$ and $K = 4$ are described for the large-sample statistic when $n \leq 5$.

It should be noted that, if a judge could not rank-order two of the wines, he would normally be told to assign midranks to the two tied wines. In the general case, midrank assignments are preferred, since they tend to produce a conservative test of hypothesis, a point of view that has been adopted throughout this book for adjusting statistical tests.

14–3. The Friedman Test as a Substitute for the Classical F Test

As suggested by the two scales reported in Figure 14–1, the Friedman statistic as defined by S can be related to a chi-square statistic; and, as suggested by the skewness of the distribution of S, the association of S with X^2 might be expected. The test statistic as defined by Friedman is indeed related to chi-square, as will be shown in this section.

EXAMPLE 14–3.1. While the Friedman test is the best test available for treating data that have been ranked by a set of judges, it can also be used for data that have been measured, such as those shown in Table 14–2. These data are derived from a study in which ten girls taking a course in high-school business math were given a test to measure their recall of 7-digit numbers. The tests were given at the end of the 4th, 8th, 12th, and 16th week of the course. It was hypothesized that, with increased exposure to arithmetic and numbers during the taking of business math, digit-span memory would also increase. The results, along with the ranked data for each girl, are summarized in Table 14–2. Note that, by ranking the data within the girls, we have created a model similar to the wine-tasting study. In this case, the four scores correspond to a ranking of four wines in which a rank of 1 is associated, not with the best wine, but with the test score associated with the maximum number of errors. In addition, once the ranks are assigned, the mathematical models for the two different experimental situations become identical.

The null hypothesis for the digit-span experiment is that there are no systematic differences between testings on digit-span scores. To test this hypothesis, let K denote the number of testings on each subject or, more generally, the number of treatments observed in each block of a randomized block design. Let n denote the number of subjects or the number of blocks, if the data are generated in a randomized block design. Let each subject's K scores be ranked, and let the ranks be used to replace the original scores.

Let r_{ik} denote the rank for the ith subject under the kth treatment, and $R_k = r_{1k} + r_{2k} + \ldots + r_{nk}$. For example, $R_1 = 13$ is the sum of the 10 ranks for the fourth-week testing in Table 14–2. Since each R_k is a sum of n random variables, each has a normal distribution under the operation. If the R_k's were independent, it would follow, under the model of Section 2–10, that:

$$U_0 = \sum_{k=1}^{K} \left[\frac{R_k - E(R_k)}{\sqrt{\mathrm{Var}(R_k)}} \right]^2$$

TABLE 14–2. *Digit-span scores on ten girls.*

Girl	Number of errors in 50 problems				Ranked data			
	4th week	8th week	12th week	16th week	4th	8th	12th	16th
Amelia	38	30	10	8	1	2	3	4
Beatrice	32	30	9	5	1	2	3	4
Carmen	37	33	15	10	1	2	3	4
Doretta	35	41	22	12	2	1	3	4
Erzebet	31	33	28	20	2	1	3	4
Fidés	36	20	8	2	1	2	3	4
Gunilla	29	5	6	1	1	3	2	4
Hedwig	46	33	32	29	1	2	3	4
Iolanthe	41	45	28	32	2	1	4	3
Jocasta	46	40	27	29	1	2	4	3
Total					13	18	31	38

would be distributed as chi-square with K degrees of freedom. Since the sum of all the rank scores is equal to $r_{11} + r_{12} + \ldots + r_{nK} = n(1 + 2 + \ldots + K) = nK(K + 1)/2$, it follows that knowledge of any $(K - 1)$ rank values $R_1, R_2, \ldots, R_K$ determines the value of the remaining R_k. Thus, the R_k values are correlated among themselves. Given that H_0 is true and that the rank assignment within a row is random, it can be shown that all correlation coefficients are equal to a common value of $\rho = -1/(K-1)$. Thus, under the model of Section 2–10:

$$X_r^2 = \frac{1}{1 - \rho} U_0$$

has an approximate chi-square distribution with $v = K - 1$ degrees of freedom.

To define the test statistic in its entirety, it is first necessary to determine $E(R_k)$, $\text{Var}(R_k)$, and the value of ρ. Utilizing the models of Section 2–6, it can be shown that:

$$E(r_{ik}) = \frac{K + 1}{2}$$

and that:

$$\text{Var}(r_{ik}) = \frac{K^2 - 1}{12}$$

Since the probability distributions of the n subjects are identical under the null hypothesis, it follows that:

1. $E(R_k) = nE(r_{ik}) = n\left(\dfrac{K + 1}{2}\right)$

and

2. $\text{Var}(R_k) = n\,\text{Var}(r_{ik}) = n\left(\dfrac{K^2 - 1}{12}\right)$

Further, since $R_1 + R_2 + \ldots + R_K = n[K(K + 1)/2]$, that is, a constant:

$$\text{Var}(R_1 + R_2 + \ldots + R_K) = \text{Var}(\text{constant}) = 0$$

As a result:

$$\text{Var}\left[\sum_{k=1}^{K}(R_k)\right] = \sum_{k=1}^{K}\text{Var}(R_k) + \sum_{k=1}^{K}\sum_{\substack{k'=1 \\ k \neq k'}}^{K'}\text{cov}(R_k, R_{k'}) = 0$$

$$= K\left[\frac{n(K^2 - 1)}{12}\right] + K(K - 1)\rho\left[\frac{n(K^2 - 1)}{12}\right] = 0$$

$$= Kn\frac{(K^2 - 1)}{12}[1 + (K - 1)\rho] = 0$$

Since $K \neq 0$ and $n \neq 0$, it follows that:

$$[1 + (K - 1)\rho] = 0$$

so that:

3. $\rho = \dfrac{-1}{K - 1}$

Making the appropriate substitutions into X_r^2, we have:

$$X_r^2 = \frac{1}{1-\rho} U_0 = \frac{1}{1-\left[-1/(K-1)\right]} \sum_{k=1}^{K} \left[\frac{R_k - (n/2)(K+1)}{\sqrt{n\left[(K^2-1)/12\right]}}\right]^2$$

Upon completion of the algebra, a simple computing formula for X_r^2 is given by:

$$X_r^2 = \frac{12}{nK(K+1)} \sum_{k=1}^{K} R_k^2 - 3n(K+1)$$

For completeness, it should be noted that S and X_r^2 are simply related in that:

$$X_r^2 = \left[\frac{K-1}{K}\right]\left[\frac{1}{(n/12)(K^2-1)}\right] S = \frac{12}{nK(K+1)} S$$

indicating that X_r^2 is a constant multiple of S and therefore has the same probability distribution spread over a different scale.

EXAMPLE 14–3.2. For the data of Table 14–2, the value of the Friedman test statistic is given by:

$$X_r^2 = \frac{12}{(10)(4)(5)}\left[13^2 + 18^2 + 31^2 + 38^2\right] - (3)(10)(5) = 23.88$$

For $\alpha = 0.05$, the region of rejection is defined by values of the test statistic greater than or equal to the 95th percentile of the chi-square distribution with $v = K - 1 = 3$ degrees of freedom, $X_{3;0.95}^2 = 7.81$. The conclusion is to reject the null hypothesis that there are no systematic differences between testings at the 0.05 level of significance. Where the difference exists is, however, not known.

Referring the Friedman test statistic, X_r^2, to the chi-square distribution provides an approximate test of the null hypothesis. As has already been demonstrated for the wine testing example, Fisher's method of randomization may be used for an exact test. Critical values of X_r^2 have been tabled for designs having 3 treatments and 2 through 9 subjects, and 4 treatments and 2 through 4 subjects. The tables are presented in the Appendix as Table A–22. For designs having greater numbers of treatments or subjects, the chi-square approximation is satisfactory, except for $\alpha \leq 0.001$.

When there are only two subjects, the Friedman test reduces to a test of significance for the Spearman correlation coefficient defined in Section 16–2. The most extreme differences between treatments result when the ranks under a given treatment are all the same. For two subjects, this is the same as perfect rank correlation, where the treatments define the pairs rather than the subjects.

While the Friedman test is the best test for objects that are compared and ranked, it is also a good nonparametric test for testing the hypothesis:

$$H_0: \text{All } K \text{ distributions are identical}$$

against the alternative:

$$H_1: \text{The distributions differ in centers}$$

If the Friedman test is performed when the classical F test is valid, there is a loss in efficiency, as expected. The asymptotic relative efficiency for this special case is given by:

$$E = \frac{3}{\pi} \frac{K}{K+1}$$

For $K = 2$, $E = 2/\pi = 0.637$, the sign-test efficiency value. For $K = 3$, $E = (9/4\pi) = 0.716$, while for $K = 10$, $E = (30/11\pi) = 0.868$, and for exceptionally large K, $E = 3/\pi = 0.955$. When there are only two subjects, the Friedman test is equivalent to the test of significance for the Spearman correlation coefficient, which has asymptotic efficiency of 0.912 when the joint distribution of the underlying variables is bivariate normal. If the distributions are uniform with equal dispersions, then $E = 1$. If normal scores are substituted for ranks, the efficiency is also given by $E = 1$, provided the underlying variable is normal. In most other cases, it will exceed 1 and this test is a reasonable competitor to the classical F test.

14–4. The Sign Test as a Friedman Test

When there are only two treatment groups, the Friedman test is equivalent to the sign test, indicating that the Friedman test is the natural extension of the sign test for $K \geq 3$. This is illustrated for the data of the first two testings of the previous example. The data are presented in Table 14–3.

EXAMPLE 14–4.1. For the data of Table 14–3, the Friedman test statistic is given by:

$$X_r^2 = \frac{12}{(10)(2)(3)} \left[13^2 + 17^2 \right] - (3)(10)(3) = 1.60$$

TABLE 14–3. Digit-span scores for the first two testings of Table 14–2.

Girl	Week 4th	Week 8th	Rank 4th	Rank 8th	Difference
Amelia	38	30	1	2	−1
Beatrice	32	30	1	2	−1
Carmen	37	33	1	2	−1
Doretta	35	41	2	1	1
Erzebet	31	33	2	1	1
Fidés	36	20	1	2	−1
Gunilla	29	5	1	2	−1
Hedwig	46	33	1	2	−1
Iolanthe	41	45	2	1	1
Jocasta	46	40	1	2	−1
Total			13	17	−4

Nonparametric
Tests for
Repeated
Measures and
Matched Samples
for Multiple
Samples: The
Friedman Model

361

TABLE 14–4. Computations for the sign test in its Karl Pearson form.

Value of difference or sign	Observed frequency	Estimated expected frequency	$T_i - \hat{E}(T_i)$	$[T_i - \hat{E}(T_i)]^2$	$\dfrac{[T_i - \hat{E}(T_i)]^2}{\hat{E}(T_i)}$
−1 (−)	7	5	+2	4	0.8
1 (+)	3	5	−2	4	0.8
Total					1.6

Computations for the sign test performed as a Karl Pearson test are summarized in Table 14–4. In the Karl Pearson form of the sign test described in Section 3–6, when uncorrected for continuity:

$$X^2 = \sum_{k=1}^{2} \frac{[T_i - \hat{E}(T_i)]^2}{\hat{E}(T_i)} = \frac{(7-5)^2}{5} + \frac{(3-5)^2}{5} = 1.6$$

Both tests have the same value for their test statistics and both are referred to a chi-square distribution with one degree of freedom. The conclusion for both forms of the test is not to reject the null hypothesis at the 0.05 level of significance.

When the Friedman type of test is used, one frequently encounters tied observations. This problem is generally solved by assigning midranks to the data. This has a tendency to change the distribution of X_r^2 by making it more compact and thereby making the probability of the stated critical region smaller than it would be if there were no tied values. In most cases, this does not create a problem, because if H_0 is rejected when no correction is made for ties, no error is made by a researcher, since the correction for ties will only make the value of X_r^2 larger. On the other hand, if X_r^2 is in the nonrejection region of the test, then a researcher is advised to correct for ties. The correction for G groups of tied ranks, $t_1, t_2, \ldots, t_g, \ldots, t_G$ is given by:

$$C = 1 - \frac{\sum_{g=1}^{G} t_g(t_g^2 - 1)}{N(K^3 - K)}$$

which is then applied to X_r^2 by simply dividing the observed value by C to give the corrected value. In addition, if H_0 is rejected, then one should make appropriate adjustments for the variance of any contrast that may be of interest.

14–5. Post Hoc Procedures for the Friedman Test

For the data of Table 14–2, the hypothesis of identical distributions for the number of errors over the four different test periods was rejected. Since the alternative hypothesis is of an òmnibus nature, possible reasons for the rejection may be explained by means of post hoc comparisons on contrasts involving the ranked values. For ranked data, contrasts of interest can be created by assigning appropriate numbers to the coefficients of the expected average ranks in:

$$\psi = a_1 E(\overline{R}_1) + a_2 E(\overline{R}_2) + \ldots + a_K E(\overline{R}_K)$$

such that $a_1 + a_2 + \ldots + a_K = 0$. These contrasts are estimated by:

$$\hat{\phi} = a_1 \overline{R}_1 + a_2 \overline{R}_2 + \ldots + a_K \overline{R}_K$$

The variance of these types of contrast has been shown by Marascuilo and McSweeney (1967) to be given by:

$$\text{Var}(\hat{\phi}) = \frac{K(K + 1)}{12} \sum_{k=1}^{K} \frac{a_k^2}{n}$$

With this model, the chi-square analog to Scheffé's theorem is as follows: In the limit, the probability is $(1 - \alpha)$ that all confidence intervals of the form:

$$\hat{\phi} - \sqrt{X^2_{K-1:1-\alpha}} \sqrt{\text{Var}(\hat{\phi})} < \phi < \hat{\phi} + \sqrt{X^2_{K-1:1-\alpha}} \sqrt{\text{Var}(\hat{\phi})}$$

are simultaneously true statements.

EXAMPLE 14–5.1. For the data of Table 14–2, visual inspection suggests that there is a decreasing relationship between the average rank and the amount of training. As pointed out elsewhere, monotonic relationships in the original metric can be investigated by means of the linear orthogonal polynomial applied to mean ranks. For these data, the appropriate contrast is:

$$\begin{aligned}
\hat{\phi}_{\text{linear}} &= -3\overline{R}_1 - 1\overline{R}_2 + 1\overline{R}_3 + 3\overline{R}_4 \\
&= -3(1.3) - 1(1.8) + 1(3.1) + 3(3.8) \\
&= 8.8
\end{aligned}$$

The variance of this contrast is:

$$\text{Var}(\hat{\phi}_{\text{linear}}) = \frac{4(4 + 1)}{12}\left[\frac{(-3)^2}{10} + \frac{(-1)^2}{10} + \frac{(+1)^2}{10} + \frac{(+3)^2}{10}\right] = 3.33$$

Thus, the 95% post hoc Scheffé-type confidence interval is given by:

$$\hat{\phi}_{\text{linear}} = 8.8 \pm \sqrt{7.81} \sqrt{3.33} = 8.8 \pm 5.1$$

Since this confidence interval does not cover zero, it follows that the relationship between the expected average ranks and weeks of training has a significant linear component. Continuing with this post hoc investigation, the corresponding confidence intervals for the quadratic and cubic components are as follows:

$$\hat{\phi}_{\text{quad}} = 0.2 \pm \sqrt{7.81} \sqrt{0.67} = 0.2 \pm 0.7$$

$$\hat{\phi}_{\text{cubic}} = -1.4 \pm \sqrt{7.81} \sqrt{3.33} = -1.4 \pm 5.1$$

Since these confidence intervals cover zero, it can be concluded that the relationship between the expected average ranks and weeks of training is linear. Furthermore, one can conclude that the relationship between number of errors and weeks of training is monotonic. As inspection of Figure 14–2 indicates, the median number of errors traces out a monotonic decreasing curve.

If a researcher were interested in making pairwise comparisons, the variance for any contrast would be given by:

$$\begin{aligned}
\text{Var}(\hat{\phi}) &= \frac{K(K + 1)}{12}\left[\frac{a_1^2}{n} + \frac{(-a_2)^2}{n}\right] \\
&= \frac{4(4 + 1)}{12}\left[\frac{(+1)^2}{10} + \frac{(-1)^2}{10}\right] = 0.333
\end{aligned}$$

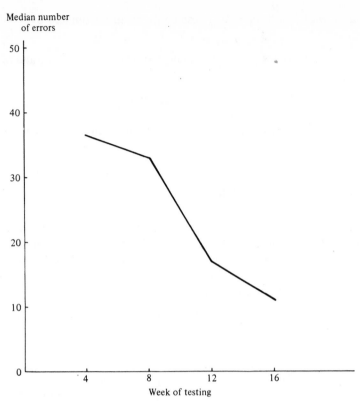

Median number
of errors

Week of testing

FIGURE 14–2.   Median number of errors for the data of Table 14–2.

Thus, any difference in ranks exceeding

$$\Delta = \sqrt{X^2_{K-1:1-\alpha}} \sqrt{\text{Var}(\hat{\psi})} = \sqrt{7.81} \sqrt{0.3333} = \sqrt{2.60} = 1.61$$

would represent a significant difference. The ordered mean rank values are given by

$$(1.3, 1.8, 3.1, 3.8)$$

Thus, 1.3 is different from 3.1 and 3.8. In addition, 1.8 differs from 3.8. This suggests that the number of errors made at week 4 is statistically different from the number made at weeks 12 and 16. Also, it appears that the number of errors made at week 8 is different from the number made at week 16.

If a researcher wishes to examine only pairwise contrasts, use can be made of Tukey's method for pairwise comparisons. If this model is adopted, then the critical value, $\underline{S}^* = \sqrt{X^2_{K-1:1-\alpha}}$, is replaced by:

$$T = \frac{q^{(\alpha)}_{K:\infty}}{\sqrt{2}}$$

where q is read from Table A–20. For Example 14–5.1, $\underline{S}^* = \sqrt{7.81} = 2.80$ is replaced by:

$$T = \frac{q^{(0.05)}_{4:\infty}}{\sqrt{2}} = \frac{3.63}{\sqrt{2}} = 2.57$$

14-6. Planned Comparisons in the Friedman Model

While Example 14–5.1 employed a post hoc trend analysis on the average ranks, planned comparison procedures for the Friedman model are as flexible as the standard procedures of classical theory. To show this, another example will be presented that does not use trend analysis even though the variable is digit-span memory. In this study, 24 children from a middle-class elementary school in a suburban California community were given a digit-span test consisting of items presented in three different ways. At the testing period, each subject was told to listen to and then repeat a series of digits of length varying from four to nine digits, on each of a number of trials. The presentation of the digits varied over trials, but was always done in such a manner that possible influencing factors were balanced. The presentation conditions of the experiment were as follows:

Condition One. Single series, immediate recall. The digits were read to the subjects one at a time. When the series was completed, subjects were expected to write the digits in their correct order on an answer sheet.

Condition Two. Repeated series, immediate recall. The digits were read to the subjects one at a time. The series of digits was then repeated two more times so that the subject heard the complete span of digits three times.

Condition Three. Single series, delayed recall. The digits were read to the subjects one at a time. When the series was completed, a ten-second delay was made before the subjects were permitted to write down their answers in correct order.

The criterion variable for the study was the number of digits recalled in the correct position for each of the three conditions. These scores are reported in Table 14–5.

Examination of the data suggests that a two-way analysis of variance repeated-measures design, with subjects treated as a blocking variable, could be used to analyze the data. In addition to assuming normality, common variance, and independence between subjects, it is necessary to assume that the intercorrelations between conditions are equal. In many repeated-measures designs, the latter assumption is false, so that the classical analysis of variance is suspect. Once the data are ranked, as shown in Table 14–5, the Friedman statistic can be computed. Since interest in specific contrasts exists, the Friedman statistic need not be computed. Thus, one can go directly to the contrasts. In this example:

$$\hat{\psi}_1 = \overline{R}_1 - \overline{R}_2 = 2.3333 - 2.4792 = -0.1459$$
$$\hat{\psi}_2 = \overline{R}_1 - \overline{R}_3 = 2.3333 - 1.1875 = 1.1458$$
$$\hat{\psi}_3 = \overline{R}_2 - \overline{R}_3 = 2.4792 - 1.1875 = 1.2917$$

Since all contrasts are algebraically equivalent:

$$\text{Var}(\hat{\psi}) = \frac{K(K+1)}{12}\left[\frac{1}{n} + \frac{1}{n}\right] = \frac{3(4)}{12}\left[\frac{1}{24} + \frac{1}{24}\right] = \frac{1}{12} = 0.0833$$

TABLE 14–5. Scores and ranked data for a digit-span test.

Subject	C_1	C_2	C_3	R_1	R_2	R_3
1	77	90	78	1	3	2
2	71	71	62	2.5	2.5	1
3	66	77	65	2	3	1
4	63	67	48	2	3	1
5	72	92	72	1.5	3	1.5
6	99	95	89	3	2	1
7	70	80	67	2	3	1
8	75	69	62	3	2	1
9	92	92	72	2.5	2.5	1
10	50	58	39	2	3	1
11	85	93	68	2	3	1
12	60	55	47	3	2	1
13	70	40	27	3	2	1
14	75	67	68	3	1	2
15	83	83	77	2.5	2.5	1
16	62	74	51	2	3	1
17	68	78	58	2	3	1
18	64	72	49	2	3	1
19	70	65	53	3	2	1
20	86	81	63	3	2	1
21	88	71	73	3	1	2
22	40	55	41	1	3	2
23	79	84	68	2	3	1
24	74	73	66	3	2	1
Average	72.5	74.3	61.0	2.3333	2.4792	1.1875

For a post hoc analysis with $(K - 1) = 3 - 1 = 2$, $X^2_{2:0.95} = 5.99$, so that $\sqrt{5.99} = 2.45$. However, since a planned pairwise analysis is being made, Tukey's method can be used. Thus, from Table A–20, we see that 2.45 should be replaced by:

$$T = \frac{q_{3:\infty}^{(0.05)}}{\sqrt{2}} = \frac{3.31}{\sqrt{2}} = 2.34$$

Thus, the 95% set of planned simultaneous pairwise confidence intervals is:

$$\psi_1 = -0.1459 \pm 2.34\sqrt{0.0833} = -0.1459 \pm 0.6753$$

$$\psi_2 = 1.1458 \pm 2.34\sqrt{0.0833} = 1.1458 \pm 0.6753$$

$$\psi_3 = 1.2917 \pm 2.34\sqrt{0.0833} = 1.2917 \pm 0.6753$$

This indicates that condition 3 differs from conditions 1 and 2, but that conditions 1 and 2 are similar. Thus, the procedure that produces the lowest set of recalled digits is the delayed recall condition. It is interesting to note that repeating the digit series three times does not improve recall significantly above that noted for one reading of the digits.

14–7. Rosenthal and Ferguson Multiple Confidence Intervals

A post hoc procedure for detecting sources of variance, following a hypothesis rejected by a test statistic based on Hotelling's T^2, has been derived by Rosenthal and Ferguson (1965). While their derived statistic and post hoc procedure is based upon Hotelling's T^2 applied to rank data, one can perform the post hoc procedure without having to compute the value of the test statistic. This is a significant advantage since the determination of the rank analog to Hotelling's T^2 requires the inversion of a K-variate variance–covariance matrix that is not easy to compute.

For the Rosenthal–Ferguson procedure, contrasts are computed in the usual manner, but instead of using $\sqrt{X^2_{K-1:1-\alpha}}$ as a multiplying coefficient, one uses:

$$S = \sqrt{\frac{(K-1)(n-1)}{(n-K+1)}F_{K-1,n-K+1:1-\alpha}}$$

Furthermore, the variances of the contrasts are estimated from the ranked data. These estimates are used in the corresponding confidence intervals of the contrasts in place of:

$$\text{Var}(\hat{\phi}) = \frac{K(K+1)}{12}\sum_{k=1}^{K}\frac{a_k^2}{n}$$

This procedure is illustrated using the data of Example 14–6.1.

EXAMPLE 14–7.1.   For the data of Example 14–6.1, the mean ranks are given by:

$$\overline{R}_1 = 2.3333, \qquad \overline{R}_2 = 2.4792, \qquad \text{and} \qquad \overline{R}_3 = 1.1875$$

The standard deviations are given by:

$$S_1 = 0.63702, \qquad S_2 = 0.63381, \qquad \text{and} \qquad S_3 = 0.38483$$

The correlation coefficients are given by:

$$r_{12} = -0.81661, \qquad r_{13} = -0.31037, \qquad \text{and} \qquad r_{23} = -0.29523$$

While general contrasts can be defined, the computations required to determine their standard errors are prohibitive. Therefore, it is suggested that this method be used only with pairwise comparisons. With this concession, the general form of the pairwise contrasts is given by:

$$\hat{\phi} = \overline{R}_k - \overline{R}_{k'}$$

The variance of a pairwise contrast is estimated as:

$$SE_{\hat{\phi}}^2 = \frac{1}{n}\left[S_{R_k}^2 + S_{R_{k'}}^2 - 2r_{kk'}S_{R_k}S_{R_{k'}}\right]$$

For these data

$$\hat{\phi}_1 = 2.3333 - 2.4792 = -0.1459$$
$$\hat{\phi}_2 = 2.3333 - 1.1875 = 1.1458$$
$$\hat{\phi}_3 = 2.4792 - 1.1875 = 1.2917$$

$$SE^2_{\hat{\psi}_1} = \frac{1}{24}\left[(0.63702)^2 + (0.63381)^2 - 2(-0.81661)(0.63702)(0.63381)\right]$$
$$= 0.06112$$

$$SE^2_{\hat{\psi}_2} = \frac{1}{24}\left[(0.63702)^2 + (0.38483)^2 - 2(-0.30137)(0.63702)(0.38483)\right]$$
$$= 0.02942$$

$$SE^2_{\hat{\psi}_3} = \frac{1}{24}\left[(0.63381)^2 + (0.38483)^2 - 2(-0.29523)(0.63381)(0.38483)\right]$$
$$= 0.02890$$

The multiplying coefficient for the corresponding set of 95% confidence intervals is given by:

$$S = \sqrt{\frac{(3-1)(24-1)}{(24-3+1)}F_{2,22;0.95}}$$
$$= \sqrt{\frac{2(23)}{22}(3.44)} = \sqrt{7.19} = 2.68$$

Thus:

$$\hat{\psi}_1 = -0.1459 \pm 2.68\sqrt{0.06112} = -0.1459 \pm 0.6629$$
$$\hat{\psi}_2 = 1.1458 \pm 2.68\sqrt{0.02942} = 1.1458 \pm 0.4600$$
$$\hat{\psi}_3 = 1.2917 \pm 2.68\sqrt{0.02890} = 1.2917 \pm 0.4550$$

The conclusions made with this procedure are the same as those made for the Scheffé-type procedure.

It is interesting to compare these intervals to the post hoc Scheffé and pre-planned Tukey-type intervals. For the Scheffé-type intervals:

$$\text{Var}(\hat{\psi}) = \frac{K(K+1)}{12}\left[\frac{1}{n} + \frac{1}{n}\right] = \frac{3(4)}{12}\left[\frac{1}{24} + \frac{1}{24}\right] = 0.0833$$

so that:

$$\Delta_S = \underline{S}^*\sqrt{\text{Var}(\hat{\psi})} = \sqrt{5.99(0.0833)} = \sqrt{0.5000} = 0.7071$$

For the Tukey intervals:

$$\Delta_T = T\sqrt{\text{Var}(\hat{\psi})} = \sqrt{5.48(0.0833)} = 0.6753$$

For the Rosenthal and Ferguson model, the average squared standard error is given by:

$$\overline{SE^2_{\hat{\psi}}} = \tfrac{1}{3}(0.06112 + 0.02942 + 0.02890) = 0.03913$$

so that the average interval has:

$$\Delta_{RF} = S\sqrt{\overline{SE^2_{\hat{\psi}}}} = \sqrt{7.19(0.03913)} = 0.5304$$

As these figures suggest, the Rosenthal–Ferguson intervals are considerably narrower. Thus, this procedure, while more time-consuming, appears to be the more efficient procedure, and for that reason, it is recommended.

14–8. Multiple Matched-Pair Wilcoxon Tests

Since the Friedman test is the logical extension of the sign test, which is known to have less power than the matched-pair Wilcoxon test, it is natural to wonder whether one can do better with a procedure based upon the Wilcoxon distribution. As might be expected, the answer is *yes*, provided one is willing to restrict the analysis to planned paired comparisons only.

EXAMPLE 14–8.1. Consider the data of Table 14–2. With these data one can perform $Q = \begin{bmatrix} 4 \\ 2 \end{bmatrix} = 6$ different matched-pair Wilcoxon tests. If each test is performed at $\alpha = 0.05/6 = 0.0083$, it is known that the probability of at least one Type I error in the set is given by $\alpha_T \leq 0.05$. Thus, if one refers to Table A–21 of the Appendix for $n = 10$, it is seen that the hypothesis of no pairwise difference should be rejected if any of the six Wilcoxon statistics is given by $T \leq 3$ or $T \geq 42$. With this rule, each comparison is made with $\alpha = 0.010$, so that across the six comparisons, $\alpha_T \leq 6(0.010) = 0.060$. With a more complete table, it would be found that one could use a decision rule that did satisfy the relationship $\alpha_T \leq 0.05$. However, with Table A–21 this is not always possible to achieve.

The results for the six tests are summarized in Table 14–6. As can be seen, four of the six paired differences are significant. This differs from the decision made by the post hoc procedure applied to the differences in mean rank for the Friedman test. For that procedure, it was seen that the mean rank for the 4th week differed from the 16th and 24th week, but not from the 12th week, as is the case for the Wilcoxon procedure. Both procedures identified the 8th week mean rank as different from the 16th week mean value. Thus, while the Friedman procedure identified three comparisons as significant, the Wilcoxon procedure identified an extra comparison for a total of four significant differences.

Multiple matched-pair Wilcoxon tests not only generate more powerful tests for this small set of specified contrasts, they also lead to confidence intervals on the scale of the original variable for the median differences, by repeated application of the procedure discussed in Section 13–6. These intervals are reported in Table 14–6. As can be seen, the two intervals that include zero are also the two intervals that have not led to a rejection of the hypothesis that the pairwise differences are different from zero.

One of the disadvantages associated with the post hoc procedures for the Friedman test is that statistical differences in mean ranks are not necessarily correlated with mean differences in the original variables. The procedure described in this section does not suffer from this difficulty, since confidence intervals are defined on the originally observed variables. Naturally, there is a price to pay for this desirable property and for the greater power: The researcher must decide beforehand that only pairwise contrasts are of interest. If this decision can be made, then a researcher is advised to perform multiple Wilcoxon tests with the correct probability level and thereby ignore the Friedman test altogether.

As the reader has surmised, this procedure is actually based on application of

TABLE 14–6. Pairwise Wilcoxon tests for the data of Table 14–2. (Rank values are reported only for the negative differences.)

Girl	Comparison 1 4 wk vs. 8 wk d_i	$|r_i|$	Comparison 2 4 wk vs. 12 wk d_i	$|r_i|$	Comparison 3 4 wk vs. 16 wk d_i	$|r_i|$	Comparison 4 8 wk vs. 12 wk d_i	$|r_i|$	Comparison 5 8 wk vs. 16 wk d_i	$|r_i|$	Comparison 6 12 wk vs. 16 wk d_i	$|r_i|$
Amelia	8		28		30		20		22		2	
Beatrice	2		23		27		21		25		4	
Carmen	4		22		27		18		23		5	
Doretta	−6	5.5	13		23		19		29		10	
Erzebet	−2	1.5	3		11		5		13		8	
Fidés	16		28		34		12		18		6	
Gunilla	24		23		28		−1	1	4		5	
Hedwig	13		14		17		1		4		3	
Iolanthe	−4	3.5	13		9		17		13		−3	3.5
Jocasta	6		19		17		13		11		−2	1.5
Value of T	10.5		0		0		1		0		5.0	
Decision	Not sig.		Signif.		Signif.		Signif.		Signif.		Not sig.	
Confidence interval	$-4 \leq \Delta \leq 16$		$13 \leq \Delta \leq 25.5$		$11 \leq \Delta \leq 30$		$2 \leq \Delta \leq 20$		$7.5 \leq \Delta \leq 25$		$-0.5 \leq \Delta \leq 8$	

the Bonferroni procedure described in Section 2–8 and also used in other sections of this book. In general, it gives rise to powerful methods and is highly recommended when appropriate.

14–9. Normal Scores in the K-Sample Matched-Pair Problem

Just as normal scores can be used for the matched-pair Wilcoxon test, they can be used for the K-matched-sample problem. For this, one assigns normal scores within each block or subject and then proceeds to generate a test statistic analogous to the Friedman statistic. For this development, let Z_{ik} denote the normal-order statistic for the ith subject or block under treatment k. Within a block, it is seen that $Z_{i1} + Z_{i2} + \ldots + Z_{iK} = 0$. Let:

$$T_k = \sum_{i=1}^{n} Z_{ik} \qquad \text{for } k = 1, 2, \ldots, K$$

Under H_0:

$$E(T_k) = E\left[\sum_{i=1}^{n} Z_{ik}\right] = \sum_{i=1}^{n} E(Z_{ik}) = \sum_{i=1}^{n} \frac{1}{K} \sum_{k=1}^{K} Z_{ik} = 0$$

Within each block:

$$\sigma^2 = \frac{1}{K} \sum_{k=1}^{K} Z_{ik}^2$$

so that:

$$\text{Var}(T_k) = \text{Var}\left[\sum_{i=1}^{n} Z_{ik}\right] = \sum_{i=1}^{n} \text{Var}(Z_{ik}) = \sum_{i=1}^{n} \frac{1}{K} \sum_{k=1}^{K} Z_{ik}^2 = n\sigma^2$$

Since $T_1 + T_2 + \ldots + T_K = 0$, it follows that:

$$\text{Var}(T_1 + T_2 + \ldots + T_K) = 0 = \sum_{i=1}^{K} \text{Var}(T_k) + \sum_{k=1}^{K} \sum_{\substack{k'=1 \\ k \neq k'}}^{K'} \text{cov}(T_k, T_{k'})$$

$$= Kn\sigma^2 + K(K - 1)\rho n\sigma^2$$

$$= 0$$

so that $1 + (K - 1)\rho = 0$ produces the expected result that:

$$\rho = -\frac{1}{K - 1}$$

Thus, under the model of Section 2–10,

$$X^2 = \frac{1}{1 - \rho} U_0 = \frac{1}{1 - [-1/(K - 1)]} \sum_{k=1}^{K} \frac{[T_k - E(T_k)]^2}{\text{Var}(T_k)}$$

$$= \frac{K - 1}{K} \sum_{k=1}^{K} \frac{T_k^2}{n\sigma^2}$$

is approximately X^2 with $v = K - 1$. The computations associated with this test are illustrated for the data of Table 14–2, in the Van der Waerden form of normal scores.

TABLE 14-7. *Normal-order statistic analysis of the data of Table 14-2.*

Girl	Normal-order statistic for			
	4th wk.	8th wk.	12th wk.	16th wk.
Amelia	−0.84	−0.25	0.25	0.84
Beatrice	−0.84	−0.25	0.25	0.84
Carmen	−0.84	−0.25	0.25	0.84
Doretta	−0.25	−0.84	0.25	0.84
Erzebet	−0.25	−0.84	0.25	0.84
Fidés	−0.84	−0.25	0.25	0.84
Gunilla	−0.84	0.25	−0.25	0.84
Hedwig	−0.84	−0.25	0.25	0.84
Iolanthe	−0.25	−0.84	0.84	0.25
Jocasta	−0.84	−0.25	0.84	0.25
T_k	−6.63	−3.77	3.18	7.22

EXAMPLE 14-9.1. For the data of Table 14-2, ranks 1, 2, 3, and 4 are replaced by normal scores −0.84, −0.25, +0.25, and +0.84. With these rankings, the basic data are as shown in Table 14-7. For these ranks:

$$\sigma^2 = \frac{1}{K} \sum_{k=1}^{K} \overline{Z}_{ik}^2 = \frac{1}{4}\left[(-0.84)^2 + (-0.25)^2 + (0.25)^2 + (0.84)^2\right]$$

$$= \frac{1.5362}{4} = 0.384$$

Thus:

$$X^2 = \frac{4-1}{4} \frac{(-6.63)^2 + (-3.77)^2 + (3.18)^2 + (7.22)^2}{10(0.384)}$$

$$= 23.52$$

With $v = K - 1 = 4 - 1 = 3$, the hypothesis of identical distributions is rejected, since $X^2_{3:0.95} = 7.82$. The conclusion reached is identical to that reached with the Friedman statistic.

14-10. Post Hoc Procedures for the Normal-Scores Matched-Sample Problem

Simultaneous confidence intervals for normal scores can be determined for contrasts in the $E(\overline{Z}_k)$ in a manner analogous to that used for the Friedman test. For this extension, let:

$$\psi = a_1 E(\overline{Z}_1) + a_2 E(\overline{Z}_2) + \ldots + a_K E(\overline{Z}_K)$$

which is estimated in the sample by:

$$\hat{\psi} = a_1 \overline{Z}_1 + a_2 \overline{Z}_2 + \ldots + a_K \overline{Z}_K$$

The variances of these estimates are given by:

$$\text{Var}(\hat{\psi}) = \frac{K}{K-1} \frac{\sigma^2}{n} \sum_{k=1}^{K} a_k^2$$

EXAMPLE 14–10.1. For the $\begin{bmatrix} 4 \\ 2 \end{bmatrix} = 6$ pairwise comparisons, $a_1 = 1$ and $a_2 = -1$, so that:

$$\text{Var}(\hat{\psi}) = \frac{4}{4-1} \left[\frac{0.384}{10} \right] \left[(+1)^2 + (-1)^2 \right] = 0.1024$$

For a post hoc analysis any pairwise difference that exceeds:

$$\Delta = \sqrt{X_{K-1:1-\alpha}^2} \sqrt{\text{Var}(\hat{\psi})} = \sqrt{7.81} \sqrt{0.1024} = \sqrt{0.8007} = 0.895$$

represents a significant source of variance.

For the observed data, the mean normal-ordered statistics are given by $-0.663, -0.377, 0.318,$ and 0.722. The six pairwise differences are summarized in Table 14–8. As can be seen, the decisions are identical to those made with the Friedman test.

If a researcher wishes to examine only pairwise contrasts, use can be made of Tukey's method for pairwise comparisons. If this model is adopted, then the critical value, $\underline{S}^* = \sqrt{X_{K-1:1-\alpha}^2}$, is replaced by:

$$T = \frac{q_{K:\infty}^{(\alpha)}}{\sqrt{2}}$$

where q is read from Table A–20. For Example 14–10.1, $\underline{S}^* = \sqrt{7.81} = 2.80$ is replaced by:

$$T = \frac{q_{4:\infty}^{(0.05)}}{\sqrt{2}} = \frac{3.63}{\sqrt{2}} = 2.57$$

14–11. Power Comparisons of the Three K-Matched-Sample Tests

The discussion presented for the matched-pair sample tests can be repeated for these tests, except that the efficiency of the Friedman tests increases from 0.637 to

TABLE 14–8. Pairwise comparisons for the data of Table 14–7.

Comparison	Value of $\hat{\psi}$	Decision*
$\overline{Z}_4 - \overline{Z}_8$	$-0.663 - (-0.377) = -0.286$	Not significant
$\overline{Z}_4 - \overline{Z}_{12}$	$-0.663 - (+0.318) = -.981$	Significant
$\overline{Z}_4 - \overline{Z}_{16}$	$-0.663 - (+0.722) = -1.385$	Significant
$\overline{Z}_8 - \overline{Z}_{12}$	$-0.377 - (+0.318) = -0.695$	Not significant
$\overline{Z}_8 - \overline{Z}_{16}$	$-0.377 - (+0.722) = -1.099$	Significant
$\overline{Z}_{12} - \overline{Z}_{16}$	$+0.318 - (+0.722) = -0.404$	Not significant

*Any $\Delta \geq 0.895$ is significant at $\alpha \leq 0.05$.

0.912 as K increases. While the normal-scores test was no better than the Friedman test for the example presented, it should not be concluded that this is always true. If $K \geq 4$, the normal-scores test should be better. Again, it should be noted that, if only pairwise comparisons are of interest, then multiple Wilcoxon tests should be considered; otherwise, thought should be given to the Rosenthal and Ferguson procedure.

14–12. The Page Test of Monotonic Ordered Treatment Effects

For data similar to those presented in Table 14–2, a number of nonparametric tests have been considered. Each of these tests has involved a test of the hypothesis H_0: All distributions are identical, versus the omnibus alternative that H_0 is false. Once rejection of H_0 was achieved, then a post hoc investigation based upon the evaluation of contrasts was required. In most cases, post hoc comparisons are sufficient, but for the data of Table 14–2, it is clear that the testing of H_0 against all alternatives is not the most efficient way to analyze the data, since an alternative similar to H_1: $E(\overline{R}_1) < E(\overline{R}_2) < E(\overline{R}_3) < E(\overline{R}_4)$ is definitely at issue. Page (1963) has developed a test that is specifically sensitive to these kinds of ordered alternatives. As will be seen, this test is identical to the test for a linear-trend component as presented in Example 14–5.1, but it is done as a planned comparison.

EXAMPLE 14–12.1. For the data of Table 14–2, a test of monotonicity was based on a post hoc investigation of the linear component. Let the analysis now be considered as a planned comparison in the mean ranks for linear trend only. For this specific case:

$$\psi_L = -3E(\overline{R}_1) - 1E(\overline{R}_2) + 1E(\overline{R}_3) + 3E(\overline{R}_4)$$

should be related to the $N(0, 1)$ distribution by way of:

$$Z = \frac{\hat{\psi}_L - \psi_L}{\sqrt{\text{Var}(\hat{\psi}_L)}}$$

Under the hypothesis of no linear trend on the mean ranks, $\psi_L = 0$, so that Z reduces to $Z = \hat{\psi}_L/\sigma_{\hat{\psi}_L}$. For the data of Table 14–2, it was seen that:

$$\hat{\psi}_L = -3\overline{R}_1 - 1\overline{R}_2 + 1\overline{R}_3 + 3\overline{R}_4$$
$$= -3(1.3) - 1(1.8) + 1(3.1) + 3(3.8)$$
$$= 8.8$$

$$\text{Var}(\hat{\psi}_L) = \frac{K(K + 1)}{12n}\left[(-3)^2 + (-1)^2 + (+1)^2 + (+3)^2\right]$$
$$= \frac{4(4 + 1)}{12(10)}(20) = 3.3333$$

so that

$$Z = \frac{8.8}{\sqrt{3.3333}} = \frac{8.8}{1.825} = 4.82$$

Thus, with $\alpha = 0.05$, the hypothesis of no linear component in the mean ranks is rejected in favor of the alternative that errors reduce as weeks of training increase, since $Z > 1.645$.

The Page test statistic is defined as:

$$L = 1R_1 + 2R_2 + \ldots + KR_K = \sum_{k=1}^{K} kR_k$$

and its table of significant values is reported in Table A–23.

EXAMPLE 14–12.2. For $K = 4$ and $n = 12$, it is seen in Table A–23 that the one-tailed $\alpha = 0.05$ value is given by $L = 266$. If the observed $L \geq 266$, the hypothesis of no monotonic trend is rejected. For the data of Table 14–2:

$$L = 1(13) + 2(18) + 3(31) + 4(38) = 294$$

Thus, H_0 is rejected and it is concluded that a monotonic relationship exists across the four test periods. As suggested by the data, it is negative.

It should be noted that the Page coefficients of $1, 2, 3, \ldots, K$ are linearly related to the coefficients derived from orthogonal polynomials, and so the two tests of monotonic trend presented in this section are identical. This identity will be illustrated by means of the large-sample approximation of the Page test.

In terms of the theory developed for the Friedman test, it can be shown that:

$$E(L) = \frac{nK(K + 1)^2}{4}$$

and

$$\mathrm{Var}(L) = \frac{nK^2(K^2 - 1)(K + 1)}{144}$$

so that

$$Z = \frac{L - E(L)}{\sqrt{\mathrm{Var}(L)}}$$

can be related to the $N(0, 1)$ distribution.

EXAMPLE 14–12.3. For the data of Table 14–2:

$$E(L) = \frac{nK(K + 1)^2}{4} = \frac{10(4)(5)^2}{4} = 250$$

and

$$\mathrm{Var}(L) = \frac{nK^2(K^2 - 1)(K + 1)}{144} = \frac{10(4)^2(15)(5)}{144} = 83.3333$$

so that

$$Z = \frac{L - 250}{\sqrt{83.3333}} = \frac{294 - 250}{9.13} = \frac{44}{9.13} = 4.82$$

the same value found for the test of linear trend on the average ranks.

The conclusion for the two procedures illustrated in this section should be clearly understood. As soon as the coefficients derived from orthogonal polynomials are used to test the hypothesis of linear trend, it is implicitly assumed that a linear component does, indeed, exist in the total relationship as defined by the *average ranks*, but not necessarily upon the *mean values of the underlying variables*. Thus, making the conclusion that a linear relationship exists on the mean ranks indirectly states that, on the underlying variable, the mean values tend to satisfy a monotonic relationship, which may also be linear but is not necessarily so.

In practice, a researcher can use either model to test for monotonicity in the original variable and linearity in the mean ranked values, since the same conclusions will be reached in both cases. If quadratic, cubic, or higher-order trend components are to be investigated, then recourse should be made to the orthogonal polynomials used in planned comparisons. Again, it should be noted that these tests are not dependent upon variables that are measured. As always, the Friedman model is best for those cases in which a group of n judges are asked to rank K objects, statements, wines, foods, people, and so on, according to some dimension. If the order can be predicted in advance, then Page's test or the corresponding linear orthogonal polynomial can be used. If the order cannot be predicted with any degree of certainty, then post hoc investigations via the Friedman test and its related simultaneous multiple confidence-interval procedure are appropriate.

14–13. Friedman Test for Two or More Observations per Experimental Unit

The Friedman test proves to be one of the most versatile of the nonparametric tests for repeated measures or randomized blocks. One of its simple extensions occurs when more than one observation is made on each experimental unit of a study. An example is provided in the data of Table 14–9.

EXAMPLE 14–13.1. In the study represented by the data in Table 14–9, 27 college sophomores were given a test to measure their degree of anxiety in an encounter group situation. On the basis of this test, they were divided into three groups of subjects with high, medium, or low levels of anxiety. A month later they participated in a study in which they were placed in a three-person group where they were told to make a policy decision concerning racial discrimination in the hiring of custodial workers on the campus.

None of the 27 target subjects knew that the remaining two group members were accomplices of the experimenter. Instead, they were led to believe that the other group members were fellow classmates. In condition 1, the accomplices played a minimal role in formulating the policy statement by offering little help. In condition 2, one accomplice adopted a negative point of view to that of the target subject, while the remaining student adopted a neutral position. In condition 3, both accomplices tried to frustrate the efforts of the target subject by defending an opposite, usually racial, point of view.

TABLE 14–9. Number of minutes required to produce a policy statement concerning racial discrimination, according to three levels of anxiety and three special anxiety-provoking situations.

Anxiety level	Original data			Ranked data		
	c_1	c_2	c_3	c_1	c_2	c_3
High	12	15	Unknown	5	6	8.5
	10	11	Unknown	3	4	8.5
	9	8	10	2	1	7
Medium	12	13	Unknown	6	7	9
	7	9	18	2.5	5	8
	6	8	7	1	4	2.5
Low	9	10	10	5.5	8	8
	5	10	9	2	8	5.5
	4	6	7	1	3	4

The dependent variable of the study was the number of minutes it took the target subject to make a firm decision concerning the statement to be offered. If no decision was reached in 20 minutes, the meeting was terminated by the experimenter, and the test subject was released after being told whether or not his group was played against his point of view.

The classical analysis for these data is the two-way analysis of variance with interaction and three replications; otherwise, an analysis based on nested comparisons within each anxiety level would be performed, depending upon the specific research questions of the experimenter. Since three subjects took more than 20 minutes, either classical procedure is invalid. To test for differences in the three treatment conditions, a modified form of the Friedman test is possible. For this modification, the three anxiety levels are treated as blocks and the data are ranked in a block in exactly the same way as they are for the Kruskal–Wallis test. Tied observations are given midranks while the extreme unknown time values are given the top rank values. The resulting ranks are as reported in Table 14–9.

If K = number of treatments, B = number of blocks, and n = number of observations for each treatment, it can be shown that for R_k = total rank sum for each treatment,

$$E(R_k) = \frac{nB(nK + 1)}{2}$$

and

$$\text{Var}(R_k) = \frac{Bn^2(nK + 1)(K - 1)}{12}$$

with

$$\rho = -\frac{1}{K - 1}$$

so that under the model of Section 2–10:

$$X^2 = \frac{1}{1 - \rho} U_0 = \frac{1}{1 - [-1/(K - 1)]} \sum_{k=1}^{K} \left[\frac{R_k - (nB(nK + 1)/2)}{\sqrt{Bn^2(nK + 1)(K - 1)/12}} \right]^2$$

is approximately X^2 with $v = K - 1$ degrees of freedom. For computational purposes, one would use:

$$X^2 = \frac{12}{BKn^2(nK + 1)} \sum_{k=1}^{K} R_k^2 - 3B(nK + 1)$$

In this form, it is seen that, for one replication per treatment, with $n = 1$, the formula reduces to the computing formula for Friedman's statistic.

EXAMPLE 14–13.2.   For the data of Table 14–9, $R_1 = 28$, $R_2 = 46$, and $R_3 = 61$, $n = 3$, $B = 3$, and $K = 3$, so that:

$$\begin{aligned} X^2 &= \frac{12}{3(3)(3)^2[3(3) + 1]} (28^2 + 46^2 + 61^2) - 3(3)[3(3) + 1] \\ &= 98.09 - 90 \\ &= 8.09 \end{aligned}$$

With $\alpha = 0.05$, H_0 is rejected, since $X^2_{2:0.95} = 5.99$.

To locate possible sources for the rejection of H_0, one would examine contrasts in the $\overline{R}_k$ on a post hoc basis. For a general contrast:

$$\psi = a_1 E(\overline{R}_1) + a_2 E(\overline{R}_2) + \ldots + a_K E(\overline{R}_K)$$

An unbiased estimate is given by:

$$\hat{\psi} = a_1 \overline{R}_1 + a_2 \overline{R}_2 + \ldots + a_K \overline{R}_K$$

with

$$\text{Var}(\hat{\psi}) = \frac{Kn(nK + 1)}{12} \sum_{k=1}^{K} \frac{a_k^2}{Bn}$$

When $n = 1$, this reduces to the result stated in Section 14–5.

EXAMPLE 14–13.3.   For the data of Table 14–9 and pairwise comparisons:

$$\text{Var}(\hat{\psi}) = \frac{3(3)[3(3 + 1)]}{12} \left[\frac{(+1)^2 + (-1)^2}{(3)(3)} \right] = 1.666$$

For a post hoc analysis any pairwise mean difference exceeding:

$$\Delta = \sqrt{X^2_{2:0.95}} \sqrt{\text{Var}(\hat{\psi})} = \sqrt{5.99}\sqrt{1.666} = \sqrt{9.9829} = 3.16$$

represents a significant source of variance. For the three simple contrasts, one has that $\hat{\psi}_1 = \overline{R}_1 - \overline{R}_2 = 3.11 - 5.11 = -2.00$ is not significant, $\hat{\psi}_2 = \overline{R}_1 - \overline{R}_3 = 3.11 - 6.78 = -3.67$ is significant, and $\hat{\psi}_3 = \overline{R}_2 - \overline{R}_3 = 5.11 - 6.78 = -1.67$ is not significant.

As a post hoc test of monotonicity one has:

$$\hat{\psi}_{\text{linear}} = -\overline{R}_1 + 0\overline{R}_2 + 1\overline{R}_3 = \overline{R}_3 - \overline{R}_1 = -\hat{\psi}_2$$

which has already been seen to be significant. Thus, the simplest explanation for the finding is that, as number of agitators increases, the amount of time it takes to reach a decision increases.

Note that the interaction of anxiety with amount of frustration produced by the agitators has not been investiaged. If one wished to make comparisons within the three levels of anxiety, three simple Kruskal–Wallis tests could be performed. In this case, that might be a sensible investigation to make, since the data are already ranked and available for analysis.

If a planned test of monotonicity is desired, then the planned one-degree-of-freedom test:

$$X_1^2 = \frac{\hat{\psi}_{\text{linear}}^2}{\text{Var}(\hat{\psi}_{\text{linear}})} = \frac{(-3.67)^2}{1.6666} = 8.08$$

can be reported in an analysis of Chi-square table, as shown in Table 14–10.

If a researcher wishes to examine only pairwise contrasts, use can be made of Tukey's method for pairwise comparisons. If this model is adopted, then the critical value, $\underline{S}^* = \sqrt{X_{K-1:1-\alpha}^2}$ is replaced by:

$$T = \frac{q_{K:\infty}^{(\alpha)}}{\sqrt{2}}$$

where q is read from Table A–20. For Example 14–13.3, $\underline{S}^* = \sqrt{5.99} = 2.45$ is replaced by:

$$T = \frac{q_{3:\infty}^{(0.05)}}{\sqrt{2}} = \frac{3.31}{\sqrt{2}} = 2.34$$

14–14. Durbin's Test for Balanced Incomplete Block Designs

Incomplete block designs are not encountered too frequently in behavioral studies since they are generally difficult to analyze, especially if mixed with other completely crossed or nested factors. One area of behavioral research where some

TABLE 14–10. Partitioning of the Friedman X_r^2 statistic for a planned test of monotonicity.

Source	d/f	Value of X^2
Monotonicity	1	8.08
Residual	1	0.01
Total	2	8.09

TABLE 14–11. *Balanced incomplete design* for comparing 8 definitions of integration measured on 14 high school students for the case in which each student rank-ordered 4 definitions.*

Student	Definition							
	F	C	A	D	H	G	E	B
Alicia	2	1	3	4				
Blonda	2	1					3	4
Carlos	1		2			3		4
Darwin	1			2		3	4	
Elena					1	2	3	4
Franklin			1	2	3	4		
Gwyneth		1		3	2		4	
Harvey		1	2		3			4
Irina	2	1			4	3		
Jackson	2		1		3		4	
Kevin	1			2	3			4
Lurella			1	2			4	3
Matthew		2		1		3		4
Natasha		1	2			3	4	
Total R_k	11	8	12	16	19	21	26	27
Mean rank	1.57	1.14	1.71	2.28	2.71	3.00	3.71	3.86

*Taken from *Design and Analysis of Industrial Experiments* (2nd. Ed.) Owen L. Davies (Ed.). New York: Hafner Publishing Co., 1956, p. 232.

of the simpler designs can find interesting applications with minimal arithmetic computations consists of studies in which subjects are asked to rank a set of K objects, statements, persons, and so on, from 1 to K. If $K > 4$, the task becomes difficult and may even become impossible with increasing K. An example of such a study is summarized in Table 14–11.

EXAMPLE 14–14.1 In this example, fourteen students were each given four of eight different definitions of integration to rank-order. Each subject was told to rank-order the definitions, giving a rank of 1 to the definition most like his own and a rank of 4 to the definition least like his own. The results were as shown. The eight definitions compared are:

A. Integration is the free association of people of different races on the basis of mutual or like interests.
B. Integration is the forced mixing of people of different races.
C. Integration is the open acceptance of another person and his racial and cultural heritage.
D. Integration is all people having equal social value (may marry outside of their own races, join social clubs, and so forth), and receiving equal justice under the law.
E. Integration is accepting the prevailing or common cultural values of the larger society.

F. Integration is all people having equal chances for all things including education, employment, and housing.
G. Integration is the voluntary mixing of people of different races.
H. Integration is the incorporation or inclusion into society, on the basis of equal membership, of people who differ in some group characteristic (like race).

Once the design was selected, the definitions were randomly assigned to the columns of the design pattern, as shown in Table 14–11. As a result, subject 1 was asked to rank definitions A, C, D, and F, while subject 14 was asked to rank definitions A, C, E, and G.

To obtain a Friedman-type statistic, let:

1. B = number of blocks or subjects.
2. K = number of treatments or conditions.
3. T = number of treatments compared in a single block.
4. M = number of times a treatment is observed in the total incomplete design.
5. $\lambda = M(T - 1)/(K - 1)$ = number of times a pair of treatments are compared against each other.

Within a block, let ranks $1, 2, \ldots, T$ be assigned to the conditions being compared. Thus within a block:

$$E(r_{ik}) = \frac{T + 1}{2} \quad \text{and} \quad \text{Var}(r_{ik}) = \frac{T^2 - 1}{12}$$

Thus, for a treatment rank sum total:

$$R_k = \sum_{i=1}^{B} r_{ik} = \sum_{i'=1}^{M} r_{i'k}$$

where i' refers to the blocks that contribute to the total of R_k. Over the M contributing blocks:

$$E(R_k) = M\left[\frac{T + 1}{2}\right] \quad \text{and} \quad \text{Var}(R_k) = M\left[\frac{T^2 - 1}{12}\right]$$

Since $R_1 + R_2 + \ldots + R_K = \dfrac{BT(T + 1)}{2} = \text{constant}$, it follows that:

$$\rho = -\frac{1}{K - 1}$$

Thus, a Friedman-type statistic is defined under the model of Section 2–10 as:

$$X^2 = \frac{1}{1 - \rho} U_0$$

$$= \frac{1}{1 - [-1/(K - 1)]} \sum_{k=1}^{K} \left[\frac{R_k - M(T + 1)/2}{\sqrt{M[(T^2 - 1)/12]}}\right]^2$$

which, when H_0 is true, is approximately X^2 with $v = (K - 1)$ degrees of freedom (Durbin, 1951). For the computational form, we may write:

$$X^2 = \frac{12(K - 1)}{M(T^2 - 1)K} \sum_{k=1}^{K} R_k^2 - \frac{3M(K - 1)(T + 1)}{T - 1}$$

Note that when $T = K$, this formula reduces to the usual Friedman statistic.
For any balanced incomplete design it is known that:

$$BT = KM$$

so that:

$$M = \frac{BT}{K}$$

EXAMPLE 14–14.2. For the design of Table 14–11, $B = 14$, $T = 4$, and $K = 8$, so that:

$$M = \frac{(14)(4)}{8} = \frac{56}{8} = 7$$

Thus, for the observed data:

$$X^2 = \frac{12(8 - 1)}{7(4^2 - 1)8} \left[(11)^2 + (8)^2 + (12)^2 + (16)^2 + (19)^2 \right.$$

$$\left. + (21)^2 + (26)^2 + (27)^2 \right] - \frac{3(7)(8 - 1)(4 + 1)}{(4 - 1)}$$

$$= 279.20 - 245.00 = 34.2$$

With $v = K - 1 = 8 - 1 = 7$, the hypothesis of no difference in mean ranking is rejected at $\alpha = 0.05$, since $X^2_{7:0.95} = 14.07$. Since H_0 has been rejected, post hoc analysis on interesting contrasts is now in order.

The contrast:

$$\psi = a_1 E(\overline{R}_1) + a_2 E(\overline{R}_2) + \ldots + a_K E(\overline{R}_K)$$

is estimated by the usual linear weighted sum:

$$\hat{\psi} = a_1 \overline{R}_1 + a_2 \overline{R}_2 + \ldots + a_K \overline{R}_K$$

with

$$\text{Var}(\hat{\psi}) = \frac{K(T^2 - 1)}{(K - 1)12M} \sum_{k=1}^{K} a_k^2$$

For a post hoc analysis, $\underline{S}^* = \sqrt{X^2_{K-1:1-\alpha}}$, and for planned pairwise comparisons, Tukey's method can be used with:

$$T = \frac{q^{(\alpha)}_{K:\infty}}{\sqrt{2}}$$

EXAMPLE 14–14.3. For planned pairwise contrasts of Table 14–11:

$$\text{Var}(\hat{\psi}) = \frac{8(4^2 - 1)}{(8 - 1)(12)(7)} \left[(+1)^2 + (-1)^2 \right] = 0.4081$$

Thus, any difference exceeding:

$$\Delta = T\sqrt{\text{Var}(\hat{\psi})} = \frac{q^{(0.05)}_{8:\infty}}{\sqrt{2}} \sqrt{\text{Var}(\hat{\psi})} = \frac{4.29}{\sqrt{2}} \sqrt{0.4081} = 2.30$$

represents a significant source of variance. If all pairwise comparisons are estimated, it is seen that $\bar{R}_C$ differs from $\bar{R}_E$ and $\bar{R}_B$. None of the other pairwise comparisons is significant. Definition C involves the idealistic elements of open acceptance of a person and his heritage, while definitions E and B involve the forced mixing of people or the acceptance of the prevailing values of the larger society, almost polar points of view concerning integration.

In many studies similar to that discussed, it would be natural to assign S subjects to each block instead of only one. For this extension, a typical rank value is given by r_{ibk}, where ibk represents the rank assigned by subject i in the bth block to treatment k. Summing across the blocks, one has that:

$$R_k = R_{.1k} + R_{.2k} + \ldots + R_{.Bk}$$

Within a block:

$$R_{.bk} = r_{1bk} + r_{2bk} + \ldots + r_{Sbk}$$

so that under H_0:

$$E(R_{.bk}) = S\left[\frac{T+1}{2}\right]$$

Thus, across the M blocks that contribute to the total rank sum:

$$E(R_k) = MS\left[\frac{T+1}{2}\right]$$

In a like manner:

$$\text{Var}(R_k) = MS\left[\frac{T^2-1}{12}\right]$$

As might be expected:

$$\rho = -\frac{1}{K-1}$$

since $R_1 + R_2 + \ldots + R_K = MS[T(T+1)/2] =$ a constant. Thus, under the model of Section 2–10:

$$X^2 = \frac{1}{1-\rho}\, U_0 = \left[\frac{1}{1-[-1/(K-1)]}\right]\sum_{k=1}^{K}\left[\frac{R_k - MS[(T+1)/2)]}{\sqrt{MS[(T^2-1)/12]}}\right]^2$$

which, when H_0 is true, is approximately X^2 with $v = K - 1$. For computational form, one has:

Nonparametric
Tests for
Repeated
Measures and
Matched Samples
for Multiple
Samples: The
Friedman Model

$$X^2 = \frac{12(K-1)}{MS(T^2-1)K}\sum_{k=1}^{K} R_k^2 - \frac{3MS(K-1)(T+1)}{T-1}$$

If H_0 were rejected, post hoc comparisons could be made using:

$$\psi = \sum_{k=1}^{K} a_k E(\bar{R}_k)$$

with

$$\hat{\psi} = \sum_{k=1}^{K} a_k \overline{R}_k$$

and

$$\text{Var}(\hat{\psi}) = \frac{K(T^2 - 1)}{(K - 1)12SM} \sum_{k=1}^{K} a_k^2$$

For the set of all possible contrasts, $\underline{S}^* = \sqrt{X^2_{K-1:1-\alpha}}$, while for pairwise contrasts, $T = q_{K:\infty}^{(\alpha)}/\sqrt{2}$ is used as the critical value.

14–15. Combined Friedman Tests for Unequal Sample Sizes

The algebra associated with the extension of the Durbin test for blocks with equal sample sizes indirectly shows how Friedman tests based on different groups but testing the same hypothesis can be combined to give a single test of the basic research hypothesis.

Across the various B groups:

$$R_k = R_{.1k} + R_{.2k} + \ldots + R_{.Bk} = \sum_{b=1}^{B} R_{.bk}$$

When H_0 is true:

$$E(R_k) = \sum_{b=1}^{B} n_b \left[\frac{K + 1}{2} \right]$$

$$\text{Var}(R_k) = \sum_{b=1}^{B} n_b \left[\frac{K^2 - 1}{12} \right]$$

with

$$\rho = - \frac{1}{K - 1}$$

Thus, the combined Friedman statistic is given by:

$$X^2 = \frac{1}{1 - \rho} U_0$$

$$= \left[\frac{1}{1 - [-1/(K - 1)]} \right] \sum_{k=1}^{K} \left[\frac{R_k - \sum_{b=1}^{B} n_b [(K + 1)/2]}{\sqrt{\sum_{b=1}^{B} n_b [(K^2 - 1)/12]}} \right]^2$$

If $N = \sum_{b=1}^{B} n_k$, this reduces to:

$$X^2 = \frac{12}{K(K + 1)N} \sum_{k=1}^{K} R_k^2 - 3N(K + 1)$$

the expected result. This model is illustrated for the study discussed in Section 14–14, where, however, subjects were asked to rank all eight definitions.

EXAMPLE 14–15.1. The three Friedman statistics for the three racial groups of the study are given by $X^2_{\text{Asians}} = 18.4$, $X^2_{\text{Blacks}} = 48.7$, and $X^2_{\text{Whites}} = 106.2$. The rank totals and sample sizes for the three groups are as shown in Table 14–12. For the observed data:

$$X^2 = \frac{12}{8(8+1)(209)}\left[(779)^2 + (1240)^2 + (801)^2 + (862)^2 \right.$$
$$\left. + (1160)^2 + (868)^2 + (924)^2 + (891)^2 \right] - 3(209)(8+1)$$
$$= 5802.0470 - 5643.0000 = 159.05$$

For $K = 8$, H_0 is rejected, since $X^2 = 159.05$ is greater than $X^2_{7:0.95} = 14.07$.

Summary

For repeated-measures designs, the Friedman statistic is an exceptionally versatile statistic for the analysis of ranked objects, statements, places, persons, and so on. In its most general form, it is given by:

$$X^2 = \frac{K-1}{K}\sum_{k=1}^{K}\left[\frac{R_k - \sum_{m=1}^{M} n_m\left[(T+1)/2\right]}{\sqrt{\sum_{m=1}^{M} n_m(T^2-1)/12}}\right]^2$$

TABLE 14–12. Rank totals and mean ranks of eight definitions of integration as rated by Asian males, black males and white males.

Race		A	B	C	D	E	F	G	H	Sample size	X^2_r
Asian	R	160	205	144	163	213	155	166	163	38	18.4
	$\overline{R}$	4.2	5.4	3.8	4.3	5.6	4.1	4.4	4.3		
Black	R	190	320	216	199	281	202	213	254	52	48.7
	$\overline{R}$	3.7	6.2	4.2	3.8	5.4	3.9	4.1	4.9		
White	R	429	715	441	500	666	511	546	475	119	106.2
	$\overline{R}$	3.6	6.0	3.7	4.2	5.6	4.3	4.6	4.0		
Total	R	779	1240	801	862	1160	868	924	891	209	159.1
	$\overline{R}$	3.7	5.9	3.8	4.1	5.6	4.2	4.4	4.3		

Nonparametric Tests for Repeated Measures and Matched Samples for Multiple Samples: The Friedman Model

where

K = Number of treatments,
T = Number of treatments compared in a block,
n_m = Number of observations on treatment k made in block m that contributes to the rank sum R_k.

Case I. If $T = K$, then every treatment is observed in each block so that $M = B$ and the test statistic reduces to the form described in Section 14–15 and is referred to as the combined form of the Friedman statistic.

Case II. If $T < K$, and if each $n_m = S$, then one has the Durbin test of Section 14–14 with S subjects or observations made on each treatment in a block.

Case III. If $T < K$, and if each $n_m = 1$, then one has the Durbin test itself, as described in Section 14–14.

Case IV. If $T = K$, and $n_m = 1$, then one has the Friedman test of Section 14–3 in its usual simple form.

Case V. If $T = K$, and n subjects are assigned to each treatment, then one has the Friedman test of Section 14–13, in which the ranks within a block are assigned as they would be for the Kruskal–Wallis model.

It should be noted that when $K = 3$ or 4, and $n \leq 5$, the Chi-square approximation may not be adequate. Under these conditions, the probabilities and test values reported in Table A–22 should be used. Unfortunately, these values are valid only for the classical form of the Friedman test. Since the generation of the correct distribution for Cases I, II, III, and V is difficult, one must rely on the large-sample approximation, even for small-sample sizes. As the test tends to be conservative at small-sample sizes, rejection of H_0 is most likely an indication that H_0 is, indeed, false. On the other hand, if H_0 is not rejected, a researcher cannot be assured that a correct decision has been made. In these cases, he must rely upon his own judgment of the situation.

Like the basic test statistic X_r^2 used to test $H_0 : E(R_1) = E(R_2) = \ldots = E(R_K)$, the post hoc procedures for the various forms of the Friedman statistic are easy to apply. In all cases, a contrast is estimated as:

$$\hat{\psi} = a_1 \overline{R}_1 + a_2 \overline{R}_2 + \ldots + a_K \overline{R}_K$$

where

$$a_1 + a_2 + \ldots + a_K = 0$$

with

$$\underline{S}^* = \sqrt{X_{K-1 : 1-\alpha}^2}$$

and variances defined as follows for the various special cases:

Case	Variance

I $\quad \mathrm{Var}(\hat{\psi}) = \dfrac{K(T^2 - 1)}{(K - 1)12M} \sum\limits_{k=1}^{K} \dfrac{a_k^2}{n_k}$ $\qquad$ IV $\quad \mathrm{Var}(\hat{\psi}) = \dfrac{K(K + 1)}{12} \sum\limits_{k=1}^{K} \dfrac{a_k^2}{n}$

II $\quad \mathrm{Var}(\hat{\psi}) = \dfrac{K(T^2 - 1)}{(K - 1)12MS} \sum\limits_{k=1}^{K} a_k^2$ $\qquad$ V $\quad \mathrm{Var}(\hat{\psi}) = \dfrac{Kn(nK + 1)}{12} \sum\limits_{k=1}^{K} \dfrac{a_k^2}{Bn}$

III $\quad \mathrm{Var}(\hat{\psi}) = \dfrac{K(T^2 - 1)}{(K - 1)12M} \sum\limits_{k=1}^{K} a_k^2$

The intervals defined under Case IV, the usual Friedman model, are wide when compared to the multiple confidence interval procedure developed by Rosenthal and Ferguson. For their method, one still computes $\hat{\psi}$ in the usual way but replaces

$$\underline{S}^* = \sqrt{X_{K-1:1-\alpha}^2}$$

by

$$\underline{S}^* = \sqrt{\frac{(K - 1)(n - 1)}{(n - K + 1)} F_{K-1, n-K+1:1-\alpha}}$$

In addition, the variances of the individual contrasts are estimated directly from the ranked data and not from the formula specified for Case IV.

If the treatment conditions represent an ordering of methods from a low quantitative level to a high quantitative level, a researcher can use the Page procedure to test for a monotonic relationship between the dependent variable and the various states of the ordered independent variable. Under the Friedman model, the Page statistic, defined as:

$$L = 1R_1 + 2R_2 + \ldots + KR_K$$

is related to the $N(0, 1)$ distribution by means of;

$$Z = \frac{L - E(L)}{\sqrt{\mathrm{Var}(L)}}$$

where

$$E(L) = \frac{nK(K + 1)^2}{4}$$

and

$$\mathrm{Var}(L) = \frac{nK^2(K^2 - 1)(K + 1)}{144}$$

If, in a K-sample repeated-measures design, a researcher is interested only in pairwise differences, then repeated matched-pair Wilcoxon tests are preferred over the familiar Friedman test, because of the preservation of both magnitude and direction of differences under the Wilcoxon model. Under this method of analysis $Q = \begin{bmatrix} K \\ 2 \end{bmatrix}$ matched-pair Wilcoxon tests are performed but with each test alpha-controlled at $\alpha \leq \alpha_T / \begin{bmatrix} K \\ 2 \end{bmatrix}$.

As indicated in this chapter, the Friedman-type tests can be improved upon by a simple substitution of normal scores. For the Friedman test, an actual gain in power is achieved if $K \geq 4$. When $K = 2$, the use of normal scores produces a test identical to the sign test, and so no increase in power is obtained. This is also true for $K = 3$, since the three normal scores are equally spaced and equivalent to the rank values 1, 2, and 3. Thus, when $K \geq 4$, thought should be given to the use of normal scores in the repeated-measures design.

Exercises

*1. Fifteen graduate students majoring in art were given six oil paintings to rank-order on the balance in use of primary colors by the artists. The subjects were told the paintings were done by outstanding art students in the local high schools. They were also told that the outstanding artist would be given a $3000 scholarship to the school attended by the fifteen judges. However, they were not told that two of the paintings were produced by two art professors under whom the students were taking courses in color composition, two other paintings were produced by schizoprenic patients, and the remaining two paintings were, indeed, produced by two outstanding students who actually were given scholarships for the following school year. Results are as shown. What do the rankings suggest about graduate students' ability to rank-order the paintings?

Type of Painter

Judge	Student one	Student two	Professor one	Professor two	Patient one	Patient two
1	5	2	1	3	4	6
2	3	2	4	1	5	6
3	4	1	2	3	6	5
4	3	1	2	5	4	6
5	4	2	1	3	6	5
6	2	3	1	4	6	5
7	4	2	1	3	5	6
8	4	3	2	5	1	6
9	4	2	1	3	6	5
10	4	1	2	3	5	6
11	3	4	1	2	6	5
12	3	1	2	5	4	6
13	5	1	2	3	4	6
14	2	1	3	5	4	6
15	4	3	1	2	5	6

*2. For the data of Exercise 1, examine the following three planned comparisons for significance by means of the techniques of Sections 14–5 and 14–7. Which of the two methods seems to have the most power?

$$\hat{\psi}_1 = \frac{1}{2}(\overline{R}_1 + \overline{R}_2) - \frac{1}{2}(\overline{R}_3 + \overline{R}_4)$$

$$\hat{\psi}_2 = \frac{1}{2}(\overline{R}_1 + \overline{R}_2) - \frac{1}{2}(\overline{R}_5 + \overline{R}_6)$$

$$\hat{\psi}_3 = \frac{1}{2}(\overline{R}_3 + \overline{R}_4) - \frac{1}{2}(\overline{R}_5 + \overline{R}_6)$$

*3. Just as the chi-square of the Kruskal–Wallis test can be decomposed into $(K - 1)$ orthogonal components, each X_1^2, so can the chi-square of the Friedman test. Demonstrate this decomposition for the data of Example 14–5.1. For the kth contrast,

$$X_k^2 = \frac{\hat{\psi}_k^2}{\text{Var}(\hat{\psi}_k)}$$

*4. Analyze the data of Exercise 1 in terms of:
   a) The Van der Waerden normal scores.
   b) The Terry-Hoeffding normal scores.

*5. In a learning study, 20 third-grade children were randomly assigned to one of two conditions. Subjects assigned to the control condition were trained by a standard program in which the teacher was the instructor. Subjects in the experimental condition were trained with computer-assisted instruction at the console of the data-input machine. Following each lesson, students were given a reading test. The number of errors made by each student over four test periods is as shown in the accompanying table. Use the rank methods of this chapter to describe what happens in the control group and in the experimental group.

	Control group					Experimental group			
Sub-ject	Trial 1	Trial 2	Trial 3	Trial 4	Sub-ject	Trial 1	Trial 2	Trial 3	Trial 4
1	12	12	8	6	11	10	4	0	0
2	13	7	10	9	12	16	12	3	1
3	10	6	6	8	13	14	10	9	5
4	15	10	10	12	14	16	12	10	6
5	10	12	2	5	15	13	15	2	0
6	8	15	12	10	16	10	8	4	6
7	14	12	6	0	17	9	12	2	2
8	15	10	12	9	18	12	16	5	4
9	16	6	14	10	19	11	13	6	0
10	8	12	11	4	20	6	9	2	0

*6. The purpose of the study in Exercise 5 is to compare teacher instruction with computer instruction. Develop a rank-test procedure based on contrasts for the testing of the hypothesis of no difference in treatment effects.

*7. Answer the questions of Exercises 5 and 6 in terms of normal scores.

*8. Analyze the data of Exercise 5 by the multiple matched-pair Wilcoxon test procedure of Section 14–8 for the experimental group of 10 students. Find the $\alpha \le 0.05$ set of simultaneous confidence intervals for the median differences.

*9. Analyze the data of Exercise 5 using the multiple matched-pair Wilcoxon test procedure of Section 14–8.

*10. Apply the Page test to the control group of Exercise 7. Repeat the analysis on the experimental group. Generate a test of identical rank order across the two groups by means of contrasts or by differences in Page's L statistic. Explain what you observe.

*11. In a study in which the effects of smoking marijuana were being examined with respect to age in months at which newborn babies began to walk without assistance, the following statistics were generated. Since age of mother at birth of child might be a contributing factor to the age of unsupported walking, statistical control was achieved by blocking. Amount of marijuana smoking was determined from a questionnaire interview conducted by public health nurses at a community child-health clinic. Use the methods of Section 14–13 to analyze these data.

Number of days marijuana smoked during pregnancy

Age of mother	More than 10 days	One to 10 days	None at all
18 to 25	16 13 12	13 12 7	12 9 8
25 to 30	17 14 9	14 13 10	13 12 12
30 to 35	15 14 10	12 12 10	14 10 9
35 and over	16 14 12	17 16 10	13 12 9

*12. The study reported in Table 14–11 was repeated on 14 boys. The results are as shown. Apply the Durbin test and post hoc procedures of Section 14–14 to the data for the boys.

Definition

Student	F	C	A	D	H	G	E	B
Adam	2	1	3	4				
Bob	2	1					4	3
Cal	1		2			4		3
Donald	1			2		4	3	
Edmund					1	3	2	4
Frank			1	2	4	3		
Gary		1		2	3		4	
Harry		1	2		3			4
Ira	2	1			4	3		
Josh	1		2		3		4	
Kenneth	2			1	3			4
Leroy			2	1			4	3
Marvin		2				1	4	3
Nick		2	3			1	4	

*13. Apply the Durbin test with $S = 2$ to the combined data of Table 14–11 and Exercise 12 for the complete set of 28 students.

*14. Analyze the data of Table 14–2 in terms of normal scores, but under a model that partitions the total alpha over $Q = \begin{bmatrix} K \\ 2 \end{bmatrix}$ different matched-pair tests. See Section 14–8. How does this method compare to that of Section 14–10 and Example 14–10.1 for pairwise comparisons?

*15. In Section 14–11, it is stated: If $K \geq 4$, the normal-scores test should be better (than the Friedman test). Explain why $K = 2$ and $K = 3$ are excluded.

*16. Replace the ranks of Table 14–9 by normal scores and re-analyze the data. Note that the test statistic has not been derived in this text.

*17. The model of Section 14–15 is of considerable use when the dependent variable of a study is different in various blocks, as in the case of this example. A program for the teaching of reading using an electronic talking typewriter was tested in three different schools. Teachers did not want to use a single standardized test across the schools, since they believed that the methods varied across the schools, in spite of serious attempts to make the treatments equal. Therefore, teachers at each school produced their own criterion test of 25 items, which was given to the students in their own school following the experimental conditions. The conditions were as follows:

School	Block	Condition 1	2	3
One	1	18	20	25
	2	20	21	24
	3	12	16	23
	4	15	18	18
	5	16	17	24
Two	1	12	23	17
	2	16	15	20
	3	13	16	19
	4	9	13	18
	5	16	12	15
	6	12	19	21
	7	12	23	18
Three	1	12	10	13
	2	13	15	12
	3	17	17	20
	4	13	12	17
	5	9	10	6
	6	7	9	8
	7	13	9	7
	8	5	4	12

C_1: Regular reading program.
C_2: Training on a talking typewriter with commercially-produced teaching aids.
C_3: Training on a talking typewriter with teacher-made teaching aids.

Pupils were assigned to the conditions on the basis of a pretest. They were rank-ordered and divided into blocks of three students each. Within a block, random assignment was used. Only data for complete blocks are shown. As the data indicate, either the school differences are large, the tests are very different, or both. Yet the combined Friedman test can be used to test for condition differences. Apply it to these data.

Block Designs and Tests
on Aligned Observations

15–1. Blocking in Experimental and Observational Studies

Researchers often introduce blocking variables in an experiment or observational study and employ generalized randomized block designs to increase the precision of their analyses. This introduction of blocking variables is desirable if large *inter*block (between) and small *intra*block (within) differences are present in the data. As such designs are usually presented within the confines of an ANOVA model, researchers who can define blocking variables that meet these criteria may feel constrained to use familiar classical parametric procedures even if the data depart appreciably from the parametric assumptions. Unfortunately, use of a parametric test when assumptions are grossly inappropriate may result in a serious decrease in power. Fortunately, other tests exist and are presented in this chapter. Some of them may be more acceptable and satisfying to a researcher who needs a robust and efficient test for the generalized randomized block design. These tests are compared with both the parametric and nonparametric tests they are designed to replace.

The use of rank-order statistics for randomized block designs goes back to the Friedman test discussed in Section 14–3, which introduced X_r^2 as a test statistic for the simple randomized block design consisting of B blocks, K treatments, and $n = 1$ subject per cell. For the Friedman test, ranks are assigned separately within blocks and then are used to test the hypothesis of equality of the treatment effects. Under this ranking, no attention is given to the fact that the distributions within a block might vary and that ranks could be assigned on different bases across blocks. Attempts to extend the Friedman test by Wilcoxon (1946) and Benard and Van Elteren (1953) to the generalized randomized block design with n_{ij} subjects per cell followed the Friedman pattern of intrablock assignment of ranks, as described in Section 14–13. Although the assignment of ranks on an intrablock basis avoids the excessively conservative test of treatment effects that would result if ranks were assigned from 1 to N, Porter and McSweeney (1970) showed that intrablock ranks do not take advantage of interblock differences in the level of performance.

Hodges and Lehmann (1962) presented a hypothesis test based on the ranks of aligned or adjusted observations in a generalized randomized block design with $K = 2$ treatments. The Hodges–Lehmann test is designed to control block differences, incorporating information about the level of performance in the various blocks by aligning or correcting the observations with respect to block means or other estimates of location, such as medians, trimmed means, or Winsorized means. Once block effects or differences have been removed in the Hodges–Lehmann manner, aligned observations are ranked as a whole, and mean treatment ranks are compared. This use of interblock information produces tests that are more efficient than those using intrablock information exclusively. Mehra and Sarangi (1967) extended the Hodges–Lehmann procedure to the generalized randomized block design with $K > 2$ treatments and $n_{ij} > 1$ observations per cell. One exceptionally desirable property of the tests discussed in this chapter is that sample sizes do not have to be equal across all blocks if main effects are examined. Unfortunately, the same statement does not apply to the tests of interaction discussed.

15–2. Combined Wilcoxon Tests for Blocked Data

One of the common problems of behavioral research studies is the investigation of two or more independent variables in a single experiment. Extra variables are often introduced into a study, not because they are of intrinsic interest in themselves, but because they can be used to increase the sensitivity of the experiment. Examples of such studies are usually reported in the literature as randomized block designs in which K treatments are assigned to B blocks of subjects so that every treatment is measured in every block. Common blocking variables in educational studies, for example, are mental age, grade, teacher, school, and the like.

One way to increase the sensitivity of the $(K = 2)$-treatment test is to employ the model of Section 14–13. For this model, one ranks the data within each block and then computes a Wilcoxon statistic, W_b, $b = 1, 2, \ldots, B$, for each of the B blocks. For the notation of this chapter, let:

1. n_b = number of observations in the bth block associated with treatment one.
2. N_b = total number of observations in the bth block.
3. W_b = Wilcoxon statistic for block b,

$$W_b = \sum_{j=1}^{n_b} r_{bi}$$

Since the ranks $1, 2, \ldots, N_b$ are uniformly distributed within block b under the truth of H_0, it follows that:

$$E(W_b) = E\left[\sum_{j=1}^{n_b} r_{bi}\right] = n_b E(r_{bi}) = n_b\left[\frac{N_b + 1}{2}\right]$$

and

$$\begin{aligned}
\text{Var}(W_b) &= \text{Var}\left[\sum_{j=1}^{n_b} r_{bi}\right] = n_b \text{Var}(r_{bi})\frac{N_b - n_b}{N_b - 1} \\
&= n_b\left[\frac{N_b^2 - 1}{12}\right]\left[\frac{N_b - n_b}{N_b - 1}\right] \\
&= \frac{n_b(N_b - n_b)(N_b + 1)}{12}
\end{aligned}$$

This last result, of course, depends upon the assignment of ranks to a sample of size n_b selected from a finite population N_b for which the finite population correction is given by $(N_b - n_b)/(N_b - 1)$.

Thus, when results are combined across blocks:

$$W = \sum_{b=1}^{B} W_b$$

$$E(W) = \sum_{b=1}^{B} E(W_b) = \sum_{b=1}^{B} \frac{n_b(N_b + 1)}{2}$$

and

$$\text{Var}(W) = \sum_{b=1}^{B} \text{Var}(W_b) = \sum_{b=1}^{B} \frac{n_b(N_b - n_b)(N_b + 1)}{12}$$

When all sample sizes are equal, so that $N_b = N$ and $n_b = n$,

$$E(W) = \frac{Bn(N + 1)}{2}$$

and

$$\text{Var}(W) = \frac{Bn(N - n)(N + 1)}{12}$$

In both cases, the test statistic uncorrected for continuity is given by:

$$Z = \frac{W - E(W)}{\sqrt{\text{Var}(W)}}$$

which, when H_0 is true, is approximately $N(0, 1)$.

EXAMPLE 15–2.1. As an illustration of the way a general blocking model can be analyzed in a nonparametric manner, consider a study in which the effectiveness of two different methods for the teaching of spelling is being compared for children of different IQ levels. Let performance be measured by the number of correct items on a 70-word spelling list. The hypothesis of interest is that performances for the two treatments are identical. Suppose the data are as reported in Table 15–1. As can be seen, test scores increase as IQ increases. If this information could be efficiently utilized, one could materially increase the sensitivity and efficiency of the study.

For the data of Table 15–1, $B = 3$, $N_b = 6$, $n_b = 3$, and:

$$W = W_1 + W_2 + W_3$$
$$= (2 + 3 + 1) + (3 + 2 + 1) + (2 + 1 + 3)$$
$$= 18$$

$$E(W) = \frac{3(3)(6 + 1)}{2} = \frac{63}{2} = 31.5$$

and

$$\text{Var}(W) = \frac{3(3)(6 - 3)(6 + 1)}{12} = \frac{189}{12} = 15.75$$

With a correction for continuity, $\frac{1}{2}$ is added to W, since $W < E(W)$. Thus,

$$Z = \frac{[W + (1/2)] - E(W)}{\sqrt{\text{Var}(W)}} = \frac{18.5 - 31.5}{\sqrt{15.75}} = \frac{-13}{3.97} = -3.27$$

Since $Z = -3.27 < -1.96$, the hypothesis of equal treatment effects is rejected with $\alpha = 0.05$.

15–3. The Two-Treatment Hodges–Lehmann Test for Aligned Observations

The Hodges–Lehmann test makes use of the *inter*block comparisons ignored by the Wilcoxon test as well as the *intra*block comparisons considered by the combined Wilcoxon test of Section 15–2. If observations differ according to their block identification and if these block differences are not considered prior

TABLE 15–1. Spelling scores by teaching method and IQ level of subjects.

Block	IQ Level	Method One Score	Rank	Method Two Score	Rank	Block mean
One	95 or less	20	2	39	5	30.33
		23	3	38	4	
		17	1	45	6	
Two	96 to 105	31	3	40	4	37.00
		28	2	47	5	
		24	1	52	6	
Three	106 or more	45	3	53	4	47.83
		29	1	59	5	
		35	2	66	6	

to ranking, the treatment and block effects will be confounded in the ranks assigned to the observations. The Hodges–Lehmann statistic eliminates the problem by aligning the observations on their own block means, or some other measure of location in the blocks, such as the medians, prior to ranking.

If the classical ANOVA model is assumed where block-by-treatment interactions are zero, $\gamma_{bk} = 0$, then:

$$X_{bki} = \mu + \alpha_{.k.} + \beta_{b..} + \ell_{bki}$$

with

$$b = 1, 2, \ldots, B$$
$$k = 1, 2,$$
$$i = 1, 2, \ldots, n_{bk}$$

Under this model, the aligned observation is given by:

$$X_{bki}^A = X_{bki} - \beta_{b..} = \mu + \alpha_{.k.} + \ell_{bki}$$

which is seen to be free of the block effect. In the sample, $\beta_{b..}$ is estimated by:

$$\hat{\beta}_{b..} = \overline{X}_{b..} - \overline{X}_{...}$$

so that X_{bki}^A is estimated by:

$$\hat{X}_{bki}^A = X_{bki} - \overline{X}_{b..} + \overline{X}_{...} = X_{bki} - \hat{\beta}_{b..}$$

EXAMPLE 15–3.1. For the data of Table 15–1, the observations aligned on their block means and the corresponding ranks are given in Table 15–2. Since the average value for block one (IQ of 95 or less) is given by $\overline{X}_{1..} = 30.33$ and $\overline{X}_{...} = 38.39$, the estimated treatment effect is given by

$$\hat{\beta}_{1..} = 30.33 - 38.39 = -8.06$$

The aligned observation for the first score in the table is $\hat{X}_{111}^A = 20 - (-8.06) = 28.06$. Proceeding in this fashion, the aligned or corrected scores for each subject are as shown in Table 15–2. Since block differences have been removed, ranks are

TABLE 15–2. Aligned test scores and ranks by teaching method and IQ level of subjects.

Block	IQ Level	Method One		Method Two	
		Score	Rank	Score	Rank
One	95 or less	28.06	5	47.06	13
		31.06	7	46.06	12
		25.06	2	53.06	16
Two	96 to 105	32.39	8	41.39	10
		29.39	6	48.39	14
		25.39	3	53.39	17
Three	106 or more	35.56	9	43.56	11
		19.56	1	49.56	15
		25.56	4	56.56	18

assigned to the two samples in the same manner as that used for the two-sample Wilcoxon test. For these rankings:

$$W = \sum_{b=1}^{3} W_b = (5 + 7 + 2) + (8 + 6 + 3) + (9 + 1 + 4) = 45$$

An exact test of the hypothesis of equality of the two treatments can be generated on a randomization basis as other tests such as the Fisher randomization t test have been. However, for an example consisting of as few as 18 observations, the numerical computations are extremely tedious because they involve determining the 200 most extreme values of W that constitute a rejection region with $\alpha = 0.05$. Since normal approximations are quickly obtained for small samples, large-sample procedures are used in place of the exact tests.

For the large-sample approximation, the independence of the observations between the blocks can be used to derive the null distribution for W. If each W_b represents the sum of the ranks of method one in block b, then $W = W_1 + W_2 + \ldots + W_B$ is the sum of B independent random variables, W_b. If r_{bi} denotes the rank of the ith aligned observation in block b ($i = 1, 2, \ldots, N_b$) and n_b denotes the number of ranks in block b that belong to method one, then, if all rank assignments within a block are equally likely:

1. $E(r_{bi}) = \dfrac{1}{N_b} \sum_{i=1}^{N_b} r_{bi} = \overline{R}_b.$

2. $\text{Var}(r_{bi}) = \dfrac{1}{N_b} \sum_{i=1}^{N_b} (r_{bi} - \overline{R}_b)^2 = \dfrac{N_b \sum_{i=1}^{N_b} r_{bi}^2 - [\sum_{i=1}^{N_b} r_{bi}]^2}{N_b^2}$

3. $E(W_b) = n_b E(r_{bi}) = n_b \sum_{i=1}^{N_b} \dfrac{r_{bi}}{N_b} = n_b \overline{R}_b$

4. $\text{Var}(W_b) = n_b \text{Var}(r_{bi}) = n_b \left[\dfrac{N_b \sum_{i=1}^{N_b} r_{bi}^2 - [\sum_{i=1}^{N_b} r_{bi}]^2}{N_b^2} \right] \left[\dfrac{N_b - n_b}{N_b - 1} \right]$

5. $E(W) = \sum E(W_b) = E(W_1) + E(W_2) + \ldots + E(W_B)$

6. $\text{Var}(W) = \sum \text{Var}(W_b) = \text{Var}(W_1) + \text{Var}(W_2) + \ldots + \text{Var}(W_B)$

As B becomes large, the null distribution,

$$Z = \frac{W - E(W)}{\sqrt{\text{Var}(W)}}$$

approaches the standard normal distribution. Since W is on a discrete scale, it is ordinarily corrected for continuity to improve the approximation so that the test statistic becomes:

$$Z = \frac{W + (\pm .5) - E(W)}{\sqrt{\text{Var}(W)}}$$

If $W < E(W)$, 0.5 is added, but if $W > E(W)$, 0.5 is subtracted. Empirical comparisons given by Hodges and Lehmann (1962) show that the error in using the normal approximation rather than the exact null distribution varies between 0.001 and 0.0001 when there are five blocks ($B = 5$).

EXAMPLE 15–3.2. The statistics required for the normal approximation in Example 15–3.1 are summarized in Table 15–3. These statistics are based on the ranks of the aligned observations from Table 15–2. In block 1:

$$E(r_{1i}) = \frac{2 + 5 + \ldots + 16}{6} = \frac{55}{6} = 9.17$$

$$\text{Var}(r_{1i}) = \frac{6(2^2 + 5^2 + \ldots + 16^2) - (2 + 5 + \ldots + 16)^2}{6^2} = 23.81$$

$$E(W_1) = 3(9.17) = 27.50$$

and

$$\text{Var}(W_1) = 3(23.81)\left[\frac{6 - 3}{6 - 1}\right] = 42.85$$

The remaining values reported in Table 15–3 are found in a similar manner. On the basis of these numbers:

$$E(W) = \sum_{b=1}^{3} E(W_b)$$
$$= 27.50 + 29.00 + 29.00$$
$$= 85.50$$

and

$$\text{Var}(W) = \sum_{b=1}^{3} \text{Var}(W_b)$$
$$= 42.85 + 40.00 + 62.20$$
$$= 145.05$$

For these data, $W = 45$ and a two-tailed test at $\alpha = 0.05$ would lead to rejection of the hypothesis of no treatment effect if $Z < -1.96$ or if $Z > 1.96$. In this example, the corresponding test statistic corrected for continuity is given by:

$$Z = \frac{45 + 0.5 - 85.50}{\sqrt{145.05}} = -3.32$$

The hypothesis under test is rejected and the investigator concludes that the methods

TABLE 15–3. Expected values and variances for the normal approximation to the null distribution of W for the data of Table 15–2.

Block, b	Block size, N_b	Number in block from treatment one, n_b	Ranks, r_{bi}	Expected value, $E(W_b)$	Variance, $\text{Var}(W_b)$
1	6	3	2, 5, 7, 12, 13, 16	27.50	42.85
2	6	3	3, 6, 8, 10, 14, 17	29.00	40.00
3	6	3	1, 4, 9, 11, 15, 18	29.00	62.20

differ in effectiveness. This conclusion agrees with that obtained on the basis of the combined Wilcoxon test.

Recent studies suggest that the use of ranks produces a powerful test of equality of K distributions when the sample histogram of the errors is platykurtic. If the distribution of errors is leptokurtic or skewed, the efficiency of this test relative to that of the F test in ANOVA can be improved by the substitution of normal scores for ranks. The use of normal scores to improve the efficiency of nonparametric tests relative to their parametric counterparts is considered in Section 15–4.

Hodges and Lehmann have shown that, for all distributions, the efficiency of the rank form of the Hodges–Lehmann test never falls below $E = 0.864$. For most distributions encountered in behavioral research, the efficiency of the Hodges–Lehmann test on aligned observations is near unity when compared with the classical F test. In the case of a design with $K = 2$ conditions, $E = 0.955$ when compared with the F test when the assumptions for the latter have been satisfied. Moreover, the asymptotic relative efficiency of the Hodges–Lehmann test increases with an increase in the number of conditions.

15–4. Normal Scores in the Two-Sample Aligned Model

The Hodges–Lehmann test for aligned observations can be improved by the substitution of normal scores in the place of ranks if it is believed that the underlying variables have distributions with long tails. This procedure is illustrated in Table 15–4 for the Van der Waerden form of the normal scores.

EXAMPLE 15–4.1. For the normal-scores model, use is made of the formulas of Section 15–3, except that the rank values are replaced by the corresponding normal scores. Thus, for the data of Table 15–4,

$$W = (-0.63 - 0.34 - 1.25) + (-20 - 0.84 - 1.00)$$
$$+ (-0.07 - 1.62 - 0.80) = -6.39$$
$$E(W) = -0.2000 + 0.1350 + 0.0650 = 0.0000$$
$$\mathrm{Var}(W) = 1.0183 + 0.9668 + 1.9713 = 3.9564$$

and

$$Z = \frac{-6.39 - 0.0000}{\sqrt{3.9546}} = -3.21$$

Since $Z < -1.96$, the hypothesis is rejected at $\alpha \leq 0.05$. This conclusion agrees with the decision reached with the combined Wilcoxon and Hodges–Lehmann aligned models based on ranks.

Note that no assumption is made that the individual ℓ_{bki} are normally distributed. All that is assumed is that all of the ℓ_{bki} are statistically independent and identically distributed. The hypothesis under test states that all of the distributions

TABLE 15–4. Normal scores assigned to the ranks of Table 15–2.

Block	Ranks	Normal scores	$E(W_b)$	$Var(W_b)$
1	2	−1.25		
	5	−0.63		
	7	−0.34	−0.2000	1.0183
	12	0.34		
	13	0.48		
	16	1.00		
2	3	−1.00		
	6	−0.48		
	8	−0.20	0.1350	0.9668
	10	0.07		
	14	0.63		
	17	1.25		
3	1	−1.62		
	4	−0.80		
	9	−0.07	0.0650	1.9713
	11	0.20		
	15	0.80		
	18	1.62		

are identical, be they normal, symmetrical, skewed, peaked, flat, or anything else. The alternative that the test is most sensitive to is that the distributions have the same shape, but with different centers. Thus, if H_0 is rejected, a reasonable conclusion is that the expected values are different. As might be expected, these assumptions and conclusions also hold for the combined Wilcoxon test of Section 15–2 and the Hodges–Lehmann aligned test of Section 15–3.

15–5. The K-Sample Rank Test for Aligned Observations for Equal-Sized Samples

Just as the sign test can be extended to the Friedman test or as the McNemar test can be extended to the Cochran Q test, the Hodges–Lehmann two-sample test can be extended to a K-sample test. Similar to the Friedman test and the Cochran Q test, the sampling distribution of the test statistic of the Hodges–Lehmann test approximates that of a chi-square variable with $v = (K - 1)$ degrees of freedom. Furthermore, post hoc comparisons for this test follow the general model of the Friedman and the Cochran Q.

EXAMPLE 15–5.1. As an illustration, consider the data of Table 15–5, which represent scores on a reading test given to seventh-grade students following one, three, or five weekly 20-minute training periods on an electric talking typewriter programmed to teach reading skills. The study was conducted across four different schools, drawing from different social strata in the community, and taught

TABLE 15–5. Scores on a reading test following one, three, or five weekly 20-minute training periods on an electric talking typewriter for four different schools.

		Number of training periods per week		
School	1	3	5	
1	110	82	118	
	87	84	96	
	79	74	104	
	102	70	126	
2	41	93	111	
	76	76	76	
	43	91	91	
	74	40	105	
3	56	102	83	
	50	40	72	
	64	39	60	
	61	62	105	
4	67	68	126	
	60	87	101	
	50	69	126	
	80	65	103	

TABLE 15–6. Aligned observations and ranks for the data of Table 15–5.

	Aligned data			Ranks		
School	1	3	5	1	3	5
1	15.67	−12.33	23.67	36	16	41
	−7.33	−10.33	1.67	19	17	29
	−15.33	−20.33	9.67	14	9	33
	7.67	−24.33	31.67	32	7	43
2	−35.42	16.58	34.58	2	37	44
	−0.42	−0.42	−0.42	27	27	27
	−33.42	14.58	14.58	4	34.5	34.5
	−2.42	−36.42	28.58	24	1	42
3	−10.17	35.83	16.83	18	45	38
	−16.17	−26.17	5.83	12	6	31
	−2.17	−27.17	−6.17	25	5	20
	−5.17	−4.17	38.83	21	22	46
4	−16.50	−15.50	42.50	11	13	47.5
	−23.50	3.50	17.50	8	30	39
	−33.50	−14.50	42.50	3	15	47.5
	−3.50	−18.50	19.50	23	10	40
Total				279.0	294.5	602.5

by four different sets of teachers in four different classroom environments. Without doubt, performance on the test is confounded with school, as can be seen by examining the data of Table 15–5. The mean scores by school are $\bar{X}_{1..} = 94.33$, $\bar{X}_{2..} = 76.42$, $\bar{X}_{3..} = 66.17$, and $\bar{X}_{4..} = 83.50$, while the grand average is given by $\bar{X}_{...} = 80.10$.

One could align the data in the manner used for the two-sample test, but since $\bar{X}_{...} = 80.10$ would be added to each score, one can simplify the computations by subtracting only the block mean from each observation. Results of this alignment are shown in Table 15–6. Since the school effects have been removed by alignment, the Kruskal–Wallis test could be used to determine whether there are performance differences associated with differences in the number of training periods.

While the Kruskal–Wallis test makes use of the interblock differences, it does not utilize the intrablock differences as does the Hodges–Lehmann test. To illustrate the K-sample Hodges–Lehmann test, let us begin with the model in which $N_{.1} = N_{.2} = \ldots = N_{.K} = N$, and where each $n_{bk} = n$. For this discussion, let:

$$X_{bki} = \text{the observation on the } i\text{th subject in the } k\text{th}$$
$$\text{treatment condition and in the } b\text{th block}$$

Thus,

$$i = 1, 2, \ldots, n$$
$$k = 1, 2, \ldots, K$$
$$b = 1, 2, \ldots, B$$

and let $N_{.k.} = N = nB$. Across the entire design, the total number of observations is given by:

$$N_T = NK = nBK$$

Under the classical ANOVA model with no treatment by block interactions:

$$X_{bki} = \mu + \alpha_{.k.} + \beta_{b..} + \ell_{bki}$$

so that aligned observations are given by:

$$X_{bki}^A = X_{bki} - \beta_{b..} = \mu + \alpha_{.k.} + \ell_{bki}$$

and which are measured in the sample by:

$$\hat{X}_{bki}^A = X_{bki} - \hat{\beta}_{b..} = X_{bki} - (\bar{X}_{b..} - \bar{X}_{...})$$

or, if $\bar{X}_{...}$ is omitted, by $X_{bki} - \bar{X}_{b..}$.

Let the rank assigned to $\hat{X}_{bki}^A$ be denoted by r_{bki}. With this notation,

$$\bar{R}_{...} = \frac{1}{nBK} \sum_{b=1}^{B} \sum_{k=1}^{K} \sum_{i=1}^{n} r_{bki} = \frac{NK + 1}{2}$$

$$\bar{R}_{b..} = \frac{1}{nK} \sum_{k=1}^{K} \sum_{i=1}^{n} r_{bki}$$

$$\bar{R}_{.k.} = \frac{1}{nB} \sum_{b=1}^{B} \sum_{i=1}^{n} r_{bki}$$

Finally, let the variance of the ranks in block b be given by:

$$S_{b..}^2 = \frac{\sum_{k=1}^{K} \sum_{i=1}^{n} (r_{bki} - \bar{R}_{b..})^2}{nK}$$

and let

$$\bar{S}_b^2 = \frac{1}{B} \sum_{b=1}^{B} S_{b..}^2$$

In terms of the mean rank, $\bar{R}_{.k.}$, the test statistic is given by:

$$W = \frac{nK - 1}{nK} \sum_{k=1}^{K} \left[\frac{\bar{R}_{.k.} - \bar{R}_{...}}{\bar{S}_b / \sqrt{nB}} \right]^2$$

$$= \frac{nK - 1}{nK} (\hat{Z}_1^2 + \hat{Z}_2^2 + \ldots + \hat{Z}_K^2)$$

In this form, it is seen what W is a sum of squares of variables that are $N(0, 1)$ and is, therefore, asymptotically chi-square. Since these variables are not statistically independent, W tends to a chi-square form with $v = K - 1$.

EXAMPLE 15–5.2. For the data of Table 15–5, the sample sizes are all equal to $N_{.k.} = 16$ per condition and $N_{b..} = 12$ per block. With the observed ranks:

$$\bar{R}_{.1.} = 17.44, \qquad \bar{R}_{.2.} = 18.41, \qquad \bar{R}_{.3.} = 37.66,$$

and

$$\bar{R}_{...} = \frac{nBK + 1}{2} = \frac{4(4)(3) + 1}{2} = 24.50$$

The block variances are given by:

$$S_{1..}^2 = 142.56, \qquad S_{2..}^2 = 211.02, \qquad S_{3..}^2 = 172.08, \qquad \text{and} \qquad S_{4..}^2 = 240.53$$

so that:

$$\bar{S}_b^2 = \frac{1}{B} \sum_{b=1}^{B} S_{b..}^2$$

$$= \frac{1}{4}(142.56 + 211.02 + 172.08 + 240.53)$$

$$= \frac{766.19}{4}$$

$$= 191.55$$

With these statistics, W is given by:

$$W = \frac{4(3) - 1}{4(3)} \left[\frac{(17.44 - 24.50)^2}{191.55/16} + \frac{(18.41 - 24.50)^2}{191.55/16} + \frac{(37.66 - 24.50)^2}{191.55/16} \right]$$

$$= \frac{11}{12}[(4.1634) + (3.0979) + (14.4660)]$$

$$= 19.92$$

Since the computed value of W exceeds $X^2_{2:0.95} = 5.99$, the hypothesis of equal $E(R_{.k.})$ is rejected.

Note that $\bar{R}_{.1.}$ is about $\sqrt{4.1634} = 2.04$ standard errors below zero, $\bar{R}_{.2.}$ is about $\sqrt{3.0979} = 1.76$ standard errors below zero, while $\bar{R}_{.3.}$ is about $\sqrt{14.4660} = 3.80$ standard errors above zero. Their individual contributions to the total chi-square as measured by W are given by:

$$X^2_{(1)} = \frac{11}{12}(-2.04)^2 = 3.81$$

$$X^2_{(2)} = \frac{11}{12}(-1.76)^2 = 2.84$$

$$X^2_{(3)} = \frac{11}{12}(3.80)^2 = 13.24$$

Thus, it appears that treatment three is mainly responsible for the rejection of H_0.

15–6. Post Hoc Procedures for the Hodges–Lehmann Test for Equal-Sized Samples

Simultaneous confidence intervals can be used to locate the source of differences among the distributions if H_0 is rejected under the Hodges–Lehmann test. The appropriate confidence intervals for pairwise comparisons in the mean ranks are given by:

$$\psi = (\bar{R}_{.k.} - \bar{R}_{.k'.}) \pm \sqrt{X^2_{K-1:1-\alpha}}\, SE_{\psi}$$

where

$$SE^2_{\psi} = \frac{2K}{B(nK-1)}\bar{S}^2_b$$

EXAMPLE 15–6.1. For the data of Example 15–1.2,

$$SE^2_{\psi} = \frac{2(3)}{4[(4)(3)-1]}(191.55) = 26.12$$

so that

$$\Delta = \sqrt{X^2_{K-1:1-\alpha}}\, SE_{\psi} = \sqrt{5.99}\,\sqrt{26.12} = \sqrt{156.46} = 12.5$$

Thus, any mean rank difference exceeding 12.5 represents a statistically significant difference among the distributions. In this case, $\bar{R}_{1.}$ differs from $\bar{R}_{3.}$ and $\bar{R}_{2.}$ also differs from $\bar{R}_{3.}$, so it appears that five sessions per week are necessary to increase the test scores and improve reading skills, assuming that an increase in the former is associated with an improvement in the latter.

If one wished to test for monotonic trend or any other complex contrast, it can be shown for:

$$\psi = a_1 E(\bar{R}_{.1.}) + a_2 E(\bar{R}_{.2.}) + \ldots + a_K E(\bar{R}_{.K.})$$

that

$$SE^2_{\psi} = \frac{K}{B(nK-1)}\sum_{k=1}^{K} a_k^2 \bar{S}^2_b$$

EXAMPLE 15–6.2. Post hoc investigation of the data of Example 15–5.2 suggests that the distribution of scores on the reading test has the same measure of central tendency for one or three sessions per week, and that, as a group, it is different from the five-sessions-per-week results. This can be tested by:

$$\hat{\psi} = \bar{R}_{.1.} + \bar{R}_{.2.} - 2\bar{R}_{.3.}$$

for which

$$SE_{\hat{\psi}}^2 = \frac{K}{B(nK-1)} \sum_{k=1}^{K} a_k^2 \bar{S}_b^2$$

$$= \frac{3}{4[4(3)-1]}[(1)^2 + (1)^2 + (-2)^2][191.55] = 78.36$$

so that

$$\psi = -39.47 \pm \sqrt{5.99}\sqrt{78.36}$$
$$= -39.47 \pm 21.66$$

indicates that the post hoc hypothesis is supported.

If a researcher wished to examine only pairwise contrasts, use can be made of Tukey's method for pairwise comparisons, provided that the sample sizes are equal. If this model is adopted, then the critical value $\underline{S}^* = \sqrt{X_{K-1:1-\alpha}^2}$ is replaced by:

$$T = \frac{q_{K:\infty}^{(\alpha)}}{\sqrt{2}}$$

where q is read from Table A–20. For Example 15–6.1, $\underline{S}^* = \sqrt{5.99} = 2.45$ is replaced by:

$$T = \frac{q_{3:\infty}^{(0.05)}}{\sqrt{2}} = \frac{3.31}{\sqrt{2}} = 2.34$$

15–7. Normal Scores in the K-Sample Alignment Model

If the distributions under study are leptokurtic, one can increase the power of the aligned K-sample test by substituting normal scores in place of ranks and then repeating the computations of Section 15–5. The test statistic and simultaneous confidence-interval procedures are identical except that normal scores are substituted for the ranks. The procedure is illustrated for the data shown in Table 15–7.

EXAMPLE 15–7.1. Twenty film paired-associates (PA) were presented to kindergarten, first-grade, and third-grade children under one of the following four conditions.

1. PP Condition   Still pictures of the PA's were presented and E read a conjunction phrase containing the names of two objects in the PA pair.

2. PS Condition   Still pictures of the PA's were presented and E read a verb phrase connecting the names of the two objects in the PA pair.

TABLE 15–7. Use of normal scores in the aligned model for main effects with alignment on the sample medians.

Block	Grade	Conditions				Aligned observations				Normal scores			
		1	2	3	4	1	2	3	4	1	2	3	4
One	Kinder-garten	14	17	12	18	-3	0	-5	1	-0.84	-0.17	-1.65	.34
		20	20	13	14	3	3	-4	-3	1.65	1.65	-1.17	-0.84
		18	12	17	19	1	-5	0	2	0.34	-1.65	-0.17	0.70
Two	One	14	17	16	18	-2.5	0.5	-0.5	1.5	-0.66	0.17	-0.50	0.46
		17	19	16	19	0.5	2.5	-0.5	2.5	0.17	1.11	-0.50	1.11
		17	14	13	19	0.5	-2.5	-3.5	2.5	0.17	-0.66	-0.99	1.11
Three	Three	13	20	19	19	-4	3	2	2	-1.17	1.65	0.70	0.70
		12	17	17	17	-5	0	0	0	-1.65	-0.17	-0.17	-0.17
		17	19	17	19	0	2	0	2	-0.17	0.70	-0.17	0.70

3. GS Condition   Still pictures of the PA's were presented and S was asked to construct and utter a sentence about the two objects of the PA pair.

4. GA Condition   Action versions of the PA film materials were used and S was asked to construct and utter a sentence about the two objects in the PA pair.

Learning efficiency was measured by the number of correct responses on the test trial. No Grade $\times$ Condition interaction was expected; however, an interaction of conditions with SES level was anticipated. This illustration considers performance on the second test trial for high SES children. The presence of a ceiling effect on the scores on this trial might suggest the use of a nonparametric analysis. The original data, the aligned observations, and the Van der Waerden form of normal scores are shown in Table 15–7.

In this example, alignment is made according to the median score of each grade level. As indicated, any measure of central tendency may be used, since the alignment procedure is not dependent upon the aligning values. Since the top possible score on the test is equal to 20, alignment on the median seems more reasonable, 11 of the 36 scores are equal to either 19 or 20. Certainly the assumption of normality is not valid for these data. For these data,

$$\hat{M}_{1..} = 17, \qquad \hat{M}_{2..} = 16.5, \qquad \text{and} \qquad \hat{M}_{3..} = 17$$

Tied values are broken by assigning mean normal scores for the tied observations. Thus, three values tied at -5 are scored as:

$$\frac{1}{3}(-1.93 - 1.61 - 1.40) = -1.65$$

For the resulting statistics, with ranks replaced by normal scores,

$$\overline{Z}_{.k.} = \frac{1}{nB} \sum_{b=1}^{B} \sum_{i=1}^{n} Z_{bki}$$

so that

$$\overline{Z}_{.1.} = \frac{-2.16}{3(3)} = \frac{-2.16}{9} = -0.2400$$

$$\overline{Z}_{.2.} = \frac{2.63}{3(3)} = \frac{2.63}{9} = 0.2922$$

$$\overline{Z}_{.3.} = \frac{-4.62}{3(3)} = \frac{-4.62}{9} = -0.5133$$

$$\overline{Z}_{.4.} = \frac{4.11}{3(3)} = \frac{4.11}{9} = 0.4567$$

Since

$$\sum_{b=1}^{B} \sum_{k=1}^{K} \sum_{i=1}^{n} Z_{bki} = 0$$

it follows that $\overline{Z}_{...} = 0$. For the observed means,

$$\overline{Z}_{.1.} + \overline{Z}_{.2.} + \overline{Z}_{.3.} + \overline{Z}_{.4.} = -0.2400 + 0.2922 - 0.5133 + 0.4567 = 0.0044$$

and

$$\overline{Z}_{...} = 0.0011$$

instead of 0.000, as a result of rounding errors when averaging the normal scores. Within each block:

$$S_{b..}^2 = \frac{1}{nK} \sum_{k=1}^{K} \sum_{i=1}^{n} (Z_{bki} - \overline{Z}_{b..})^2$$

$$= \frac{nK \sum_{k=1}^{K} \sum_{i=1}^{n} Z_{bki}^2 - \left[\sum_{k=1}^{K} \sum_{i=1}^{n} Z_{bki} \right]^2}{(nK)^2}$$

so that

$$S_{1..}^2 = \frac{12(14.4491) - (-1.81)^2}{(12)^2} = 1.1813$$

$$S_{2..}^2 = \frac{12(6.3459) - (0.99)^2}{(12)^2} = 0.5220$$

$$S_{3..}^2 = \frac{12(8.9184) - (0.78)^2}{(12)^2} = 0.7390$$

and

$$\overline{S}_b^2 = \frac{1}{B} \sum_{b=1}^{B} S_{b..}^2$$

$$= \frac{1}{3}(1.1813 + 0.5220 + 0.7390)$$

$$= 0.8141$$

Finally,

$$W = \frac{nK - 1}{nK} \sum_{k=1}^{K} \left[\frac{(\overline{Z}_{.k.} - \overline{Z}_{...})^2}{\overline{S}_b^2/nB} \right]$$

$$= \frac{3(4) - 1}{3(4)} \left[\frac{(-0.2400)^2}{0.8141} + \frac{(0.2922)^2}{0.8141} + \frac{(-0.5133)^2}{0.8141} + \frac{(0.4567)^2}{0.8141} \right]$$

$$= \frac{11}{12}(0.6367 + 0.9430 + 2.9119 + 2.3049)$$

$$= 6.23$$

Since $W = 6.23 < 7.82$, the hypothesis of identical distribution is not rejected at $\alpha \leq 0.05$ with $v = K - 1 = 4 - 1 = 3$. Since the test is most sensitive to shifts in centers, it is concluded that the mean scores are not different from one another.

15–8. Planned and Post Hoc Comparisons for the K-Sample Aligned Normal-Scores Test

Both planned and post hoc comparisons for the model of Section 15–7 follow the procedures described for other K-sample tests. In this case, a contrast is defined as:

$$\psi = a_1 E(\overline{Z}_{.1.}) + a_2 E(\overline{Z}_{.2.}) + \ldots + a_K E(\overline{Z}_{.K.})$$

and estimated as

$$\hat{\psi} = a_1 \overline{Z}_{.1.} + a_2 \overline{Z}_{.2.} + \ldots + a_K \overline{Z}_{.K.}$$

with squared standard error given as:

$$SE_{\hat{\psi}}^2 = \frac{K}{B(nK-1)} \overline{S}_b^2 \sum_{k=1}^{K} a_k^2$$

For a post hoc analysis, $\underline{S}^* = \sqrt{X_{K-1;1-\alpha}^2}$ is used to set limits for the confidence intervals about the individual ψ. For a planned analysis, the figures in the last column of Table A-1 are called on. For illustrative purposes, a planned analysis is demonstrated in Example 15-8.1 for the data of Table 15-7. For planned pairwise comparisons, Tukey's method can be used if desired.

EXAMPLE 15-8.1. Suppose the researcher was most interested in the following three contrasts:

$$\psi_1 = E(\overline{Z}_{.1.}) - E(\overline{Z}_{.2.})$$
$$\psi_2 = E(\overline{Z}_{.3.}) - E(\overline{Z}_{.4.})$$

and

$$\psi_3 = \left[E(\overline{Z}_{.1.}) + E(\overline{Z}_{.2.}) \right] - \left[E(\overline{Z}_{.3.}) + E(\overline{Z}_{.4.}) \right]$$

For these contrasts and $\alpha = 0.05$, the value read from Table A-1 is 2.39. With this number:

$$\psi_1 = -0.5322 \pm 2.39\sqrt{0.1973} = -0.5322 \pm 1.0621$$
$$\psi_2 = -0.9700 \pm 2.39\sqrt{0.1973} = -0.9700 \pm 1.0621$$

and

$$\psi_3 = -0.1088 \pm 2.39\sqrt{0.3946} = -0.1088 \pm 1.5014$$

Since each confidence interval covers zero, none of the three comparisons suggests significant differences in the parent populations.

15-9. The K-Sample Test for Aligned Observations for Unequal-Sized Samples

The analysis of the K-sample problem in a randomized block design, as described in Sections 15-5 and 15-7, required that the number of observations for the kth treatment be the same regardless of the block considered. That restriction led to a simplification in the computational formula for the test statistic. If such a restriction is not imposed, computation for the test statistic requires the evaluation of two determinants. Since knowledge of the evaluation of determinants is not assumed for the use of this book, the computations for the use of this test are not presented. Instead, the confidence-interval procedure for contrasts is illustrated.

Let n_{bk} denote the number of observations in block b receiving treatment k, $n_{b.} = \sum_{k=1}^{K} n_{bk}$ be the block size for block b, and $n_{.k} = \sum_{b=1}^{B} n_{bk}$ be the size of treatment group k. Then,

$$\text{Var}(R_{.k.}) = \sum_{b=1}^{B} \frac{n_{bk}(n_{b.} - n_{bk})s_{b..}^2}{n_{b.} - 1}$$

and

$$\text{Cov}(R_{.k.}R_{.k'.}) = -\sum_{b=1}^{B} \frac{n_{bk}n_{bk'}s_{b..}^2}{n_{b.} - 1}$$
$$k \neq k'$$

Under the model of Section 2–7 for correlated measures, confidence intervals for contrasts:

$$\psi = a_1 E(\overline{R}_{.1.}) + a_2 E(\overline{R}_{.2.}) + \ldots + a_K E(\overline{R}_{.K.})$$

are estimated by $\hat\psi = a_1\overline{R}_{.1.} + a_2\overline{R}_{.2.} + \cdots + a_K\overline{R}_{.K.}$. With $\underline{S}^* = \sqrt{X_{K-1:1-\alpha}^2}$, simultaneous confidence intervals for the ψ are given by:

$$\psi = \hat\psi \pm \underline{S}^* SE_{\hat\psi}$$

where

$$SE_{\hat\psi}^2 = \sum_{k=1}^{K} \frac{a_k^2}{n_k^2}\text{Var}(R_{.k.}) + \sum_{k=1}^{K}\sum_{R'=1}^{K} \frac{a_k a_{k'}}{n_k n_{k'}}\text{Cov}(R_{.k.}R_{.k'.})$$
$$k \neq k'$$

For a planned analysis $\underline{S}^* = \sqrt{X_{K-1:1-\alpha}^2}$ is replaced by the corresponding value from Table A–1.

EXAMPLE 15–9.1.   To illustrate the computations for data with unequal block sizes, consider the data of Table 15–8, which are taken from the study of Section 15–7. The data and the corresponding ranks of the observations aligned on their respective block means are reported in Table 15–8. The rank sums for conditions and blocks are reported in Table 15–9, and the variances and covariances of the treatment conditions are given in the 4 × 4 variance–covariance matrix of Table 15–10. The variances appear on the upper-left-to-lower-right diagonal of this array. The covariances appear off the diagonal.

All of the variances and covariances of Table 15–10 are determined from the values of $S_{1..}^2$, $S_{2..}^2$, and $S_{3..}^2$, the individual block variances. In block one, the sum of the ranks is given by:

$$17.5 + 68.5 + \ldots + 10.5 = 798$$

while the sum of the squares of the ranks is given by:

$$17.5^2 + 68.5^2 + \ldots + 10.5^2 = 37421$$

Treating the 24 ranks in block one as a population of 24 values, we have:

$$S_{1..}^2 = \frac{24(37421) - 798^2}{24(24)} = 453.65$$

In the remaining two blocks:

$$S_{2..}^2 = 409.04 \quad \text{and} \quad S_{3..}^2 = 302.54$$

TABLE 15–8. Observations and ranks of aligned observations for unequal block sizes. Data are taken from Table 15–7.

Grade	Observations				Ranks of observations aligned on their respective block means			
	PP	PS	GS	GA	PP	PS	GS	GA
K	14	17	12	18	17.5	45	6.5	57.5
	20	20	13	14	68.5	68.5	10.5	17.5
	18	12	17	19	57.5	6.5	45	66.5
	13	14	14	16	10.5	17.5	17.5	32.5
	15	19	16	13	23	66.5	32.5	10.5
		13	17			10.5	45	
		16	16			32.5	32.5	
1	14	17	16	18	14	40	29.5	54.5
	17	19	16	19	40	63.5	29.5	63.5
	17	14	13	19	40	14	8	63.5
	19	17	17		63.5	40	40	
	15	17	11		22	40	2.5	
	17	18	18		40	54.5	54.5	
	18	12			54.5	5		
	11	14			2.5	14		
3	13	20	19	19	4	60	49.5	49.5
	12	17	17	17	1	26	26	26
	17	19		19	26	49.5		49.5
	16	19		20	20.5	49.5		60
		16		17		20.5		26
				18				35.5
				18				35.5
				20				60
				19				49.5

TABLE 15–9. Rank sums for the data of Table 15–8 with unequal block sizes.

	PP	PS	GS	GA	Total
K	177.0	247.0	189.5	184.5	798.0
1	276.5	271.0	164.0	181.5	893.0
3	51.5	205.5	75.5	391.5	724.0
Total	505.0	723.5	429.0	757.5	2415.0

TABLE 15–10. Variance-covariance matrix for condition rank sums for data with unequal block sizes.

	PP	PS	GS	GA
PP	5210.55	−2099.50	−1635.73	−1147.53
PS	−2099.50	5859.03	−1194.37	−1815.84
GS	−1635.73	−1194.37	4863.08	−1283.66
GA	−1147.53	−1815.84	−1283.66	4574.81

Thus,

$$\text{Var}(R_{.1.}) = \frac{5(24-5)(453.65)}{23} + \frac{8(25-8)(409.04)}{24} + \frac{4(20-4)(302.54)}{19}$$
$$= 5210.55$$

and

$$\text{Cov}(R_{.1.}, R_{.2.}) = -\left[\frac{5(7)(453.65)}{23} + \frac{8(8)(409.04)}{24} + \frac{4(5)(302.54)}{19}\right] = -2099.50$$

The remaining variances and covariances are computed in a similar manner.

For a planned analysis, let the contrasts of interest be:

$$\psi_1 = E(\bar{R}_{.1.}) - E(\bar{R}_{.2.})$$

and

$$\psi_2 = E(\bar{R}_{.1.}) + E(\bar{R}_{.2.}) + E(\bar{R}_{.3.}) - 3E(\bar{R}_{.4.})$$

For two contrasts, the constant value read from Table A–1 for $\alpha = 0.05$ is 2.24. Contrast ψ_1 compares conjunctions against verb connectives for still-picture presentation, under the condition in which the experimenter read the connective aloud to the subject. Contrast ψ_2 compares the still-picture presentation against the active-picture presentation. These contrasts are estimated in the usual fashion as:

$$\hat{\psi}_1 = \bar{R}_{.1.} - \bar{R}_{.2.} = \frac{505.0}{17} - \frac{723.5}{20} = -6.47$$

and

$$\hat{\psi}_2 = \bar{R}_{.1.} + \bar{R}_{.2.} + \bar{R}_{.3.} - 3\bar{R}_{.4.}$$
$$= \frac{505.0}{17} + \frac{723.5}{20} + \frac{429.0}{15} - \frac{3(757.5)}{17} = -39.19$$

For the first contrast:

$$SE^2_{\hat{\psi}_1} = \frac{(+1)^2}{n^2_{.1}}\text{Var}(R_{.1.}) + \frac{(-1)^2}{n^2_{.2}}\text{Var}(R_{.2.}) + \frac{2(+1)(-1)}{n_{.1}n_{.2}}\text{Cov}(R_{.1.}R_{.2.})$$

$$= \frac{(+1)^2}{17^2}(5210.55) + \frac{(-1)^2}{20^2}(5859.03) + \frac{2(+1)(-1)}{(17)(20)}(-2099.50)$$

$$= 45.0272$$

so that

$$\hat{\psi}_1 = -6.47 \pm 2.24\sqrt{45.0272} = -6.47 \pm 15.03$$

Since zero is in the interval, the difference is not significant.

For the second contrast:

$$SE^2_{\hat{\psi}_2} = \frac{(+1)^2}{n^2_{.1}}\text{Var}(R_{.1.}) + \frac{(+1)^2}{n^2_{.2}}\text{Var}(R_{.2.}) + \frac{(+1)^2}{n^2_{.3}}\text{Var}(R_{.3.})$$

$$+ \frac{(-3)^2}{n^2_{.4}}\text{Var}(R_{.4.}) + \frac{2(+1)(+1)}{n_{.1}n_{.2}}\text{Cov}(R_{.1.}R_{.2.})$$

$$+ \frac{2(+1)(+1)}{n_{.1}n_{.3}}\text{Cov}(R_{.1.}R_{.3.}) + \frac{2(+1)(+1)}{n_{.2}n_{.3}}\text{Cov}(R_{.2.}R_{.3.})$$

$$+ \frac{2(+1)(-3)}{n_{.1}n_{.4}}\text{Cov}(R_{.1.}R_{.4.}) + \frac{2(+1)(-3)}{n_{.2}n_{.4}}\text{Cov}(R_{.2.}R_{.4.})$$

$$+ \frac{2(+1)(-3)}{n_{.3}n_{.4}}\text{Cov}(R_{.3.}R_{.4.})$$

This formidable expression can be easily evaluated by direct substitution of terms from Table 15–10. The resulting value of $SE^2_{\psi_2} = 249.6887$, so that:

$$\psi_2 = -39.19 \pm 2.24\sqrt{249.6887} = -39.19 \pm 35.39$$

This difference is statistically significant, since zero is not in the interval.

15–10. Tests of Interaction in Replicated Factorial Designs Based on Alignment

The alignment procedures introduced in the previous sections for the analysis of main effects in a randomized block design can be extended in a direct manner to the study of interactions in factorial experiments. Such an extension was made by Mehra and Sen (1969) for the model given by:

$$X_{bjk} = \mu_{b..} + \alpha_{.j.} + \beta_{..k} + \gamma_{.jk} + \ell_{bjk}$$

where

$\mu_{b..}$ = Effect of replication b on the criterion variable.
$\alpha_{.j.}$ = Effect of condition j of the row variable on the criterion variable.
$\beta_{..k}$ = Effect of condition k of the column variable on the criterion variable.
$\gamma_{.jk}$ = Joint interaction effect of condition j of the row variable and condition k of the column variable on the criterion variable.
ℓ_{bjk} = Error made in replication b for the observation made on treatment combination jk. Errors are independently distributed with $E(\ell_{bjk}) = 0$.

With this notation:

$$b = 1, 2, \ldots, B, \qquad j = 1, 2, \ldots, J, \qquad k = 1, 2, \ldots, K$$

The null hypothesis of interest is:

$$H_0: \gamma_{.jk} = 0$$

for all j, k. Reinach (1965) has shown that a rank test of such a hypothesis in the presence of nonnull main effects will lead to a confounding of interaction and main effects. To avoid such confounding, the main effects may be estimated from sample data and removed from the observations prior to ranking. If

$$\hat{\mu}_{b..} = \overline{X}_{b..} - \overline{X}_{...}$$
$$\hat{\alpha}_{.j.} = \overline{X}_{.j.} - \overline{X}_{...}$$

and

$$\hat{\beta}_{..k} = \overline{X}_{..k} - \overline{X}_{...}$$

are the estimated replication, row, and column effects, respectively, then the aligned observations:

$$\hat{X}^A_{bjk} = X_{bjk} - \hat{\mu}_{b..} - \hat{\alpha}_{.j.} - \hat{\beta}_{..k}$$

are free of the confounding influence of main effects to the extent that $\hat{\mu}_{b..}$, $\hat{\alpha}_{.j.}$, and $\hat{\beta}_{..k}$ are good estimators of $\mu_{b..}$, $\alpha_{.j.}$, and $\beta_{..k}$, respectively. Let r_{bjk} represent the rank of $\hat{X}^A_{bjk}$ in the entire set of $N = BJK$ observations. Under the hypothesis of no interaction effects, the test statistic:

$$W = \frac{B \sum_{j=1}^{J} \sum_{k=1}^{K} \left[\frac{1}{B}\sum_{b=1}^{B}(r_{bjk} - \bar{R}_{b.k} - \bar{R}_{bj.} + \bar{R}_{b..})\right]^2}{\left[1/(B(J-1)(K-1))\right]\sum_{b=1}^{B}\sum_{j=1}^{J}\sum_{k=1}^{K}(r_{bjk} - \bar{R}_{b.k} - \bar{R}_{bj.} + \bar{R}_{b..})^2}$$

has a sampling distribution that is asymptotically chi-square with $v = (J-1)(K-1)$ degrees of freedom. If

$$g_{bjk} = r_{bjk} - \bar{R}_{b.k} - \bar{R}_{bj.} + \bar{R}_{b..}$$

and

$$\bar{g}_{.jk} = \frac{1}{B}\sum_{b=1}^{B} g_{bjk}$$

then the test statistic may be written in simplified form as:

$$W = \frac{B^2(J-1)(K-1)\sum_{j=1}^{J}\sum_{k=1}^{K}\bar{g}_{.jk}^2}{\sum_{b=1}^{B}\sum_{j=1}^{J}\sum_{k=1}^{K} g_{bjk}^2}$$

Although the test for interaction has been presented in the context of a design in which replicates constitute a separate main effect, or blocking variable of interest, the test for interaction based on aligned observations is not restricted to this case. McSweeney (1967) used the same principle of alignment to remove the estimated main effects of rows and columns before testing for interaction in a completely random two-way ANOVA design. The aligned test for interaction is illustrated for the data of Table 15–7, which is taken from the study discussed in Section 15–7.

EXAMPLE 15–10.1. Since no obvious blocking variable exists for the data of Table 15–11, one can create an artificial replication by treating the three rows for each grade as a separate replication or, better still, one could use a table of random numbers to create three blocks of size four. The results of using complete rows as replications are shown in Table 15–12. For the observed data, the replication means are:

$$\bar{X}_{1..} = 16.42, \qquad \bar{X}_{2..} = 16.75, \qquad \text{and} \qquad \bar{X}_{3..} = 16.75$$

Note that, if a researcher creates artificial blocks when there is no natural replication, and observations appear at random, then the replication alignment figures will tend to be close together in numerical value, and the effects of the artificial replications will not lead to biases in the resulting statistics.

Across the three grades

$$\bar{X}_{.1.} = 16.17, \qquad \bar{X}_{.2.} = 16.58, \qquad \text{and} \qquad \bar{X}_{.3.} = 17.17$$

and across the four conditions

$$\bar{X}_{..1} = 15.78, \qquad \bar{X}_{..2} = 17.22, \qquad \bar{X}_{..3} = 15.56, \qquad \text{and} \qquad \bar{X}_{..4} = 18.00$$

For the entire set of values, $\bar{X}_{...} = 16.64$. The aligned data, along with the rank scores, are reported in Table 15–11. For example, the aligned score for $X_{111} = 14$ is given by:

$$\hat{X}_{111}^{A} = X_{111} - (\bar{X}_{1..} - \bar{X}_{...}) - (\bar{X}_{.1.} - \bar{X}_{...}) - (\bar{X}_{..1} - \bar{X}_{...})$$
$$= 14.00 - (16.42 - 16.64) - (16.17 - 16.64) - (15.78 - 16.64)$$
$$= 15.55$$

TABLE 15–11. Use of the aligned model for testing a two-factor interaction hypothesis.

	Condition				Aligned data				Rank scores				Mean
	1	2	3	4	1	2	3	4	1	2	3	4	
Replication 1													
K	14	17	12	18	15.55	17.11	13.77	17.33	11	17	6	19.5	13.38
1	14	17	16	18	15.14	16.70	17.36	16.92	10	13	21	14	14.50
3	13	20	19	19	13.55	19.11	19.77	17.33	4	32	34	19.5	22.38
Mean									8.33	20.67	20.33	17.67	16.75
Replication 2													
K	20	20	13	14	21.22	19.78	14.44	13.00	36	35	8	3	20.50
1	17	19	16	19	17.81	18.37	17.03	17.59	27.5	30	16	24.5	24.50
3	12	17	17	17	12.22	15.78	17.44	15.00	2	12	22.5	9	11.38
Mean									21.83	25.67	15.50	12.17	18.79
Replication 3													
K	18	12	17	19	19.22	11.78	18.44	18.00	33	1	31	29	23.50
1	17	14	13	19	17.81	13.66	14.03	17.59	27.5	5	7	24.5	16.00
3	17	19	17	19	17.22	17.77	17.44	17.00	18	26	22.5	15	20.38
Mean									26.17	10.67	20.17	22.83	19.96

TABLE 15–12. Values of $g_{bjk} = R_{bjk} - \bar{R}_{b.k} - \bar{R}_{bj.} + \bar{R}_{b..}$ for the data of Table 15–11.

		Condition 1	Condition 2	Condition 3	Condition 4
Replication 1	K	6.04	−0.30	−10.96	5.20
	1	3.92	−5.42	2.92	−1.42
	3	−9.96	5.70	8.04	−3.80
Replication 2	K	12.46	7.62	−9.21	−10.88
	1	−0.04	−1.38	−5.21	6.62
	3	−12.42	−6.26	14.41	4.24
Replication 3	K	3.29	−13.21	7.29	2.63
	1	5.29	−1.71	−9.21	5.63
	3	−8.59	14.91	1.91	−8.25

The remaining values are found in a similar fashion. Ties are broken by averaging across the r_{bjk} values. The values for

$$g_{bjk} = r_{bjk} - \bar{R}_{b.k} - \bar{R}_{bj.} + \bar{R}_{b..}$$

are reported in Table 15–12 and the $\bar{g}_{.jk}$ are reported in Table 15–13. For example,

$$g_{111} = r_{111} - \bar{R}_{1.1} - \bar{R}_{.11} + \bar{R}_{1..}$$
$$= 11 - 8.33 - 13.38 + 16.75 = 6.04$$

and

$$\bar{g}_{.11} = \frac{1}{3}(g_{111} + g_{211} + g_{311})$$

$$= \frac{1}{3}(6.04 + 12.46 + 3.29) = 7.26$$

Except for rounding errors, the totals should add to 0.00. Thus, on the basis of these values:

$$W = \frac{B^2(J-1)(K-1)\sum_{j=1}^{J}\sum_{k=1}^{K}\bar{g}_{.jk}^2}{\sum_{b=1}^{B}\sum_{j=1}^{J}\sum_{k=1}^{K}g_{bjk}^2}$$

$$= \frac{3^2(3-1)(4-1)[(7.26)^2 + (3.06)^2 + \dots + (-2.60)^2]}{(6.04)^2 + (3.92)^2 + \dots + (-8.25)^2}$$

$$= 8.22$$

TABLE 15–13. Values of $\bar{g}_{.jk} = \frac{1}{B}\sum_{b=1}^{B} R_{bjk}$ for the data of Table 15–11.

Grade	Condition 1	Condition 2	Condition 3	Condition 4	Total
K	7.26	−1.96	−4.29	−1.02	−0.01
1	3.06	−2.84	−3.83	3.61	0.00
3	−10.32	4.78	8.12	−2.60	−0.02
Total	0.00	−0.02	0.00	−0.01	−0.03

Since $W = 8.22 < 12.59$, the 95th percentile value of X_6^2, the hypothesis of no inter-action is retained.

15–11. Post Hoc Confidence Intervals for the $E(\bar{g}_{jk})$ of the Aligned Test for Interaction

If statistically significant interactions are found, confidence intervals for the rank interaction statistic $\bar{g}_{.jk}$ can be examined in a manner analogous to that suggested by Marascuilo and Levin (1970) for the classical ANOVA model. A set of simultaneous $(1 - \alpha)\%$ confidence intervals for the $E(\bar{g}_{.jk})$ would be given by:

$$E(\bar{g}_{.jk}) = \bar{g}_{.jk} \pm \underline{S}^*SE_{\bar{g}.jk}$$

where:

$$\underline{S}^* = \sqrt{X_{(J-1)(K-1):1-\alpha}^2}$$

and

$$SE_{\bar{g}.jk}^2 = \frac{\sum_{b=1}^{B}\sum_{j=1}^{J}\sum_{k=1}^{K}g_{bjk}^2}{B^2JK}$$

In addition, complex contrasts can be examined, if desired. Since they will, in general, pose problems in interpretation on the original metric, it is recommended that only confidence intervals in the individual $\bar{g}_{.jk}$ be examined. Finally, $\underline{S}^*$ can be replaced by figures from Table A-1 for a planned analysis.

EXAMPLE 15–11.1. If H_0 for the data of Table 15–11 had been rejected, confidence intervals in the $\bar{g}_{.jk}$ would be of interest. For these data:

$$\underline{S}^* = \sqrt{X_{6:0.95}^2} = \sqrt{12.59} = 3.55$$

and

$$SE_{\bar{g}.jk}^2 = \frac{2118.8759}{3^2(3)(4)} = 19.62$$

Thus, any $\bar{g}_{.jk}$ exceeding

$$\Delta = \underline{S}^* SE_{\bar{g}.jk} = 3.55\sqrt{19.62} = 14.84$$

represents a significant measure of interaction. Since none of the $\bar{g}_{.jk}$ exceeds 14.84 in absolute value, none of the interaction measures is significant. This agrees with the nonsignificance of the corresponding chi-square value. For a planned analysis with $Q = 12$, $\underline{S}^* = 3.55$ is replaced by 2.84.

15–12. Normal Scores in the Aligned Test for Interaction

Normal scores may be substituted for ranks in the test described in Section 15–10. Once this substitution has been made, the corresponding estimated interaction effects, g_{bjk}, can be written in terms of the normal scores, Z_{bjk}, as

$$g_{bjk} = Z_{bjk} - \overline{Z}_{b.k} - \overline{Z}_{bj.} + \overline{Z}_{b..}$$

The formulas of Sections 15–10 and 15–11 can be used to obtain the appropriate test statistics and simultaneous confidence intervals, respectively. If the underlying variable has a leptokurtic distribution with heavy tails, a gain in statistical power will be observed.

15–13. Efficiency Measures of Aligned Tests

Rank tests for main effects and interaction effects in a generalized randomized block design have been presented in this chapter. The tests of main effects were applied to the model:

$$X_{bki} = \mu_{...} + \alpha_{.k.} + \beta_{b..} + \ell_{bki}$$

and tests for interaction effects were applied to the model:

$$X_{bjk} = \mu_{b..} + \alpha_{.j.} + \beta_{..k} + \gamma_{.jk} + \ell_{bjk}$$

The confounding influence of other main effects was removed by alignment of the observations on the estimated "nuisance" effects prior to ranking. This use of alignment circumvents the problem of confounding, while retaining *inter*block as well as *intra*block comparisons of the observations. Consequently, retention of interblock information produces a test statistic that is more efficient than the Friedman type of test, which employs only intrablock comparisons. The asymptotic efficiency of the test on aligned observations relative to the Friedman test is given by $E = (K + 1)/K > 1$, where K denotes the number of treatments and $n_{bi} = 1$; for the generalized randomized block design, the asymptotic efficiency of the aligned observations test relative to the Friedman type of test is a function of block size and is given by:

$$E = \frac{N_{.k} + 1}{N_{.k}} = \frac{\sum_{k=1}^{K} n_{bk} + 1}{\sum_{k=1}^{K} n_{bk}} > 1$$

For randomized block designs consisting of a large number of relatively *small blocks*, the test on aligned observations is noticeably more efficient than the Friedman type of test. For the extreme case of blocks of size 2, the asymptotic efficiency of the aligned observations test relative to the Friedman test is $\frac{3}{2}$.

The preceding expressions for asymptotic relative efficiency have been reported for the case of samples drawn from normally distributed populations. Although the expressions for the efficiency of the test on aligned observations relative to the Friedman type of test are more complex for samples drawn from other types of distributions, the relative advantage of the test on aligned observations as a function of block size is maintained.

Despite the less restrictive assumptions made by the tests on aligned observations, the asymptotic efficiency of these tests relative to the F test is high. When the assumptions for the F test have been satisfied:

$$E = \frac{3}{\pi} = 0.955$$

Sen (1968) suggested that the lower limit on the asymptotic relative efficiency for tests for main effects based on aligned observations will be 0.864, as it is for the Mann–Whitney and Kruskal–Wallis tests relative to their parametric analogs. Moreover, this minimum value applies to a highly atypical distribution. For samples from the most commonly encountered nonnormal distributions such as uniform, logistic, and exponential, efficiency equals or exceeds 1. The substitution of normal scores for ranks in any of the tests on aligned observations will produce tests for which the asymptotic efficiency relative to that of the classical F test has a lower bound of 1.

Unlike the Friedman-type tests and the classical F tests, the tests on aligned observations can easily be adjusted to take into consideration the presence of extreme skewness or extreme observations in the data. For example, the effects of extreme skewness can be modified by aligning the observations on the basis of estimated medians rather than on the unweighted sample means. The presence of gross errors or extreme observations can be compensated for by aligning the observations on the basis of trimmed or Winsorized means, in preference to the unweighted sample means. Increased efficiency results from a judicious choice of a more appropriate estimator of location on which to align observations. The computational formulas for the test statistics are unaltered by this change in location parameters for alignment.

The repetitive nature of the computations involved in alignment, ranking and, in the case of interaction tests, estimating $\gamma_{.jk}$ by means of the:

$$g_{bjk} = r_{bjk} - \overline{R}_{b.k} - \overline{R}_{bj.} + \overline{R}_{b..}$$

makes the tests easily adaptable to machine computation. Moreover, major components of the computational process can be accomplished by the use of existing computer programs for ANOVA, since the test statistics are typically defined in terms of estimated treatment effects, as in classical ANOVA. Thus, the computational chores associated with the tests on aligned observations are more apparent than real.

15–14. Winsorized and Trimmed Means

In the alignment procedures of this chapter, it was suggested that alignment could be made on the basis of sample means, medians, Winsorized means, or trimmed means. While the first of these two estimates of population centers are familiar to most researchers, the latter two are less familiar and so a word of introduction is required. If a researcher believes that the smallest or largest values in the sample are not valid observations from the population under study, he can:

I. Replace these extreme values by their nearest neighbors.
II. Eliminate the extreme values.

If model I is used, the resulting mean is called a Winsorized mean. If model II is used, the resulting mean is called a trimmed mean.

If the original population is normally distributed and Winsorization is adopted, the loss in estimate efficiency is not large. If one observation is replaced at each end of the ordered sample, the efficiency of the Winsorized mean relative to the complete sample mean is given approximately by:

$$E = 1 - \frac{1}{3(N-2)}$$

For $N = 5$, $E = 0.89$, and for $N = 10$, $E = 0.96$. If two observations are replaced at each end of the ordered sample:

$$E = 1 - \frac{2}{3(N-2)}$$

For $N = 5$, $E = 0.81$, and for $N = 10$, $E = 0.92$. For trimmed means, the efficiencies are also quite high. For the elimination of one observation from each end of the sample, for $N = 5$, $E = 0.88$, and for $N = 10$, $E = 0.95$. The determination of Winsorized and trimmed means is illustrated in the following example.

EXAMPLE 15–14.1. Consider the following sample of ordered values:
$$8, \quad 12, \quad 23, \quad 26, \quad 27, \quad 27, \quad 28, \quad 30, \quad 55, \quad 69$$
The Winsorized mean involving the replacement of 8 by 12 and 69 by 55 is given by:

$$\overline{X}_W = \frac{12 + 12 + 23 + 26 + 27 + 27 + 28 + 30 + 55 + 55}{10} = 29.5$$

The corresponding trimmed mean is given by:

$$\overline{X}_T = \frac{12 + 23 + 26 + 27 + 27 + 28 + 30 + 55}{8} = 28.5$$

If the two extreme values are replaced, then:

$$\overline{X}_W = \frac{23 + 23 + 23 + 26 + 27 + 27 + 28 + 30 + 30 + 30}{10} = 26.7$$

and

$$\overline{X}_T = \frac{23 + 26 + 27 + 27 + 28 + 30}{6} = 26.8$$

As these examples indicate, Winsorization or trimming can be employed when the extreme values appear to be too small, or too large, or, as is frequently the case, are missing.

Summary

In this chapter, a number of efficient competitors to the classical ANOVA model based on blocking techniques were introduced. The first of these, based on combined Wilcoxon statistics across the blocks, is actually the two-treatment model discussed in Section 14–13 as the Friedman test for two or more observations per experimental unit. Thus, for $K = 2$, a researcher can use the model of Section 14–13 or that of Section 15–2 to analyze the data of a $2 \times B$-way factorial design with N_b subjects per block, with n_b observations made on treatment 1 to test the hypothesis of no difference in treatment effect. For this test, a simple assignment of ranks within each block is made, as one would do for the Wilcoxon two-sample test. Within each block, the corresponding Wilcoxon statistic, W_b, is computed for the observations that constitute treatment 1. With the resulting rank assignments, one sums across the blocks to obtain:

$$W = \sum_{b=1}^{B} W_b$$

$$E(W) = \sum_{b=1}^{B} \frac{n_b(N_b + 1)}{2}$$

$$\text{Var}(W) = \sum_{b=1}^{B} \frac{n_b(N_b - n_b)(N_b + 1)}{12}$$

and for a two-tailed test of no treatment effect, rejects H_0 if:

$$Z = \frac{W - E(W)}{\sqrt{\text{Var}(W)}}$$

is in the region defined by:

$$Z < Z_{\alpha/2}$$

or if

$$Z > Z_{1-\alpha/2}$$

where $Z_{\alpha/2}$ and $Z_{1-\alpha/2}$ are the $\alpha/2$ and $(1 - \alpha/2)$ percentile values of the standard normal distribution. Since the distribution of W is discrete, a correction for continuity may be incorporated into the determination of Z by subtracting $\frac{1}{2}$ from W if $W > E(W)$ or by adding $\frac{1}{2}$ to W if $W < E(W)$.

Hodges and Lehmann have shown that the analysis of the combined Wilcoxon model can be improved upon by:

1. Alignment of the data to remove the differences between the blocks

   and by

2. Taking advantage of the differential variances that exist within each block.

If it is assumed that the latent structure of each observation is given by:

$$X_{bki} = \mu + \alpha_{.k.} + \beta_{b..} + \ell_{bki}$$

the aligned X_{bki}^A is given by:

$$X_{bki}^A = X_{bki} - \beta_{b..} = \mu + \alpha_{.k.} + \ell_{bki}$$

and is estimated by:

$$\hat{X}_{bki}^A = X_{bki} - \hat{\beta}_{b..} = X_{bki} - \overline{X}_{b..} + \overline{X}_{...}$$

With the subtraction of $\hat{\beta}_{b..}$ from each observation, only the treatment effects and errors remain to account for the variance in the total set of observations. Thus, with the alignment, a researcher can rank the *entire* set of data as would be done for the Wilcoxon test. This ranking extends across the block boundaries. For this ranking, the ordinary two-sample Wilcoxon test is performed on the rank total for treatment 1. For this summation over the N_1 observations in treatment 1,

$$W = \sum_{b=1}^{B} \sum_{i=1}^{N_b} r_{bi}$$

$$E(W) = N_1 \left[\frac{N+1}{2} \right]$$

$$\mathrm{Var}(W) = N_1 N_2 \left[\frac{N+1}{12} \right]$$

and

$$Z = \frac{W - E(W)}{\sqrt{\mathrm{Var}(W)}}$$

Since this model removes only block differences, it was not illustrated in this chapter; yet it is the appropriate model if the variances within the blocks are essentially the same. If the variances are not the same, then the second modification suggested by Hodges and Lehmann is called for. To take advantage of the differences in variations within each block, separate means and variances are computed in each block, based upon the ranks that are assigned to the aligned observation. In the bth block,

$$E(W_b) = n_b \sum_{i=1}^{N_b} \frac{r_{bi}}{N_b} = n_b \overline{R}_b$$

$$\mathrm{Var}(W_b) = n_b \left[\frac{N_b - n_b}{N_b - 1} \right] \left[\frac{N_b \sum_{i=1}^{N_b} r_{bi}^2 - \left[\sum_{i=1}^{N_b} r_{bi} \right]^2}{N_b^2} \right]$$

so that, across the blocks,

$$E(W) = \sum_{b=1}^{B} E(W_b)$$

$$\mathrm{Var}(W) = \sum_{b=1}^{B} \mathrm{Var}(W_b)$$

and

$$Z = \frac{W - E(W)}{\sqrt{\mathrm{Var}(W)}}$$

is referred to the $N(0, 1)$ distribution, corrected for continuity, if desired.

The efficiency of the latter version of the combined Wilcoxon test never falls below 0.864, and, if the original variables are normal, $E = 0.955$.

The three described models can be further improved upon by substituting normal scores for the assigned ranks. No new theory is required to justify these forms since they involve only a transformation of ranks to another monotonically related variable.

The K-sample form of the three-rank and three-normal-scores tests can be obtained by a direct application of the models of Chapter 12. The first extension is described in detail in Section 14–13. The second extension takes advantage of the differences between the blocks. The data are aligned on the basis of the block mean, median, Winsorized mean, or trimmed mean, and the aligned data are ranked across the block boundaries. Since the block differences have been removed from the observed scores, the Kruskal–Wallis test:

$$H = \frac{12}{N(N + 1)} \sum_{k=1}^{K} \frac{R_{.k}^2}{n_k} - 3(N + 1)$$

is performed on the ranks. The hypothesis of no treatment effects is rejected if $H > X_{K-1:1-\alpha}^2$.

Finally, to take advantage of the within-block differences in variances, one computes separate means and variances for the ranks that are assigned to the aligned observations. Within a block

$$\overline{R}_{b..} = \frac{1}{nK} \sum_{k=1}^{K} \sum_{i=1}^{n} r_{bki}$$

and

$$S_{b..}^2 = \frac{\sum_{k=1}^{K} \sum_{i=1}^{n} (r_{bki} - \overline{R}_{b..})^2}{nK}$$

Across the blocks, the treatment rank totals are given by:

$$R_{.k.} = \sum_{b=1}^{B} R_{bk.}$$

with

$$E(R_{.k.}) = nB \frac{nBK + 1}{2}$$

$$\text{Var}(R_{.k.}) = \frac{Bn^2(K - 1)}{nK - 1} \sum_{b=1}^{B} \frac{S_b^2}{B} = \frac{Bn^2(K - 1)}{nK - 1} \overline{S_b^2}$$

so that, under the model of Section 2–10,

$$W = \frac{nK - 1}{nK} \sum_{k=1}^{K} \left[\frac{\overline{R}_{.k.} - \overline{R}_{...}}{\overline{S_b}/\sqrt{nB}} \right]^2$$

H_0 is rejected if $W > X_{K-1:1-\alpha}^2$.

Post hoc procedures for aligned rank tests with two or more observations per block involve the estimation of contrasts of the form:

$$\psi = a_1 E(R_1) + a_2 E(R_2) + \ldots + a_K E(R_K)$$

For the aligned model that does not consider the differences in block variances,

$$\text{Var}(\hat{\psi}) = \frac{n(N + 1)}{12} \sum_{k=1}^{K} \frac{a_k^2}{Bn}$$

For the Hodges–Lehmann model, which considers both intra- and interblock differences:

$$\text{Var}(\hat{\psi}) = \frac{K\overline{S_b^2}}{B(nK - 1)} \sum_{k=1}^{K} a_k^2$$

For both models, post hoc comparisons are made with:

$$\underline{S}^* = \sqrt{X_{K-1:1-\alpha}^2}$$

If each block in a randomized block design contains a two-factor, fully crossed set of conditions, one can test the hypothesis of no interaction for the two crossed factors. This test is based on the model:

$$X_{bjk} = \mu_{b..} + \alpha_{.j.} + \beta_{..k} + \gamma_{.jk} + \ell_{bjk}$$

For this test, alignment is made on the block effect and the main effects of the two crossed factors. This alignment gives rise to:

$$X^A_{bjk} = X_{bjk} - \mu_{b..} - \alpha_{.j.} - \beta_{..k} = \gamma_{.jk} + \ell_{bjk}$$

which is seen to be a function only of the interaction parameters and the errors. If ranks are assigned to the aligned observations, then

$$W = \frac{B\sum_{j=1}^{J}\sum_{k=1}^{K}\bar{g}^2_{.jk}}{\left[1/(B(J-1)(K-1))\right]\sum_{b=1}^{B}\sum_{j=1}^{J}\sum_{k=1}^{K}g^2_{bjk}}$$

where

$$g_{bjk} = r_{bjk} - \bar{R}_{b.k} - \bar{R}_{bj.} + \bar{R}_{b..}$$

is used to test H_0: All $\gamma_{.jk} = 0$ against the omnibus alternative H_1: H_0 is false. H_0 is rejected if $W > X^2_{(J-1)(K-1):1-\alpha}$.

If H_0 is rejected, one can examine contrasts in the individual rank estimates of the $\gamma_{.jk}$, which are defined as:

$$\bar{g}_{.jk} = \frac{1}{B}\sum_{b=1}^{B}g_{bjk}$$

Confidence intervals for the $E(\bar{g}_{.jk})$ are given by:

$$E(\bar{g}_{.jk}) = \bar{g}_{.jk} \pm \underline{S}^* \, SE_{\bar{g}.jk}$$

where

$$\underline{S}^* = \sqrt{X^2_{(J-1)(K-1):1-\alpha}}$$

and

$$SE^2_{\bar{g}.jk} = \frac{1}{B^2JK}\sum_{b=1}^{B}\sum_{j=1}^{J}\sum_{k=1}^{K}g^2_{bjk}$$

Finally, normal scores can be substituted for ranks in all of the preceding tests. No new theory is needed, and the formulas for the rank tests can be applied directly to the normal scores.

Exercises

*1. Use the combined Wilcoxon test on the data of Exericse 10 in Chapter 10 for the paragraph-meaning test scores, by defining blocks in terms of the six combinations of SES and sex.

*2. Repeat the analysis of Exercise 1 in terms of:
   a) Terry–Hoeffding normal scores.
   b) Van der Waerden normal scores.
   c) Compare the two methods of this exercise with those of Exercise 1.

*3. Answer the question of Exercise 1 in terms of the two Hodges–Lehmann alignment procedures described in Section 15–3 for only the paragraph-meaning score.

*4. Answer the question of Exercise 3 in terms of Van der Waerden normal scores.

*5. Analyze the data of Exercise 11 of Chapter 14 in terms of the methods described in Sections 15–5 and 15–6. How do these results compare to the Friedman-type analysis of the earlier exercise?

*6. Analyze the data of Exercise 11 of Chapter 14 in terms of the methods described in Section 15–7.

*7. Analyze the data of Exercise 11 of Chapter 14 by performing three combined Wilcoxon tests, each at $\alpha = 0.05/3 = 0.0167$. Repeat the analysis, using the alignment procedure of Hodges and Lehmann. Compare these results to those of Exercise 5 and Exercise 6 above. Which of these four methods has the most power?

*8. Is there an interaction of age of mother with amount of marijuana smoked for the data of Exercise 11 of Chapter 14? Use the methods of Sections 15–10 and 15–11.

*9. Is there an interaction of age of mother with amount of marijuana smoked for the data of Exercise 11 of Chapter 14? Use the Van der Waerden normal scores and the methods of Section 15–12.

*10. Analyze the data of Exercises 8 and 9 of Chapter 3, in terms of the model of Sections 15–2 and 15–3, for both ranks and normal scores.
  a) Why are these procedures justified for these data, in which different tests were used in the two schools?
  b) What is the hypothesis under test in (a)?
  c) How do the analyses of (a) compare to that used in Exercises 8 and 9 of Chapter 3? Of the methods used, which would you recommend? Why?

*11. Use the methods of this chapter to analyze the following data: Let A_1 and A_2 correspond to two levels of anxiety. Within each level, subjects are randomly assigned to two treatments B_1 and B_2. Each subject is observed over four trials, C_1, C_2, C_3, and C_4. The outcomes of the experiment are as shown in the accompanying table. Conditions of the

			C_1	C_2	C_3	C_4
A_1	B_1	S_1	5	7	8	10
		S_2	6	7	11	12
		S_3	6	10	11	12
	B_2	S_4	3	4	5	7
		S_5	3	4	5	7
		S_6	0	2	7	8
A_2	B_1	S_7	4	5	6	7
		S_8	5	6	8	9
		S_9	2	4	7	9
	B_2	S_{10}	0	1	2	2
		S_{11}	1	2	3	5
		S_{12}	0	2	3	6

study are as follows:

A_1: High-anxiety subjects
A_2: Low-anxiety subjects
B_1: High-threat condition by a *student plant* in a group-therapy situation
B_2: Low-threat condition by a *student plant* in a group-therapy situation
C_1: Observation Time One
C_2: Observation Time Two
C_3: Observation Time Three
C_4: Observation Time Four

The dependent variable is the number of times the target subject verbally assaulted the *student plant*.

*12. Twelve subjects are divided at random into three groups of four subjects each. Each subject is seated before a complicated stylus maze, which is wired to an electric-powered horn that is activated every time the subject allows the stylus to touch the walls of the maze. The subjects are told to take the stylus and learn the maze. There is only one path that can be taken without operating the horn. One group of subjects is told that ability to learn the maze is closely related to intelligence. Another group is told that the average college student makes only twenty errors on the fifth trial. The third group is told that they are simply to make as few errors as possible. Each group of subjects is given five trials. The errors are as shown in the table. Use the methods of this chapter to analyze these data.

	Subject	Trial				
		1	2	3	4	5
Intelligence group	1	40	39	33	33	20
	2	40	33	31	23	22
	3	38	34	30	28	26
	4	38	32	28	25	21
Average-20 group	1	34	27	26	25	23
	2	35	34	27	23	18
	3	35	27	23	21	21
	4	32	24	24	21	22
Few-errors group	1	40	40	30	30	29
	2	38	37	33	37	32
	3	39	38	35	34	34
	4	31	30	27	26	24

*13. In a survey of married female graduates' attitudes toward marriage and careers, 87 women at a large midwestern university were given an attitude inventory to measure their Role Satisfaction in marriage. The Role Satisfaction scores for a sample of 72 women out of the total of 87 were as shown in the table below.

So as to equalize the sample sizes, 15 women were randomly excluded from the study. Low scores are correlated with Role Satisfaction. Top score on the inventory is 28. Use the methods of this chapter to analyze these data.

	Years of marriage					
	Less than 5		5 to 10		More than 10	
Occupation	Housewife	Career	Housewife	Career	Housewife	Career
	7	12	8	22	7	22
	12	19	20	21	8	14
	8	13	13	18	5	28
	14	10	19	6	6	28
	10	7	15	19	7	28
	16	14	8	23	13	28
	11	6	7	17	9	17
	11	20	12	15	8	19
	9	9	9	19	12	25
	13	7	10	19	10	28
	11	8	14	28	10	12
	12	3	17	17	4	28

*14. Thirty-six students were given a reading comprehension test and then ranked according to total scores. They were then grouped into nine achievement levels and randomly assigned to one of four experimental conditions. The results of the ranking and testing were as shown in the accompanying table.

Block	C	M_1	M_2	M_3
1	26	24	24	30
2	18	25	26	34
3	21	28	22	30
4	24	33	28	34
5	27	34	32	28
6	26	40	37	42
7	36	36	44	48
8	41	44	48	57
9	49	46	48	59

The four conditions of the study are:

1. Control: Posttest was given one week later.
2. Method 1: Posttest was given one week later but students were told to study for it.
3. Method 2: Posttest was given one week later, but students were told that their pretest scores were very low.
4. Method 3: Posttest was given one week later, but students were told that their pretest scores were very high.

Since there may have been a block by treatment interaction, it was decided to combine the blocks in groups of three to produce three superblocks of Low-, Medium-, and High-ability subjects. Use the methods of this chapter to analyze these data.

*15. Perform the Kruskal–Wallis test on the aligned data of Table 15–6. Compare the results to the Hodges–Lehmann procedures described in Example 15–5.2.

Tests of Independence and Measures of Association for Quantitative Variables

16–1. Exact Tests of Independence for Two Quantitative Variables: The Pitman Correlation Coefficient

Assume that a single random sample of size n has been selected from a universe of interest. On each element of the sample, let measurements be simultaneously recorded relative to two quantitative variables. Let the two variables be denoted by Y_1 and Y_2. Let the sample of n ordered pairs be denoted by:

$$S: \quad \{(y_{11}, y_{12}), (y_{21}, y_{22}), \ldots, (y_{n1}, y_{n2})\}$$

For this observed sample, the Pearson product-moment correlation coefficient can be evaluated by means of the familiar computing formula:

$$r = \frac{n\left[\sum_{i=1}^n y_{i1} y_{i2}\right] - \left[\sum_{i=1}^n y_{i1}\right]\left[\sum_{i=1}^n y_{i2}\right]}{\sqrt{n\left[\sum_{i=1}^n y_{i1}^2\right] - \left[\sum_{i=1}^n y_{i1}\right]^2} \sqrt{n\left[\sum_{i=1}^n y_{i2}^2\right] - \left[\sum_{i=1}^n y_{i2}\right]^2}}$$

If Y_1 and Y_2 have a joint bivariate normal distribution, r can be used to test H_0: $\rho = 0$ against $H_1: \rho \neq 0$, or $\rho < 0$, or $\rho > 0$, depending upon the alternative of interest. If Y_1 and Y_2 are not bivariate normal, then H_0 can be tested by means of a technique described by Pitman and related to Fisher's method of randomization discussed in a number of different contexts in previous chapters. Focusing on the particular sample observed, Fisher's randomization procedure is applied to the observed sample values to obtain an exact conditional distribution of r. The distribution of r generated in this fashion is referred to as the Pitman distribution of r.

To determine the Pitman distribution of r, the n paired observations are permuted so as to generate all possible values of r that can be computed from the sample values. For each permutation, r is computed. To obtain the complete permutation distribution of r, the values of Y_1 are ordered according to numerical values. Next, the Y_2 sample values are permuted against the ordered Y_1 values. The number of unique permutations is given by $T = n!$. For each of these $n!$ permutations, r is determined.

Actually the computations, though tedious, are much simpler than suggested by this description. The sums

$$\sum_{i=1}^{n} y_{i1}, \quad \sum_{i=1}^{n} y_{i2}, \quad \sum_{i=1}^{n} y_{i1}^2, \quad \text{and} \quad \sum_{i=1}^{n} y_{i2}^2$$

are each constant over the $n!$ permutations. Thus, the only random variable over the sample values of r is $\sum_{i=1}^{n} y_{i1} y_{i2}$. As a result, a researcher need only compute these summed products over the permutation set. Under the assumption of zero correlation between Y_1 and Y_2, these $n!$ summed products are equally likely, so that the observed value of r can be evaluated for significance with a Type I error of size α by comparing the observed value of $\sum_{i=1}^{n} y_{i1} y_{i2}$ to the $\alpha n!$ extreme critical values in the Pitman distribution of $\sum_{i=1}^{n} y_{i1} y_{i2}$.

EXAMPLE 16–1.1. As an example of the use of the Pitman procedure, consider the data of Table 16–1, which a researcher expected to show a positive correlation.

For these data,

$$\sum_{i=1}^{5} y_{i1} = 267, \quad \sum_{i=1}^{5} y_{i2} = 286, \quad \sum_{i=1}^{5} y_{i1}^2 = 14313, \quad \text{and} \quad \sum_{i=1}^{5} y_{i2}^2 = 16582$$

across all $T = n! = 5! = 120$ permutations of the Y_2 values. For the observed sample,

$$\sum_{i=1}^{5} y_{i1} y_{i2} = (48)(48) + (54)(56) + (52)(62) + (55)(67) + (58)(53) = 15311$$

so that $r = 0.348$. The hypothesis that the variables are positively correlated is tested on the basis of these data. In standard statistical form, this experimental model can be stated as:

$$H_0: \rho = 0 \quad \text{and} \quad H_1: \rho > 0$$

TABLE 16–1. *Standard scores on a vocabulary and arithmetic-reasoning test made by a sample of five children.*

Subject	Y_1: Score on vocabulary test	Y_2: Score on arithmetic-reasoning test
Adam	48	48
Byron	54	56
Carl	52	62
Daniel	55	67
Edward	58	53

Y_1	Permutations of Y_2					
48	48	48	48	48	53	53
52	53	56	53	53	48	48
54	56	53	62	56	56	56
55	62	62	56	67	62	67
58	67	67	67	62	67	62
$\sum_{i=1}^{n} y_{i1} y_{i2}$	15380	15374	15374	15365	15360	15345
r	0.970	0.916	0.916	0.835	0.790	0.654

Since large values of r are compatible with H_1, the $\alpha = 0.05$ critical region consists of the $\alpha n! = 0.05(120) = 6$ largest values of $\sum_{i=1}^{5} y_{i1} y_{i2}$. These six extreme outcomes are listed in Table 16–2 along with the corresponding values of $\sum_{i=1}^{5} y_{i1} y_{i2}$ and r. Since the observed sample is not included in the set of six critical samples, the hypothesis of zero correlation is not rejected.

The Pitman test of significance has the same disadvantages as any randomization, permutation, or Fisher-type test. Since the test is conditional upon the observed data, a separate computation of the null distribution or its critical region for each different set of sample values is required. However, the asymptotic efficiency of the Pitman test relative to the classical bivariate normal test of independence, when the assumptions are satisfied, equals 1.00. In this sense, the Pitman test is just as good a test as the classical test. If bivariate normality is satisfied, then the Pitman test of no association is actually a test of independence between Y_1 and Y_2 against the alternative hypothesis that the expected association between Y_1 and Y_2 is linear. Otherwise, the test is one of no association versus monotonic relationship. For this less restrictive test, the only assumption that must be satisfied is that the n paired observations are statistically independent. Operationally, this means that the researcher must have a random sample of paired observations from the bivariate population of interest. For emphasis, it should be recalled that the hypothesis under test is one of no association and not one of statistical independence. Statistical independence of the quantitative variables Y_1 and Y_2 can be tested only if Y_1 and Y_2 are bivariate normal.

16–2. The Spearman Rank-Correlation Coefficient

Just as the Fisher randomization tests can be transformed from conditional to unconditional tests, so can the Pitman test be transformed. This transformation is accomplished by ordering the Y_1 and Y_2 variables from 1 to n separately and then computing the ordinary Pearson product-moment correlation coefficient on the ranked data. This is illustrated in Table 16–3 for the data of Table 16–1. The cor-

Tests of
Independence
and Measures of
Association for
Quantitative
Variables

431

Student	Y_1: Score on vocabulary test	r_1: Rank value	Y_2: Score on arithmetic-reasoning test	r_2: Rank value	$d = r_1 - r_2$
Adam	48	1	48	1	0
Byron	54	3	56	3	0
Carl	52	2	62	4	-2
Daniel	55	4	67	5	-1
Edward	58	5	53	2	3

relational coefficient computed in this way is called the Spearman rank-correlation coefficient, and in the literature is generally denoted by r_S.

EXAMPLE 16–2.1. For the rank data of Table 16–3:

$$\sum_{i=1}^{5} r_{i1} = 1 + 3 + 2 + 4 + 5 = 15$$

$$\sum_{i=1}^{5} r_{i2} = 1 + 3 + 4 + 5 + 2 = 15$$

$$\sum_{i=1}^{5} r_{i1}^2 = 1^2 + 3^2 + 2^2 + 4^2 + 5^2 = 55$$

$$\sum_{i=1}^{5} r_{i2}^2 = 1^2 + 3^2 + 4^2 + 5^2 + 2^2 = 55$$

$$\sum_{i=1}^{5} r_{i1} r_{i2} = (1)(1) + (3)(3) + (2)(4) + (4)(5) + (5)(2) = 48$$

so that

$$r_S = \frac{5(48) - (15)(15)}{\sqrt{5(55) - (15)^2} \sqrt{5(55) - (15)^2}} = 0.30$$

When there are no tied ranks for Y_1 or Y_2, an easier computational formula using $d_i = r_{i1} - r_{i2}$ is available. If there are no errors in assigning ranks, the d_i should sum to zero. If, after the data are ranked, paired differences in the ranks, $d_i = r_{i1} - r_{i2}$, are computed, then a simple computing formula for r_S is given by:

$$r_S = 1 - \frac{6\sum_{i=1}^{n} d_i^2}{n^3 - n}$$

This formulation is easy to derive by noting that:

$$S_d^2 = S_{r_1}^2 + S_{r_2}^2 - 2rS_{r_1}S_{r_2}$$

so that

$$r = \frac{S_{r_1}^2 + S_{r_2}^2 - S_d^2}{2S_{r_1}S_{r_2}}$$

For a set of n ranks it can be shown that:

$$S_{r_1}^2 = S_{r_2}^2 = S_{r_1} S_{r_2} = \frac{n(n + 1)}{12}$$

Thus

$$r = \frac{(n(n + 1)/12) + (n(n + 1)/12) - S_d^2}{2n(n + 1)/12} = 1 - \frac{6 S_d^2}{n(n + 1)}$$

By definition,

$$S_d^2 = \frac{\sum_{i=1}^{n} (d_i - \bar{d})^2}{n - 1} = \frac{\sum_{i=1}^{n} d_i^2}{n - 1}$$

since $\bar{d} = 0$. Thus,

$$r_S = 1 - \frac{6 \sum_{i=1}^{n} d_i^2/(n - 1)}{n(n + 1)} = 1 - \frac{6 \sum_{i=1}^{n} d_i^2}{n^3 - n}$$

EXAMPLE 16–2.2. For the data of Table 16–3,

$$r_S = 1 - \frac{6\left[(0)^2 + (0)^2 + (-2)^2 + (-1)^2 + (3)^2\right]}{5^3 - 5}$$

$$= 1 - \frac{6(14)}{120} = 0.30$$

The exact sampling distribution of r_S is found in exactly the same way used to determine the sampling distribution of the Pitman correlation coefficient, except that ranks are used instead of the original observations. Under the hypothesis of no correlation, all $n!$ permutations of the n rank values are equally likely. Thus, for a test with a critical region of size alpha, one need only compute the $\alpha n!$ extreme correlations. If the observed correlation is included in this set, the hypothesis of zero correlation is rejected. With $\alpha = 0.05$ and $n = 5$, the critical region is defined by the $K = \alpha n! = 0.05(5!) = 6$ largest values of r_S.

EXAMPLE 16–2.3. The null distribution of r_S for the data of Table 16–1 is shown in Table 16–4. It is symmetric about zero and somewhat jagged in appearance. An exact test of size 0.05 is not available for these data, since values of r_S appear with multiple frequency. Three different permutations produce an $r_S = 0.80$ and the test of $\alpha \le 0.05$ is given by the exact test with $\alpha = 5/120 = 0.042 < 0.05$. For this α, the hypothesis of no correlation is rejected if $r \ge 0.90$. For completeness, the five extreme positive rank samples are shown in Table 16–5 along with the values of $\sum_{i=1}^{5} d_i^2$ and r_S.

Fortunately, tables of the distribution of r_S exist, so a researcher does not have to determine the critical region each time the test of no correlation is performed. For small sample sizes, use can be made of Table A–24, which gives the two-tailed probabilities of the null distribution of r_S. For a one-tailed test, the tabled α value is reduced to $\frac{1}{2}\alpha$.

Tests of
Independence
and Measures of
Association for
Quantitative
Variables

433

TABLE 16–4. *The null distribution of* r_S *for* $n = 5$.

Value of $\sum_{i=1}^{5} d_i^2$	Value of r_S	Frequency
40	−1.0	1
38	−0.9	4
36	−0.8	3
34	−0.7	6
32	−0.6	7
30	−0.5	6
28	−0.4	4
26	−0.3	10
24	−0.2	6
22	−0.1	10
20	0.0	6
18	0.1	10
16	0.2	6
14	0.3	10
12	0.4	4
10	0.5	6
8	0.6	7
6	0.7	6
4	0.8	3
2	0.9	4
0	1.0	1

EXAMPLE 16–2.4. For the one-tailed test of Example 16–2.2, H_0 should be rejected if $r_S \geq 0.900$. Since $r_S = 0.300$, the hypothesis that $\rho > 0$ is not rejected.

Employment of the Spearman rank-correlation coefficient is based upon the same assumptions required for the Pitman test of correlation. It must be assumed that paired observations are statistically independent. The hypothesis of no association is being tested against the alternative of a *monotonic* relationship and not a linear relationship, as tested in the classical bivariate normal model. If, however, the

TABLE 16–5. *The five most extreme permutations of ranks for the ordered* Y_1 *values of Table 16–1.*

Y_1	r_1	Permutations of r_2				
48	1	1	2	1	1	1
52	2	2	1	3	2	2
54	3	3	3	2	4	3
55	4	4	4	4	3	5
58	5	5	5	5	5	4
$\sum_{i=1}^{5} d_i^2$		0	2	2	2	2
r_S		1.0	0.9	0.9	0.9	0.9

classical bivariate normal theory is appropriate, little harm is done in using the Spearman rank-correlation coefficient to test for independence between two variables. In this case, substitution of the Spearman rank correlation for the Pearson product-moment correlation is acceptable since, under bivariate normality, the asymptotic relative efficiency of the rank procedure to the classical procedure is given by

$$E = \left(\frac{3}{\pi}\right)^2 = 0.912$$

If the Y_2 variable is normally distributed, then the asymptotic relative efficiency of the Spearman test against the univariate normal test of $H_0: \beta = 0$ in a linear regression model is given by

$$E = \left(\frac{3}{\pi}\right)^{1/3} = 0.98$$

provided the values of Y_1 represent unit increases in the independent variable. This would arise if y_1 were a variable such as time, trial, or other variable that would lead to a linear trend. The Spearman rank-correlation ceofficient is a valid measure of strength of association if the underlying variables are originally ranked and not measured. This might happen when a subject is given a set of n objects and is asked to rank-order them on some dimension from 1 to n, on two different occasions. As a measure of his consistency in performing this task, r_S is acceptable.

Even though the Spearman rank-correlation coefficient has intuitive appeal, Kendall's tau, which is also a measure of correlation, may be preferred as a measure of correlation since it has exactly the same ARE properties as Spearman's r_S. The major reasons for this preference are that the distribution of tau approaches normality faster than does the distribution of r_S and that tau has wider applicability than does r_S to behavioral data (Kendall, 1962; Ferguson, 1965). This greater flexibility is illustrated in a number of the following sections.

16–3. Tied Ranks and r_S

As was seen in Section 16–2, the null distribution of r_S is based on all possible $n!$ permutations of the rank values $1, 2, \ldots, n$. If tied observations appear in either Y_1 or Y_2, then the number of unique permutations is some number less than $n!$.

EXAMPLE 16–3.1. If, in a sample of $n = 8$, there are three values tied at one value and two values tied at some other value, then the number of unique permutations is not given by $n! = 8! = 40,320$, but is given instead by $8!/(3!2!) = 3,360$. This reduction in the number of different values of r_S produces a reduction in the variance of the sampling distribution of r_S, so that Table A–24 is, in theory, no longer applicable. If, in addition, there are ties in the Y_2 values, further reductions in the variance occur. When ties appear, the usual procedure is to assign midranks to the tied values, and then compute r_S in the usual fashion. This is illustrated in the next example.

EXAMPLE 16–3.2. Consider the following set of data:

$$Y_1: \quad 18, \quad 23, \quad 23, \quad 25, \quad 27, \quad 27, \quad 27, \quad 31$$
$$Y_2: \quad 12, \quad 10, \quad 15, \quad 16, \quad 10, \quad 17, \quad 12, \quad 15$$

In the Y_1 set, there are two values tied at 23 and three values tied at 27, while in the Y_2 set there are three sets of two tied values at 10, 12, and 15. When midranks are assigned to the tied values, the ranks for these two sets of data, along with their d_i and d_i^2, are as shown.

r_1:	1	2.5	2.5	4	6	6	6	8
r_2:	3.5	1.5	5.5	7	1.5	8	3.5	5.5
d_i:	−2.5	1.0	−3.0	−3.0	4.5	−2	2.5	2.5
d_i^2:	6.25	1.00	9.00	9.00	20.25	4.00	6.25	6.25

Thus

$$r_S = 1 - \frac{6\sum_{i=1}^{n} d_i^2}{n^3 - n} = 1 - \frac{6(62)}{8^3 - 8} = 0.262$$

In this case, if $r_S = 0.262$ is referred to Table A–24 for $n = 8$ and $\alpha = 0.05$, it is seen that $r_{S_{0.025}} = -0.738$ and $r_{S_{0.975}} = 0.738$, indicating that H_0 should not be rejected.

Kendall has shown that a better approximation for tied ranks is based on using a corrected r_S defined by:

$$r_S^C = \frac{\frac{1}{6}(n^3 - n) - \sum_{i=1}^{n} d_i^2 - T - U}{\sqrt{\frac{1}{6}(n^3 - n) - 2T}\,\sqrt{\frac{1}{6}(n^3 - n) - 2U}}$$

where

$$T = \frac{1}{12}\sum_j (t_j^3 - t_j)$$

$$U = \frac{1}{12}\sum_j (u_j^3 - u_j)$$

t_j = Number of Y_1 values tied to the same value

and

u_j = Number of Y_2 values tied to the same value

EXAMPLE 16–3.3. For the data of Example 16–3.2, $t_1 = 2$ and $t_2 = 3$, so that:

$$T = \frac{1}{12}\left[(2^3 - 2) + (3^3 - 3)\right] = 2.5$$

and for the Y_2 data, $u_1 = 2$, $u_2 = 2$, and $u_3 = 2$, so that:

$$U = \frac{1}{12}\left[(2^3 - 2) + (2^3 - 2) + (2^3 - 2)\right] = 1.5$$

Finally, the corrected r_S is given by:

$$r_S^C = \frac{\frac{1}{6}(8^3 - 8) - (62) - 2.5 - 1.5}{\sqrt{\frac{1}{6}(8^3 - 8) - 2(2.5)} \sqrt{\frac{1}{6}(8^3 - 8) - 2(1.5)}}$$

$$= \frac{18}{\sqrt{80}\sqrt{81}} = 0.224$$

As is seen, the correction doesn't make much difference when the number of tied values is small and, as a result, is not necessary if the t_j and u_j are small. However, if the t_j or u_j are large, then it might be advisable to use r_S^C as an estimator in place of r_S.

When testing for significance, it appears that no simple methods exist for dealing with ties; and so when the exact tables or approximate normal-curve tests are used, no clear-cut rules can be given. Since the true variances are smaller than estimated, it must follow that the usual tests are conservative, so that a finding significant at a Type I error level of size α most likely represents a significant finding.

16–4. The Large-Sample Test of $\rho_S = 0$

Under permutation theory, it can be shown that the mean and variance of the null distribution of the Pearson product-moment correlation coefficient are given by:

$$E(r) = 0$$

and

$$\text{Var}(r) = \frac{1}{n - 1}$$

Since the Spearman rank correlation is a Pearson product-moment correlation coefficient, and since its distribution is based on permutation theory, one can use these results to generate a large-sample test of $H_0: \rho_S = 0$ against $H_1: \rho_S \neq 0$. The test statistic is simply:

$$Z = \frac{r_S - E(r_S)}{\sqrt{\text{Var}(r_S)}} = \frac{r_S - 0}{1/\sqrt{n - 1}} = r_S\sqrt{n - 1}$$

which, when H_0 is true, has an approximate normal distribution with $E(Z) = 0$ and $\text{Var}(Z) = 1$.

EXAMPLE 16–4.1. Suppose the rank correlation between two variables is given by $r_S = 0.36$ for a sample of 26 subjects. To test $H_0: \rho_S = 0$ against $H_1: \rho_S > 0$, compute:

$$Z = r\sqrt{n-1} = 0.36\sqrt{26-1} = 1.80$$

Reject H_0 since $Z > Z_{0.95} = 1.645$, the upper 5% point of the $N(0, 1)$ distribution.

16–5. Normal Scores in the Pearson Product-Moment Correlation Coefficient

In addition to the use of ranks, normal scores can be used to measure the association between two variables. Under the permutation model, one can use the expected value and variance of the permutation distribution to test for no association.

EXAMPLE 16–5.1. In Table 16–6 normal scores of the Van der Waerden form have been determined for each of the original observations of Table 16–1. Since $\sum_{i=1}^{n} Z_{i1} = \sum_{i=1}^{n} Z_{i2} = 0$, and $\sum_{i=1}^{n} Z_{i1}^2 = \sum_{i=1}^{n} Z_{i2}^2$:

$$r = \frac{\sum_{i=1}^{n} Z_{i1} Z_{i2}}{\sum_{i=1}^{n} Z_i^2}$$

For the observed data,

$$\sum_{i=1}^{n} Z_{i1} Z_{i2} = 0.7560 \quad \text{and} \quad \sum_{i=1}^{n} Z_i^2 = 2.2516$$

so that:

$$r = \frac{0.7560}{2.2516} = 0.335$$

To test $H_0: \rho = 0$ against $H_1: \rho > 0$, one computes:

$$Z = \frac{r - E(r)}{\sqrt{\text{Var}(r)}} = \frac{r - 0}{1/\sqrt{n-1}} = r\sqrt{n-1}$$

and rejects H_0 if Z is too large. For the observed data, $Z = 0.335\sqrt{5-1} = 0.670$, so H_0 is not rejected.

As might be expected, the ARE of the normal-scores correlation to the classical measure is given by $E = 1.00$, provided that the joint distribution of Y_1

TABLE 16–6. Normal-score correlation for the data of Table 16–1.

Subject	Y_1	Y_2	Z_1	Z_2
Adam	48	48	−0.97	−0.97
Byron	54	56	0.00	0.00
Carl	52	62	−0.43	0.43
Daniel	55	67	0.43	0.97
Edward	58	53	0.97	−0.43

and Y_2 is bivariate normal. If the bivariate normal assumption is not satisfied, then the test of H_0: $\rho = 0$ is tested against the alternative that Y_1 and Y_2 are monotonically related to one another. While Van der Waerden inverse normal scores were used to illustrate the procedures, use could have been made of expected normal-order statistics.

16–6. Measures of Concordance and Discordance as Measures of Correlation

EXAMPLE 16–6.1. Consider the rank data of Table 16–3, reproduced here:

Subject	A	B	C	D	E
Rank on Y_1	1	3	2	4	5
Rank on Y_2	1	3	4	5	2

Consider the $\begin{bmatrix} n \\ 2 \end{bmatrix} = \begin{bmatrix} 5 \\ 2 \end{bmatrix} = 10$ ordered pairs of subjects, and for each pair consider the rankings of Y_1 and Y_2 individually. If the ranks are in proper order, score the pair $(+1)$, but if the rank orders are reversed, score the pair (-1). Do this for both Y_1 and Y_2 separately. Now multiply the scores. If the multiplied scores are $(+1)(+1)$ or $(-1)(-1)$, the product is equal to $(+1)$, and the pairs are said to be *concordant*. If the multiplied scores are $(+1)(-1)$ or $(-1)(+1)$, the product is equal to (-1), and the pairs are said to be *discordant*. Next, count the number of concordant and discordant pairs. Let these totals be N_C and N_D. Let their proportions in the sample be $\hat{p}_C$ and $\hat{p}_D$. Since the number of pairs is given by $\begin{bmatrix} n \\ 2 \end{bmatrix}$:

$$\tau = \hat{p}_C - \hat{p}_D = \frac{N_C}{\begin{bmatrix} n \\ 2 \end{bmatrix}} - \frac{N_D}{\begin{bmatrix} n \\ 2 \end{bmatrix}}$$

measures the degree of correlation in the data. Following the scoring procedure described, the determination of τ is as shown in Table 16–7. For these data, $N_C = 6$ and $N_D = 4$, so that

$$\tau = \frac{6}{\begin{bmatrix} 5 \\ 2 \end{bmatrix}} - \frac{4}{\begin{bmatrix} 5 \\ 2 \end{bmatrix}} = \frac{2}{10} = 0.20$$

The sample difference in proportions has been termed τ (tau) by Kendall and is a measure of the difference of the proportion of concordant and discordant pairs. If $\hat{p}_D = 0$, all pairs are concordant and $\tau = 1$. At the same time, the Spearman rank-correlation coefficient equals $+1$ or is close to it in value. If $\hat{p}_C = 0$, then all pairs are in exact disagreement, $\tau = -1$, and the Spearman rank-correlation coefficient equals -1 or is close to it in value. When $\hat{p}_C = \hat{p}_D$, $\tau = 0$ and, in general, so does r_S. Thus, tau, as a measure of concordance and discordance, is also a measure of correlation, but not as a Pearson product-moment correlation measure. As might be expected, the correlation between these two measures is quite high. As shown by

Tests of
Independence
and Measures of
Association for
Quantitative
Variables

439

TABLE 16-7. Determination of Kendall's τ for the data of Table 16-1.

Pair	Score for Y_1	Score for Y_2	Product	State
A B	+1	+1	+1	Concordant
A C	+1	+1	+1	Concordant
A D	+1	+1	+1	Concordant
A E	+1	+1	+1	Concordant
B C	−1	+1	−1	Discordant
B D	+1	+1	+1	Concordant
B E	+1	−1	−1	Discordant
C D	+1	+1	+1	Concordant
C E	+1	−1	−1	Discordant
D E	+1	−1	−1	Discordant
			+2	

Kendall,

$$\rho_{r_S \tau} = \frac{2(n + 1)}{\sqrt{2n(2n + 5)}}$$

tends to unity as n increases. Even for small samples, $\rho_{r_S \tau}$ is close to one.

Note that, if $E(\hat{p}_C) = p_C$ and $E(\hat{p}_D) = p_D$, then τ is an unbiased estimate of $p_C - p_D$, the proportion of concordant pairs minus the proportion of discordant pairs. In this sense, τ has a very simple intuitive interpretation as a measure of disarray or array. Under perfect positive correlation, all pairs are concordant, while, under perfect negative correlation, all pairs are discordant. Under no correlation, 50% of the pairs are expected to be concordant, while the remaining 50% are expected to be discordant.

Often Kendall's τ is written as:

$$\tau = \frac{S}{\begin{bmatrix} n \\ 2 \end{bmatrix}} = \frac{2S}{n(n - 1)}$$

where $S = N_C - N_D$. In general, this notation will be used in the remainder of this book, since tables prepared by Kendall are tabulated in terms of S. Since $N_C + N_D = \begin{bmatrix} n \\ 2 \end{bmatrix}$, τ can be written strictly in terms of N_D. By definition:

$$\tau = \frac{S}{\begin{bmatrix} n \\ 2 \end{bmatrix}} = \frac{N_C - N_D}{\begin{bmatrix} n \\ 2 \end{bmatrix}}$$

so that

$$\tau = \frac{\left[\begin{bmatrix} n \\ 2 \end{bmatrix} - N_D\right] - N_D}{\begin{bmatrix} n \\ 2 \end{bmatrix}} = 1 - \frac{2N_D}{\begin{bmatrix} n \\ 2 \end{bmatrix}} = 1 - \frac{4N_D}{n(n - 1)}$$

Another way to view Kendall's correlation coefficient is to consider inversions of rankings, as discussed in connection with the Mann–Whitney form of the

Wilcoxon test. The connection between counting inversions and using the scoring method described is easy to understand.

EXAMPLE 16–6.2. Consider the following set of data, which has been ranked according to the value of Y_1 in each pair:

Score on Pretest Y_1:	4	6	7	8	12	13	14	16
Score on Posttest Y_2:	9	8	10	12	15	20	28	22

To determine τ, rank the Y_2 sample observations from 1 to n, with a 1 being assigned to the smallest observation and n being assigned to the largest observation. For these data, $n = 8$. The assigned rank values are:

$$R_2: \quad 2 \quad 1 \quad 3 \quad 4 \quad 5 \quad 6 \quad 8 \quad 7$$

If the variables were perfectly correlated, the ranked values for the Y_2 sample would be identical to the ranked values of the Y_1 sample, and would be given by:

$$R_1: \quad 1 \quad 2 \quad 3 \quad 4 \quad 5 \quad 6 \quad 7 \quad 8$$

The number of inversions for this perfectly ordered ranking is zero. For the observed Y_2 ranking, the number of inversions equals two. This number is identical to N_D. The number of correctly ordered pairs is 24. This number is identical to N_C.

This method of counting N_C and N_D is identical to that used in Example 16–6.1 of this section. Since the Y_1 values are already ordered, every Y_1 pair is scored $(+1)$. Thus, multiplication with the Y_2 pair score is unnecessary, since if the Y_2 pair is scored $(+1)$, the product would remain $(+1)$, or if the Y_2 pair is scored (-1), the product would remain (-1). As a result, one need only count the number of $(+1)$ and (-1) pairs for the Y_2 ranking, to obtain N_C and N_D directly.

For the data of this example, $N_D = 2$, $N_C = 26$, so that $S = 26 - 2 = 24$. Thus,

$$\tau = \frac{2S}{n(n-1)} = \frac{2(24)}{8(7)} = \frac{6}{7} = 0.857$$

or, since $N_D = 2$, tau is also given by:

$$\tau = 1 - \frac{4N_D}{n(n-1)} = 1 - \frac{4(2)}{8(7)} = \frac{6}{7} = 0.857$$

The distribution of S for small samples is presented in Table A–25. As will be shown, the distribution of τ is symmetrical about zero, so that the approximate 0.005, 0.01, 0.025, 0.05, and 0.10 percentile values are the simple negatives of the table values. Tables of τ for $n > 10$ are not necessary, since the distribution of τ tends to a normal form for relatively small sample sizes. When $n > 10$, a good normal approximation exists for both τ and S. Because S has greater statistical use than τ, discussion will focus on S as a test statistic.

EXAMPLE 16–6.3. From the table, it is seen that for $n = 8$, $S = 24$, and $\tau = 0.857$, the two-tailed $\alpha = 0.05$ decision rule indicates that a statistically significant correlation exists between Y_1 and Y_2, since the approximate $S_{0.025} = -18$ and $S_{0.975} = 18$.

16–7. Distribution Theory of Tau

To generate the distribution of tau when Y_1 and Y_2 are uncorrelated, let a random sample of size n be selected from the universe of interest and then let the sample observations be ordered on the basis of the Y_1 values obtained in the sample. So as to avoid tied values, let it also be assumed that the joint distribution of Y_1 and Y_2 is continuous in both variables. If Y_1 and Y_2 are uncorrelated, then all possible arrangements of the Y_2 sample values are equally likely provided that the Y_1 values are ordered. The number of such equally likely arrangements of the Y_2's is given by $T = n!$. Thus, the probability of any one arrangement is given by $p = 1/n!$. To find the distribution of S or τ, one need only determine the $n!$ equally likely permutations of $\{1, 2, 3, \ldots, n\}$, compute S and τ for each permutation, and tabulate the results. This procedure is illustrated for $n = 4$. For $n = 4$, $T = 4! = (4)(3)(2)(1) = 24$. These permutations, along with S and τ, are summarized in Table 16–8. From this table, the distribution of tau and S is determined. These distribu-

TABLE 16–8. The complete set of 24 permutations of the integers 1, 2, 3, and 4, along with their corresponding S and τ values.

Permutation	Value of S	Value of τ
1 2 3 4	6	1
1 2 4 3	4	$\frac{2}{3}$
1 3 2 4	4	$\frac{2}{3}$
1 3 4 2	2	$\frac{1}{3}$
1 4 2 3	2	$\frac{1}{3}$
1 4 3 2	0	0
2 1 3 4	4	$\frac{2}{3}$
2 1 4 3	2	$\frac{1}{3}$
2 3 1 4	2	$\frac{1}{3}$
2 3 4 1	0	0
2 4 1 3	0	0
2 4 3 1	-2	$-\frac{1}{3}$
3 1 2 4	2	$\frac{1}{3}$
3 1 4 2	0	0
3 2 1 4	0	0
3 2 4 1	-2	$-\frac{1}{3}$
3 4 1 2	-2	$-\frac{1}{3}$
3 4 2 1	-4	$-\frac{2}{3}$
4 1 2 3	0	0
4 1 3 2	-2	$-\frac{1}{3}$
4 2 1 3	-2	$-\frac{1}{3}$
4 2 3 1	-4	$-\frac{2}{3}$
4 3 1 2	-4	$-\frac{2}{3}$
4 3 2 1	-6	-1

TABLE 16–9. *The probability distribution of S and τ for n = 4.*

Value of S	Value of τ	Number	Probability
-6	-1	1	$\frac{1}{24}$
-4	$-\frac{2}{3}$	3	$\frac{3}{24}$
-2	$-\frac{1}{3}$	5	$\frac{5}{24}$
0	0	6	$\frac{6}{24}$
2	$\frac{1}{3}$	5	$\frac{5}{24}$
4	$\frac{2}{3}$	3	$\frac{3}{24}$
6	1	1	$\frac{1}{24}$
		24	$\frac{24}{24}$

tions are shown in Table 16–9. As can be seen, the distribution of S is symmetrical about zero, so that $E(S) = 0$. In addition, it is seen that the distance between the possible values of S is two complete units.

16–8. Large-Sample Distribution of τ and Nonparametric Tests for Monotonic Relationships

Since τ is a measure of correlation, it might be assumed that it, or some variable related to it, can be used to test for regression or monotonic trend. As is recalled, if Y_2 increases as Y_1 increases, the relationship between Y_1 and Y_2 is monotonic increasing. If Y_2 decreases as Y_1 increases, the relationship is said to be monotonic decreasing.

When Y_1 and Y_2 are uncorrelated, so that no trend relationship exists between Y_1 and Y_2, one can show, with some tortuous algebra, that:

$$E(S) = 0$$

and

$$\text{Var}(S) = \frac{n(n-1)(2n+5)}{18}$$

Since large positive values of S correspond to positive relationship, and large negative values of S correspond to negative relationship, tests for trend or regression are performed by comparing the observed S to the tabled S values, or by means of the large-sample normal-distribution approximation:

$$Z = \frac{S - E(S)}{\sqrt{\text{Var}(S)}} = \frac{S}{\sqrt{n(n-1)(2n+5)/18}}$$

which approaches a $N(0, 1)$ form as n increases. Since S is a discrete random variable, a correction for continuity is advisable before computing Z. In general, most continuity corrections involve the addition or subtraction of $\frac{1}{2}$ unit from the observed statistic. For S, the continuity corrections involve the addition or subtraction of the number *one*, since the units separating unique values of S are of size two. When S is positive, one should be subtracted. When S is negative, 1 should be added.

EXAMPLE 16–8.1. For the data of Example 16–6.2, $S = 24$, and $n = 8$. Thus, to test H_0: Y_1 and Y_2 are unrelated, versus the alternative H_1: Y_1 and Y_2 are correlated and monotonically related:

$$Z = \frac{S - 1}{\sigma_S} = \frac{24 - 1}{\sqrt{(8)(7)(17)/18}} = \frac{23}{\sqrt{52.89}} = 3.16$$

For a two-sided test with $\alpha = 0.05$, H_0 should be rejected if $Z < -1.96$ or if $Z > 1.96$. Since $Z = 3.16$, there is reason to believe that a relationship exists between Y_1 and Y_2. Since S is positive, there is further reason to believe that Y_2 increases as Y_1 increases. This agrees with the decision of Example 16–6.3, in which exact probabilities and significance values of Table A–25 were used. Even though the normal approximation is quite good for small sample sizes, it is best to use the exact distribution if $n \leq 10$.

16–9. Correction for τ Where There Are Tied Observations

The basic assumption in the derivation of the probability distribution of τ is continuity of the underlying joint distribution of Y_1 and Y_2. This means that the probability of tied observations is zero. In behavioral research, tied values often occur as a result of the crudeness of the measurements, and an adjustment for ties is a necessity. Fortunately, this measure of association and its corresponding test of significance can be adjusted when ties are present. The corrected τ is defined by:

$$\tau = \frac{S}{\sqrt{\binom{n}{2} - U_1} \sqrt{\binom{n}{2} - U_2}}$$

where

$$U_1 = \frac{1}{2} \sum_j t_j (t_j - 1)$$

and

$$U_2 = \frac{1}{2} \sum_j u_j (u_j - 1)$$

where t_j refers to the tied values on the Y_1 variable and u_j refers to the tied values on the Y_2 variable.

When ties occur, it is not advisable to determine N_D and N_C separately, because it is easy to make counting errors since tied values do not correspond to a correct ordering or inversion. To reduce the possibility of error, one can determine S directly by counting $(+1)$ for each correctly ordered Y_2 pair, (-1) for each incorrectly ordered Y_2 pair, and (0) for all pairs in which the Y_1 or Y_2 values are tied.

EXAMPLE 16–9.1. Consider the following set of data, which has been ranked according to the Y_1 variable and which contains tied values in both the Y_1 and Y_2 variables:

$$Y_1:\ 5\ \ 5\ \ 8\ \ \ 8\ \ 9\ \ 10\ \ 12\ \ 12\ \ 12\ \ 15\ \ 18\ \ 23$$
$$Y_2:\ 6\ \ 7\ \ 4\ \ 10\ \ 9\ \ \ 4\ \ 10\ \ 10\ \ 10\ \ 20\ \ 13\ \ 25$$

If average ranks are assigned to corresponding tied observations, the following rankings are obtained:

$$R_1:\ \ 1.5\ \ 1.5\ \ 3.5\ \ 3.5\ \ 5\ \ 6\ \ \ \ 8\ \ \ \ 8\ \ \ \ 8\ \ \ \ 10\ \ 11\ \ 12$$
$$R_2:\ \ 3\ \ \ \ 4\ \ \ \ 1.5\ \ 7.5\ \ 5\ \ 1.5\ \ 7.5\ \ 7.5\ \ 7.5\ \ 11\ \ 10\ \ 12$$

For these rankings:

$$U_1 = \frac{1}{2}[2(2-1) + 2(2-1) + 3(3-1)] = \frac{1}{2}[2 + 2 + 6] = 5$$

$$U_2 = \frac{1}{2}[2(2-1) + 4(4-1)] = \frac{1}{2}[2 + 12] = 7$$

For these data, a (0) is assigned to the first pair (3, 4), since the corresponding Y_1 values are tied at (1.5, 1.5). The next pair, (3, 1.5), is scored as a (-1), since the corresponding Y_1 values (1.5, 3.5), are not tied. The third pair, (3, 7.5) is scored as a $(+1)$, since the Y_1 pairs (1.5, 3.5), are different. A little reflection shows that these three scored values correspond to $(0)(+1)$, $(+1)(-1)$, and $(+1)(+1)$ and are in agreement with original scoring procedures described in Section 16–6. Since the Y_1 values are already ordered, one need only count the concordant and discordant Y_2 pairs and scores zero if either the Y_1 or Y_2 pair is tied. Continuing according to this rule, it follows that:

$$
\begin{aligned}
S = &\left[(0) + (-1) + (1) + (1) + (-1) + (1) + (1) + (1) + (1) + (1) + (1)\right] \\
&+ \left[(-1) + (1) + (1) + (-1) + (1) + (1) + (1) + (1) + (1) + (1)\right] \\
&+ \left[(0) + (1) + (0) + (1) + (1) + (1) + (1) + (1) + (1)\right] \\
&+ \left[(-1) + (-1) + (0) + (0) + (0) + (1) + (1) + (1)\right] \\
&+ \left[(-1) + (1) + (1) + (1) + (1) + (1) + (1)\right] \\
&+ \left[(1) + (1) + (1) + (1) + (1) + (1)\right] \\
&+ \left[(0) + (0) + (1) + (1) + (1)\right] \\
&+ \left[(0) + (1) + (1) + (1)\right] \\
&+ \left[(1) + (1) + (1)\right] \\
&+ \left[(-1) + (1)\right] \\
&+ \left[(1)\right] \\
= &\ 49 - 8 \\
= &\ 41
\end{aligned}
$$

so that

$$\tau = \frac{41}{\sqrt{\binom{12}{2} - 5}\ \sqrt{\binom{12}{2} - 7}} = \frac{41}{\sqrt{(61)(59)}} = 0.683$$

Tests of
Independence
and Measures of
Association for
Quantitative
Variables

445

When ranks are tied, not only is τ affected, but $\text{Var}(S)$ is also affected. For tied values:

$$\text{Var}(S) = \frac{n(n-1)(2n+5)}{18}$$

$$- \frac{1}{18}\left[\left\{\sum_j t_j(t_j - 1)(2t_j + 5)\right\} + \left\{\sum_j u_j(u_j - 1)(2u_j + 5)\right\}\right]$$

$$+ \frac{1}{9n(n-1)(n-2)}\left[\sum_j t_j(t_j - 1)(t_j - 2)\right]\left[\sum_j u_j(u_j - 1)(u_j - 2)\right]$$

$$+ \frac{2}{n(n-1)}U_1 U_2$$

EXAMPLE 16–9.2. For the data of Example 16–9.1:

$$\text{Var}(S) = \frac{(12)(11)(29)}{18}$$

$$- \frac{1}{18}\left[\{(2)(1)(9) + (2)(1)(9) + (3)(2)(11)\} + \{(2)(1)(9) + (4)(3)(13)\}\right]$$

$$+ \frac{1}{(9)(12)(11)(10)}\left[(2)(1)(0) + (2)(1)(0) + (3)(2)(1)\right]\left[(2)(1)(0) + (4)(3)(2)\right]$$

$$+ \frac{2}{(12)(11)}(5)(7)$$

$$= 212.6667 - 15.3333 + 0.0061 + 0.5300$$
$$= 197.8695$$

If there were no tied rankings, $\text{Var}(S) = 212.6667$. As can be seen, the correction for ties decreases σ_S and increases Z, so as to make rejection of H_0 easier. In this case:

$$Z = \frac{S - 1}{\sigma_S} = \frac{41 - 1}{\sqrt{197.8695}} = 2.84$$

With $\alpha = 0.05$, H_0 is rejected since $Z = 2.84$ is in the upper region of the two-sided critical region of $Z < -1.96$ or $Z > 1.96$. Since $Z > 1.96$, there is reason to believe that the correlation is positive. The point estimates of p_C and p_D are given, respectively, by $\hat{p}_C = 49/66 = 0.74$ and $\hat{p}_D = 8/66 = 0.12$. In addition, the proportion of tied values is given by $\hat{p}_T = 9/66 = 0.14$.

16–10. Ordered Contingency Tables: Test for Monotonic Trend for Two Ordered Qualitative Variables

Tests of trend for qualitative variables are quite uncommon even though hypotheses involving qualitative variables are quite common.

EXAMPLE 16–10.1. Consider the data of Table 16–10, which were obtained in a study in which adults were asked to express their attitudes toward the integration of schools in an urban school district.

Attitude toward integration of elementary schools

Attitude toward the integration of junior high schools	Strongly agree	Moderately agree	Moderately disagree	Strongly disagree	Total
Strongly agree	1	2	12	10	25
Moderately agree	4	2	8	14	28
Moderately disagree	5	10	8	2	25
Strongly disagree	6	8	1	7	22
Total	16	22	29	33	100

Many researchers would analyze the data of Table 16–10 as though it represented a 4 by 4 contingency table. The usual procedure would be based on Pearson's X^2 statistic and correlation theory associated with the mean-square contingency coefficient. In this case, such procedures are not advisable, since the response categories are ordered. Permuting rows or columns would destroy the ordered relationships that exist in the data. Chi-square tests of independence should be performed only if the permutation of rows or columns is permissible. When they cannot be permuted, the method of this section can be used.

For both questions, the response categories define an ordering of attitudes. Consider responses to the question about the integration of elementary schools. The 16 individuals who selected "Strongly agree" are at the opposite end of the scale from the 33 individuals who selected "Strongly disagree." While it is impossible to rank-order the 16 individuals who selected "Strongly agree," they can be distinguished as a group from the 33 who selected "Strongly disagree." If the responses were ranked, the first 16 responses of "Strongly agree" would be ranked {1, 2, 3, . . . , 15, 16}, so that the average rank would be 8.5. The next 22 responses would be ranked {17, 18, . . . , 37, 38}, so that the average rank would be 27.5. Following this procedure, the rankings of the tied responses, along with their frequencies, is as follows:

R_1	R_2	f	R_1	R_2	f
8.5	13	1	53	13	12
8.5	39.5	4	53	39.5	8
8.5	66	5	53	66	8
8.5	89.5	6	53	89.5	1
27.5	13	2	83.5	13	10
27.5	39.5	2	83.5	39.5	14
27.5	66	10	83.5	66	2
27.5	89.5	8	83.5	89.5	7

For these rankings:

$$
\begin{aligned}
S = {} & 1\big[0 + 0 + 0 + 0 + 2 + 10 + 8 + 0 + 8 + 8 + 1 + 0 + 14 + 2 + 7\big] \\
& + 4\big[0 + 0 - 2 + 0 + 10 + 8 - 12 + 0 + 8 + 1 - 10 + 0 + 2 + 7\big] \\
& + 5\big[0 - 2 - 2 + 0 + 8 - 12 - 8 + 0 + 1 - 10 - 14 + 0 + 7\big] \\
& + 6\big[-2 - 2 - 10 + 0 - 12 - 8 - 8 + 0 - 10 - 14 - 2 + 0\big] \\
& + 2\big[0 + 0 + 0 + 0 + 8 + 8 + 1 + 0 + 14 + 2 + 7\big] \\
& + 2\big[0 + 0 - 12 + 0 + 8 + 1 - 10 + 0 + 2 + 7\big] \\
& + 10\big[0 - 12 - 8 + 0 + 1 - 10 - 14 + 0 + 7\big] \\
& + 8\big[-12 - 8 - 8 + 0 - 10 - 14 - 2 + 0\big] \\
& + 12\big[0 + 0 + 0 + 0 + 14 + 2 + 7\big] \\
& + 8\big[0 + 0 - 10 + 0 + 2 + 7\big] + 8\big[0 - 10 - 14 + 0 + 7\big] \\
& + 1\big[-10 - 14 - 2 + 0\big] + 10\big[0 + 0 + 0\big] + 14\big[0 + 0\big] + 2\big[0\big] \\
= {} & 1(60) + 4(12) + 5(-32) + 6(-68) + 2(40) + 2(-4) + 10(-36) + 8(-54) \\
& + 12(23) + 8(-1) + 8(-17) + 1(-26) + 10(0) + 14(0) + 2(0) \\
= {} & -1074
\end{aligned}
$$

The uncorrected value of τ is given by:

$$
\tau = \frac{-1074}{\begin{bmatrix}100\\2\end{bmatrix}} = -0.217
$$

This suggests that the correlation is negative. Since there are an exceptionally large number of ties, U_1 and U_2 must be evaluated. For these data:

$$
U_1 = \frac{1}{2}\sum_j t_j(t_j - 1)
$$

$$
= \frac{1}{2}\big[(16)(15) + (22)(21) + (29)(28) + (33)(32)\big] = 1285
$$

and

$$
U_2 = \frac{1}{2}\sum_j u_j(u_j - 1)
$$

$$
= \frac{1}{2}\big[(25)(24) + (28)(27) + (25)(24) + (22)(21)\big] = 1209
$$

Finally,

$$
\tau = \frac{S}{\sqrt{\begin{bmatrix}n\\2\end{bmatrix} - U_1}\ \sqrt{\begin{bmatrix}n\\2\end{bmatrix} - U_2}} = \frac{-1074}{\sqrt{\begin{bmatrix}100\\2\end{bmatrix} - 1285}\ \sqrt{\begin{bmatrix}100\\2\end{bmatrix} - 1209}} = -0.290
$$

There is evidence that the correlation between the response categories for the two questions is negative. To test this result for statistical significance, one can use:

$$
Z = \frac{S - 1}{\sigma_S}
$$

Since the number of ties is very large, the correction for ties in σ_S is also mandatory.

For the observed table:

$$\text{Var}(S) = \frac{(100)(99)(205)}{18}$$

$$- \frac{1}{18}\left[\{(16)(15)(37) + (22)(21)(47) + (29)(28)(63) + (33)(32)(71)\}\right.$$

$$+ \{(25)(24)(55) + (28)(27)(61) + (25)(24)(55) + (22)(21)(47)\}\right]$$

$$+ \frac{1}{9(100)(99)(98)}$$

$$\times \left[(16)(15)(14) + (22)(21)(20) + (29)(28)(27) + (33)(32)(31)\right]$$

$$\times \left[(25)(24)(23) + (28)(27)(26) + (25)(24)(23) + (22)(21)(20)\right]$$

$$+ \frac{2}{(100)(99)}(1285)(1209)$$

$$= 112750.0000 - 16142.0000 + 435.1819 + 313.8515$$

$$= 97357.0335$$

so that

$$\sigma_S = \sqrt{97357.0335} = 312.02$$

is considerably less than $\sqrt{112750.0000} = 336$. Thus, to test the hypothesis that Y_1 and Y_2 are correlated, one uses:

$$Z = \frac{S - 1}{\sigma_S} = \frac{-1074 - 1}{312.02} = \frac{-1075}{312.02} = -3.44$$

Since $Z = -3.44 < -1.96$, it is concluded that Y_1 and Y_2 are correlated. As suggested by the data, the correlation is negative.

16–11. Test for Trend in the Kruskal–Wallis Model

In educational research, data similar to those of Table 16–11 are frequently generated. Some researchers would perform a classical analysis of variance on such data, in which orthogonal polynomials for trend are employed to preserve the ordered relationships in the independent variable. If the sample sizes are equal and if the distances between the response choices are equal intervals, the procedure has much to recommend it. However, if sample sizes are unequal or if distances between response choices are unequal, the procedure of the next example can be applied.

EXAMPLE 16–11.1. For the data of Table 16–11, one would like to know whether attitude toward school integration is independent of the number of years of completed schooling. Visual inspection of the data suggests that favorable attitudes toward school integration increase as number of years of education increases.

As a first step in determining S and τ, tied ranks are assigned to the qualitative variable response categories. Then the Y_2 variable is ranked by ignoring the

Tests of
Independence
and Measures of
Association for
Quantitative
Variables

449

	Attitude toward elementary school integration			
	Strongly disagree	Moderately disagree	Moderately agree	Strongly agree
	5	9	12	16
	4	10	13	18
	10	7	9	12
	12	12	12	19
	3	12	16	14
		10	15	
			14	
Number of subjects	5	6	7	5

attitude response. The result of the ranking is given by:

Sample 1

R_1:   3   3   3   3   3
R_2:   3   2   8   12.5   1

Sample 2

R_1:   8.5   8.5   8.5   8.5   8.5   8.5
R_2:   5.5   8   4   12.5   12.5   8

Sample 3

R_1:   15   15   15   15   15   15   15
R_2:   12.5   16   5.5   12.5   20.5   19   17.5

Sample 4

R_1:   21   21   21   21   21
R_2:   20.5   22   12.5   23   17.5

To determine S, one compares each R_2 of Sample 1 with the R_2's of Samples 2, 3, and 4. This is then repeated for Sample 2 and Sample 3 but not for Sample 4. A little reflection shows that these simplified rules correspond to the original scoring procedures discussed in Section 16–6 in which the formulation of Kendall's tau was presented. For these data:

$$S = 18 + 18 + 10 + 4 + 18 + 11 + 10 + 12 + 7 + 7 + 10$$
$$+ 4 + 3 + 5 + 4 + 0 + 1 + 2$$
$$= 144$$

so that the uncorrected tau is given by:

$$\tau = \frac{144}{\begin{bmatrix} 23 \\ 2 \end{bmatrix}} = 0.569$$

To determine the corrected tau:

$$U_1 = \frac{1}{2} \sum_j t_j(t_j - 1)$$

$$= \frac{1}{2}[(5)(4) + (6)(5) + (7)(6) + (5)(4)] = 56$$

and

$$U_2 = \frac{1}{2} \sum_j u_j(u_j - 1)$$

$$= \frac{1}{2}[(6)(5) + (3)(2) + (2)(1) + (2)(1) + (2)(1)] = 21$$

so that

$$\tau = \frac{S}{\sqrt{\begin{bmatrix} N \\ 2 \end{bmatrix} - U_1} \ \sqrt{\begin{bmatrix} N \\ 2 \end{bmatrix} - U_2}}$$

$$= \frac{144}{\sqrt{\begin{bmatrix} 23 \\ 2 \end{bmatrix} - 56} \ \sqrt{\begin{bmatrix} 23 \\ 2 \end{bmatrix} - 21}}$$

$$= 0.674$$

To test this observed measure of correlation against no correlation, one must determine σ_S corrected for ties. For these data:

$$\begin{aligned}
\text{Var}(S) &= \frac{(23)(24)(51)}{18} - \frac{1}{18}[\{(5)(4)(15) + (6)(5)(17) + (7)(6)(19) + (5)(4)(15)\} \\
&\quad + \{(6)(5)(17) + (3)(2)(11) + (2)(1)(9) + (2)(1)(9) + (2)(1)(9)\}] \\
&\quad + \frac{1}{9(23)(22)(21)}[(5)(4)(3) + (6)(5)(4) + (7)(6)(5) + (5)(4)(3)] \\
&\quad \times [(6)(5)(4) + (3)(2)(1) + (2)(1)(0) + (2)(1)(0) + (2)(1)(0)] \\
&\quad + \frac{2}{(23)(22)}[(56)(21)] \\
&= 1564.000 - 141.000 + 0.5929 + 4.6482 \\
&= 1428.2411
\end{aligned}$$

so that

$$Z = \frac{S - 1}{\sigma_S} = \frac{144 - 1}{\sqrt{1428.2411}} = 3.78$$

Since $Z = 3.78 > 1.96$, there is reason to believe that correlation exists between attitudes toward integration of schools and the number of years of schooling. It appears that the most favorable attitudes toward integration are held by those people who have had the most schooling.

16–12. *Test for Trend in the Friedman Model*

Consider the data of Table 14–2, which represents the error scores made by 10 girls on a digit-span memory test given after 4, 8, 12, and 16 weeks of training. Some researchers would analyze these data as a repeated measures analysis-of-variance design employing orthogonal polynomials for trend. This model requires that the variances across the treatments be equal and the correlations between the treatments be equal. If these conditions cannot be satisfied, then the methods of this section can be applied.

EXAMPLE 16–12.1. For each girl of Table 14–2, one computes S_i and then sums the resulting values. For these 10 girls,

$$S_1 = 6, \quad S_2 = 6, \quad S_3 = 6, \quad S_4 = 4, \quad S_5 = 4,$$
$$S_6 = 6, \quad S_7 = 4, \quad S_8 = 6, \quad S_9 = 2, \quad \text{and} \quad S_{10} = 4$$

Across the 10 girls, the total S is given by:

$$S = \sum_{i=1}^{10} S_i = 48$$

Since the variance of S_i for an individual girl is given by:

$$\text{Var}(S_i) = \frac{K(K-1)(2K+5)}{18} = \frac{(4)(3)(13)}{18} = \frac{26}{3}$$

it follows that, since the girls' performances are statistically independent, the $\text{Var}(S)$ is given by:

$$\text{Var}(S) = \sum_{i=1}^{n} \text{Var}(S_i) = n\,\text{Var}(S)$$
$$= n\left[\frac{K(K-1)(2K+5)}{18}\right]$$
$$= 10\left[\frac{26}{2}\right]$$
$$= 86.6667$$

Thus, a test of no trend across the four weeks of training is given by:

$$Z = \frac{(S-1)}{\sigma_S} = \frac{48-1}{\sqrt{86.6667}} = 5.05$$

Since $Z = 5.05 > 1.96$, there is reason to doubt the hypothesis of no trend with $\alpha = 0.05$. It can be concluded that errors decrease as practice increases. The average tau for these data is given by:

$$\bar{\tau} = \frac{S}{\left[\dfrac{n}{2}\right]\left[\dfrac{4}{2}\right]} = \frac{\frac{1}{10}(48)}{\left[\dfrac{4}{2}\right]} = \frac{4.8}{6} = 0.80$$

16–13. Kendall's Tau as a Nonparametric Point-Biserial Correlation

Kendall's tau can be used to measure the correlation that exists between a dichotomous variable and a measured or quantitative variable, as illustrated in the next example.

EXAMPLE 16–13.1. Consider the data of Table 11–7 for scores made by 16 boys and 11 girls on a questionnaire involving sex stereotyping of various jobs. Under classical theory, mean differences between the boys and girls would be assessed by means of the two-sample t test. If H_0 were rejected, the strength of the association would be measured by the point-biserial correlation coefficient. In the nonparametric case, the Wilcoxon two-sample or Mann–Whitney test would be used to assess the significance of the median difference, and Kendall's tau would be used to estimate the correlation.

For this procedure, the scores would be rank-ordered as shown.

Y_1	Y_2	Y_1	Y_2	Y_1	Y_2
0	B	5	B	13	G
0	B	5	G	18	B
0	B	6	G	19	G
0	B	7	B	20	G
0	G	7	B	21	G
1	B	7	G	22	B
3	B	10	B	22	G
4	B	12	B	30	G
4	B	12	G	39	B

Assuming that sex represents a ranking, the 16 boys are assigned a midrank value of 8.5, while the 11 girls are assigned a midrank value of 22. The Y_1 scores are ranked in the usual fashion as shown:

R_1	R_2	R_1	R_2	R_1	R_2
3	8.5	10.5	8.5	19	22
3	8.5	10.5	22	20	8.5
3	8.5	12	22	21	22
3	8.5	14	8.5	22	22
3	22	14	8.5	23	22
6	8.5	14	22	24.5	8.5
7	8.5	16	8.5	24.5	22
8.5	8.5	17.5	8.5	26	22
8.5	8.5	17.5	22	27	8.5

For these data:

$$S = 10 + 10 + 10 + 10 - 12 + 10 + 10 + 10 + 10 + 9 - 7 - 7 + 7 + 7$$
$$\quad -5 + 7 + 6 - 3 - 3 + 5 - 2 - 2 - 2 + 1 - 1 - 1$$
$$\quad = 122 - 45$$
$$\quad = 77$$

so that the uncorrected tau is equal to:

$$\tau = \frac{77}{\begin{bmatrix} 27 \\ 2 \end{bmatrix}} = 0.219$$

a positive, but weak, correlation. To correct tau for ties, one has that:

$$U_1 = \frac{1}{2}\left[(5)(4) + (2)(1) + (2)(1) + (3)(2) + (2)(1) + (2)(1)\right]$$
$$\quad = 17$$

and

$$U_2 = \frac{1}{2}\left[(16)(15) + (11)(10)\right] = 175$$

Thus, the corrected tau is given by:

$$\tau = \frac{77}{\sqrt{\begin{bmatrix} 27 \\ 2 \end{bmatrix} - 17} \sqrt{\begin{bmatrix} 27 \\ 2 \end{bmatrix} - 175}} = 0.318$$

and a test for H_0: $\tau = 0$ is given by:

$$Z = \frac{S-1}{\sigma_S} = \frac{77-1}{40.36} = 1.88$$

The hypothesis that $\tau = 0$ cannot be rejected at $\alpha = 0.05$ on the basis of these data. When these data were tested for sex differences in ratings by means of the Mann–Whitney test, U, the number of inversions corrected for ties equaled 49.5 and $Z = -1.90$. When N_D is similarly corrected for ties by counting one-half of the ties as discordances,

$$N_D + 0.5(\text{ties}) = 45 + 4.5 = 49.5$$

Thus, despite the apparent differences in the counting procedures and descriptive statistics used to summarize the counting, tau and the Mann–Whitney statistic lead to identical results within the limits of rounding error and application of a correction for continuity.

16–14. Tau and Phi for 2 × 2 Contingency Tables

If Y_1 and Y_2 each take on only two values, then the joint sample distribution of Y_1 and Y_2 can be represented by the 2 × 2 contingency table shown in Table 8–1. It should come as no surprise that if one computes tau as shown in Section 16–6, one obtains a value for tau that is identical to the value of phi for the same data.

EXAMPLE 16–14.1. Consider the data of Table 16–12, which show the joint responses to two questions concerned with the integration of elementary and secondary schools by 212 adults. For these data, the Karl Pearson $X^2 = 33.06$, so that:

$$\hat{\phi}^2 = \frac{X^2}{N} = \frac{33.06}{212} = 0.1559$$

and

$$\hat{\phi} = \sqrt{0.1559} = 0.3950$$

The ranked data and frequency count for these data are given by:

$$\begin{array}{lcccc}
R_1: & 30.5 & 30.5 & 106.5 & 106.5 \\
R_2: & 52 & 158 & 52 & 158 \\
X_{12}: & 48 & 12 & 55 & 97
\end{array}$$

For these rankings:

$$\begin{aligned}
S &= (48)\big[0 + 0 + 97\big] + (12)\big[-55 + 0\big] + (55)\big[0\big] \\
&= (48)(97) - (12)(55) = 3996
\end{aligned}$$

$$\begin{aligned}
U_1 &= \frac{1}{2}\sum_j t_j(t_j - 1) \\
&= \frac{1}{2}\big[(60)(59) + (152)(151)\big] \\
&= 13246
\end{aligned}$$

and

$$\begin{aligned}
U_2 &= \frac{1}{2}\sum_j u_j(u_j - 1) \\
&= \frac{1}{2}\big[(103)(102) + (109)(108)\big] \\
&= 11139
\end{aligned}$$

so that

$$\tau = \frac{3996}{\sqrt{\left[\dfrac{212}{2}\right] - 13246}\ \sqrt{\left[\dfrac{212}{2}\right] - 11139}}$$

$$= 0.3950$$

the same value as $\hat{\phi}$.

TABLE 16–12. *Joint responses to two questions concerning the integration of elementary and secondary schools.*

	Question 1		
Question 2	Agree	Disagree	Total
Agree	48	55	103
Disagree	12	97	109
Total	60	152	212

16–15. Kendall's Measure of Partial Correlation

Whenever two variables Y_1 and Y_2 are correlated, a researcher may wish to determine whether the variables are correlated with each other directly or whether the variables are correlated because they are actually associated with a third variable Y_3. A problem of this nature is illustrated in the data of Table 16–13.

EXAMPLE 16–15.1. For the data of Table 16–13, $\tau_{12} = \frac{15}{21}$, $\tau_{13} = \frac{17}{21}$, and $\tau_{23} = \frac{15}{21}$. Since Y_1 and Y_2 each show considerable correlation with Y_3, it is reasonable to question the correlation between Y_1 and Y_2, which is of considerable magnitude. To make this evaluation, proceed as follows.

Since the effects of Y_3 are to be partialed out of the correlation, one begins by rank-ordering the Y_3 variable and then records the ranks of Y_1 and Y_2, as shown. Following this procedure, one has:

$$Y_3: \quad 1 \quad 2 \quad 3 \quad 4 \quad 5 \quad 6 \quad 7$$
$$Y_1: \quad 1 \quad 2 \quad 5 \quad 3 \quad 4 \quad 6 \quad 7$$
$$Y_2: \quad 1 \quad 3 \quad 4 \quad 2 \quad 5 \quad 7 \quad 6$$

Next, write down all possible ordered pairs from 1 to 7 and record a $(+)$ if the pair is concordant with the Y_3 pair, and a $(-)$ if the pair is discordant with the Y_3 pair. Following this rule, one has the set of pluses and minuses reported in Table 16–14. Next, the 2 by 2 contingency table shown as Table 16–15 is created from the 21 triplets of plus and minus signs.

By definition, the partial rank-correlation coefficient is given by:

$$\tau_{12.3} = \hat{\phi} = \sqrt{\frac{X^2}{\left[\dfrac{n}{2}\right]}}$$

where X^2 is the Pearson chi-square statistic for a 2 by 2 contingency table. For these

TABLE 16–13. Scores made by seven boys on a reading test and arithmetic test, related to their scores on a standard intelligence test.

	Test scores			Ranked scores		
Subject	Y_1: Reading test	Y_2: Arithmetic test	Y_3: IQ test	R_1	R_2	R_3
Andrew	53	48	105	3	2	4
Bentley	47	55	103	2	3	2
Charles	56	57	104	5	4	3
Denver	69	63	118	7	6	7
Edmund	32	41	92	1	1	1
Farley	55	58	110	4	5	5
Gerald	63	64	113	6	7	6

TABLE 16–14. *Table of concordant and discordant pairs for the determination of Kendall's* $\tau_{12.3}$ *for Example 16–15.1.*

Pair	Y_3	Y_1	Y_2	Pair	Y_3	Y_1	Y_2
1 2	+	+	+	3 4	+	−	−
1 3	+	+	+	3 5	+	−	+
1 4	+	+	+	3 6	+	+	+
1 5	+	+	+	3 7	+	+	+
1 6	+	+	+	4 5	+	+	+
1 7	+	+	+	4 6	+	+	+
2 3	+	+	+	4 7	+	+	+
2 4	+	+	−	5 6	+	+	+
2 5	+	+	+	5 7	+	+	+
2 6	+	+	+	6 7	+	+	−
2 7	+	+	+				

data:

$$X^2 = 21 \left[\frac{17^2}{18 \cdot 19} + \frac{2^2}{3 \cdot 19} + \frac{1^2}{2 \cdot 18} + \frac{1^2}{2 \cdot 3} \right] - 21 = 2.3037$$

so that

$$\tau_{12.3} = \sqrt{\frac{2.3037}{21}} = \sqrt{0.1097} = 0.3311$$

This suggests that the major part of the correlation between the reading and arithmetic test scores can be attributed to their individual high correlations with the intelligence test scores.

It should be noted that an algebraic sign can be attached to the partial rank-correlation coefficient if it is computed in terms of τ_{12}, τ_{13}, and τ_{23} directly. As shown by Kendall:

$$\tau_{12.3} = \frac{\tau_{12} - \tau_{13}\tau_{23}}{\sqrt{1 - \tau_{13}^2}\,\sqrt{1 - \tau_{23}^2}}$$

TABLE 16–15. *2 by 2 contingency table relating the correlation of* Y_1 *and* Y_2 *after* Y_3 *is removed.*

	Ranking of Y_1		
Ranking of Y_2	Pairs concordant with Y_3	Pairs discordant with Y_3	Total
Pairs concordant with Y_3	17	1	18
Pairs discordant with Y_3	2	1	3
Total	19	2	21

for these data

$$\tau_{12.3} = \frac{(15/21) - (17/21)(15/21)}{\sqrt{1 - (17/21)^2} \sqrt{1 - (15/21)^2}} = 0.3311$$

It is easy to see that $\tau_{12.3}$ is a measure of partial association by noting that, as a phi coefficient, it measures the correlation between Y_1 and Y_2 relative to their concordance and discordance with Y_3. If $\tau_{12.3} = 0$, it follows that the probability of a Y_1 pair concordant with Y_3 is independent of a Y_2 pair concordant with Y_3, while if $\tau_{12.3} = 1$, it follows that if a Y_1 pair is concordant (or discordant) with Y_3, then the corresponding Y_2 pair is also concordant (or discordant) with Y_3. Thus, if $\tau_{12.3} = 1$, corresponding pairs of Y_1 with Y_3 and Y_2 with Y_3 are in complete agreement. In a like manner, if $\tau_{12.3} = -1$, corresponding pairs of Y_2 with Y_3 and Y_2 with Y_3 are in complete disagreement. When one pair is concordant, the other pair is discordant.

Even though $\tau_{12.3}$ can be equated in a computational form to a phi coefficient and is structurally similar to $r_{12.3}$, it should not be concluded that the statistical theory for $\hat{\phi}$ or $r_{12.3}$ can be attached to $\tau_{12.3}$. That it cannot should be obvious. In the theory associated with $\hat{\phi}$, it is assumed that the n pairs of observations are statistically independent of one another. For the Kendall partial rank-correlation measure, this assumption is clearly violated, since the $\binom{n}{2}$ different pairs are determined from only n triplets of observations. For the observed sample, there were exactly $n = 7$ subjects measured, but the number of pairs that were generated for the tabulations of Table 16–15 is given by $\binom{n}{2} = \binom{7}{2} = 21$ interdependent pairs. It should also be noted that a statistical test of $H_0: \tau_{12.3} = 0$ is not available, since the sampling distribution of $\tau_{12.3}$ has not yet been derived. This means that a researcher can only interpret $\tau_{12.3}$ on a subjective basis.

16–16. Kendall's Coefficient of Concordance

Up to this point, the discussion has focused on estimating the degree of correlation that exists between two variables Y_1 and Y_2 by means of rank orderings. Let us now consider the estimation of the average correlation between $Y_1, Y_2, \ldots, Y_K$ as measured over n subjects or experimental units in terms of their rank orderings. Basically, this corresponds to the model used in deriving the Friedman and related tests described in Chapter 14. In the discussion of Section 14–2, it is recalled that four subjects were asked to rank-order three different wines according to bouquet. The results of the ranking were as reported in Table 14–1. In addition to asking whether there are differences in ranking between the wines, one could ask whether the testers agree among themselves or, in the terminology of this chapter, whether the testers are concordant or discordant among themselves in evaluating the wines. This degree of agreement is measured by a statistic, W, also derived by Kendall and called Kendall's coefficient of concordance. In terms of the notation presented in Section 14–2, this coefficient is defined simply as $W = S/\max S$.

EXAMPLE 16–16.1. In the discussion of the wine discrimination study, it was noted that $S = 24$ and max $S = 32$. Thus, $W = 24/32 = 0.75$ suggests that the testers are in basic agreement with one another in rating the wines.

In a more formal statement, Kendall's coefficient of concordance is a measure of the agreement in the ranking of K conditions or objects by n subjects or experimental units. If all subjects rank the conditions in the same order, then average differences between conditions are at a maximum and the coefficient of concordance is 1. As discrepancies exist between subjects with regard to the ranking, W will fluctuate somewhere between 0 and 1.

EXAMPLE 16–16.2. Consider the data of Table 14–2, which are based on a study in which ten girls taking a course in high-school business mathematics were given a test to measure their recall of 7-digit numbers. The tests were given at the 4th, 8th, 12th, and 16th week of the course. It was hypothesized that digit-span memory would increase as experience with numbers during the taking of business math also increased. One criterion variable used to measure the increase in digit-span memory was the number of errors made in 50 problems. The average τ for these data is given by $\bar{\tau} = 0.80$.

As stated in the derivation of the Friedman test, a measure of the observed sum of squared deviations between the rank totals is:

$$S = \sum_{k=1}^{K} (R_k - \overline{R})^2$$

where

$$\overline{R} = \frac{\sum_{k=1}^{K} R_k}{K}$$

If there are no differences between the measurements taken at different times, then this measure of dispersion (S) should be equal to zero, since $R_1 = R_2 = \ldots = R_K = \overline{R}$. In this particular study, if no differences existed between the number of errors across the test trials, then each R_k would be equal to 25, since for any one girl the sum of the ranks is given by $1 + 2 + 3 + 4 = 10$. Across the ten girls, the total sum is $(10)(10) = 100$. Since there are four experimental conditions, the column totals under no difference should equal $100/4 = 25$. In order for a maximum separation to exist between the four conditions, the following must be true:

$$R_1^M = n(\text{smallest rank}) = 10(1) = 10$$
$$R_2^M = n(\text{second rank}) = 10(2) = 20$$
$$R_3^M = n(\text{third rank}) = 10(3) = 30$$
$$R_4^M = n(\text{largest rank}) = 10(4) = 40$$

where R_k^M equals the maximum total rank for the k ordered conditions. Thus, the measure of maximum dispersion would be given by:

$$
\begin{aligned}
S_M &= \sum_{k=1}^{K} (R_k^M - \overline{R})^2 \\
&= (10 - 25)^2 + (20 - 25)^2 + (30 - 25)^2 + (40 - 25)^2 \\
&= (-15)^2 + (-5)^2 + (5)^2 + (15)^2 \\
&= 225 + 25 + 25 + 225 = 500
\end{aligned}
$$

For the observed data,

$$
\begin{aligned}
S &= \sum_{k=1}^{K} (R_k - \overline{R})^2 \\
&= (13 - 25)^2 + (18 - 25)^2 + (31 - 25)^2 + (38 - 25)^2 \\
&= (-12)^2 + (-7)^2 + (6)^2 + (13)^2 \\
&= 144 + 49 + 36 + 169 = 398
\end{aligned}
$$

The ratio of S to S_M will give a measure of agreement in the ranking of K conditions:

$$W = \frac{S}{S_M} = \frac{398}{500} = 0.796$$

which is seen to be very close in numerical value to the average tau for the ranked data.

The value of S will lie somewhere between zero and S_M, indicating complete disagreement or implying unanimous agreement, respectively. The observed differences in average ranks between the four experimental conditions are 79.6% of the maximum deviation possible. This ratio of S to S_M is called Kendall's coefficient of concordance. It can also be determined from the following formula:

$$W = \frac{12}{n^2 K (K^2 - 1)} \sum_{k=1}^{K} R_k^2 - \frac{3(K + 1)}{(K - 1)}$$

Since the models for Kendall's W and Friedman's statistic are identical, it is reasonable to expect some algebraic connection between W and X_r^2. According to the computation formula:

$$\begin{aligned}
W &= \frac{12}{n^2 K (K^2 - 1)} \sum_{k=1}^{K} R_k^2 - \frac{3(K + 1)}{(K - 1)} \\
&= \frac{1}{n(K - 1)} \left[\frac{12}{nK(K + 1)} \sum_{k=1}^{K} R_k^2 - 3n(K + 1) \right] \\
&= \frac{1}{n(K - 1)} X_r^2
\end{aligned}$$

Thus, a convenient way to compute W is first to compute the Friedman statistic, X_r^2, and then compute W.

EXAMPLE 16–16.3. For the data of Example 16–16.2:

$$\begin{aligned}
W &= \frac{12(13^2 + 18^2 + 31^2 + 38^2)}{(10)^2(4)(4^2 - 1)} - \frac{3(4 + 1)}{(4 - 1)} \\
&= \frac{12(2898)}{100(4)(15)} - 5 = 5.796 - 5 \\
&= 0.796
\end{aligned}$$

or, since $X_r^2 = 23.88$,

$$W = \frac{1}{10(4 - 1)}(23.88) = \frac{23.88}{30} = 0.796$$

A surprising property of W is its connection to Spearman's rank-correlation coefficient. The connection is illustrated in the following example.

EXAMPLE 16–16.4. If one considers each pair of subjects in the study of Example 16–16.2, the number of unique pairs is given by:

$$T = \begin{bmatrix} n \\ 2 \end{bmatrix} = \begin{bmatrix} 10 \\ 2 \end{bmatrix} = 45$$

For the Amelia and Beatrice pair, Spearman's rank-correlation coefficient is equal to 1. If desired, all 45 rank-correlation coefficients could be computed and then averaged. A simpler way to determine this average value is to compute Kendall's coefficient of concordance and then determine $\bar{r}_S$ by means of:

$$\bar{r}_S = \frac{nW - 1}{n - 1}$$

For the observed data,

$$\bar{r}_S = \frac{10(0.796) - 1}{9} = 0.773$$

While the bounds on W are $0 \leq W \leq 1$, the formula defining $\bar{r}_S$ in terms of W shows that bounds on $\bar{r}_S$ are $-1/(n - 1) \leq \bar{r}_S \leq 1$.

16–17. Sampling Distribution of W

The sampling distribution of W can be found by the usual permutation procedures applied to the ranks $1, 2, \ldots, K$ in each of the n experimental units. The final distribution will be identical to that obtained for the Friedman test, except that the scales will differ. Because W is a linear function of X_r^2, the Friedman test can be used to test H_0: $W = 0$ versus H_1: $W \neq 0$. If the Friedman test leads to a rejection of H_0: $E(R_1) = E(R_2) = \ldots = E(R_K)$, then it follows that W is significantly different from zero.

When sample sizes are small, the chi-square approximation may not be adequate. In that case, Table A–22 can be used to test the significance of W by way of X_r^2 as a test statistic.

EXAMPLE 16–17.1.   For the wine-tasting study of Section 14–2, $S = 24$. With $n = 4$ and $K = 3$, it is seen in Table A–22 that H_0: $W = 0$ should be rejected at $\alpha = 0.05$ if $X_r^2 \geq 6.50$. In this case, the hypothesis cannot be rejected even though the value of $W = 0.75$ is large, since $X_r^2 = n(K - 1)W = 4(2)(0.75) = 6.00$. Failure to reject H_0 obviously reflects the small sample size. When $n = 4$ and $K = 3$, the sampling distribution of W is as shown in Figure 14–1.

16–18. Tied Values and W

One of the assumptions required in the use of W is that within an experimental unit there are no tied values. When ties occur, a modification must be made in the determination of W. For this adjustment:

$$W = \frac{S}{\max S - T}$$

where

$$T = n \sum_{i=1}^{n} T_i$$

and

$$T_i = \frac{1}{12} \Sigma (t^3 - t)$$

is the usual correction for ties in the ith experimental unit of the Freidman model.

16–19. Coefficient of Concordance for the Durbin Model

As was shown in Chapter 14, the Friedman model could be extended in a number of different directions. One of these is to the Durbin model, discussed in Section 14–14. Since the Friedman test has been shown to be related to Kendall's coefficient of concordance, it might be assumed that Durbin's test is related to a similar measure of concordance. That this is true is easy to demonstrate. The derivation parallels that used in defining W.

EXAMPLE 16–19.1. Consider the data of Table 14–11, which shows how 14 high-school students rank-ordered eight definitions of integration, but where each student ranked only four definitions. For any one subject, the sum of the four rank values is given by $1 + 2 + 3 + 4 = 10$, so that across all 14 subjects, the total rank sum is given by 140.

If there were no differences across the eight definitions, each column total would equal $140/8 = 17.5$. Thus, for the observed totals S is given by:

$$S = (11 - 17.5)^2 + (8 - 17.5)^2 + \ldots + (27 - 17.5)^2$$
$$= 342$$

If this value of S could be related to the maximum value of S, then a measure of concordance directly similar to Kendall's coefficient would be given by:

$$W = \frac{S}{\max S}$$

Fortunately, the maximum value of S is easy to obtain.

For the rankings of Table 14–11, maximum correlation exists if the column totals are some permutation of:

$$7, \quad 7 + \Delta, \quad 7 + 2\Delta, \quad 7 + 3\Delta, \quad 7 + 4\Delta, \quad 7 + 5\Delta, \quad 7 + 6\Delta, \quad \text{and} \quad 7 + 7\Delta$$

Since these column sums must total to 140, it follows that:

$$7 + (7 + \Delta) + (7 + 2\Delta) + \ldots + (7 + 7\Delta) = 140$$

so that $\Delta = 3$. This means that the rank totals must be some permutation of 7, 10, 13, 16, 19, 22, 25, and 28. Thus:

$$\max S = (7 - 17.5)^2 + (10 - 17.5)^2 + \ldots + (28 - 17.5)^2$$
$$= 378$$

and, as a result,

$$W = \frac{342}{378} = 0.9045$$

This large value for W suggests that the 14 high-school students polled are in accord in their rankings of the eight definitions of integration.

For the general model,

$$S = \sum_{k=1}^{K} \left[R_k - \frac{M(T+1)}{2} \right]^2$$

where

K = Number of treatments
M = Number of times a treatment is observed in the total incomplete design
T = Number of treatments compared in a single block

With a little effort it can be shown that:

$$\max S = \frac{M^2 K(K+1)(T-1)^2}{12(K-1)}$$

so that the coefficient of concordance is given by:

$$W = \frac{S}{\max S} = \frac{12(K-1)\sum_{k=1}^{K}[R_k - (M(T+1)/2)]^2}{M^2 K(K+1)(T-1)^2}$$

EXAMPLE 16–19.2.   For the data of Table 14–11, $K = 8$, $T = 4$, $B = 14$, and $M = 7$. Thus:

$$W = \frac{12(8-1)}{(7)^2(8)(8+1)(4-1)^2}\left[(11-17.5)^2 + (8-17.5)^2 \right.$$
$$\left. + (12-17.5)^2 + \ldots + (27-17.5)^2\right]$$
$$= \frac{342}{378} = 0.9045$$

the value obtained by definition.

As might be expected, W can be computed directly from the value of X^2, just as Kendall's W can be determined from the simpler Friedman statistic. Since the Durbin test statistic is given by:

$$X^2 = \frac{12(K-1)}{M(T^2-1)K} \sum_{k=1}^{K}\left[R_k - \frac{M(T+1)}{2}\right]^2$$
$$= \frac{M(K+1)(T-1)}{(T+1)}\left[\frac{12(K-1)S}{M^2 K(K+1)(T-1)^2}\right]$$
$$= \frac{M(K+1)(T-1)}{T+1}W$$

it follows that:

$$W = \frac{(T+1)X^2}{M(K+1)(T-1)}$$

Tests of
Independence
and Measures of
Association for
Quantitative
Variables

EXAMPLE 16–19.3.   For the data of Table 14–11, $X^2 = 34.2$. Thus:

$$W = \frac{(4+1)(34.2)}{(7)(9)(3)} = 0.9048$$

Except for fourth-place accuracy, the three different computing methods produce the same result.

16–20. Paired Comparisons as a Durbin-Type Test

A special case of the coefficient of concordance, as related to the Durbin model of Section 16–19, occurs with some frequency in psychological research. In these and related studies, a subject is given all possible pairs of K objects and is asked to state, for each pair, which member is preferred or which has more of a particular property. The purpose of the study is to obtain a rank-ordering of the objects. In addition, the researcher will want to know whether or not the subject has shown consistency in the choices. The method is easily illustrated by an example.

Suppose one of the high-school students of Table 14–11 was given $\begin{bmatrix} 8 \\ 2 \end{bmatrix} =$ 28 sheets of paper, each containing two definitions of integration, and asked to select the definition he preferred. Assume that the results were as shown in Table 16–16, where a 1 is assigned to the more preferred definition. For this model, the total rank sum is given by $28(1 + 2) = 84$, so that if the subject were inconsistent, column totals would equal $84/8 = 10.5$. Thus, for these data:

$$S = (9 - 10.5)^2 + (13 - 10.5)^2 + \ldots + (11 - 10.5)^2 = 32$$

To find the maximum value of S, it is first noted that the smallest possible rank total is 7. Thus:

$$7 + (7 + \Delta) + (7 + 2\Delta) + \ldots + (7 + 7\Delta) = 84$$

so that

$$\Delta = 1$$

Thus, the maximum value of S is given by:

$$\max S = (7 - 10.5)^2 + (8 - 10.5)^2 + (9 - 10.5)^2 + \ldots + (14 - 10.5)^2 = 42$$

so that the coefficient of concordance for this subject is given by:

$$W = \frac{32}{42} = 0.7619$$

indicating a high degree of concordance. For the general model:

$$W = \frac{12S}{K(K^2 - 1)}$$

Since this is a Durbin-type model, one can test $H_0: W = 0$ by means of a chi-square statistic. In this case, in which K objects are compared:

1. $B = \begin{bmatrix} K \\ 2 \end{bmatrix} = \frac{K(K - 1)}{2}$
2. $K = K$
3. $T = 2$
4. $M = K - 1$
5. $\lambda = 1$

TABLE 16–16. Results of making 28 paired comparisons of eight different definitions of integration by one student.

Definitions

Pair	A	B	C	D	E	F	G	H
A B	1	2						
A C	2		1					
A D	1			2				
A E	1				2			
A F	2					1		
A G	1						2	
A H	1							2
B C		2	1					
B D		2		1				
B E		1			2			
B F		2				1		
B G		2					1	
B H		2						1
C D			1	2				
C E			1		2			
C F			1			2		
C G			1				2	
C H			1					2
D E				1	2			
D F				1		2		
D G				1			2	
D H				2				1
E F					2	1		
E G					2		1	
E H					1			2
F G						1	2	
F H						1		2
G H							2	1
Rank totals	9	13	7	10	13	9	12	11

so that

$$X^2 = \frac{12(K-1)}{(K-1)(2^2-1)n} \sum_{k=1}^{K} (R_k - \overline{R})^2$$

$$= \frac{4}{K} \sum_{k=1}^{K} (R_k - \overline{R})^2$$

The computational form of the test statistic is given by:

$$X^2 = \frac{4}{K} \sum_{k=1}^{K} R_k^2 - 9(K-1)^2$$

EXAMPLE 16–20.1.   For the data of Table 16–16:

$$X^2 = \frac{4}{8}\left[9^2 + 13^2 + 7^2 + 10^2 + 13^2 + 9^2 + 12^2 + 11^2\right] - 9(8-1)^2$$

$$= 457 - 441$$

$$= 16$$

Tests of
Independence
and Measures of
Association for
Quantitative
Variables

465

With $v = K - 1 = 8 - 1 = 7$ degrees of freedom, the hypothesis of no difference in mean rankings is rejected at $\alpha = 0.05$, since $X^2_{7:0.95} = 14.07$.

Extension of W to the case in which comparisons are replicated across m different subjects is straightforward, as is the corresponding Durbin-type statistic. In this special case,

$$W = \frac{12S}{n^2 K(K^2 - 1)} = \frac{12 \sum_{k=1}^{K} (R_k - \overline{R})^2}{n^2 K(K^2 - 1)}$$

while

$$X^2 = \frac{4}{Kn} \sum_{i=1}^{K} (R_k - \overline{R})^2$$

and where

$$R_k = \sum_{i=1}^{n} R_{ik}$$

The hypotheses $H_0: W = 0$ or $H_0: E(R_1) = E(R_2) = \ldots = E(R_K)$ are rejected if $X^2 > X^2_{K-1:1-\alpha}$.

16–21. Goodman and Kruskal's Gamma: A Measure of Association for Ordered Contingency Tables

In Section 16–10, the use of Kendall's tau as a measure of association for ordered contingency tables was illustrated and implicitly recommended. Another measure of association for ordered contingency tables that has been widely adopted by researchers in the social sciences is a measure of association proposed by Goodman and Kruskal (1954, 1963), which they named γ (gamma). This measure, unlike the γ of Section 8–9, is closely allied to Kendall's tau. In fact, it is a Kendall tau, but where tied rankings are removed from the set of complete paired observations and where each observation is also paired with itself. Thus, under the Kendall model, $\binom{n}{2} = (n(n - 1)/2)$ pairs are examined for concordance, while under the Goodman and Kruskal model, n^2 pairs are examined. By definition:

$$\gamma = \frac{P_C - P_D}{P_C + P_D}$$

In the sample, one estimates γ as:

$$G = \frac{N_C - N_D}{N_C + N_D}$$

Except for the difference in sampling with and without replacement, τ is simply the numerator of γ, since:

$$\tau = P_C - P_D$$

This means that if P(tied pairs) is different from zero, then $|\gamma| > |\tau|$, and if a large number of pairs are tied, $|\gamma|$ will be considerably larger than $|\tau|$. For those researchers who operate under a conservative philosophy concerning statistical significance and decision-making, the use of τ will be preferred to the use of γ. The computations involved in the determination of γ are illustrated in the following two examples.

EXAMPLE 16–21.1. For the data of Table 16–10, it was shown that $S = -1074$ under sampling without replacement. For the same data under the sampling-*without*-replacement model one may use the counting procedure of Section 16–6 to determine N_C and N_D; however, the following method is much simpler:

$$N_C = \sum_{r=1}^{R} \sum_{c=1}^{C} N_{rc} \sum_{r>r'} \sum_{c>c'} N_{r'c'}$$

$$\begin{aligned}
&= 1\big[2 + 10 + 8 + 8 + 8 + 1 + 14 + 2 + 7\big] \\
&\quad + 4\big[10 + 8 + 8 + 1 + 2 + 7\big] + 5\big[8 + 1 + 7\big] \\
&\quad + 2\big[8 + 8 + 1 + 14 + 2 + 7\big] + 2\big[8 + 1 + 2 + 7\big] \\
&\quad + 10\big[1 + 7\big] + 12\big[14 + 2 + 7\big] + 8\big[2 + 7\big] + 8\big[7\big] \\
&= 1(60) + 4(36) + 5(16) + 2(40) + 2(18) + 10(8) + 12(23) \\
&= 884
\end{aligned}$$

and

$$N_D = \sum_{r=1}^{R} \sum_{c=1}^{C} N_{rc} \sum_{r>r'} \sum_{c>c'} N_{r'c'}$$

$$\begin{aligned}
&= 4\big[2 + 12 + 10\big] + 5\big[2 + 2 + 12 + 8 + 10 + 14\big] \\
&\quad + 6\big[2 + 2 + 10 + 12 + 8 + 8 + 10 + 14 + 2\big] \\
&\quad + 2\big[12 + 10\big] + 10\big[12 + 8 + 12 + 14\big] \\
&\quad + 8\big[12 + 8 + 8 + 10 + 14 + 2\big] + 8\big[10\big] + 8\big[10 + 14\big] \\
&\quad + 1\big[10 + 14 + 2\big] \\
&= 4(24) + 5(48) + 6(68) + 2(22) + 10(44) + 8(54) \\
&\quad + 8(10) + 8(24) + 1(26) \\
&= 1958
\end{aligned}$$

so that

$$G = \frac{N_C - N_D}{N_C + N_D} = \frac{884 - 1958}{884 + 1958} = \frac{-1074}{2842} = -0.378$$

As expected, $G = -0.378$ is considerably larger in absolute value than $\tau = -0.217$ uncorrected for ties and $\tau = -0.291$ corrected for ties. For the Goodman–Kruskal model:

$$\hat{P}_C = \frac{884}{2842} = 0.311$$

and

$$\hat{P}_D = \frac{1958}{2842} = 0.689$$

while for the Kendall model,

$$\hat{P}_C = \frac{884}{4950} = 0.179$$

and

$$\hat{P}_D = \frac{1958}{4950} = 0.396$$

corresponding to an inverse relationship among the ordered paired observations.

EXAMPLE 16–21.2. Reconsider the data of Table 16–10, but under the model of sampling *with* replacement. Under this model:

$$N_C = 2 \sum_{r=1}^{R} \sum_{c=1}^{C} N_{rc} \left[\sum_{r>r'} \sum_{c>c'} N_{r'c'} \right]$$

$$N_D = 2 \sum_{r=1}^{R} \sum_{c=1}^{C} N_{rc} \left[\sum_{r>r'} \sum_{c>c'} N_{r'c'} \right]$$

and

$$N_T = \sum_{r=1}^{R} N_{r.}^2 + \sum_{c=1}^{C} N_{.c}^2 - \sum_{r=1}^{R} \sum_{c=1}^{C} N_{rc}^2$$

It will be immediately noted, upon initiation of the computations, that:

$$N_C = 2(884) = 1768 \quad \text{and} \quad N_D = 2(1958) = 3916$$

where 884 and 1958 are the number of concordant and discordant pairs under the Kendall model. Thus:

$$G = \frac{N_C - N_D}{N_C + N_D} = \frac{1768 - 3916}{1768 + 3916} = \frac{-2148}{5684} = -0.378$$

the same value found under the Kendall model. Note that:

$$\begin{aligned}
N_T &= \left[25^2 + 28^2 + 25^2 + 22^2\right] + \left[16^2 + 22^2 + 29^2 + 33^2\right] \\
&\quad - \left[1^2 + 4^2 + 5^2 + 6^2 + 2^2 + 2^2 + 10^2 + 8^2 + 12^2 \right. \\
&\quad \left. + 8^2 + 8^2 + 1^2 + 10^2 + 14^2 + 2^2 + 7^2\right] \\
&= 4316
\end{aligned}$$

so that among the untied pairs:

$$\hat{P}_C = \frac{1768}{5684} = 0.311$$

and

$$\hat{P}_D = \frac{3916}{5684} = 0.689$$

These examples illustrate some important properties of γ:

1. If the frequencies of the $R \times C$ table are concentrated in a single row or column, N_T will tend to be close to n^2 or $\left[\begin{smallmatrix}n\\2\end{smallmatrix}\right]$, depending upon whether sampling with or without replacement is assumed. In either case, the value of G is inflated, since most of the pairs will be tied and removed from the analysis. This means that the value of G will be essentially indeterminate.
2. If the frequencies are concentrated in a diagonal, $G = \pm 1$ depending upon whether the diagonal relates increasing r to increasing c or to decreasing c.
3. For a 2 by 2 table:

$$\gamma = \frac{p_{11} p_{22} - p_{12} p_{21}}{p_{11} p_{22} + p_{12} p_{21}}$$

so that in the sample:

$$G = \frac{n_{11}n_{22} - n_{12}n_{21}}{n_{11}n_{22} + n_{12}n_{21}}$$

4. If one cell of a 2 by 2 table is empty, $G = \pm 1$, depending upon which cell is empty.

Whereas Kendall's tau reduces to an ordinary ϕ coefficient, γ does not. This is illustrated in the following example.

EXAMPLE 16–21.3. As shown in Section 16–14, $\tau = \hat{\phi} = 0\ 3950$ for the data of Table 16–12. For the same data:

$$\begin{aligned} G &= \frac{n_{11}n_{22} - n_{12}n_{21}}{n_{11}n_{22} + n_{12}n_{21}} \\ &= \frac{(48)(97) - (12)(55)}{(48)(97) + (12)(55)} = \frac{3996}{5316} \\ &= 0.752 \end{aligned}$$

Clearly, this large value for G is a reflection of the small frequency associated with $n_{21} = 12$. This example illustrates that large values of G can occur in a 2 by 2 table simply by having one cell with a low or minimal frequency. As this example suggests, large values of G should be viewed and evaluated with caution. This same statement does not apply to Kendall's tau.

In 1963, Goodman and Kruskal determined the standard error of G for large samples. For a moderate-sized contingency table, such as that of Table 16–10, the computations become unwieldy; however, they identified an upper bound for the standard error of G, which is easy to compute. This upper bound, which is based on sampling with replacement theory, yields very conservative tests and broad confidence intervals. It is given by:

$$SE_G = \sqrt{\frac{2n(1 - G^2)}{n^2 - N_T}}$$

Thus, $Z = (G - \gamma)/SE_G$ can be used to test $H_0: \gamma = 0$ by use of the $N(0, 1)$ distribution. In addition, a $(1 - \alpha)\%$ confidence interval for γ is given by:

$$\gamma = G \pm Z_{\alpha/2} SE_G$$

The use of this upper bound is illustrated for the data of Example 16–21.3.

EXAMPLE 16–21.4. For the data of Example 16–21.3, $G = -0.378$, $n = 100$, and $N_T = 4316$. Thus:

$$\begin{aligned} SE_G &= \sqrt{\frac{2(100)[1 - (-0.378)^2]}{100^2 - 4316}} \\ &= 0.173 \end{aligned}$$

Tests of
Independence
and Measures of
Association for
Quantitative
Variables

469

The 95% confidence interval for γ is given by:

$$\gamma = G \pm Z_{0.025} SE_G$$
$$= -0.378 \pm 1.96(0.173)$$
$$= -0.378 \pm 0.339$$

Since $\gamma = 0$ is not included in the interval, it is concluded that $\gamma \neq 0$.

For these data one can test $H_0: \gamma = 0$ against $H_1: \gamma \neq 0$ by means of:

$$Z = \frac{G - 0}{SE_G} = \frac{-0.378}{0.173} = -2.18$$

In this case, H_0 is rejected, as it is under the confidence interval model. However, for the test of $H_0: \tau = 0$ against $H_1: \tau \neq 0$ based on the same data, it has been shown that $Z = -3.44$, suggesting that the test for τ is more powerful than the test for γ when the upper bound on the standard error is used in the latter test.

While there appears to be no simple way for testing $H_0: \tau_1 = \tau_2$, the same is not true for the testing of $H_0: \gamma_1 = \gamma_2$. For a two-sided test, one need only compute:

$$Z = \frac{G_1 - G_2}{\sqrt{SE_{G_1}^2 + SE_{G_2}^2}}$$

and reject H_0 if $Z < Z_{\alpha/2}$ or $Z > Z_{1-\alpha/2}$. Of course, the same statistic can be used for a one-tailed test with the appropriate one-sided decision rule. However, one must ensure that the two contingency tables have the same number of rows and columns and the same categories for the rows and columns of each table. Also, the sample sizes must be large enough to ensure the normal approximation.

16–22. A Partial Coefficient for Goodman and Kruskal's Gamma

Davis (1967) provided a measure of partial association for Goodman and Kruskal's gamma. Davis defines the partial gamma for two ordered qualitative variables Y_1 and Y_2 when the effects of a third factor Y_3, defined by categories $(A_1, A_2, \ldots, A_K)$, are eliminated:

$$G_{12.3} = \frac{\sum_{k=1}^{K} N_{Ck} - \sum_{k=1}^{K} N_{Dk}}{\sum_{k=1}^{K} N_{Ck} + \sum_{k=1}^{K} N_{Dk}}$$

The evaluation of this measure is illustrated for the data of Table 9–7.

EXAMPLE 16–22.1. For the sample of Whites of Table 9–7,

$$N_{CW} = 230[478 + 83 + 47 + 54] + 130[83 + 54] + 246[47 + 54] + 478[54]$$
$$= 230(662) + 130(137) + 246(101) + 478(54)$$
$$= 220728$$

$$N_{DW} = 130[246 + 9] + 15[246 + 478 + 9 + 47] + 478[9] + 83[9 + 47]$$
$$= 130(255) + 15(780) + 478(9) + 83(56)$$
$$= 53800$$

so that, for the Whites,

$$G_{12}^{W} = \frac{N_{CW} - N_{DW}}{N_{CW} + N_{DW}}$$

$$= \frac{220728 - 53800}{220728 + 53800} = \frac{166928}{274528}$$

$$= 0.608$$

For the sample of Blacks of Table 9–7,

$$N_{CB} = 244[259 + 59 + 49 + 37] + 109[59 + 37] + 191[49 + 37] + 259[37]$$
$$= 244(404) + 109(96) + 191(86) + 259(37)$$
$$= 135049$$
$$N_{DB} = 109[191 + 19] + 12[191 + 259 + 19 + 49] + 259[19] + 59[19 + 49]$$
$$= 109(210) + 12(518) + 259(19) + 59(68)$$
$$= 38039$$

so that, for the Blacks,

$$G_{12}^{B} = \frac{N_{CB} - N_{DB}}{N_{CB} + N_{DB}}$$

$$= \frac{135049 - 38039}{135049 + 38039} = \frac{97010}{173088}$$

$$= 0.560$$

Finally, if the effects of race are removed,

$$G_{12.3} = \frac{(N_{CW} + N_{CB}) - (N_{DW} + N_{DB})}{(N_{CW} + N_{CB}) + (N_{DW} + N_{DB})}$$

$$= \frac{(220728 + 135049) - (53800 + 38039)}{(220728 + 135049) + (53800 + 38039)}$$

$$= \frac{355777 - 91839}{355777 + 91839} = \frac{263938}{477616}$$

$$= 0.553$$

Since the partial G is not essentially different from the unconditional G value, 0.608 and 0.560, it would be concluded that the correlation between perceived social mixing and number of new friends made from the other racial groups is independent of the race of the perceiver. Thus, among both Whites and Blacks, it would be concluded that the amount of interracial social mixing that a student reports having seen is related in a positive fashion with the number of new friends that he or she made among the other race; and furthermore, the correlation between the perception and the behavior is independent of the race of the perceptor.

Summary

In this chapter, a number of assumption-freer models were presented as competitors to the classical correlation and regression models. Three of these models serve as direct extensions of the Karl Pearson product-moment correlation, where it is not assumed that the two dependent variables Y_1 and Y_2 are distributed in a

Tests of
Independence
and Measures of
Association for
Quantitative
Variables

471

joint bivariate normal distribution. The first of these procedures, based upon Fisher's method of randomization, is referred to as a Pitman correlation. For this model, one computes the familiar Pearson product-moment correlation coefficient and concludes that $\rho \neq 0$ if $Z = r\sqrt{n-1}$ is too large or too small, depending upon the alpha that is selected as the probability of a Type I error. For $\alpha = 0.05$, it is concluded that $\rho \neq 0$ if $Z < -1.96$ or if $Z > 1.96$.

While the classical procedure is used to test the hypothesis of linear relationship, the Pitman test is not so restrictive. Under the Pitman model, the hypothesis of no association is tested against the alternative of monotonic relationship, be it linear or curvilinear. The Pitman test, like the normal-scores or Spearman test, is insensitive to deviation from linearity. If the relationship is linear and if the underlying variables are bivariate normal, then both the Pitman test and the normal-scores test have Asymptotic Relative Efficiency values of 1.00, while the ARE for the Spearman rho is given by 0.912 for the bivariate normal model, and 0.98 for the normal regression model, where Y_1 represents unit increases in the independent variable.

While the Pitman r:

$$r = \frac{n\left[\sum_{i=1}^{n} y_{i1} y_{i2}\right] - \left[\sum_{i=1}^{n} y_{i1}\right]\left[\sum_{i=1}^{n} y_{i2}\right]}{\sqrt{n\left[\sum_{i=1}^{n} y_{i1}^2\right] - \left[\sum_{i=1}^{n} y_{i1}\right]^2} \sqrt{n\left[\sum_{i=1}^{n} y_{i2}^2\right] - \left[\sum_{i=1}^{n} y_{i2}\right]^2}}$$

is computed from the original observations, the Spearman rho is computed from the rank values assigned to the original observations, and the normal-scores r is computed from the normal scores that are substituted for the ranks. While the Pearson formula may be used directly for all three correlation coefficients, the Spearman r is usually computed as:

$$r_S = 1 - \frac{6 \sum_{i=1}^{n} d_i^2}{n^3 - n}$$

and the normal-scores correlation is computed as:

$$r = \frac{\sum_{i=1}^{n} Z_{i1} Z_{i2}}{\sum_{i=1}^{n} Z_i^2}$$

Under these formulations,

d_i = difference in rank values for the ith pairs of (Y_1, Y_2)
N = number of paired observations
Z_{i1} = ith normal score assigned to Y_1
Z_{i2} = ith normal score assigned to Y_2

In all three cases, the hypothesis $H_0: \rho = 0$ is rejected with the probability of a Type I error controlled at α if $Z < Z_{\alpha/2}$ or if $Z > Z_{1-\alpha/2}$, where $Z = r\sqrt{n-1}$. If n is small, one can generate the exact sampling distribution of r to define the critical region of the test.

Perhaps of greater utility than any of the three Pearson product-moment correlation coefficients are the measures of correlation based on concordant and discordant pairs of measures. These measures have greater flexibility and can therefore be used in a larger number of contexts than can the corresponding correlation coefficients. To help understand what these measures of association measure, consider the set of pairs that are rank-ordered on the basis of the Y_1 variable. For the moment, assume that no values are tied with one another:

$$Y_1: \{y_{11} \; y_{21} \; y_{31} \; \ldots \; y_{n1}\}$$
$$Y_2: \{y_{12} \; y_{22} \; y_{32} \; \ldots \; y_{n2}\}$$

Consider the first two pairs of observations (y_{11}, y_{12}) and (y_{21}, y_{22}). If $y_{12} < y_{22}$, it is said that the two pairs of observations are concordant, but if $y_{12} > y_{22}$, the two pairs are said to be discordant. If N_C equals the number of concordant pairs and N_D equals the number of discordant pairs, then among the complete set of $\begin{bmatrix} n \\ 2 \end{bmatrix}$ ordered pairs:

$$\hat{p}_C = \frac{N_C}{\begin{bmatrix} n \\ 2 \end{bmatrix}} = \text{Percent of concordant pairs}$$

$$\hat{p}_D = \frac{N_D}{\begin{bmatrix} n \\ 2 \end{bmatrix}} = \text{Percent of discordant pairs}$$

The difference in these proportions:

$$\tau = \hat{p}_C - \hat{p}_D = \frac{N_C}{\begin{bmatrix} n \\ 2 \end{bmatrix}} - \frac{N_D}{\begin{bmatrix} n \\ 2 \end{bmatrix}} = \frac{N_C - N_D}{\begin{bmatrix} n \\ 2 \end{bmatrix}}$$

measures the tendency of the Y_1 values to vary with the Y_2 values. If $\hat{p}_D = 0$, all pairs are concordant, $\tau = 1$, and r_S tends to one in value. If $\hat{p}_C = 0$, all pairs are discordant, $\tau = -1$, and r_S tends to minus one.

For $S = N_C - N_D$, Kendall's tau is usually computed as:

$$\tau = \frac{2S}{n(n-1)}$$

When Y_1 and Y_2 are uncorrelated, $E(S) = 0$; thus $E(\tau) = 0$ and:

$$\text{Var}(S) = \frac{n(n-1)(2n+5)}{18}$$

so that:

$$\text{Var}(\tau) = \frac{2(2n+5)}{9n(n-1)}$$

In terms of S, the hypothesis $H_0: \tau = 0$ is rejected if $Z < Z_{\alpha/2}$ or if $Z > Z_{1-\alpha/2}$, where:

$$Z = \frac{S - E(S)}{\sqrt{\text{Var}(S)}} = \frac{S}{\sqrt{\dfrac{n(n-1)(2n+5)}{18}}}$$

Since the distribution of S is discrete, a correction for continuity can be made by subtracting 1 if S is positive and adding 1 if S is negative.

If there are many ties in either the set of Y_1 or Y_2 observations, a correction is recommended since τ will tend to be too small. The corrected τ is defined as:

$$\tau = \frac{S}{\sqrt{\left[\begin{matrix}n\\2\end{matrix}\right] - U_1}\sqrt{\left[\begin{matrix}n\\2\end{matrix}\right] - U_2}}$$

where

$$U_1 = \frac{1}{2}\sum_j t_j(t_j - 1)$$

$$U_2 = \frac{1}{2}\sum_j u_j(u_j - 1)$$

where

t_j = Number of observations tied at the same value on the Y_1 variable
u_j = Number of observations tied at the same value on the Y_2 variable

and the corrected variance of S is defined as:

$$\begin{aligned}
\text{Var}(S) = {} & \frac{n(n-1)(2n+5)}{18} \\
& - \frac{1}{18}\left(\left[\sum_j t_j(t_j-1)(2t_j+5)\right] + \left[\sum_j u_j(u_j-1)(2u_j+5)\right]\right) \\
& + \frac{1}{9n(n-1)(n-2)}\left[\sum_j t_j(t_j-1)(t_j-2)\right]\left[\sum_j u_j(u_j-1)(u_j-2)\right] \\
& + \frac{2}{n(n-1)}U_1 U_2
\end{aligned}$$

Under the correction for ties, Kendall's tau may be used to:

1. Test for correlation and monotonic relationships in ordered contingency tables.
2. Test for monotonic trend in the Kruskal–Wallis model.
3. Test for monotonic trend in the Friedman model.
4. Serve as a point-biserial correlation coefficient for the Mann–Whitney model.
5. Estimate the phi coefficient of a 2 by 2 contingency table.

In many research studies, subjects are asked to rank-order K objects, statements, foods, wines, and so on, according to some criteria specified by the researcher. One question that immediately arises in such studies concerns how well the subjects agree or are concordant in their rankings. The tendency to agree or disagree is measured by Kendall's coefficient of concordance, which is usually computed as:

$$W = \frac{1}{n(K-1)}X_r^2$$

where X_r^2 is the familiar Friedman statistic described in Section 14–2. Under the Durbin model of Section 14–14, in which each subject is asked to rank T of the K

objects:

$$W = \frac{(T + 1)X^2}{M(K + 1)(T - 1)}$$

where X^2 is the value of the Durbin statistic and M is the number of times each object is ranked across the n subjects of the study.

In 1954, Goodman and Kruskal introduced a measure of association for ordered contingency tables that has gained wide acceptance by researchers in the social sciences. This measure, called gamma, is computed like Kendall's tau, except that tied pairs are removed from the count of total pairs examined. By definition, γ is estimated in the sample by:

$$G = \frac{N_C - N_D}{N_C + N_D}$$

Since $N_C + N_D$ is generally smaller than the number of pairs, $G > \tau$ if $N_C - N_D$ is positive and $G < \tau$ if $N_C - N_D$ is negative. In almost all situations, G tends to exceed τ in absolute value and thereby may lead a researcher to believe that the correlation between two ordered qualitative variables is actually stronger than it is in reality.

With $N_T = n^2 - N_C - N_D$ and where N_C and N_D are as defined in Example 16–21.2, the upper bound on the standard error of G is estimated as:

$$SE_G = \sqrt{\frac{2n(1 - G^2)}{n^2 - N_T}}$$

With this estimate, one can test $H_0: \gamma = \gamma_0$ or set up a confidence interval for γ. If $Z < Z_{\alpha/2}$ or $Z > Z_{1-\alpha/2}$, where

$$Z = \frac{G - \gamma_0}{SE_G}$$

the hypothesis that $\gamma = \gamma_0$ is rejected. The $(1 - \alpha)\%$ confidence interval for γ is given by:

$$\gamma = G \pm Z_{\alpha/2}\, SE_G$$

In addition, the hypothesis $H_0: \gamma_1 = \gamma_2$ can be tested by referring:

$$Z = \frac{G_1 - G_2}{\sqrt{SE_{G_1}^2 + SE_{G_2}^2}}$$

to tables of the $N(0, 1)$ distribution.

Finally, the Goodman and Kruskal model can be used to define a partial correlation coefficient between two ordered qualitative variables when the effects of a third, not necessarily ordered, variable are removed. This coefficient defined across the categories $A_1, A_2, \ldots, A_K$ is computed as:

$$G_{12.3} = \frac{\sum_{k=1}^{K} N_{Ck} - \sum_{k=1}^{K} N_{Dk}}{\sum_{k=1}^{K} N_{Ck} + \sum_{k=1}^{K} N_{Dk}}$$

In addition, Kendall's tau can be used to measure the partial correlation between two quantitative variables when the effects of a third quantitative variable are held constant. For this model,

$$\tau_{12.3} = \frac{\tau_{12} - \tau_{13}\tau_{23}}{\sqrt{1 - \tau_{13}^2}\sqrt{1 - \tau_{23}^2}}$$

Exercises

*1. Determine the value of both Spearman's rho and Kendall's tau for the paragraph meaning scores and mental-age values of the data of Exercise 10 of Chapter 10 for the males.

*2. Is there any reason to believe that $\rho = 0$ or $\tau = 0$ for the data of Exercise 1?

*3. Determine $\rho_{23.1}$ for the males of Exercise 10 of Chapter 10.

*4. Analyze the data of Exercise 1 in terms of Van der Waerden inverse normal order scores. Repeat the analysis for expected normal order scores.

*5. Determine the value of both Spearman's rho and Kendall's tau for the data of Exercise 4 of Chapter 3.

*6. Is there any reason to believe that $\rho = 0$ or $\tau = 0$ for the data of Exercise 5?

*7. Determine the value of Spearman's rho and Kendall's tau for the data of Exercise 10 of Chapter 3.

*8. Is there any reason to believe that $\rho = 0$ or $\tau = 0$ for the data of Exercise 7?

*9. Analyse the data of Table 7–8 according to the methods of Sections 16–10 and 16–22. What is the hypothesis being tested under both models? Which model do you prefer? Why?

*10. Analyze the data of Table 6–7 according to the methods of Sections 16–10 and 16–22. What is the hypothesis being tested?

*11. Analyze the data of Exercise 4 of Chapter 6 by testing the hypothesis that $\tau = 0$ and $\gamma = 0$. Compare the results to those of part (a) in which the Karl Pearson statistic is used. Which method or methods would you recommend? Why?

*12. Analyze the data of Table 8–11 according to the methods of this chapter. What is the hypothesis under test?

*13. Determine Kendall's tau for the data of Table 11–1. What relationship do Z_1 and Z_2 have to each other where:

$$Z_1 = \frac{\tau - 0}{\sigma_\tau} \quad \text{and} \quad Z_2 = \frac{U - E(U)}{\sigma_U}$$

and where $\tau =$ Kendall's tau and $U =$ Mann–Whitney statistic.

*14. Answer the questions of Exercise 13 for the data of Table 11–15 for the rank statistics.

*15. Analyze the data of Table 11–18 according to the methods of this chapter. What is the hypothesis being tested?

*16. Analyze the data of Table 11–19 with the methods of this chapter. What is the hypothesis under test?

*17. For the data of Table 13–1, use the Pitman correlation model to test the hypothesis that $\rho = 0$.

*18. Use the model of Section 16–11 to examine the data in the accompanying table, which were obtained in an attitude survey of career police officers in a large Eastern city. In this study, each officer was given an attitude inventory designed to measure his feelings about arresting adults who participated in victimless crimes involving sexual deviation. High scores are indicative of acceptance of sexual deviation. The results are shown by number of years on the police force.

Less than 5 years	5 Years to 10 years	10 years to 15 years	More than 15 years
35	31	22	17
38	38	27	27
38	39	35	29
40	39	36	30
47	52	37	30
47		49	36
50			42
55			
56			
57			

*19. For the 10 officers of Exercise 18 who had less than 5 years service, the statistics given below were obtained on another attitude test concerning victimless crimes. In this test inventory, 15 yes–no items appeared for each of the four victimless crimes. High scores correspond to a belief that the police should not arrest adults for such behavior.

Officer	Homosexuality	Prostitution	Gambling	Drunkenness
1	13	9	10	12
2	12	10	3	13
3	8	6	5	10
4	12	10	8	12
5	11	13	11	10
6	14	12	8	10
7	15	15	3	14
8	14	12	14	10
9	14	10	12	15
10	13	15	8	14

a) Is there any agreement among the 10 officers as to how they view these four victimless crimes?

b) Is there any reason to believe that Kendall's coefficient of concordance is different from zero?

c) What is the average Spearman rho across the 10 officers?

*20. In the study of Exercise 19, each officer was asked to compare each victimless crime against the others by means of a pairwise comparison. Results are as shown in the

Tests of
Independence
and Measures of
Association for
Quantitative
Variables

477

table below for one officer. A rank of one is assigned to the least serious victimless crime.

a) On the basis of these data, would you conclude that this officer has an ordering of the seriousness of these victimless crimes?
b) Estimate W for these data.
c) Is there reason to believe that $W \neq 0$?

Compari-son	Homosexuality	Prostitu-tion	Gambling	Drunken-ness
H, P	2	1		
H, G	1		2	
H, D	2			1
P, G		1	2	
P, D		1		2
G, D			2	1

Compari-son	Homosexuality	Prostitu-tion	Gambling	Drunken-ness
H, P	1	2		
	1	2		
	1	2		
	1	2		
	2	1		
H, G	1		2	
	1		2	
	1		2	
	1		2	
	2		1	
H, D	2			1
	2			1
	1			2
	2			1
	1			2
P, G		1	2	
		1	2	
		1	2	
		1	2	
		1	2	
P, D		1		2
		1		2
		1		2
		1		2
		2		1
G, D			2	1
			2	1
			2	1
			2	1
			2	1

*21. For the five officers who served on the police force for five to ten years, the results of the pairwise comparisons are as shown below. Answer (a), (b), and (c) of Exercise 20 for these five officers.

*22. Determine Kendall's tau for the data of Table 3–11. Is there any reason to believe $E(\tau) = 0$?

*23. Use normal scores to evaluate the correlation between the paired observations of Table 3–11.

*24. Use Kendall's tau and the Mann–Whitney test to evaluate the data of Table 5–12.

*25. Use Kendall's tau to determine whether the two sets of data of Exercise 14 of Chapter 6 are monotonically related.

*26. Determine Goodman and Kruskal's gamma for each religion level of Exercise 12 of Chapter 5. Determine gamma for the case in which the effects of religion are held constant, or removed.

*27. Is the relationship between sex and success independent of grade for the data of Table 5–10?

*28. Determine Kendall's tau and Goodman and Kruskall's gamma for the data of Table 5–9. Compare the two measures.

*29. Is the relationship between mobility and interest in job independent of age for the data of Exercise 6 of Chapter 6?

*30. For the data of Exercise 13 of Chapter 6, find G_{Males} and G_{Females}. Is there any reason to believe that attitude toward Negroes and toward protest are independent of sex?

*31. For the data of Table 8–19, is the relationship between the use of marijuana and grade-point ratio independent of father's income?

*32. Determine Goodman and Kruskal's gamma for the two groups of students in Exercise 11 of Chapter 8. Is there any reason to believe that the correlation between the pre- and posttests is independent of strength of message?

*33. For the data of Table 9–1, determine G_1, G_2, and G_3. Is the correlation between race and attitude independent of school?

*34. Determine W for the data of Exercise 1 of Chapter 14. What does this tell you about the ranking of the painters across the 15 judges?

*35. Determine W for the control group and the experimental group of Exercise 5 of Chapter 14. What questions would you like to ask about W_C and W_E?

*36. Determine W for the data of Exercises 12 and 13 of Chapter 14.

*37. Analyze the data of Exercise 11 of Chapter 3 in terms of Spearman's rank correlation. Repeat the analysis with Kendall's tau.

*38. Analyze the data of Exercise 13 of Chapter 3 in terms of the Spearman rank correlation. Repeat the analysis with Kendall's tau.

*39. The analysis of Example 16–12.1 serves as a competitor to Page's test for monotonic trend. Perform the large-sample form of the test and compare the resulting Z to the Z value for Kendall's model. Which method would you recommend? Why?

Tables

Number of Comparisons Q	α	Error df											
		5	7	10	12	15	20	24	30	40	60	120	∞
2	.05	3.17	2.84	2.64	2.56	2.49	2.42	2.39	2.36	2.33	2.30	2.27	2.24
	.01	4.78	4.03	3.58	3.43	3.29	3.16	3.09	3.03	2.97	2.92	2.86	2.81
3	.05	3.54	3.13	2.87	2.78	2.69	2.61	2.58	2.54	2.50	2.47	2.43	2.39
	.01	5.25	4.36	3.83	3.65	3.48	3.33	3.26	3.19	3.12	3.06	2.99	2.94
4	.05	3.81	3.34	3.04	2.94	2.84	2.75	2.70	2.66	2.62	2.58	2.54	2.50
	.01	5.60	4.59	4.01	3.80	3.62	3.46	3.38	3.30	3.23	3.16	3.09	3.02
5	.05	4.04	3.50	3.17	3.06	2.95	2.85	2.80	2.75	2.71	2.66	2.62	2.58
	.01	5.89	4.78	4.15	3.93	3.74	3.55	3.47	3.39	3.31	3.24	3.16	3.09
6	.05	4.22	3.64	3.28	3.15	3.04	2.93	2.88	2.83	2.78	2.73	2.68	2.64
	.01	6.15	4.95	4.27	4.04	3.82	3.63	3.54	3.46	3.38	3.30	3.22	3.15
7	.05	4.38	3.76	3.37	3.24	3.11	3.00	2.94	2.89	2.84	2.79	2.74	2.69
	.01	6.36	5.09	4.37	4.13	3.90	3.70	3.61	3.52	3.43	3.34	3.27	3.19
8	.05	4.53	3.86	3.45	3.31	3.18	3.06	3.00	2.94	2.89	2.84	2.79	2.74
	.01	6.56	5.21	4.45	4.20	3.97	3.76	3.66	3.57	3.48	3.39	3.31	3.23
9	.05	4.66	3.95	3.52	3.37	3.24	3.11	3.05	2.99	2.93	2.88	2.83	2.77
	.01	6.70	5.31	4.53	4.26	4.02	3.80	3.70	3.61	3.51	3.42	3.34	3.26
10	.05	4.78	4.03	3.58	3.43	3.29	3.16	3.09	3.03	2.97	2.92	2.86	2.81
	.01	6.86	5.40	4.59	4.32	4.07	3.85	3.74	3.65	3.55	3.46	3.37	3.29
15	.05	5.25	4.36	3.83	3.65	3.48	3.33	3.26	3.19	3.12	3.06	2.99	2.94
	.01	7.51	5.79	4.86	4.56	4.29	4.03	3.91	3.80	3.70	3.59	3.50	3.40
20	.05	5.60	4.59	4.01	3.80	3.62	3.46	3.38	3.30	3.23	3.16	3.09	3.02
	.01	8.00	6.08	5.06	4.73	4.42	4.15	4 04	3.90	3.79	3.69	3.58	3.48
25	.05	5.89	4.78	4.15	3.93	3.74	3.55	3.47	3.39	3.31	3.24	3.16	3.09
	.01	8.37	6.30	5.20	4.86	4.53	4.25	4.1*	3.98	3.88	3.76	3.64	3.54
30	.05	6.15	4.95	4.27	4.04	3.82	3.63	3.54	3.46	3.38	3.30	3.22	3.15
	.01	8.68	6.49	5.33	4.95	4.61	4.33	4.2*	4.13	3.93	3.81	3.69	3.59
35	.05	6.36	5.09	4.37	4.13	3.90	3.70	3.61	3.52	3.43	3.34	3.27	3.19
	.01	8.95	6.67	5.44	5.04	4.71	4.39	4.3*	4.26	3.97	3.84	3.73	3.63
40	.05	6.56	5.21	4.45	4.20	3.97	3.76	3.66	3.57	3.48	3.39	3.31	3.23
	.01	9.19	6.83	5.52	5.12	4.78	4.46	4.3*	4.1*	4.01	3.89	3.77	3.66
45	.05	6.70	5.31	4.53	4.26	4.02	3.80	3.70	3.61	3.51	3.42	3.34	3.26
	.01	9.41	6.93	5.60	5.20	4.84	4.52	4.3*	4.2*	4.1*	3.93	3.80	3.69
50	.05	6.86	5.40	4.59	4.32	4.07	3.85	3.74	3.65	3.55	3.46	3.37	3.29
	.01	9.68	7.06	5.70	5.27	4.90	4.56	4.4*	4.2*	4.1*	3.97	3.83	3.72
100	.05	8.00	6.08	5.06	4.73	4.42	4.15	4.04	3.90	3.79	3.69	3.58	3.48
	.01	11.04	7.80	6.20	5.70	5.20	4.80	4.7*	4.4*	4.5*		4.00	3.89
250	.05	9.68	7.06	5.70	5.27	4.90	4.56	4.4*	4.2*	4.1*	3.97	3.83	3.72
	.01	13.26	8.83	6.9*	6.3*	5.8*	5.2*	5.0*	4.9*	4.8*			4.11

*Obtained by graphical interpolation. Table reproduced from Multiple comparisons among means, *Journal of the American Statistical Association*, 1961, **56**, 52–64, with permission of the author, O. J. Dunn, and the editor.

z	X	Area	z	X	Area
-3.25	$\mu - 3.25\sigma$	.0006	-1.00	$\mu - 1.00\sigma$	.1587
-3.20	$\mu - 3.20\sigma$	.0007	$-.95$	$\mu - .95\sigma$	.1711
-3.15	$\mu - 3.15\sigma$	.0008	$-.90$	$\mu - .90\sigma$	.1841
-3.10	$\mu - 3.10\sigma$	.0010	$-.85$	$\mu - .85\sigma$	.1977
-3.05	$\mu - 3.05\sigma$	.0011	$-.80$	$\mu - .80\sigma$	.2119
-3.00	$\mu - 3.00\sigma$	.0013	$-.75$	$\mu - .75\sigma$	.2266
-2.95	$\mu - 2.95\sigma$	.0016	$-.70$	$\mu - .70\sigma$	.2420
-2.90	$\mu - 2.90\sigma$	.0019	$-.65$	$\mu - .65\sigma$	.2578
-2.85	$\mu - 2.85\sigma$	.0022	$-.60$	$\mu - .60\sigma$	.2743
-2.80	$\mu - 2.80\sigma$	.0026	$-.55$	$\mu - .55\sigma$	.2912
-2.75	$\mu - 2.75\sigma$	.0030	$-.50$	$\mu - .50\sigma$	.3085
-2.70	$\mu - 2.70\sigma$	.0035	$-.45$	$\mu - .45\sigma$	.3264
-2.65	$\mu - 2.65\sigma$	.0040	$-.40$	$\mu - .40\sigma$	.3446
-2.60	$\mu - 2.60\sigma$	.0047	$-.35$	$\mu - .35\sigma$	.3632
-2.55	$\mu - 2.55\sigma$	.0054	$-.30$	$\mu - .30\sigma$	.3821
-2.50	$\mu - 2.50\sigma$	.0062	$-.25$	$\mu - .25\sigma$	.4013
-2.45	$\mu - 2.45\sigma$	.0071	$-.20$	$\mu - .20\sigma$	.4207
-2.40	$\mu - 2.40\sigma$	.0082	$-.15$	$\mu - .15\sigma$	.4404
-2.35	$\mu - 2.35\sigma$	.0094	$-.10$	$\mu - .10\sigma$	.4602
-2.30	$\mu - 2.30\sigma$	.0107	$-.05$	$\mu - .05\sigma$	.4801
-2.25	$\mu - 2.25\sigma$	.0122			
-2.20	$\mu - 2.20\sigma$	.0139			
-2.15	$\mu - 2.15\sigma$	.0158	.00	μ	.5000
-2.10	$\mu - 2.10\sigma$	.0179			
-2.05	$\mu - 2.05\sigma$	.0202			
-2.00	$\mu - 2.00\sigma$	.0228	.05	$\mu + .05\sigma$	.5199
-1.95	$\mu - 1.95\sigma$	.0256	.10	$\mu + .10\sigma$	.5398
-1.90	$\mu - 1.90\sigma$	.0287	.15	$\mu + .15\sigma$	.5596
-1.85	$\mu - 1.85\sigma$	.0322	.20	$\mu + .20\sigma$	.5793
-1.80	$\mu - 1.80\sigma$	.0359	.25	$\mu + .25\sigma$	.5987
-1.75	$\mu - 1.75\sigma$	.0401	.30	$\mu + .30\sigma$	.6179
-1.70	$\mu - 1.70\sigma$	.0446	.35	$\mu + .35\sigma$	.6368
-1.65	$\mu - 1.65\sigma$	.0495	.40	$\mu + .40\sigma$	.6554
-1.60	$\mu - 1.60\sigma$	.0548	.45	$\mu + .45\sigma$	.6736
-1.55	$\mu - 1.55\sigma$	.0606	.50	$\mu + .50\sigma$	.6915
-1.50	$\mu - 1.50\sigma$	.0668	.55	$\mu + .55\sigma$	.7088
-1.45	$\mu - 1.45\sigma$	.0735	.60	$\mu + .60\sigma$	.7257
-1.40	$\mu - 1.40\sigma$	.0808	.65	$\mu + .65\sigma$	.7422
-1.35	$\mu - 1.35\sigma$	.0885	.70	$\mu + .70\sigma$	.7580
-1.30	$\mu - 1.30\sigma$	.0968	.75	$\mu + .75\sigma$	.7734
-1.25	$\mu - 1.25\sigma$	.1056	.80	$\mu + .80\sigma$	.7881
-1.20	$\mu - 1.20\sigma$	.1151	.85	$\mu + .85\sigma$	.8023
-1.15	$\mu - 1.15\sigma$	.1251	.90	$\mu + .90\sigma$	.8159
-1.10	$\mu - 1.10\sigma$	.1357	.95	$\mu + .95\sigma$	.8289
-1.05	$\mu - 1.05\sigma$	.1469	1.00	$\mu + 1.00\sigma$	.8413

z	X	Area	z	X	Area
1.05	$\mu + 1.05\sigma$	.8531	−4.265	$\mu − 4.265\sigma$	.00001
1.10	$\mu + 1.10\sigma$	.8643	−3.719	$\mu − 3.719\sigma$	.0001
1.15	$\mu + 1.15\sigma$	.8749	−3.090	$\mu − 3.090\sigma$	.001
1.20	$\mu + 1.20\sigma$	.8849	−2.576	$\mu − 2.576\sigma$	.005
1.25	$\mu + 1.25\sigma$	.8944	−2.326	$\mu − 2.326\sigma$	.01
1.30	$\mu + 1.30\sigma$	.9032	−2.054	$\mu − 2.054\sigma$	.02
1.35	$\mu + 1.35\sigma$	.9115	−1.960	$\mu − 1.960\sigma$	.025
1.40	$\mu + 1.40\sigma$	.9192	−1.881	$\mu − 1.881\sigma$	.03
1.45	$\mu + 1.45\sigma$	.9265	−1.751	$\mu − 1.751\sigma$	.04
1.50	$\mu + 1.50\sigma$	.9332	−1.645	$\mu − 1.645\sigma$	.05
1.55	$\mu + 1.55\sigma$	.9394	−1.555	$\mu − 1.555\sigma$	.06
1.60	$\mu + 1.60\sigma$	.9452	−1.476	$\mu − 1.476\sigma$	.07
1.65	$\mu + 1.65\sigma$	.9505	−1.405	$\mu − 1.405\sigma$	.08
1.70	$\mu + 1.70\sigma$	.9554	−1.341	$\mu − 1.341\sigma$	.09
1.75	$\mu + 1.75\sigma$	.9599	−1.282	$\mu − 1.282\sigma$	.10
1.80	$\mu + 1.80\sigma$	.9641	−1.036	$\mu − 1.036\sigma$	.15
1.85	$\mu + 1.85\sigma$	.9678	− .842	$\mu − .842\sigma$	.20
1.90	$\mu + 1.90\sigma$	.9713	− .674	$\mu − .674\sigma$	.25
1.95	$\mu + 1.95\sigma$	.9744	− .524	$\mu − .524\sigma$	.30
2.00	$\mu + 2.00\sigma$	.9772	− .385	$\mu − .385\sigma$	.35
2.05	$\mu + 2.05\sigma$	.9798	− .253	$\mu − .253\sigma$	.40
2.10	$\mu + 2.10\sigma$	.9821	− .126	$\mu − .126\sigma$	.45
2.15	$\mu + 2.15\sigma$	.9842	0	μ	.50
2.20	$\mu + 2.20\sigma$	.9861	.126	$\mu + .126\sigma$	.55
2.25	$\mu + 2.25\sigma$	.9878	.253	$\mu + .253\sigma$	.60
2.30	$\mu + 2.30\sigma$	.9893	.385	$\mu + .385\sigma$	.65
2.35	$\mu + 2.35\sigma$	.9906	.524	$\mu + .524\sigma$	.70
2.40	$\mu + 2.40\sigma$	.9918	.674	$\mu + .674\sigma$	.75
2.45	$\mu + 2.45\sigma$	.9929	.842	$\mu + .842\sigma$	.80
2.50	$\mu + 2.50\sigma$	.9938	1.036	$\mu + 1.036\sigma$	.85
2.55	$\mu + 2.55\sigma$	.9946	1.282	$\mu + 1.282\sigma$	.90
2.60	$\mu + 2.60\sigma$	.9953	1.341	$\mu + 1.341\sigma$	.91
2.65	$\mu + 2.65\sigma$	.9960	1.405	$\mu + 1.405\sigma$	.92
2.70	$\mu + 2.70\sigma$	.9965	1.476	$\mu + 1.476\sigma$	.93
2.75	$\mu + 2.75\sigma$	.9970	1.555	$\mu + 1.555\sigma$	.94
2.80	$\mu + 2.80\sigma$	.9974	1.645	$\mu + 1.645\sigma$	.95
2.85	$\mu + 2.85\sigma$	.9978	1.751	$\mu + 1.751\sigma$	.96
2.90	$\mu + 2.90\sigma$	.9981	1.881	$\mu + 1.881\sigma$	.97
2.95	$\mu + 2.95\sigma$	.9984	1.960	$\mu + 1.960\sigma$	.975
3.00	$\mu + 3.00\sigma$	.9987	2.054	$\mu + 2.054\sigma$	.98
3.05	$\mu + 3.05\sigma$	.9989	2.326	$\mu + 2.326\sigma$	.99
3.10	$\mu + 3.10\sigma$	.9990	2.576	$\mu + 2.576\sigma$	.995
3.15	$\mu + 3.15\sigma$	.9992	3.090	$\mu + 3.090\sigma$	.999
3.20	$\mu + 3.20\sigma$	.9993	3.719	$\mu + 3.719\sigma$	.9999
3.25	$\mu + 3.25\sigma$	.9994	4.265	$\mu + 4.265\sigma$	.99999

TABLE A–3. Critical values of the X^2 distribution

df	$P_{0.5}$	P_{01}	$P_{02.5}$	P_{05}	P_{10}	P_{90}	P_{95}	$P_{97.5}$	P_{99}	$P_{99.5}$
1	.000039	.00016	.00098	.0039	.0158	2.71	3.84	5.02	6.63	7.88
2	.0100	.0201	.0506	.1026	.2107	4.61	5.99	7.38	9.21	10.60
3	.0717	.115	.216	.352	.584	6.25	7.81	9.35	11.34	12.84
4	.207	.297	.484	.711	1.064	7.78	9.49	11.14	13.28	14.86
5	.412	.554	.831	1.15	1.61	9.24	11.07	12.83	15.09	16.75
6	.676	.872	1.24	1.64	2.20	10.64	12.59	14.45	16.81	18.55
7	.989	1.24	1.69	2.17	2.83	12.02	14.07	16.01	18.48	20.28
8	1.34	1.65	2.18	2.73	3.49	13.36	15.51	17.53	20.09	21.96
9	1.73	2.09	2.70	3.33	4.17	14.68	16.92	19.02	21.67	23.59
10	2.16	2.56	3.25	3.94	4.87	15.99	18.31	20.48	23.21	25.19
11	2.60	3.05	3.82	4.57	5.58	17.28	19.68	21.92	24.73	26.76
12	3.07	3.57	4.40	5.23	6.30	18.55	21.03	23.34	26.22	28.30
13	3.57	4.11	5.01	5.89	7.04	19.81	22.36	24.74	27.69	29.82
14	4.07	4.66	5.63	6.57	7.79	21.06	23.68	26.12	29.14	31.32
15	4.60	5.23	6.26	7.26	8.55	22.31	25.00	27.49	30.58	32.80
16	5.14	5.81	6.91	7.96	9.31	23.54	26.30	28.85	32.00	34.27
18	6.26	7.01	8.23	9.39	10.86	25.99	28.87	31.53	34.81	37.16
20	7.43	8.26	9.59	10.85	12.44	28.41	31.41	34.17	37.57	40.00
24	9.89	10.86	12.40	13.85	15.66	33.20	36.42	39.36	42.98	45.56
30	13.79	14.95	16.79	18.49	20.60	40.26	43.77	46.98	50.89	53.67
40	20.71	22.16	24.43	26.51	29.05	51.81	55.76	59.34	63.69	66.77
60	35.53	37.48	40.48	43.19	46.46	74.40	79.08	83.30	88.38	91.95
120	83.85	86.92	91.58	95.70	100.62	140.23	146.57	152.21	158.95	163.64

From *Introduction to Statistical Analysis* (3rd ed.), by W. J. Dixon and F. J. Massey, Jr. Copyright © 1969 by McGraw-Hill, Inc. Used with permission of McGraw-Hill Book Company.

TABLE A–4. Percentage points of student's t distribution

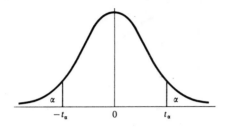

df	α .25 2α .50	.20 .40	.15 .30	.10 .20	.05 .10	.025 .05	.01 .02	.005 .01	.0005 .001
1	1.000	1.376	1.963	3.078	6.314	12.706	31.821	63.657	636.619
2	.816	1.061	1.386	1.886	2.920	4.303	6.965	9.925	31.598
3	.765	.978	1.250	1.638	2.353	3.182	4.541	5.841	12.924
4	.741	.941	1.190	1.533	2.132	2.776	3.747	4.604	8.610
5	.727	.920	1.156	1.476	2.015	2.571	3.365	4.032	6.869
6	.718	.906	1.134	1.440	1.943	2.447	3.143	3.707	5.959
7	.711	.896	1.119	1.415	1.895	2.365	2.998	3.499	5.408
8	.706	.889	1.108	1.397	1.860	2.306	2.896	3.355	5.041
9	.703	.883	1.100	1.383	1.833	2.262	2.821	3.250	4.781
10	.700	.879	1.093	1.372	1.812	2.228	2.764	3.169	4.587
11	.697	.876	1.088	1.363	1.796	2.201	2.718	3.106	4.437
12	.695	.873	1.083	1.356	1.782	2.179	2.681	3.055	4.318
13	.694	.870	1.079	1.350	1.771	2.160	2.650	3.012	4.221
14	.692	.868	1.076	1.345	1.761	2.145	2.624	2.977	4.140
15	.691	.866	1.074	1.341	1.753	2.131	2.602	2.947	4.073
16	.690	.865	1.071	1.337	1.746	2.120	2.583	2.921	4.015
17	.689	.863	1.069	1.333	1.740	2.110	2.567	2.898	3.965
18	.688	.862	1.067	1.330	1.734	2.101	2.552	2.878	3.922
19	.688	.861	1.066	1.328	1.729	2.093	2.539	2.861	3.883
20	.687	.860	1.064	1.325	1.725	2.086	2.528	2.845	3.850
21	.686	.859	1.063	1.323	1.721	2.080	2.518	2.831	3.819
22	.686	.858	1.061	1.321	1.717	2.074	2.508	2.819	3.792
23	.685	.858	1.060	1.319	1.714	2.069	2.500	2.807	3.767
24	.685	.857	1.059	1.318	1.711	2.064	2.492	2.797	3.745
25	.684	.856	1.058	1.316	1.708	2.060	2.485	2.787	3.725
26	.684	.856	1.058	1.315	1.706	2.056	2.479	2.779	3.707
27	.684	.855	1.057	1.314	1.703	2.052	2.473	2.771	3.690
28	.683	.855	1.056	1.313	1.701	2.048	2.467	2.763	3.674
29	.683	.854	1.055	1.311	1.699	2.045	2.462	2.756	3.659
30	.683	.854	1.055	1.310	1.697	2.042	2.457	2.750	3.646
40	.681	.851	1.050	1.303	1.684	2.021	2.423	2.704	3.551
60	.679	.848	1.046	1.296	1.671	2.000	2.390	2.660	3.460
120	.677	.845	1.041	1.289	1.658	1.980	2.358	2.617	3.373
∞	.674	.842	1.036	1.282	1.645	1.960	2.326	2.576	3.291

From Table iii of Fisher and Yates, *Statistical Tables for Biological, Agricultural and Medical Research*, published by Longman Group Ltd., London (previously published by Oliver & Boyd, Edinburgh). Reprinted by permission of the authors and publishers.

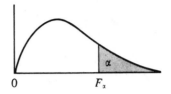

$$\alpha = .05$$

Degrees of Freedom

ν_1

ν_2	1	2	3	4	5	6	7	8	9
1	161.4	199.5	215.7	224.6	230.2	234.0	236.8	238.9	240.5
2	18.51	19.00	19.16	19.25	19.30	19.33	19.35	19.37	19.38
3	10.13	9.55	9.28	9.12	9.01	8.94	8.89	8.85	8.81
4	7.71	6.94	6.59	6.39	6.26	6.16	6.09	6.04	6.00
5	6.61	5.79	5.41	5.19	5.05	4.95	4.88	4.82	4.77
6	5.99	5.14	4.76	4.53	4.39	4.28	4.21	4.15	4.10
7	5.59	4.74	4.35	4.12	3.97	3.87	3.79	3.73	3.68
8	5.32	4.46	4.07	3.84	3.69	3.58	3.50	3.44	3.39
9	5.12	4.26	3.86	3.63	3.48	3.37	3.29	3.23	3.18
10	4.96	4.10	3.71	3.48	3.33	3.22	3.14	3.07	3.02
11	4.84	3.98	3.59	3.36	3.20	3.09	3.01	2.95	2.90
12	4.75	3.89	3.49	3.26	3.11	3.00	2.91	2.85	2.80
13	4.67	3.81	3.41	3.18	3.03	2.92	2.83	2.77	2.71
14	4.60	3.74	3.34	3.11	2.96	2.85	2.76	2.70	2.65
15	4.54	3.68	3.29	3.06	2.90	2.79	2.71	2.64	2.59
16	4.49	3.63	3.24	3.01	2.85	2.74	2.66	2.59	2.54
17	4.45	3.59	3.20	2.96	2.81	2.70	2.61	2.55	2.49
18	4.41	3.55	3.16	2.93	2.77	2.66	2.58	2.51	2.46
19	4.38	3.52	3.13	2.90	2.74	2.63	2.54	2.48	2.42
20	4.35	3.49	3.10	2.87	2.71	2.60	2.51	2.45	2.39
21	4.32	3.47	3.07	2.84	2.68	2.57	2.49	2.42	2.37
22	4.30	3.44	3.05	2.82	2.66	2.55	2.46	2.40	2.34
23	4.28	3.42	3.03	2.80	2.64	2.53	2.44	2.37	2.32
24	4.26	3.40	3.01	2.78	2.62	2.51	2.42	2.36	2.30
25	4.24	3.39	2.99	2.76	2.60	2.49	2.40	2.34	2.28
26	4.23	3.37	2.98	2.74	2.59	2.47	2.39	2.32	2.27
27	4.21	3.35	2.96	2.73	2.57	2.46	2.37	2.31	2.25
28	4.20	3.34	2.95	2.71	2.56	2.45	2.36	2.29	2.24
29	4.18	3.33	2.93	2.70	2.55	2.43	2.35	2.28	2.22
30	4.17	3.32	2.92	2.69	2.53	2.42	2.33	2.27	2.21
40	4.08	3.23	2.84	2.61	2.45	2.34	2.25	2.18	2.12
60	4.00	3.15	2.76	2.53	2.37	2.25	2.17	2.10	2.04
120	3.92	3.07	2.68	2.45	2.29	2.17	2.09	2.02	1.96
∞	3.84	3.00	2.60	2.37	2.21	2.10	2.01	1.94	1.88

	ν_1									
10	**12**	**15**	**20**	**24**	**30**	**40**	**60**	**120**	∞	ν_2
241.9	243.9	245.9	248.0	249.1	250.1	251.1	252.2	253.3	254.3	1
19.40	19.41	19.43	19.45	19.45	19.46	19.47	19.48	19.49	19.50	2
8.79	8.74	8.70	8.66	8.64	8.62	8.59	8.57	8.55	8.53	3
5.96	5.91	5.86	5.80	5.77	5.75	5.72	5.69	5.66	5.63	4
4.74	4.68	4.62	4.56	4.53	4.50	4.46	4.43	4.40	4.36	5
4.06	4.00	3.94	3.87	3.84	3.81	3.77	3.74	3.70	3.67	6
3.64	3.57	3.51	3.44	3.41	3.38	3.34	3.30	3.27	3.23	7
3.35	3.28	3.22	3.15	3.12	3.08	3.04	3.01	2.97	2.93	8
3.14	3.07	3.01	2.94	2.90	2.86	2.83	2.79	2.75	2.71	9
2.98	2.91	2.85	2.77	2.74	2.70	2.66	2.62	2.58	2.54	10
2.85	2.79	2.72	2.65	2.61	2.57	2.53	2.49	2.45	2.40	11
2.75	2.69	2.62	2.54	2.51	2.47	2.43	2.38	2.34	2.30	12
2.67	2.60	2.53	2.46	2.42	2.38	2.34	2.30	2.25	2.21	13
2.60	2.53	2.46	2.39	2.35	2.31	2.27	2.22	2.18	2.13	14
2.54	2.48	2.40	2.33	2.29	2.25	2.20	2.16	2.11	2.07	15
2.49	2.42	2.35	2.28	2.24	2.19	2.15	2.11	2.06	2.01	16
2.45	2.38	2.31	2.23	2.19	2.15	2.10	2.06	2.01	1.96	17
2.41	2.34	2.27	2.19	2.15	2.11	2.06	2.02	1.97	1.92	18
2.38	2.31	2.23	2.16	2.11	2.07	2.03	1.98	1.93	1.88	19
2.35	2.28	2.20	2.12	2.08	2.04	1.99	1.95	1.90	1.84	20
2.32	2.25	2.18	2.10	2.05	2.01	1.96	1.92	1.87	1.81	21
2.30	2.23	2.15	2.07	2.03	1.98	1.94	1.89	1.84	1.78	22
2.27	2.20	2.13	2.05	2.01	1.96	1.91	1.86	1.81	1.76	23
2.25	2.18	2.11	2.03	1.98	1.94	1.89	1.84	1.79	1.73	24
2.24	2.16	2.09	2.01	1.96	1.92	1.87	1.82	1.77	1.71	25
2.22	2.15	2.07	1.99	1.95	1.90	1.85	1.80	1.75	1.69	26
2.20	2.13	2.06	1.97	1.93	1.88	1.84	1.79	1.73	1.67	27
2.19	2.12	2.04	1.96	1.91	1.87	1.82	1.77	1.71	1.65	28
2.18	2.10	2.03	1.94	1.90	1.85	1.81	1.75	1.70	1.64	29
2.16	2.09	2.01	1.93	1.89	1.84	1.79	1.74	1.68	1.62	30
2.08	2.00	1.92	1.84	1.79	1.74	1.69	1.64	1.58	1.51	40
1.99	1.92	1.84	1.75	1.70	1.65	1.59	1.53	1.47	1.39	60
1.91	1.83	1.75	1.66	1.61	1.55	1.50	1.43	1.35	1.25	120
1.83	1.75	1.67	1.57	1.52	1.46	1.39	1.32	1.22	1.00	∞

489

$$\alpha = .01$$

Degrees of Freedom

v_1

v_2	1	2	3	4	5	6	7	8	9
1	4052	4999.5	5403	5625	5764	5859	5928	5982	6022
2	98.50	99.00	99.17	99.25	99.30	99.33	99.36	99.37	99.39
3	34.12	30.82	29.46	28.71	28.24	27.91	27.67	27.49	27.35
4	21.20	18.00	16.69	15.98	15.52	15.21	14.98	14.80	14.66
5	16.26	13.27	12.06	11.39	10.97	10.67	10.46	10.29	10.16
6	13.75	10.92	9.78	9.15	8.75	8.47	8.26	8.10	7.98
7	12.25	9.55	8.45	7.85	7.46	7.19	6.99	6.84	6.72
8	11.26	8.65	7.59	7.01	6.63	6.37	6.18	6.03	5.91
9	10.56	8.02	6.99	6.42	6.06	5.80	5.61	5.47	5.35
10	10.04	7.56	6.55	5.99	5.64	5.39	5.20	5.06	4.94
11	9.65	7.21	6.22	5.67	5.32	5.07	4.89	4.74	4.63
12	9.33	6.93	5.95	5.41	5.06	4.82	4.64	4.50	4.39
13	9.07	6.70	5.74	5.21	4.86	4.62	4.44	4.30	4.19
14	8.86	6.51	5.56	5.04	4.69	4.46	4.28	4.14	4.03
15	8.68	6.36	5.42	4.89	4.56	4.32	4.14	4.00	3.89
16	8.53	6.23	5.29	4.77	4.44	4.20	4.03	3.89	3.78
17	8.40	6.11	5.18	4.67	4.34	4.10	3.93	3.79	3.68
18	8.29	6.01	5.09	4.58	4.25	4.01	3.84	3.71	3.60
19	8.18	5.93	5.01	4.50	4.17	3.94	3.77	3.63	3.52
20	8.10	5.85	4.94	4.43	4.10	3.87	3.70	3.56	3.46
21	8.02	5.78	4.87	4.37	4.04	3.81	3.64	3.51	3.40
22	7.95	5.72	4.82	4.31	3.99	3.76	3.59	3.45	3.35
23	7.88	5.66	4.76	4.26	3.94	3.71	3.54	3.41	3.30
24	7.82	5.61	4.72	4.22	3.90	3.67	3.50	3.36	3.26
25	7.77	5.57	4.68	4.18	3.85	3.63	3.46	3.32	3.22
26	7.72	5.53	4.64	4.14	3.82	3.59	3.42	3.29	3.18
27	7.68	5.49	4.60	4.11	3.78	3.56	3.39	3.26	3.15
28	7.64	5.45	4.57	4.07	3.75	3.53	3.36	3.23	3.12
29	7.60	5.42	4.54	4.04	3.73	3.50	3.33	3.20	3.09
30	7.56	5.39	4.51	4.02	3.70	3.47	3.30	3.17	3.07
40	7.31	5.18	4.31	3.83	3.51	3.29	3.12	2.99	2.89
60	7.08	4.98	4.13	3.65	3.34	3.12	2.95	2.82	2.72
120	6.85	4.79	3.95	3.48	3.17	2.96	2.79	2.66	2.56
∞	6.63	4.61	3.78	3.32	3.02	2.80	2.64	2.51	2.41

TABLE A–5 (continued)

ν_1

10	12	15	20	24	30	40	60	120	∞	ν_2
6056	6106	6157	6209	6235	6261	6287	6313	6339	6366	1
99.40	99.42	99.43	99.45	99.46	99.47	99.47	99.48	99.49	99.50	2
27.23	27.05	26.87	26.69	26.60	26.50	26.41	26.32	26.22	26.13	3
14.55	14.37	14.20	14.02	13.93	13.84	13.75	13.65	13.56	13.46	4
10.05	9.89	9.72	9.55	9.47	9.38	9.29	9.20	9.11	9.02	5
7.87	7.72	7.56	7.40	7.31	7.23	7.14	7.06	6.97	6.88	6
6.62	6.47	6.31	6.16	6.07	5.99	5.91	5.82	5.74	5.65	7
5.81	5.67	5.52	5.36	5.28	5.20	5.12	5.03	4.95	4.86	8
5.26	5.11	4.96	4.81	4.73	4.65	4.57	4.48	4.40	4.31	9
4.85	4.71	4.56	4.41	4.33	4.25	4.17	4.08	4.00	3.91	10
4.54	4.40	4.25	4.10	4.02	3.94	3.86	3.78	3.69	3.60	11
4.30	4.16	4.01	3.86	3.78	3.70	3.62	3.54	3.45	3.36	12
4.10	3.96	3.82	3.66	3.59	3.51	3.43	3.34	3.25	3.17	13
3.94	3.80	3.66	3.51	3.43	3.35	3.27	3.18	3.09	3.00	14
3.80	3.67	3.52	3.37	3.29	3.21	3.13	3.05	2.96	2.87	15
3.69	3.55	3.41	3.26	3.18	3.10	3.02	2.93	2.84	2.75	16
3.59	3.46	3.31	3.16	3.08	3.00	2.92	2.83	2.75	2.65	17
3.51	3.37	3.23	3.08	3.00	2.92	2.84	2.75	2.66	2.57	18
3.43	3.30	3.15	3.00	2.92	2.84	2.76	2.67	2.58	2.49	19
3.37	3.23	3.09	2.94	2.86	2.78	2.69	2.61	2.52	2.42	20
3.31	3.17	3.03	2.88	2.80	2.72	2.64	2.55	2.46	2.36	21
3.26	3.12	2.98	2.83	2.75	2.67	2.58	2.50	2.40	2.31	22
3.21	3.07	2.93	2.78	2.70	2.62	2.54	2.45	2.35	2.26	23
3.17	3.03	2.89	2.74	2.66	2.58	2.49	2.40	2.31	2.21	24
3.13	2.99	2.85	2.70	2.62	2.54	2.45	2.36	2.27	2.17	25
3.09	2.96	2.81	2.66	2.58	2.50	2.42	2.33	2.23	2.13	26
3.06	2.93	2.78	2.63	2.55	2.47	2.38	2.29	2.20	2.10	27
3.03	2.90	2.75	2.60	2.52	2.44	2.35	2.26	2.17	2.06	28
3.00	2.87	2.73	2.57	2.49	2.41	2.33	2.23	2.14	2.03	29
2.98	2.84	2.70	2.55	2.47	2.39	2.30	2.21	2.11	2.01	30
2.80	2.66	2.52	2.37	2.29	2.20	2.11	2.02	1.92	1.80	40
2.63	2.50	2.35	2.20	2.12	2.03	1.94	1.84	1.73	1.60	60
2.47	2.34	2.19	2.03	1.95	1.86	1.76	1.66	1.53	1.38	120
2.32	2.18	2.04	1.88	1.79	1.70	1.59	1.47	1.32	1.00	∞

491

From "Tables of Percentage Points of the Inverted Beta (F) Distribution," *Biometrika*, Vol. 33 (1943), pp. 73–88, by Maxine Merrington and Catherine M. Thompson. Reproduced by permission of Professor E. S. Pearson.

TABLE A−6. Binomial coefficients $\binom{N}{x}$.

N	$\binom{N}{0}$	$\binom{N}{1}$	$\binom{N}{2}$	$\binom{N}{3}$	$\binom{N}{4}$	$\binom{N}{5}$	$\binom{N}{6}$	$\binom{N}{7}$	$\binom{N}{8}$	$\binom{N}{9}$	$\binom{N}{10}$
0	1										
1	1	1									
2	1	2	1								
3	1	3	3	1							
4	1	4	6	4	1						
5	1	5	10	10	5	1					
6	1	6	15	20	15	6	1				
7	1	7	21	35	35	21	7	1			
8	1	8	28	56	70	56	28	8	1		
9	1	9	36	84	126	126	84	36	9	1	
10	1	10	45	120	210	252	210	120	45	10	1
11	1	11	55	165	330	462	462	330	165	55	11
12	1	12	66	220	495	792	924	792	495	220	66
13	1	13	78	286	715	1287	1716	1716	1287	715	286
14	1	14	91	364	1001	2002	3003	3432	3003	2002	1001
15	1	15	105	455	1365	3003	5005	6435	6435	5005	3003
16	1	16	120	560	1820	4368	8008	11440	12870	11440	8008
17	1	17	136	680	2380	6188	12376	19448	24310	24310	19448
18	1	18	153	816	3060	8568	18564	31824	43758	48620	43758
19	1	19	171	969	3876	11628	27132	50388	75582	92378	92378
20	1	20	190	1140	4845	15504	38760	77520	125970	167960	184756

From *Statistical Methods for Behavioral Science Research*, by L. A. Marascuilo. Copyright © 1971 by McGraw-Hill, Inc. Used with permission of McGraw-Hill Book Company.

TABLE A−7. Critical values of X for the sign test

(Two-tail percentage points are given for the binomial for $p = .5$)

N	1%	5%	10%	25%	N	1%	5%	10%	25%
1					51	15	18	19	20
2					52	16	18	19	21
3				0	53	16	18	20	21
4				0	54	17	19	20	22
5			0	0	55	17	19	20	22
6		0	0	1	56	17	20	21	23
7		0	0	1	57	18	20	21	23
8	0	0	1	1	58	18	21	22	24
9	0	1	1	2	59	19	21	22	24
10	0	1	1	2	60	19	21	23	25
11	0	1	2	3	61	20	22	23	25
12	1	2	2	3	62	20	22	24	25
13	1	2	3	3	63	20	23	24	26
14	1	2	3	4	64	21	23	24	26
15	2	3	3	4	65	21	24	25	27
16	2	3	4	5	66	22	24	25	27
17	2	4	4	5	67	22	25	26	28
18	3	4	5	6	68	22	25	26	28
19	3	4	5	6	69	23	25	27	29
20	3	5	5	6	70	23	26	27	29
21	4	5	6	7	71	24	26	28	30
22	4	5	6	7	72	24	27	28	30
23	4	6	7	8	73	25	27	28	31
24	5	6	7	8	74	25	28	29	31
25	5	7	7	9	75	25	28	29	32
26	6	7	8	9	76	26	28	30	32
27	6	7	8	10	77	26	29	30	32
28	6	8	9	10	78	27	29	31	33
29	7	8	9	10	79	27	30	31	33
30	7	9	10	11	80	28	30	32	34
31	7	9	10	11	81	28	31	32	34
32	8	9	10	12	82	28	31	33	35
33	8	10	11	12	83	29	32	33	35
34	9	10	11	13	84	29	32	33	36
35	9	11	12	13	85	30	32	34	36
36	9	11	12	14	86	30	33	34	37
37	10	12	13	14	87	31	33	35	37
38	10	12	13	14	88	31	34	35	38
39	11	12	13	15	89	31	34	36	38
40	11	13	14	15	90	32	35	36	39
41	11	13	14	16	91	32	35	37	39
42	12	14	15	16	92	33	36	37	39
43	12	14	15	17	93	33	36	38	40
44	13	15	16	17	94	34	37	38	40
45	13	15	16	18	95	34	37	38	41
46	13	15	16	18	96	34	37	39	41
47	14	16	17	19	97	35	38	39	42
48	14	16	17	19	98	35	38	40	42
49	15	17	18	19	99	36	39	40	43
50	15	17	18	20	100	36	39	41	43

For values of N larger than 100, approximate values of r may be found by taking the nearest integer less than $(N - 1)/2 - k \sqrt{N + 1}$, where k is 1.2879, 0.9800, 0.8224, 0.5752 for the 1, 5, 10, 25% values, respectively.

From *Introduction to Statistical Analysis* (3rd ed.), by W. J. Dixon and F. J. Massey, Jr. Copyright © 1969 by McGraw-Hill, Inc. Used with permission of McGraw-Hill Book Company.

493

TABLE A–8. Probabilities for hypergeometric probabilities and fourfold tables for $N \leq 15$ or $N_1 + N_2 \leq 15$.

N	S_1	S_2	X	Obs.	Other	Total	N	S_1	S_2	X	Obs.	Other	Total	N	S_1	S_2	X	Obs.	Other	Total
2	1	1	0	.500	.500	1.000	7	3	3	0	.114	.029	.143	9	2	3	1	.583	.417	1.000
2	1	1	1	.500	.500	1.000	7	3	3	1	.628	.372	1.000	9	2	3	2	.083	.000	.083
3	1	1	0	.667	.333	1.000	7	3	3	2	.372	.114	.486	9	2	4	0	.278	.167	.444
3	1	1	1	.333	.000	.333	7	3	3	3	.029	.000	.029	9	2	4	1	.722	.278	1.000
4	1	1	0	.750	.250	1.000	8	1	1	0	.875	.125	1.000	9	2	4	2	.167	.000	.167
4	1	1	1	.250	.000	.250	8	1	1	1	.125	.000	.125	9	3	3	0	.238	.226	.464
4	1	2	0	.500	.500	1.000	8	1	2	0	.750	.250	1.000	9	3	3	1	1.000	.000	1.000
4	1	2	1	.500	.500	1.000	8	1	2	1	.250	.000	.250	9	3	3	2	.226	.238	.464
4	2	2	0	.167	.167	.333	8	1	3	0	.625	.375	1.000	9	3	3	3	.012	.000	.012
4	2	2	1	1.000	.000	1.000	8	1	3	1	.375	.000	.375	9	3	4	0	.012	.048	.060
4	2	2	2	.167	.167	.333	8	1	4	0	.500	.500	1.000	9	3	4	1	.488	.512	1.000
5	1	1	0	.800	.200	1.000	8	1	4	1	.500	.500	1.000	9	3	4	2	.405	.012	.417
5	1	1	1	.200	.000	.200	8	2	2	0	.536	.464	1.000	9	3	4	3	.048	.000	.048
5	1	2	0	.600	.400	1.000	8	2	2	1	.464	.536	1.000	9	4	4	0	.040	.008	.048
5	1	2	1	.400	.000	.400	8	2	2	2	.035	.000	.035	9	4	4	1	.357	.167	.524
5	2	2	0	.300	.100	.400	8	2	3	0	.357	.107	.464	9	4	4	2	.643	.357	1.000
5	2	2	1	.700	.300	1.000	8	2	3	1	.643	.357	1.000	9	4	4	3	.167	.040	.206
5	2	2	2	.100	.000	.100	8	2	3	2	.107	.000	.107	9	4	4	4	.008	.000	.008
6	1	1	0	.833	.167	1.000	8	2	4	0	.214	.214	.428	10	1	1	0	.900	.100	1.000
6	1	1	1	.167	.000	.167	8	2	4	1	1.000	.000	1.000	10	1	1	1	.100	.000	.100
6	1	2	0	.667	.333	1.000	8	2	4	2	.214	.214	.428	10	1	2	0	.800	.200	1.000
6	1	2	1	.333	.000	.333	8	3	3	0	.179	.018	.197	10	1	2	1	.200	.000	.200
6	1	3	0	.500	.500	1.000	8	3	3	1	.715	.286	1.000	10	1	3	0	.700	.300	1.000
6	1	3	1	.500	.500	1.000	8	3	3	2	.286	.179	.465	10	1	3	1	.300	.000	.300
6	2	2	0	.400	.067	.467	8	3	3	3	.018	.000	.018	10	1	4	0	.600	.400	1.000
6	2	2	1	.533	.467	1.000	8	3	4	0	.071	.071	.143	10	1	4	1	.400	.000	.400
6	2	2	2	.067	.000	.067	8	3	4	1	.500	.500	1.000	10	1	5	0	.500	.500	1.000
6	2	3	0	.200	.200	.400	8	3	4	2	.500	.500	1.000	10	1	5	1	.500	.500	1.000
6	2	3	1	1.000	.000	1.000	8	3	4	3	.071	.071	.143	10	2	2	0	.622	.378	1.000
6	2	3	2	.200	.200	.400	8	4	4	0	.014	.014	.029	10	2	2	1	.378	.000	.378
6	3	3	0	.050	.050	.100	8	4	4	1	.243	.243	.486	10	2	2	2	.022	.000	.022
6	3	3	1	.500	.500	1.000	8	4	4	2	1.000	.000	1.000	10	2	3	0	.467	.067	.533
6	3	3	2	.500	.500	1.000	8	4	4	3	.243	.243	.486	10	2	3	1	.533	.467	1.000
6	3	3	3	.050	.050	.100	8	4	4	4	.014	.014	.029	10	2	3	2	.067	.000	.067
7	1	1	0	.857	.143	1.000	9	1	1	0	.889	.111	1.000	10	2	4	0	.333	.133	.467
7	1	1	1	.143	.000	.143	9	1	1	1	.111	.000	.111	10	2	4	1	.667	.333	1.000
7	1	2	0	.714	.286	1.000	9	1	2	0	.778	.222	1.000	10	2	4	2	.133	.000	.133
7	1	2	1	.286	.000	.286	9	1	2	1	.222	.000	.222	10	2	5	0	.222	.222	.444
7	1	3	0	.571	.429	1.000	9	1	3	0	.667	.333	1.000	10	2	5	1	.778	.778	1.000
7	1	3	1	.429	.000	.429	9	1	3	1	.333	.000	.333	10	2	5	2	.222	.222	.444
7	2	2	0	.476	.524	1.000	9	1	4	0	.556	.444	1.000	10	3	3	0	.292	.183	.475
7	2	2	1	.524	.000	.524	9	1	4	1	.444	.000	.444	10	3	3	1	.708	.292	1.000
7	2	2	2	.048	.000	.048	9	2	2	0	.583	.417	1.000	10	3	3	2	.183	.000	.183
7	2	3	0	.286	.143	.429	9	2	2	1	.417	.000	.417	10	3	3	3	.008	.000	.008
7	2	3	1	.714	.286	1.000	9	2	2	2	.028	.000	.028	10	3	4	0	.167	.033	.200
7	2	3	2	.143	.000	.143	9	2	3	0	.417	.083	.500	10	3	4	1	.667	.333	1.000

Cumulative probabilities are given for deviations in the observed direction from equality and for deviation of the same size or greater in the opposite direction. The total probabilities can be used for two-tail tests. Tables are extracted from more extensive tables prepared by Donald Goyette and M. Ray Mickey, Health Sciences Computing Facility, UCLA. In the probability columns "Obs." refers to the probability of a deviation as large or larger in the observed direction and "Other" refers to the probability of a deviation as large or larger in the opposite direction.

S_1 is the smallest marginal total and S_2 is the next smallest; X is the frequency in the cell corresponding to the two smallest totals.

TABLE A–8 (continued)

N	S_1	S_2	X	Obs.	Other	Total	N	S_1	S_2	X	Obs.	Other	Total	N	S_1	S_2	X	Obs.	Other	Total
10	3	4	2	.333	.167	.500	11	3	4	2	.279	.212	.491	12	3	3	1	.618	.382	1.000
10	3	4	3	.033	0	.033	11	3	4	3	.024	0	.024	12	3	3	2	.127	0	.127
10	3	5	0	.083	.083	.167	11	3	5	0	.121	.061	.182	12	3	3	3	.005	0	.005
10	3	5	1	.500	.500	1.000	11	3	5	1	.576	.424	1.000	12	3	4	0	.255	.236	.491
10	3	5	2	.500	.500	1.000	11	3	5	2	.424	.121	.545	12	3	4	1	.764	.745	1.000
10	3	5	3	.083	.083	.167	11	3	5	3	.061	0	.061	12	3	4	2	.236	.255	.491
10	4	4	0	.071	.005	.076	11	4	4	0	.106	.088	.194	12	3	4	3	.018	0	.018
10	4	4	1	.452	.119	.571	11	4	4	1	.530	.470	1.000	12	3	5	0	.159	.045	.205
10	4	4	2	.548	.452	1.000	11	4	4	2	.470	.106	.576	12	3	5	1	.636	.364	1.000
10	4	4	3	.119	.071	.190	11	4	4	3	.088	0	.088	12	3	5	2	.364	.159	.523
10	4	4	4	.005	0	.005	11	4	4	4	.003	0	.003	12	3	5	3	.045	0	.045
10	4	5	0	.024	.024	.048	11	4	5	0	.045	.015	.061	12	3	6	0	.091	.091	.182
10	4	5	1	.262	.262	.524	11	4	5	1	.348	.197	.545	12	3	6	1	.500	.500	1.000
10	4	5	2	.738	.738	1.000	11	4	5	2	.652	.348	1.000	12	3	6	2	.500	.500	1.000
10	4	5	3	.262	.262	.524	11	4	5	3	.197	.045	.242	12	3	6	3	.091	.091	.182
10	4	5	4	.024	.024	.048	11	5	5	0	.013	.002	.015	12	4	4	0	.141	.067	.208
10	5	5	0	.004	.004	.008	11	5	5	1	.175	.067	.242	12	4	4	1	.594	.406	1.000
10	5	5	1	.103	.103	.206	11	5	5	2	.608	.392	1.000	12	4	4	2	.406	.141	.547
10	5	5	2	.500	.500	1.000	11	5	5	3	.392	.175	.567	12	4	4	3	.067	0	.067
10	5	5	3	.500	.500	1.000	11	5	5	4	.067	.013	.080	12	4	4	4	.002	0	.002
10	5	5	4	.103	.103	.206	11	5	5	5	.002	0	.002	12	4	5	0	.071	.010	.081
10	5	5	5	.004	.004	.008	12	1	1	0	.917	.083	1.000	12	4	5	1	.424	.152	.576
11	1	1	0	.909	.091	1.000	12	1	1	1	.083	0	.083	12	4	5	2	.576	.424	1.000
11	1	1	1	.091	0	.091	12	1	2	0	.833	.167	1.000	12	4	5	3	.152	.071	.222
11	1	2	0	.818	.182	1.000	12	1	2	1	.167	0	.167	12	4	5	4	.010	0	.010
11	1	2	1	.182	0	.182	12	1	3	0	.750	.250	1.000	12	4	6	0	.030	.030	.061
11	1	3	0	.727	.273	1.000	12	1	3	1	.250	0	.250	12	4	6	1	.273	.273	.545
11	1	3	1	.273	0	.273	12	1	4	0	.667	.333	1.000	12	4	6	2	.727	.727	1.000
11	1	4	0	.636	.364	1.000	12	1	4	1	.333	0	.333	12	4	6	3	.273	.273	.545
11	1	4	1	.364	0	.364	12	1	5	0	.583	.417	1.000	12	4	6	4	.030	.030	.061
11	1	5	0	.545	.455	1.000	12	1	5	1	.417	0	.417	12	5	5	0	.027	.001	.028
11	1	5	1	.455	0	.455	12	1	6	0	.500	.500	1.000	12	5	5	1	.247	.045	.293
11	2	2	0	.655	.345	1.000	12	1	6	1	.500	.500	1.000	12	5	5	2	.689	.311	1.000
11	2	2	1	.345	0	.345	12	2	2	0	.682	.318	1.000	12	5	5	3	.311	.247	.558
11	2	2	2	.018	0	.018	12	2	2	1	.318	0	.318	12	5	5	4	.045	.027	.072
11	2	3	0	.509	.055	.564	12	2	2	2	.015	0	.015	12	5	5	5	.001	0	.001
11	2	3	1	.491	.509	1.000	12	2	3	0	.545	.455	1.000	12	5	6	0	.008	.008	.015
11	2	3	2	.055	0	.055	12	2	3	1	.455	.545	1.000	12	5	6	1	.121	.121	.242
11	2	4	0	.382	.109	.491	12	2	3	2	.045	0	.045	12	5	6	2	.500	.500	1.000
11	2	4	1	.618	.382	1.000	12	2	4	0	.424	.091	.515	12	5	6	3	.500	.500	1.000
11	2	4	2	.109	0	.109	12	2	4	1	.576	.424	1.000	12	5	6	4	.121	.121	.242
11	2	5	0	.273	.182	.455	12	2	4	2	.091	0	.091	12	5	6	5	.008	.008	.015
11	2	5	1	.727	.273	1.000	12	2	5	0	.318	.152	.470	12	6	6	0	.001	.001	.002
11	2	5	2	.182	0	.182	12	2	5	1	.682	.318	1.000	12	6	6	1	.040	.040	.080
11	3	3	0	.339	.152	.491	12	2	5	2	.152	0	.152	12	6	6	2	.284	.284	.567
11	3	3	1	.661	.339	1.000	12	2	6	0	.227	.227	.455	12	6	6	3	1.000	.000	1.000
11	3	3	2	.152	0	.152	12	2	6	1	.773	.773	1.000	12	6	6	4	.284	.284	.567
11	3	3	3	.006	0	.006	12	2	6	2	.227	.227	.455	12	6	6	5	.040	.040	.080
11	3	4	0	.212	.024	.236	12	3	3	0	.382	.127	.509	12	6	6	6	.001	.001	.002
11	3	4	1	.721	.279	1.000	13	4	5	3	.119	.098	.217	13	1	1	0	.923	.077	1.000
13	1	1	1	.077	0	.077	13	4	5	4	.007	0	.007	14	2	5	1	.604	.396	1.000
13	1	2	0	.846	.154	1.000	13	4	6	0	.049	.021	.070	14	2	5	2	.110	0	.110
13	1	2	1	.154	0	.154	13	4	6	1	.343	.217	.559	14	2	6	0	.308	.165	.473
13	1	3	0	.769	.231	1.000	13	4	6	2	.657	.343	1.000	14	2	6	1	.692	.308	1.000
13	1	3	1	.231	0	.231	13	4	6	3	.217	.049	.266	14	2	6	2	.165	0	.165
13	1	4	0	.692	.308	1.000	13	4	6	4	.021	0	.021	14	2	7	0	.231	.231	.462
13	1	4	1	.308	0	.308	13	5	5	0	.044	.032	.075	14	2	7	1	.769	.769	1.000
13	1	5	0	.615	.385	1.000	13	5	5	1	.315	.249	.565	14	2	7	2	.231	.231	.462
13	1	5	1	.385	0	.385	13	5	5	2	.685	.315	1.000	14	3	3	0	.453	.093	.547
13	1	6	0	.538	.462	1.000	13	5	5	3	.249	.044	.293	14	3	3	1	.547	.453	1.000
13	1	6	1	.462	0	.462								14	3	3	2	.093	0	.093

PROBABILITY

N	S₁	S₂	X	Obs.	Other	Total
13	2	2	0	.705	.295	1.000
13	2	2	1	.295	0	.295
13	2	2	2	.013	0	.013
13	2	3	0	.577	.423	1.000
13	2	3	1	.423	0	.423
13	2	3	2	.038	0	.038
13	2	4	0	.462	.077	.538
13	2	4	1	.538	.462	1.000
13	2	4	2	.077	0	.077
13	2	5	0	.359	.128	.487
13	2	5	1	.641	.359	1.000
13	2	5	2	.128	0	.128
13	2	6	0	.269	.192	.462
13	2	6	1	.731	.269	1.000
13	2	6	2	.192	0	.192
13	3	3	0	.420	.108	.528
13	3	3	1	.580	.420	1.000
13	3	3	2	.108	0	.108
13	3	3	3	.003	0	.003
13	3	4	0	.294	.203	.497
13	3	4	1	.706	.294	1.000
13	3	4	2	.203	0	.203
13	3	4	3	.014	0	.014
13	3	5	0	.196	.035	.231
13	3	5	1	.685	.315	1.000
13	3	5	2	.315	.196	.510
13	3	5	3	.035	0	.035
13	3	6	0	.122	.070	.192
13	3	6	1	.563	.437	1.000
13	3	6	2	.437	.122	.559
13	3	6	3	.070	0	.070
13	4	4	0	.176	.052	.228
13	4	4	1	.646	.354	1.000
13	4	4	2	.354	.176	.530
13	4	4	3	.052	0	.052
13	4	4	4	.001	0	.001
13	4	5	0	.098	.007	.105
13	4	5	1	.490	.119	.608
13	4	5	2	.510	.490	1.000
14	5	5	2	.622	.378	1.000
14	5	5	3	.203	.063	.266
14	5	5	4	.023	0	.023
14	5	5	5	.000	0	.000
14	5	6	0	.028	.003	.031
14	5	6	1	.238	.063	.301
14	5	6	2	.657	.343	1.000
14	5	6	3	.343	.238	.580
14	5	6	4	.063	.028	.091
14	5	6	5	.003	0	.003
14	5	7	0	.010	.010	.021
14	5	7	1	.133	.133	.266
14	5	7	2	.500	.500	1.000
14	5	7	3	.500	.500	1.000
14	5	7	4	.133	.133	.266
14	5	7	5	.010	.010	.021
14	6	6	0	.009	.000	.010
14	6	6	1	.121	.016	.138
14	6	6	2	.471	.156	.627
14	6	6	3	.529	.471	1.000
14	6	6	4	.156	.121	.277
14	6	6	5	.016	.009	.026

PROBABILITY

N	S₁	S₂	X	Obs.	Other	Total
13	5	5	4	.032	0	.032
13	5	5	5	.001	0	.001
13	5	6	0	.016	.005	.021
13	5	6	1	.179	.086	.266
13	5	6	2	.587	.413	1.000
13	5	6	3	.413	.179	.592
13	5	6	4	.086	.016	.103
13	5	6	5	.005	0	.005
13	6	6	0	.004	.001	.005
13	6	6	1	.078	.025	.103
13	6	6	2	.383	.209	.592
13	6	6	3	.617	.383	1.000
13	6	6	4	.209	.078	.286
13	6	6	5	.025	.004	.029
13	6	6	6	.001	0	.001
14	1	1	0	.929	.071	1.000
14	1	1	1	.071	0	.071
14	1	2	0	.857	.143	1.000
14	1	2	1	.143	0	.143
14	1	3	0	.786	.214	1.000
14	1	3	1	.214	0	.214
14	1	4	0	.714	.286	1.000
14	1	4	1	.286	0	.286
14	1	5	0	.643	.357	1.000
14	1	5	1	.357	0	.357
14	1	6	0	.571	.429	1.000
14	1	6	1	.429	0	.429
14	1	7	0	.500	.500	1.000
14	1	7	1	.500	.500	1.000
14	2	2	0	.725	.275	1.000
14	2	2	1	.275	0	.275
14	2	2	2	.011	0	.011
14	2	3	0	.604	.396	1.000
14	2	3	1	.396	0	.396
14	2	3	2	.033	0	.033
14	2	4	0	.495	.066	.560
14	2	4	1	.505	.495	1.000
14	2	4	2	.066	0	.066
14	2	5	0	.396	.110	.505
15	1	7	0	.533	.467	1.000
15	1	7	1	.467	0	.467
15	2	2	0	.743	.257	1.000
15	2	2	1	.257	0	.257
15	2	2	2	.010	0	.010
15	2	3	0	.629	.371	1.000
15	2	3	1	.371	0	.371
15	2	3	2	.029	0	.029
15	2	4	0	.524	.057	.581
15	2	4	1	.476	.524	1.000
15	2	4	2	.057	0	.057
15	2	5	0	.429	.095	.524
15	2	5	1	.571	.429	1.000
15	2	5	2	.095	0	.095
15	2	6	0	.343	.143	.486
15	2	6	1	.657	.343	1.000
15	2	6	2	.143	0	.143
15	2	7	0	.267	.200	.467
15	2	7	1	.733	.267	1.000
15	2	7	2	.200	0	.200
15	3	3	0	.484	.081	.565
15	3	3	1	.516	.484	1.000

PROBABILITY

N	S₁	S₂	X	Obs.	Other	Total
14	3	3	3	.003	0	.003
14	3	4	0	.330	.176	.505
14	3	4	1	.670	.330	1.000
14	3	4	2	.176	0	.176
14	3	4	3	.011	0	.011
14	3	5	0	.231	.027	.258
14	3	5	1	.725	.275	1.000
14	3	5	2	.275	.231	.505
14	3	5	3	.027	0	.027
14	3	6	0	.154	.055	.209
14	3	6	1	.615	.385	1.000
14	3	6	2	.385	.154	.538
14	3	6	3	.055	0	.055
14	3	7	0	.096	.096	.192
14	3	7	1	.500	.500	1.000
14	3	7	2	.500	.500	1.000
14	3	7	3	.096	.096	.192
13	4	4	0	.210	.041	.251
14	4	4	1	.689	.311	1.000
14	4	4	2	.311	.210	.520
14	4	4	3	.041	0	.041
14	4	4	4	.001	0	.001
14	4	5	0	.126	.095	.221
14	4	5	1	.545	.455	1.000
14	4	5	2	.455	.126	.580
14	4	5	3	.095	0	.095
14	4	5	4	.005	0	.005
14	4	6	0	.070	.015	.085
14	4	6	1	.406	.175	.580
14	4	6	2	.594	.406	1.000
14	4	6	3	.175	.070	.245
14	4	6	4	.015	0	.015
14	4	7	0	.035	.035	.070
14	4	7	1	.280	.280	.559
14	4	7	2	.720	.720	1.000
14	4	7	3	.280	.280	.559
14	4	7	4	.035	.035	.070
14	5	5	0	.063	.023	.086
14	5	5	1	.378	.203	.580
15	4	6	0	.092	.011	.103
15	4	6	1	.462	.143	.604
15	4	6	2	.538	.462	1.000
15	4	6	3	.143	.092	.235
15	4	6	4	.011	0	.011
15	4	7	0	.051	.026	.077
15	4	7	1	.338	.231	.569
15	4	7	2	.662	.338	1.000
15	4	7	3	.231	.051	.282
15	4	7	4	.026	0	.026
15	5	5	0	.084	.017	.101
15	5	5	1	.434	.167	.600
15	5	5	2	.566	.434	1.000
15	5	5	4	.017	0	.017
15	5	5	5	.000	0	.000
15	5	6	0	.042	.047	.089
15	5	6	1	.294	.287	.580
15	5	6	2	.713	.706	1.000
15	5	6	3	.287	.294	.580
15	5	6	4	.047	.042	.089
15	5	6	5	.002	0	.002

N	S_1	S_2	X	Obs.	Other	Total	N	S_1	S_2	X	Obs.	Other	Total	N	S_1	S_2	X	Obs.	Other	Total
14	6	6	6	.000	0	.000	15	3	3	2	.081	0	.081	15	5	7	0	.019	.007	.026
14	6	7	0	.002	.002	.005	15	3	3	3	.002	0	.002	15	5	7	1	.182	.100	.282
14	6	7	1	.051	.051	.103	15	3	4	0	.363	.154	.516	15	5	7	2	.573	.427	1.000
14	6	7	2	.296	.296	.592	15	3	4	1	.637	.363	1.000	15	5	7	3	.427	.182	.608
14	6	7	3	.704	.704	1.000	15	3	4	2	.154	0	.154	15	5	7	4	.100	.019	.119
14	6	7	4	.296	.296	.592	15	3	4	3	.009	0	.009	15	5	7	5	.007	0	.007
14	6	7	5	.051	.051	.103	15	3	5	0	.264	.242	.505	15	6	6	0	.017	.011	.028
14	6	7	6	.002	.002	.005	15	3	5	1	.758	.736	1.000	15	6	6	1	.168	.119	.287
14	7	7	0	.000	.000	.001	15	3	5	2	.242	.264	.505	15	6	6	2	.545	.455	1.000
14	7	7	1	.015	.015	.029	15	3	5	3	.022	0	.022	15	6	6	3	.455	.168	.622
14	7	7	2	.143	.143	.286	15	3	6	0	.185	.044	.229	15	6	6	4	.119	.017	.136
14	7	7	3	.500	.500	1.000	15	3	6	1	.659	.341	1.000	15	6	6	5	.011	0	.011
14	7	7	4	.500	.500	1.000	15	3	6	2	.341	.185	.525	15	6	6	6	.000	0	.000
14	7	7	5	.143	.143	.286	15	3	6	3	.044	0	.044	15	6	7	0	.006	.001	.007
14	7	7	6	.015	.015	.029	15	3	7	0	.123	.077	.200	15	6	7	1	.084	.035	.119
14	7	7	7	.000	.000	.001	15	3	7	1	.554	.446	1.000	15	6	7	2	.378	.231	.608
15	1	1	0	.933	.067	1.000	15	3	7	2	.446˙	.123	.569	15	6	7	3	.622	.378	1.000
15	1	1	1	.067	0	.067	15	3	7	3	.077	0	.077	15	6	7	4	.231	.084	.315
15	1	2	0	.867	.133	1.000	15	4	4	0	.242	.033	.275	15	6	7	5	.035	.006	.041
15	1	2	1	.133	0	.133	15	4	4	1	.725	.275	1.000	15	6	7	6	.001	0	.001
15	1	3	0	.800	.200	1.000	15	4	4	2	.275	.242	.516	15	7	7	0	.001	.000	.001
15	1	3	1	.200	0	.200	15	4	4	3	.033	0	.033	15	7	7	1	.032	.009	.041
15	1	4	0	.733	.267	1.000	15	4	4	4	.001	0	.001	15	7	7	2	.214	.100	.315
15	1	4	1	.267	0	.267	15	4	5	0	.154	.077	.231	15	7	7	3	.595	.405	1.000
15	1	5	0	.667	.333	1.000	15	4	5	1	.593	.407	1.000	15	7	7	4	.405	.214	.619
15	1	5	1	.333	0	.333	15	4	5	2	.407	.154	.560	15	7	7	5	.100	.032	.132
15	1	6	0	.600	.400	1.000	15	4	5	3	.077	0	.077	15	7	7	6	.009	.001	.010
15	1	6	1	.400	0	.400	15	4	5	4	.004	0	.004	15	7	7	7	.000	0	.000

From *Introduction to Statistical Analysis* (3rd ed.), by W. J. Dixon and F. J. Massey, Jr. Copyright © 1969 by McGraw-Hill, Inc. Used with permission of McGraw-Hill Book Company.

k	Polynomial				Coefficients							Σc_{ij}^2
3	Linear	−1	0	1								2
	Quadratic	1	−2	1								6
4	Linear	−3	−1	1	3							20
	Quadratic	1	−1	−1	1							4
	Cubic	−1	3	−3	1							20
5	Linear	−2	−1	0	1	2						10
	Quadratic	2	−1	−2	−1	2						14
	Cubic	−1	2	0	−2	1						10
	Quartic	1	−4	6	−4	1						70
6	Linear	−5	−3	−1	1	3	5					70
	Quadratic	5	−1	−4	−4	−1	5					84
	Cubic	−5	7	4	−4	−7	5					180
	Quartic	1	−3	2	2	−3	1					28
7	Linear	−3	−2	−1	0	1	2	3				28
	Quadratic	5	0	−3	−4	−3	0	5				84
	Cubic	−1	1	1	0	−1	−1	1				6
	Quartic	3	−7	1	6	1	−7	3				154
8	Linear	−7	−5	−3	−1	1	3	5	7			168
	Quadratic	7	1	−3	−5	−5	−3	1	7			168
	Cubic	−7	5	7	3	−3	−7	−5	7			264
	Quartic	7	−13	−3	9	9	−3	−13	7			616
	Quintic	−7	23	−17	−15	15	17	−23	7			2184
9	Linear	−4	−3	−2	−1	0	1	2	3	4		60
	Quadratic	28	7	−8	−17	−20	−17	−8	7	28		2772
	Cubic	−14	7	13	9	0	−9	−13	−7	14		990
	Quartic	14	−21	−11	9	18	9	−11	−21	14		2002
	Quintic	−4	11	−4	−9	0	9	4	−11	4		468
10	Linear	−9	−7	−5	−3	−1	1	3	5	7	9	330
	Quadratic	6	2	−1	−3	−4	−4	−3	−1	2	6	132
	Cubic	−42	14	35	31	12	−12	−31	−35	−14	42	8580
	Quartic	18	−22	−17	3	18	18	3	−17	−22	18	2860
	Quintic	−6	14	−1	−11	−6	6	11	1	−14	6	780

TABLE A–10. Arcsin transformation

$$\phi = 2 \arcsin \sqrt{X}$$

X	ϕ	X	ϕ	X	ϕ	X	ϕ	X	ϕ
.001	.0633	.041	.4078	.36	1.2870	.76	2.1177	.971	2.7993
.002	.0895	.042	.4128	.37	1.3078	.77	2.1412	.972	2.8053
.003	.1096	.043	.4178	.38	1.3284	.78	2.1652	.973	2.8115
.004	.1266	.044	.4227	.39	1.3490	.79	2.1895	.974	2.8177
.005	.1415	.045	.4275	.40	1.3694	.80	2.2143	.975	2.8240
.006	.1551	.046	.4323	.41	1.3898	.81	2.2395	.976	2.8305
.007	.1675	.047	.4371	.42	1.4101	.82	2.2653	.977	2.8371
.008	.1791	.048	.4418	.43	1.4303	.83	2.2916	.978	2.8438
009	.1900	.049	.4464	.44	1.4505	.84	2.3186	.979	2.8507
.010	.2003	.050	.4510	.45	1.4706	.85	2.3462	.980	2.8578
.011	.2101	.06	.4949	.46	1.4907	.86	2.3746	.981	2.8650
.012	.2195	.07	.5355	.47	1.5108	.87	2.4039	.982	2.8725
.013	.2285	.08	.5735	.48	1.5308	.88	2.4341	.983	2.8801
.014	.2372	.09	.6094	.49	1.5508	.89	2.4655	.984	2.8879
.015	.2456	.10	.6435	.50	1.5708	.90	2.4981	.985	2.8960
.016	.2537	.11	.6761	.51	1.5908	.91	2.5322	.986	2.9044
.017	.2615	.12	.7075	.52	1.6108	.92	2.5681	.987	2.9131
.018	.2691	.13	.7377	.53	1.6308	.93	2.6062	.988	2.9221
.019	.2766	.14	.7670	.54	1.6509	.94	2.6467	.989	2.9315
.020	.2838	.15	.7954	.55	1.6710	.95	2.6906	.990	2.9413
.021	.2909	.16	.8230	.56	1.6911	.951	2.6952	.991	2.9516
.022	.2978	.17	.8500	.57	1.7113	.952	2.6998	.992	2.9625
.023	.3045	.18	.8763	.58	1.7315	.953	2.7045	.993	2.9741
.024	.3111	.19	.9021	.59	1.7518	.954	2.7093	.994	2.9865
.025	.3176	.20	.9273	.60	1.7722	.955	2.7141	.995	3.0001
.026	.3239	.21	.9521	.61	1.7926	.956	2.7189	.996	3.0150
.027	.3301	.22	.9764	.62	1.8132	.957	2.7238	.997	3.0320
.028	.3363	.23	1.0004	.63	1.8338	.958	2.7288	.998	3.0521
.029	.3423	.24	1.0239	.64	1.8546	.959	2.7338	.999	3.0783
.030	.3482	.25	1.0472	.65	1.8755	.960	2.7389		
.031	.3540	.26	1.0701	.66	1.8965	.961	2.7440		
.032	.3597	.27	1.0928	.67	1.9177	.962	2.7492		
.033	.3654	.28	1.1152	.68	1.9391	.963	2.7545		
.034	.3709	.29	1.1374	.69	1.9606	.964	2.7598		
.035	.3764	.30	1.1593	.70	1.9823	.965	2.7652		
.036	.3818	.31	1.1810	.71	2.0042	.966	2.7707		
.037	.3871	.32	1.2025	.72	2.0264	.967	2.7762		
.038	.3924	.33	1.2239	.73	2.0488	.968	2.7819		
.039	.3976	.34	1.2451	.74	2.0715	.969	2.7876		
.040	.4027	.35	1.2661	.75	2.0944	.970	2.7934		

TABLE A–11. Quantiles of the Kolmogorov test statistic

One-Sided Test											
$p = .90$	.95	.975	.99	.995		$p = .90$	.95	.975	.99	.995
Two-Sided Test											
$p = .80$	.90	.95	.98	.99		$p = .80$	.90	.95	.98	.99
$n = 1$	.900	.950	.975	.990	.995	$n = 21$	.226	.259	.287	.321	.344
2	.684	.776	.842	.900	.929	22	.221	.253	.281	.314	.337
3	.565	.636	.708	.785	.829	23	.216	.247	.275	.307	.330
4	.493	.565	.624	.689	.734	24	.212	.242	.269	.301	.323
5	.447	.509	.563	.627	.669	25	.208	.238	.264	.295	.317
6	.410	.468	.519	.577	.617	26	.204	.233	.259	.290	.311
7	.381	.436	.483	.538	.576	27	.200	.229	.254	.284	.305
8	.358	.410	.454	.507	.542	28	.197	.225	.250	.279	.300
9	.339	.387	.430	.480	.513	29	.193	.221	.246	.275	.295
10	.323	.369	.409	.457	.489	30	.190	.218	.242	.270	.290
11	.308	.352	.391	.437	.468	31	.187	.214	.238	.266	.285
12	.296	.338	.375	.419	.449	32	.184	.211	.234	.262	.281
13	.285	.325	.361	.404	.432	33	.182	.208	.231	.258	.277
14	.275	.314	.349	.390	.418	34	.179	.205	.227	.254	.273
15	.266	.304	.338	.377	.404	35	.177	.202	.224	.251	.269
16	.258	.295	.327	.366	.392	36	.174	.199	.221	.247	.265
17	.250	.286	.318	.355	.381	37	.172	.196	.218	.244	.262
18	.244	.279	.309	.346	.371	38	.170	.194	.215	.241	.258
19	.237	.271	.301	.337	.361	39	.168	.191	.213	.238	.255
20	.232	.265	.294	.329	.352	40	.165	.189	.210	.235	.252
			Approximation for $n > 40$			$\dfrac{1.07}{\sqrt{n}}$	$\dfrac{1.22}{\sqrt{n}}$	$\dfrac{1.36}{\sqrt{n}}$	$\dfrac{1.52}{\sqrt{n}}$	$\dfrac{1.63}{\sqrt{n}}$

The entries in this table are selected quantiles w_p of the Kolmogorov test statistics T_1, T_1^+, and T_1^- as defined by (6.1.1) for two-sided tests and by (6.1.2) and (6.1.3) for one-sided tests. Reject H_0 at the level α if T exceeds the $1 - \alpha$ quantile given in this table. These quantiles are exact for $n \leq 20$ in the two-tailed test. The other quantiles are approximations which are equal to the exact quantiles in most cases.

From "Table of Percentage Points of Kolmogorov Statistics," by L. H. Miller, *Journal of the American Statistical Association*, 1956, Vol. 51, pp. 111–121, as adapted by Conover (1971). Reprinted by permission.

TABLE A−12. *Quantiles of the Lilliefors test statistic*

	$p = .80$	.85	.90	.95	.99
Sample size $n = 4$	.300	.319	.352	.381	.417
5	.285	.299	.315	.337	.405
6	.265	.277	.294	.319	.354
7	.247	.258	.276	.300	.348
8	.233	.244	.261	.285	.331
9	.223	.233	.249	.271	.311
10	.215	.224	.239	.258	.294
11	.206	.217	.230	.249	.284
12	.199	.212	.223	.242	.275
13	.190	.202	.214	.234	.268
14	.183	.194	.207	.227	.261
15	.177	.187	.201	.220	.257
16	.173	.182	.195	.213	.250
17	.169	.177.	.189	.206	.245
18	.166	.173	.184	.200	.239
19	.163	.169	.179	.195	.235
20	.160	.166	.174	.190	.231
25	.142	.147	.158	.173	.200
30	.131	.136	.144	.161	..187
Over 30	$\dfrac{.736}{\sqrt{n}}$	$\dfrac{.768}{\sqrt{n}}$	$\dfrac{.805}{\sqrt{n}}$	$\dfrac{.886}{\sqrt{n}}$	$\dfrac{1.031}{\sqrt{n}}$

The entries in this table are the approximate quantiles w_p of the Lilliefors test statistic T_2 as defined by equation (6.1.11). Reject H_0 at the level α if T_2 exceeds $w_{1-\alpha}$ for the particular sample size n.

From Table 1 of "On the Kolmogorov-Smirnov Test for Normality with Mean and Variance Unknown," by H. W. Lilliefors, *Journal of the American Statistical Association*, 1967, Vol. 62, pp. 399–402, as adapted by Conover (1971). Reprinted by permission.

TABLE A–13. Percentiles of the Kolmogorov–Smirnov test statistic

		One-Sided Test: $\alpha =$				
		.90	.95	.975	.99	.995
		Two-Sided Test: $\alpha =$				
		.80	.90	.95	.98	.99
n_1	n_2					
3	3	.667	.667			
3	4	.750	.750			
3	5	.667	.800	.800		
3	6	.667	.667	.833		
3	7	.667	.714	.857	.857	
3	8	.625	.750	.750	.875	
3	9	.667	.667	.778	.889	.889
3	10	.600	.700	.800	.900	.900
3	12	.583	.667	.750	.833	.917
4	4	.750	.750	.750		
4	5	.600	.750	.800	.800	
4	6	.583	.667	.750	.833	.833
4	7	.607	.714	.750	.857	.857
4	8	.625	.625	.750	.875	.875
4	9	.556	.667	.750	.778	.889
4	10	.550	.650	.700	.800	.800
4	12	.583	.667	.667	.750	.833
4	16	.563	.625	.688	.750	.812
5	5	.600	.600	.800	.800	.800
5	6	.600	.667	.667	.833	.833
5	7	.571	.657	.714	.829	.857
5	8	.550	.625	.675	.800	.800
5	9	.556	.600	.689	.778	.800
5	10	.500	.600	.700	.700	.800
5	15	.533	.600	.667	.733	.733
5	20	.500	.550	.600	.700	.750
6	6	.500	.667	.667	.833	.833
6	7	.548	.571	.690	.714	.833
6	8	.500	.583	.667	.750	.750
6	9	.500	.556	.667	.722	.778
6	10	.500	.567	.633	.700	.733
6	12	.500	.583	.583	.667	.750
6	18	.444	.556	.611	.667	.722
6	24	.458	.500	.583	.625	.667
7	7	.571	.571	.714	.714	.714
7	8	.482	.589	.625	.732	.750
7	9	.492	.556	.635	.714	.746
7	10	.471	.557	.614	.700	.714
7	14	.429	.500	.571	.643	.714
7	28	.429	.464	.536	.607	.643
8	8	.500	.500	.625	.625	.750
8	9	.444	.542	.625	.667	.750
8	10	.475	.525	.575	.675	.700
8	12	.458	.500	.583	.625	.667

n_1	n_2					
8	16	.438	.500	.563	.625	.625
8	32	.406	.438	.500	.563	.594
9	9	.444	.556	.556	.667	.667
9	10	.467	.500	.578	.667	.689
9	12	.444	.500	.556	.611	.667
9	15	.422	.489	.533	.600	.644
9	18	.389	.444	.500	.556	.611
9	36	.361	.417	.472	.528	.556
10	10	.400	.500	.600	.600	.700
10	15	.400	.467	.500	.567	.633
10	20	.400	.450	.500	.550	.600
10	40	.350	.400	.450	.500	.576
11	11	.454	.454	.545	.636	.636
12	12	.417	.417	.500	.583	.583
12	15	.383	.450	.500	.550	.583
12	16	.375	.438	.479	.542	.583
12	18	.361	.417	.472	.528	.556
12	20	.367	.417	.467	.517	.567
13	13	.385	.462	.462	.538	.615
14	14	.357	.429	.500	.500	.571
15	15	.333	.400	.467	.467	.533
16	16	.375	.375	.438	.500	.563
17	17	.353	.412	.412	.471	.529
18	18	.333	.389	.444	.500	.500
19	19	.316	.368	.421	.473	.473
20	20	.300	.350	.400	.450	.500
21	21	.286	.333	.381	.429	.476
22	22	.318	.364	.364	.454	.454
23	23	.304	.348	.391	.435	.435
24	24	.292	.333	.375	.417	.458
25	25	.280	.320	.360	.400	.440

For other sample sizes, let $C = \sqrt{\dfrac{n_1 + n_2}{n_1 n_2}}$, and use as an approximation:

		$1.07C$	$1.22C$	$1.36C$	$1.52C$	$1.63C$

Adapted from "Distribution Table for the Deviation between Two Sample Cumulatives," by F. J. Massey, Jr., *Annals of Mathematical Statistics*, 1952, Vol. 23, pp. 435–441, as adapted by Conover (1971). Reprinted by permission.

TABLE A–14. Distribution of the Rank Sum T

The values of T_1, T_2, and α are such that if the n_1 and n_2 observations are chosen at random from the same population the chance that the rank sum T of the n_1 observations in the smaller sample is equal to or less than T_1 is α and the chance that T is equal to or greater than T_2 is α. The sample sizes are shown in parentheses (n_1, n_2).

T_1	T_2	α	T_1	T_2	α	T_1	T_2	α	T_1	T_2	α
(1,1)			(2,2)			(2,8) (Cont.)			(3,5) (Cont.)		
1	2	.500	3	7	.167	8	14	.267	8	19	.071
(1,2)			4	6	.333	9	13	.356	9	18	.125
1	3	.333	5	5	.667	10	12	.444	10	17	.196
2	2	.667	(2,3)			11	11	.556	11	16	.286
(1,3)			3	9	.100	(2,9)			12	15	.393
1	4	.250	4	8	.200	3	21	.018	13	14	.500
2	3	.500	5	7	.400	4	20	.036	(3,6)		
(1,4)			6	6	.600	5	19	.073	6	24	.012
1	5	.200	(2,4)			6	18	.109	7	23	.024
2	4	.400	3	11	.067	7	17	.164	8	22	.048
3	3	.600	4	10	.133	8	16	.218	9	21	.083
(1,5)			5	9	.267	9	15	.291	10	20	.131
1	6	.167	6	8	.400	10	14	.364	11	19	.190
2	5	.333	7	7	.600	11	13	.455	12	18	.274
3	4	.500	(2,5)			12	12	.545	13	17	.357
(1,6)			3	13	.047	(2,10)			14	16	.452
1	7	.143	4	12	.095	3	23	.015	15	15	.548
2	6	.286	5	11	.190	4	22	.030	(3,7)		
3	5	.428	6	10	.286	5	21	.061	6	27	.008
4	4	.571	7	9	.429	6	20	.091	7	26	.017
(1,7)			8	8	.571	7	19	.136	8	25	.033
1	8	.125	(2,6)			8	18	.182	9	24	.058
2	7	.250	3	15	.036	9	17	.242	10	23	.092
3	6	.375	4	14	.071	10	16	.303	11	22	.133
4	5	.500	5	13	.143	11	15	.379	12	21	.192
(1,8)			6	12	.214	12	14	.455	13	20	.258
1	9	.111	7	11	.321	13	13	.545	14	19	.333
2	8	.222	8	10	.429	(3,3)			15	18	.417
3	7	.333	9	9	.571	6	15	.050	16	17	.500
4	6	.444	(2,7)			7	14	.100	(3,8)		
5	5	.556	3	17	.028	8	13	.200	6	30	.006
(1,9)			4	16	.056	9	12	.350	7	29	.012
1	10	.100	5	15	.111	10	11	.500	8	28	.024
2	9	.200	6	14	.167	(3,4)			9	27	.042
3	8	.300	7	13	.250	6	18	.028	10	26	.067
4	7	.400	8	12	.333	7	17	.057	11	25	.097
5	6	.500	9	11	.444	8	16	.114	12	24	.139
(1,10)			10	10	.556	9	15	.200	13	23	.188
1	11	.091	(2,8)			10	14	.314	14	22	.248
2	10	.182	3	19	.022	11	13	.429	15	21	.315
3	9	.273	4	18	.044	12	12	.571	16	20	.387
4	8	.364	5	17	.089	(3,5)			17	19	.461
5	7	.455	6	16	.133	6	21	.018	18	18	.539
6	6	.545	7	15	.200	7	20	.036			

T_1	T_2	α	T_1	T_2	α	T_1	T_2	α	T_1	T_2	α
(3,9)			(4,5) (Cont.)			(4,8) (Cont.)			(5,5) (Cont.)		
6	33	.005	17	23	.278	24	28	.404	18	37	.028
7	32	.009	18	22	.365	25	27	.467	19	36	.048
8	31	.018	19	21	.452	26	26	.533	20	35	.075
9	30	.032	20	20	.548	(4,9)			21	34	.111
10	29	.050	(4,6)			10	46	.001	22	33	.155
11	28	.073	10	34	.005	11	45	.003	23	32	.210
12	27	.105	11	33	.010	12	44	.006	24	31	.274
13	26	.141	12	32	.019	13	43	.010	25	30	.345
14	25	.186	13	31	.033	14	42	.017	26	29	.421
15	24	.241	14	30	.057	15	41	.025	27	28	.500
16	23	.300	15	29	.086	16	40	.038	(5,6)		
17	22	.363	16	28	.129	17	39	.053	15	45	.002
18	2i	.432	17	27	.176	18	38	.074	16	44	.004
19	20	.500	18	26	.238	19	37	.099	17	43	.009
(3,10)			19	25	.305	20	36	.130	18	42	.015
6	36	.003	20	24	.381	21	35	.165	19	41	.026
7	35	.007	21	23	.457	22	34	.207	20	40	.041
8	34	.014	22	22	.545	23	33	.252	21	39	.063
9	33	.024	(4,7)			24	32	.302	22	38	.089
10	32	.038	10	38	.003	25	31	.355	23	37	.123
11	31	.056	11	37	.006	26	30	.413	24	36	.165
12	30	.080	12	36	.012	27	29	.470	25	35	.214
13	29	.108	13	35	.021	28	28	.530	26	34	.268
14	28	.143	14	34	.036	(4,10)			27	33	.331
15	27	.185	15	33	.055	10	50	.001	28	32	.396
16	26	.234	16	32	.082	11	49	.002	29	31	.465
17	25	.287	17	31	.115	12	48	.004	30	30	.535
18	24	.346	18	30	.158	13	47	.007	(5,7)		
19	23	.406	19	29	.206	14	46	.012	15	50	.001
20	22	.469	20	28	.264	15	45	.018	16	49	.003
21	2i	.531	21	27	.324	16	44	.026	17	48	.005
(4,4)			22	26	.394	17	43	.038	18	47	.009
10	26	.014	23	25	.464	18	42	.053	19	46	.015
11	25	.029	24	24	.538	19	41	.071	20	45	.024
12	24	.057	(4,8)			20	40	.094	21	44	.037
13	23	.100	10	42	.002	21	39	.120	22	43	.053
14	22	.171	11	41	.004	22	38	.152	23	42	.074
15	21	.243	12	40	.008	23	37	.187	24	41	.101
16	20	.343	13	39	.014	24	36	.227	25	40	.134
17	19	.443	14	38	.024	25	35	.270	26	39	.172
18	18	.557	15	37	.036	26	34	.318	27	38	.216
(4,5)			16	36	.055	27	33	.367	28	37	.265
10	30	.008	17	35	.077	28	32	.420	29	36	.319
11	29	.016	18	34	.107	29	31	.473	30	35	.378
12	28	.032	19	33	.141	30	30	.527	31	34	.438
13	27	.056	20	32	.184	(5,5)			32	33	.500
14	26	.095	21	31	.230	15	40	.004	(5,8)		
15	25	.143	22	30	.285	16	39	.008	15	55	.001
16	24	.206	23	29	.341	17	38	.016	16	54	.002

TABLE A–14 (continued)

T_1	T_2	α	T_1	T_2	α	T_1	T_2	α	T_1	T_2	α
(5,8) (Cont.)			(5,10) (Cont.)			(6,7) (Cont.)			(6,9) (Cont.)		
17	53	.003	20	60	.006	28	56	.026	28	68	.009
18	52	.005	21	59	.010	29	55	.037	29	67	.013
19	51	.009	22	58	.014	30	54	.051	30	66	.018
20	50	.015	23	57	.020	31	53	.069	31	65	.025
21	49	.023	24	56	.028	32	52	.090	32	64	.033
22	48	.033	25	55	.038	33	51	.117	33	63	.044
23	47	.047	26	54	.050	34	50	.147	34	62	.057
24	46	.064	27	53	.065	35	49	.183	35	61	.072
25	45	.085	28	52	.082	36	48	.223	36	60	.091
26	44	.111	29	51	.103	37	47	.267	37	59	.112
27	43	.142	30	50	.127	38	46	.314	38	58	.136
28	42	.177	31	49	.155	39	45	.365	39	57	.164
29	41	.217	32	48	.185	40	44	.418	40	56	.194
30	40	.262	33	47	.220	41	43	.473	41	55	.228
31	39	.311	34	46	.257	42	42	.527	42	54	.264
32	38	.362	35	45	.297	(6,8)			43	53	.303
33	37	.416	36	44	.339	21	69	.000	44	52	.344
34	36	.472	37	43	.384	22	68	.001	45	51	.388
35	35	.528	38	42	.430	23	67	.001	46	50	.432
(5,9)			39	41	.477	24	66	.002	47	49	.477
15	60	.000	40	40	.523	25	65	.004	48	48	.523
16	59	.001	(6,6)			26	64	.006	(6,10)		
17	58	.002	21	57	.001	27	63	.010	21	81	.000
18	57	.003	22	56	.002	28	62	.015	22	80	.000
19	56	.006	23	55	.004	29	61	.021	23	79	.000
20	55	.009	24	54	.008	30	60	.030	24	78	.001
21	54	.014	25	53	.013	31	59	.041	25	77	.001
22	53	.021	26	52	.021	32	58	.054	26	76	.002
23	52	.030	27	51	.032	33	57	.071	27	75	.004
24	51	.041	28	50	.047	34	56	.091	28	74	.005
25	50	.056	29	49	.066	35	55	.114	29	73	.008
26	49	.073	30	48	.090	36	54	.141	30	72	.011
27	48	.095	31	47	.120	37	53	.172	31	71	.016
28	47	.120	32	46	.155	38	52	.207	32	70	.021
29	46	.149	33	45	.197	39	51	.245	33	69	.028
30	45	.182	34	44	.242	40	50	.286	34	68	.036
31	44	.219	35	43	.294	41	49	.331	35	67	.047
32	43	.259	36	42	.350	42	48	.377	36	66	.059
33	42	.303	37	41	.409	43	47	.426	37	65	.074
34	41	.350	38	40	.469	44	46	.475	38	64	.090
35	40	.399	39	39	.531	45	45	.525	39	63	.110
36	39	.449	(6,7)			(6,9)			40	62	.132
37	38	.500	21	63	.001	21	75	.000	41	61	.157
(5,10)			22	62	.001	22	74	.000	42	60	.184
15	65	.000	23	61	.002	23	73	.001	43	59	.214
16	64	.001	24	60	.004	24	72	.001	44	58	.246
17	63	.001	25	59	.007	25	71	.002	45	57	.281
18	62	.002	26	58	.011	26	70	.004	46	56	.318
19	61	.004	27	57	.017	27	69	.006	47	55	.356

T_1	T_2	α	T_1	T_2	α	T_1	T_2	α	T_1	T_2	α
(6,10) (Cont.)			(7,8) (Cont.)			(7,10) (Cont.)			(8,8) (Cont.)		
48	54	.396	46	66	.140	32	94	.001	52	84	.052
49	53	.437	47	65	.168	33	93	.001	53	83	.065
50	52	.479	48	64	.198	34	92	.001	54	82	.080
51	51	.521	49	63	.232	35	91	.002	55	81	.097
(7,7)			50	62	.268	36	90	.003	56	80	.117
28	77	.000	51	61	.306	37	89	.005	57	79	.139
29	76	.001	52	60	.347	38	88	.007	58	78	.164
30	75	.001	53	59	.389	39	87	.009	59	77	.191
31	74	.002	54	58	.433	40	86	.012	60	76	.221
32	73	.003	55	57	.478	41	85	.017	61	75	.253
33	72	.006	56	56	.522	42	84	.022	62	74	.287
34	71	.009	(7,9)			43	83	.028	63	73	.323
35	70	.013	28	91	.000	44	82	.035	64	72	.360
36	69	.019	29	90	.000	45	81	.044	65	71	.399
37	68	.027	30	39	.000	46	80	.054	66	70	.439
38	67	.036	31	88	.001	47	79	.067	67	69	.480
39	66	.049	32	87	.001	48	78	.081	68	68	.520
40	65	.064	33	86	.002	49	77	.097	(8,9)		
41	64	.082	34	85	.003	50	76	.115	36	108	.000
42	63	.104	35	84	.004	51	75	.135	40	104	.000
43	62	.130	36	83	.006	52	74	.157	41	103	.001
44	61	.159	37	82	.008	53	73	.182	42	102	.001
45	60	.191	38	81	.011	54	72	.209	43	101	.002
46	59	.228	39	80	.016	55	71	.237	44	100	.003
47	58	.267	40	79	.021	56	70	.268	45	99	.004
48	57	.310	41	78	.027	57	69	.300	46	98	.006
49	56	.355	42	77	.036	58	68	.335	47	97	.008
50	55	.402	43	76	.045	59	67	.370	48	96	.010
51	54	.451	44	75	.057	60	66	.406	49	95	.014
52	53	.500	45	74	.071	61	65	.443	50	94	.018
(7,8)			46	73	.087	62	64	.481	51	93	.023
28	84	.000	47	72	.105	63	63	.519	52	92	.030
29	83	.000	48	71	.126	(8,8)			53	91	.037
30	82	.001	49	70	.150	36	100	.000	54	90	.046
31	81	.001	50	69	.175	37	99	.000	55	89	.057
32	80	.002	51	68	.204	38	98	.000	56	88	.069
33	79	.003	52	67	.235	39	97	.001	57	87	.084
34	78	.005	53	66	.268	40	96	.001	58	86	.100
35	77	.007	54	65	.303	41	95	.001	59	85	.118
36	76	.010	55	64	.340	42	94	.002	60	84	.138
37	75	.014	56	63	.379	43	93	.003	61	83	.161
38	74	.020	57	62	.419	44	92	.005	62	82	.185
39	73	.027	58	61	.459	45	91	.007	63	81	.212
40	72	.036	59	60	.500	46	90	.010	64	80	.240
41	71	.047	(7,10)			47	89	.014	65	79	.271
42	70	.060	28	98	.000	48	88	.019	66	78	.303
43	69	.076	29	97	.000	49	87	.025	67	77	.336
44	68	.095	30	96	.000	50	86	.032	68	76	.371
45	67	.116	31	95	.000	51	85	.041	69	75	.407

T_1	T_2	α	T_1	T_2	α	T_1	T_2	α	T_1	T_2	α
(8,9) (Cont.)				(9,9)		(9,10) (Cont.)			(10,10) (Cont.)		
70	74	.444	45	126	.000	54	126	.001	65	145	.001
71	73	.481	50	121	.000	55	125	.001	66	144	.001
72	72	.519	51	120	.001	56	124	.002	67	143	.001
(8,10)			52	119	.001	57	123	.003	68	142	.002
36	116	.000	53	118	.001	58	122	.004	69	141	.003
41	111	.000	54	117	.002	59	121	.005	70	140	.003
42	110	.001	55	116	.003	60	120	.007	71	139	.004
43	109	.001	56	115	.004	61	119	.009	72	138	.006
44	108	.002	57	114	.005	62	118	.011	73	137	.007
45	107	.002	58	113	.007	63	117	.014	74	136	.009
46	106	.003	59	112	.009	64	116	.017	75	135	.012
47	105	.004	60	111	.012	65	115	.022	76	134	.014
48	104	.006	61	110	.016	66	114	.027	77	133	.018
49	103	.008	62	109	.020	67	113	.033	78	132	.022
50	102	.010	63	108	.025	68	112	.039	79	131	.026
51	101	.013	64	107	.031	69	111	.047	80	130	.032
52	100	.017	65	106	.039	70	110	.056	81	129	.038
53	99	.022	66	105	.047	71	109	.067	82	128	.045
54	98	.027	67	104	.057	72	108	.078	83	127	.053
55	97	.034	68	103	.068	73	107	.091	84	126	.062
56	96	.042	69	102	.081	74	106	.106	85	125	.072
57	95	.051	70	101	.095	75	105	.121	86	124	.083
58	94	.061	71	100	.111	76	104	.139	87	123	.095
59	93	.073	72	99	.129	77	103	.158	88	122	.109
60	92	.086	73	98	.149	78	102	.178	89	121	.124
61	91	.102	74	97	.170	79	101	.200	90	120	.140
62	90	.118	75	96	.193	80	100	.223	91	119	.157
63	89	.137	76	95	.218	81	99	.248	92	118	.176
64	88	.158	77	94	.245	82	98	.274	93	117	.197
65	87	.180	78	93	.273	83	97	.302	94	116	.218
66	86	.204	79	92	.302	84	96	.330	95	115	.241
67	85	.230	80	91	.333	85	95	.360	96	114	.264
68	84	.257	81	90	.365	86	94	.390	97	113	.289
69	83	.286	82	89	.398	87	93	.421	98	112	.315
70	82	.317	83	88	.432	88	92	.452	99	111	.342
71	81	.348	84	87	.466	89	91	.484	100	110	.370
72	80	.381	85	86	.500	90	90	.516	101	109	.398
73	79	.414	(9,10)			(10,10)			102	108	.427
74	78	.448	45	135	.000	55	155	.000	103	107	.456
75	77	.483	52	128	.000	63	147	.000	104	106	.485
76	76	.517	53	127	.001	64	146	.001	105	105	.515

For sample sizes greater than 10 the chance that the statistic T will be less than or equal to an integer k is given approximately by the area under the standard normal curve to the left of

$$z = \frac{k + \frac{1}{2} - n_1(n_1 + n_2 + 1)/2}{\sqrt{n_1 n_2 (n_1 + n_2 + 1)/12}}$$

From *Introduction to Statistical Analysis* (3rd ed.), by F. J. Dixon and W. J. Massey, Jr. Copyright © 1969 by McGraw-Hill, Inc. Used with permission of McGraw-Hill Book Company.

TABLE A-15. *Expected values of order statistics of the Terry–Hoeffding form* $E(V^{(i)})$

[Number of standard deviations above $(+)$ or below $(-)$ the mean]

Numbers in left margin are the numbers of the order statistics taken from the right—greatest to least. These numbers are values of $n - i + 1$; the $n - i +$ 1st order statistic from the right is the ith from the left, and vice versa.

Example. Find the mean difference between the 18th and 7th order statistic in a sample of size 20 from the standard normal.

Solution. Under $n = 20$, the number listed for 7 is 0.45, which gives -0.45 for the 7th smallest; $20 - 18 + 1 = 3$, and so $+1.13$ is the mean for the 18th order statistic. The difference is $1.13 - (-0.45) = 1.58$ standard deviations.

$n-i+1$ \\ n	1	2	3	4	5	6	7	8	9	10
1	0	0.56	0.85	1.03	1.16	1.27	1.35	1.42	1.49	1.54
2		−0.56	0.00	0.30	0.50	0.64	0.76	0.85	0.93	1.00
3			−0.85	−0.30	0.00	0.20	0.35	0.47	0.57	0.66
4				−1.03	−0.50	−0.20	0.00	0.15	0.27	0.38
5					−1.16	−0.64	−0.35	−0.15	0.00	0.12
6						−1.27	−0.76	−0.47	−0.27	−0.12

$n-i+1$ \\ n	11	12	13	14	15	16	17	18	19	20
1	1.59	1.63	1.67	1.70	1.74	1.77	1.79	1.82	1.84	1.87
2	1.06	1.12	1.16	1.21	1.25	1.28	1.32	1.35	1.38	1.41
3	0.73	0.79	0.85	0.90	0.95	0.99	1.03	1.07	1.10	1.13
4	0.46	0.54	0.60	0.66	0.71	0.76	0.81	0.85	0.89	0.92
5	0.22	0.31	0.39	0.46	0.52	0.57	0.62	0.66	0.71	0.75
6	0.00	0.10	0.19	0.27	0.34	0.40	0.45	0.50	0.55	0.59
7	−0.22	−0.10	0.00	0.09	0.17	0.23	0.30	0.35	0.40	0.45
8	−0.46	−0.31	−0.19	−0.09	0.00	0.08	0.15	0.21	0.26	0.31
9	−0.73	−0.54	−0.39	−0.27	−0.17	−0.08	0.00	0.07	0.13	0.19
10	−1.06	−0.79	−0.60	−0.46	−0.34	−0.23	−0.15	−0.07	0.00	0.06
11	−1.59	−1.12	−0.85	−0.66	−0.52	−0.40	−0.30	−0.21	−0.13	−0.06

$n - i + 1$ \ n	21	22	23	24	25	26	27	28	29	30
1	1.89	1.91	1.93	1.95	1.97	1.98	2.00	2.01	2.03	2.04
2	1.43	1.46	1.48	1.50	1.52	1.54	1.56	1.58	1.60	1.62
3	1.16	1.19	1.21	1.24	1.26	1.29	1.31	1.33	1.35	1.36
4	0.95	0.98	1.01	1.04	1.07	1.09	1.11	1.14	1.16	1.18
5	0.78	0.82	0.85	0.88	0.91	0.93	0.96	0.98	1.00	1.03
6	0.63	0.67	0.70	0.73	0.76	0.79	0.82	0.85	0.87	0.89
7	0.49	0.53	0.57	0.60	0.64	0.67	0.70	0.73	0.75	0.78
8	0.36	0.41	0.45	0.48	0.52	0.55	0.58	0.61	0.64	0.67
9	0.24	0.29	0.33	0.37	0.41	0.44	0.48	0.51	0.54	0.57
10	0.12	0.17	0.22	0.26	0.30	0.34	0.38	0.41	0.44	0.47
11	0.00	0.06	0.11	0.16	0.20	0.24	0.28	0.32	0.35	0.38
12	−0.12	−0.06	0.00	0.05	0.10	0.14	0.19	0.22	0.26	0.29
13	−0.24	−0.17	−0.11	−0.05	0.00	0.05	0.09	0.13	0.17	0.21
14	−0.36	−0.29	−0.22	−0.16	−0.10	−0.05	0.00	0.04	0.09	0.12
15	−0.49	−0.41	−0.33	−0.26	−0.20	−0.14	−0.09	−0.04	0.00	0.04
16	−0.63	−0.53	−0.45	−0.37	−0.30	−0.24	−0.19	−0.13	−0.09	−0.04

$n - i + 1$ \ n	31	32	33	34	35	36	37	38	39	40
1	2.06	2.07	2.08	2.09	2.11	2.12	2.13	2.14	2.15	2.16
2	1.63	1.65	1.66	1.68	1.69	1.70	1.72	1.73	1.74	1.75
3	1.38	1.40	1.42	1.43	1.45	1.46	1.48	1.49	1.50	1.52
4	1.20	1.22	1.23	1.25	1.27	1.28	1.30	1.32	1.33	1.34
5	1.05	1.07	1.09	1.11	1.12	1.14	1.16	1.17	1.19	1.20
6	0.92	0.94	0.96	0.98	1.00	1.02	1.03	1.05	1.07	1.08
7	0.80	0.82	0.85	0.87	0.89	0.91	0.92	0.94	0.96	0.98
8	0.69	0.72	0.74	0.76	0.79`	0.81	0.83	0.85	0.86	0.88
9	0.60	0.62	0.65	0.67	0.69	0.71	0.73	0.75	0.77	0.79
10	0.50	0.53	0.56	0.58	0.60	0.63	0.65	0.67	0.69	0.71
11	0.41	0.44	0.47	0.50	0.52	0.54	0.57	0.59	0.61	0.63
12	0.33	0.36	0.39	0.41	0.44	0.47	0.49	0.51	0.54	0.56
13	0.24	0.28	0.31	0.34	0.36	0.39	0.42	0.44	0.46	0.49
14	0.16	0.20	0.23	0.26	0.29	0.32	0.34	0.37	0.39	0.42
15	0.08	0.12	0.15	0.18	0.22	0.24	0.27	0.30	0.33	0.35
16	0.00	0.04	0.08	0.11	0.14	0.17	0.20	0.23	0.26	0.28
17	−0.08	−0.04	0.00	0.04	0.07	0.10	0.14	0.16	0.19	0.22
18	−0.16	−0.12	−0.08	−0.04	0.00	0.03	0.07	0.10	0.13	0.16
19	−0.24	−0.20	−0.15	−0.11	−0.07	−0.03	0.00	0.03	0.06	0.09
20	−0.33	−0.28	−0.23	−0.18	−0.14	−0.10	−0.07	−0.03	0.00	0.03
21	−0.41	−0.36	−0.31	−0.26	−0.22	−0.17	−0.14	−0.10	−0.06	−0.03

TABLE A–16. The Van der Waerden inverse-normal scores for n = 1 to n = 40

i	n	1	2	3	4	5	6	7	8	9	10
1		0	−.44	−.67	−.82	−.98	−1.07	−1.15	−1.22	−1.28	−1.34
2			.44	0	−.25	−.44	−.57	−.67	−.76	−.84	−.91
3				.67	.25	0	−.18	−.32	−.43	−.52	−.60
4					.82	.44	.18	0	−.14	−.25	−.35
5						.98	.57	.32	.14	0	−.11
6								.67	.43	.25	.11
7										.52	.35

i	n	11	12	13	14	15	16	17	18	19	20
1		−1.38	−1.43	−1.46	−1.50	−1.53	−1.56	−1.59	−1.62	−1.64	−1.67
2		−.97	−1.02	−1.07	−1.11	−1.15	−1.19	−1.22	−1.25	−1.28	−1.31
3		−.67	−.74	−.79	−.84	−.89	−.93	−.97	−1.00	−1.04	−1.07
4		−.43	−.50	−.57	−.62	−.67	−.72	−.76	−.80	−.84	−.88
5		−.21	−.29	−.37	−.43	−.49	−.54	−.59	−.63	−.67	−.71
6		0	−.10	−.18	−.25	−.32	−.38	−.43	−.48	−.52	−.57
7		.21	.10	0	−.09	−.16	−.22	−.28	−.34	−.39	−.43
8		.43	.29	.18	.09	0	−.07	−.14	−.20	−.25	−.30
9				.37	.25	.16	.07	0	−.07	−.13	−.18
10						.32	.22	.14	.07	0	−.06
11								.28	.20	.13	.06
12										.25	.18

i	n	21	22	23	24	25	26	27	28	29	30
1		−1.69	−1.71	−1.73	−1.75	−1.77	−1.79	−1.80	−1.82	−1.83	−1.85
2		−1.34	−1.36	−1.38	−1.41	−1.43	−1.45	−1.47	−1.48	−1.50	−1.52
3		−1.10	−1.12	−1.15	−1.17	−1.20	−1.22	−1.24	−1.26	−1.28	−1.30
4		−.91	−.94	−.97	−.99	−1.02	−1.04	−1.07	−1.09	−1.11	−1.13
5		−.75	−.78	−.81	−.84	−.87	−.90	−.92	−.94	−.97	−.99
6		−.60	−.64	−.67	−.71	−.74	−.76	−.79	−.82	−.84	−.86
7		−.47	−.51	−.55	−.58	−.62	−.65	−.67	−.70	−.73	−.75
8		−.35	−.39	−.43	−.47	−.50	−.54	−.57	−.60	−.62	−.65
9		−.23	−.28	−.32	−.36	−.40	−.43	−.46	−.49	−.52	−.55
10		−.11	−.16	−.21	−.25	−.29	−.33	−.37	−.40	−.43	−.46
11		0	−.05	−.10	−.15	−.19	−.23	−.27	−.31	−.34	−.37
12		.11	.05	0	−.05	−.10	−.14	−.18	−.22	−.25	−.29
13		.23	.16	.10	.05	0	−.05	−.09	−.13	−.17	−.20
14				.21	.15	.10	.05	0	−.04	−.08	−.12
15						.19	.14	.09	.04	0	−.04
16								.18	.13	.08	.04
17										.17	.12

i n	31	32	33	34	35	36	37	38	39	40
1	−1.86	−1.88	−1.89	−1.90	−1.91	−1.93	−1.94	−1.95	−1.96	−1.97
2	−1.53	−1.55	−1.56	−1.58	−1.59	−1.61	−1.62	−1.63	−1.64	−1.66
3	−1.32	−1.34	−1.35	−1.37	−1.38	−1.40	−1.41	−1.43	−1.44	−1.45
4	−1.15	−1.17	−1.19	−1.20	−1.22	−1.24	−1.25	−1.27	−1.28	−1.30
5	−1.01	−1.03	−1.05	−1.07	−1.09	−1.10	−1.12	−1.13	−1.15	−1.17
6	−.89	−.91	−.93	−.95	−.97	−.99	−1.00	−1.02	−1.04	−1.05
7	−.77	−.80	−.82	−.84	−.86	−.88	−.90	−.92	−.93	−.95
8	−.67	−.70	−.72	−.74	−.76	−.79	−.80	−.82	−.84	−.86
9	−.58	−.60	−.63	−.65	−.67	−.70	−.72	−.74	−.76	−.77
10	−.49	−.52	−.54	−.57	−.59	−.61	−.63	−.65	−.67	−.69
11	−.40	−.43	−.46	−.48	−.51	−.53	−.55	−.58	−.60	−.62
12	−.32	−.35	−.38	−.40	−.43	−.46	−.48	−.50	−.52	−.55
13	−.24	−.27	−.30	−.33	−.36	−.38	−.41	−.43	−.45	−.48
14	−.16	−.19	−.22	−.25	−.28	−.31	−.34	−.36	−.39	−.41
15	−.08	−.11	−.15	−.18	−.21	−.24	−.27	−.29	−.32	−.34
16	0	−.04	−.07	−.11	−.14	−.17	−.20	−.23	−.25	−.28
17	.08	.04	0	−.04	−.07	−.10	−.13	−.16	−.19	−.22
18	.16	.11	.07	.04	0	−.03	−.07	−.10	−.13	−.15
19			.15	.11	.07	.03	0	−.03	−.06	−.09
20					.14	.10	.07	.03	0	−.03
21							.13	.10	.06	.03
22									.13	.09

Adapted from Table V in *Nonparametric Statistics*, by J. Hájek. Copyright 1969 by Holden-Day, Inc. Reprinted by permission.

01	02	03	04	05	06	07	08	09	10
0.464	0.137	2.455	−0.323	−0.068	0.296	−0.288	1.298	0.241	−0.957
0.060	−2.526	−0.531	−0.194	0.543	−1.558	0.187	−1.190	0.022	0.525
1.486	−0.354	−0.634	0.697	0.926	1.375	0.785	−0.963	−0.853	−1.865
1.022	−0.472	1.279	3.521	0.571	−1.851	0.194	1.192	−0.501	−0.273
1.394	−0.555	0.046	0.321	2.945	1.974	−0.258	0.412	0.439	−0.035
0.906	−0.513	−0.525	0 595	0.881	−0.934	1.579	0.161	−1.885	0.371
1.179	−1.055	0.007	0.769	0.971	0.712	1.090	−0.631	−0.255	−0.702
−1.501	−0.488	−0.162	−0.136	1.033	0.203	0.448	0.748	−0.423	−0.432
−0.690	0.756	−1.618	−0.345	−0.511	−2.051	−0.457	−0.218	0.857	−0.465
1.372	0.225	0.378	0.761	0.181	−0.736	0.960	−1.530	−0.260	0.120
−0.482	1.678	−0.057	−1.229	−0.486	0.856	−0.491	−1.983	−2.830	−0.238
−1.376	−0.150	1.356	−0.561	−0.256	−0.212	0.219	0.779	0.953	−0.869
−1.010	0.598	−0.918	1.598	0.065	0.415	−0.169	0.313	−0.973	−1.016
−0.005	−0.899	0.012	−0.725	1.147	−0.121	1.096	0.481	−1.691	0.417
1.393	−1.163	−0.911	1.231	−0.199	−0.246	1.239	−2.574	−0.558	0.056
−1.787	−0.261	1.237	1.046	−0.508	−1.630	−0.146	−0.392	−0.627	0.561
−0.105	−0.357	−1.384	0.360	−0.992	−0.116	−1.698	−2.832	−1.108	−2.357
−1.339	1.827	−0.959	0.424	0.969	−1.141	−1.041	0.362	−1.726	1.956
1.041	0.535	0.731	1.377	0.983	−1.330	1.620	−1.040	0.524	−0.281
0.279	−2.056	0.717	−0.873	−1.096	−1.396	1.047	0.089	−0.573	0.932
−1.805	−2.008	−1.633	0.542	0.250	−0.166	0.032	0.079	0.471	−1.029
−1.186	1.180	1.114	0.882	1.265	−0.202	0.151	−0.376	−0.310	0.479
0.658	−1.141	1.151	−1.210	−0.927	0.425	0.290	−0.902	0.610	2.709
−0.439	0.358	−1.939	0.891	−0.227	0.602	0.873	−0.437	−0.220	−0.057
−1.399	−0.230	0.385	−0.649	−0.577	0.237	−0.289	0.513	0.738	−0.300
0.199	0.208	−1.083	−0.219	−0.291	1.221	1.119	0.004	−2.015	−0.594
0.159	0.272	−0.313	0.084	−2.828	−0.439	−0.792	−1.275	−0.623	−1.047
2.273	0.606	0.606	−0.747	0.247	1.291	0.063	−1.793	−0.699	−1.347
0.041	−0.307	0.121	0.790	−0.584	0.541	0.484	−0.986	0.481	0.996
−1.132	−2.098	0.921	0.145	0.446	−1.661	1.045	−1.363	−0.586	−1.023
0.768	0.079	−1.473	0.034	−2.127	0.665	0.084	−0.880	−0.579	0.551
0.375	−1.658	−0.851	0.234	−0.656	0.340	−0.086	−0.158	−0.120	0.418
−0.513	−0.344	0.210	−0.736	1.041	0.008	0.427	−0.831	0.191	0.074
0.292	−0.521	1.266	−1.206	−0.899	0.110	−0.528	−0.813	0.071	0.524
1.026	2.990	−0.574	−0.491	−1.114	1.297	−1.433	−1.345	−3.001	0.479
−1.334	1.278	−0.568	−0.109	−0.515	−0.566	2.923	0.500	0.359	0.326
−0.287	−0.144	−0.254	0.574	−0.451	−1.181	−1.190	−0.318	−0.094	1.114
0.161	−0.886	−0.921	−0.509	1.410	−0.518	0.192	−0.432	1.501	1.068
−1.346	0.193	−1.202	0.394	−1.045	0.843	0.942	1.045	0.031	0.772
1.250	−0.199	−0.288	1.810	1.378	0.584	1.216	0.733	0.402	0.226
0.630	−0.537	0.782	0.060	0.499	−0.431	1.705	1.164	0.884	−0.298
0.375	−1.941	0.247	−0.491	0.665	−0.135	−0.145	−0.498	0.457	1.064
−1.420	0.489	−1.711	−1.186	0.754	−0.732	−0.066	1.006	−0.798	0.162
−0.151	−0.243	−0.430	−0.762	0.298	1.049	1.810	2.885	−0.768	−1.204
−0.309	0.531	0.416	−1.541	1.456	2.040	−0.124	0.196	0.023	−1.204
0.424	−0.444	0.593	0.993	−0.106	0.116	0.484	−1.272	1.066	1.097
0.593	0.658	−1.127	−1.407	−1.579	−1.616	1.458	1.262	0.736	−0.916
0.862	−0.885	−0.142	−0.504	0.532	1.381	0.022	−0.281	−0.342	1.222
0.235	−0.628	−0.023	−0.463	−0.899	−0.394	−0.538	1.707	−0.188	−1.153
−0.853	0.402	0.777	0.833	0.410	−0.349	−1.094	0.580	1.395	1.298

11	12	13	14	15	16	17	18	19	20
−1.329	−0.238	−0.838	−0.988	−0.445	0.964	−0.266	−0.322	−1.726	2.252
1.284	−0.229	1.058	0.090	0.050	0.523	0.016	0.277	1.639	0.554
0.619	0.628	0.005	0.973	−0.058	0.150	−0.635	−0.917	0.313	−1.203
0.699	−0.269	0.722	−0.994	−0.807	−1.203	1.163	1.244	1.306	−1.210
0.101	0.202	−0.150	0.731	0.420	0.116	−0.496	−0.037	−2.466	0.794
−1.381	0.301	0.522	0.233	0.791	−1.017	−0.182	0.926	−1.096	1.001
−0.574	1.366	−1.843	0.746	0.890	0.824	−1.249	−0.806	−0.240	0.217
0.096	0.210	1.091	0.990	0.900	−0.837	−1.097	−1.238	0.030	−0.311
1.389	−0.236	0.094	3.282	0.295	−0.416	0.313	0.720	0.007	0.354
1.249	0.706	1.453	0.366	−2.654	−1.400	0.212	0.307	−1.145	0.639
0.756	−0.397	−1.772	−0.257	1.120	1.188	−0.527	0.709	0.479	0.317
−0.860	0.412	−0.327	0.178	0.524	−0.672	−0.831	0.758	0.131	0.771
−0.778	−0.979	0.236	−1.033	1.497	−0.661	0.906	1.169	−1.582	1.303
0.037	0.062	0.426	1.220	0.471	0.784	−0.719	0.465	1.559	−1.326
2.619	−0.440	0.477	1.063	0.320	1.406	−0.701	−0.128	0.518	−0.676
−0.420	−0.287	−0.050	−0.481	1.521	−1.367	0.609	0.292	0.048	0.592
1.048	0.220	1.121	−1.789	−1.211	−0.871	−0.740	0.513	−0.558	−0.395
1.000	−0.638	1.261	0.510	−0.150	0.034	0.054	−0.055	0.639	−0.825
0.170	−1.131	−0.985	0.102	−0.939	−1.457	1.766	1.087	−1.275	2.362
0.389	−0.435	0.171	0.891	1.158	1.041	1.048	−0.324	−0.404	1.060
−0.305	0.838	−2.019	−0.540	0.905	1.195	−1.190	0.106	0.571	0.298
−0.321	−0.039	1.799	−1.032	−2.225	−0.148	0.758	−0.862	0.158	−0.726
1.900	1.572	−0.244	−1.721	1.130	0.495	−0.484	0.014	−0.778	−1.483
−0.778	−0.288	−0.224	−1.324	−0.072	0.890	−0.410	0.752	0.376	−0.224
0.617	−1.718	−0.183	−0.100	1.719	0.696	−1.339	−0.614	1.071	−0.386
−1.430	−0.953	0.770	−0.007	−1.872	1.075	−0.913	−1.168	1.775	0.238
0.267	−0.048	0.972	0.734	−1.408	−1.955	−0.848	2.002	0.232	−1.273
0.978	−0.520	−0.368	1.690	−1.479	0.985	1.475	−0.098	−1.633	2.399
−1.235	−1.168	0.325	1.421	2.652	−0.486	−1.253	0.270	−1.103	0.118
−0.258	0.638	2.309	0.741	−0.161	−0.679	0.336	1.973	0.370	−2.277
0.243	0.629	−1.516	−0.157	0.693	1.710	0.800	−0.265	1.218	0.655
−0.292	−1.455	−1.451	1.492	−0.713	0.821	−0.031	−0.780	1.330	0.977
−0.505	0.389	0.544	−0.042	1.615	−1.440	−0.989	−0.580	0.156	0.052
0.397	−0.287	1.712	0.289	−0.904	0.259	−0.600	−1.635	−0.009	−0.799
−0.605	−0.470	0.007	0.721	−1.117	0.635	0.592	−1.362	−1.441	0.672
1.360	0.182	−1.476	−0.599	−0.875	0.292	−0.700	0.058	−0.340	−0.639
0.480	−0.699	1.615	−0.225	1.014	−1.370	−1.097	0.294	0.309	−1.389
−0.027	−0.487	−1.990	−0.015	0.119	−1.990	−0.687	−1.964	0.366	1.759
−1.482	−0.815	−0.121	1.884	−0.185	0.601	0.793	0.430	−1.181	0.426
−1.256	−0.567	−0.994	1.011	−1.071	−0.623	−0.420	−0.309	1.362	0.863
−1.132	2.039	1.934	−0.222	0.386	1.100	0.284	1.597	−1.718	−0.560
−0.780	−0.239	−0.497	−0.434	−0.284	−0.241	−0.333	1.348	−0.478	−0.169
−0.859	−0.215	0.241	1.471	0.389	−0.952	0.245	0.781	1.093	−0.240
0.447	1.479	0.067	0.426	−0.370	−0.675	−0.972	0.225	0.815	0.389
0.269	0.735	−0.066	−0.271	−1.439	1.036	−0.306	−1.439	−0.122	−0.336
0.097	−1.883	−0.218	0.202	−0.357	0.019	1.631	1.400	0.223	−0.793
−0.686	1.596	−0.286	0.722	0.655	−0.275	1.245	−1.504	0.066	−1.280
0.957	0.057	−1.153	0.701	−0.280	1.747	−0.745	1.338	−1.421	0.386
−0.976	−1.789	−0.696	−1.799	−0.354	0.071	2.355	0.135	−0.598	1.883
0.274	0.226	−0.909	−0.572	0.181	1.115	0.496	0.453	−1.218	−0.115

514

TABLE A–18. Critical values of the Klotz Test, for

$$K = \sum_{i=1}^{n_1} \left[\phi^{-1} \left[\frac{r_i}{N + 1} \right] \right]^2 \times 100$$

Percentile

α		.005	.01	.025	.05	.95	.975	.99	.995
n_1	n_2	K_α	K_α	K_α	K_α	K_α	K_α	K_α	K_α
6	6	99	115	149	178	614	643	677	693
7	7	143	161	199	241	727	769	807	825
8	8	192	216	257	301	845	889	930	954
9	9	236	265	314	364	962	1012	1061	1090
10	10	287	320	375	429	1079	1133	1188	1221
6	7	96	114	145	177	642	673	721	734
6	8	92	117	142	175	664	702	741	773
6	9	92	114	144	177	683	729	770	806
6	10	92	111	140	177	702	751	800	830
7	8	141	163	199	238	753	794	837	861
7	9	139	158	197	235	776	820	869	901
7	10	133	158	198	234	797	847	902	934
8	9	184	214	256	298	870	919	966	996
8	10	181	207	250	296	891	943	995	1028
9	10	234	264	313	362	986	1039	1094	1125

Adapted from Tables XII and XIII in *Nonparametric Statistics*, by J. Hájek. Copyright 1969 by Holden-Day, Inc. Reprinted by permission.

TABLE A–19. *Percentage points for the Kruskal–Wallis Test for K = 3 and n ≤ 5*

Sample sizes			$\alpha \leq .10$	$\alpha \leq .05$	$\alpha \leq .01$
n_1	n_2	n_3			
2	2	2	4.57	—	—
3	2	1	4.29	—	—
3	2	2	—	4.71	—
3	3	1	4.57	5.14	—
3	3	2	4.56	5.36	—
3	3	3	4.62	5.60	7.20
4	2	1	4.50	—	—
4	2	2	4.46	5.33	—
4	3	1	4.06	5.21	—
4	3	2	4.51	5.44	6.44
4	3	3	4.71	5.73	6.75
4	4	1	4.17	4.97	6.67
4	4	2	4.55	5.45	7.04
4	4	3	4.55	5.60	7.14
4	4	4	4.65	5.69	7.66
5	2	1	4.20	5.00	—
5	2	2	4.36	5.16	6.53
5	3	1	4.02	4.96	—
5	3	2	4.65	5.25	6.82
5	3	3	4.53	5.65	7.08
5	4	1	3.99	4.99	6.95
5	4	2	4.54	5.27	7.12
5	4	3	4.55	5.63	7.44
5	4	4	4.62	5.62	7.76
5	5	1	4.11	5.13	7.31
5	5	2	4.62	5.34	7.27
5	5	3	4.54	5.71	7.54
5	5	4	4.53	5.64	7.77
5	5	5	4.56	5.78	7.98
Large samples			4.61	5.99	9.21

Adapted from *Sturdy Statistics*, by F. Mosteller and R. E. K. Rourke. Copyright 1973 by Addison-Wesley, Reading, Mass. Reprinted by permission.

Error df	α	\multicolumn{10}{c}{r = number of means or number of steps between ordered means}
		2	3	4	5	6	7	8	9	10	11
5	.05	3.64	4.60	5.22	5.67	6.03	6.33	6.58	6.80	6.99	7.17
	.01	5.70	6.98	7.80	8.42	8.91	9.32	9.67	9.97	10.24	10.48
6	.05	3.46	4.34	4.90	5.30	5.63	5.90	6.12	6.32	6.49	6.65
	.01	5.24	6.33	7.03	7.56	7.97	8.32	8.61	8.87	9.10	9.30
7	.05	3.34	4.16	4.68	5.06	5.36	5.61	5.82	6.00	6.16	6.30
	.01	4.95	5.92	6.54	7.01	7.37	7.68	7.94	8.17	8.37	8.55
8	.05	3.26	4.04	4.53	4.89	5.17	5.40	5.60	5.77	5.92	6.05
	.01	4.75	5.64	6.20	6.62	6.96	7.24	7.47	7.68	7.86	8.03
9	.05	3.20	3.95	4.41	4.76	5.02	5.24	5.43	5.59	5.74	5.87
	.01	4.60	5.43	5.96	6.35	6.66	6.91	7.13	7.33	7.49	7.65
10	.05	3.15	3.88	4.33	4.65	4.91	5.12	5.30	5.46	5.60	5.72
	.01	4.48	5.27	5.77	6.14	6.43	6.67	6.87	7.05	7.21	7.36
11	.05	3.11	3.82	4.26	4.57	4.82	5.03	5.20	5.35	5.49	5.61
	.01	4.39	5.15	5.62	5.97	6.25	6.48	6.67	6.84	6.99	7.13
12	.05	3.08	3.77	4.20	4.51	4.75	4.95	5.12	5.27	5.39	5.51
	.01	4.32	5.05	5.50	5.84	6.10	6.32	6.51	6.67	6.81	6.94
13	.05	3.06	3.73	4.15	4.45	4.69	4.88	5.05	5.19	5.32	5.43
	.01	4.26	4.96	5.40	5.73	5.98	6.19	6.37	6.53	6.67	6.79
14	.05	3.03	3.70	4.11	4.41	4.64	4.83	4.99	5.13	5.25	5.36
	.01	4.21	4.89	5.32	5.63	5.88	6.08	6.26	6.41	6.54	6.66
15	.05	3.01	3.67	4.08	4.37	4.59	4.78	4.94	5.08	5.20	5.31
	.01	4.17	4.84	5.25	5.56	5.80	5.99	6.16	6.31	6.44	6.55
16	.05	3.00	3.65	4.05	4.33	4.56	4.74	4.90	5.03	5.15	5.26
	.01	4.13	4.79	5.19	5.49	5.72	5.92	6.08	6.22	6.35	6.46
17	.05	2.98	3.63	4.02	4.30	4.52	4.70	4.86	4.99	5.11	5.21
	.01	4.10	4.74	5.14	5.43	5.66	5.85	6.01	6.15	6.27	6.38
18	.05	2.97	3.61	4.00	4.28	4.49	4.67	4.82	4.96	5.07	5.17
	.01	4.07	4.70	5.09	5.38	5.60	5.79	5.94	6.08	6.20	6.31
19	.05	2.96	3.59	3.98	4.25	4.47	4.65	4.79	4.92	5.04	5.14
	.01	4.05	4.67	5.05	5.33	5.55	5.73	5.89	6.02	6.14	6.25
20	.05	2.95	3.58	3.96	4.23	4.45	4.62	4.77	4.90	5.01	5.11
	.01	4.02	4.64	5.02	5.29	5.51	5.69	5.84	5.97	6.09	6.19
24	.05	2.92	3.53	3.90	4.17	4.37	4.54	4.68	4.81	4.92	5.01
	.01	3.96	4.55	4.91	5.17	5.37	5.54	5.69	5.81	5.92	6.02
30	.05	2.89	3.49	3.85	4.10	4.30	4.46	4.60	4.72	4.82	4.92
	.01	3.89	4.45	4.80	5.05	5.24	5.40	5.54	5.65	5.76	5.85
40	.05	2.86	3.44	3.79	4.04	4.23	4.39	4.52	4.63	4.73	4.82
	.01	3.82	4.37	4.70	4.93	5.11	5.26	5.39	5.50	5.60	5.69
60	.05	2.83	3.40	3.74	3.98	4.16	4.31	4.44	4.55	4.65	4.73
	.01	3.76	4.28	4.59	4.82	4.99	5.13	5.25	5.36	5.45	5.53
120	.05	2.80	3.36	3.68	3.92	4.10	4.24	4.36	4.47	4.56	4.64
	.01	3.70	4.20	4.50	4.71	4.87	5.01	5.12	5.21	5.30	5.37
∞	.05	2.77	3.31	3.63	3.86	4.03	4.17	4.29	4.39	4.47	4.55
	.01	3.64	4.12	4.40	4.60	4.76	4.88	4.99	5.08	5.16	5.23

12	13	14	15	16	17	18	19	20	α	Error df
7.32	7.47	7.60	7.72	7.83	7.93	8.03	8.12	8.21	.05	5
10.70	10.89	11.08	11.24	11.40	11.55	11.68	11.81	11.93	.01	
6.79	6.92	7.03	7.14	7.24	7.34	7.43	7.51	7.59	.05	6
9.48	9.65	9.81	9.95	10.08	10.21	10.32	10.43	10.54	.01	
6.43	6.55	6.66	6.76	6.85	6.94	7.02	7.10	7.17	.05	7
8.71	8.86	9.00	9.12	9.24	9.35	9.46	9.55	9.65	.01	
6.18	6.29	6.39	6.48	6.57	6.65	6.73	6.80	6.87	.05	8
8.18	8.31	8.44	8.55	8.66	8.76	8.85	8.94	9.03	.01	
5.98	6.09	6.19	6.28	6.36	6.44	6.51	6.58	6.64	.05	9
7.78	7.91	8.03	8.13	8.23	8.33	8.41	8.49	8.57	.01	
5.83	5.93	6.03	6.11	6.19	6.27	6.34	6.40	6.47	.05	10
7.49	7.60	7.71	7.81	7.91	7.99	8.08	8.15	8.23	.01	
5.71	5.81	5.90	5.98	6.06	6.13	6.20	6.27	6.33	.05	11
7.25	7.36	7.46	7.56	7.65	7.73	7.81	7.88	7.95	.01	
5.61	5.71	5.80	5.88	5.95	6.02	6.09	6.15	6.21	.05	12
7.06	7.17	7.26	7.36	7.44	7.52	7.59	7.66	7.73	.01	
5.53	5.63	5.71	5.79	5.86	5.93	5.99	6.05	6.11	.05	13
6.90	7.01	7.10	7.19	7.27	7.35	7.42	7.48	7.55	.01	
5.46.	5.55	5.64	5.71	5.79	5.85	5.91	5.97	6.03	.05	14
6.77	6.87	6.96	7.05	7.13	7.20	7.27	7.33	7.39	.01	
5.40	5.49	5.57	5.65	5.72	5.78	5.85	5.90	5.96	.05	15
6.66	6.76	6.84	6.93	7.00	7.07	7.14	7.20	7.26	.01	
5.35	5.44	5.52	5.59	5.66	5.73	5.79	5.84	5.90	.05	16
6.56	6.66	6.74	6.82	6.90	6.97	7.03	7.09	7.15	.01	
5.31	5.39	5.47	5.54	5.61	5.67	5.73	5.79	5.84	.05	17
6.48	6.57	6.66	6.73	6.81	6.87	6.94	7.00	7.05	.01	
5.27	5.35	5.43	5.50	5.57	5.63	5.69	5.74	5.79	.05	18
6.41	6.50	6.58	6.65	6.73	6.79	6.85	6.91	6.97	.01	
5.23	5.31	5.39	5.46	5.53	5.59	5.65	5.70	5.75	.05	19
6.34	6.43	6.51	6.58	6.65	6.72	6.78	6.84	6.89	.01	
5.20	5.28	5.36	5.43	5.49	5.55	5.61	5.66	5.71	.05	20
6.28	6.37	6.45	6.52	6.59	6.65	6.71	6.77	6.82	.01	
5.10	5.18	5.25	5.32	5.38	5.44	5.49	5.55	5.59	.05	24
6.11	6.19	6.26	6.33	6.39	6.45	6.51	6.56	6.61	.01	
5.00	5.08	5.15	5.21	5.27	5.33	5.38	5.43	5.47	.05	30
5.93	6.01	6.08	6.14	6.20	6.26	6.31	6.36	6.41	.01	
4.90	4.98	5.04	5.11	5.16	5.22	5.27	5.31	5.36	.05	40
5.76	5.83	5.90	5.96	6.02	6.07	6.12	6.16	6.21	.01	
4.81	4.88	4.94	5.00	5.06	5.11	5.15	5.20	5.24	.05	60
5.60	5.67	5.73	5.78	5.84	5.89	5.93	5.97	6.01	.01	
4.71	4.78	4.84	4.90	4.95	5.00	5.04	5.09	5.13	.05	120
5.44	5.50	5.56	5.61	5.66	5.71	5.75	5.79	5.83	.01	
4.62	4.68	4.74	4.80	4.85	4.89	4.93	4.97	5.01	.05	∞
5.29	5.35	5.40	5.45	5.49	5.54	5.57	5.61	5.65	.01	

r = number of means or number of steps between ordered means

The percentiles listed cover the range $\alpha = .005$ to $.125$ for every sample size up to $n = 20$. Values $T_{(+)}$ are such that the probability is α that the signed rank statistic is less than or equal to $T_{(+)}$. The values $T_{(-)}$ are such that the probability is α that T is greater than or equal to $T_{(-)}$.

$T_{(+)}$	$T_{(-)}$	α	$T_{(+)}$	$T_{(-)}$	α	$T_{(+)}$	$T_{(-)}$	α	$T_{(+)}$	$T_{(-)}$	α
n=1			n=9 (Cont.)			n=12 (Cont.)			n=14 (Cont.)		
0	1	.500	4	41	.014	9	69	.008	17	88	.012
n=2			5	40	.020	10	68	.010	18	87	.015
0	3	.250	6	39	.027	11	67	.013	19	86	.018
n=3			7	38	.037	12	66	.017	20	85	.021
0	6	.125	8	37	.049	13	65	.021	21	84	.025
n=4			9	36	.064	14	64	.026	22	83	.029
0	10	.062	10	35	.082	15	63	.032	23	82	.034
1	9	.125	11	34	.102	16	62	.039	24	81	.039
n=5			12	33	.125	17	61	.046	25	80	.045
0	15	.031	n=10			18	60	.055	26	79	.052
1	14	.062	3	52	.005	19	59	.065	27	78	.059
2	13	.094	4	51	.007	20	58	.076	28	77	.068
3	12	.156	5	50	.010	21	57	.088	29	76	.077
n=6			6	49	.014	22	56	.102	30	75	.086
0	21	.016	7	48	.019	23	55	.117	31	74	.097
1	20	.031	8	47	.024	24	54	.133	32	73	.108
2	19	.047	9	46	.032	n=13			33	72	.121
3	18	.078	10	45	.042	9	82	.004	34	71	.134
4	17	.109	11	44	.053	10	81	.005	n=15		
5	16	.156	12	43	.065	11	80	.007	15	105	.004
n=7			13	42	.080	12	79	.009	16	104	.005
0	28	.008	14	41	.097	13	78	.011	17	103	.006
1	27	.016	15	40	.116	14	77	.013	18	102	.008
2	26	.023	16	39	.138	15	76	.016	19	101	.009
3	25	.039	n=11			16	75	.020	20	100	.011
4	24	.055	5	61	.005	17	74	.024	21	99	.013
5	23	.078	6	60	.007	18	73	.029	22	98	.015
6	22	.109	7	59	.009	19	72	.034	23	97	.018
7	21	.148	8	58	.012	20	71	.040	24	96	.021
n=8			9	57	.016	21	70	.047	25	95	.024
0	36	.004	10	56	.021	22	69	.055	26	94	.028
1	35	.008	11	55	.027	23	68	.064	27	93	.032
2	34	.012	12	54	.034	24	67	.073	28	92	.036
3	33	.020	13	53	.042	25	66	.084	29	91	.042
4	32	.027	14	52	.051	26	65	.095	30	90	.047
5	31	.039	15	51	.062	27	64	.108	31	89	.053
6	30	.055	16	50	.074	28	63	.122	32	88	.060
7	29	.074	17	49	.087	29	62	.137	33	87	.068
8	28	.098	18	48	.103	n=14			34	86	.076
9	27	.125	19	47	.120	12	93	.004	35	85	.084
n=9			20	46	.139	13	92	.005	36	84	.094
1	44	.004	n=12			14	91	.007	37	83	.104
2	43	.006	7	71	.005	15	90	.008	38	82	.115
3	42	.010	8	70	.006	16	89	.010	39	81	.126

$T_{(+)}$	$T_{(-)}$	α	$T_{(+)}$	$T_{(-)}$	α	$T_{(+)}$	$T_{(-)}$	α	$T_{(+)}$	$T_{(-)}$	α
	$n = 16$			$n = 17$ (Cont.)			$n = 18$ (Cont.)			$n = 19$ (Cont.)	
19	117	.005	36	117	.028	51	120	.071	64	126	.113
20	116	.005	37	116	.032	52	119	.077	65	125	.121
21	115	.007	38	115	.036	53	118	.084	66	124	.129
22	114	.008	39	114	.040	54	117	.091		$n = 20$	
23	113	.009	40	113	.044	55	116	.098	37	173	.005
24	112	.011	41	112	.049	56	115	.106	38	172	.005
25	111	.012	42	111	.054	57	114	.114	39	171	.006
26	110	.014	43	110	.060	58	113	.123	40	170	.007
27	109	.017	44	109	.066	59	112	.132	41	169	.008
28	108	.019	45	108	.073		$n = 19$		42	168	.009
29	107	.022	46	107	.080	32	158	.005	43	167	.010
30	106	.025	47	106	.087	33	157	.005	44	166	.011
31	105	.029	48	105	.095	34	156	.006	45	165	.012
32	104	.033	49	104	.103	35	155	.007	46	164	.013
33	103	.037	50	103	.112	36	154	.008	47	163	.015
34	102	.042	51	102	.122	37	153	.009	48	162	.016
35	101	.047	52	101	.132	38	152	.010	49	161	.018
36	100	.052		$n = 18$		39	151	.011	50	160	.020
37	99	.058	27	144	.004	40	150	.013	51	159	.022
38	98	.065	28	143	.005	41	149	.014	52	158	.024
39	97	.072	29	142	.006	42	148	.016	53	157	.027
40	96	.080	30	141	.007	43	147	.018	54	156	.029
41	95	.088	31	140	.008	44	146	.020	55	155	.032
42	94	.096	32	139	.009	45	145	.022	56	154	.035
43	93	.106	33	138	.010	46	144	.025	57	153	.038
44	92	.116	34	137	.012	47	143	.027	58	152	.041
45	91	.126	35	136	.013	48	142	.030	59	151	.045
46	90	.137	36	135	.015	49	141	.033	60	150	.049
	$n = 17$		37	134	.017	50	140	.036	61	149	.053
23	130	.005	38	133	.019	51	139	.040	62	148	.057
24	129	.005	39	132	.022	52	138	.044	63	147	.062
25	128	.006	40	131	.024	53	137	.048	64	146	.066
26	127	.007	41	130	.027	54	136	.052	65	145	.071
27	126	.009	42	129	.030	55	135	.057	66	144	.077
28	125	.010	43	128	.033	56	134	.062	67	143	.082
29	124	.012	44	127	.037	57	133	.067	68	142	.088
30	123	.013	45	126	.041	58	132	.072	69	141	.095
31	122	.015	46	125	.045	59	131	.078	70	140	.101
32	121	.017	47	124	.049	60	130	.084	71	139	.108
33	120	.020	48	123	.054	61	129	.091	72	138	.115
34.	119	.022	49	122	.059	62	128	.098	73	137	.123
35	118	.025	50	121	.065	63	127	.105	74	136	.131

TABLE A–22. *Percentage points for the Friedman Test for K = 3 and n ≤ 15, and for K = 4 and n ≤ 8*

	K = 3			K = 4		
n	$\alpha \leq .10$	$\alpha \leq .05$	$\alpha \leq .01$	$\alpha \leq .10$	$\alpha \leq .05$	$\alpha \leq .01$
2	—	—	—	6.00	6.00	—
3	6.00	6.00	—	6.60	7.40	9.00
4	6.00	6.50	8.00	6.30	7.80	9.60
5	5.20	6.40	8.40	6.36	7.80	9.96
6	5.33	7.00	9.00	6.40	7.60	10.00
7	5.43	7.14	8.86	6.26	7.80	10.37
8	4.75	6.25	9.00	6.30	7.65	10.50
9	5.56	6.22	8.67			
10	5.00	6.20	9.60			
11	4.91	6.54	9.46			
12	5.17	6.50	9.50			
13	4.77	6.00	9.39			
14	—	6.40	9.00			
15	—	6.40	8.93			
∞	4.61	5.99	9.21	6.25	7.82	11.34

Adapted from Table A–15 in *Sturdy Statistics*, by F. Mosteller and R. E. K. Rourke, copyright 1973 by Addison-Wesley, Reading, Mass., and from Table A–15 in *Nonparametric Statistical Methods*, by H. Hollander and D. A. Wolfe, copyright © 1973 by John Wiley & Sons, Inc. Reprinted by permission.

For given K, n, and α, the tabled entry is $L(\alpha, K, n)$ satisfying $P_0\{L \geq L(\alpha, K, n)\} \approx \alpha$.

K

	3			4			5		
		α			α			α	
n	.001	.01	.05	.001	.01	.05	.001	.01	.05
2			28		60	58	109	106	103
3		42	41	89	87	84	160	155	150
4	56	55	54	117	114	111	210	204	197
5	70	68	66	145	141	137	259	251	244
6	83	81	79	172	167	163	307	299	291
7	96	93	91	198	193	189	355	346	338
8	109	106	104	225	220	214	403	393	384
9	121	119	116	252	246	240	451	441	431
10	134	131	128	278	272	266	499	487	477
11	147	144	141	305	298	292	546	534	523
12	160	156	153	331	324	317	593	581	570
13	172	169	165						
14	185	181	178						
15	197	194	190						
16	210	206	202						
17	223	218	215						
18	235	231	227						
19	248	243	239						
20	260	256	251						

K

	6			7			8		
		α			α			α	
n	.001	.01	.05	.001	.01	.05	.001	.01	.05
2	178	173	166	269	261	252	388	376	362
3	260	252	244	394	382	370	567	549	532
4	341	331	321	516	501	487	743	722	701
5	420	409	397	637	620	603	917	893	869
6	499	486	474	757	737	719	1,090	1,063	1,037
7	577	563	550	876	855	835	1,262	1,232	1,204
8	655	640	625	994	972	950	1,433	1,401	1,371
9	733	717	701	1,113	1,088	1,065	1,603	1,569	1,537
10	811	793	777	1,230	1,205	1,180	1,773	1,736	1,703
11	888	869	852	1,348	1,321	1,295	1,943	1,905	1,868
12	965	946	928	1,465	1,437	1,410	2,112	2,072	2,035

TABLE A-24. Critical values of Spearman's rank correlation coefficient

n	α = .05	α = .025	α = .01	α = .005
5	0.900	—	—	—
6	0.829	0.886	0.943	—
7	0.714	0.786	0.893	—
8	0.643	0.738	0.833	0.881
9	0.600	0.683	0.783	0.833
10	0.564	0.648	0.745	0.794
11	0.523	0.623	0.736	0.818
12	0.497	0.591	0.703	0.780
13	0.475	0.566	0.673	0.745
14	0.457	0.545	0.646	0.716
15	0.441	0.525	0.623	0.689
16	0.425	0.507	0.601	0.666
17	0.412	0.490	0.582	0.645
18	0.399	0.476	0.564	0.625
19	0.388	0.462	0.549	0.608
20	0.377	0.450	0.534	0.591
21	0.368	0.438	0.521	0.576
22	0.359	0.428	0.508	0.562
23	0.351	0.418	0.496	0.549
24	0.343	0.409	0.485	0.537
25	0.336	0.400	0.475	0.526
26	0.329	0.392	0.465	0.515
27	0.323	0.385	0.456	0.505
28	0.317	0.377	0.448	0.496
29	0.311	0.370	0.440	0.487
30	0.305	0.364	0.432	0.478

From "Distribution of Sums of Squares of Rank Differences for Small Numbers of Individuals," E. G. Olds, *Annals of Mathematical Statistics*, Volume 9 (1938). Reproduced with the kind permission of the Editor, *Annals of Mathematical Statistics*.

TABLE A–25. *Critical upper-tail values of S for Kendall's rank-order correlation test*

n	α = .005	α = .010	α = .025	α = .050	α = .100
4	8	8	8	6	6
5	12	10	10	8	8
6	15	13	13	11	9
7	19	17	15	13	11
8	22	20	18	16	12
9	26	24	20	18	14
10	29	27	23	21	17
11	33	31	27	23	19
12	38	36	30	26	20
13	44	40	34	28	24
14	47	43	37	33	25
15	53	49	41	35	29
16	58	52	46	38	30
17	64	58	50	42	34
18	69	63	53	45	37
19	75	67	57	49	39
20	80	72	62	52	42
21	86	78	66	56	44
22	91	83	71	61	47
23	99	89	75	65	51
24	104	94	80	68	54
25	110	100	86	72	58
26	117	107	91	77	61
27	125	113	95	81	63
28	130	118	100	86	68
29	138	126	106	90	70
30	145	131	111	95	75
31	151	137	117	99	77
32	160	144	122	104	82
33	166	152	128	108	86
34	175	157	133	113	89
35	181	165	139	117	93
36	190	172	146	122	96
37	198	178	152	128	100
38	205	185	157	133	105
39	213	193	163	139	109
40	222	200	170	144	112

*Body of table is reproduced from Table III in L. Kaarsemaker and A. van Wijngaarden's "Tables for Use in Rank Correlation," *Statistica Neerlandica*, 7 (1953), 41–54 (reproduced as Report R73 of the Computation Department of the Mathematical Centre, Amsterdam), with permission of the authors, the Mathematical Centre, and the editor of *Statistica Neerlandica*.

TABLE A–26. Fisher's r to Z transformation

r	Z	r	Z
.01	.010	.51	.563
.02	.020	.52	.577
.03	.030	.53	.590
.04	.040	.54	.604
.05	.050	.55	.618
.06	.060	.56	.633
.07	.070	.57	.648
.08	.080	.58	.663
.09	.090	.59	.678
.10	.100	.60	.693
.11	.110	.61	.709
.12	.121	.62	.725
.13	.131	.63	.741
.14	.141	.64	.758
.15	.151	.65	.775
.16	.161	.66	.793
.17	.172	.67	.811
.18	.181	.68	.829
.19	.192	.69	.848
.20	.203	.70	.867
.21	.214	.71	.887
.22	.224	.72	.908
.23	.234	.73	.929
.24	.245	.74	.950
.25	.256	.75	.973
.26	.266	.76	.996
.27	.277	.77	1.020
.28	.288	.78	1.045
.29	.299	.79	1.071
.30	.309	.80	1.099
.31	.321	.81	1.127
.32	.332	.82	1.157
.33	.343	.83	1.188
.34	.354	.84	1.221
.35	.366	.85	1.256
.36	.377	.86	1.293
.37	.389	.87	1.333
.38	.400	.88	1.376
.39	.412	.89	1.422
.40	.424	.90	1.472
.41	.436	.91	1.528
.42	.448	.92	1.589
.43	.460	.93	1.658
.44	.472	.94	1.738
.45	.485	.95	1.832
.46	.497	.96	1.946
.47	.510	.97	2.092
.48	.523	.98	2.298
.49	.536	.99	2.647
.50	.549		

From *Statistics for Psychology*, by W. Mendenhall and M. Ramey. Copyright © 1973 by Wadsworth Publishing Company, Inc. Reprinted by permission of the publisher, Duxbury Press.

TABLE A-27. Table of common logarithms

N	0	1	2	3	4	5	6	7	8	9
10	0000	0043	0086	0128	0170	0212	0253	0294	0334	0374
11	0414	0453	0492	0531	0569	0607	0645	0682	0719	0755
12	0792	0828	0864	0899	0934	0969	1004	1038	1072	1106
13	1139	1173	1206	1239	1271	1303	1335	1367	1399	1430
14	1461	1492	1523	1553	1584	1614	1644	1673	1703	1732
15	1761	1790	1818	1847	1875	1903	1931	1959	1987	2014
16	2041	2068	2095	2122	2148	2175	2201	2227	2253	2279
17	2304	2330	2355	2380	2405	2430	2455	2480	2504	2529
18	2553	2577	2601	2625	2648	2672	2695	2718	2742	2765
19	2788	2810	2833	2856	2878	2900	2923	2945	2967	2989
20	3010	3032	3054	3075	3096	3118	3139	3160	3181	3201
21	3222	3243	3263	3284	3304	3324	3345	3365	3385	3404
22	3424	3444	3464	3483	3502	3522	3541	3560	3579	3598
23	3617	3636	3655	3674	3692	3711	3729	3747	3766	3784
24	3802	3820	3838	3856	3874	3892	3909	3927	3945	3962
25	3979	3997	4014	4031	4048	4065	4082	4099	4116	4133
26	4150	4166	4183	4200	4216	4232	4249	4265	4281	4298
27	4314	4330	4346	4362	4378	4393	4409	4425	4440	4456
28	4472	4487	4502	4518	4533	4548	4564	4579	4594	4609
29	4624	4639	4654	4669	4683	4698	4713	4728	4742	4757
30	4771	4786	4800	4814	4829	4843	4857	4871	4886	4900
31	4914	4928	4942	4955	4969	4983	4997	5011	5024	5038
32	5051	5065	5079	5092	5105	5119	5132	5145	5159	5172
33	5185	5198	5211	5224	5237	5250	5263	5276	5289	5302
34	5315	5328	5340	5353	5366	5378	5391	5403	5416	5428
35	5441	5453	5465	5478	5490	5502	5514	5527	5539	5551
36	5563	5575	5587	5599	5611	5623	5635	5647	5658	5670
37	5682	5694	5705	5717	5729	5740	5752	5763	5775	5786
38	5798	5809	5821	5832	5843	5855	5866	5877	5888	5899
39	5911	5922	5933	5944	5955	5966	5977	5988	5999	6010
40	6021	6031	6042	6053	6064	6075	6085	6096	6107	6117
41	6128	6138	6149	6160	6170	6180	6191	6201	6212	6222
42	6232	6243	6253	6263	6274	6284	6294	6304	6314	6325
43	6335	6345	6355	6365	6375	6385	6395	6405	6415	6425
44	6435	6444	6454	6464	6474	6484	6493	6503	6513	6522
45	6532	6542	6551	6561	6571	6580	6590	6599	6609	6618
46	6628	6637	6646	6656	6665	6675	6684	6693	6702	6712
47	6721	6730	6739	6749	6758	6767	6776	6785	6794	6803
48	6812	6821	6830	6839	6848	6857	6866	6875	6884	6893
49	6902	6911	6920	6928	6937	6946	6955	6964	6972	6981
50	6990	6998	7007	7016	7024	7033	7042	7050	7059	7067
51	7076	7084	7093	7101	7110	7118	7126	7135	7143	7152
52	7160	7168	7177	7185	7193	7202	7210	7218	7226	7235
53	7243	7251	7259	7267	7275	7284	7292	7300	7308	7316
54	7324	7332	7340	7348	7356	7364	7372	7380	7388	7396
N	0	1	2	3	4	5	6	7	8	9

N	0	1	2	3	4	5	6	7	8	9
55	7404	7412	7419	7427	7435	7443	7451	7459	7466	7474
56	7482	7490	7497	7505	7513	7520	7528	7536	7543	7551
57	7559	7566	7574	7582	7589	7597	7604	7612	7619	7627
58	7634	7642	7649	7657	7664	7672	7679	7686	7694	7701
59	7709	7716	7723	7731	7738	7745	7752	7760	7767	7774
60	7782	7789	7796	7803	7810	7818	7825	7832	7839	7846
61	7853	7860	7868	7875	7882	7889	7896	7903	7910	7917
62	7924	7931	7938	7945	7952	7959	7966	7973	7980	7987
63	7993	8000	8007	8014	8021	8028	8035	8041	8048	8055
64	8062	8069	8075	8082	8089	8096	8102	8109	8116	8122
65	8129	8136	8142	8149	8156	8162	8169	8176	8182	8189
66	8195	8202	8209	8215	8222	8228	8235	8241	8248	8254
67	8261	8267	8274	8280	8287	8293	8299	8306	8312	8319
68	8325	8331	8338	8344	8351	8357	8363	8370	8376	8382
69	8388	8395	8401	8407	8414	8420	8426	8432	8439	8445
70	8451	8457	8463	8470	8476	8482	8488	8494	8500	8506
71	8513	8519	8525	8531	8537	8543	8549	8555	8561	8567
72	8573	8579	8585	8591	8597	8603	8609	8615	8621	8627
73	8633	8639	8645	8651	8657	8663	8669	8675	8681	8686
74	8692	8698	8704	8710	8716	8722	8727	8733	8739	8745
75	8751	8756	8762	8768	8774	8779	8785	8791	8797	8802
76	8808	8814	8820	8825	8831	8837	8842	8848	8854	8859
77	8865	8871	8876	8882	8887	8893	8899	8904	8910	8915
78	8921	8927	8932	8938	8943	8949	8954	8960	8965	8971
79	8976	8982	8987	8993	8998	9004	9009	9015	9020	9025
80	9031	9036	9042	9047	9053	9058	9063	9069	9074	9079
81	9085	9090	9096	9101	9106	9112	9117	9122	9128	9133
82	9138	9143	9149	9154	9159	9165	9170	9175	9180	9186
83	9191	9196	9201	9206	9212	9217	9222	9227	9232	9238
84	9243	9248	9253	9258	9263	9269	9274	9279	9284	9289
85	9294	9299	9304	9309	9315	9320	9325	9330	9335	9340
86	9345	9350	9355	9360	9365	9370	9375	9380	9385	9390
87	9395	9400	9405	9410	9415	9420	9425	9430	9435	9440
88	9445	9450	9455	9460	9465	9469	9474	9479	9484	9489
89	9494	9499	9504	9509	9513	9518	9523	9528	9533	9538
90	9542	9547	9552	9557	9562	9566	9571	9576	9581	9586
91	9590	9595	9600	9605	9609	9614	9619	9624	9628	9633
92	9638	9643	9647	9652	9657	9661	9666	9671	9675	9680
93	9685	9689	9694	9699	9703	9708	9713	9717	9722	9727
94	9731	9736	9741	9745	9750	9754	9759	9763	9768	9773
95	9777	9782	9786	9791	9795	9800	9805	9809	9814	9818
96	9823	9827	9832	9836	9841	9845	9850	9854	9859	9863
97	9868	9872	9877	9881	9886	9890	9894	9899	9903	9908
98	9912	9917	9921	9926	9930	9934	9939	9943	9948	9952
99	9956	9961	9965	9969	9974	9978	9983	9987	9991	9996
N	0	1	2	3	4	5	6	7	8	9

TABLE A–28. Table of squares and square roots

N	N²	√N	N	N²	√N
1	1	1	51	2,601	7.141
2	4	1.414	52	2,704	7.211
3	9	1.732	53	2,809	7.280
4	16	2	54	2,916	7.348
5	25	2.236	55	3,025	7.416
6	36	2.449	56	3,136	7.483
7	49	2.646	57	3,249	7.550
8	64	2.828	58	3,364	7.616
9	81	3	59	3,481	7.681
10	100	3.162	60	3,600	7.746
11	121	3.317	61	3,721	7.810
12	144	3.464	62	3,844	7.874
13	169	3.606	63	3,969	7.937
14	196	3.742	64	4,096	8
15	225	3.873	65	4,225	8.062
16	256	4	66	4,356	8.124
17	289	4.123	67	4,489	8.185
18	324	4.243	68	4,624	8.246
19	361	4.359	69	4,761	8.307
20	400	4.472	70	4,900	8.367
21	441	4.583	71	5,041	8.426
22	484	4.690	72	5,184	8.485
23	529	4.796	73	5,329	8.544
24	576	4.899	74	5,476	8.602
25	625	5	75	5,625	8.660
26	676	5.099	76	5,776	8.718
27	729	5.196	77	5,929	8.775
28	784	5.292	78	6,084	8.832
29	841	5.385	79	6,241	8.888
30	900	5.477	80	6,400	8.944
31	961	5.568	81	6,561	9
32	1,024	5.657	82	6,724	9.055
33	1,089	5.745	83	6,889	9.110
34	1,156	5.831	84	7,056	9.165
35	1,225	5.916	85	7,225	9.220
36	1,296	6	86	7,396	9.274
37	1,369	6.083	87	7,569	9.327
38	1,444	6.164	88	7,744	9.381
39	1,521	6.245	89	7,921	9.434
40	1,600	6.325	90	8,100	9.487
41	1,681	6.403	91	8,281	9.539
42	1,764	6.481	92	8,464	9.592
43	1,849	6.557	93	8,649	9.644
44	1,936	6.633	94	8,836	9.695
45	2,025	6.708	95	9,025	9.747
46	2,116	6.782	96	9,216	9.798
47	2,209	6.856	97	9,409	9.849
48	2,304	6.928	98	9,604	9.899
49	2,401	7	99	9,801	9.950
50	2,500	7.071	100	10,000	10

References

Chapter 1

Bradley, J. V. *Distribution-free statistical tests*. Englewood Cliffs, New Jersey: Prentice-Hall, Inc., 1968, p. 15.
Ury, H. In response to Noether's Letter, "Needed—a new name." *The American Statistician*, 1967, **21**: 53.

Chapter 2

Anderson, N. H. Scales and statistics: Parametric and nonparametric. *Psychological Bulletin*, 1961, **58**: 305–316.
Baker, B. O., C. D. Hardyck, and L. F. Petrinovich. Weak measurement vs. strong statistics: An empirical critique of S. S. Stevens' proscriptions on statistics. *Educational and Psychological Measurement*, 1966, **26**: 291–309.
Dunn, O. J. Multiple comparisons among means. *Journal of the American Statistical Association*, 1961, **56**: 52–64.
Gardner, P. L. Scales and statistics. *Review of Educational Research*, 1975, **45**: 43–57.
Grizzle, J. E. Continuity correction in the X^2 test for 2×2 tables. *The American Statistician*, 1967, **21**: 28–32.
Lord, F. M. On the statistical treatment of football numbers. *American Psychologist*, 1953, **8**: 750–751.
Savage, I. R. Nonparametric statistics. *Journal of the American Statistical Association*, 1957, **52**: 331–344.
Siegel, S. *Nonparametric statistics for the behavioral sciences*. New York: McGraw-Hill, 1956.
Stevens, S. S. On the theory of scales of measurement. *Science*, 1946, **103**: 677–680.
Stevens, S. S. Measurement, statistics, and the schempiric view. *Science*, 1968, **101**, 849–856.

Chapter 3

Arbuthnott, J. An argument for Divine Providence taken from the constant regularity observed in the birth of both sexes. *Philosophical Transactions*, 1710, **27**: 186–190.

Bradley, J. V. *Distribution-free statistical tests*. Englewood Cliffs, New Jersey: Prentice-Hall, Inc., 1968.

Cox, D. R., and A. Stuart. Some quick sign tests for trend in location and dispersion. *Biometrika*, 1955, **42**: 80–95.

Noether, G. E. Two sequential tests against trend. *Journal of the American Statistical Association*, 1956, **51**: 440–450.

Chapter 4

Festinger, L., and D. Katz. (Eds.) *Research methods in the behavioral sciences*. New York: Dryden Press, 1953.

Glass, G. V., P. D. Peckham, and J. R. Sanders. Consequences of failure to meet assumptions underlying the fixed effects analysis of variance and covariance. *Review of Educational Research*, 1972, **42**: 237–288.

Klotz, J. Small-sample power and efficiency of the one-sample Wilcoxon and normal-scores tests. *Annals of Mathematical Statistics*, 1963, **34**: 624–632.

Koch, G. G. Some aspects of the statistical analysis of split-plot experiments in completely randomized layouts. *Journal of the American Statistical Association*, 1969, **64**: 485–505.

Koch, G. G., and P. K. Sen. Some aspects of the statistical analysis of the mixed model. *Biometrics*, 1968, **24**: 27–47.

Puri, M. L., and P. K. Sen. *Nonparametric methods in multivariate analysis*. New York: Wiley, 1971.

Siegel, S. *Nonparametric statistics for the behavioral sciences*. New York: McGraw-Hill, 1956.

Chapter 5

Cochran, W. G. Some methods for strengthening the common X^2 tests. *Biometrics*, 1954, **10**: 417–451.

Grizzle, J. E. Continuity correction in the X^2 test for 2×2 tables. *The American Statistician*, 1967, **21**: 28–32.

Mantel, N., and S. W. Greenhouse. What is the continuity correction? *The American Statistician*, 1968, **22**: 27–30.

Maxwell, A. E. *Analysing qualitative data*. London: Methuen and Company, 1961.

Chapter 6

Cohen, J. An Alternative to Marascuilo's "Large-sample multiple comparisons" for proportions. *Psychological Bulletin*, 1967, **67**: 199–201.

Coleman, J. S., *et al. Equality of educational opportunity*. Washington, D.C.: U.S. Government Printing Office, 1966.

Light, R. J., and B. H. Margolin. An analysis of variance for categorical data. *Journal of the American Statistical Association*, 1971, **66**: 534–544.

Maxwell, A. E. *Analysing qualitative data*. London: Methuen and Company, 1961.

Chapter 7

Bishop, Y. M. M., S. E. Fienberg, and P. W. Holland. *Discrete multivariate analysis: Theory and practice*. Cambridge, Massachusetts: MIT Press, 1975.

Bowker, A. H. A test for symmetry in contingency tables. *Journal of the American Statistical Association*, 1948, **43**: 572–574.

Cochran, W. G. The comparison of percentages in matched samples. *Biometrika*, 1950, **37**: 256–266.

Cochran, W. G. The X^2 test of goodness of fit. *Annals of Mathematical Statistics*, 1952, **23**: 315–345.

Cochran, W. G. Some methods for strengthening the common X^2 tests. *Biometrics*, 1954, **10**: 417–451.

D'Agostino, R. B. A second look at analysis of variance on dichotomous data. *Journal of Educational Measurement*, 1971, **8**: 327–333.

Grizzle, J. E., C. F. Starmer, and G. G. Koch. Analysis of categorical data by linear models. *Biometrics*, 1969, **25**: 489–504.

Koch, G. G., J. L. Freeman, D. H. Freeman, and R. G. Lehnen. A general methodology for the analysis of experiments with repeated measurement of categorical data. *Institute of Statistics Mimeo Series No. 961*. Chapel Hill, North Carolina: University of North Carolina, 1974.

Koch, G. G., and D. W. Reinfurt. The analysis of categorical data from mixed models. *Biometrics*, 1971, **27**: 157–173.

Kullback, S. *Information theory and statistics*. New York: Dover, 1968.

Kullback, S. Marginal homogeneity of multidimensional contingency tables. *Annals of Mathematical Statistics*, 1971, **42**: 594–606.

Lewontin, R. C., and J. Felsenstein. The robustness of homogeneity tests in $2 \times n$ tables. *Biometrics*, 1965, **21**: 19–33.

Lunney, G. H. Using analysis of variance with a dichotomous dependent variable: an empirical study. *Journal of Educational Measurement*, 1970, **4**: 263–269.

McNemar, Q. Note on the sampling error of the difference between correlated proportions or percentages. *Psychometrika*, 1947, **12**: 153–157.

Slakter, M. J. Comparative validity of the chi-square and two modified chi-square goodness-of-fit tests for small but equal expected frequencies. *Biometrika*, 1966, **53**: 619–623.

Stuart, A. A test for homogeneity of the marginal distributions in a two-way classification. *Biometrika*, 1955, **42**: 412–416.

Stuart, A. The comparison of frequencies in matched samples. *British Journal of Statistical Psychology*, 1957, **10**: 29–32.

Tate, M. W., and S. M. Brown. Note on the Cochran Q test. *Journal of the American Statistical Association*, 1970, **65**: 155–160.

Chapter 8

Blomqvist, N. Some tests based on dichotomization. *Annals of Mathematical Statistics*, 1951, **27**: 362–371.

Cramer, H. *Mathematical methods of statistics*. Princeton, New Jersey: Princeton University Press, 1946.

Goodman, L. A. Simultaneous confidence limits for cross-product ratios in contingency tables. *Journal of the Royal Statistical Society, Series B*, 1964, **26**: 86–102.

Light, R. J., and B. H. Margolin. Analysis of variance for categorical data. *Journal of the American Statistical Association*, 1971, **66**: 534–544.

Margolin, B. H., and R. J. Light. An analysis of variance for categorical data, II: Small-sample comparisons with chi-square and other competitors. *Journal of the American Statistical Association*, 1974, **69**: 755–764.

Maxwell, A. E. *Analysing qualitative data*. London: Methuen and Company, 1961.

Chapter 9

Bartlett, M. S. Contingency-table interactions. *Journal of the Royal Statistical Society Supplement*, 1935, **2**: 248–252.

Goodman, L. A. On methods of comparing contingency tables. *Journal of the Royal Statistical Society, Series A*, 1963a, **126**: 94–108.

Goodman, L. A. On Plackett's test for contingency-table interactions. *Journal of the Royal Statistical Society, Series B*, 1963b, **25**: 179–188.

Goodman, L. A. Interactions in multidimensional contingency tables. *Annals of Mathematical Statistics*, 1964a, **35**: 632–646.

Goodman, L. A. Simple methods for analyzing three-factor interaction in contingency tables. *Journal of the American Statistical Association*, 1964b, **59**: 319–352.

Goodman, L. A. On partitioning chi-square and detecting partial association in three-way contingency tables. *Journal of the Royal Statistical Society, Series B*, 1969, **31**: 486–498.

Goodman, L. A. The multivariate analysis of qualitative data: Interactions among multiple classifications. *Journal of the American Statistical Association*, 1970, **65**: 226–256.

Grizzle, J. E., C. F. Starmer, and G. G. Koch. Analysis of categorical data by linear models. *Biometrics*, 1969, **25**: 489–504.

Lancaster, H. O. Complex contingency tables treated by partition of X^2. *Journal of the Royal Statistical Society, Series B*, 1951, **13**: 242–249.

Lewis, B. N. On the analysis of interaction in multidimensional contingency tables. *Journal of the Royal Statistical Society, Series A*, 1962, **125**: 88–117.

Mosteller, F. Association and estimation in contingency tables. *Journal of the American Statistical Association*, 1968, **63**: 1–28.

Chapter 10

Lilliefors, H. W. On the Kolmogorov–Smirnov test for normality with mean and variance unknown. *Journal of the American Statistical Association*, 1967, **62**: 399–402.

Massey, F. J. The Kolmogorov–Smirnov test for goodness of fit. *Journal of the American Statistical Association*, 1951, **46**: 68–78.

Chapter 11

Bell, C. B., and K. A. Doksum. Some new distribution-free statistics. *Annals of Mathematical Statistics*, 1965, **36**: 203–214.

Hollander, M. A distribution-free test for parallelism. *Journal American Statistical Association*, 1970, **65**: 387–394.

Klotz, J. Nonparametric tests for scale. *Annals of Mathematical Statistics*, 1962, **33**: 498–512.

Mann, H. B., and D. R. Whitney. On a test of whether one of two random variables is stochastically larger than the other. *Annals of Mathematical Statistics*, 1947, **18**: 50–60.

Mood, A. M. On the asymptotic efficiency of certain nonparametric two-sample tests. *Annals of Mathematical Statistics*, 1954, **25**: 514–522.

Siegel, S., and J. Tukey. A nonparametric sum of ranks procedure for relative spread in unpaired samples. *Journal of the American Statistical Association*, 1960, **55**: 429–445.

Terry, M. E. Some rank-order tests, which are most powerful against specific parametric alternatives. *Annals of Mathematical Statistics*, 1952, **23**: 346–366.

Van der Waerden, B. L. Order tests for the two-sample problem and their power. *Proceedings: Koninklijke Nederlandse Akademie van Wetenschappen, Series A*, 1953, **56**: 303–316.

Wilcoxon, F. *Some rapid approximate statistical procedures*. Stamford, Connecticut: Stamford Research Laboratories, American Cyanamid Company, 1949.

Chapter 12

Hodges, J. L., Jr., and E. L. Lehmann. Estimates of location based on rank tests. *Annals of Mathematical Statistics*, 1963, **34**: 598–611.

Kruskal, W. H., and W. A. Wallis. Use of ranks in one-criterion variance analysis. *Journal of the American Statistical Association*, 1952, **47**: 583–621.

Marascuilo, L. A., and M. McSweeney. Nonparametric post hoc comparisons for trend. *Psychological Bulletin*, 1967, **67**: 401–412.

McSweeney, M., and D. A. Penfield. The normal scores test for the c-sample problem. *British Journal of Mathematical and Statistical Psychology*, 1969, **22**: 177–192.

Spjøtvoll, E. A note on robust estimation in analysis of variance. *Annals of Mathematical Statistics*, 1968, **39**: 1486–1492.

Srisukho, D. "Monte Carlo Study of the power of *H*-test compared to *F*-test when population distributions are different in form." Doctoral dissertation. Berkeley: University of California, 1970.

Steel, R. G. D. A rank-sum test comparing all pairs of treatments. *Technometrics*, 1960, **2**: 197–207.

Chapter 13

Hodges, J. L., Jr., and E. L. Lehmann. Estimates of location based on rank tests. *Annals of Mathematical Statistics*, 1963, **34**: 598–611.

Tukey, J. W. The simplest signed-rank tests. *Mimeographed report 17 of the Statistical Research Group*. Princeton, New Jersey: Princeton University, 1949.

Wilcoxon, F. *Some rapid approximate statistical procedures*. Stamford, Connecticut: Stamford Research Laboratories, American Cyanamid Company, 1949.

Chapter 14

Davies, O. L. (Ed.) *Design and analysis of industrial experiments*. New York: Hafner Publishing Company, 1956, p. 232.

Durbin, J. Incomplete blocks in ranking experiments. *British Journal of Statistical Psychology*, 1951, **4**: 85–90.

Friedman, M. The use of ranks to avoid the assumption of normality implied in the analysis of variance. *Journal of the American Statistical Association*, 1937, **32**: 675–701.

Marascuilo, L. A., and M. McSweeney. Nonparametric post hoc comparisons for trend. *Psychological Bulletin*, 1967, **67**: 401–412.

Page, E. B. Ordered hypotheses for multiple treatments: A significance test for linear ranks. *Journal of the American Statistical Association*, 1963, **58**: 216–230.

Rosenthal, I., and T. S. Ferguson. An asymptotically distribution-free multiple-comparison method with application to the problem of *n* rankings of *m* objects. *The British Journal of Mathematical and Statistical Psychology*, 1965, **18**: 243–254.

Scheffé, H. *The analysis of variance*. New York: John Wiley and Sons, 1959.

Chapter 15

Benard, A., and P. H. Van Elteren. A generalization of the method of *m*-rankings. *Indagationes Mathematicae*, 1953, **15**: 358–369.

Hodges, J. L., Jr., and E. L. Lehmann. Rank methods for combination of independent experiments in analysis of variance. *Annals of Mathematical Statistics*, 1962, **33**: 482–497.

Marascuilo, L. A., and J. R. Levin. Appropriate post hoc comparisons for interaction and nested hypotheses in analysis-of-variance designs: The elimination of Type IV errors. *American Educational Research Journal*, 1970, **7**: 397–421.

McSweeney, M. *An empirical study of two proposed nonparametric tests for main effects and interaction*. Doctoral dissertation. Berkeley, California: University of California, 1967.

Mehra, K. L., and J. Sarangi. Asymptotic efficiency of certain rank tests for comparative experiments. *Annals of Mathematical Statistics*, 1967, **38**: 90–107.

Mehra, K. L., and P. K. Sen. On a class of conditionally distribution-free tests for interaction in factorial experiments. *Annals of Mathematical Statistics*, 1969, **40**: 658–664.

Porter, A. C., and M. McSweeney. Randomized blocks design and nonparametric statistics. Occasional Paper No. 8, Office of Research Consultation, Michigan State University, East Lansing, Michigan, 1970.

Reinach, S. G. A nonparametric analysis for a multiway classification with one element per cell. *South African Journal of Agricultural Science*, 1965, **8**: 941–960.

Wilcoxon, F. Individual comparisons of grouped data by ranking methods. *Journal of Entomology*, 1946, **39**: 269–270.

Chapter 16

Davis, J. A. A partial coefficient for Goodman and Kruskal's gamma. *Journal of the American Statistical Association*, 1967, **62**: 189–193.

Ferguson, G. A. *Nonparametric trend analysis: A practical guide for research workers.* Montreal: McGill University Press, 1965.

Goodman, L. A., and W. H. Kruskal. Measures of association for cross classifications. *Journal of the American Statistical Association*, 1954, **49**: 732–764.

Goodman, L. A., and W. H. Kruskal. Measures of association for cross classifications. III: Approximate sampling theory. *Journal of the American Statistical Association*, 1963, **58**: 310–364.

Kendall, M. G. *Rank-correlation methods* (Third Ed.). London: Griffin, 1962.

Answers to Selected Exercises

Chapter 2

2. a) H_0: The death of 4 adjacent dead trees is a chance event.
   b) H_1: The death of 4 adjacent dead trees is not a chance event.
   c) $T = \begin{bmatrix} 15 \\ 4 \end{bmatrix} = 1365$ d) 12 e) $\dfrac{12}{1365} = 0.0087$ f) Yes

3. a) H_0: The death of 2 or more adjacent dead trees is a chance event.
   b) H_1: The death of 2 or more adjacent dead trees is not a chance event.
   c) $T = 2^{15} = 32768$
   d) $1 + 2 + 3 + 4 + 5 + 6 + 7 + 8 + 9 + 10 + 11 + 12 + 13 + 14 = 105$
   e) $\dfrac{105}{32768} = 0.0032$ f) Yes

5. a) $7! = 5040$ b) $7!/(7 - 4)! = 840$ c) $10, 11, 12, \ldots, 20, 21, 22$
   d) $\dfrac{7!}{4!3!} = \begin{bmatrix} 7 \\ 4 \end{bmatrix} = 35$ e) $10, 11, 12, \ldots, 20, 21, 22$ f) Combinations

6. a) $\frac{1}{35}$ b) $\frac{1}{35}$ c) $\frac{2}{35}$ d) $\frac{3}{35}$
   e) $\alpha = \frac{2}{35}$, if the rejection region contains $T = 10$ and $T = 22$.

7. a) $\frac{29}{34}$ b) $\frac{12}{34}$ c) $\frac{7}{34}$ d) $\frac{0}{34}$ e) $\frac{12}{34} + \frac{29}{34} - \frac{7}{34} = 1$ f) $\frac{7}{12}$

8. a) $\frac{40}{100}$ b) $\frac{20}{100}$ c) $\frac{70}{100}$ d) $\frac{40}{60}$
   e) No, since $P(A|B) = \frac{40}{50}$, $P(A|\overline{B}) = \frac{20}{50}$, and $P(A) = \frac{60}{100}$.

f) P(One student will fail at least one item) $= \frac{50}{100} + \frac{40}{100} - \frac{30}{100} = \frac{60}{100}$.
P(all five fail) $= (\frac{60}{100})^5 = 0.0778$.

11. a) $\frac{5}{10}$ b) $\frac{3}{10}$ c) $\frac{7}{10}$ d) $\frac{3}{5}$ e) $\frac{3}{5}$ f) No   g) $\frac{2}{9}$ h) $\frac{5}{9}$ i) $\frac{1}{15}$
    j) $\frac{1}{5}$ k) $\frac{1}{5}$ l) $\frac{1}{12}$ m) $\frac{1}{2}$ n) $\frac{1}{6}$ o) $\frac{19}{120}$ p) 0

12. a) 0.1587   b) 0.7888

13. a) $Z \geq 1.41$, $P = 0.08$;   b) $Z \geq 0.44$, $P = 0.33$

14. a) $Z = -1.5625$. Do not reject.   b) $Z = -1.7953$. Reject.

Chapter 3

1. Let $T = \{$Number who report Worse$\}$ and consider a one-tailed H_1.
   a) $T = 3$. Reject H_0 if $T \leq 2$.
   b) $T = 7$. Reject H_0 if $T \leq 4$.
   c) $T = 3 + r$. Reject H_0 if $T \leq 4$.

2. For a two-tailed interval, $p = \frac{7}{16} \pm 1.645\sqrt{(\frac{7}{16})(\frac{9}{16})(\frac{1}{16})}$; for a one-tailed interval, replace ± 1.645 with $+1.282$.

3. For a two-tailed interval, $t_1 = 2$, $t_2 = 8$, $X^{(3)} = -1$, $X^{(8)} = 16$, $-1 \leq M_d \leq 16$, $M_d = \frac{1}{2}(X^{(5)} + X^{(6)}) = 9.5$.

4. $H_0: M_d = 0$, $H_1: M_d > 0$. Reject H_0 if $T \leq 3$, $T = 3$.

5. For a two-tailed test at $\alpha = 0.10$, $t_1 = 4$, $t_2 = 10$, and $1 \leq M_d \leq 5$.

7. $T = 35$, $p = 0.25$, $Z = 2.40$. Reject H_0.

8. Procedure One: $N = 27$, $p = \frac{1}{2}$, $T = 18$. Reject H_0 if $T \leq 7$ or if $T \geq 20$. $Z = -1.54$. Do not reject. Procedure Two: $Z = 1.77$. Do not reject.

11. $N = 32$, $S = 7$, $Z = -3.01$. Reject H_0.

12. No.

13. a) $N = 12$, $S = 2$. Reject H_0 if $S \leq 2$ or $S \geq 10$.

Chapter 4

1. For $\alpha = 0.10$:
    $E_{\text{Sign/normal}} = 0.8006$; normal-curve power $= 0.7088$; binomial power $= 0.5675$.
    For $\alpha = 0.01$:
    $E_{\text{Sign/normal}} = 0.5831$; normal-curve power $= 0.3085$; binomial power $= 0.1789$.

2. For $\mu_1 - \mu_2 = 6$:
    $E_{\text{Sign/normal}} = 0.7142$; normal-curve power $= 0.3936$; binomial power $= 0.2811$.
    For $\mu_1 - \mu_2 = 10$:
    $E_{\text{Sign/normal}} = 0.7467$; normal-curve power $= 0.7389$; binomial power $= 0.5517$.

5. $N = 79$.

Answers to
Selected
Exercises

Chapter 5

1. $H_0: p_1 = p_2$ versus $H_1: p_1 \neq p_2$. Let $t_1 = $ {Number of operated-upon cats who remember}. Reject H_0 if $t_1 = 0$ or 5. Do not reject.

2. $H_0: p_1 = p_2$ versus $H_1: p_1 < p_2$. Let $t_1 = $ {Number of operated-upon cats who remember}. Reject H_0 if $t_1 = 0, 1, 2, 3$. $P(t_1 \leq 3) = 0.0456$. Reject H_0.

3. a) 0.0202   b) 0.152.

4. $H_0: p = 0.75$ versus $H_1: p \neq 0.75$. $n = 40$. $Z = -1.68$. Do not reject. One should not be surprised.

6. $H_0: p_1 = p_2$. $H_1: p_1 \neq p_2$. $\hat{p}_1 = \frac{47}{141}, \hat{p}_2 = \frac{41}{53}, \hat{p}_0 = \frac{88}{194}$, $Z = -5.51$. Reject $H_0: (p_1 - p_2) = 0.441 \pm 0.137$.

7. For $n_1 = n_2 = 75$: Power $= P(Z \leq 0.5) = 0.6915$.
   For $n_1 = n_2 = 100$: Power $= P(Z \leq 0.866) = 0.8068$.
   $n_1 = n_2 = 99$.

8. Without a correction for continuity, $Z_1 = -1.36$, $Z_2 = 2.67$, $Z_3 = 0.65$, $Z_4 = 1.79$, $Z = 1.875$. As a two-tailed test, H_0 is not rejected at $\alpha = 0.05$.

9. Method One: $Z_1 = 2.29$, $Z_2 = 1.71$, $Z_3 = 1.58$, $Z = 3.22$. Reject H_0.
   Method Two: $X^2 = 13.93$. Reject H_0.
   Method Three:
   $d_1 = 0.349$, $d_2 = 0.277$, $d_3 = 0.242$; $W_1 = 10.31$, $W_2 = 9.39$, $W_3 = 8.03$; $\bar{d} = 0.293$, $SE_{\bar{d}}^2 = 0.008$, $Z = 3.30$. Reject H_0.
   Method Four:
   $p_1 = P(X^2 > 5.24) = .024$
   $p_2 = P(X^2 > 2.91) = .091$
   $p_3 = P(X^2 > 2.49) = .143$
   $\lambda = 16.14$, $v = 6$, $X^2_{6:95} = 12.59$. Reject H_0.

10. $X^2 = 1.69$.

16. Method One: $Z_1 = 4.56$, $Z_2 = 2.31$, $Z_3 = .65$, $Z = 4.34$.   Reject H_0.
    Method Two: $X^2 = 10.24$. Reject H_0.
    Method Three:
    $d_1 = .196$, $d_2 = .076$, $d_3 = -.031$,
    $\bar{d} = .078$, $SE_{\bar{d}} = .023$, $Z = 3.39$. Reject H_0.

Chapter 6

1. $X^2 = 23.28$, $v_1 = 4$, $X^2_{4:0.95} = 9.49$. H_0 is rejected.
   $\hat{R}^2_{LM} = 0.0371$, $v_1 = 4$, $X^2_{LM} = 19.14$. H_0 is rejected.

   Pairwise contrasts. $\sqrt{9.49} = 3.08$.

	$\hat{\psi}$	$SE_{\hat{\psi}}$	
Very much	−.160	0.0756	N.S.
Much	−.250	0.0963	N.S.
A medium amount	+.030	0.0960	N.S.
Little	+.173	0.0624	N.S.
Very little	+.207	0.0538	Significant

2. For a planned analysis, replace 3.08 by 2.58. Contrasts involving Much, Little, and Very little are significant:

$$\psi_{Much} = -0.250 \pm 0.248; \qquad \psi_{Little} = 0.173 \pm 0.161; \qquad \psi_{Very\ little} = 0.207 \pm 0.139.$$

4. $X^2 = 322.83$, $v = 4$, $X^2_{4:0.95} = 9.49$. H_0 is rejected. Study is invalid: Observations within a rater are not independent.

5. $\hat{R}^2_{LM} = 0.2736$, $X^2 = 327.75$, $X^2_{4:0.95} = 9.49$. H_0 is rejected.

6. $X^2 = 45.12$, $v = 5$, $X^2_{5:0.95} = 11.07$. H_0 is rejected. Post hoc analysis use $\underline{S}^* = 3.33$. Planned analysis use $Z = 2.94$.

Contrast	$\hat{\psi}$	$SE\hat{\psi}$	Planned	Post hoc
1 vs. 2	0.203	0.1218		
1 vs. 3	0.341	0.1097	Sig	
1 vs. 4	-0.066	0.0934		
1 vs. 5	0.444	0.0961	Sig	Sig
1 vs. 6	0.390	0.0983	Sig	Sig
2 vs. 3	0.139	0.1250		
2 vs. 4	-0.269	0.1109		
2 vs. 5	0.241	0.1131		
2 vs. 6	0.187	0.1149		
3 vs. 4	-0.407	0.0974	Sig	Sig
3 vs. 5	0.103	0.1000		
3 vs. 6	0.049	0.1020		
4 vs. 5	0.510	0.0818	Sig	Sig
4 vs. 6	0.456	0.0843	Sig	Sig
5 vs. 6	-0.054	0.0872		

7. $\hat{\psi}_{Under\ 35} = \hat{p}_1 - \hat{p}_3 = 0.3414$, $SE_{\hat{\psi}} = 0.1101$,

$$\underline{S}^* = 2.45, \quad X^2 = \frac{\hat{\psi}^2}{SE^2_{\hat{\psi}}} = \frac{0.3414^2}{0.1101^2} = 9.61.$$

$\hat{\psi}_{Over\ 35} = \hat{p}_4 - \hat{p}_6 = 0.4559$, $SE_{\hat{\psi}} = 0.0848$,

$$\underline{S}^* = 2.45, \quad X^2 = \frac{\hat{\psi}^2}{SE^2_{\hat{\psi}}} = \frac{0.4559^2}{0.0848^2} = 28.90.$$

8. Pairwise contrasts, $\underline{S}^* = \sqrt{9.49} = 3.08$.

Contribution	Contrast		$SE\hat{\psi}$	Decision
Low	$\hat{p}_1 - \hat{p}_2 =$	0.390	0.046	Sig
	$\hat{p}_1 - \hat{p}_3 =$	0.665	0.035	Sig
	$\hat{p}_2 - \hat{p}_3 =$	0.275	0.035	Sig
Medium	$\hat{p}_1 - \hat{p}_2 =$	-0.485	0.040	Sig
	$\hat{p}_1 - \hat{p}_3 =$	-0.170	0.036	Sig
	$\hat{p}_2 - \hat{p}_3 =$	0.315	0.046	Sig
High	$\hat{p}_1 - \hat{p}_2 =$	0.095	0.038	N.S.
	$\hat{p}_1 - \hat{p}_3 =$	-0.495	0.043	Sig
	$\hat{p}_2 - \hat{p}_3 =$	-0.590	0.040	Sig

9. Analysis of chi-square table:

df		Source	Chi-square
Under 35	2	8.63	
Mono	1		8.51
Residual	1		0.12
Over 35	2	35.46	
Mono	1		23.00
Residual	1		12.46
Under 35 vs. Over 35	1	0.98	
Total	5	45.05	

10. $\hat{\psi} = 0.3414 - 0.4559 = -0.1145$; $SE_{\hat{\psi}}^2 = 0.1101^2 + 0.0848^2 = 0.0193$;
$X^2 = \dfrac{-0.1145^2}{0.0193} = 0.68$.

11. $\hat{R}_{LM}^2 = 0.1728$, $X^2 = 44.93$.

12. Under 35: $\hat{R}_{LM}^2 = 0.086$, $X^2 = 8.53$.
Over 35: $\hat{R}_{LM}^2 = 0.222$, $X^2 = 35.54$.
Under 35 vs. Over 35: $\hat{R}_{LM}^2 = 0.004$, $X^2 = 0.97$.

13. Analysis of chi-square table:

Favorable vs. unfavorable:	1	24.21
Between sex in favorable:	1	2.47
Between sex in unfavorable:	1	5.04
Total	3	31.72

Chapter 7

1. In terms of Table A–7, reject H_0 if $X \leq 6$, since $m = 22$ and $X_{21} = 7$. H_0 is not rejected. As a one-tailed Z-test of $p_{21} < p_{12}$, $Z = -1.49$. Do not reject, since $Z = -1.49 > -1.645$.

2. $SE_{\hat{\psi}_1}^2 = 0.003641$, $SE_{\hat{\psi}_2}^2 = 0.003082$.

$$Z = \frac{\hat{\psi}_1 - \hat{\psi}_2}{\sqrt{SE_{\hat{\psi}_1}^2 + SE_{\hat{\psi}_2}^2}} = \frac{0.2629}{0.0820} = 3.21$$

Reject H_0, since $Z = 3.21 > 1.96$.

3. Bowker's test is used to examine internal shift. $X^2 = 43.10$, $v = 3$, $X_{3:0.95}^2 = 7.81$.
Reject H_0. There is a shift to higher job status.
Stuart test on margins:

$$\hat{\Delta} \pm \underline{S}^* SE_{\hat{\Delta}}$$

Low	-0.2092 ± 0.0832	Sig
Medium	-0.0306 ± 0.0998	N.S.
High	0.2398 ± 0.0949	Sig

6. Six subjects were noninformative. Thus $n = 24$.
$T_{.1} = 13$, $T_{.2} = 5$, $T_{.3} = 15$, $T_{.4} = 19$, $Q = 14.51$, $v = 3$, $X_{3:0.95}^2 = 7.81$, H_0 is rejected.
$\underline{S}^* = \sqrt{7.81} = 2.80$, $\text{Var}(\hat{\psi}) = 0.1577$.

Pairwise comparisons:

$$\hat{\psi} \pm S\underline{S}^*\sigma_{\hat{\psi}}$$

1 vs. 2	0.267 ± 0.442	N.S.
1 vs. 3	-0.067 ± 0.442	N.S.
1 vs. 4	-0.200 ± 0.442	N.S.
2 vs. 3	-0.333 ± 0.442	N.S.
2 vs. 4	-0.467 ± 0.442	Sig
3 vs. 4	-0.133 ± 0.442	N.S.

7. For $C = 4$, $\alpha = 0.05$, $Z = \pm 2.50$.

$$\psi_1 = \left[\tfrac{9}{31} - \tfrac{13}{24}\right] \pm 2.50\sqrt{\tfrac{9}{31}\left[\tfrac{22}{31}\right]\left[\tfrac{1}{31}\right] + \tfrac{13}{24}\left[\tfrac{11}{24}\right]\left[\tfrac{1}{24}\right]}$$

$\psi_1 = -0.251 \pm 0.326$ N.S.

$\psi_2 = -0.047 \pm 0.265$ N.S.

$\psi_3 = -0.044 \pm 0.332$ N.S.

$\psi_4 = 0.047 \pm 0.265$ N.S.

Chapter 8

3. $X^2 = 7.29$. Reject H_0. $\phi^2 = 0.0333$.

4. $g = 10.2804$, $\hat{\gamma} = 2.3303$, $\text{Var}(\hat{\gamma}) = 1.1103$, $Z = 2.21$, $\gamma = 2.3303 \pm 2.0652$, $Z^2 = (2.21)^2 = 4.88 < 7.29$.

5. $X^2 = 62.99$, $\phi^2 = 0.2086$, $\phi'^2 = 0.1043$.

6. Significant γ values for $\underline{S}^* = \sqrt{X^2_{6:0.95}} = 3.55$ involve:
   (Brown and Blue) with (Black and Blonde)
   (Brown and Other) with (Black and Blonde)
   (Brown and Blue) with (Brown and Blonde)
   (Brown and Blue) with (Red and Blonde)

7. $\hat{\beta} = 1.0394$, $SE_{\hat{\beta}} = 0.1414$, $X^2 = 54.02$, $X^2 = 60.75$

Analysis of chi-square table:

Source of variance	d/f	Value of X^2
Regression	1	54.02
Departure from regr.	2	6.73
Total	3	60.75

8. $\hat{\psi} = -2.1243$, $SE^2_{\hat{\psi}} = 0.0554$, $Z^2 = 81.46$

10. None of the γ's is significant with $\underline{S}^* = 3.55$.

11. For code values $(-1 \quad 0 \quad +1)$:
   $\hat{\beta}_1 = -0.3336$, $SE_{\hat{\beta}_1} = 0.1797$, $X^2_1 = 3.46$, $X^2_1 = 5.15$.
   $\hat{\beta}_2 = -0.7857$, $SE_{\hat{\beta}_2} = 0.1334$, $X^2_2 = 34.68$, $X^2_2 = 58.30$.
   For code values $(3.5 \quad 11 \quad 14.5)$:
   $\hat{\beta}_1 = -0.3219$, $SE_{\hat{\beta}_1} = 0.1600$, $X^2_1 = 4.05$.
   $\hat{\beta}_2 = -0.7335$, $SE_{\hat{\beta}_2} = 0.1300$, $X^2_2 = 31.84$.

19. $X^2 = 3.24$, $\phi^2 = 0.0108$, for $n = 300$.
   $X^2 = 12.96$, $\phi^2 = 0.0108$, for $n = 1200$.

Chapter 9

1. $\gamma_1 = -0.7341$, $\gamma_2 = -0.4487$, $\gamma_3 = -0.3091$.
   $\psi_1 = \gamma_1 - \gamma_2 = -1.1828 \pm 2.395(0.4003) = -1.1828 \pm 0.9587$ Sig
   $\psi_2 = \gamma_1 - \gamma_3 = -1.0433 \pm 2.395(0.4098) = -1.0433 \pm 0.9815$ Sig
   $\psi_3 = \gamma_2 - \gamma_3 = 0.1394 \pm 2.395(0.3862) = 0.1394 \pm 0.9247$ N.S.

2. $\hat{\beta}_{\text{White}} = 0.3478$, $SE_{\hat{\beta}}^2 = 0.0006052$, $X^2 = 199.88$, $\phi^2 = 0.077$.
   $\hat{\beta}_{\text{Black}} = 0.3596$, $SE_{\hat{\beta}}^2 = 0.0009323$, $X^2 = 138.63$, $\phi^2 = 0.071$.

3. $\hat{\Delta}_2 = 0.3557$, $\hat{\Delta}_5 = 0.3333$, $\hat{\Delta}_8 = 0.3385$, $\hat{\Delta}_{11} = 0.2588$, $\hat{\Delta}_0 = 0.3208$.
   $SE_{\hat{\Delta}_2}^2 = 0.0244$, $SE_{\hat{\Delta}_5}^2 = 0.0366$, $SE_{\hat{\Delta}_8}^2 = 0.0351$, $SE_{\hat{\Delta}_{11}}^2 = 0.0273$. $U_0 = 0.2039$, $v = 3$.

4. Catholic vs. Protestant: $\psi = -0.3128 \pm 2.395(0.9576)$
   Catholic vs. Others: $\psi = -0.1542 \pm 2.395(1.0739)$
   Protestant vs. Others: $\psi = 0.1586 \pm 2.395(1.1916)$

6. Catholic vs. Protestant: $\psi = 0.6323 \pm 2.635(0.2990)$
   Catholic vs. Jewish: $\psi = 2.4551 \pm 2.635(0.7420)$
   Catholic vs. Other: $\psi = 1.6734 \pm 2.635(0.4836)$
   Protestant vs. Jewish: $\psi = 1.8229 \pm 2.635(0.7321)$
   Protestant vs. Other: $\psi = 0.1770 \pm 2.635(0.4682)$
   Jewish vs. Other: $\psi = -1.9954 \pm 2.635(0.8249)$

8. Under 30 vs. 30 to 45: $\psi = -0.7068 \pm 2.395(0.5452)$
   Under 30 vs. over 45: $\psi = -0.0602 \pm 2.395(0.6798)$
   30 to 45 vs. over 45: $\psi = 0.6466 \pm 2.395(0.6354)$
   $\hat{\beta}_{\text{Catholic}} = 0.3296$, $SE_{\hat{\beta}}^2 = 0.00356$, $X^2 = 30.54$.
   $\hat{\beta}_{\text{Protestant}} = 0.3495$, $SE_{\hat{\beta}}^2 = 0.00250$, $X^2 = 48.86$.

Chapter 10

1. a) Means: $X^2 = 8.77$, $X^2_{9:0.95} = 16.92$. Do not reject.
   Medians: $X^2 = 9.90$, $X^2_{9:0.95} = 16.92$. Do not reject.

   b) Lilliefors: Means: $L = 0.0396$, $L_{0.95} > \dfrac{0.886}{\sqrt{300}} = 0.0512$. Do not reject.

   Medians: $L = 0.0369$, $L_{0.95} > 0.0512$. Do not reject.

   Kolmogorov: Means: $K = 0.0396$, $K_{0.95} > \dfrac{1.36}{\sqrt{300}} = 0.0785$. Do not reject.

   Medians: $K = 0.0369$, $K_{0.95} = 0.0785$. Do not reject.

2. KS $= 0.0600$, $KS_{300, 300:0.95} \geq 1.36 \sqrt{\dfrac{600}{300(300)}} = 0.1110$. Do not reject.

3. $X^2 = 16.00$, $X^2_{9:0.95} = 16.92$. Do not reject.

5. Samples are not independent.

11. $v = 2$, $X^2 = 3.20$, $X^2_{2:0.95} = 5.99$. Do not reject.

13. $v = 1$, $X^2 = 0.74$, $X^2_{1:0.95} = 3.84$. Model fits, but $p \neq 0.54$.

Chapter 11

1. $R_{Old} = 216.5$, $R_{New} = 449.5$, $N(N + 1)/2 = 666$. Corrected for continuity, but not for ties, $Z = -3.37$ with $SE = 31.607$. Reject H_0. Corrected for continuity and for ties, $Z = -3.39$ with $SE = 31.464$. Reject H_0.

2. a) $\overline{X}_{Old} = 7.167$, $\overline{X}_{New} = 11.833$, $S^2_{Old} = 10.147$, $S^2_{New} = 7.088$, $t = -4.77$, $S^2_{Pooled} = 8.618$, $v_2 = 34$. Reject H_0.
   b) Terry–Hoffding: $Z = -3.67$, $T_1 = -10.75$, $SE_{T_1} = 2.93$.
   Van der Waerden: $Z = -3.69$, $X_1 = -10.25$, $SE_{X_1} = 2.78$.
   c) $M = 10$

	Old	New	Total
Less than 10	13	3	16
Above 10	4	12	16
Total	17	15	32

$X^2 = 10.25$, $Z = \sqrt{10.25} = 3.20$, $X^2_{1:0.95} = 3.84$. Reject H_0.

3. $\hat{M}_d = 5$. 95% confidence interval: $2 \leq M_d \leq 7$;
   $D^{(101)} \leq M_d \leq D^{(224)}$; $D^{(101)} = 2$; $D^{(224)} = 7$.

4. a) $Z = \dfrac{302 + 0.5 - 333}{31.61} = -0.97$. Do not reject.

   b) $Z = \dfrac{2362.5 - 1942.5}{293.34} = 1.43$. Do not reject.

   c) $Z = \dfrac{20.5341 - 15.0957}{3.0502} = 1.78$. Do not reject.

Chapter 12

1. a) $H = 26.56$

2. a)

Contrast	Coefficients							
1	1	1	1	−1	−1	−1	Males vs. Females
2	1	0	−1	0	0	0	Linear in Males
3	0	0	0	1	0	−1	Linear in Females
4	1	−2	1	0	0	0	Quadratic in Males
5	0	0	0	1	−2	1	Quadratic in Females

	Analysis on Rank				Analysis on Normal Scores			
	$\hat{\phi}$	L.L.	U.L.	Sig.	$\hat{\phi}$	L.L.	U.L.	Sig.
1	28.6	−6.3	63.5	No	1.45	−0.44	3.35	No
2	22.0	1.8	42.2	Yes	1.22	0.13	2.32	Yes
3	17.0	−3.2	37.1	No	.95	−0.15	2.04	No
4	−4.3	−39.2	30.6	No	−.38	−2.28	1.51	No
5	21.6	−13.4	56.5	No	1.02	−0.88	2.91	No

b) Significant pairwise differences with $Z = \pm 2.94$ are:

Ranks:

1 vs. 5	L.L. = 4.04	U.L. = 49.96
1 vs. 6	L.L. = 1.74	U.L. = 47.66

Normal Scores:

1 vs. 5	L.L. = .12	U.L. = 2.62
1 vs. 6	L.L. = .09	U.L. = 2.58

6. $H = 11.24$. Reject H_0.

7.

Contrast	Coefficients				
1	1	1	−1	−1	Mothers vs. Nurses
2	1	−1	1	−1	Trained vs. Untrained
3	1	−1	−1	1	Interaction

Contrast	$\hat\psi \pm 2.39 SE_{\hat\psi}$	Sig.
1	5.40 ± 12.65	No
2	16.80 ± 12.65	Yes
3	1.80 ± 12.65	No

$$H = \frac{5.40^2}{28} + \frac{16.80^2}{28} + \frac{1.80^2}{28} = 11.24$$

9. $H = 22.91$

10.

Contrast	Coefficients				
1	1	1	−1	−1	Cool vs. Warm
2	1	−1	0	0	Blue vs. Green
3	0	0	1	−1	Yellow vs. Red

Contrast	$\hat\psi$	L.L.	U.L.	Sig.
1	30.4	12.7	48.1	Yes
2	−4.5	−17.0	8.0	No
3	12.0	−.5	24.5	No

14. $H = 2.53$

15.

Contrast	Coefficients				
1	1	1	−1	−1	Males vs. Females
2	1	−1	1	−1	10 minutes vs. 1 minute
3	1	−1	−1	1	Interaction

Contrast	$\hat\psi \pm ZSE_{\hat\psi}$	Sig.
1	.05 ± 14.21	No
2	−8.14 ± 14.21	No
3	4.34 ± 14.21	No

$$\frac{0.05^2}{35.36} + \frac{8.14^2}{35.36} + \frac{4.34^2}{35.36} = 2.41 \neq H,$$

because sample sizes are unequal.

16. Test for monotonicity. $\psi = 3.2 \pm 14.40$ is significant.

19. $H = 182.58$, $C = 0.8865$, $H^* = 200.07$. Test for monotonic trend. $X_1^2 = (-224.79)^2/300.5 = 168.15$ and $X_1^{*2} = 168.15/0.8865 = 189.68$.

20. $H = 58.36$, $C = 0.8847$, $H^* = 65.96$.

Chapter 13

1. Wilcoxon statistic $= 10$. One-tailed decision rule is to reject H_0 if $T \le 10$.
   Van der Waerden: $Z = 1.78$. One-tailed decision rule is to reject H_0 if $Z \ge 1.645$.
   Sign-test statistic $= 7$. One-tailed decision rule is to reject H_0 if $T \ge 9$.

3. Two-tailed 95% confidence interval for:
   Wilcoxon model: $-1.5 \le M_d \le 23.5$;
   Sign-test model: $-3 \le M_d \le 36$.

4. Wilcoxon model: $\hat{M}_d = 3$;   Sign-test model: $\hat{M}_d = 2$

11. $\hat{\beta} = 0.355$, $0.14 \le \beta \le 0.56$.

12. $\hat{\beta}_{Old} = 0.2552$, $0.1104 \le \beta_{Old} \le 0.3870$.
    $\hat{\beta}_{New} = 0.3148$, $0.1112 \le \beta_{New} \le 0.6042$.

Chapter 14

1. $X_r^2 = 50.70$.

2. $\psi_1 = 0.233 \pm 1.607$, $\psi_2 = -2.430 \pm 1.607$, $\psi_3 = -2.667 \pm 1.607$.
   $\psi_1 = 0.233 \pm 1.612$, $\psi_2 = -2.430 \pm 1.073$, $\psi_3 = -2.667 \pm 1.446$.

3.

Source	d/f	X^2
Linear	1	23.23
Quadratic	1	.06
Cubic	1	.59
Total	3	23.88

4. For Van der Waerden scores, $\sigma^2 = 0.5294$, $X^2 = 50.36$.

5. $X_{Control}^2 = 7.53$. $X_{Experimental}^2 = 25.08$, $\psi_{Linear}^{Experimental} = -9.800 \pm 2.795\sqrt{3.33}$.

8. For T_1 vs. T_2, $W_1 = 7$; T_1 vs. T_3, $W_2 = 12$; T_1 vs. T_4, $W_3 = 0$;
   T_2 vs. T_3, $W_4 = 0$; T_2 vs. T_4, $W_5 = 2$; T_3 vs. T_4, $W_6 = 2$.

9. Trial 1. $W_1 = 102.5$.   Trial 2. $W_2 = 95.5$.   Trial 3. $W_3 = 70.5$.
   Trial 4. $W_4 = 70.0$.
   With $\alpha = 0.05/4 = 0.0125$; reject H_0 if $W \le 75$ or $W \ge 135$.

11. $B = 4$, $K = 3$, $n = 3$, $R_1 = 75.5$, $R_2 = 61$, $R_3 = 43.5$, $X^2 = 5.70$.
    For the linear contrast $\hat{\psi} = -2.67$, $SE_{\hat{\psi}}^2 = 1.25$, and $X_{Linear}^2 = (-2.67)^2/1.25 = 5.70$.

12. $B = 14$, $K = 8$, $T = 4$, $M = 7$, $\lambda = 3$, $X^2 = 29$. Any pairwise contrast larger than 2.40 is significant.

13. $B = 14$, $K = 8$, $T = 4$, $M = 7$, $S = 2$, and $X^2 = 60.90$.

17. $R_1 = 30.5$, $R_2 = 40.0$, $R_3 = 49.5$, $X^2 = 9.03$.
$\hat{\phi}_1 = \overline{R}_1 - \overline{R}_2 = -0.475$, $\hat{\phi}_2 = \overline{R}_1 - \overline{R}_3 = -0.9500$, $\hat{\phi}_3 = \overline{R}_2 - \overline{R}_3 = -0.475$, $\Delta = 0.774$.

Chapter 15

1. $W_1 = 6.5$, $W_2 = 6$, $W_3 = 9$, $W_4 = 6$, $W_5 = 6$, $W_6 = 6$, and $W = 6.5 + 6 + 9 + 6 + 6 + 6 = 39.5$.
   Values of Z for:
   1. Corrected for ties and continuity: $Z = -3.00$
   2. Corrected for ties only: $Z = -3.09$
   3. Corrected for continuity only: $Z = -2.94$
   4. No correction: $Z = -3.03$

2. a) Terry–Hoeffding statistics are:
   $-1.27, -0.64, -0.20, 0.20, 0.64, 1.27$.

$$W_1 = -1.91, \; \sigma^2_{W_1} = 3\left[0.64109\left[\frac{6-3}{6-1}\right]\right] = 1.1537;$$

$$W_2 = -2.11, \; \sigma^2_{W_2} = 3\left[0.68970\left[\frac{6-3}{6-1}\right]\right] = 1.2415;$$

$$W_3 = -0.64, \; \sigma^2_{W_3} = 3\left[0.64109\left[\frac{6-3}{6-1}\right]\right] = 1.1537;$$

$$W_4 = -2.11, \; \sigma^2_{W_4} = 3\left[0.63163\left[\frac{6-3}{6-1}\right]\right] = 1.1369;$$

$$W_5 = -2.11, \; \sigma^2_{W_5} = 3\left[0.63829\left[\frac{6-3}{6-1}\right]\cdot\right] = 1.1489;$$

$$W_6 = -2.11, \; \sigma^2_{W_6} = 3\left[0.68750\left[\frac{6-3}{6-1}\right]\right] = 1.2375;$$

$$W = -10.99, \quad \sigma^2_W = 7.0722, \quad Z = \frac{-10.99}{\sqrt{7.0722}} = -4.13.$$

3. $W_{\text{Old}} = 187.5$, $W_{\text{New}} = 478$.
   If within-block variances are ignored:

$$E(W_{\text{Old}}) = n_1\left[\frac{N+1}{2}\right] = 18\left[\frac{36+1}{2}\right] = 333;$$

$$\text{Var}(W_{\text{Old}}) = \frac{n_1 n_2}{12}(N+1) = \frac{18(18)}{12}(37) = 999; \quad Z = -4.59.$$

If within-block variance is taken into account:

$$\overline{R}_1 = \frac{115}{6} = 19.1667, \quad \text{Var}(r_{1i}) = 111.4722;$$

$$\overline{R}_2 = \frac{109}{6} = 18.1667, \quad \text{Var}(r_{2i}) = 102.4722;$$

$$\overline{R}_3 = \frac{115}{6} = 19.1667, \quad \text{Var}(r_{3i}) = 106.3056;$$

$$\overline{R}_4 = \frac{105}{6} = 17.5000, \quad \text{Var}(r_{4i}) = 64.7500;$$

$$\overline{R}_5 = \frac{107}{6} = 17.8333, \quad \mathrm{Var}(r_{5i}) = 71.1389;$$

$$\overline{R}_6 = \frac{115}{6} = 19.1667, \quad \mathrm{Var}(r_{6i}) = 186.8889.$$

$$E(W_{\mathrm{Old}}) = 3(19.1667) + 3(18.1667) + \ldots + 3(19.1667) = 333;$$

$$\mathrm{Var}(W_{\mathrm{Old}}) = 3(111.4722)\left[\frac{6-3}{6-1}\right] + \ldots + 3(186.8889)\left[\frac{6-3}{6-1}\right] = 1157.45;$$

$$Z = \frac{(187.5 + 0.5) - 333}{\sqrt{1157.45}} = -4.26.$$

4. $\overline{Z}_1 = 0.045/6 = 0.0075, \qquad \mathrm{Var}(Z_{1i}) = 0.9468;$
$\overline{Z}_2 = 0.05/6 = 0.0083, \qquad \mathrm{Var}(Z_{2i}) = 0.8036;$
$\overline{Z}_3 = 0.45/6 = 0.0750, \qquad \mathrm{Var}(Z_{3i}) = 0.7179;$
$\overline{Z}_4 = -0.56/6 = -0.0933, \qquad \mathrm{Var}(Z_{4i}) = 0.3697;$
$\overline{Z}_5 = -0.29/6 = -0.0483, \qquad \mathrm{Var}(Z_{5i}) = 0.3850;$
$\overline{Z}_6 = 0.295/6 = 0.0492, \qquad \mathrm{Var}(Z_{6i}) = 1.7668.$
$E(Z_{\mathrm{Old}}) = 3(0.0075) + \ldots + 3(0.0492) = -0.0048;$

$$\mathrm{Var}(Z_{\mathrm{Old}}) = 3(0.9468)\left[\frac{6-3}{6-1}\right] + \ldots + 3(1.7668)\left[\frac{6-3}{6-1}\right] = 8.9816;$$

$$Z_{\mathrm{Old}} = -12.005, \quad Z = \frac{-12.005 + 0.0048}{\sqrt{8.9816}} = -4.00.$$

5.

	Aligned scores			Ranked data		
	4.67	1.67	0.67	36	27.5	22
$\overline{X}_1 = 11.33$	1.67	0.67	-2.33	27.5	22	8
	0.67	-4.33	-3.33	22	1	4
	4.33	1.33	0.33	35	25.5	19.5
$\overline{X}_2 = 12.67$	1.33	0.33	-0.67	25.5	19.5	14.5
	-3.67	-2.67	-0.67	3	7	14.5
	3.22	0.22	2.22	33	17.5	29.5
$\overline{X}_3 = 11.78$	2.22	0.22	-1.78	29.5	17.5	10
	-1.78	-1.78	-2.78	10	10	6
	2.78	3.78	-0.22	31.5	34	16
$\overline{X}_4 = 13.22$	0.78	2.78	-1.22	24	31.5	12.5
	-1.22	-3.22	-4.22	12.5	5	2
				289.5	218	158.5

H test on aligned ranks without a correction for ties:

$$H = \frac{12}{36(37)}\left[\frac{289.5^2}{12} + \frac{218^2}{12} + \frac{158.5^2}{12}\right] - 3(37) = 6.46$$

For the Hodges–Lehmann test:

$$\overline{R}_{1..} = \frac{170}{9} = 18.8889, \quad S_{1..}^2 = 125.5988.$$

$$\overline{R}_{2..} = \frac{164}{9} = 18.2222, \quad S_{2..}^2 = 86.2284.$$

$$\bar{R}_{3..} = \frac{163}{9} = 18.1111, \quad S^2_{3..} = 91.7654.$$

$$\bar{R}_{4..} = \frac{169}{9} = 18.7778, \quad S^2_{4..} = 126.7284.$$

$$\bar{S}^2_b = \frac{1}{4}(125.5988 + \ldots + 126.7284) = 107.5803.$$

$n = 3, \quad K = 3, \quad B = 4.$

$$W = \frac{3(3) - 1}{3(3)} \left[\frac{(24.1250 - 18.5)^2}{107.5803/12} + \frac{(18.1667 - 18.5)^2}{107.5803/12} + \frac{(13.2083 - 18.5)^2}{107.5803/12} \right] = 5.92$$

For pairwise contrasts $T = 2.34$; any pairwise difference exceeding $\Delta = \pm 2.34 \sqrt{2(107.5803)/12}$ $= 9.91$ is significant.

$$\begin{aligned}
\psi_1 &= 24.1250 - 18.1667 = 5.9583 & \text{N.S.} \\
\psi_2 &= 24.1250 - 13.2083 = 10.9167 & \text{Sig.} \\
\psi_3 &= 18.1667 - 13.2083 = 4.9584 & \text{N.S.}
\end{aligned}$$

Contrast ψ_2 also is the test for monotonicity. As a test statistic:

$$X^2_1 = \frac{10.9167^2}{2(107.5803)/12} = 6.65.$$

6. $W = 5.675$; do not reject H_0. Post hoc contrasts with $\underline{S}^* = \sqrt{5.99} = 2.45$.

$$\begin{aligned}
\bar{Z}_{.1.} - \bar{Z}_{.2.} &= 0.563 & \text{N.S.} \\
\bar{Z}_{.1.} - \bar{Z}_{.3.} &= 0.938 & \text{N.S.} \\
\bar{Z}_{.2.} - \bar{Z}_{.3.} &= 0.375 & \text{N.S.}
\end{aligned}$$

as $\Delta = 0.969$

7.
Group	>10 vs. 1–10	>10 vs. None	1–10 vs. None
Z	0.87	2.29	1.09
Decision	N.S.	N.S.	N.S.
Aligned	1.19	2.38	1.08

8. $W = 7.12$; H_0 is not rejected, since $X^2_{6:0.95} = 12.59$.

9. $W = 4.12 < 12.59 = X^2_{6:0.95}$. Hypothesis of no interaction is retained.

Chapter 16

1.
	Value of ρ	Value of τ
Uncorrected for ties	.573	.399
Corrected for ties	.559	.418

2.
	Value of Z for ρ	Value of Z for τ
Uncorrected for ties	2.36	2.27
Corrected for ties	2.30	2.30

3. $\tau_{23.1} = .33$.

4. Inverse normal: $r = .593$, $Z = 2.44$. Expected normal order: $r = .592$, $Z = 2.44$.

9. Uncorrected for ties: $\tau = .41$. Corrected for ties: $\tau = .58$; $Z = 8.24$. $G = .76$, $SE_G = .14$, $Z = 5.27$.

13. $\tau = \dfrac{20}{45} = \dfrac{S}{\begin{bmatrix} n \\ 2 \end{bmatrix}}$. $\text{Var}(S) = \dfrac{10(9)(25)}{18} - \dfrac{1}{18}\big[4(3)(13) + 6(5) + 17\big] = 88$. $Z = \dfrac{S - 0}{\sqrt{\text{Var}(S)}} =$

$\dfrac{20 - 0}{\sqrt{88}} = \dfrac{20}{9.38} = 2.12$. $U = 2$, $E(U) = 12$, $\text{Var}(U) = 22$. $Z = \dfrac{U - E(U)}{\sqrt{\text{Var}(Z)}} = \dfrac{2 - 12}{\sqrt{22}} =$

$\dfrac{-10}{4.69} = -2.12$.

15. In terms of Spearman's rho with no correction for ties: $r_{\text{Males}} = .6966$, $Z_{\text{Males}} = 2.86$; $r_{\text{Females}} = .7389$, $Z_{\text{Females}} = 3.05$. For testing H_0: $\rho_M = \rho_F$, $Z = -.12$.

18. $S = -170$, $\tau = -.52$.

19. $W = .273$, $X_r^2 = 8.19$, $\bar{r}_s = .19$.

20. $W = 1$.

Name Index

Subject Index